Computing Essentials

2006
Complete Edition

The O'Leary Series

Computing Concepts

- *Computing Essentials 2005* Introductory & Complete Editions
- *Computing Essentials 2006* Introductory & Complete Editions

Microsoft Office Applications

- *Microsoft Office 2003* Volume 1
- *Microsoft Office 2003* Volume 2
- *Microsoft Office Word 2003* Introductory & Complete Editions
- *Microsoft Office Excel 2003* Introductory & Complete Editions
- *Microsoft Office Access 2003* Introductory & Complete Editions
- *Microsoft Office PowerPoint 2003* Introductory & Complete Editions

Computing Essentials
2006
Complete Edition

Timothy J. O'Leary
Arizona State University

Linda I. O'Leary

McGraw Hill **Technology Education**

Boston   Burr Ridge, IL   Dubuque, IA   Madison, WI   New York   San Francisco   St. Louis
Bangkok   Bogotá   Caracas   Kuala Lumpur   Lisbon   London   Madrid   Mexico City
Milan   Montreal   New Delhi   Santiago   Seoul   Singapore   Sydney   Taipei   Toronto

Technology Education

COMPUTING ESSENTIALS 2006, COMPLETE EDITION

Published by McGraw-Hill/Technology Education, a business unit of The McGraw-Hill Companies, Inc. 1221 Avenue of the Americas, New York, NY, 10020. Copyright © 2006 by The McGraw-Hill Companies, Inc. All rights reserved. No part of this publication may be reproduced or distributed in any form or by any means, or stored in a database or retrieval system, without the prior written consent of The McGraw-Hill Companies, Inc., including, but not limited to, in any network or other electronic storage or transmission, or broadcast for distance learning. Some ancillaries, including electronic and print components, may not be available to customers outside the United States.

This book is printed on acid-free paper.

1 2 3 4 5 6 7 8 9 0 QPD/QPD 0 9 8 7 6 5

ISBN 0-07-226110-2

Editor-in-chief: *Robert Woodbury, Jr.*
Senior sponsoring editor: *Donald J. Hull*
Freelance developmental editor: *Jane Ducham*
Director of sales and marketing: *Paul Murphy*
Marketing manager: *Sankha Basu*
Lead media project manager: *Edward Przyzycki*
Lead project manager: *Lori Koetters*
Manager, new book production: *Heather Burbridge*
Coordinator freelance design: *Artemio Ortiz Jr.*
Photo research coordinator: *Jeremy Chesherack*
Photo researcher: *Keri Johnson*
Supplement producer: *Matthew Perry*
Senior digital content specialist: *Brian Nacik*
Cover design and interior icons: *Asylum Studios*
Interior design: *Artemio Ortiz, Jr.*
Typeface: *10/12 New Aster*
Compositor: *Cenveo*
Printer: *Quebecor World Dubuque Inc.*

Library of Congress Cataloging-in-Publication Data

O'Leary, Timothy J., 1947–
    Computing essentials 2006 / Timothy J. O'Leary, Linda I. O'Leary.—Complete ed.
      p. cm   (The O'Leary series)
    ISBN 0-07-226110-2 (alk. paper)
    1. Computers. 2. Electronic data processing. I. O'Leary, Linda I. II. Title.
QA76.5.O425 2006
004—dc22

                                     2004059280

www.mhhe.com

Brief Contents

Contents

15

YOUR FUTURE AND INFORMATION TECHNOLOGY *432*

Preface

INTRODUCTION

The 20th century not only brought us the dawn of the information age, but it also continued to bring us rapid changes in information technology. There is no indication that this rapid rate of change will be slowing—it may even be increasing. As we begin the 21st century, computer literacy will undoubtedly become a prerequisite in whatever career a student chooses. The goal of *Computing Essentials* is to provide students with the basis for understanding the concepts necessary for success in the information age. *Computing Essentials* also endeavors to instill in students an appreciation for the effect of information technology on people and our environment and to give students a basis for building the necessary skill set to succeed in this new 21st century.

ABOUT THE AUTHORS

Tim and Linda O'Leary live in the American Southwest and spend much of their time engaging instructors and students in conversation about learning. In fact, they have been talking about learning for over 25 years. Some-

thing in those early conversations convinced them to write a book, to bring their interest in the learning process to the printed page. Today, they are as concerned as ever about learning, about technology, and about the challenges of presenting material in new ways, both in terms of content and the method of delivery.

A powerful and creative team, Tim combines his years of classroom teaching experience with Linda's background as a consultant and corporate trainer. Tim has taught courses at Stark Technical College in Canton, Ohio, and at Rochester Institute of Technology in upstate New York, and is currently a professor at Arizona State University in Tempe, Arizona. Tim and Linda have talked to and taught students from 8 to 80, all of them with a desire to learn something about computers and the applications that make their lives easier, more interesting, and more productive.

Each new edition of an O'Leary text, supplement, or learning aid has benefited from these students and their instructors who daily stand in front of them (or over their shoulders). *Computing Essentials* is no exception.

A WORD FROM THE AUTHORS

Times are changing, technology is changing, and this text is changing, too. Do you think the students of today are different from those of yesterday? Mine are, and I'll wager that yours are as well. On the positive side, I am amazed how much effort students put toward things that interest them and things they are convinced are relevant to them. Their effort directed at learning application programs and exploring the Web seems, at times, limitless. On the other hand, it is difficult to engage them in other equally important topics, such as personal privacy and technological advances.

I've changed the way I teach, and this book reflects that. I no longer lecture my students about how important certain concepts like microprocessors, input devices, and utility programs are. Rather, I begin by engaging their interest by presenting practical tips related to the key concepts, by demonstrating interesting applications that are relevant to their lives, and by focusing on outputs rather than processes. Then, I discuss the concepts and processes.

Motivation and relevance are the keys. This text has several features specifically designed to engage students and to demonstrate the relevance of technology in their lives. These elements are combined with a thorough coverage of the concepts and sound pedagogical devices.

SELECTED FEATURES OF THIS BOOK

- **Visual Chapter Openers** Each chapter begins with a two-page Visual Chapter Opener with large graphics and brief text. The graphics present the structure and organization of the chapter. The text relates the graphics to topics that are covered in the chapter and discusses their importance. The objective of the visual chapter openers is to engage students and provide relevancy and motivation.

- **On the Web Explorations** Within many of the chapters, two or more On the Web Explorations are presented as marginal elements. These explorations encourage students to connect to carefully selected Web sites that provide additional information on key topics. The objective of the Web Explorations is to encourage students to expand their knowledge by using Web resources.

On the Web Explorations

To learn more about one of the leaders in developing continuous-speech systems, visit our Web site at

www.olearyseries.com/CE06
and select On the Web Explorations.

- **Tips** Within many of the chapters, Tips are provided that offer advice on a variety of chapter-related issues, such as how to efficiently locate information on the Web, how to speed up computer operations, and how to protect against computer viruses. One objective of the Tips is to provide students with assistance on common technology-related problems or issues. The other objective is to motivate students by showing that the concepts presented in the chapter are relevant to their everyday lives.

TIPS
Have you ever bought anything online? If not, it's likely that in the future you will join the millions who have. Here are a few suggestions on how to shop online:

1. **Consult product review sites.** To get evaluations or opinions on products, visit one of the many review sites on the Web such as www.consumersearch.com and www.epinions.com.

2. **Use a shopping bot.** Once you have selected a specific product, enlist a shopping bot or automated shopping assistants to compare prices. Two well-known shopping bots are located at www.mysimon.com and www.shopping.yahoo.com.

3. **Consult vendor review sites.** Of course, price is not everything. Before placing an order with a vendor, check their reputation by visiting vendor review sites such as www.gomez.com and www.bizrate.com.

4. **Select payment option.** Once you have selected the product and the vendor, the final step is to order and pay. Security of your credit card number is critical. Consider payment options available from www.private.buy.com and www.americanexpress.com/privatepayments.

- **Concept Checks** Every chapter contains strategically placed Concept Check boxes. Each box contains questions related to the material just presented. The objective of these Concept Checks is to provide students the opportunity to test their retention of key chapter concepts.

▼ CONCEPT CHECK

▶ What is a information system?

▶ What is required of a competent end user?

- **Making IT Work for You** Based on student surveys, 11 special interest topics have been identified. These topics include downloading music from the Internet, creating personal Web sites, and using the Internet to place free long-distance telephone calls. Each of these 11 special interest topics is presented in a two-page Making IT Work for You section within the relevant chapter. The objective is to engage students by presenting high-interest topics and to motivate them to learn about related concepts in the chapter.

- **Using IT at DVD Direct** Many students find information systems concepts to be very challenging. A series of four cases focused on DVD Direct, a fictitious Web-based movie rental company, have been created. The cases are introduced at the end of Chapters 11, 12, 13, and 14. The complete cases are on the *Computing Essentials* CD and at our Web site, www.olearyseries.com/CE06. They have been written to allow instructors to skip all or some of the cases without losing continuity. The objective of the cases is to engage students in an interesting current application of technology and to demon-

strate the relevance and importance of information systems, databases, systems analysis and design, and programming.

- **A Look to the Future** Each chapter concludes with a brief discussion of a specific recent technological advancement related to material presented in the chapter. The objective of this feature is to remind students that technology is always changing and to reinforce the importance of staying informed of recent changes.

- **Visual Chapter Summaries** Each chapter ends with a multipage visual chapter summary. Like the chapter openers, the summaries use graphics to present the structure of the chapter and text to provide specifics. Using a columnar arrangement, major concepts are represented by graphics followed by detailed text summaries. The objective of the visual chapter summaries is to provide a detailed summary of key concepts and terms in an engaging and meaningful way.

- **Using Technology** Every chapter has Web-related end-of-chapter exercises that direct students to explore current popular uses of technology. In most cases, the first question requires the student to review the chapter's Making IT Work for You features and to respond to a series of related questions. Other questions require Web research. One objective of the Using Technology feature is to provide support for instructors who would like to expose their students to the Making IT Work for You features without using class time. The other objective is to provide a powerful tool that engages and motivates students with assignments related to technology that is directly applicable to them.

- **Expanding Your Knowledge** Every chapter has Web-related end-of-chapter exercises directing students to enhance their depth of knowledge on specific technologies introduced in the chapter. In most cases, one question requires the students to use their free *Computing Essentials* CD and to respond to a series of related questions. Other questions require Web research into carefully selected topics. One objective of the Expanding Your Knowledge feature is to provide support for instructors who want their students to effectively use the *Computing Essentials* CD and one Web site. The other objective is to support instructors who want their students to obtain greater indepth understanding of key technologies.

- **Building Your Portfolio** Every chapter has Web-related end-of-chapter exercises directing students to prepare and to write a one- or two-page paper on critical technology-related issues. Some questions require students to summarize and analyze select emerging technologies addressed in the chapter. Other questions focus on a critical chapter-related privacy, security, and/or ethical issue. Students are required to consider, evaluate, and formulate a position. One objective of the Building Your Portfolio feature is to support instructors who want their students to develop critical thinking and writing skills. Another objective is to provide support for instructors who want their students to create written document(s) recording their technology knowledge. A third objective is to provide support for instructors who want their students to recognize, understand, and analyze key privacy, security, and ethical issues relating to technology.

- **Engaging Students** Having all these features is one thing. Making the students aware of them is another. As in almost all textbooks, Chapter 1 of this textbook provides an overview and framework for the following chapters. Unlike other textbooks, our Chapter 1 also provides a discussion and overview of each of the above engaging features. One objective of this approach is to support instructors who want to focus their students' attention on any one or on a combination of features. The other objective is to motivate students by highlighting features that are visually interesting and relevant to their lives.

- **Computing Essentials CD** Throughout the pages of the text you will see references to *Computing Essentials* CD. This is a set of reference materials including *tips, animations, videos, self tests, careers in IT,* and more. The materials can be accessed from either of two sources. One source is from the *Computing Essentials* CD. The other source is our Web site at www.olearyseries.com/CE06. Students have the flexibility to use either or both of these sources. For example, a student who does not have convenient access to a high speed Internet connection would likely choose to view videos from the *Computing Essentials* CD. If a student were to lose the *Computing Essentials* CD, he or she would still have access to all materials from our Web site.

Instructor's Guide

RESOURCES FOR INSTRUCTORS

We understand that in today's teaching environment offering a textbook alone is not sufficient to meet the needs of the many different instructors who use our books. To teach effectively, instructors must have a full complement of supplemental resources to assist them in every facet of teaching from preparing for class, to presenting lectures, to assessing students' comprehension. *Computing Essentials* offers a complete, fully integrated supplements package as described below.

Instructor's Resource Kit

The Instructor's Resource Kit CD-ROM contains the Instructor's Manual, PowerPoint slides, and Examview Pro test generation software with accompanying test item files for each chapter and 20 video clips (with summaries) from G4techTV. The distinctive features of each component of the Instructor's Resource Kit are described below.

- **Instructor's Manual** The Instructor's Manual has been prepared by William Hitchcock, associate professor of accounting & business and department chair at Loras College. The manual contains lecture outlines with teaching notes and page references. It contains definitions of key terms and answers to the various end-of-chapter questions such as multiple choice, matching, and open-ended. It also summarizes the concept checks and key figures in each chapter. Professor Hitchcock also assisted with selection of the G4techTV video clips that accompany this text, and he prepared the user summaries for these clips.

- **PowerPoint Presentation** The PowerPoint slides, by Brenda Nielsen of Mesa Community College–Red Mountain, are designed to provide instructors with a com-prehensive resource for use during lecture. They include a review of key terms and definitions, figures from the text, new illustrations, anticipated student questions with answers, and additional resources. Also included with the slides are comprehensive speaker's notes.

- **Testbank** The *Computing Essentials* testbank, carefully prepared by Margaret Trenholm-Edmonds of Mt. Allison University, contains over 2,200 questions categorized by level of learning (definition, concept, and application). This is the same learning scheme that is introduced in the text to provide a valuable testing and reinforcement tool. The test questions are identified by text page number to assist you in planning your exams, and rationales for each answer are also included. Additional quizzes, which can be used as pretests and posttests in class, can be found on the Online Learning Center at www.olearyseries.com/CE06.

G4techTV—Video Series from McGraw-Hill Technology Education

McGraw-Hill Technology Education is pleased to continue its relationship with G4techTV. Through this partnership, we are able to offer instructors and  students new video content directly related to computing that enhances the classroom or lab experience with technology programming from business and society. Video selections from G4techTV programs such as "The Screen Savers" and "Pulse" are sometimes edgy and always informative. Use of these videos will help students understand how computing interacts with and contributes to business and society and will also offer an advance look at emerging technology and devices. These new videos have been developed with the guidance of professors Donald L. Amoroso of Appalachian State University and William Hitchcock of Loras College. Professors Amoroso and Hitchcock are active teachers of large sections and have selected video segments from G4techTV that they know will work in the classroom. Written guidance on how to best use these videos is included in the Instructor's Resource Kit to facilitate learning. This series gives instructors and students more power for teaching and learning in the computing classroom!

SimNet Concepts 1.5

SimNet is an interactive program for student learning and assessment on 77 key computer concepts. SimNet includes a learning or tutorial presentation of each of these 77 concepts and includes both practice and assessment exam questions for each one. Students gain a greater understanding of the wide range of computer concepts using this learning and assessment program by employing a learning sequence of "Teach Me," "Show Me," "Let Me Try." SimNet Concepts 1.5 is available in an optional bundle with the text for a modest additional charge.

Computing Essentials Student CD & Web Site www.olearyseries.com/CE06

The *Computing Essentials* Student CD contains animations of key concepts, videos relating to select Making IT Work for You applications, and in-depth coverage of select topics. *Computing Essentials* Interactive icons are located in the margins throughout the book to alert students that expanded coverage of the material in the text can be found on their *Computing Essentials* CD and on the *Computing Essentials* Web site.

Digital Solutions to Help You Manage Your Course

Online Learning Centers—The Online Learning Center that accompanies *Computing Essentials* is accessible at www.olearyseries.com/CE06. This site provides additional learning and instructional tools developed using the same three-level approach found in the text and supplements. This offers a consistent method for students to enhance their comprehension of the concepts presented in the text. The student section also houses the G4techTV video clips.

Online Courses Available—OLCs are your perfect solutions for Internet-based content. Simply put, these courses are digital cartridges that contain a book's pedagogy and supplements. As students read the book, they can go online and take self-grading quizzes or work through interactive exercises. These also provide students with appropriate access to lecture materials and other key supplements.

Blackboard.com

WebCT (a product of Universal Learning Technology)

O'Leary Series Applications Textbooks

The O'Leary Series computer applications textbooks for Microsoft Office are available separately, or packaged with *Computing Essentials*. The O'Leary Series offers a step-by-step approach to developing computer applications skills and is available in both brief and introductory versions. The introductory books are MOS Certified and prepare students for the Microsoft Office User Certification Exam.

Skills Assessment for Office Applications

SimNet (Simulated Network Assessment Product) provides a way for you to test students' software skills in a simulated environment. SimNet is available for Microsoft Office 2003. SimNet provides flexibility for you in your applications course by offering:

Pretesting options

Posttesting options

Course placement testing

Diagnostic capabilities to reinforce skills

Proficiency testing to measure skills

Web or LAN delivery of tests

Computer-based training tutorials (new for Office XP)

MOS preparation exams

Learning verification reports

Spanish version

For more information on skills assessment software, please contact your local sales representative, or visit us at www.mhhe.com.

Student's Guide

STUDENT'S GUIDE TO THE O'LEARY LEARNING SYSTEM

Recently, at the end of the semester, some of my students stopped by my office to say they enjoyed the class and that they "learned something that they could actually use." High praise indeed for a professor! Actually, I had mixed feelings. Of course, it felt good to learn that my students had enjoyed the course. However, it hurt a bit that they were surprised that they learned something useful.

As you read the text, notice the Tips scattered throughout the book. These tips offer suggestions on a variety of topics from the basics of cleaning a monitor to how to make your computer run faster and smoother. Also, notice the Making IT Work for You sections that demonstrate some specific computer applications you might find interesting. For example, one demonstrates how to capture and use television video clips for electronic presentations

> **Here's my promise to you:**
> *In the following pages you will find things that you can actually use now and that will provide a foundation for understanding future technological advances.*

and another shows how to capture, save, and play music from the Internet.

Many learning aids are built into the text to ensure your success with the material and to make the process of learning rewarding. In the pages that follow, we call your attention to the key features in the text. We also show you supplemental materials, such as the student Online Learning Center, that you should take advantage of to ensure your success in this course.

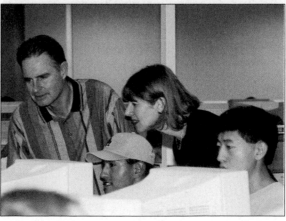

What makes *Computing Essentials* such a powerful tool?

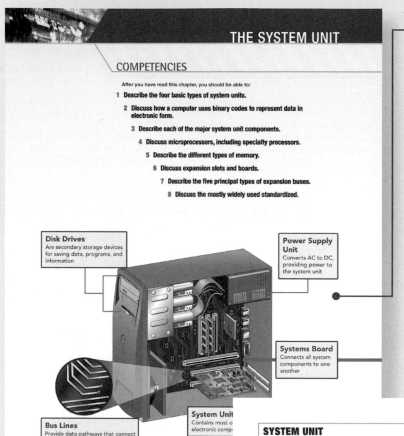

Visual Chapter Openers

Each chapter begins with a two-page opening spread that provides the Chapter Competencies and a brief introduction to the chapter. Graphics present the structure and organization of the chapter visually, while text discusses the topics that will be covered and their importance.

Key Terms

Throughout the text, the most important terms are presented in bold type and are defined within the text. You will also find a list of key terms at the end of each chapter and in the glossary at the end of the book.

THE SYSTEM UNIT

COMPETENCIES

After you have read this chapter, you should be able to:

1 Describe the four basic types of system units.

2 Discuss how a computer uses binary codes to represent data in electronic form.

3 Describe each of the major system unit components.

4 Discuss microprocessors, including specialty processors.

5 Describe the different types of memory.

6 Discuss expansion slots and boards.

7 Describe the five principal types of expansion buses.

8 Discuss the mostly widely used standardized.

Disk Drives
Are secondary storage devices for saving data, programs, and information

Power Supply Unit
Converts AC to DC, providing power to the system unit

Systems Board
Connects all system components to one another

Bus Lines
Provide data pathways that connect various system components

System Unit
Contains most o[...] electronic comp[...]

SYSTEM UNIT

System components are housed within the system unit or system cabinet. Desktop, notebook, tablet PC, and handheld are four types of system units.

The **system unit,** also known as the **system cabinet** or **chassis,** is a container that houses most of the electronic components that make up a computer system. All computer systems have a system unit. For microcomputers, there are four basic types (see Figure 6-1):

- **Desktop system units** typically contain the system's electronic components and selected secondary storage devices. Input and output devices, such as a mouse, keyboard, and monitor, are located outside the system unit. This type of system unit is design to be placed either horizontally or vertically. Vertical units are often called **tower models.**
- **Notebook system units** are portable and much smaller. These system units contain the electronic components, selected secondary storage devices, and input devices (keyboard and pointing device). Located outside the system unit, the monitor is attached by hinges. Notebook system units are often called **laptops.**

Figure 6–1 Basic types of system units

How does *Computing Essentials* use the Web and provide practical real world tips?

Tips

Tips appear within nearly every chapter and are provided to offer advice on a variety of chapter-related issues, such as how to efficiently locate information on the Web, how to speed up computer operations, and how to protect against computer viruses. Tips assist you with common technology-related problems or issues and motivate you by showing the relevance of concepts presented in the chapter to everyday life.

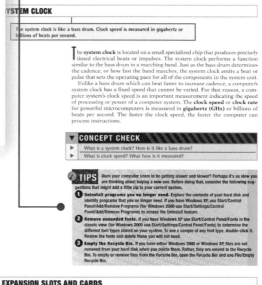

On the Web Explorations

Two or more On the Web Explorations appear within nearly every chapter and are presented as marginal elements. These explorations ask you to connect to carefully selected Web sites that provide additional information on key topics, encouraging you to expand your knowledge by using Web resources.

Computing Essentials Web site

Throughout the text, the *Computing Essentials* Web site at www.olearyseries.com/CE06 is referenced. The text directs you to this Web site for additional material, Web links, and exercises to boost interest and enhance your comprehension of the material.

How does *Computing Essentials* get you involved in current technologies?

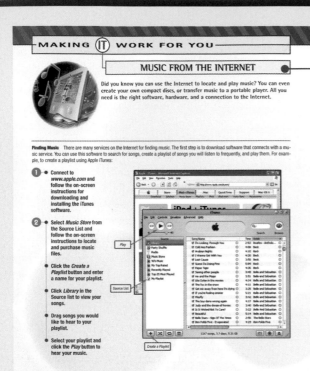

Making IT Work for You

Special interest topics are presented in a two-page Making IT Work for You section within the chapter relating to that topic. These topics include protecting against computer viruses, downloading music from the Internet, and using the Internet to place free long-distance telephone calls.

Making IT Work Figures

Several critical technologies are presented in full page figures. These figures show how the technologies work and how they are used. These figures include How Digital Cameras Work, How Instant Messenging Works, How Home Networks Work, and more. Additionally, several of these topics are animated and presented on the Computing Essentials CD or on our Web site.

How does *Computing Essentials* teach you about the future in information technology?

Careers in IT

Some of the fastest growing career opportunities in information technology are presented in the *Computing Essentials* CD. These descriptions include job titles, responsibilities, educational requirements, and salary ranges. Among the careers covered are Webmaster, software engineer, and database administrator. You will learn how the material you are studying relates directly to a potential career path.

A Look to the Future

Each chapter concludes with a brief discussion of a recent technological advancement related to the chapter material, reinforcing the importance of staying informed.

A Look to the Future

Xybernaut Corporation Makes Wearable Computers a Reality

Wouldn't it be nice if you could conveniently access the Internet wirelessly at any time during the day? What if you could send and receive e-mail from your waist-mounted computer? What if you could maintain your personal schedule book, making new appointments with others on the fly? What if you could play interactive games, and surf the Web from anywhere?

Of course you can do all this and more using wireless technology and PDAs. Many people currently use this technology when they are away from their home or office. What if these users could accomplish these tasks with an even smaller, more portable, and less intrusive system? Will people be wearing computers rather than carrying them? What if your computer featured a head-mounted display?

Xybernaut Corporation is currently marketing a personal wearable computer called POMA™. The device is described as a personal multimedia appliance. It is composed of a processor that runs Windows CE, a wireless pointing device, and a head-mounted display. The display allows you to see the equivalent of a desktop monitor via a small screen that is worn in front of one eye. This screen is only one inch square and weighs a mere 3 ounces. The device includes an MP3 player that plays songs and displays videos, and abridged versions of Windows Office programs.

Devices made by Xybernaut® are currently being evaluated for use in airports by security personal. These devices are currently being used by the U.S. Department of Defense for military applications and by the Toronto Blue Jays to end long lines at ticket windows. When coupled with face recognition technology, Xybernaut's Mobile Assistant® V provides security personnel portable and instant communication with the command center. Police and security officers may someday use this technology to check IDs and verify your identity. Experts say that wearable computers will be used by surgeons in operating rooms to "view" their patients.

Will we be wearing computers soon? Some of us already are. And some experts predict the majority of us will employ a wearable computer before the end of the decade. Many computer manufacturers are currently working on wearable computers, and there is even a wearable computer fashion show that showcases the latest designs. Many people are already wearing their computers, and making use of this mobile technology to read e-mail while waiting in lines or even studying their notes for the next exam. What do you think? Will Americans someday grab their keys and their computers before they leave the house? Will your computer one day be housed in your jacket?

How does *Computing Essentials* reinforce key concepts?

Visual Chapter Summaries

These summaries appear in at least two pages at the end of each chapter. Using a columnar arrangement, major concepts are presented by graphics followed by detailed text summaries, providing a summary of key concepts and terms in an engaging and meaningful way.

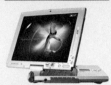

VISUAL SUMMARY
THE SYSTEM UNIT

SYSTEM UNIT

System unit (system cabinet or chassis) contains electronic components. Four basic types are: **desktop** (tower models positioned vertically), **notebook**, **tablet PC** (convertible and slate), and **handheld**. **PDA** (personal digital assistant) most widely used handheld computer.

Electronic Representation
Our voices create continuous **analog** signals. A conversion to **digital** signals is necessary before processing. Data and instructions can be represented electronically with a **two-state** or **binary** system of numbers (0 and 1). Each 0 or 1 is called a **bit**. A **byte** consists of eight bits and represents one character.

Binary Coding Schemes
Binary coding schemes convert binary data into characters. Three such schemes are:
- **ASCII**—the most widely used for microcomputers.
- **EBCDIC**—developed by IBM; used primarily by large computers.
- **Unicode**—16-bit code; designed to support international languages like Chinese and Japanese.

SYSTEM BOARD

The **system board** (main board or motherboard) connects all system components and allows input and output devices to communicate with the system unit. It is a flat circuit board covered with these electronic components:
- **Sockets** provide connection points for chips (silicon chips, semiconductors, integrated circuits). Chips mounted on carrier packages.
- **Slots** provide connection points for specialized cards or circuit boards.
- **Bus lines** provide pathways to support communication.

A Look to the Future

Information Overload

Have you ever questioned the value of technology? Has it really helped us and made us more productive? Is it possible that the various devices intended to increase our productivity have actually had the opposite effect?

E-mail, cell phones, notebook computers, and the Web are great. They allow us to communicate, work almost anywhere, and have access to vast amounts of data. However, unless we are careful, they can create "information overload" and have a negative effect on our ability to get work done.

Several recent studies have found that e-mail is the major source of information overload. It was recently reported that a typical knowledge worker in a large corporation sends and receives over 100 e-mail messages a day. Furthermore, the study concluded that the majority of these messages are not necessary. Here are some tips to control e-mail overload:

- **Be selective.** Look first at the subject line in an e-mail—read only those of direct and immediate interest to you. Look next at the sender line—read only those from people important to you; postpone or ignore the others.

- Remove. After reading an e-mail, respond if necessary; then either file it in the appropriate folder or delete it.
- Protect. Limit your e-mail by giving your address only to those who need it.
- Be brief. When responding, be concise and direct.
- Stop spam. Spam is unwanted e-mail advertisements. Avoid mailing lists, complain to those who send spam, and ask to have your name removed from their mailing list.
- Don't respond. You do not have to respond to an e-mail. Be selective; respond only to those worthy of your time.

Is information overload part of your future? If you are like today's busy executives, it probably will be. Don't let it get you down!

─── USING (IT) AT DVD DIRECT—A CASE STUDY ───

INFORMATION SYSTEMS AT DVD DIRECT

DVD Direct, a factitious organization, is an entirely Web-oriented movie rental business. Unlike traditional movie rental businesses like Blockbuster, DVD Direct conducts all business over the Web at its Web storefront. For a monthly fee, their customers are able to order up to three movies at a time from a listing posted at the company Web site. The movies the customers select are delivered to them on DVD disks by mail within three working days. After viewing, customers return one or more disks by mail. They are allowed to keep the disks as long as they wish but can never have more than three disks in their possession at one time.

Although in operation for only three years, DVD Direct has experienced rapid growth. To help manage and to accelerate this growth, the company has just hired Alice, a recent college graduate. To follow Alice on her first day and to learn about DVD Direct's information systems, consult your Computing Essentials CD or visit us on the Web at www.olearyseries.com/CE06 and select DVD Direct and then select Information Systems at DVD Direct from Tim's Toolbox.

CD icon here

Using IT at DVD Direct—A Case Study

Beginning in Chapter 11 and continuing through Chapter 15, Using IT at DVD Direct—A Case Study is an up-close look at what you might expect to find on the job in the real world. You will follow Alice, a recent college graduate hired as a marketing analyst, as she navigates her way through Accounting, Marketing, Production, Human Resources and Research, gathering and processing data to help manage and accelerate the growth of the three-year-old company. This case study is supported with end-of-chapter exercises and the *Computing Essentials* CD.

▼ CONCEPT CHECK
- ▶ What is a bus and what is its function?
- ▶ What are ports? What do they do? Describe four standard ports.
- ▶ What is a power supply unit? What is an AC adaptor?

Concept Check

Located at points throughout each chapter, the Concept Check cues you to note which topics have been covered and to self-test your understanding of the material.

How does *Computing Essentials* help you to evaluate your knowledge of the material in each chapter?

Chapter Review

Following the Visual Summary, the chapter Review includes material designed to review and reinforce chapter content. It includes a **Key Terms List** that reiterates the terms presented in the chapter, a **Crossword Puzzle** to challenge your understanding of the chapter material, **Multiple Choice** questions to help test your recall of information presented in the chapter. **Matching** exercises to test your recall of terminology presented in the chapter, and **Open-Ended** questions or statements to help review your understanding of the key concepts presented in the chapter.

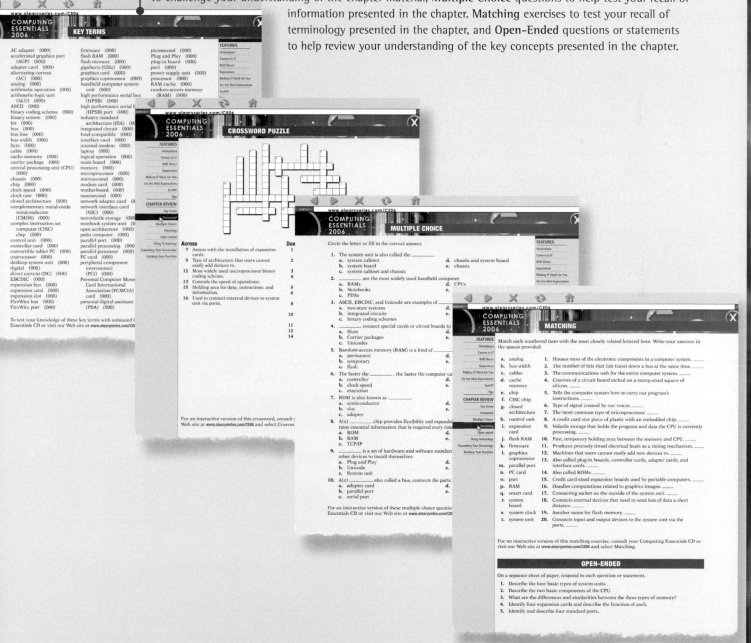

How does *Computing Essentials* encourage you to develop and utilize critical thinking skills?

Using Technology

In each chapter, Using Technology presents two questions designed to help you gain a better understanding of how technology is being used today. One question typically relates the chapter's Making IT Work for You topics. The other question focuses on interesting applications of technology that relate directly to you. Topics include: Online Auctions, Online Personal Information Managers, and Desktop and Notebook Computers.

Expanding Your Knowledge

In each chapter, Expanding Your Knowledge presents two questions that help you gain a deeper understanding of select topics. Typically, one question relates to a topic contained on your *Computing Essentials* CD, such as How Instant Messaging Works, How Streaming Media Works, and How Virus Protection Works. The other question in Expanding Your Knowledge typically relates to Web research into carefully selected topics including robotics, multimedia, HDTV, and Internet hard drives.

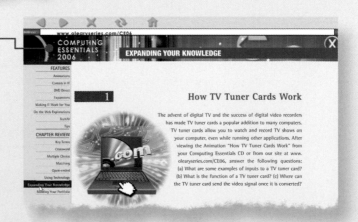

How does *Computing Essentials* help you create a portfolio that demonstrates your knowledge of technology?

Building Your Portfolio

The first question in Building Your Portfolio relates to key technologies. Topics include electronic commerce, artificial intelligence, Linux, microprocessors, digital input, and firewalls. The second question in Building Your Portfolio relates to security, privacy, and ethical issues. The issues presented include: HTML source code, antitrust legislation, processor serial numbers, CD-R and music files, and electronic monitoring. One objective of the Building Your Portfolio feature is to help you develop critical thinking and writing skills. Another objective is to help you create written documents recording your technology knowledge. A third objective is to help you recognize, understand, and analyze key privacy, security, and ethical issues relating to technology.

How do the *Computing Essentials* Interactive Web site and CD that accompany *Computing Essentials* work with the text to enhance learning?

Computing Essentials Interactive

Throughout the book you will find numerous references to *Computing Essentials* Interactive. This feature provides a variety of interesting and valuable reference materials. For your convenience, you can access these materials either from your *Computing Essentials* CD or from our Web site at www.olearyseries.com/CE06. Some of the features are Animations, Expansions, and Videos as discussed below.

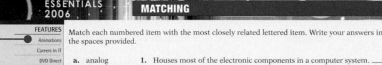

Address: www.olearyseries.com/CE06

COMPUTING ESSENTIALS 2006

MATCHING

FEATURES
- Animations
- Careers in IT
- DVD Direct
- Expansions
- Making IT Work for You
- On the Web Explorations
- Videos
- Tips

CHAPTER REVIEW
- Key Terms
- Crossword
- Multiple Choice
- Matching
- Open-ended
- Using Technology
- Expanding Your Knowledge
- Building Your Portfolio

Match each numbered item with the most closely related lettered item. Write your answers in the spaces provided.

a. analog
b. bus width
c. cables
d. cache memory
e. chip
f. CISC chip
g. closed architecture
h. control unit
i. expansion card
j. flash RAM
k. firmware
l. graphics coprocessor
m. parallel port
n. PC card
o. port
p. RAM

1. Houses most of the electronic components in a computer system. _____
2. The number of bits that can travel down a bus at the same time. _____
3. The communications web for the entire computer system. _____
4. Consists of a circuit board etched on a stamp-sized square of silicon. _____
5. Tells the computer system how to carry out program's instructions. _____
6. Type of signal created by our voices. _____
7. The most common type of microprocessor. _____
8. A credit card size piece of plastic with an embedded chip. _____
9. Volatile storage that holds the program and data the CPU is currently processing. _____
10. Fast, temporary holding area between the memory and CPU. _____
11. Produces precisely timed electrical beats as a timing mechanism. _____
12. Machines that users cannot easily add new devices to. _____
13. Also called plug-in boards, controller cards, adapter cards, and interface cards. _____
14. Also called ROMs. _____
15. Credit card-sized expansion boards used by portable computers. _____
    Handle: tions   graphics images.

Animations

Numerous Animations depicting how select technologies work and how they are used are provided. Animations cover such topics as digital video cameras, virus protection programs, and Spyware.

Expansions

The coverage of several critical topics from the book has been expanded. These Expansions include digital video editing, virtual memory, and identity theft.

Videos

Several current and interesting Videos are provided. Video topics include identity theft, cyber crime, and Internet scams.

Computing Essentials

2006
Complete Edition

COMPETENCIES

After you have read this chapter, you should be able to:

1 **Explain the five parts of an information system: people, procedures, software, hardware, and data.**

2 **Distinguish between system software and application software.**

3 **Discuss the three kinds of system software programs.**

4 **Distinguish between basic and specialized application software.**

5 **Identify the four types of computers and the four types of microcomputers.**

6 **Describe the different types of computer hardware including the system unit, input, output, storage, and communication devices.**

7 **Define data and describe document, worksheet, database, and presentation files.**

8 **Explain computer connectivity, the wireless revolution, and the Internet.**

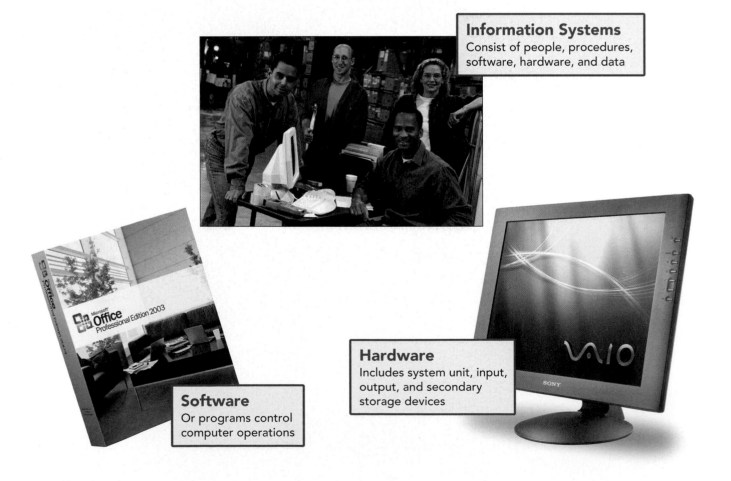

Information Systems
Consist of people, procedures, software, hardware, and data

Software
Or programs control computer operations

Hardware
Includes system unit, input, output, and secondary storage devices

Just as the Internet and the Web have affected all of us, they have affected computer technology as well. Today, communication links to the Internet are a common feature of almost all computer systems. Information technology (IT) is a modern term that describes this combination of traditional computer and communication technologies.

The purpose of this book is to help you become competent with computer technology. **Computer competency** refers to acquiring computer-related skills. These skills are indispensable tools for today. They include how to efficiently and effectively use popular application packages and the Internet.

In this chapter, we first present an overview of an information system: people, procedures, software, hardware, and data. It is essential to understand these basic parts and how connectivity through the Internet and the Web expands the role of information technology in our lives. In subsequent chapters, we will describe these parts of an information system in detail.

Fifteen years ago, most people had little to do with computers, at least directly. Of course, they filled out computerized forms, took computerized tests, and paid computerized bills. But the real work with computers was handled by specialists—programmers, data entry clerks, and computer operators.

Then microcomputers came along and changed everything. Today it is easy for nearly everybody to use a computer.

- Microcomputers are common tools in all areas of life. Writers write, artists draw, engineers and scientists calculate—all on microcomputers. Students and businesspeople do all this, and more.
- New forms of learning have developed. People who are homebound, who work odd hours, or who travel frequently may take courses on the Web. A college course need not fit within the usual time of a quarter or a semester.
- New ways to communicate, to find people with similar interests, and to buy goods are available. All kinds of people are using electronic mail, electronic commerce, and the Internet to meet and to share ideas and products.

What about you? How are you using information technology? Many interesting and practical uses have recently surfaced to make our personal lives richer and more entertaining. These applications range from recording digital video clips to creating personalized Web sites.

To be competent with IT, you need to know the five parts of an information system: people, procedures, software, hardware, and data. Additionally, you need to understand connectivity, the wireless revolution, the Internet, and the Web and to recognize the role of information technology in your personal and professional life.

Wireless revolution is dramatically affecting communications and computing

INFORMATION SYSTEMS

An information system has five parts: people, procedures, software, hardware, and data. Connectivity allows computers to connect and share information, thereby greatly expanding the capability and usefulness of an information system.

When you think of a microcomputer, perhaps you think of just the equipment itself. That is, you think of the monitor or the keyboard. Yet, there is more to it than that. The way to think about a microcomputer is as part of an information system. An **information system** has five parts: *people, procedures, software, hardware,* and *data.* (See Figure 1-1.)

- **People:** It is easy to overlook people as one of the five parts of an information system. Yet this is what microcomputers are all about—making **people, end users** like you, more productive.
- **Procedures:** The rules or guidelines for people to follow when using software, hardware, and data are **procedures.** These procedures are typically documented in manuals written by computer specialists. Software and hardware manufacturers provide manuals with their products. These manuals are provided either in printed or electronic form.
- **Software:** A **program** consists of the step-by-step instructions that tell the computer how to do its work. **Software** is another name for a program or programs. The purpose of software is to convert **data** (unprocessed facts) into **information** (processed facts). For example, a payroll program would instruct the computer to take the number of hours you worked in a week (data) and multiply it by your pay rate (data) to determine how much you are paid for the week (information).

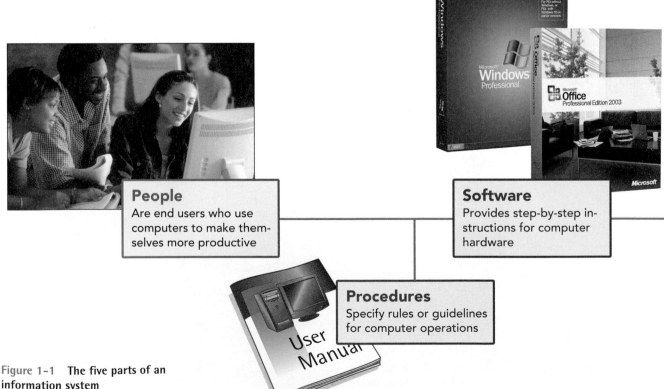

People
Are end users who use computers to make themselves more productive

Software
Provides step-by-step instructions for computer hardware

Procedures
Specify rules or guidelines for computer operations

Figure 1–1 **The five parts of an information system**

- **Hardware:** The equipment that processes the data to create information is called **hardware.** It includes the keyboard, mouse, monitor, system unit, and other devices. Hardware is controlled by software.
- **Data:** The raw, unprocessed facts, including text, numbers, images, and sounds, are called data. Processed, data yields information. Using the previous example, the data (number of hours worked and pay rate) are processed (multiplied) to yield information (weekly pay).

Almost all of today's computer systems add an additional part to the information system. This part, called **connectivity,** allows computers to connect and to share information. These connections, including Internet connections, can be by telephone lines, by cable, or through the air. Connectivity allows users to greatly expand the capability and usefulness of their information systems.

In large computer systems, there are specialists who write procedures, develop software, and capture data. In microcomputer systems, however, end users often perform these operations. To be a competent end user, you must understand the essentials of **information technology (IT),** including software, hardware, and data.

▼ CONCEPT CHECK

▶ What are the five parts of an information system?

▶ What is the difference between data and information?

▶ What is connectivity?

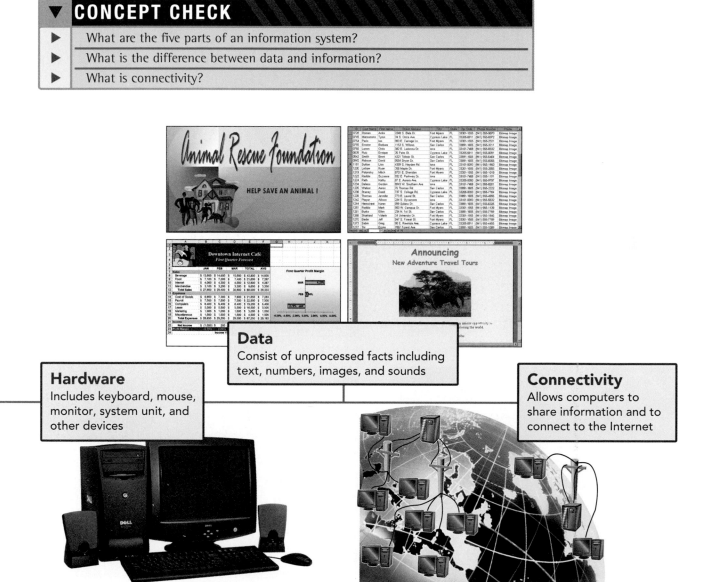

Data
Consist of unprocessed facts including text, numbers, images, and sounds

Hardware
Includes keyboard, mouse, monitor, system unit, and other devices

Connectivity
Allows computers to share information and to connect to the Internet

PEOPLE

Although easy to overlook, people are surely the most important part of any information system. Our lives are touched every day by computers and information systems. Many times the contact is direct and obvious, such as when we create documents using a word processing program or when we connect to the Internet. Other times, the contact is not as obvious. Consider just the four examples in Figure 1-2.

Throughout this book you will find a variety of features designed to help you become computer competent and knowledgeable. These features include Making IT Work for You, Tips, and the Computing Essential CD.

- **Making IT Work for You.** In the chapters that follow, you will find Making IT Work for You features that present interesting and practical IT applications. Using a step-by-step procedure, you are provided with specific instructions on how to use each application. Figure 1-3 presents a list of these applications.

Figure 1–2 Computers in entertainment, business, education, and medicine

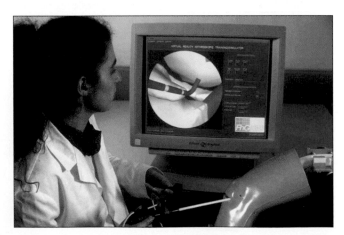

INFORMATION TECHNOLOGY TOPICS

Information technology touches our lives every day in a personal way. Many interesting and practical uses of IT have recently surfaced to make our lives richer and more entertaining. In the following chapters, you will find these applications presented in detail.

 Blocking Spam Are you tired of unwanted e-mail in your Inbox? Do you frequently spend valuable time sorting through junk e-mail? Installing spam blocking software can help. One of the best known is Spam Bully. See page 38.

 Speech Recognition Tired of using your keyboard to type term papers? Have you ever thought about using your voice to control application software? Perhaps speech recognition is just what you are looking for. See page 62.

 Digital Video Editing Do you want to make your own movie? Would you like to edit some home movies and distribute them to family and friends on DVDs? It's easy with the right equipment and software. See page 100.

 Virus Protection and Internet Security Worried about computer viruses? Did you know that others could be intercepting your private e-mail? It is even possible for them to gain access and control of your computer system. Fortunately, Internet security suites are available to help ensure your safety while you are on the Internet. See page 134.

 TV Tuner Cards and Video Clips Want to watch your favorite television program while you work? Perhaps you would like to include a video clip from a television program or from a DVD in a class presentation. It's easy using a TV tuner card. See page 162.

 Web Cams and Instant Messaging Do you enjoy chatting with your friends? Are you working on a project and need to collaborate with others in your group? What if you could see and hear your group online? Perhaps instant messaging is just what you're looking for. See page 188.

 Music from the Internet Did you know that you can use the Internet to locate music, download it to your computer, and create your own compact discs? All it takes is the right software, hardware, and a connection to the Internet. See page 222.

 Home Networking Computer networks are not just for corporations and schools anymore. If you have more than one computer, you can use a wireless home network to share files and printers, to allow multiple users access to the Internet at the same time, and to play interactive computer games. See page 252.

 Spyware Removal Are you concerned about maintaining your privacy while you are surfing the Web? Did you know that programs known as spyware could be monitoring your every move? Fortunately, these programs are relatively easy to detect and remove. See page 280.

 Job Opportunities Did you know that you can use the Internet to find a job? You can browse through job openings, post your resume, and even use special programs that will search for the job that's just right for you. See page 440.

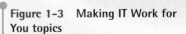

Figure 1–3   Making IT Work for You topics

TIPS

- **Controlling spam.** Do you get a lot of unwanted e-mail advertisements? Americans receive over 200 billion spam e-mails every year. There are some basic steps that you can take to keep your inbox spam-free. See page 35.
- **Online shopping.** Have you ever bought anything online? If not, it's likely that in the future you will join the millions who have. Consider a few guidelines to make your shopping easier and safer. See page 43.
- **Creating and updating Web sites.** Are you thinking about creating your own Web site? Perhaps you already have one and would like to spruce it up a bit. Here are a few suggestions that might help. See page 105.
- **Improving slow computer operations.** Does your computer seem to be getting slower and slower? Consider a few suggestions that might add a little zip to your current system. See page 160.
- **Improving hard disk performance.** Does your internal hard-disk drive run a lot and seem slow? Are you having problems with lost or corrupted files? To clean up the disk and speed up access, consider defragging. See page 216.
- **Protecting your privacy.** Are you concerned about your privacy while on the Web? Consider some suggestions for protecting your identity online. See page 278.

Figure 1-4 Selected Tips

- **Tips.** We all can benefit from a few tips or suggestions. Throughout this book you will find numerous Tips ranging from the basics of keeping your computer system running smoothly to how to protect your privacy while surfing the Web. For a partial list of the Tips presented in the following chapters, see Figure 1-4. For a complete list, select Tips from your Computing Essentials CD or from our Web site at www.olearyseries.com/CE06.
- **Computing Essentials CD.** Throughout this book you will find numerous references to this CD. It contains videos, animations, tips, career information, and a variety of test preparation activities including flash cards, crosswords, and self tests. (See Figure 1-5.)

Figure 1-5 The Computing Essentials CD

SOFTWARE

> There are two kinds of software: system software and application software. System software includes operating systems, utilities, and device drivers. Application software is categorized as basic and specialized.

Software, as we mentioned, is another name for programs. Programs are the instructions that tell the computer how to process data into the form you want. In most cases, the words software and programs are interchangeable. There are two major kinds of software—*system software* and *application software*. You can think of application software as the kind you use. Think of system software as the kind the computer uses.

SYSTEM SOFTWARE

The user interacts primarily with application software. **System software** enables the application software to interact with the computer hardware. System software is "background" software that helps the computer manage its own internal resources.

System software is not a single program. Rather it is a collection of programs, including the following:

- **Operating systems** are programs that coordinate computer resources, provide an interface between users and the computer, and run applications. Windows XP and the Mac OS X are two of the best-known operating systems for today's microcomputer users. (See Figure 1-6.)

- **Utilities,** also known as **service programs,** perform specific tasks related to managing computer resources. For example, the Windows utility called Disk Defragmenter locates and eliminates unnecessary file fragments and rearranges files and unused disk space to optimize computer operations.

- **Device drivers** are specialized programs designed to allow particular input or output devices to communicate with the rest of the computer system.

APPLICATION SOFTWARE

Application software might be described as end user software. These programs can be categorized as either *basic* or *specialized applications*.

Basic applications, or **general-purpose applications** are widely used in nearly all career areas. They are the kinds of programs you have to know to be considered computer competent. One of these basic applications is a browser to

Figure 1-6   Windows and Mac operating systems

TIPS Have you used the Internet? If so, then you probably already know how to use a browser. For those of you who do not, here are a few tips to get you started.

1. **Start browser.** Typically, all you need to do is double-click the browser's icon on the desktop.
2. **Enter URL.** In the browser's location box, type the URL (uniform resource locator, or address) of the Internet or Web location (site) that you want to visit.
3. **Press ENTER.** On your keyboard, press the ENTER key to connect to the site.
4. **Read and explore.** Once connected to the site, read the information displayed on your monitor. Using the mouse, move the pointer on the monitor. When the pointer changes from an arrow to a hand, click the mouse button to explore other locations.
5. **Close browser.** Once you are done exploring, click on your browser's CLOSE button.

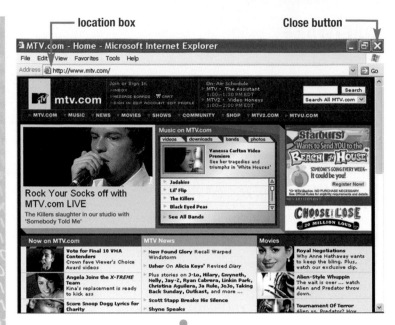

Figure 1-7 Internet Explorer browser

Type	Description
Browser	Connect to Web sites and display Web pages
Word processor	Prepare written documents
Spreadsheet	Analyze and summarize numerical data
Database management system	Organize and manage data and information
Presentation graphics	Communicate a message or persuade other people

Figure 1-8 Basic applications

navigate, explore, and find information on the Internet. (See Figure 1-7.) The two most widely used browsers are Microsoft's Internet Explorer and Netscape's Navigator. For a summary of the basic applications, see Figure 1-8.

Specialized applications, also known as **special-purpose applications,** include thousands of other programs that are more narrowly focused on specific disciplines and occupations. Some of the best known are graphics, audio, video, multimedia, Web authoring, and artificial intelligence programs.

CONCEPT CHECK

- Describe the two major kinds of software.
- Describe three types of system software programs.
- Define and compare basic and specialized applications.

HARDWARE

> Four types of computers are supercomputer, mainframe computer, minicomputer, and microcomputer. Desktop, notebook, tablet PC, and handheld are types of microcomputers. Microcomputer hardware consists of the system unit, input/output, secondary storage, and communications devices.

Computers are electronic devices that can follow instructions to accept input, process that input, and produce information. This book focuses principally on microcomputers. However, it is almost certain that you will come in contact, at least indirectly, with other types of computers.

TYPES OF COMPUTERS

There are four types of computers: supercomputers, mainframe computers, minicomputers, and microcomputers.

- **Supercomputers** are the most powerful type of computer. These machines are special high-capacity computers used by very large organizations. For example, NASA uses supercomputers to track and control space explorations.
- **Mainframe computers** occupy specially wired, air-conditioned rooms. Although not nearly as powerful as supercomputers, mainframe computers are capable of great processing speeds and data storage. For example, insurance companies use mainframes to process information about millions of policyholders.
- **Minicomputers,** also known as **midrange computers,** are refrigerator-sized machines. Medium-sized companies or departments of large companies typically use them for specific purposes. For example, production departments use minicomputers to monitor certain manufacturing processes and assembly line operations.
- **Microcomputers** are the least powerful, yet the most widely used and fastest-growing, type of computer. There are four types of microcomputers: *desktop, notebook, tablet PC,* and *handheld computers.* (See Figure 1-9.) **Desktop computers** are small enough to fit on top of or alongside a desk yet are too big to carry around. **Notebook computers,** also known as **laptop computers,** are portable, lightweight, and fit into most briefcases. A **tablet PC** is a type of notebook computer that accepts your handwriting. This input is digitized and converted to standard text that can be further processed by programs such as a word processor. **Handheld computers** are the smallest and are designed to fit into the palm of one hand. Also known as **palm computers,** these systems typically combine pen input, writing recognition, personal organizational tools, and communications capabilities in a very small package. **Personal digital assistants (PDA)** are the most widely used handheld computer.

MICROCOMPUTER HARDWARE

Hardware for a microcomputer system consists of a variety of different devices. See Figure 1-10 for a typical desktop system. This physical equipment falls into four basic categories: system unit, input/output, secondary storage, and communication. Because we discuss hardware in detail later in this book, here we will present just a quick overview of the four basic categories.

Desktop

Notebook

Handheld

Tablet PC

Figure 1-9   Microcomputers

- **System unit:** The **system unit,** also known as the **system cabinet** or **chassis,** is a container that houses most of the electronic components that make up a computer system. (See Figure 1-11.) Two important components of the system unit are the *microprocessor* and *memory.* The **microprocessor** controls and manipulates data to produce information. Many times the microprocessor is contained within a protective cartridge. **Memory,** also known as **primary storage** or **random access memory (RAM),** holds data and program instructions for processing the data. It also holds the processed information before it is output. Memory is sometimes referred to as **temporary storage** because its contents will typically be lost if the electrical power to the computer is disrupted.

- **Input/output: Input devices** translate data and programs that humans can understand into a form that the computer can process. The most common input devices are the **keyboard** and the **mouse. Output devices** translate the processed information from the computer into a form that humans can understand. The most common output devices are **monitors** or **video display screens** (see Figure 1-12) and **printers.**

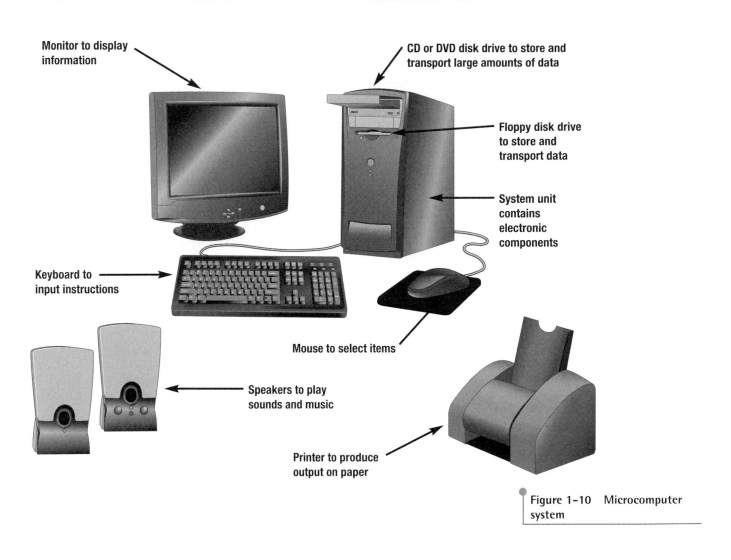

Monitor to display
information

CD or DVD disk drive to store and
transport large amounts of data

Floppy disk drive
to store and
transport data

System unit
contains
electronic
components

Keyboard to
input instructions

Mouse to select items

Speakers to play
sounds and music

Printer to produce
output on paper

Figure 1–10   Microcomputer
system

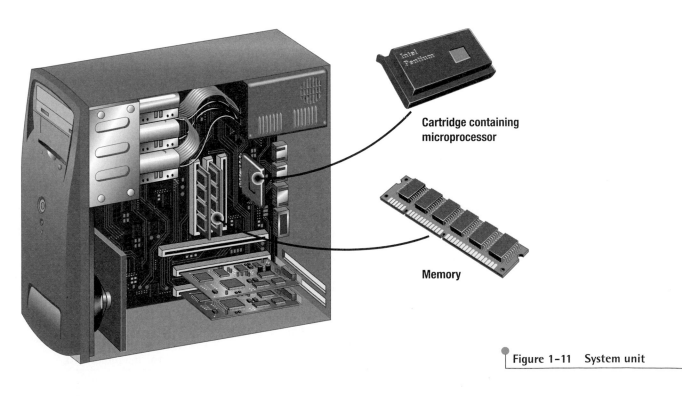

Cartridge containing
microprocessor

Memory

Figure 1–11   System unit

Information Technology, the Internet, and You

- **Secondary storage:** Unlike memory, **secondary storage devices** hold data and programs even after electrical power to the computer system has been turned off. The most important kinds of secondary media are *floppy, hard,* and *optical disks.* **Floppy disks** are widely used to store and transport data from one computer to another. (See Figure 1-13.) They are called floppy because data is stored on a very thin flexible, or floppy, plastic disk. **Hard disks** are typically used to store programs and very large data files. Using a rigid metallic platter, hard disks have a much greater capacity and are able to access information much faster than floppy disks. **Optical disks** use laser technology and have the greatest capacity. (See Figure 1-14.) The two basic types of optical disks are **compact discs (CDs)** and **digital versatile (or video) discs (DVDs).**

- **Communication:** At one time, it was uncommon for a microcomputer system to communicate with other computer systems. Now, using **communication devices,** a microcomputer can communicate with other computer systems located as near as the next office or as far away as halfway around the world using the Internet. The most widely used communication device is a **modem**, which modifies telephone communications into a form that can be processed by a computer. Modems also modify computer output into a form that can be transmitted across standard telephone lines.

▼ CONCEPT CHECK

▶ What are the four types of computers?

▶ Describe the four types of microcomputers.

▶ Describe the four basic categories of microcomputer hardware.

Figure 1-12   Monitor

Figure 1-13   A 3½-inch floppy disk

Figure 1-14   An optical disk

> Data is unprocessed facts. Processing data creates information. Four common file types are document, worksheet, database, and presentation.

Data is raw, unprocessed facts, including text, numbers, images, and sounds. As we have mentioned earlier, processed data becomes information. When stored electronically in files, data can be used directly as input for the system unit.

Four common types of files (see Figure 1-15) are:

- **Document files,** created by word processors to save documents such as memos, term papers, and letters.
- **Worksheet files,** created by electronic spreadsheets to analyze things like budgets and to predict sales.
- **Database files,** typically created by database management programs to contain highly structured and organized data. For example, an employee database file might contain all the workers' names, social security numbers, job titles, and other related pieces of information.
- **Presentation files,** created by presentation graphics programs to save presentation materials. For example, a file might contain audience handouts, speaker notes, and electronic slides.

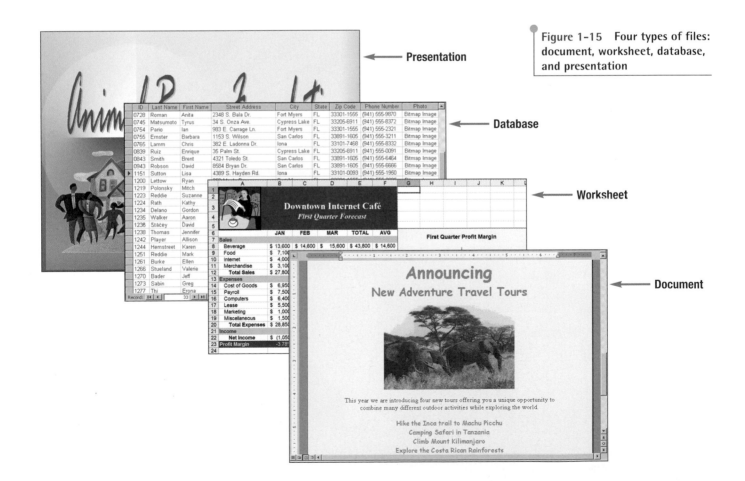

Figure 1-15   Four types of files: document, worksheet, database, and presentation

CONNECTIVITY, THE WIRELESS REVOLUTION, AND THE INTERNET

> Connectivity allows sharing of information worldwide. The wireless revolution is expected to alter communications and computer systems. Networks connect computers. The Internet is the largest network in the world.

Connectivity is the capability of your microcomputer to share information with other computers. The single most dramatic change in connectivity in the past five years has been the widespread use of mobile or wireless communication devices. For just a few of these devices, see Figure 1-16. Many experts predict that these wireless applications are just the beginning of the **wireless revolution,** a revolution that is expected to dramatically affect the way we communicate and use computer technology.

Central to the concept of connectivity is the **network** or **computer network.** A network is a communications system connecting two or more computers. The largest network in the world is the **Internet.** It is like a giant highway that connects you to millions of other people and organizations located throughout the world. The **Web,** also known as the **World Wide Web** or **WWW,** provides a multimedia interface to the numerous resources available on the Internet.

▼ CONCEPT CHECK

▶   Define data. List four common types of files.

▶   Define connectivity and the wireless revolution. What is a network?

Figure 1-16   Wireless communication devices

A Look to the Future

Using and Understanding Information Technology Means Being Computer Competent

The purpose of this book is to help you use and understand information technology. We want to help you become computer competent in today's world and to provide you with a foundation of knowledge so that you can understand how technology is being used today and anticipate how technology will be used in the future. This will enable you to benefit from four important information technology developments.

THE INTERNET AND THE WEB
The Internet and the Web are considered by most to be the two most important technologies for the 21st century. Understanding how to efficiently and effectively use the Internet to browse the Web, communicate with others, and locate information are indispensable computer competencies. These issues are presented in Chapter 2, The Internet, the Web, and Electronic Commerce.

POWERFUL SOFTWARE
The software now available can do an extraordinary number of tasks and help you in an endless number of ways. You can create professional looking documents, analyze massive amounts of data, create dynamic multimedia Web pages, and much more. Today's employers are expecting the people they hire to be able to effectively and efficiently use a variety of different types of software. Basic and specialized applications are presented in Chapters 3 and 4. System software is presented in Chapter 5.

POWERFUL HARDWARE
Microcomputers are now much more powerful than they used to be. New communication technologies such as wireless networks are dramatically changing the ways to connect to other computers, networks, and the Internet. However, despite the rapid change of specific equipment, their essential features remain unchanged. Thus, the competent end user should focus on these features. Chapters 6 through 9 explain what you need to know about hardware. A Buyer's Guide and an Upgrader's Guide are presented at the end of this book for those considering the purchase or upgrade of a microcomputer system.

SECURITY AND PRIVACY
What about people? Experts agree that we as a society must be careful about the potential of technology to negatively impact our personal privacy and security. Additionally, we need to be aware of potential physical and mental health risks associated with using technology. Finally, we need to be aware of negative effects on our environment caused by the manufacture of computer-related products. Thus, Chapter 10 explores each of these critical issues in detail.

ORGANIZATIONS
Almost all organizations rely on the quality and flexibility of their information systems to stay competitive. As a member or employee of an organization, you will undoubtedly be involved in these information systems. Therefore, you need to be knowledgeable about the different types of organizational information systems and how they are used. Accordingly, we devote Chapters 11 through 14 to detail what you need to know about information systems and how to develop, modify, and maintain these systems.

CHANGING TIMES
Are the times changing any faster now than they ever have? Most people think so. Whatever the answer, it is clear we live in a fast-paced age. The Evolution of the Computer Age section presented at the end of this book tracks the major developments since computers were first introduced.

After reading this book, you will be in a very favorable position compared with many other people in industry today. You will learn not only the basics of hardware, software, connectivity, the Internet, and the Web, but you will also learn the most current technology. You will be able to use these tools to your advantage.

INFORMATION TECHNOLOGY, THE INTERNET, AND YOU

INFORMATION SYSTEMS

The way to think about a microcomputer is to realize that it is one part of an **information system.** There are five parts of an information system:

1. **People** are an essential part of the system. The purpose of information systems is to make people, or **end users** like you, more productive.
2. **Procedures** are rules or guidelines to follow when using software, hardware, and data. They are typically documented in manuals written by computer professionals.
3. **Software (programs)** provides step-by-step instructions to control the computer to convert data into information.
4. **Hardware** consists of the physical equipment. It is controlled by software and processes data to create information.
5. **Data** consists of unprocessed facts including text, numbers, images, and sound. **Information** is data that has been processed by the computer.

Connectivity is an additional part to today's information systems. It allows computers to connect and share information. To be **computer competent,** end users need to understand **information technology (IT).**

PEOPLE

People are the most important part of an information system. People are touched hundreds of times daily by computers. This book contains several features to demonstrate how people just like you use computers. These features include:

- **Making IT Work for You** presents several interesting and practical applications. Topics include creating personal Web sites, using digital photography, and searching for job opportunities.
- **Tips** offer a variety of suggestions on such practical matters as how to improve slow computer performance and how to protect your privacy while on the Web.
- **Computing Essentials CD** contains videos, animations, tips, career information, and test preparation activities.

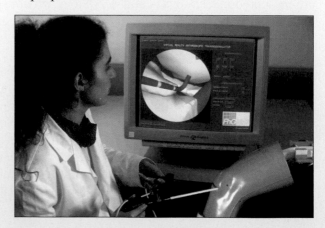

To prepare for your future as a competent end user, you need to understand the basic parts of an information system: people, procedures, software, hardware, and data. Also you need to understand connectivity through the Internet and the Web and to recognize the role of technology in your professional and personal life.

SOFTWARE

Software, or programs, consists of system and application software.

System Software

System software enables application software to interact with computer hardware. It consists of a variety of programs including:

- **Operating systems** coordinate resources, provide an interface for users and computer hardware, and run applications. Windows XP and Mac OS X are operating systems.
- **Utilities (service programs)** perform specific tasks to manage computer resources.
- **Device drivers** are specialized programs to allow input and output devices to communicate with the rest of the computer system.

Application Software

Application software includes basic and specialized applications.

- **Basic (general-purpose) applications** are widely used in nearly all career areas. Programs include browsers, word processors, spreadsheets, database management systems, and presentation graphics.
- **Specialized (special-purpose) applications** focus on specific disciplines and occupations. These programs include graphics, audio, video, multimedia, Web authoring, and artificial intelligence programs.

HARDWARE

Hardware is the physical equipment in an information system.

Types of Computers

Supercomputer, mainframe, minicomputer (midrange), and microcomputer are four types of computers. Microcomputers can be desktop, notebook (laptop), tablet PC, or handheld (palm). PDAs are the most widely used handheld computer.

Microcomputer Hardware

There are four basic categories of hardware devices:

- **System unit (system cabinet or chassis)** contains the electronic circuitry, including the microprocessor and memory (primary storage, random access memory [RAM], temporary storage).
- **Input/output devices** are translators between humans and computers. Input devices include the keyboard and mouse. Output devices include monitors (video display screens) and printers.
- **Secondary storage devices** store data and programs. Typical media include floppy, hard, and optical disks (CD and DVD).
- **Communication devices** connect the system unit to other computers and the Internet. A modem modifies signals for processing and communication.

DATA

Data is the raw facts unprocessed about something. Common file types include:

- **Document files** created by word processors.

- **Worksheet files** created by spreadsheet programs.

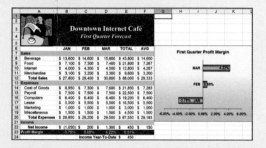

- **Database files** created by database management programs.

- **Presentation files** created by presentation graphics programs.

CONNECTIVITY AND THE INTERNET

Connectivity

Connectivity is a concept describing the ability of end users to tap into resources well beyond their desktops. **Computer networks (networks)** are connected computers that share data and resources.

The Wireless Revolution

The **wireless revolution** is the widespread and increasing use of mobile (wireless) communication devices.

Internet

The **Internet** is the world's largest computer network. The **Web,** also known as the **World Wide Web (WWW),** provides a multimedia interface to resources available on the Internet.

application software   (9)
basic application   (9)
chassis   (12)
communication device   (14)
compact disc (CD)   (14)
computer competency   (3)
computer network   (16)
connectivity   (5)
data   (4)
database file   (15)
device driver   (9)
desktop computer   (11)
digital versatile disc (DVD)   (14)
digital video disc (DVD)   (14)
document file   (15)
end user   (4)
floppy disk   (14)
general-purpose application   (9)
handheld computer   (11)
hard disk   (14)
hardware   (5)
information   (4)
information system   (4)
information technology (IT)   (5)
input device   (12)
Internet   (16)
keyboard   (12)
laptop computer   (11)
mainframe computer   (11)
memory   (12)
microcomputer   (11)
microprocessor   (12)
midrange computer   (11)
minicomputer   (11)

modem   (14)
monitor   (12)
mouse   (12)
network   (16)
notebook computer   (11)
operating system   (9)
optical disk   (14)
output device   (12)
palm computer   (11)
people   (4)
personal digital assistant (PDA)   (11)
presentation file   (15)
primary storage   (12)
printer   (12)
procedures   (4)
program   (4)
random access memory (RAM)   (12)
secondary storage device   (14)
service program   (9)
software   (4)
specialized application   (9)
special-purpose application   (9)
supercomputer   (11)
system cabinet   (12)
system software   (9)
system unit   (12)
tablet PC   (11)
temporary storage   (12)
utility   (9)
video display screen   (12)
Web   (16)
wireless revolution   (16)
worksheet file   (15)
World Wide Web (WWW)   (16)

FEATURES

Animations
Careers in IT
DVD Direct
Expansions
Making IT Work for You
On the Web Explorations
TechTV
Tips

CHAPTER REVIEW

Key Terms
Crossword
Multiple Choice
Matching
Open-ended
Using Technology
Expanding Your Knowledge
Building Your Portfolio

To test your knowledge of these key terms with animated flash cards, consult your Computing Essentials CD or visit our Web site at www.olearyseries.com/CE06 and select Key Terms.

Across

4 The most widely used handheld computer.

6 The world's largest computer network.

7 The physical equipment of a microcomputer.

10 Rules or guidelines to follow when using software, hardware, and data.

11 Provides step-by-step instructions to the computer.

12 Uses computers to become more productive.

14 Coordinates computer resources.

15 Created by database management programs.

16 The most essential part of an information system.

17 Contains the system's electronic circuitry.

Down

1 Modifies signals for processing.

2 Unprocessed facts.

3 Specialized programs that allow input and output devices to communicate.

5 Provides multimedia interface to the Internet.

8 Created by word processors.

9 Data that has been processed by the computer.

13 Type of microcomputer.

For an interactive version of this crossword, consult your Computing Essentials CD or visit our Web site at **www.olearyseries.com/CE06** and select Crossword.

COMPUTING ESSENTIALS 2006

MULTIPLE CHOICE

Circle the letter or fill in the correct answer.

1. Computer _____ refers to acquiring computer related skills.
   a. competency
   b. aware
   c. connectivity
   d. networked
   e. active

2. The _____ consist(s) of the following equipment: keyboard, mouse, monitor, system unit, and other devices.
   a. people
   b. procedures
   c. hardware
   d. system unit
   e. information

3. The _____ is one of the system software programs.
   a. word processor
   b. database management system
   c. operating system
   d. application software
   e. information system

4. Browsers, word processors, and spreadsheets are _____ applications.
   a. specialized
   b. basic
   c. advanced
   d. artificial intelligence
   e. multimedia

5. A _____ computer is another name for a notebook computer.
   a. PDA
   b. laptop
   c. midrange
   d. DVD
   e. handheld

6. _____ is sometimes referred to as temporary storage.
   a. PDA
   b. CD
   c. RAM
   d. DVD
   e. Secondary storage

7. _____ disks use laser technology.
   a. Concentric
   b. Layered
   c. Hard
   d. Floppy
   e. Optical

8. A _____ file might contain audience handouts, speaker notes, and electronic slides.
   a. document
   b. database
   c. worksheet
   d. presentation
   e. floppy disk

9. The term _____ refers to the widespread use of mobile communication devices.
   a. IT
   b. wireless revolution
   c. PDA
   d. RAM
   e. WWW

10. The largest network in the world is called the _____.
    a. Internet
    b. WWW
    c. World Wide Web
    d. Web
    e. DVD

For an interactive version of these multiple choice questions, consult your Computing Essentials CD or visit our Web site at www.olearyseries.com/CE06 and select Multiple Choice.

COMPUTING ESSENTIALS 2006

MATCHING

Match each numbered item with the most closely related lettered item. Write your answers in the spaces provided.

a. application software

b. computer network

c. connectivity

d. database files

e. document file

f. hard disks

g. information

h. input device

i. mainframe computer

j. microcomputers

k. optical disks

l. output device

m. primary storage

n. procedures

o. program

p. secondary storage device

q. supercomputers

r. system software

s. system unit

t. the Internet

1. Guidelines people follow when using software. _____
2. Consists of the step-by-step instructions that tell the computer how to do its work. _____
3. Although not the most powerful, this type of computer is capable of great processing speeds and data storage. _____
4. Allows sharing of information worldwide. _____
5. Software that enables the application software to interact with the computer hardware. _____
6. End user software. _____
7. The most powerful type of computer. _____
8. Data that has been processed through the computer. _____
9. Translates processed information from the computer into a form that humans can understand. _____
10. Container that houses most of the electronic components that make up a computer system. _____
11. The least powerful and most widely used type of computer. _____
12. Translates data and programs that humans can understand into a form that the computer can process. _____
13. Created by database management programs. _____
14. Holds data and programs even after electrical power to the system has been turned off. _____
15. Typically used to store programs and very large data files. _____
16. Uses laser technology. _____
17. Created by word processors to save documents. _____
18. Holds data and program instructions for processing data. _____
19. Communications system connecting two or more computers. _____
20. The largest network in the world. _____

For an interactive version of this matching exercise, consult your Computing Essentials CD or visit our Web site at **www.olearyseries.com/CE06** and select Matching.

OPEN-ENDED

On a separate sheet of paper, respond to each question or statement.

1. Explain the five parts of an information system. What part do people play in this system?
2. What is system software? What kinds of programs are included in system software?
3. Define and compare basic and specialized application software. Describe some different types of basic applications. Describe some types of specialized applications.
4. Describe the different types of computers. What is the most common type? What are the types of microcomputers?
5. What is connectivity? How are the wireless revolution and connectivity related? What is a computer network? What is the Internet? What is the Web?

Making a habit of keeping current with technology trends is a key to your success with information technology. In each of this book's chapters, the Using Technology feature will present two questions designed to help you gain a better understanding of how technology is being used today.

The first question in Using Technology typically relates to one of the Making IT Work for You topics. Some of these topics are listed below. Select the two that you find the most interesting and then describe why they are of interest to you and how you might use (or, are using) those applications.

- **Web Cams and Instant Messaging** Do you enjoy chatting with your friends? Have you ever worked on a group project and had problems getting everyone together for a meeting? Perhaps instant messaging is just what you're looking for. See page 207.

- **TV Tuner Cards and Video Clips** Want to watch your favorite television program while you work? Perhaps you would like to include a video clip from a television program or from a VHS tape in a class presentation. It's easy using a TV tuner card. See page 175.

- **Digital Video Editing** Want to make your own movie? Would you like to edit and distribute home movies to friends and family? It's easy with the right equipment and software. See page 117.

- **Home Networking** Computer networks are not just for corporations and schools anymore. If you have more than one computer, you can use a wireless home network to share files and printers, to allow multiple users access to the Internet at the same time, and to play interactive computer games. See page 267.

- **Job Opportunities** Did you know that you can use the Internet to find a job? You can browse through job openings, post your resume, and even use special programs that will search for the job that's just right for you. See page 453.

EXPANDING YOUR KNOWLEDGE

A deeper knowledge of select topics can greatly enhance your understanding of information technology. In each of the following chapters, the Expanding Your Knowledge feature presents two questions designed to help you gain a deeper understanding of select topics.

The first question in Expanding Your Knowledge typically relates to a topic contained on your **Computing Essentials CD** and at our Web site at www.olearyseries.com/CE06. Some of those topics are listed below. Select the two that you find the most interesting and then describe why they are of interest to you and why they are important.

- **How Instant Messaging Works** One of the fastest growing applications on the Internet is instant messaging. This extension to e-mail provides a way for friends and colleagues to communicate and share information from almost anywhere in the world. See page 56.

- **How Web-based Applications Work** Some predict that many organizations will be using Web-based applications in the near future. These organizations will not be required to own, install, upgrade, or store applications. Additionally, applications and application files can be accessed from almost anywhere in the world. See page 90.

- **How Computer Virus Protection Programs Work** Computer viruses are destructive and dangerous programs that can migrate through networks and operating systems. They often attach themselves to other programs, e-mail messages, and databases. It is essential to protect your computer systems from computer viruses. See page 145.

- **How Digital Cameras Work** While traditional cameras capture images on film, digital cameras capture images and convert them into a digital form. These images can be viewed immediately and saved to a disk or into the camera's memory. See page 208.

- **How Internet Telephones Work** Internet telephones offer a low-cost alternative to making long distance calls. Using the Internet telephone (or other appropriate audio input and output devices), the Internet, a special service provider, a sound card, and special software you can place long distance calls to almost anywhere in the world. See page 208.

- **How Wireless Home Networks Work** Wireless home networks are becoming very popular. They are easy to set up and use. They allow different computers to share resources including a common Internet connection and printer. See page 268.

- **How Web Bugs Work** Web bugs are often distributed through infected e-mail messages. One type of Web bug effectively wiretaps all communication between infected individuals. This bug secretly copies all outgoing e-mail messages and sends them to a predefined server on the Web. See page 304.

A portfolio typically consists of printed material that documents an individual's skills and knowledge. The process of creating a portfolio helps individuals to recognize and to organize their accomplishments. In the following chapters, the Building Your Portfolio feature presents two questions designed to help you create a portfolio to document your computer competency.

(a) One question relates to key technologies. Two of these technologies are listed below. Select one and then describe why it is of interest to you and why a prospective employer would be impressed with this knowledge.

- **Electronic Commerce** Electronic commerce is one of the most exciting Web applications. Different types include business to consumer (B2C), consumer to consumer (C2C), and business to business (B2B). Each of these has significant economic potential for nearly all organizations. See page 57.

- **Artificial Intelligence** A technology that promises widespread implications is artificial intelligence. This technology attempts to simulate human senses, thought processes, and actions. Many software manufacturing companies are producing programs with built-in artificial intelligence. See page 119.

(b) The other question relates to security, privacy, and ethical issues. Two of these issues are listed below. Select one and then describe why it is of interest to you and why it is an important issue.

- **HTML Source Code** A common way to create interesting and dynamic Web pages is to examine how professionals create their sites. Once connected to most Web sites, you can display the HTML source code used to create that site. Additionally, you can make a copy of the code and save it on your computer system. Some argue that this is unethical and illegal. Others argue that this is an acceptable way to create personal and professional sites. See page 119.

- **Electronic Monitoring** Surveillance of individuals occurs more frequently today than ever before. For example, the FBI has proposed the widespread use of a technology known as Carnivore to help them track terrorists. This technology supports widespread monitoring of individual Internet activity and e-mail. Privacy advocates claim that this would be an unnecessary and unneeded invasion of personal privacy. See page 209.

COMPETENCIES

After you have read this chapter, you should be able to:

1 **Discuss the origins of the Internet and the Web.**

2 **Describe how to access the Web using providers and browsers.**

3 **Discuss Internet communications, including e-mail, instant messaging, and discussion groups.**

4 **Describe search tools, including search engines and metasearch engines.**

5 **Discuss electronic commerce, including B2C, C2C, B2B, and security issues.**

6 **Describe these Web utilities: Telnet, FTP, plug-ins, and filters.**

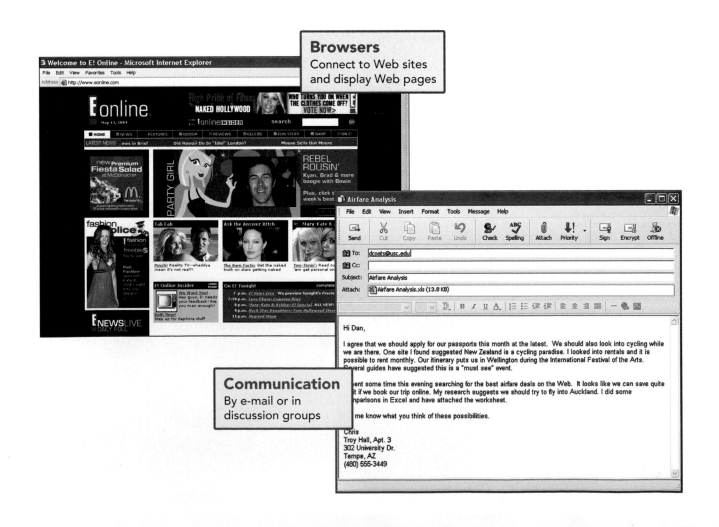

Browsers
Connect to Web sites and display Web pages

Communication
By e-mail or in discussion groups

CHAPTER

Want to communicate with a friend across town, in another state, or even in another country? Perhaps you would like to send a drawing, a photo, or just a letter. Looking for travel or entertainment information? Perhaps you're researching a term paper or exploring different career paths. Where do you start? For these and other information-related activities, try the Internet and the Web.

The Internet is often referred to as the Information Superhighway. In a sense, it is like a highway that connects you to millions of other people and organizations. Unlike typical highways that move people and things from one location to another, the Internet moves your ideas and information. Rather than moving through geographic space, you move through cyberspace—the space that moves ideas and information electronically. The Web provides an easy-to-use, exciting, multimedia interface to connect to the Internet and to access the resources available in cyberspace. It has become an everyday tool for all of us to use. For example, you can create personal Web sites to share information with others and use instant messaging to chat with friends and collaborate on group projects.

Competent end users need to be aware of the resources available on the Internet and the Web. Additionally, they need to know how to access these resources, to effectively communicate electronically, to efficiently locate information, to understand electronic commerce, and to use Web utilities.

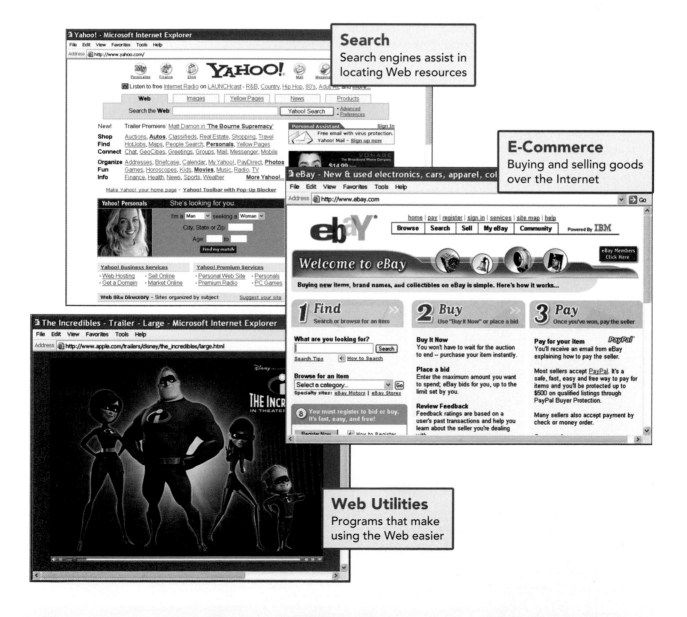

Search
Search engines assist in locating Web resources

E-Commerce
Buying and selling goods over the Internet

Web Utilities
Programs that make using the Web easier

THE INTERNET AND THE WEB

The Internet is a worldwide network. The Web, introduced at CERN, is a multimedia interface. Internet uses include communication, shopping, searching, entertainment, and education.

On the Web Explorations

Many individuals and institutions played a part in the development of the Internet and the Web. To learn more about the history of the Internet and Web visit our site at www.olearyseries.com/CE06 and select On the Web Explorations.

The **Internet,** or **Net,** was launched in 1969 when the United States funded a project that developed a national computer network called **Advanced Research Project Agency Network (ARPANET).** The Internet is a large network that connects together smaller networks all over the globe. The **Web,** also known as **WWW** and the **World Wide Web,** was introduced in 1992 at the **Center for European Nuclear Research (CERN)** in Switzerland. Prior to the Web, the Internet was all text—no graphics, animations, sound, or video. The Web made it possible to include these elements. It provided a multimedia interface to resources available on the Internet. From these early research beginnings, the Internet and the Web have evolved into one of the most powerful tools of the 21st century.

It is easy to get the Internet and the Web confused, but they are not the same thing. The Internet is the actual physical network. It is made up of wires, cables, and satellites. Being connected to this network is often described as being **online.** The Internet connects millions of computers and resources throughout the world. The Web is a multimedia interface to resources available on the Internet. Every day over a billion users from every country in the world use the Internet and the Web. What are they doing? The most common uses are the following:

- **Communicating** is by far the most popular Internet activity. You can exchange e-mail with your family and friends almost anywhere in the world. You can join and listen to discussions and debates on a wide variety of special-interest topics. You can even create your own personal Web page for friends and family to visit.
- **Shopping** is one of the fastest-growing Internet applications. You can visit individual stores or a **cybermall,** which provides access to a variety of different stores. You can window shop, look for the latest fashions, search for bargains, and make purchases. (See Figure 2-1.) You can purchase goods using checks, credit cards, or electronic cash.

Figure 2-1   Shopping over the Internet is one of the Web's fastest growing activities

- **Searching** for information has never been more convenient. You can access some of the world's largest libraries directly from your home computer. You can visit **virtual libraries,** search through their stacks, read selected items, and even check out books. You will also find the latest local, national, and international news. Most newspapers maintain an online presence and include interactive and multimedia presentations related to current news stories.

- **Entertainment** options are nearly endless. You can find music, movies, magazines, and computer games. You will find live concerts, movie previews, book clubs, and interactive live games. (See Figure 2-2.)

Figure 2-2 Entertainment site

- **Education** or **e-learning** is another rapidly emerging Web application. You can take classes on almost any subject. There are courses just for fun and there are courses for high school, college, and graduate school credit. Some cost nothing to take and others cost a lot.

The first step to using the Internet and Web is to get connected, or to gain access to the Internet.

▼ CONCEPT CHECK

▶ Describe how the Internet and the Web started.

▶ What is the difference between the Internet and the Web?

▶ List and describe five of the most common uses of the Internet and the Web.

ACCESS

Providers give us access to the Internet. National, regional, and wireless are three types of ISPs. Browsers provide access to Web resources.

The Internet and the telephone system are similar—you can connect a computer to the Internet much like you connect a phone to the telephone system. Once you are on the Internet, your computer becomes an extension of what seems like a giant computer—a computer that branches all over the world. When provided with a connection to the Internet, you can use a browser program to search the Web.

PROVIDERS

The most common way to access the Internet is through an **Internet service provider (ISP).** The providers are already connected to the Internet and provide a path or connection for individuals to access the Internet. Your college or university most likely provides you with free access to the Internet either through its local area networks or through a dial-up or telephone connection. There are also some companies that offer free Internet access.

Figure 2-3   America Online ISP

Commercial Internet service providers offer national, regional, and wireless service.

- **National service providers** like America Online (AOL) are the most widely used. They provide access through standard telephone connections. Users can access the Internet from almost anywhere within the country for a standard fee without incurring long-distance telephone charges. (See Figure 2-3.)

- **Regional service providers** also use telephone lines. Their service area, however, is smaller, typically consisting of several states. If users access the Internet from outside the regional area, they incur long-distance connection charges in addition to the service's standard fees.

- **Wireless service providers** do not use telephone lines. They provide Internet connections for computers with wireless modems and a wide array of wireless devices.

As we will discuss in Chapter 9, users connect to ISPs using one of a variety of connection technologies including **dial-up, DSL, cable,** and **wireless modems.** This creates a **client-server network.** The user's computer is the **client** that requests services from the provider's computer or **server.**

BROWSERS

Browsers are programs that provide access to Web resources. This software connects you to remote computers, opens and transfers files, displays text and images, and provides in one tool an uncomplicated interface to the Internet and Web documents. Browsers allow you to explore, or to **surf,** the Web by easily moving from one Web site to another. Two well-known browsers are Netscape Navigator and Microsoft Internet Explorer. (See Figure 2-4.)

For browsers to connect to resources, the **location** or **address** of the resources must be specified. These addresses are called **uniform resource locators (URLs).** All URLs have at least two basic parts. (See Figure 2-5.) The first part presents the protocol used to connect to the resource. As we will

Figure 2-4   Internet Explorer

protocol —
domain code —
http://www.mtv.com
— domain name

Figure 2-5   Two basic parts of a URL

discuss in Chapter 9, **protocols** are rules for exchanging data between computers. The protocol *http://* is the most widely used Web protocol. The second part presents the **domain name,** also know as the **top level domain,** it is the name of the server where the resource is located. In Figure 2-5 the server is identified as www.mtv.com. (Many URLs have additional parts specifying directory paths, file names, and pointers.) The last part of the domain name following the dot (.) is the **domain code.** It identifies the type of organization. For example, *.com* indicates a commercial site. The URL *http:// www.mtv.com* connects your computer to a computer that provides information about MTV.

Once the browser has connected to the Web site, a document file is sent back to your computer. This document contains **Hypertext Markup Language (HTML)** commands. The browser interprets the HTML commands and displays the document as a **Web page.** For example, when your browser first connects to the Internet, it opens up to a Web page specified in the browser settings. This page presents information about the site along with references and **hyperlinks** or **links** that connect to other documents containing related information—text files, graphic images, audio, and video clips. (See Figure 2-6.)

These documents may be located on a nearby computer system or on one halfway around the world. The computer that stores and shares these documents is called a **Web server.** The references appear as underlined and colored text and/or images on the Web page. To access the referenced material, all you do is click on the highlighted text or image. A connection is automatically made to the computer containing the material, and the referenced material appears on your display screen.

Web pages also can contain special programs called **applets** that are typically written in a programming language called **Java.** (Java and other programming languages will be presented in Chapter 14.) These programs can be downloaded quickly and run by most browsers. Java applets are widely used to add interest and activity to a Web site by presenting animation, displaying graphics, providing interactive games, and much more.

To learn more about browsers, consult your Computing Essentials CD or visit our site at www.olearyseries.com/CE06 and select Expansions.

Figure 2-6   MTV Web site

On the Web Explorations

Popup ads often appear while you surf the Web. They can be a real annoyance. There are many programs available to eliminate these ads. To learn more about getting rid of popup ads, visit our Web site at

www.olearyseries.com/CE06 and select On the Web Explorations.

▼ CONCEPT CHECK

▶   What is the function of an ISP? Describe three types of ISPs.

▶   What is the function of a browser?

▶   What are URLs, HTML, Web pages, hyperlinks, applets, and Java?

E-mail is the transmission of electronic messages, and it is the most popular Internet activity. Instant messaging extends e-mail to direct, live communication. Discussion groups include mailing lists, news groups, and chat groups.

As previously mentioned, communication is the most popular Internet activity, and its impact cannot be overestimated. At a personal level, friends and family can stay in contact with one another even when separated by thousands of miles. At a business level, electronic communication has become a standard, and many times preferred, way to stay in touch with suppliers, employees, and customers. The three most popular types of Internet communication are e-mail, instant messaging, and discussion groups.

E-MAIL

E-mail or **electronic mail** is the transmission of electronic messages over the Internet. At one time, e-mail consisted only of basic text messages. Now e-mail routinely includes graphics, photos, and many different types of file attachments. People all over the world send e-mail to each other. You can e-mail your family, your co-workers, and even your senator. All you need to send and receive e-mail is an e-mail account, access to the Internet, and an e-mail program. Two of the most widely used e-mail programs are Microsoft's Outlook Express and AOL's Netscape Mail.

A typical e-mail message has three basic elements: header, message, and signature. (See Figure 2-7.) The **header** appears first and typically includes the following information:

- **Addresses:** Addresses of the persons sending, receiving, and, optionally, anyone else who is to receive copies. E-mail addresses have two basic parts. (See Figure 2-8.) The first part is the user's name and the second part is the domain name, which includes the domain code. In our example e-mail, *dcoats* is Dan's user name. The server providing e-mail service for Dan is *usc.edu.* The domain code indicates that the provider is an educational institution.

- **Subject:** A one-line description, used to present the topic of the message. Subject lines typically are displayed when a person checks his or her mailbox.

- **Attachments:** Many e-mail programs allow you to attach files such as documents and worksheets. If a message has an attachment, the file name appears on the attachment line.

The letter or **message** comes next. It is typically short and to the point. Finally, the **signature line** provides additional information about the sender. Typically, this information includes the sender's name, address, and telephone number.

E-mail can be a valuable asset in your personal and professional life. However, like many other valuable technologies, there are drawbacks too. Americans receive billions of unwanted and unsolicited e-mails every year. This unwelcome mail is called **spam.** While spam is indeed a distraction and nuisance, it also can be dangerous. For example, **computer viruses** or destructive programs are often attached to unsolicited e-mail. Computer viruses and ways to protect against them will be discussed in Chapter 5.

In an attempt to control spam, anti-spam laws have been added to our legal system. This approach, however, has had minimal impact since over 50 percent

On the Web Explorations

Almost all ISPs and online service providers offer e-mail service to their customers. But you can get this service for free from several sources. To learn more about these free services, visit our site at:

www.olearyseries.com/CE06 and select On the Web Explorations.

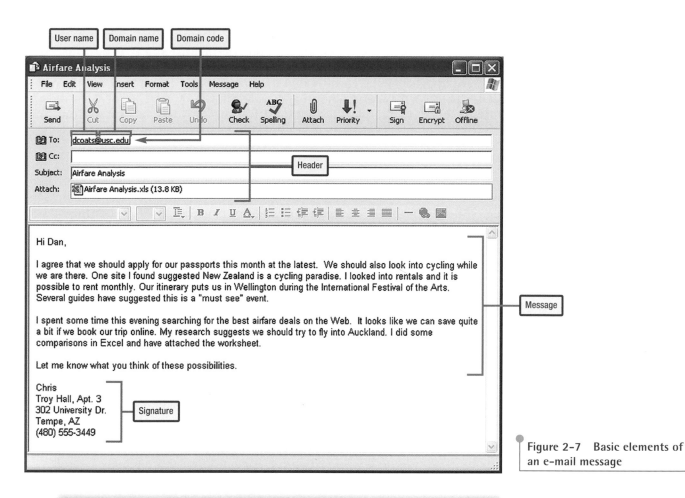

Figure 2-7 Basic elements of an e-mail message

Figure 2-8 Two parts of an e-mail address

Are you tired of sorting through an inbox full of spam? Americans receive over 200 billion spam e-mails every year. Here are a few simple tips to help ensure that your inbox is spam-free:

1 **Choose a complex address.** sally_smith@hotmail.com is much more likely to get spam than 4it3scoq2@hotmail.com. Consider using a more complicated, and less personal, user name.

2 **Keep a low profile.** Many spammers collect e-mail addresses from personal Web sites, chat rooms, and message boards. Use caution when handing out your address and be sure to read the privacy policy of a site before you hand over your address.

3 **Don't ever respond to spam.** Once you respond to spam, either in interest or to opt out of a list, you have confirmed the address is valid. Valid addresses are worth more to spammers, who then sell the address to others.

4 **Use ez-mail filter options.** Most e-mail programs have a filter option that screens incoming e-mail based on a set of preferences you choose. You can set up your inbox to accept only mail from certain addresses or to block mail from others.

5 **Use anti-spam.** There are plenty of programs available to help protect your inbox. For example, MailWasher provides an effective and free program available at www.mailwasher.com.

The Internet, the Web, and Electronic Commerce

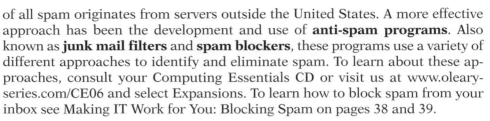

of all spam originates from servers outside the United States. A more effective approach has been the development and use of **anti-spam programs**. Also known as **junk mail filters** and **spam blockers**, these programs use a variety of different approaches to identify and eliminate spam. To learn about these approaches, consult your Computing Essentials CD or visit us at www.oleary-series.com/CE06 and select Expansions. To learn how to block spam from your inbox see Making IT Work for You: Blocking Spam on pages 38 and 39.

INSTANT MESSAGING

Instant messaging (IM) is an extension of e-mail that allows two or more people to contact each other via direct, live communication. To use instant messaging, you specify a list of **friends** (also known as **buddies** or **contacts**) and register with an instant messaging server. Whenever you connect to the Internet, special software informs your messaging server that you are online. In response, the server will notify you if any of your contacts are online. At the same time, it notifies your contacts that you are online. You can then send messages directly back and forth to one another. Many new instant messaging programs also include videoconferencing features, file sharing, and remote assistance. To see how Instant Messaging works, consult your Computing Essentials CD or visit us at www.olearyseries.com/CE06 and select Animations.

The most widely used instant messaging services are AOL's Instant Messenger, Microsoft's MSN Messenger, and Yahoo Messenger. One limitation, however, is that many instant messaging services do not support communication with other services. For example, at the time of this writing, a user registered with AOL cannot use AOL's Instant Messenger software to communicate with a user registered with Yahoo Messenger. Recently, however, some software companies have started providing **universal instant messenger** programs that overcome this limitation. For example, Gain, Odigo, and Trillian provide instant messaging services that do support communication with other services.

▼ CONCEPT CHECK

▶ Define e-mail. What are the three basic elements of a typical e-mail message?

▶ What is SPAM? What are anti-spam programs?

▶ Define instant messaging. What is a universal instant messenger?

DISCUSSION GROUPS

You can also use e-mail to communicate in **discussion groups** with people you do not know but with whom you wish to share ideas and interests. You can participate in forums and debates that range from general topics like current events and movies to specialized forums like computer troubleshooting and Hollywood animations. Discussion groups include mailing lists, newsgroups, and chat groups.

Description	Subscription Address
Music and bands	dbird@netinfo.com.au
Movies	moviereview@cuenet.com
Jokes	jokeaday.com
Travel	tourbus@listserv.aol.com

Figure 2-9 **Popular mailing lists**

- **Mailing lists** allow members to communicate by sending messages to a **list address.** Each message is then copied and sent via e-mail to every member of the mailing list. To participate in a mailing list, you must first subscribe by sending an e-mail request to the mailing list **subscription address.** (See Figure 2-9.) Once you are a member of a list, you can expect to receive e-mail from others on the list. You may find the number of messages to be overwhelming. If you want to cancel a mailing list, send an e-mail request to "unsubscribe" to the subscription address.

- **Newsgroups,** unlike mailing lists, use a special network of computers called the **UseNet.** Each of these computers maintains the newsgroup listing. There are over 10,000 different newsgroups organized into major topic areas that are further subdivided into subtopics. (See Figure 2-10.) Contributions to a particular newsgroup are sent to one of the computers on the UseNet. This computer saves the messages on its system and periodically shares all its recent messages with the other computers on the UseNet. Unlike mailing lists, a copy of each message is not sent to each member of a list. Rather, interested individuals check contributions to a particular newsgroup, reading only those of interest. There are thousands of newsgroups covering a wide variety of topic areas. (See Figure 2-11.)

Figure 2-10   Google Groups connects you to UseNet

- **Chat groups,** like IM, allow direct live communication. Unlike IM, chat groups typically connect individuals who have never met face-to-face. To participate, you join a chat group, select a **channel** or topic, and communicate live with others by typing words on your computer. Other members of your channel immediately see those words on their computers and can respond in the same manner. One popular chat service is called **Internet Relay Chat (IRC).** This software is available free from several locations on the Internet. Using the chat-client software, you log on to the server, select a channel or topic in which you are interested, and begin chatting. To participate, you need access to a server or computer that supports IRC. This is done using special chat-client software.

Description	Newsgroups
Aerobics fitness	misc.fitness.aerobic
Cinema	rec.arts.movies
Mountain biking	rec.bicycles.off-road
Music	rec.music.hip-hop
Clip art	alt.binaries.clip-art

Figure 2-11   Popular newsgroups

Before you submit a contribution to a discussion group, it is recommended that you observe or read the communications from others. This is called **lurking.** By lurking, you can learn about the culture of a discussion group. For example, you can observe the level and style of the discussions. You may decide that a particular discussion group is not what you were looking for—in which case, unsubscribe. If the discussions are appropriate and you wish to participate, try to fit into the prevailing culture. Remember that your contributions will likely be read by hundreds of people.

For a list of commonly used discussion group terms, see Figure 2-12.

Term	Description
Flaming	Insulting, putting down, or attacking
Lurking	Reading news but not joining in to contribute
RFD	Request for discussion
Saint	Someone who aids new users by answering questions
Thread	A sequence of ongoing messages on the same subject
Wizard	Someone who has comprehensive knowledge about a subject

Figure 2-12   Common discussion group terms

▼ CONCEPT CHECK

▶ What is a discussion group? Discuss mailing lists, newsgroups, and chat groups.

▶ Compare and contrast mailing lists and newsgroups.

▶ What is a chat group? What are channels?

MAKING IT WORK FOR YOU

BLOCKING SPAM

Are you tired of unwanted e-mail in your inbox? Do you frequently spend valuable time sorting through junk e-mail? Installing spam blocking software can help. One of the best known spam blockers is Spam Bully, available from www.spambully.com, which integrates with Microsoft Outlook. Once Spam Bully has been installed, the Spam Bully toolbar will be displayed each time Outlook is started.

Training the Software   Before Spam Bully can detect spam for you automatically, it needs to be trained to recognize unwanted messages. As you follow the steps below for several weeks, Spam Bully should become more and more accurate at categorizing your incoming e-mail and moving it to the correct folder automatically. After opening Outlook, you can begin training Spam Bully.

1 ● Select each spam message in your inbox and click the *Spam* button.

2 ● Open the Spam folder and review the new messages.

● For any nonspam message, select the message and click the *Not Spam* button to return it to your inbox.

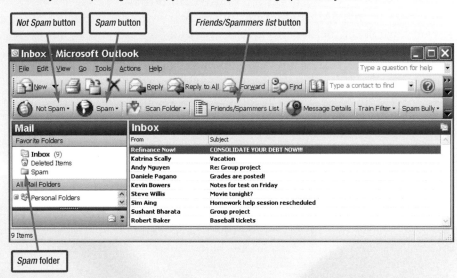

Specifying Friends and Spammers   To ensure that e-mail messages from certain senders are never accidentally categorized as spam, you can add them to a list of friends. Likewise, you can also maintain a list of addresses that should always be considered spam. To specify friends and spammers:

1 ● Click the *Friends/Spammers List* button to open the Email address lists.

2 ● Click within the Friends List to select it.

● To specify a friend, click the *Add* button and enter the friend's address.

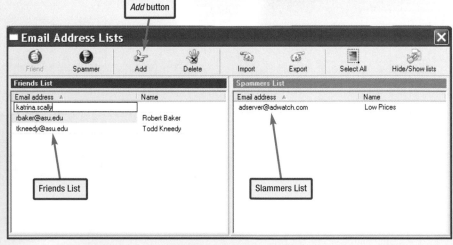

Messages from the Friends List will always be delivered to your inbox. Repeat the above procedures for the Spammers List to specify addresses for messages that should always be considered spam.

Sending Challenge Messages   Challenge messages increase the effectiveness of spam-blocking software. Unknown senders are required to respond to an automated e-mail with a password or phrase before their original message is delivered to you. This minimizes the chances that the e-mail came from a spam program. To enable challenge messages in Spam Bully:

1 ● Click the *Spam Bully* button, and select *Configure Spam Bully*.

2 ● Select *Customize Filter* from the list on the left.

● Check the *Send Challenge emails* box in the list on the right.

● Click OK.

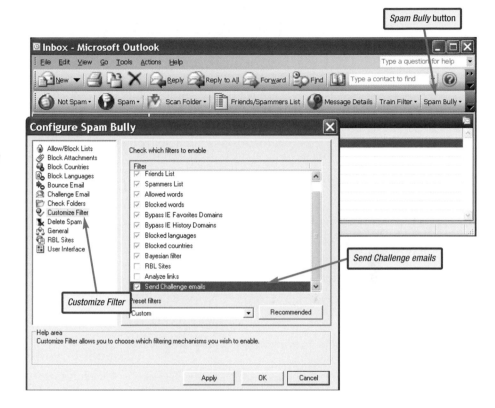

Spam-blocking programs are continually changing and some of the specifics presented in this Making IT Work for You may have changed. To learn about other ways to make information technology work for you, consult your Computing Essentials CD or visit us at www.oleary-series.com/CE06 and select Making IT Work for You.

> Search engines locate information. Metasearch engines submit search requests to several search engines simultaneously. Specialized search engines focus on subject-specific Web sites.

The Web can be an incredible resource, providing information on nearly any topic imaginable. Are you planning a trip? Writing an economics paper? Looking for a movie review? Trying to locate a long-lost friend? Information sources related to these questions, and much, much more are available on the Web.

With over 2 billion pages and more being added daily, the Web is a massive collection of interrelated pages. With so much available information, locating the precise information you need can be difficult. Fortunately, a number of organizations called **search services** or **search providers** operate Web sites that can help you locate the information you need. They maintain huge databases relating to information provided on the Web and the Internet. The information stored at these databases includes addresses, content descriptions or classifications, and keywords appearing on Web pages and other Internet informational resources. Special programs called **spiders,** or **Webcrawlers** continually look for new information and update the search services' databases. Additionally, search services provide special programs called search engines that you can use to locate specific information on the Web.

SEARCH ENGINES

Search engines are specialized programs that assist you in locating information on the Web and the Internet. To find information, you go to a search service's Web site and use its search engine. For example, see Figure 2-13 for Yahoo's search engine. This search engine, like most others, provides two different search approaches.

TIPS Are you going to use a search tool to locate some information? Here are a few tips that might help.

1 Start with the right approach. For general information, use a direct search. For specific information, use a key word search.

2 Be as precise as possible. Use specific key words that relate directly to the topic.

3 Use multiple words. Use quotation marks to identify key words.

4 Use Boolean operators. Typically, these include words such as "and," "not," "or."

5 Check your spelling. Misspelling is one of the most common problems.

6 Keep moving. Look only at the first page of search results. If necessary, try another search using different key words.

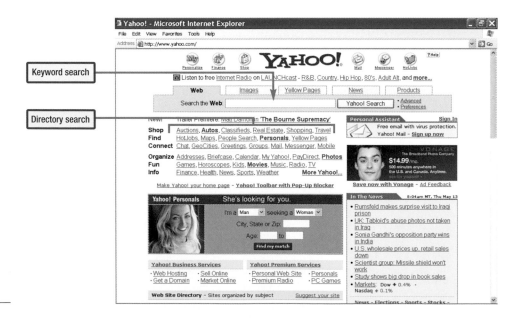

Figure 2-13 Yahoo's search engine provides keyword and directory search

- **Keyword search:** In a **keyword search,** you enter a keyword or phrase reflecting the information you want. The search engine compares your entry against its database and returns a list of **hits,** or sites that contain the keywords. Each hit includes a hyperlink to the referenced Web page (or other resource) along with a brief discussion of the information contained at that location. Many searches result in a large number of hits. For example, if you were to enter the keyword *travel,* you would get thousands of hits. Search engines order the hits according to those sites that most likely contain the information requested and present the list to you in that order, usually in groups of 10.

- **Directory search:** Most search engines also provide a directory or list of categories or topics such as Finance, Health, and News. In a **directory search,** also known as an **index search,** you select a category or topic that fits the information that you want. Another list of subtopics related to the topic you selected appears. You select the subtopic that best relates to your topic and another subtopic list appears. You continue to narrow your search in this manner until a list of Web sites appears. This list corresponds to the hit list previously discussed.

As a rule, if you are searching for general information, use the directory search approach. For example, to find general information about music, use a directory search beginning with the category Entertainment and then select the subtopic Music. If you are searching for specific information, use the keyword approach. For example, if you were looking for a specific music file, you would use a keyword search that includes the album title and/or the artist's name.

A recent study by the NEC Research Institute found that any one search engine includes only a fraction of the informational sources on the Web. Therefore, it is highly recommended that you use more than one search engine when researching important topics. See Figure 2-14 for a list of some of the most widely used search engines. Or, you could use a special type of search engine called a metasearch engine.

METASEARCH ENGINES

One way to research a topic is to visit the Web sites for several individual search engines. At each site, you would enter the search instructions, wait for the hits to appear, review the list, and visit selected sites. This process can be quite time-consuming and duplicate responses from different search engines are inevitable. Metasearch engines offer an alternative.

Metasearch engines are programs that automatically submit your search request to several search engines simultaneously. The metasearch engine receives the results, eliminates duplicates, orders the hits, and then provides the edited list to you. See Figure 2-15 for a list of several metasearch engines available on the Web. One of the best known is Dogpile, see Figure 2-16.

SPECIALIZED SEARCH ENGINES

Specialized search engines focus on subject-specific Web sites. Specialized sites can potentially save you time by narrowing your search. For a list of just a few selected specialized search engines, see Figure 2-17. For example, let's say you are researching a paper about the fashion industry. You could begin with a general search engine like Yahoo! Or you could go to a search engine that specializes specifically in fashion, such as infomat.com.

Search Service	Site
Alta Vista	www.altavista.com
Excite	www.excite.com
Google	www.google.com
Ask Jeeves	www.ask.com
Teoma	www.teoma.com
Yahoo!	www.yahoo.com

Figure 2-14 Search engines

Metasearch Service	Site
Dogpile	www.dogpile.com
Ixquick	www.ixquick.com
Mamma	www.mamma.com
MetaCrawler	www.metacrawler.com
ProFusion	www.profusion.com
Search	www.search.com
Vivisimo	www.vivisimo.com

Figure 2-15 Metasearch sites

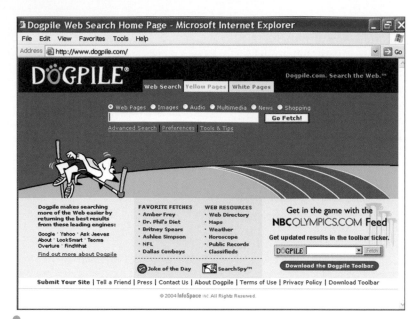

Figure 2-16 Dogpile search site

Topic	Site
Environment	www.eco-web.com
Fashion	www.infomat.com
History	www.historynet.com
Law	www.llrx.com/guide
Medicine	www.medsite.com

Figure 2-17 Select specialized search engines

▼ CONCEPT CHECK

▶ What is the difference between a search engine and a metasearch engine?

▶ What is a specialized search engine? When would a specialized search engine be useful?

ELECTRONIC COMMERCE

E-commerce is buying and selling over the Internet. B2C, C2C, and B2B are types of e-commerce. Web storefronts are B2C. Web auctions are C2C. The greatest challenge to e-commerce development is security.

Electronic commerce, also known as **e-commerce,** is the buying and selling of goods over the Internet. Have you ever bought anything over the Internet? If you have not, there is a very good chance that you will within the next year or two. Shopping on the Internet is growing rapidly and there seems to be no end in sight. Just like any other type of commerce, electronic commerce involves two parties: businesses and consumers. There are three basic types of electronic commerce:

- **Business-to-consumer (B2C)** involves the sale of a product or service to the general public or end users. Oftentimes this arrangement eliminates the middleman by allowing manufacturers to sell directly to customers. Other times, existing retail stores use B2C e-commerce to create a presence on the Web as another way to reach customers.

- **Consumer-to-consumer (C2C)** involves individuals selling to individuals. This often takes the form of an electronic version of the classified ads or an auction. Goods are described and interested buyers contact sellers to negotiate prices. Unlike traditional sales via classified ads and auctions, buyers and sellers typically never meet face-to-face.

- **Business-to-business (B2B)** involves the sale of a product or service from one business to another. This is typically a manufacturer–supplier relationship. For example, a furniture manufacturer requires raw materials such as wood, paint, and varnish. In B2B e-commerce, manufacturers electronically place orders with suppliers and many times payment is made electronically. The most popular B2B e-commerce is for automobile parts, electronics including computers, and health care.

WEB STOREFRONTS

Web storefronts are virtual stores for B2C electronic commerce. Shoppers visit the stores on the Web to inspect merchandise and make purchases. A new type of program called **Web storefront creation packages** or **commerce servers** has recently evolved to help businesses create virtual stores. These programs create Web sites that allow visitors to register, browse, place products into virtual shopping carts, and purchase goods and services. And they do even more behind the scenes. They calculate taxes and shipping costs, handle a variety of payment options, update and replenish inventory, and ensure reliable and safe communications. Additionally, the storefront sites collect data about visitors and generate reports to evaluate the site's profitability. (See Figure 2-18.)

Using commerce servers, a start-up company can become operational with a Web storefront in just a few weeks for as little as $2,000 and monthly server costs of $100.

WEB AUCTIONS

A recent trend in C2C e-commerce is the growing popularity of Web auctions. **Web auctions** are similar to traditional auctions except that buyers and sellers seldom, if ever, meet face-to-face. Sellers post descriptions of products at a Web site and buyers submit bids electronically. Like traditional auctions, sometimes the bidding becomes highly competitive and enthusiastic. There are two basic types of Web auction sites:

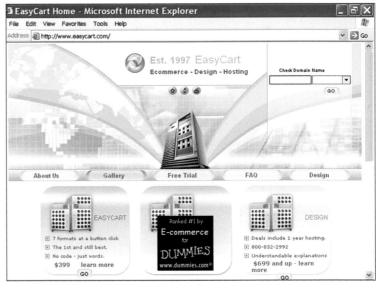

Figure 2-18   Web storefront creation package site

- **Auction house sites** sell a wide range of merchandise directly to bidders. The auction house owner presents merchandise that is typically from a company's surplus stock. These sites operate like a traditional auction, and bargain prices are not uncommon. Auction house sites are generally considered safe places to shop.

- **Person-to-person auction sites** operate more like flea markets. The owner of the site provides a forum for numerous buyers and sellers to gather. While the owners of these sites typically facilitate the bidding process, they are not involved in completing transactions or in verifying the authenticity of the goods sold. (See Figure 2-19.) As with purchases at a flea market, buyers and sellers need to be cautious.

For a list of the most popular Web auction sites, see Figure 2-20.

The Internet, the Web, and Electronic Commerce

Figure 2-19   Person-to-person
Web auction site

Organization	Site
Amazon	www.auctions.amazon.com
eBay	www.ebay.com
uBid.com	www.ubid.com
Sotheby's	www.sothebys.com
Yahoo!	www.auctions.yahoo.com

Figure 2-20   Auction sites

SECURITY

The single greatest challenge for e-commerce is the development of fast, secure, and reliable payment methods for purchased goods. The three basic payment options are check, credit card, and electronic cash.

- Checks are the most traditional and perhaps the safest. Unfortunately, check purchases require the longest time to complete. After selecting an item, the buyer sends a check through the mail. Upon receipt of the check, the seller verifies that the check is good. If it is good, then the purchased item is sent out.

- Credit card purchases are faster and more convenient than check purchases. Credit card fraud, however, is a major concern for both buyers and sellers. Criminals known as **carders** specialize in stealing, trading, and using stolen credit cards over the Internet. We will discuss this and other privacy and security issues related to the Internet in Chapter 10.

- **Electronic cash,** or **e-cash,** is the Internet's equivalent to traditional cash. It is also known as **cybercash** and **digital cash.** Buyers purchase e-cash from a third party (a bank that specializes in electronic currency) by transferring funds from their banks. (See Figure 2-21.) Buyers purchase goods using e-cash. Sellers convert the e-cash to traditional currency through the third party. Although not as convenient as credit card purchases, e-cash is more secure. For a list of e-cash providers, see Figure 2-22.

Figure 2-21   PayPal offers electronic payment

Organization	Site
ECash	www.ecash.com
EmoneyMail	www.emoneymail.com
World Pay	www.worldplay.com
PayPal	www.paypal.com

Figure 2-22   Electronic cash providers

WEB UTILITIES

> **Web utilities are programs that make working with the Web and the Internet easier and safer. Telnet and FTP are Internet standards. Plug-ins operate as part of a browser. Filters block access and monitor use of selected Web sites.**

Utilities are programs that make computing easier. **Web utilities** are specialized utility programs that make using the Internet and the Web easier and safer. Some of these utilities are Internet services for connecting and sharing resources over the Internet. Others are browser-related programs that either become part of your browser or are executed from your browser.

TELNET

Many computers on the Internet will allow you to connect to them and to run selected programs on them. **Telnet** is an Internet standard that allows you to connect to another computer (host) on the Internet and to log on to that computer as if you were on a terminal in the next room. There are hundreds of computers on the Internet that you can connect to. Some allow limited free access, and others charge fees for their use.

FTP

File transfer protocol (FTP) is an Internet standard for transferring files. Many computers on the Internet allow you to copy files to your computer. This is called **downloading.** You also can use FTP to copy files from your computer to another computer on the Internet. This is called **uploading.**

PLUG-INS

Plug-ins are programs that are automatically started and operate as a part of your browser. Many Web sites require you to have one or more plug-ins to fully experience their content. Some widely used plug-ins include:

- Acrobat Reader from Adobe—for viewing and printing a variety of standard forms and other documents saved in a special format called PDF.
- Cosmos from Silicon Graphics—for displaying three-dimensional graphics.
- Windows Media Player from Microsoft—for playing audio files, video files, and much more.
- QuickTime from Apple—for playing audio and video files. (See Figure 2-23.)

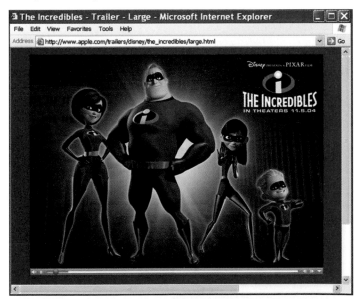

Figure 2-23   QuickTime movie at Apple.com

Plug-in	Source
Acrobat Reader	www.adobe.com
Media Player	www.microsoft.com
QuickTime	www.apple.com
RealPlayer	www.real.com
Shockwave	www.macromedia.com

Figure 2-24 Plug-in sites

- RealPlayer from RealNetworks—for playing audio and video files.
- Shockwave from Macromedia—for playing Web-based games and viewing concerts and dynamic animations.

Some of these utilities are included in many of today's browsers and operating systems. Others must be installed before they can be used by your browser. To learn more about plug-ins and how to download them, visit some of the sites listed in Figure 2-24.

FILTERS

Filters block access to selected sites. The Internet is an interesting and multifaceted arena. But one of those facets is a dark and seamy one. Parents, in particular, are concerned about children roaming unrestricted across the Internet. (See Figure 2-25.) Filter programs allow parents as well as organizations to block out selected sites and set time limits. (See Figure 2-26.) Additionally, these programs can monitor use and generate reports detailing the total time spent on the Internet and the time spent at individual Web sites, chat groups, and newsgroups. Three well-known filters are CyberPatrol, Cybersitter, and Net Nanny.

Figure 2-25 Parents play an important role in Internet supervision

▼ **CONCEPT CHECK**

▶ What are Web utilities?

▶ Describe Telnet and FTP.

▶ What are plug-ins and filters used for?

Figure 2-26 CyberPatrol is a Web filter

A Look to the Future

Internet2 Is a High-Performance Network

Have you ever been unable to connect to the Internet? Have you ever waited a long time for a graphic to download? Would you like to have high-speed access to multimedia content? What if you could work in a virtual science lab? Internet2 is a project designed to develop the software and resources needed to meet these bandwidth-heavy services.

Internet2 is a collaborative project between an assembly of universities, the government, and private research groups. Over 60 private companies and 200 universities are currently working together to develop the technology and applications they believe will power the Internet in the future. Internet2 is currently 100 times faster than the Internet. Students and faculty at participating universities are currently using Internet2 to collaborate on very media-intensive files and projects. In fact, exchange of digital video is expected to become a major component of Internet2. In order to supply large and uninterrupted digital video files, Internet2 must be a high-bandwidth connect with little delay.

Faster downloads and less waiting are the ultimate goal of this group, but the main objective of their combined efforts is to provide access to new applications. For example, it is anticipated that Internet2 will provide

individuals access to virtual libraries and science labs. Internet2 is also expected to enhance the distance learning experience. Current tests are allowing music students to use audio and video equipment to have music lessons with instructors in other countries. Students are using Internet2 to examine atoms with electron microscopes. Doctors are participating in video surgeries.

Internet2 is not a separate network; it is designed to use advanced networking technology and is not expected to replace the current Internet. It is a super-fast connection over a fiber-optic network that is less likely to lose data or be interrupted. It is nearly 3,000 times faster than a modem connection to the Internet. Private industry is using university experiences with Internet2 to develop products for public use later. For example, Cisco Systems is currently working with universities on the next generation of network hardware.

Do you think developments like these will eventually benefit the public? What are the benefits of such collaboration between the public and private sectors? The original Internet and e-mail are the result of private and public partnership. What do you think? Will students one day attend university courses virtually? Some experts suggest the applications currently in development may make it possible.

VISUAL SUMMARY

THE INTERNET, THE WEB, AND ELECTRONIC COMMERCE

INTERNET AND WEB

ACCESS

Internet

Launched in 1969 with **ARPANET,** the **Internet (Net)** consists of the actual physical network made up of wires, cables, and satellites. Being connected to this network is often described as being **online.**

Web

Introduced in 1992 at **CERN,** the **Web** (**WWW** and **World Wide Web**) provides a multimedia interface to Internet resources.

Common Uses

The most common uses of the Internet and Web include:

- Communication—the most popular Internet activity.
- Shopping—**cybermalls** provide access to a variety of stores.
- Searching—**virtual libraries** provide access to a variety of resources.
- Entertainment—music, movies, magazines, and computer games.
- Education—**e-learning** or taking online courses.

Once connected to the Internet, our computer seemingly becomes an extension of a giant computer that branches all over the world.

Providers

Internet service providers are connected to the Internet. **ISPs** may be **national, regional,** or **wireless.**

Connection technologies include **dial-up, DSL, cable,** and **wireless modems.** User's computer **(client)** requests services from ISP **(server)** forming **client-server network.**

Browsers

Browsers access the Web allowing you to **surf** or explore. Some related terms are:

- **URLs**—**locations** or **addresses** to Web resources; two parts are **protocol** and **domain name (top level domain); domain code** identifies type of organization.
- **HTML**—commands to display **Web pages; hyperlinks (links)** are connections.
- **Web server**—computer on Internet that stores and shares documents.
- **Applets**—special programs linked to Web pages; typically written in **Java.**

To be a competent end user you need to be aware of resources available on the Internet and Web, to be able to access these resources, to effectively communicate electronically, to efficiently locate information, to understand electronic commerce, and to use Web browsers and utilities.

COMMUNICATION

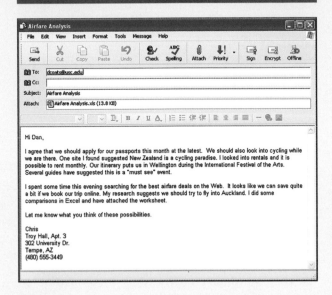

E-mail

E-mail (electronic mail) is the transmission of electronic messages. Basic elements: **header** (including **addresses, subject,** and **attachments**), **message,** and **signature line. Spam** is unwanted and unsolicited e-mail that may include a **computer virus. Anti-spam programs (junk mail filters, spam blockers)** identify and eliminate spam.

Instant Messaging

Instant messaging (IM) extends e-mail to support live communication with **friends (buddies** or **contacts). Universal instant messengers** support communication with other services.

Discussion Groups

Discussion groups use e-mail to communicate with people who may have never met face-to-face.

- Includes **mailing lists** (using **list** and **subscription addresses**), **newsgroups** (using the **UseNet**), and **chat groups** (using **channels; IRC** is a popular chat service).
- Associated terms include flaming, lurking, RFD, saint, thread, and wizard.

SEARCH TOOLS

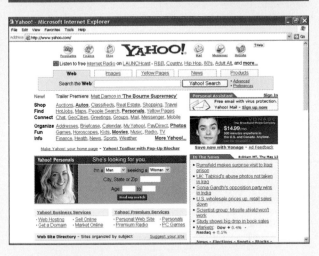

Search services (search providers) maintain huge Web site databases to locate information. **Spiders (Webcrawlers)** are programs that update these databases.

Search Engines

Search engines locate information. Most provide two search approaches:

- **Keyword search**—keyword(s) entered and list of **hits** returns. Good for locating specific information.
- **Directory search (index search)**—selections made from a list of topics. Good for locating general information.

Metasearch Engines

Metasearch engines submit search requests to several search engines simultaneously. Duplicate sites eliminated, hits ordered, and composite hit list presented.

Specialized Search Engines

Specialized search engines focus on subject-specific Web sites.

ELECTRONIC COMMERCE

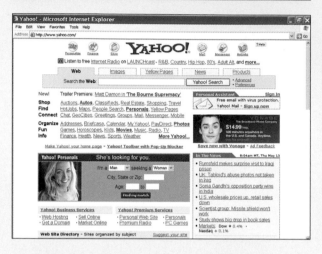

Electronic commerce, or **e-commerce,** is the buying and selling of goods over the Internet. Three basic types of e-commerce are **Business-to-consumer (B2C), Consumer-to-consumer (C2C), Business-to-business (B2B).**

Web Storefronts
Web storefronts are B2C virtual stores. **Web storefront creation packages (commerce servers)** are programs for creating virtual stores.

Web Auctions
Web auctions are a growing C2C application of e-commerce. Similar to traditional auctions except that buyers and sellers rarely meet. Two basic types are **auction house sites** and **person-to-person auction sites**.

Security
Security is the greatest challenge for e-commerce development. Three basic payment options are: **check, credit card (carders** specialize in stealing, trading, and using credit cards over the Internet), and **electronic cash (e-cash, cyber-cash, digital cash).**

WEB UTILITIES

Organization	Site
ECash	www.ecash.com
EmoneyMail	www.emoneymail.com
World Pay	www.worldplay.com
PayPal	www.paypal.com

Web utilities are specialized utility programs that make using the Internet and the Web easier and safer.

Telnet
Telnet is an Internet standard that helps you connect to another computer on the Internet and use that computer as if you were on a terminal in the next room.

FTP
FTP (file transfer protocol) is an Internet standard for transferring files. **Downloading** is the process of receiving a file from another computer. **Uploading** is the process of sending a file to another computer.

Plug-ins
Plug-ins are automatically loaded and operate as part of a browser. Many Web sites require specific plug-ins to fully experience their content. Some plug-ins are included in many of today's browsers; others must be installed.

Filters
Filters are used by parents and organizations to block certain sites and to monitor use of the Internet and the Web.

KEY TERMS

address (32)
Advanced Research Project Agency Network (ARPANET) (30)
anti-spam program (36)
applets (33)
attachment (34)
auction house site (43)
browser (32)
buddy (36)
business-to-business (B2B) (42)
business-to-consumer (B2C) (42)
cable (32)
carder (44)
Center for European Nuclear Research (CERN) (30)
channel (37)
chat group (37)
client (32)
client-server network (32)
commerce server (43)
computer virus (34)
contact (36)
contacts (36)
consumer-to-consumer (C2C) (42)
cybercash (44)
cybermall (30)
dial-up (32)
digital cash (44)
directory search (41)
discussion group (36)
domain code (33)
domain name (33)
downloading (45)
DSL (32)
e-cash (44)
e-commerce (42)

e-learning (31)
electronic cash (44)
electronic commerce (42)
electronic mail (34)
e-mail (34)
file transfer protocol (FTP) (45)
filter (46)
friend (36)
header (34)
hit (41)
hyperlink (33)
Hypertext Markup Language (HTML) (33)
index search (41)
instant messaging (IM) (36)
Internet (30)
Internet Relay Chat (IRC) (37)
Internet Service Provider (ISP) (31)
Java (33)
junk mail filter (36)
keyword search (41)
link (33)
list address (36)
location (32)
lurking (37)
mailing list (36)
message (34)
metasearch engine (41)
national service provider (32)
Net (30)
newsgroup (37)
online (30)
person-to-person auction site (43)
plug-in (45)
protocol (33)

regional service provider (32)
search engine (40)
search provider (40)
search service (40)
server (32)
signature line (34)
spam (34)
spam blocker (36)
specialized search engine (41)
spider (40)
subject (34)
subscription address (36)
surf (32)
Telnet (45)
top level domain (33)
uniform resource locator (URL) (32)
universal instant messenger (36)
uploading (45)
UseNet (37)
virtual library (31)
Web (30)
Web auction (43)
Webcrawler (40)
Web page (33)
Web server (33)
Web storefront (43)
Web storefront creation package (43)
Web utility (45)
wireless modem (32)
wireless service provider (32)
World Wide Web (30)
WWW (30)

FEATURES
Animations
Careers in IT
DVD Direct
Expansions
Making IT Work for You
On the Web Explorations
TechTV
Tips

CHAPTER REVIEW
Key Terms
Crossword
Multiple Choice
Matching
Open-ended
Using Technology
Expanding Your Knowledge
Building Your Portfolio

To test your knowledge of these key terms with animated flash cards, consult your Computing Essentials CD or visit us at www.olearyseries.com/CE06 and select Key Terms.

COMPUTING ESSENTIALS 2006

CROSSWORD PUZZLE

Across

6 Program that provides access to Web resources.

8 Observation of a discussion group.

9 Special program written in Java.

10 Locates information online.

12 Connections to Web resources.

14 Internet standard for connecting and logging onto remote computers.

15 Provide users a connection to the Internet.

17 Location of Web resource.

Down

1 Involves the sale of a product to another business.

2 Steals credit card information.

3 Being connected to the Internet.

4 The last part of the domain name.

5 Friends or Buddies.

7 Explore the Web.

11 Used to block certain sites.

13 Internet standard for transferring files.

16 Unwelcome e-mail.

For an interactive version of this crossword, consult your Computing Essentials CD or visit our Web site at **www.olearyseries.com/CE06** and select Crossword.

MULTIPLE CHOICE

Circle the letter or fill in the correct answer.

1. The Internet was launched in 1969 when the United States funded a project to develop a national computer network called _____.
   a. ARPANET
   b. CERN
   c. the Web
   d. WWW
   e. IRC

2. _____ use telephone lines and service an area limited to several states.
   a. Wireless service providers
   b. National service providers
   c. Local service providers
   d. Regional service providers
   e. Commercial ISPs

3. _____ connect(s) to remote computers, open(s) and transfer(s) files, display(s) text and images, and provide(s) in one tool an uncomplicated interface to the Internet and Web.
   a. Bots
   b. Browsers
   c. Java
   d. Web utilities
   e. Wizards

4. The computer that stores and shares Web page resources is called a _____.
   a. Web portal
   b. Web server
   c. Telnet
   d. ISP
   e. applet

5. _____ are often attached to unsolicited e-mail.
   a. Spam e-mails
   b. Addresses
   c. Web pages
   d. Computer viruses
   e. Applets

6. _____ programs identify and eliminate unwanted and unsolicited e-mails.
   a. Media
   b. Anti-spam
   c. Search
   d. DSL
   e. Meta

7. To participate in a chat group, select a _____ and communicate live with others.
   a. signal
   b. index
   c. engine
   d. list
   e. channel

8. In a directory or _____ search, you select a category that fits the information you want.
   a. packet
   b. keyword
   c. index
   d. specialized
   e. subject

9. In _____ commerce, individuals typically sell to other individuals without ever meeting face-to-face.
   a. C2C
   b. B2C
   c. B2B
   d. C2I
   e. I2I

10. _____ are programs that are automatically loaded and operate as part of a browser.
    a. Plug-ins
    b. Add-ons
    c. Providers
    d. Agents
    e. Applets

For an interactive version of these multiple-choice questions, consult your Computing Essentials CD or visit our Web site at www.olearyseries.com/CE06 and select Multiple Choice.

FEATURES
Animations
Careers in IT
DVD Direct
Expansions
Making IT Work for You
On the Web Explorations
TechTV
Tips

CHAPTER REVIEW
Key Terms
Crossword
Multiple Choice
Matching
Open-ended
Using Technology
Expanding Your Knowledge
Building Your Portfolio

MATCHING

Match each numbered item with the most closely related lettered item. Write your answers in the spaces provided.

a. applets

b. buddy

c. carders

d. computer virus

e. DSL

f. e-cash

g. e-commerce

h. header

i. hits

j. hyperlinks

k. lurking

l. metasearch engine

m. plug-in

n. signature line

o. subscription address

p. surfing

q. URLs

r. Web auction

s. Web page

t. Web storefronts

1. Connection technology used by ISPs. ____

2. Another name for an IM friend. ____

3. Addresses of Web resources. ____

4. Moving from one Web site to another. ____

5. Special programs written in Java. ____

6. HTML document displayed by a browser. ____

7. Part of an e-mail message that includes the subject, address, and attachments. ____

8. Typically includes the sender's name, address, and telephone number. ____

9. To participate in a mailing list, you must send a request to this address. ____

10. Links that connect to other documents. ____

11. Reading and observing discussions without participating. ____

12. Program that starts and operates as part of a browser. ____

13. The list of sites that contain the keywords of a keyword search. ____

14. Program that automatically submits a search request to several search engines simultaneously. ____

15. Buying and selling goods over the Internet. ____

16. Destructive program often attached to unsolicited e-mail. ____

17. Virtual stores for B2C electronic commerce. ____

18. Similar to a traditional auction, but buyers and sellers typically interact only on the Web. ____

19. Criminals that specialize in stealing, trading, and using stolen credit cards over the Internet. ____

20. Internet equivalent to traditional cash. ____

For an interactive version of this matching exercise, consult your Computing Essentials CD or visit our Web site at www.olearyseries.com/CE06 and select Matching.

OPEN-ENDED

On a separate sheet of paper, respond to each question or statement.

1. Discuss the uses of the Internet. Which activities have you participated in? Which one do you think is the most popular?

2. Explain the differences between the three types of providers.

3. What are the basic elements of an e-mail message?

4. What are the types of discussion groups? Describe any groups you participate in.

5. Describe the different types of search engines. Give an example of the type of search each engine is best for.

1

Blocking Spam

Are you tired of unwanted e-mail in your inbox? Do you frequently spend valuable time sorting through junk e-mail? Spam can mean anything from a minor annoyance to a serious loss of productivity. Installing spam-blocking software can help. To learn more about spam-blocking software, review Making IT Work for You: Blocking Spam, on pages 38 and 39. Then complete the following questions: (a) Describe the procedure for categorizing spam e-mail messages with the Spam Bully program. (b) What is the name for the list of e-mail addresses that should never be considered spammers? (c) What is the "challenge e-mail"? Why is it sent?

2

Online Shopping

Shopping on the Internet can be fast and convenient. Connect to our Web site at www.olearyseries.com/CE06 and select Using Technology to link to a popular shopping site. Once there, try shopping for one or two products, and answer the following questions: (a) What product(s) did you shop for? Could you find the product(s) at the site? If not, then search for another product that you can locate at the site. (b) Describe your experience. Was the site easy to use? Did you find it easy to locate the product(s)? What are the pros and cons of shopping online versus at a traditional store? Are there any products or circumstances in which you would more likely shop online? (c) Have you ever purchased anything online? If you have, describe what you bought and why you bought it online. If you have not, do you expect to in the near future? Why or why not?

1   How Spam Filters Work

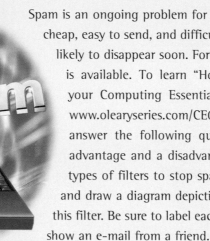

Spam is an ongoing problem for e-mail users everywhere. Spam is cheap, easy to send, and difficult to track, so the problem is unlikely to disappear soon. Fortunately, spam-blocking software is available. To learn "How Spam Filters Work," consult your Computing Essentials CD or visit our Web site at www.olearyseries.com/CE06 and select Expansions. Then answer the following questions: (a) Briefly describe an advantage and a disadvantage to using each of the three types of filters to stop spam. (b) Choose one of the filters and draw a diagram depicting a spam e-mail going through this filter. Be sure to label each step. (c) Modify the diagram to show an e-mail from a friend.

2   How Instant Messaging Works

One of the fastest growing applications on the Internet is instant messaging. This extension to e-mail provides a way for friends and colleagues to communicate and share information from almost anywhere in the world. To learn "How Instant Messenging Works," consult your Computing Essentials CD or visit our Web site at www.olearyseries.com/CE06 and select Animations. Then answer the following:

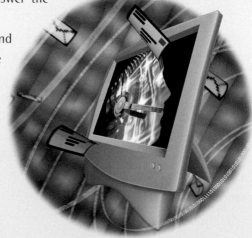

As described in Step 4: Communicate, Linda, Steve, and Chris agree to meet for a movie. Then Chris tells them that he has to leave for school and disconnects. Linda and Steve continue talking with Linda asking Steve, "Have you seen any good movies lately?" On a single page of paper, create a drawing based on the animation that describes these events beginning with Step 5 when Chris says, "Bye for now—I have to leave for school."

1

Electronic Commerce

Electronic commerce is one of the most exciting Web applications. Write a one-page paper titled "Electronic Commerce" that addresses the following: (a) Define electronic commerce including B2C, C2C, and B2B. Provide examples. (b) What types of businesses and consumers are most affected by electronic commerce today? What types will be affected in the future? Discuss and justify your positions. (c) What are the greatest challenges to future developments in electronic commerce? Discuss and justify your conclusions.

2

Free Speech Online

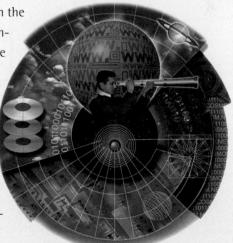

Some feel that there is too much objectionable material allowed on the Internet, whereas others argue that the Internet should be completely uncensored. Consider these two viewpoints and answer the following questions in a one-page paper: (a) Should religious groups be allowed to distribute information over the Internet? What about groups that advocate hatred or oppression? (b) Is there any material you feel should not be freely available on the Web? What about child pornography? (c) If you think some regulation is required, who should determine what restrictions should be imposed? (d) The Internet is not owned by a particular group or country. What limitations does this impose on enforcement of restrictions?

COMPETENCIES

After you have read this chapter, you should be able to:

1 **Discuss common features of most software applications.**

2 **Discuss word processors and word processing features.**

3 **Describe spreadsheets and spreadsheet features.**

4 **Discuss database management systems and database management features.**

5 **Describe presentation graphics and presentation graphics features.**

6 **Discuss integrated software and software suites.**

7 **Describe ways to share data between applications.**

Word Processing Software
Create text-based documents

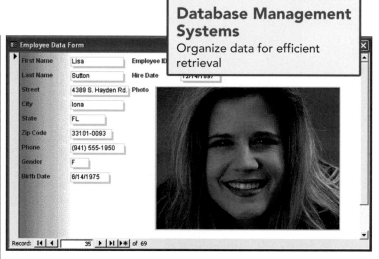

Database Management Systems
Organize data for efficient retrieval

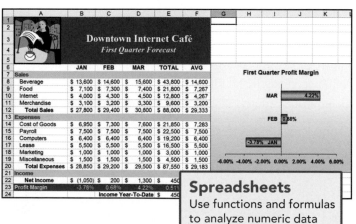

Spreadsheets
Use functions and formulas to analyze numeric data

Not long ago, trained specialists were required to perform many of the operations you can now do with a microcomputer. Secretaries used typewriters to create business correspondence. Market analysts used calculators to project sales. Graphic artists created designs by hand. Data processing clerks created electronic files to be stored on large computers. Now you can do all these tasks—and many others—with a microcomputer and the appropriate application software.

Think of the microcomputer as an electronic tool. You may not consider yourself very good at typing, calculating, organizing, presenting, or managing information. However, a microcomputer can help you do all these things and much more. All it takes is the right kinds of software.

You are probably most familiar with the software available for sale in retail stores. You purchase these programs, store them on your hard disk, and run them. An emerging trend, however, is to use Web-based applications. These are programs you access from the Internet and run on your microcomputer.

Competent end users need to understand the capabilities of basic application software, which includes word processors, spreadsheets, database management systems, and presentation programs. They need to know how to use application programs effectively and how to share data between applications.

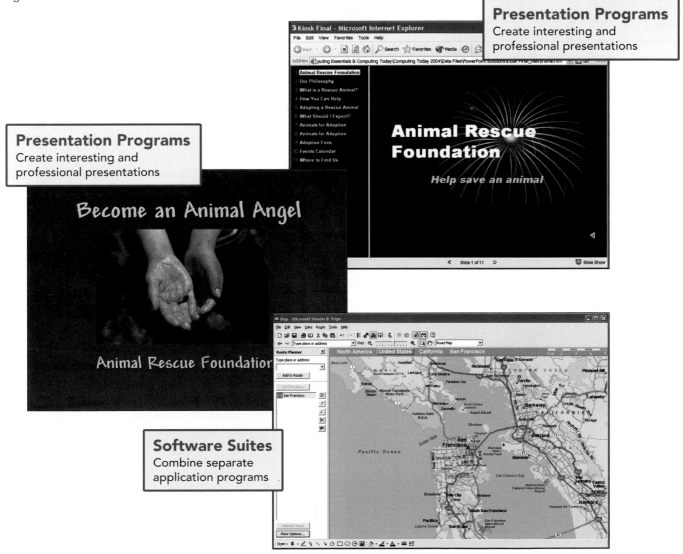

Presentation Programs
Create interesting and professional presentations

Presentation Programs
Create interesting and professional presentations

Software Suites
Combine separate application programs

APPLICATION SOFTWARE

There are two categories of application software: basic and specialized. Common interface features include icons, windows, menus, dialog boxes, Help, toolbars, and buttons. Speech recognition accepts voice input. ASPs provide access to Web-based applications.

On the Web Explorations

Microsoft is one of the leaders in creating software applications. To learn more about the company, visit our Web site at

www.olearyseries.com/CE06 and select On the Web Explorations.

As we discussed in Chapter 1, there are two kinds of software. **System software** works with end users, application software, and computer hardware to handle the majority of technical details. **Application software** can be described as end user software and is used to accomplish a variety of tasks.

Application software, in turn, can be divided into two categories. One category, **basic applications,** is the focus of this chapter. These programs, also known as **general-purpose applications** and **productivity applications,** are widely used in nearly every discipline and occupation. They include word processors, spreadsheets, database management systems, and presentation graphics. The other category, **specialized applications,** also known as **special-purpose applications,** includes thousands of other programs that are more narrowly focused on specific disciplines and occupations. Some of the best known are graphics programs, audio and video editors, multimedia creation programs, Web authoring, and virtual reality programs. (A detailed discussion of these specialized applications is presented in Chapter 4.)

COMMON FEATURES

A **user interface** is the portion of the application that you work with. Most applications use a **graphical user interface (GUI)** that displays graphical elements called **icons** to represent familiar objects and a mouse. The mouse controls a **pointer** on the screen that is used to select items such as icons. Another feature is the use of windows to display information. A **window** is simply a rectangular area that can contain a document, program, or message. (Do not confuse the term *window* with the various versions of Microsoft's Windows operating systems, which are programs.) More than one window can be opened and displayed on the computer screen at one time.

Almost all software programs have **menus** to present commands. Typically, menus are displayed in a **menu bar** at the top of the screen. When one of the menu items is selected, a **pull-down** or **drop-down menu** appears. This is a list of options or commands associated with the selected menu. Selecting one of these options may display an additional list of menu options or a **dialog box** that provides additional information and requests user input. One of the commands on the menu bar is **Help.** This option provides access to a variety of Help features and acts as an online reference manual.

Toolbars typically are below the menu bar. They contain small outlined areas called **buttons** that provide shortcuts for quick access to commonly used commands. For example, the **standard toolbar** contains a variety of buttons that are common to most applications, including those to open, save, and print files. (See Figure 3-1.) All Microsoft Office applications have a common user interface, including similar commands and menu structures. (See Figure 3-2.) The newest version of Microsoft Office provides **speech recognition** or the ability to accept voice input to select menu options and dictate text. See Making IT Work for You: Speech Recognition on pages 62 and 63. To learn more about how speech recognition works, consult your Computing Essentials CD or visit our Web site at www.olearyseries.com/CE06 and select Expansions.

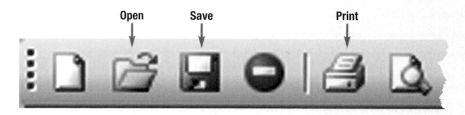

Open   Save   Print

Figure 3-1   Buttons on the standard toolbar

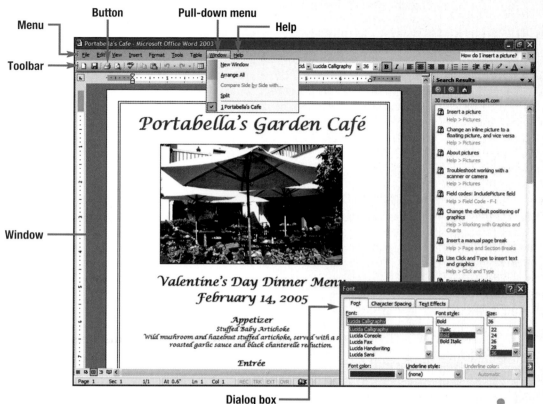

Menu —   Button   Pull-down menu

Help

Toolbar —

Window —

Dialog box —

Figure 3-2   Common features

WEB-BASED APPLICATIONS

Typically, application programs are owned by individuals or organizations and stored on their computer system's hard disks. For the application to be used, a copy of the program (or part of the program) is read into the computer system's memory. An emerging trend, however, is to free users from owning and storing applications by using Web-based applications.

Special Web sites, called **application service providers (ASPs),** allow access to their application programs. To use one of these **Web-based applications,** you connect to the ASP, copy the application program to your computer system's memory, and then run the application. Most ASPs provide access to a wide range of application programs and charge a fee for their service. To see how Web-based applications work, consult your Computing Essentials CD or visit our Web site at www.olearyseries.com/CE06 and select Animations.

▼ CONCEPT CHECK

▶   What is the difference between basic and specialized applications?

▶   List some common features of application software.

▶   What are Web-based applications?

MAKING (IT) WORK FOR YOU

SPEECH RECOGNITION

Tired of using your keyboard to type term papers? Have you ever thought about using your voice to control application software? Perhaps speech recognition is just what you are looking for.

Training the Software   The first step is to set up your microphone and train your software to recognize your voice. Start any Microsoft Office 2003 application:

1 ● Select *Speech* from the *Tools* menu.

   ● Follow the on-screen instructions to test your microphone.

2 ● Read the text presented to teach the software your unique speech patterns.

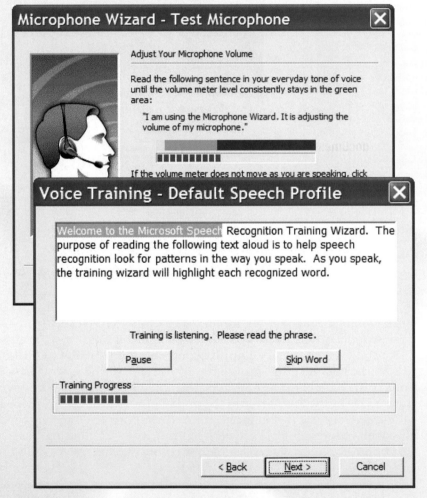

Microphone Wizard - Test Microphone ⊠

Adjust Your Microphone Volume

Read the following sentence in your everyday tone of voice until the volume meter level consistently stays in the green area:

"I am using the Microphone Wizard. It is adjusting the volume of my microphone."

If the volume meter does not move as you are speaking, click

Voice Training - Default Speech Profile ⊠

Welcome to the Microsoft Speech Recognition Training Wizard. The purpose of reading the following text aloud is to help speech recognition look for patterns in the way you speak. As you speak, the training wizard will highlight each recognized word.

Training is listening. Please read the phrase.

Pause   Skip Word

Training Progress

< Back   Next >   Cancel

Controlling a Program Once the software is trained, you can control many computer operations with just your voice by using the Language bar. For example, to insert the picture "Tiger" into a Microsoft Word document:

1
- Click the *Microphone* button on the Language bar.

- Click the *Voice Command* button on the Language bar.

- Say the names of the menus and commands you wish to perform.

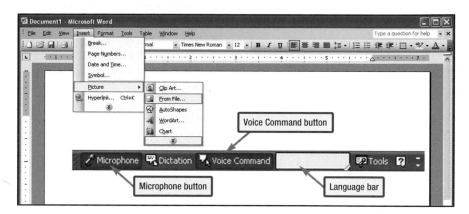

Dictating a Document You can also dictate text using the Language bar. For example, to insert text into a Microsoft Word document:

1
- Click the *Dictation* button on the Language bar.

- Dictate the text you want to appear in the Word document.

"...find out how you can experience..."

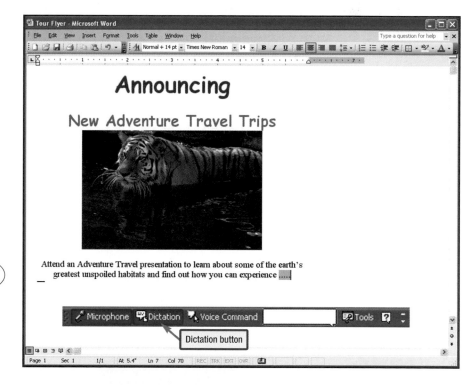

Although speech recognition technology continues to improve, speech recognition is not yet ready for completely hands-free operation. You will get the best results if you use a combination of your voice and the mouse or keyboard.

The Web is continually changing, and some of the specifics presented in the Making IT Work for You section may have changed. To learn about other ways to make information technology work for you, visit our Web site at www.olearyseries.com/CE06 and select Making IT Work for You.

> Word processing software creates text-based documents. Features support entering, editing, and formatting text.

Word processors create text-based **documents** and are one of the most flexible and widely used software tools. All types of people and organizations use word processors to create memos, letters, and faxes. Organizations create newsletters, manuals, and brochures to provide information to their customers. Students and researchers use word processors to create reports. Word processors can even be used to create personalized Web pages.

The three most widely used word processing programs are Microsoft Word, Corel WordPerfect, and Lotus Word Pro.

FEATURES

Word processors provide a variety of features to make entering, editing, and formatting documents easy. One of the most basic features for entering text is **word wrap.** This feature automatically moves the insertion point to the next line once the current line is full. As you type, the words wrap around to the next line.

There are numerous features designed to support **editing** or modifying a document. One of these is a **Thesaurus** that provides synonyms, antonyms, and related words for a selected word or phrase. You can quickly locate and replace selected words using the **find and replace** feature. **Spelling** and **grammar checkers** look for misspelled words and problems with capitalization, punctuation, and sentence structure. Other features are designed to improve the **format** or appearance of a document. One of the most basic is the **font** or design of the characters. (See Figure 3-3.) The height of a character is its **font size.** The appearance of characters can be enhanced using such **character effects** as **bold,** *italic,* shadow, and colors. **Bulleted** and **numbered lists** can make a sequence of topics easy to read.

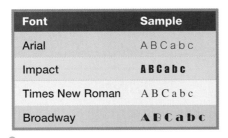

Font	Sample
Arial	A B C a b c
Impact	**ABCabc**
Times New Roman	A B C a b c
Broadway	**A B C a b c**

Figure 3-3 Sample fonts

CASE

Assume that you have accepted a job as an advertising coordinator for Adventure Travel Tours, a travel agency specializing in active adventure vacations. Your primary responsibilities are to create and coordinate the company's promotional materials, including flyers and travel reports. To see how you could use Microsoft Word, the most widely used word processing program, as the advertising coordinator for the Adventure Travel Tours, see Figures 3-4 and 3-5.

▼ CONCEPT CHECK

▶ What do word processors do?

▶ Describe the following editing features: Thesaurus, find and replace, spelling and grammar checkers.

▶ Describe the following formatting features: font, font size, character effects, numbered and bulleted lists.

Spelling Checker
Correcting spelling and typing errors identified by the **spelling checker** creates an error-free and professional-looking document.

Fonts and Font Size
Using interesting **fonts** and a large **font size** in the flyer's title grabs the reader's attention.

Announcing
New Adventure Travel Trips

Center Aligning
Center aligning all of the text in the flyer creates a comfortable, balanced appearance.

Attend an Adventure Travel presentation to learn about some of the earth's greatest unspoiled habitats and find out how you can experience the adventure of a lifetime. This year we are introducing four new tours and offering you a unique opportunity to combine many different outdoor activities while exploring the world.

Hike the Inca trail to Machu Picchu
Camp on safari in Tanzania
Climb Mt. Kilimanjaro
Explore the Costa Rican rain forests

Presentation dates and times are January 5 at 7 PM, February 3 at 7:30 PM, and March 8 at 7 PM. All presentations are held at convenient hotel locations. The hotels are located in downtown Los Angeles, Santa Clara and at the airport.

Call 1-800-777-0004 for presentation locations, a full color brochure, and itinerary information, costs, and trip dates.

Word Wrap
The automatic **word wrap** feature frees you to focus your attention on the content of the flyer.

Character Effects
Adding **character effects** such as bold and color makes important information stand out and makes the flyer more visually interesting.

Grammar Checker
Incomplete sentences, awkward wording, and incorrect punctuation are identified and corrections are offered by the **grammar checker**.

CREATING A FLYER

You have been asked to create an advertising flyer for upcoming promotional presentations. After discussing the flyer's contents and basic structure with your supervisor, you start to enter the flyer's text. As you enter, the text, *words wrap* automatically at the end of each line. Also, while entering the text, the *spelling checker* and *grammar checker* catch spelling and grammatical errors. Once the text has been entered, you focus your attention on enhancing the visual aspects of the flyer. You add an interesting graphic and experiment with different character and paragraph formats including *fonts, font sizes, colors,* and *alignments.*

Figure 3–4 Flyer

CREATING A REPORT

Your next assignment is to create a report on Tanzania and Peru. After conducing your research, you start writing your paper. As you enter the text for the report, you notice that the *AutoCorrect* feature automatically corrects some grammar and punctuation errors. Your report includes several figures and *tables*. You use the *captions* feature to keep track of figure and table numbers, to enter the caption text, and to position the captions. When referencing figures or tables from the text, you use the *cross reference* feature. You then carefully document your sources using *footnotes*. Finally, you prepare the report for printing by adding *header* and *footer* information.

AutoCorrect

As you enter text, you occasionally forget to capitalize the first word in a sentence. Fortunately, **AutoCorrect** recognizes the error and automatically capitalizes the word.

Header or Footer

Page numbers and other document-related information can be included in a **header** or **footer**.

Footnote

To include a note about Lake Titicaca, you use the **footnote** feature. This feature inserts the footnote superscript number and automatically formats the bottom of the page to contain the footnote text.

Captions and Cross References

Identifying figures with **captions** and using **cross-references** in a report makes the report easier to read and more professional.

Table

To concisely present and organize the weather information, you use a **table**.

- 1 -

Peru

Geography and Climate

Peru, located in South America, borders the Pacific Ocean on its west and shares common borders with the countries of Ecuador, Colombia, Brazil, and Bolivia. Peru is subdivided into three regions – La Costa, La Sierra, and La Selva — based on differing climate and geographical features. Though entirely within the tropics, Peru's climate varies from region to region, ranging from tropical to arctic. Its varied climate corresponds to the sharply contrasting geographical features of seafront, mountains, and rainforests.

La Costa

Occupying the slender area along Peru's western coastline, La Costa, provides a division between the mountains and sea. Although some of this area is fertile, mostly it is extremely dry and arid. The Andes Mountains prevent greater annual precipitation coming from the east. Some areas in the south are considered drier than the Sahara. Conversely, there are a few areas in this region where mountain rivers meet the ocean that are green with life and do not give the impression of being in a desert at all.

La Sierra

Inland and to the east is the mountainous region called La Sierra, encompassing Peru's share of the Andes mountain range. The southern portion of this region is prone to

volcanic activity, and some volcanoes are active today. La Sierra is subject to a dry season from May to September, which is winter in that part of the world. The weather is typically sunny, with moderate annual precipitation. The former Incan capital Cuzco is in this region, as well as the Sacred Valley of the Incas. This region also contains Lake Titicaca, the world's highest navigable lake.[1]

Figure 1-Sacred Valley

La Selva

La Selva, a region of tropical rainforest, is the easternmost region in Peru. This region, with the eastern foot of the Andes Mountains, forms the Amazon Basin, into which numerous rivers flow. La Selva is extremely wet, with some areas exceeding an annual precipitation of 137 inches. Its wettest season occurs from November to April. The weather here is humid and extremely hot.

Region	Annual Rainfall (Inches)	Average Temperature (Fahrenheit)
La Costa	2	68
La Sierra	35	54
La Selva	137	80

[1] Lake Titicaca is 12,507 feet above sea level.

Figure 3-5   Report

SPREADSHEETS

> Spreadsheet programs manipulate numeric data. Features include workbooks, worksheets, rows, columns, ranges, text and numeric entries, formulas, functions, cells, charts, recalculation, and what–if analysis.

Spreadsheet programs organize, analyze, and graph numeric data such as budgets and financial reports. Once used exclusively by accountants, spreadsheets are widely used by nearly every profession. Marketing professionals analyze sales trends. Financial analysts evaluate and graph stock market trends. Students and teachers record grades and calculate grade point averages.

The three most widely used spreadsheet programs are Microsoft Excel, Corel Quattro Pro, and Lotus 1-2-3.

FEATURES

Unlike word processors, which manipulate text and create text documents, spreadsheet programs manipulate numeric data and create workbook files. **Workbook files** consist of one or more related worksheets. A **worksheet,** also known as a **spreadsheet** or **sheet,** is a rectangular grid of **rows** and **columns.** For example in Figure 3-6, the columns are identified by letters and the rows are identified by numbers. The intersection of a row and column creates a **cell.** For example the cell D8 is formed by the intersection of column D and row 8.

A cell can contain text or numeric entries. **Text entries** or **labels** provide structure to a worksheet by describing the contents of rows and columns. For example in Figure 3-6, cell B8 contains the label Food. The cell in D8 contains a number identified as the food expense.

A **numeric entry** can be a number or a formula. A **formula** is an instruction to calculate or process. For example the cell F15 contains the formula =E5−E13. This formula will calculate a value and display that value in cell F15 (Net). The value is calculated by taking the value in cell E5 (Wages) and subtracting the value in cell E13 (Total Expenses). **Functions** are prewritten formulas provided by the spreadsheet program that perform calculations such as adding a series of cells. For example, the cell E13 contains the function

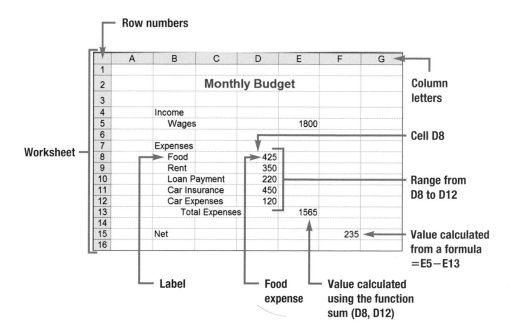

Figure 3-6   Monthly budget worksheet

SUM(D8:D12), which adds the values in the range from D8 to D12. A **range** is a series of continuous cells. In this case the range includes D8, D9, D10, D11, and D12. The sum of the values in this range is displayed in cell E13. Spreadsheet programs typically provide a variety of different types of functions, including financial, mathematical, statistical, and logical functions. Some of these functions are presented in Figure 3-7.

Analytical graphs or **charts** are visual representations of data in a worksheet. You can readily create graphs in a spreadsheet program by selecting the cells containing the data to be charted and then selecting the type of chart to display. If you change one or more numbers in your spreadsheet, all related formulas will automatically recalculate and charts will be recreated. This is called **recalculation.** The process of observing the effect of changing one or more cells is often referred to as **what-if analysis.** For example, to analyze the effect of a rent increase in the Monthly Budget worksheet in Figure 3-6, all you would need to do is replace the contents in cell D9. The entire worksheet, including any charts that had been created, would be recalculated automatically.

TIPS Have you ever wanted to draw attention to a cell in a spreadsheet? AutoShapes make it easy to emphasize the contents of your worksheet. If you are using Excel:

1 **Open the Drawing Toolbar.** Right click a toolbar and select the Drawing toolbar from the menu.

2 **Open the AutoShapes Menu.** Click the AutoShapes button on the Drawing toolbar to open the AutoShapes menu.

3 **Choose and Insert an AutoShape.** Select an AutoShape click on the worksheet and drag to create the shape.

CASE

Assume that you have just accepted a job as manager of the Downtown Internet Café. This cafe provides a variety of flavored coffees as well as Internet access. One of your responsibilities is to create a financial plan for the next year. To see how you could use Microsoft Excel, the most widely used spreadsheet program, as the manager for the Downtown Internet Café, see Figures 3-8 through 3-10.

▼ CONCEPT CHECK

▶ What are spreadsheets used for? What is a workbook? What is a worksheet?

▶ Define rows, columns, cells, ranges, text, and numeric entries.

▶ Describe the following spreadsheet features: formulas, functions, charts, recalculation, and what-if analysis.

Type	Function	Calculates
Financial	PMT	Size of loan payments
	PV	Present value for an investment
Mathematical	SUM	Sum of the numbers in a range of cells
	ABS	Absolute value of a number
Statistical	AVERAGE	Average or mean of the numbers in a range of cells
	MAX	Largest numbers in a range of cells
Logical	IF	Whether a condition is true; if true, a specified value is displayed; if not true, then a different specified value is displayed
	AND	Whether two conditions are true; if both are true, then a specified value is displayed, if either one or both are not true, then a different specified value is displayed

Figure 3-7 Selected spreadsheet functions

CREATING A SALES FORECAST

Your first project is to develop a first quarter sales forecast for the cafe. You begin by studying the sales at the Downtown Internet Café and talking with several managers. After obtaining sales and expense estimates, you are ready to create the first quarter forecast. You start structuring the *worksheet* by inserting descriptive *text entries* for the row and column headings. Next, you insert *numeric entries,* including *formulas* and *functions* to perform calculations. To test the accuracy of the worksheet, you change the values in some cells and compare the recalculated spreadsheet results with hand calculations.

Figure 3-8   Worksheet

Worksheets

Worksheets are used for a wide range of different applications. One of the most common uses is to create, analyze, and forecast budgets.

Text Entries

Text entries provide meaning to the values in the worksheet. The rows are labeled to identify the various sales and expense items. The columns are labeled to specify the months.

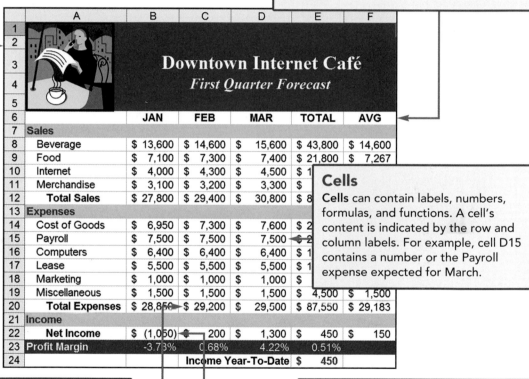

Cells

Cells can contain labels, numbers, formulas, and functions. A cell's content is indicated by the row and column labels. For example, cell D15 contains a number or the Payroll expense expected for March.

Functions

One advantage of using **functions** rather than entering formulas is that they are easier to enter. In this case, cell C20 (Total Expenses for February) contains the function SUM(C14: C19) rather than the formula =C14+C15+ C16+C17+C18+C19.

Formulas

Formulas provide a way to perform calculations in the worksheet. In this case Cell B22 (Net Income for January) contains the formula = B12 (Total Sales for January) −B20 (Total Expenses for January).

CREATING A CHART

After completing the First Quarter Forecast for the Downtown Internet Café, you decide to *chart* the sales data to better visualize the projected growth in sales. You select the 3D column *chart type* to show each month's projected sales category. Using a variety of chart options, you enter descriptive *titles* for the chart, the x-axis, and the y-axis. Then you use *data labels* to focus attention on the growing Internet sales. Finally, you insert a *legend* to define the chart's different columns.

Figure 3–9 Chart

Chart Types
To display the monthly expenses over the quarter, you consider several different **chart types** before selecting the 3D column chart. The 3D variation of the chart provides an interesting depth perception to the columns.

Chart
Once data is in the worksheet, it is very easy to **chart** the data. All you need to do is to select the data to chart, select the chart types, and add some descriptive text.

Titling
Clearly **titling** the chart as well as the x-axis and y-axis makes the chart easier to read and understand.

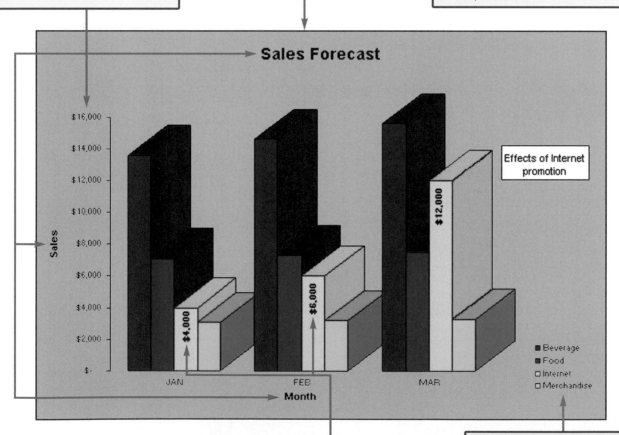

Data Labels
Data labels draw the viewer's attention to selected pieces of information in the chart.

Legend
The **legend** defines each sales expense by a color. Legends are essential to charts that depict more than one set of data.

Goal Seek

A common goal in many financial workbooks is to achieve a certain level of profit. **Goal seek** allows you to set a goal and then will analyze other parts of the workbook that would need to be adjusted to meet that goal.

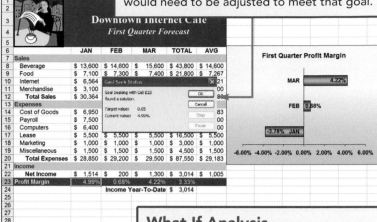

What-If Analysis

What-if analysis is a very powerful and simple tool to test the effects of different assumptions in a spreadsheet.

Workbook

The first worksheet in a **workbook** is often a summary of the following worksheets. In this case, the first workbook presents the entire year's forecast. The subsequent worksheets provide the details.

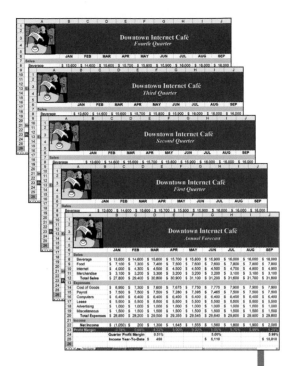

Downtown Internet Café
Annual Forecast

	JAN	FEB	MAR	APR	MAY	JUN	JUL	AUG	SEP
Sales									
Beverage	$ 13,600	$ 14,600	$ 15,600	$ 15,700	$ 15,800	$ 15,900	$ 16,000	$ 16,000	$ 16,000
Food	$ 7,100	$ 7,300	$ 7,400	$ 7,500	$ 7,600	$ 7,600	$ 7,800	$ 7,800	$ 7,800
Internet	$ 4,000	$ 4,300	$ 4,500	$ 4,500	$ 4,500	$ 4,500	$ 4,700	$ 4,800	$ 4,900
Merchandise	$ 3,100	$ 3,200	$ 3,300	$ 3,200	$ 3,200	$ 3,200	$ 3,100	$ 3,100	$ 3,100
Total Sales	$ 27,800	$ 29,400	$ 30,800	$ 30,900	$ 31,100	$ 31,200	$ 31,600	$ 31,700	$ 31,800
Expenses									
Cost of Goods	$ 6,950	$ 7,300	$ 7,600	$ 7,675	$ 7,750	$ 7,775	$ 7,900	$ 7,900	$ 7,900
Payroll	$ 7,500	$ 7,500	$ 7,500	$ 7,280	$ 7,395	$ 7,465	$ 7,500	$ 7,500	$ 7,500
Computers	$ 6,400	$ 6,400	$ 6,400	$ 6,400	$ 6,400	$ 6,400	$ 6,400	$ 6,400	$ 6,400
Lease	$ 5,500	$ 5,500	$ 5,500	$ 5,500	$ 5,500	$ 5,500	$ 5,500	$ 5,500	$ 5,500
Advertising	$ 1,000	$ 1,000	$ 1,000	$ 1,000	$ 1,000	$ 1,000	$ 1,000	$ 1,000	$ 1,000
Miscellaneous	$ 1,500	$ 1,500	$ 1,500	$ 1,500	$ 1,500	$ 1,500	$ 1,500	$ 1,500	$ 1,500
Total Expenses	$ 28,850	$ 29,200	$ 29,500	$ 29,355	$ 29,545	$ 29,640	$ 29,800	$ 29,800	$ 29,800
Income									
Net Income	$ (1,050)	$ 200	$ 1,300	$ 1,545	$ 1,555	$ 1,560	$ 1,800	$ 1,900	$ 2,000
Profit Margin	-3.78%	0.68%	4.22%	5.00%	5.00%	5.00%	5.70%	5.99%	6.29%
		Quarter Profit Margin	0.51%			5.00%			5.99%
		Income Year-To-Date	$ 450			$ 5,110			$ 10,810

Sheet Name

Each worksheet has a unique **sheet name**. To make the workbook easy to navigate, it is a good practice to always use simple yet descriptive names for each worksheet.

ANALYZING YOUR DATA

After presenting the First Quarter Forecast to the owner, you revise the format and expand the *workbook* to include worksheets for each quarter and an annual forecast summary. You give each worksheet a descriptive *sheet name*. At the request of the owner, you perform a *what-if analysis* to test the effect of different estimates for payroll, and you use *Goal Seek* to determine how much Internet Sales would have to increase to produce a profit margin of 5.00 percent for January.

Figure 3–10 Workbook

DATABASE MANAGEMENT SYSTEMS

> A database is like an electronic file cabinet. DBMS structures data and provides tools. Relational databases use tables, records, and fields. Features include tools for sorting, filtering, defining criteria, querying, creating forms, and reports.

A **database** is a collection of related data. It is the electronic equivalent of a file cabinet. A **database management system (DBMS)** or **database manager** is a program that sets up, or structures, a database. It also provides tools to enter, edit, and retrieve data from the database. All kinds of individuals use databases, from teachers recording grades to police officers checking criminal histories. Colleges and universities use databases to keep records on their students, instructors, and courses. Organizations of all types maintain employee databases.

Three of the most widely used database management systems designed for microcomputers are Microsoft Access, Corel Paradox, and Lotus Approach.

FEATURES

The **relational database** is the most widely used database structure. Data is organized into related **tables.** Each table is made up of rows called **records** and columns called **fields.** Each record contains fields of data about some specific person, place, or thing.

DBMS provides a variety of tools to create and use databases. A **sort** tool will quickly rearrange a table's records according to a selected field.

The greatest power of a DBMS, however, comes from its ability to quickly find and bring together information stored in separate tables using queries, forms, and reports. A **query** is a question or a request for specific data contained in a database. Database **forms** look similar to traditional printed forms. These electronic forms are displayed on the computer monitor and typically reflect the contents for one record in a table. They are primarily used to enter new records and to make changes to existing records. Data from tables and queries can be printed in a variety of different types of **reports** from a simple listing of an entire field in a table to a list of selected fields based on a query involving several tables.

CASE

Assume that you have accepted a job as an employment administrator for the Lifestyle Fitness Club. One of your responsibilities is to create a database management system to replace the club's manual system for recording employee information. To see how you could use Microsoft Access, one of the most widely used relational DBMS programs, as the employment administrator for the Lifestyle Fitness Club, see Figures 3-11 and 3-12.

▼ CONCEPT CHECK

▶ What is a database? What is a DBMS? A relational database?

▶ What are tables, records, and fields?

▶ Describe the following DBMS features: sort, query, form, and report.

CREATING A DATABASE

The first step in creating the database management system is to plan. You study the existing manual system focusing on how and what data is collected and how it is used. Next, you design the basic structure or organization of the new database system to have two related *tables*, which will make entering data and using the database more efficient. Focusing on the first table, Employees, you create the table structure by specifying the *fields*, and *primary key* field. To make the process faster and more accurate, you create a *form* and use the form to enter the data for each employee as a *record* in the table.

Figure 3-11   Table and form

Primary Key
The **primary key** is the unique employee identification number. You considered using the last name field as the primary key but realized that more than one employee could have the same last name. Primary keys are often used to link tables.

Fields
Fields are given field names that are displayed at the top of each table. You select the field names to describe their contents.

Table
Tables make up the basic structure of a relational database with columns containing field data and rows containing record information. This table records basic information about each employee, including name, address, and telephone number.

Record
Each **record** contains information about one employee. A record often includes a combination of numeric, text, and object data types.

Form
Like printed paper forms, electronic **forms** should be designed to be easy to read and use. This form makes it easy to enter and view all employees' data, including their photograph.

Query
Your **query** requests the names, addresses, and telephone numbers of all employees living in Iona or Cypress Lake who work in Fort Myers.

Joined
Since the query involves two tables, they must be linked or **joined** by common fields. You chose to link the tables by the key field ID.

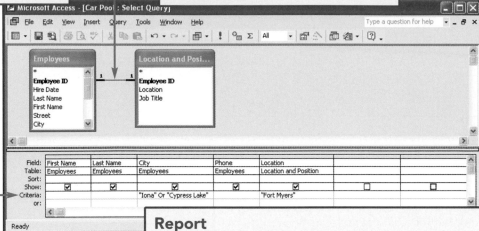

Microsoft Access - [Car Pool : Select Query]

File　Edit　View　Insert　Query　Tools　Window　Help　　Type a question for help

Employees
*
Employee ID
Hire Date
Last Name
First Name
Street
City

Location and Posi...
*
Employee ID
Location
Job Title

Field:	First Name	Last Name	City	Phone	Location		
Table:	Employees	Employees	Employees	Employees	Location and Position		
Sort:							
Show:	✓	✓	✓	✓	✓	☐	☐
Criteria:			"Iona" Or "Cypress Lake"		"Fort Myers"		
or:							

Ready

Criteria
The query **criteria** to produce the car pool list require that both the Employees table and the Location and Position table be consulted. The criteria identify all employees who work at Fort Myers and live either in Iona or Cypress Lake.

Report
From a variety of different **report** formats, you selected this format to display the names, addresses, and telephone numbers of all employees who might commute from either Cypress Lake or Iona to the Fort Myers plant.

Iona to Fort Myers Car Pool Report

Last Name	First Name	Street Address	City	Phone Number
Delucchi	Bill	950 S. Terrace Dr.	Cypress Lake	(941) 555-8195
Fromthart	Lisa	32 Redcoat Rd.	Cypress Lake	(941) 555-0110
Helfand	Eric	4601 E. Willow Dr.	Iona	(941) 555-9101
Lawrence	Nichol	433 S. Gaucho Dr.	Cypress Lake	(941) 555-7656
Lopez	Mina	4290 E. Alameda Dr.	Cypress Lake	(941) 555-5050
Nichols	Cathy	75 Brooklea Dr.	Cypress Lake	(941) 555-0001
Reddie	Suzanne	932 E. Parkway Dr.	Iona	(941) 555-1191
Schiff	Marc	235 N. Cactus Dr.	Cypress Lake	(941) 555-0010
Sutton	Lisa	4389 S. Hayden Rd.	Iona	(941) 555-1950

Sorted
To make the report easier for employees to locate their name and the names of others, you **sorted** the query results alphabetically by last name.

CREATING A QUERY

You have continued to build the database by creating a second table containing information about each employee's work location and job title. This table is linked or *joined* with the Employee table by the common field, ID. After you completed this second table, you received a request to create car pool information for those employees who live in either Iona or Cypress Lake and work in Fort Meyers. You created a *query* using the appropriate *criteria* to create the car pool list. After *sorting* the resulting list alphabetically according to last name, you created a *report* to distribute to interested employees.

Figure 3-12　Query and report

PRESENTATION GRAPHICS

Presentation graphics create interesting and professional presentations. Features include slides, AutoContent wizard, color schemes, slide layouts, special effects, design templates, and master slides.

Research shows that people learn better when information is presented visually. A picture is indeed worth a thousand words or numbers. **Presentation graphics** are programs that combine a variety of visual objects to create attractive, visually interesting presentations. They are excellent tools to communicate a message and to persuade people.

People in a variety of settings and situations use presentation graphics programs to make their presentations more interesting and professional. For example, marketing managers use presentation graphics to present proposed marketing strategies to their superiors. Sales people use these programs to demonstrate products and encourage customers to make purchases. Students use presentation graphics programs to create high-quality class presentations.

Three of the most widely used presentation graphics programs are Microsoft PowerPoint, Corel Presentations, and Lotus Freelance Graphics.

On the Web Explorations

Lotus is one of the leaders in developing presentation graphics. To learn more about the company, visit our Web site at

www.olearyseries.com/CE06 and select On the Web Explorations.

FEATURES

An electronic presentation consists of a series of **slides.** Presentation programs include a variety of features to help you create effective dynamic presentations. Most include a wizard such as Microsoft's **AutoContent wizard** that steps you through the process of creating a presentation. Other features include tools to select alternative color schemes, slide layouts, special effects, design templates, and master slides. **Design templates** provide professionally selected combinations of color schemes, slide layouts, and special effects.

Every presentation has a **master slide.** It is a special slide that does not appear in a presentation but controls the format and placement of all slides in a presentation. For example, the design for a presentation can be changed easily for the entire presentation using the master slide.

Planning a presentation for school or work? Here are a few tips from professionals to make it the best ever:

1. **Be prepared.** Know your audience, equipment, and presentation room.

2. **Practice and time** your presentation by giving it to a friend.

3. **Begin and end well.** Begin with a joke or story. End with a summary.

4. **Know when to move.** Move around to focus attention on you. Remain still to focus attention on your slides.

5. **Relax.** Prior to a presentation, take a short walk, stretch, or just take a few quiet moments to breathe deeply.

CASE

Assume that you have volunteered for the Animal Rescue Foundation, a local animal rescue agency. You have been asked to create a powerful and persuasive presentation to encourage other members from your community to volunteer. To see how you could use Microsoft PowerPoint, one of the most widely used presentation graphics programs, as a volunteer for the Animal Rescue Foundation, see Figures 3-13 through 3-14.

▼ CONCEPT CHECK

- ▶ What are presentation graphics programs? What are they used for?
- ▶ What are slides? What is a master slide? What are design templates?
- ▶ What is the AutoContent Wizard? What is it used for?

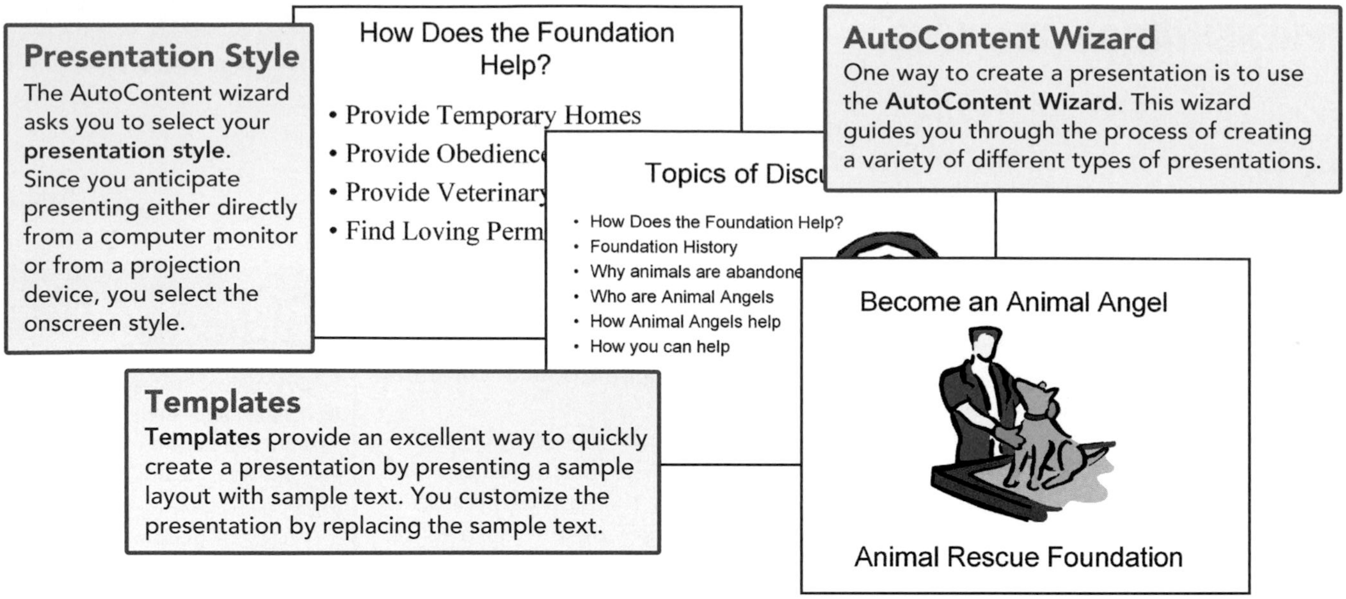

Presentation Style

The AutoContent wizard asks you to select your **presentation style**. Since you anticipate presenting either directly from a computer monitor or from a projection device, you select the onscreen style.

How Does the Foundation Help?

- Provide Temporary Homes
- Provide Obedience
- Provide Veterinary
- Find Loving Perm

AutoContent Wizard

One way to create a presentation is to use the **AutoContent Wizard**. This wizard guides you through the process of creating a variety of different types of presentations.

Topics of Discu

- How Does the Foundation Help?
- Foundation History
- Why animals are abandone
- Who are Animal Angels
- How Animal Angels help
- How you can help

Become an Animal Angel

Animal Rescue Foundation

Templates

Templates provide an excellent way to quickly create a presentation by presenting a sample layout with sample text. You customize the presentation by replacing the sample text.

Figure 3-13   Presentation

CREATING A PRESENTATION

You start creating the presentation using the *AutoContent Wizard* and specify the *template* and *presentation style* to use. The wizard creates a sample presentation containing suggested content in each slide and uses a consistent design style throughout. After replacing the sample content with the information for your presentation, you are on your way to the director's office to show him what you have.

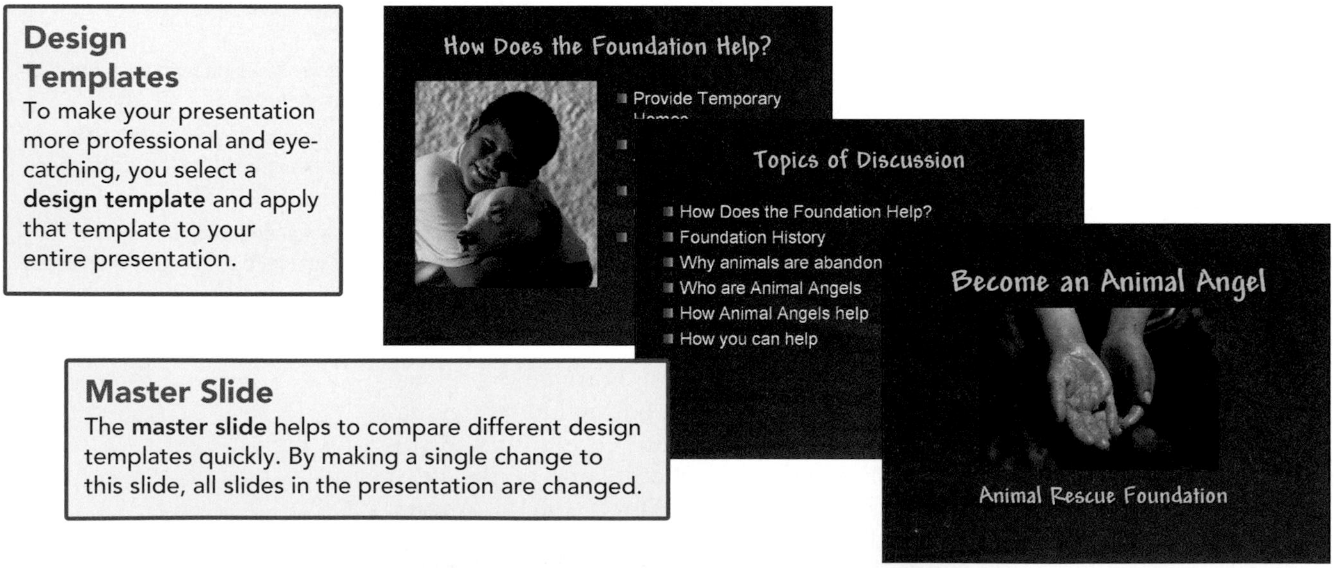

Design Templates

To make your presentation more professional and eye-catching, you select a **design template** and apply that template to your entire presentation.

How Does the Foundation Help?

- Provide Temporary Homes

Topics of Discussion

- How Does the Foundation Help?
- Foundation History
- Why animals are abandon
- Who are Animal Angels
- How Animal Angels help
- How you can help

Become an Animal Angel

Animal Rescue Foundation

Master Slide

The **master slide** helps to compare different design templates quickly. By making a single change to this slide, all slides in the presentation are changed.

Figure 3-14   Revised presentation

UPDATING A PRESENTATION

After discussing the presentation with the director, you have some ideas to enhance the effectiveness of the message. First, you improve the color of selected items and add more graphics. Next, you select one of the *design templates* and make some other changes. You apply these changes to all the slides by simply adjusting the *master slide*. Finally, you practice or rehearse the presentation, create speaker notes, and print out audience handouts. You're ready to give a professionally designed, dynamic presentation.

INTEGRATED PACKAGES

> Integrated packages provide the functionality of several separate application programs within a single program. Also known as personal or home software, they provide limited capability at low cost.

An **integrated package** is a single program that provides the *functionality* of a word processor, spreadsheet, database manager, and more. The primary disadvantage of an integrated package is that the capabilities of each function (such as word processing) are not as extensive as in the individual programs (such as Microsoft Word). The primary advantages are cost and simplicity. The cost of an integrated package is much less than the cost of the individual powerful, professional-grade application programs discussed thus far in this chapter.

Integrated packages are popular with many home users and are sometimes classified as **personal** or **home software.** The most widely used integrated packages are Microsoft Works and AppleWorks. See Figure 3-15.

Figure 3-15   AppleWorks

CASE

Assume that you publish a gardening newsletter that you distribute to members of the Desert Gardening Club. Using the word processing function, you entered text, formatted titles and subtitles, and inserted several photographs. (See Figure 3-16.) Using the spreadsheet function, you analyzed daily rainfall for the feature article and included a chart. After completing the newsletter, you will use the database function and the membership database to print mailing labels.

▼ CONCEPT CHECK

▶ What is an integrated package?

▶ Describe the advantages and disadvantages of an integrated package.

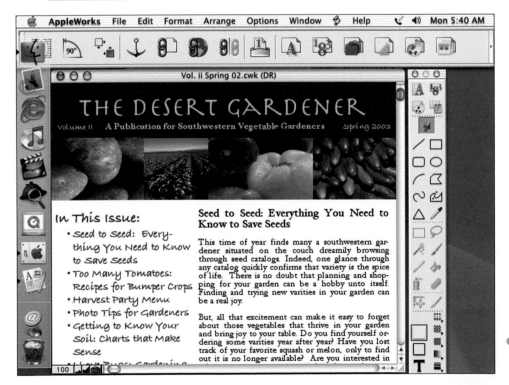

Figure 3-16   Integrated package (AppleWorks)

SOFTWARE SUITES

A software suite is a group of application programs. The four types of software suites are productivity, personal, specialized, and utility.

Figure 3-17   Microsoft Office

A **software suite** is a collection of separate application programs bundled together and sold as a group. While the applications function exactly the same whether purchased in a suite or separately, it is significantly less expensive to buy a suite of applications than to buy each application separately. There are four types of suites:

- **Productivity suite**   Productivity suites, also known as **business suites,** contain professional-grade application programs, including a word processor, spreadsheet, database manager, and more. The best known is Microsoft Office. (See Figure 3-17.) Two other well-known productivity suites are Corel WordPerfect OfficeSuite and Lotus SmartSuite.

- **Personal suite**   Also known as **home suites,** these contain personal software applications or programs intended for home use. The best known is Microsoft Works Suite, which includes the Works integrated package along with Works Calendar, Streets & Trips, and more. (See Figure 3-18.)

- **Specialized suite**   Specialized suites focus on specific applications. These include graphics suites, financial planning suites, and many others. (Graphics suites will be discussed in Chapter 4.)

- **Utility suite**   These suites include a variety of programs designed to make computing easier and safer. One of the best known is Norton System Works and Norton Internet Security Suite. (Utility suites will be discussed in detail in Chapter 5.)

▼ CONCEPT CHECK

▶   What is a software suite? What are the advantages of purchasing a suite?

▶   What are the four types of software suites?

▶   What is the best-known productivity suite? What is the best-known personal suite?

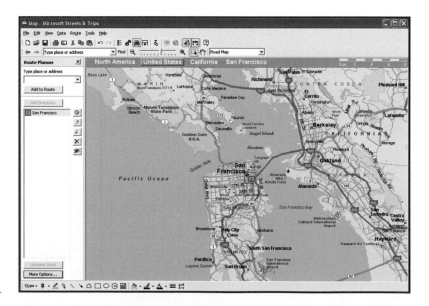

Figure 3-18   Streets & Trips from Microsoft Works Suite

SHARING DATA BETWEEN APPLICATIONS

> Ways to share data include copy and paste, object linking, and object embedding. Copy and paste is static. OLE is dynamic.

Many times it is convenient to share data between applications. For example, when writing a report it may be useful to include a chart from a spreadsheet or data from a database. Data created by one application can be shared with another application in a variety of different ways, including copying and pasting, object linking, and object embedding.

COPY AND PASTE

The most straightforward way to share data is to copy and then paste. From the file that contains the data to be shared, you would select the item and then select the copy command. Next, go to the file where the selected data is to be inserted. Position the insertion pointer at the location where the data is to be inserted and select the paste command. The data will be inserted into this file.

This is a static copy in that any changes to one file will not affect the other file. Object linking and object embedding, however, create more dynamic relationships.

OBJECT LINKING AND EMBEDDING

Object linking and embedding (OLE) is a feature that makes it easy to dynamically share and exchange data between applications. For example, you could create a text document using a word processing program that includes a chart created by a spreadsheet program and a presentation created by a graphics program. Whenever the text document is opened, the most up-to-date version of the chart would appear in the document and the presentation could be run. (See Figure 3-19.)

With **object linking,** a copy of the object from a **source file** (the file containing the object) is inserted in a **destination file** (the file receiving the object) and a *link* or connection between the two files is established. In our example, the object is a chart from a spreadsheet (source) file. If a change occurs in the spreadsheet file that affects the chart, the link between the two files will automatically update the chart in the word processing file. Object linking is useful if you want the destination document to always contain the most up-to-date data.

With **object embedding,** the object from the source file is *embedded* or added to the destination document and becomes part of the destination document. In our example, the embedded object is a presentation created by a presentation graphics program. The presentation (embedded object) can be run and edited from within the destination document. However, changes you make to the embedded object are not reflected in the original source file.

Object linking and embedding is a powerful and useful feature to support sharing and exchanging data between files.

▼ CONCEPT CHECK

- ▶ Discuss the three ways to share data between applications.
- ▶ What are OLE, source files, and destination files?
- ▶ What is the difference between object linking and object embedding?

How Object Linking and Embedding Work

Destination File
A **destination file** receives objects (the Excel chart and the PowerPoint presentation) from source files.

Linked Object
A **linked object** (the Excel chart) from the source file appears in the destination file. Any changes in the source file affecting the linked object are automatically made in the destination file.

Embedded Object
An **embedded object** (presentation) is part of the destination file. Double-clicking the object in the destination file causes the object to run.

Source Files
Source files (Excel and PowerPoint files) provide objects that are either linked or embedded into a destination file.

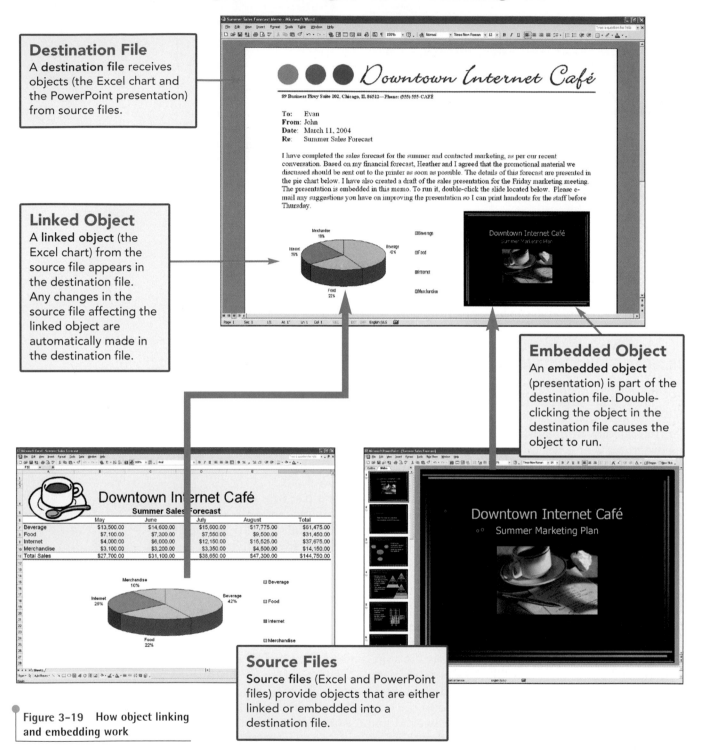

Figure 3-19   How object linking and embedding work

A Look to the Future

Web-based Application Software Updates Ease Maintenance

Wouldn't it be great if you never had to buy software again? What if you could pay as you go, only paying for those parts of a software suite that you actually use? These options sound terrific to end users eager to avoid the high cost and difficulties of software maintenance. They sound even better to large and small corporations, where the costs of maintaining software and the information systems department can be huge expenditures.

Of course, that is what Web-based application service providers, ASPs, are all about. As we discussed earlier, you can use the Web to connect to an ASP and use its software. A major advantage of using an ASP is that others do all the administration work—there are no programs for you to install and configure, and you never have to worry about the hassle of upgrades.

With an ASP you can access your data from any Internet-connected computer in the world. This means that if a computer is lost or damaged, no data or time has been wasted. And because any computer that can access the Internet can connect to an ASP, any platform can be used. For example, PCs and Apple computers could share data and applications in the same office. Finally using an ASP allows for a simpler and cheaper computer system, because you don't have to worry about hardware requirements or storage space.

These considerations may sound tempting to individuals who dislike installing and maintaining software, and some experts predict that eventually all software may be distributed this way. However, ASPs are currently very valuable to smaller companies with fewer dollars to spend on these labor intensive maintenance and installation tasks. ASPs allow them to customize their software in ways that would otherwise be too expensive for them.

Some experts have even suggested ASPs may become widely used by large corporations with IT departments that decide to outsource these projects. They predict that software may become a service that companies receive from an outside company. For example, a large company in the future may have a software contract with a company that agrees to supply a word processing program over the Internet. In fact, some traditional software developers are slowly moving toward Web deployment. Microsoft's .NET program is believed to be a step by the corporation toward providing Web services of their popular software programs.

Do you think you and other end users will use ASPs for these new services? Will we be using ASPs to create customized programs for our personal use?

VISUAL SUMMARY

APPLICATION SOFTWARE

There are two basic types of software. **System software** focuses on handling technical details. **Application software** focuses on completing specific tasks or applications. Two categories are **basic applications (general-purpose applications, productivity applications) and specialized applications (special-purpose applications).**

Common Features

Common features of most application programs include:

- **User interface**—most have **graphical user interfaces (GUI)** that display **icons.**
- **Windows**—rectangular areas that can contain documents, programs, and messages.
- **Menus**—present commands listed on the menu bar; use **pull-down (drop-down)** menus. **Help** menu provides access to online assistance.
- **Dialog box**—provides additional information or requests user input.
- **Toolbars**—contain **buttons** and menus; **standard toolbar** is common to most applications.
- New versions of Microsoft Office provide **speech recognition.**

Web-based Applications

Web-based applications from Web sites called **application service providers (ASP).**

WORD PROCESSORS

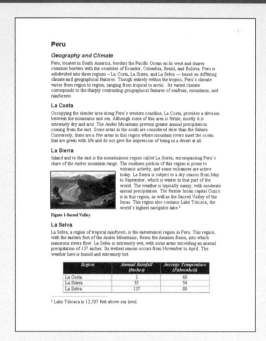

Word processors allow you to create, edit, save, and print text-based **documents,** including flyers, reports, newsletters, and Web pages.

Features

Word wrap is a basic feature that automatically moves the insertion point to the next line.

Editing features include:

- **Thesaurus** provides synonyms, antonyms, and related words.
- **Find** and **Replace,** which locates (finds), removes, and inserts (replace) another word(s).
- **Spelling** and **grammar checkers** automatically locate misspelled words and grammatical problems.

Formatting features include:

- **Font**—design of characters. **Font size** is height of characters.
- **Character effects**—include **bold,** *italic,* shadow, and colors.
- **Bulleted** and **numbered lists**—used to present sequences of topics or steps.

To be a competent end user, you need to understand the capabilities of basic application software, which includes word processors, spreadsheets, database management systems, and presentation programs. You need to know how to use these applications and how data can be shared between them.

SPREADSHEET

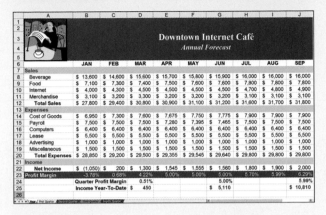

Spreadsheet programs are used to organize, analyze, and graph numeric data.

Features
Principal spreadsheet features include the following:

- **Workbook files** consist of one or more related worksheets.
- **Worksheets,** also known as **spreadsheets** or **sheets,** are rectangular grids of **rows** and **columns.** Rows are identified by numbers, columns by letters.
- **Cells** formed by intersection of a row and column; used to hold text and numeric entries.
- **Text entries (labels)** provide structure and **numeric entries** can be numbers or formulas.
- **Formulas** are instructions for calculations. **Functions** are prewritten formulas.
- **Range** is a series of cells.
- **Analytical graphs (charts)** represent data visually.
- **Recalculation** occurs whenever a value changes in one cell that affects another cell(s).
- **What-if analysis** is the process of observing the effect of changing one or more values.

DATABASE MANAGEMENT SYSTEMS

A **database** is a collection of related data. A **database management system (DBMS),** also known as a **database manager,** structures a database and provides tools for entering, editing, and retrieving data.

Features
Principal database management system features include the following:

- **Relational database** organizes data into related tables.
- **Tables** have rows **(records)** and columns **(fields).**
- **Sort** is a tool to rearrange records using a particular field.
- **Query** is a question or request for specific data contained in a database.
- **Forms** are used to enter new records or edit existing records.
- **Reports** are printed output in a variety of forms.

PRESENTATION GRAPHICS

Presentation graphics combine a variety of visual objects to create attractive, visually interesting presentations. They are excellent tools to communicate a message and to persuade people.

Features
Principal presentation graphics features include: **slides, AutoContent wizard, and master slides.**

INTEGRATED PACKAGES

An **integrated package,** also known as **personal** or **home software,** is a single program that provides the functionality of several application packages. Some important characteristics include:

- Functions typically include word processing, spreadsheet, database manager, and more.
- Each function is not as extensive or powerful as a single function application program.
- Less expensive than purchasing several individual application programs.
- Simple to use and switch between functions.
- Popular with home users who are willing to sacrifice some advanced features for cost and simplicity.

SOFTWARE SUITES

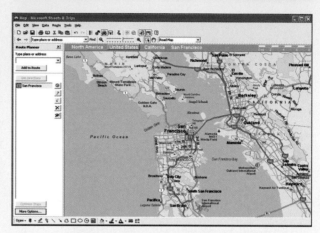

A **software suite** is a collection of individual application packages sold together. While functionally identical, application packages purchased in a suite are significantly less expensive than those purchased separately.

Four types of suites are **productivity (business), personal (home), specialized, and utility.**

SHARING DATA

Sharing data between files created with different applications is often convenient.

Copy and Paste
Copy and paste is the most straightforward way to share between files. This creates a static copy.

OLE
Object linking and embedding (OLE) is a feature to dynamically share and exchange data.
- With **object linking** a copy of an **object** from a **source file** is inserted into a **destination file** and a *link* between the two files is made.
- With **object embedding,** the object is embedded into the destination file and the embedded object can be run from that file.

analytical graph   (68)
application service provider (ASPs)   (61)
application software   (60)
AutoContent wizard   (75)
basic application   (60)
bulleted list   (64)
business suite   (77)
button   (60)
cell   (67)
character effect   (64)
chart   (68)
column   (67)
database   (72)
database management system (DBMS)   (72)
database manager   (72)
design template   (75)
destination file   (79)
dialog box   (60)
document   (64)
drop-down menu   (60)
editing   (64)
field   (72)
find and replace   (64)
font   (64)
font size   (64)
form   (72)
format   (64)
formula   (67)
function   (67)
general-purpose application   (60)
grammar checker   (64)
graphical user interface (GUI)   (60)
Help   (60)
home software   (77)
home suite   (77)
icons   (60)
integrated package   (77)
label   (67)
master slide   (75)
menu   (60)
menu bar   (60)
numbered list   (64)
numeric entry   (67)

object embedding   (79)
object linking   (79)
object linking and embedding (OLE)   (79)
personal software   (77)
personal suite   (77)
pointer   (60)
presentation graphics   (75)
productivity application   (60)
productivity suite   (77)
pull-down menu   (60)
query   (72)
range   (68)
recalculation   (68)
record   (72)
relational database   (72)
report   (72)
row   (67)
sheet   (67)
slide   (75)
software suite   (77)
sort   (72)
source file   (79)
specialized application   (60)
specialized suite   (77)
special-purpose application   (60)
speech recognition   (60)
spelling checker   (64)
spreadsheet   (67)
standard toolbar   (60)
system software   (60)
table   (72)
text entry   (67)
Thesaurus   (64)
toolbar   (60)
user interface   (60)
utility suite   (77)
Web-based application   (61)
what-if analysis   (68)
window   (60)
word processor   (64)
word wrap   (64)
workbook file   (67)
worksheet   (67)

To test your knowledge of these key terms with animated flash cards, consult your Computing Essentials CD or visit our Web site at www.olearyseries.com/CE06 and select Key Terms.

COMPUTING ESSENTIALS 2006

CROSSWORD PUZZLE

Across

4 Database Manager.

6 Series of cells.

7 Dynamically shares data between files.

9 Collection of related data.

13 Collection of individual applications.

15 Contain buttons and menus.

16 Question or request for data in a database.

17 Flyer, report, newsletter, Web page.

18 Menu that provides access to online assistance.

Down

1 Requests user input.

2 Has records and fields.

3 Formed by intersection of row and column.

5 Rearranges records using a field.

8 Controls format and placement of slides.

10 Make up a presentation.

11 List of commands.

12 Rectangular area that contains messages.

14 Moves insertion point to next line.

For an interactive version of this crossword, consult your Computing Essentials CD or visit our Web site at **www.olearyseries.com/CE06** and select Crossword.

MULTIPLE CHOICE

Circle the letter or fill in the correct answer.

1. General-purpose applications are also known as _____.
   a. software suites
   b. advanced applications
   c. basic applications
   d. special-purpose applications
   e. integrated applications

2. Graphics, multimedia, Web authoring, and virtual reality programs are examples of _____.
   a. special-purpose applications
   b. general-purpose applications
   c. basic applications
   d. occupational applications
   e. system software

3. _____ are prewritten formulas that perform calculations automatically.
   a. Functions
   b. Macros
   c. Templates
   d. Calculators
   e. Tables

4. In a relational database, data is organized into _____.
   a. fields
   b. columns
   c. records
   d. tables
   e. rows

5. _____ is a DBMS tool that arranges records according to a selected field.
   a. Align
   b. Range
   c. Report
   d. Form
   e. Sort

6. Most presentation graphics programs have design _____ that provide color schemes, slide layouts, and special effects.
   a. layout files
   b. templates
   c. samples
   d. records
   e. formatting

7. A(n) _____ is a single program that provides the functionality of a word processor, spreadsheet, database manager, and more.
   a. general-purpose application
   b. software suite
   c. integrated package
   d. program manager
   e. OLE

8. A _____ suite is also known as a productivity suite.
   a. personal
   b. utility
   c. specialized
   d. home
   e. business

9. To have an object automatically updated in a destination file when a change is made to the source file, the object must be _____.
   a. embedded
   b. linked
   c. replaced
   d. resolved
   e. amended

10. With object linking, the object is contained in the _____.
    a. destination file
    b. origin file
    c. layout file
    d. support file
    e. source file

For an interactive version of these multiple choice questions, consult your Computing Essentials CD or visit our Web site at www.olearyseries.com/CE06 and select Multiple Choice.

FEATURES
Animations
Careers in IT
DVD Direct
Expansions
Making IT Work for You
On the Web Explorations
TechTV
Tips

CHAPTER REVIEW
Key Terms
Crossword
Multiple Choice
Matching
Open-ended
Using Technology
Expanding Your Knowledge
Building Your Portfolio

COMPUTING
ESSENTIALS
2006

MATCHING

Match each numbered item with the most closely related lettered item. Write your answers in the spaces provided.

a. ASP
b. cell
c. find
d. formulas
e. general-purpose applications
f. grammar checker
g. integrated package
h. OLE
i. presentation graphics
j. range
k. relational database
l. software suite
m. sort
n. spelling checker
o. templates
p. Thesaurus
q. utility
r. what-if analysis
s. window
t. word processor

1. Word processors are one type. ____
2. Area that contains a document, program, or message. ____
3. A feature that contains buttons. ____
4. Site that provides access to Web-based applications. ____
5. Type of suite that makes computing easier and safer. ____
6. Checks for problems with capitalization and punctuation. ____
7. Includes the functionality of a word processor, spreadsheet, database manager, and more. ____
8. Software that creates text-based documents such as reports. ____
9. Identifies incorrectly spelled words and suggests alternatives. ____
10. Locates any character, word, or phrase in a document. ____
11. The intersection of a row and column in a spreadsheet. ____
12. A collection of two or more cells in a spreadsheet. ____
13. Instructions for calculations. ____
14. Spreadsheet feature in which changing one or more numbers results in the automatic recalculation of all related fields. ____
15. Database structure that organizes data into related tables. ____
16. Arranging objects numerically or alphabetically. ____
17. Programs used to communicate a message or to persuade. ____
18. Provides synonyms, antonyms, and related words. ____
19. Individual applications that are sold as a group. ____
20. Feature used to share information between applications. ____

For an interactive version of this matching exercise, consult your Computing Essentials CD or visit our Web site at **www.olearyseries.com/CE06** and select Matching.

OPEN-ENDED

On a separate sheet of paper, respond to each question or statement.

1. Explain the difference between general-purpose and special-purpose applications.
2. What is the difference between a function and a formula? How is a formula related to what-if analysis?
3. What are presentation graphics programs? How are they used?
4. Explain the difference between a linked object and an embedded object? What are the advantages of OLE?
5. What is the difference between an integrated package and a software suite? What are the advantages and disadvantages of each?

1 Speech Recognition

Tired of using your keyboard to type term papers? Have you ever thought about speaking to your computer? Perhaps speech recognition is just what you are looking for. It is easy with the right software and hardware. To learn more about speech recognition, review Making IT Work for You: Speech Recognition on pages 62 and 63. Then answer the following questions: (a) What menu item is selected to begin training the software? (b) What are the verbal commands to insert a picture into a Microsoft Word document? (c) What button must you press to speak text into a Word document? (d) Have you ever used speech recognition? If you have, describe how you used it and discuss how effective it was for you. If you have not used speech recognition, discuss how you might use it in the future. Be specific.

2 Presentation Graphics

For presentations, having the right software can help grab your audience's attention and improve your effectiveness as a speaker. Connect to our Web site at www.olearyseries.com/CE06 and select Using Technology to link to a presentation graphics software package. Once connected, review the product's features, and answer the following questions: (a) What computer hardware and software is required to use the presentation graphics product? (b) List and describe three features that could help you organize or present your ideas. (c) What types of files can be embedded with a presentation using this software?

1   How Speech Recognition Works

Speech recognition is an emerging technology. As speech recognition systems become more accurate at interpreting the voice commands of users, new applications of this technology will become more widely available. Study the "How Speech Recognition Works" Expansion on your Computing Essentials CD or visit our Web site at www.olearyseries.com/CE06. Then answer the following questions: (a) Create a drawing similar to the one in the Expansion that would represent dictating a mailing address for an address label. Be sure to include and number the appropriate steps. (b) What hardware is required to use voice recognition software? (c) Describe how speech recognition could enhance your use of each of the following types of applications: word processing, spreadsheet, and presentation. (d) Describe a profession that could benefit from speech recognition software. Be specific.

2   How Web-based Applications Work

Some predict that many organizations will be using Web-based applications in the near future. These organizations will not be required to own, install, upgrade, or store applications. Additionally, applications and application files can be accessed from almost anywhere in the world. To learn more about "How Web-based Applications Work" consult your Computing Essentials CD or visit our Web site at www. olearyseries.com/CE06 and select Animations. Then consider the following case.

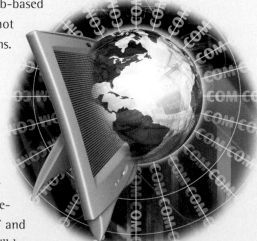

Assume that you are about to give a presentation at your company's national sales meeting. Earlier in the week you created the presentation using a Web ASP's program PRESENT and saved the presentation at the ASP's site. This presentation will be run from your notebook computer and will be displayed on a projection screen large enough for everyone at the sales meeting to see. To run the program, you need access to the presentation file and the PRESENT program.

On a single page of paper, create a drawing similar to the figure on the CD and on the Web that describes how you will use the Web-based application to give the presentation.

1   Software Suites

Software suites offer both end users and businesses some unique advantages. In a one-page paper titled "Software Suites," address the following questions: (a) Define software suites. (b) Which suites are the most popular today? Why? (c) New versions of software suites are coming out all the time. As a user, how can you know when it's time to upgrade?

2   Acquiring Software

There are three common ways to obtain new software: use public domain software, use shareware, buy commercial software. In addition to these three ways, two others are to copy programs from a friend or to purchase unauthorized copies of programs. Investigate each of these five options, and then answer the following questions in a one-page paper: (a) Define and discuss each option. Be sure to discuss both the advantages and disadvantages of each. (b) Which seems like the best method to you? Why? (c) Do you think there is anything wrong with obtaining and using unauthorized software? Identify and explore the key issues.

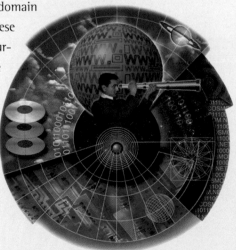

COMPETENCIES

After you have read this chapter, you should be able to:

1 **Describe graphics software, including desktop publishing, image editors, illustration programs, image galleries, and graphics suites.**

2 **Discuss audio and video editing software.**

3 **Describe multimedia, including story boards and multimedia authoring programs.**

4 **Explain Web authoring, Web site design, and Web authoring programs.**

5 **Describe virtual reality and VRML.**

6 **Discuss knowledge-based (expert) systems.**

7 **Describe robotics including perception systems, industrial robots, and mobile robots.**

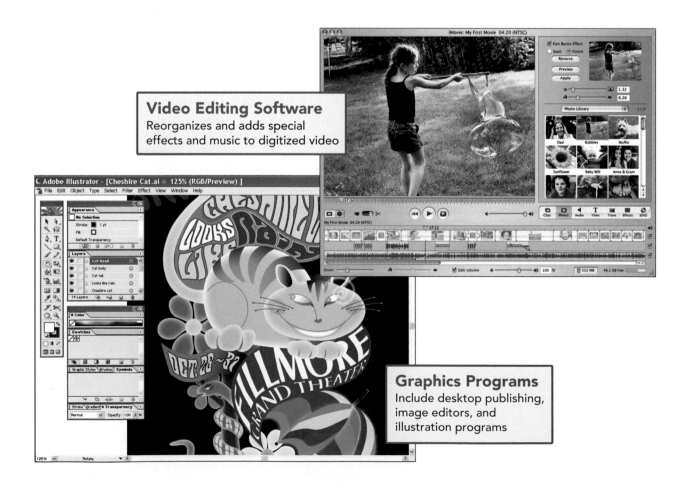

Video Editing Software
Reorganizes and adds special effects and music to digitized video

Graphics Programs
Include desktop publishing, image editors, and illustration programs

E xpect surprises—exciting and positive opportunities. The latest technological developments offer you new opportunities to extend your range of computer competency. As we show in this chapter, software that for years was available only for mainframes has recently become available for microcomputers. A whole new generation of software only recently available for microcomputers, called specialized applications, now makes it possible to perform advanced tasks at home.

The latest technological developments have created an opportunity for home users to take advantage of software previously used only in professional environments. For example, it is now possible, and quite common, for people to create their own Web sites. Home users also have access to software that helps manipulate and create graphic images. Many musicians and artists work from home to create complex and beautiful work using specialized applications.

Some of these same technological advances have allowed researchers and computer scientists to make advances in the field of artificial intelligence that previously were envisioned only in science fiction. Robots now provide security and assistance in homes. Virtual reality is providing opportunities in the fields of medicine and science but also commonly appears in video games.

Competent end users need to be aware of specialized applications. They need to know who uses them, what they are used for, and how they are used. These advanced applications include graphics programs, audio and video editing software, multimedia, Web authoring, and artificial intelligence, including virtual reality, knowledge-based systems, and robotics.

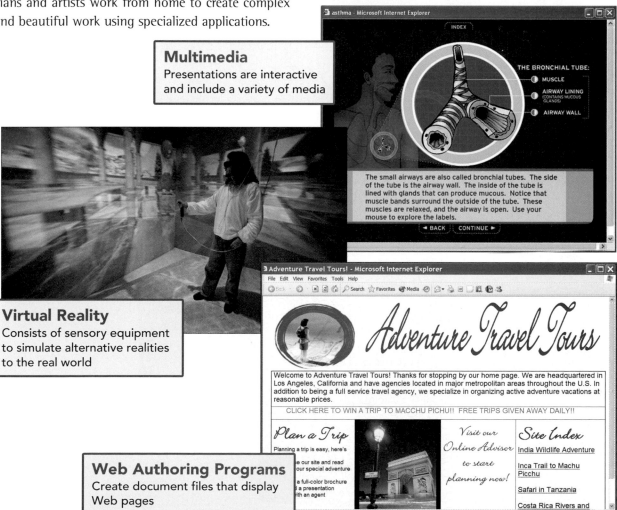

Multimedia
Presentations are interactive and include a variety of media

Virtual Reality
Consists of sensory equipment to simulate alternative realities to the real world

Web Authoring Programs
Create document files that display Web pages

SPECIALIZED APPLICATIONS

Specialized applications are widely used within specific professions. Applications include graphics, audio, video, multimedia, Web authoring, and emerging applications.

In the previous chapter, we discussed basic applications that are widely used in nearly every profession. This chapter focuses on specialized applications that are widely used within specific professions. (See Figure 4-1.) Specifically, we will examine:

- Graphics programs for creating professional-looking published documents, for creating and editing images, and for locating and inserting graphics.
- Audio and video software to create, edit, and play music and videos.
- Multimedia programs to create dynamic interactive presentations.
- Web authoring programs to create, edit, and design Web sites.
- Emerging applications that merge artificial intelligence into a variety of different types of applications, including virtual reality, knowledge-based systems, and robotics.

Figure 4–1 Specialized applications

94   CHAPTER 4

GRAPHICS

Desktop publishers mix text and graphics. Image editors modify bitmap image files. Illustrators modify vector files. Image galleries are libraries of electronic images. Graphics suites bundle separate programs.

In Chapter 3, we discussed analytical and presentation graphics, which are widely used to analyze data and to create professional-looking presentations. Here we focus on more specialized graphics programs used by professionals in the graphic arts profession.

DESKTOP PUBLISHING

Desktop publishing programs, or **page layout programs,** allow you to mix text and graphics to create publications of professional quality. While word processors focus on creating text and have the ability to combine text and graphics, desktop publishers focus on page design and layout and provide greater flexibility. Professional graphic artists use desktop publishing programs to create documents such as brochures, newsletters, newspapers, and textbooks.

Popular desktop publishing programs include Adobe PageMaker, Microsoft Publisher, and QuarkXPress. While these programs provide the capability to create text and graphics, typically graphic artists import these elements from other sources, including word processors, digital cameras, scanners, image editors, illustration programs, and image galleries.

IMAGE EDITORS

One of the most common types of graphic files is bitmap. **Bitmap images,** also known as **raster images,** use thousands of dots or **pixels** to represent images. Each dot has a specific location, color, and shade. One limitation of bitmap images, however, is that when they are expanded, the images can become pixilated or jagged on the edges. For example, when the letter A in Figure 4-2 is expanded, the borders of the letter appear jagged, as indicated by the expanded view.

Popular professional image editors include Microsoft Paint, Adobe Photoshop, Corel PhotoPaint, and Paint Shop Pro. (See Figure 4-3.)

Letter A

Expanded view

Figure 4-2   Bitmap image

ILLUSTRATION PROGRAMS

Vector is another common type of graphic file. While bitmap images use pixels to represent images, **vector images,** also known as **vector illustrations,** use geometric shapes or objects. (See Figure 4-4.) These objects are created by connecting lines and curves. Because these objects can be defined by mathematical equations, they can be rapidly and easily resized, colored, textured, and manipulated. An image is a combination of several objects. **Illustration programs,** also known as **drawing programs,** are used to create and to edit vector images.

Popular professional illustration programs include Adobe Illustrator, Corel-Draw, Macromedia FreeHand, and Micrografx Designer. (See Figure 4-5.)

IMAGE GALLERIES

Image galleries are libraries of electronic images. These images are used for a wide variety of applications from illustrating textbooks to providing visual

Paint Tools

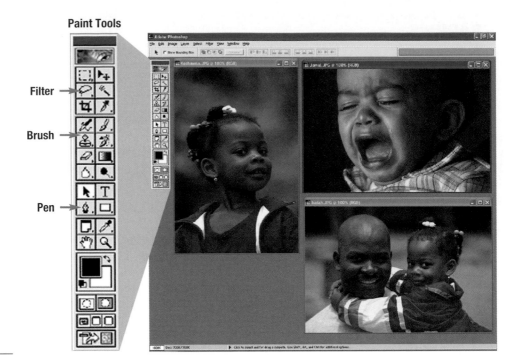

Filter

Brush

Pen

Figure 4-3 Adobe Photoshop

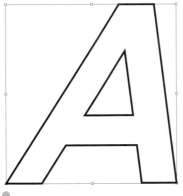

Figure 4-4   Vector Image

interest to presentations. There are two basic types of electronic images in these galleries.

- **Stock photographs**—photographs on a variety of subject material from professional models to natural landscapes.
- **Clip art**—graphic illustrations representing a wide range of topics. Most applications provide access to a limited selection of free clip art. For example in Microsoft Word, you can gain access to several pieces of clip art by issuing the command Insert>Pictures>Clip Art.

Figure 4-5   Adobe Illustrator

There are numerous Web image galleries. (See Figure 4-6.) Some of these sites offer free images and clip art while others charge a fee.

GRAPHICS SUITES

Some companies are combining or bundling their separate graphics programs in groups called **graphics suites.** The advantage of the graphics suites is that you can buy a larger variety of graphics programs at a lower cost than if purchased separately.

One of the most popular suites is from the Corel Corporation. The suite, called CorelDraw Graphics Suite, includes five individual Corel graphics programs plus a large library of clip art, media clips, and fonts. (See Figure 4-7.) Two other popular suites are Adobe's Creative Suites and Macromedia's Studio.

Organization	Site
Classroom Clipart	www.classroomclipart.com
Broderbund	www.broderbund.com
MS Office clip art	office.microsoft.com/clipart
GifArt	www.gifart.com
ClipArt.com	www.clipart.com

Figure 4-6 Selected Web image galleries

Figure 4-7 CorelDraw

▼ CONCEPT CHECK

► What is desktop publishing?

► What is the difference between an image editor and an illustration program?

► Describe image galleries. What are graphics suites?

AUDIO AND VIDEO

Digital video editing software makes it easy to make digital video into professional quality home movies. Audio editing software makes it easy to record and edit music at home.

In the past, professional quality editing of home audio and video was a job for professional photo labs or studios. For example, if you wanted to assemble footage from all your Fourth of July picnics, you sent all the tapes to a lab and waited for a compilation tape. Now, using audio and video editing software, you can create your own compilation movies.

- **Video editing software** allows you to reorganize, add effects, and more to your digital video footage. Two commonly used video editing software programs are Apple's iMovie and Windows Movie Maker. (See Figure 4-8.) These programs are designed to allow you to assemble and edit new home videos and movies from raw digital video footage. To see how digital video editors work, consult your Computing Essentials CD or visit our Web site at www.olearyseries.com/CE06 and select Expansions. To learn how to use a digital video editor, see Making IT Work for You: Digital Video Editing on pages 100 and 101.

- **Audio editing software** allows you to create and edit audio clips. Most audio editing software also has features that allow you to add audio effects, like filters, to your tracks. For example, you can use this type of software to filter out pops or scratches in an old recording. You can even use this software to create your own MP3s. Some commonly used audio editing software programs are Ableton's Live and Sony's ACID. (See Figure 4-9.)

Specialized Application Software

Figure 4–8   Apple iMovie

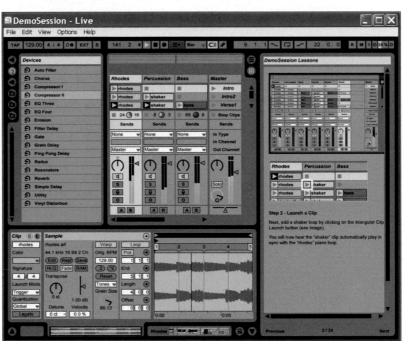

Figure 4–9   Live audio editing
software

MULTIMEDIA

Multimedia presentations can include a variety of media and should include
interactivity. Pages are linked by buttons. Plan and analyze, design, create,
and support are the steps in developing multimedia presentations. Multimedia
authoring programs create presentations.

Multimedia is the integration of all sorts of media into one presentation. For
example, a multimedia presentation may include video, music, voice,
graphics, and text. You may have seen multimedia applied in video games,

Web presentations, or even a word processing document. Many of the basic application software programs you learned about in Chapter 3 include features that make the incorporation of multimedia in documents easy. Although these applications include multimedia features, they create documents that are generally accessed in a linear fashion and provide very limited user interaction.

Effective multimedia presentations incorporate user participation or interactivity. **Interactivity** allows the user to choose the information to view, to control the pace and flow of information, and to respond to items and receive feedback. When experiencing an interactive multimedia presentation, users customize the presentation to their needs. For example Figure 4-10 presents an opening page of a multimedia presentation titled "About Asthma." Users are able to select the language to be used and decide whether to include sound.

Once used almost exclusively for computer games, interactive multimedia is now widely used in business, education, and the home. Business uses include high-quality interactive presentations, product demonstrations, and Web page design. In education, interactive multimedia is used for in-class presentations and demonstrations, long-distance learning, and online testing over the Internet. In the home, multimedia is primarily used for entertainment.

LINKS AND BUTTONS

An interactive multimedia presentation is typically organized as a series of related pages. Each page presents information and provides **links** or connections to related information. These links can be to video, sound, graphics, and text files, and to other pages and resources. By clicking special areas called **buttons** on a page, you can make appropriate links and navigate through a presentation to locate and discover information. Typically, there are several buttons on a page. You can select one, several, or none of them. You are in control. You direct the flow and content of the presentation. (See Figure 4-11.)

DEVELOPING MULTIMEDIA PRESENTATIONS

To create interactive multimedia presentations, follow these steps: Plan and Analyze, Design, Create, and Support. Follow the same development process regardless of the complexity and size of the project.

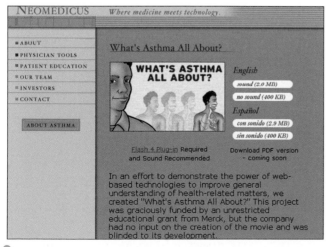

Figure 4-10   Opening page of a multimedia presentation "About Asthma"

Buttons

Figure 4-11   Links and buttons are used to navigate the "About Asthma" multimedia presentation

DIGITAL VIDEO EDITING

Do you want to make your own movie? Would you like to edit some home movies and distribute them to family and friends on DVDs? It's easy with the right equipment and software.

Capturing Video   You can capture video to your computer from a device such as a digital camcorder. Once captured, the video can be edited using digital video editing software. Follow the steps below to capture video from a digital camcorder using Windows Movie Maker.

1 ● **Connect the digital camcorder to your computer. The *Video Capture Wizard* starts automatically.**

● **Enter a file name for your captured video and select a location to save it to.**

2 ● **Follow the on-screen instructions to select a video setting and capture method for your video.**

3 ● **Preview the video as it is captured from your camera to the file you specified.**

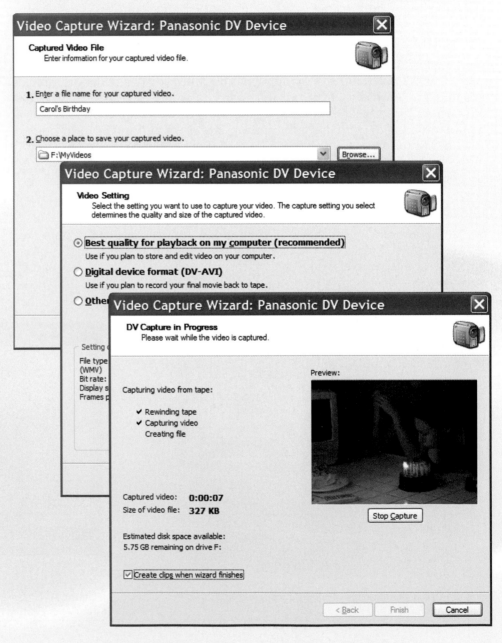

Video Capture Wizard: Panasonic DV Device

Captured Video File
Enter information for your captured video file.

1. Enter a file name for your captured video.

Carol's Birthday

2. Choose a place to save your captured video.

F:\MyVideos   Browse...

Video Capture Wizard: Panasonic DV Device

Video Setting
Select the setting you want to use to capture your video. The capture setting you select determines the quality and size of the captured video.

⊙ **Best quality for playback on my computer (recommended)**
Use if you plan to store and edit video on your computer.

○ **Digital device format (DV-AVI)**
Use if you plan to record your final movie back to tape.

○ **Other**

Setting
File type
(WMV)
Bit rate:
Display s
Frames p

Video Capture Wizard: Panasonic DV Device

DV Capture in Progress
Please wait while the video is captured.

Capturing video from tape:

✔ Rewinding tape
✔ Capturing video
    Creating file

Preview:

Captured video: **0:00:07**
Size of video file: **327 KB**

Estimated disk space available:
5.75 GB remaining on drive F:

☑ Create clips when wizard finishes

Stop Capture

< Back   Finish   Cancel

Editing a Movie   Windows Movie Maker divides your captured video into *clips*, or scenes that make up your movie. Follow the steps below to create a movie by arranging clips and adding special effects.

1
- Drag movie clips from the Collection Pane and arrange them in the Timeline.
- Use the options in the Movie Tasks Pane to add a soundtrack to your movie.
- Use the options in the Movie Tasks Pane to add effects, titles, and credits.
- Use the Monitor to preview your movie.

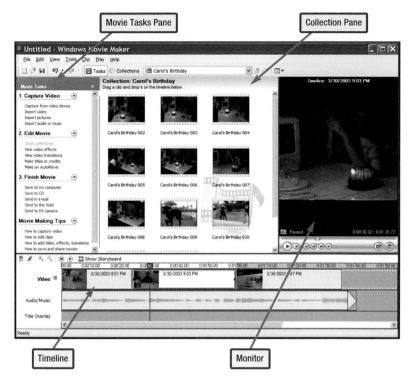

Movie Tasks Pane

Collection Pane

Timeline

Monitor

Creating a DVD   Once you have edited your movies, you can create a DVD to share with friends and family. You will need a DVD writer and some special software, such as Sonic MyDVD. Follow the steps below to design a menu, add movies, and create your DVD.

1
- Open Sonic MyDVD and select *Create or Modify a DVD-Video Project*.

2
- Click the title text to change the title of your DVD menu.
- Click *Get Movies* to add your movie files.
- Click the Burn button to create your DVD.

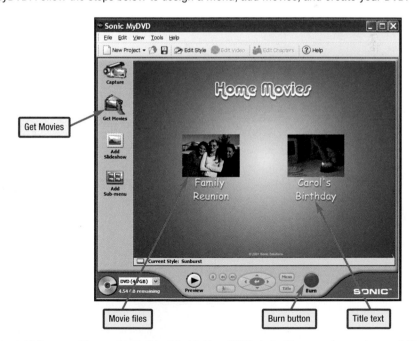

Get Movies

Movie files

Burn button

Title text

The Web is continually changing, and some of the specifics presented in this Making IT Work for You may have changed. To learn more about other ways to make information technology work for you, visit our site at www.olearyseries.com/CE06 and select Making IT Work for You.

- **Plan and analyze:** Determine the overall objective of the project, the resources required, and the person or team of people who will work on the project.
- **Design:** The creation of a story board is essential to the development of the project. A **story board** is a design tool used to record the intended overall logic, flow, and structure of a multimedia presentation. Figure 4-12 presents a partial overall story board. The highlighted path indicates just one of the many different paths a user could take. Each rectangle represents a single page in the presentation. Each page has a detailed story board associated with it that specifies the content, style, and design along with the links to video, audio, graphics, text, or any other media for that particular page.
- **Create:** Use a multimedia authoring program to create the interactive multimedia presentation. For example, see a selection of pages from "About Asthma" in Figure 4-13. This sequence of pages matches the highlighted story board elements in Figure 4-12 and represents just one possible path through the presentation.
- **Support:** Evaluate effectiveness, identify errors, and revise as needed.

MULTIMEDIA AUTHORING PROGRAMS

Multimedia authoring programs are special programs used to create multimedia presentations. They bring together all the video, audio, graphics, and text elements into an interactive framework. Widely used authoring programs include Macromedia Director, Authorware, and Toolbook. (See Figure 4-14.)

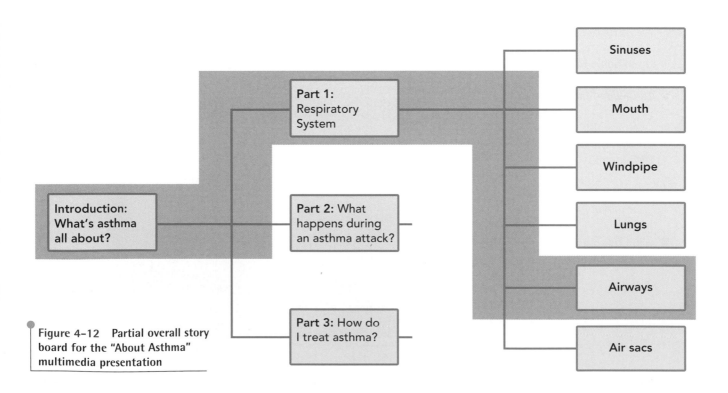

Figure 4–12   Partial overall story board for the "About Asthma" multimedia presentation

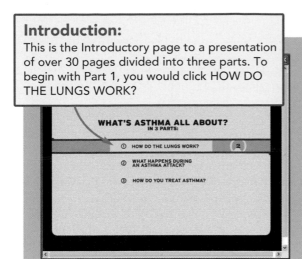

Introduction:
This is the Introductory page to a presentation of over 30 pages divided into three parts. To begin with Part 1, you would click HOW DO THE LUNGS WORK?

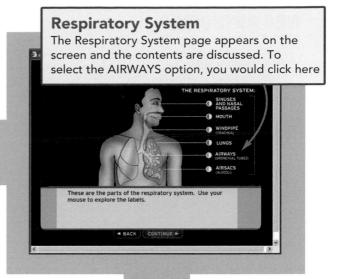

Respiratory System
The Respiratory System page appears on the screen and the contents are discussed. To select the AIRWAYS option, you would click here

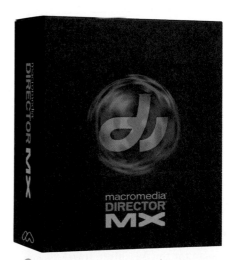

Airways
The Airways page appears with audio and an animation begins

Figure 4-13 One path through the completed "About Asthma" multimedia presentation

▼ CONCEPT CHECK

► What is digital video editing software? What is audio editing software?

► What are multimedia and interactivity? What are multimedia authoring programs?

► Describe the steps to create an interactive multimedia presentation.

Figure 4-14 Macromedia Director

WEB AUTHORING

Creating Web sites is called Web authoring. Graphical maps present overall Web site design. Web authoring programs support design and HTML coding.

On the Web Explorations

To learn more about some of the leading companies that develop multimedia authoring programs, visit our Web site at

www.olearyseries.com/CE06 and select On the Web Explorations.

You have probably interacted with a multimedia presentation on a Web site. There are over half a million commercial Web sites on the Internet, and hundreds more are being added every day. Corporations use the Web to reach new customers and to promote their products. (See Figure 4-15.) Many individuals create their own personal sites, called **Web logs** or **blogs,** to keep in touch with friends and family. Creating a site is called **Web authoring.** It begins with site design followed by creation of a document file that displays the Web site's content.

WEB SITE DESIGN

A Web site is an interactive multimedia form of communication. Designing a Web site begins with determining the site's overall content. The content is then broken down into a series of related pieces of information. The overall site design is commonly represented in a **graphical map.** (See Figure 4-16.)

Notice that the graphical map shown in Figure 4-16 is very similar to the story board depicted in Figure 4-12. In this case, however, each block in the map represents a Web page. Lines joining the blocks represent links to related pages of information that make up the Web site. The first page typically serves as an introduction and supplies a table of contents. The following pages present the specific pieces or blocks of information.

Multimedia elements are added to individual pages to enhance interest and interactivity. One common multimedia element found on most Web sites is moving graphics called **animations.** These animations can be simple moving text or complicated interactive features. There are many specialized programs available to aid in the creation of animation. One type of interactive animation is produced using software from Macromedia Inc. This type of animation, called **Flash,** is usually full-screen, highly dynamic, and interactive. (See Figure 4-17.) Another common visual effect found on the Web is morphing. **Morphing** is a special effect in which one image seems to melt into another.

Figure 4-15 Adventure Travel Tours Web site

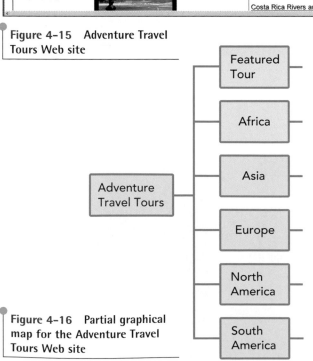

Figure 4-16 Partial graphical map for the Adventure Travel Tours Web site

WEB AUTHORING PROGRAMS

As we mentioned in Chapter 2, Web pages are displayed using HTML documents. With knowledge of HTML and a simple text editor, you can create Web pages. Even without knowledge of HTML you can create Web pages using a word processing package like Microsoft Word.

Name	Address
Ben & Jerry's	www.benjerry.com
Disney	www.disney.com
Red Bull	www.redbull.com
Hard Rock Hotel	www.hardrockhotel.com
Sony Classical	www.sonyclassical.com

Figure 4-17 Web sites that use Flash animation

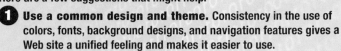
More specialized and powerful programs, called **Web authoring programs,** are typically used to create sophisticated commercial sites. Also known as **Web page editors** and **HTML editors,** these programs provide support for Web site design and HTML coding. Widely used Web authoring programs include Macromedia Dreamweaver, NetObjects Fusion, and Microsoft FrontPage. (See Figure 4-18.) The Web site depicted in Figures 4-15 and 4-16 was created using Microsoft FrontPage. (See Figure 4-19.)

To learn more about creating your own personal Web site, consult your Computing Essentials CD or visit our Web site at www.olearyseries.com/CE06 and select Expansions.

▼ **CONCEPT CHECK**

► Describe Web authoring.

► What are graphical maps, animation, Flash, and morphing?

► What are Web authoring programs?

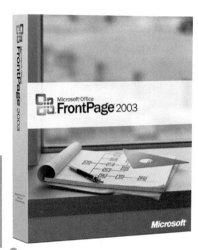

Figure 4-18 Microsoft FrontPage

EMERGING APPLICATIONS

> Artificial intelligence attempts to simulate human senses, thought processes, and actions. Three areas are virtual reality, knowledge-based (expert) systems, and robotics.

New and revised applications programs are appearing every day. A common thread with most of these emerging applications is the inclusion, however subtle, of artificial intelligence concepts. Clearly, artificial intelligence and its applications are one of the most exciting developments in the 21st century. You have probably seen a portrayal of a robot with the intelligence, sensibilities, and capabilities of a human in a movie or on television. Depictions of robots and computers with artificial intelligence are common. In the past such depictions were pure fiction, but computer science has made great strides in the creation of artificial intelligence and the integration of this intelligence into a wide range of applications.

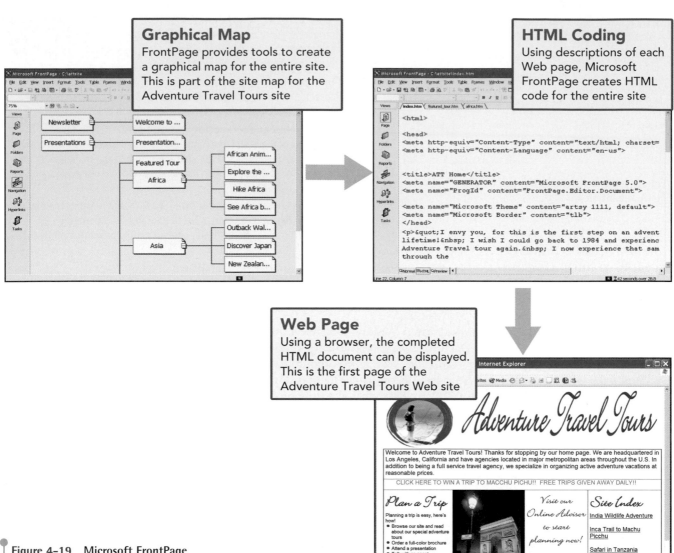

Graphical Map
FrontPage provides tools to create a graphical map for the entire site. This is part of the site map for the Adventure Travel Tours site

HTML Coding
Using descriptions of each Web page, Microsoft FrontPage creates HTML code for the entire site

Web Page
Using a browser, the completed HTML document can be displayed. This is the first page of the Adventure Travel Tours Web site

Figure 4-19 Microsoft FrontPage and the Adventure Travel Tours

On the Web Explorations

Many people believe that the next big leap forward in computing will involve artificial intelligence. To learn about a leading developer of artificial intelligence software, visit our Web site at

www.olearyseries.com/CE06 and select On the Web Explorations.

The field of computer science known as **artificial intelligence (AI)** attempts to develop computer systems that can mimic or simulate human senses, thought processes, and actions. These include reasoning, learning from past actions, and using senses such as vision and touch. Artificial intelligence that corresponds to human intelligence is still a long way off. However, several tools that emulate human senses, problem solving, and information processing have been developed.

These modern applications of artificial intelligence are designed to help people and organizations become more productive. Many of these tools have practical applications for business, medicine, law, and so on. In the past, computers used calculating power to solve **structured problems,** which can be broken down into a series of well-defined steps. People—using intuition, reasoning, and memory—were better at solving **unstructured problems,** whether building a product or approving a loan. Organizations have long been able to computerize the tasks once performed by clerks. Now knowledge-intensive work and unstructured problems, such as activities performed by many managers, is being automated. Let us now consider three areas in which human talents and abilities have been enhanced with "computerized intelligence": virtual reality, knowledge-based systems, and robotics.

VIRTUAL REALITY

Suppose you could create and virtually experience any new form of reality you wished. You could see the world through the eyes of a child, a robot—or even a lobster. You could explore faraway resorts, the moon, or inside a nuclear waste dump, without leaving your chair. This simulated experience is possible with virtual reality.

Virtual reality is an artificial, or simulated, reality generated in 3-D by a computer. Virtual reality is also commonly known as **VR, artificial reality,** or **virtual environments.** To navigate in a virtual space you use virtual reality hardware including headgear and gloves. The headgear has earphones and three-dimensional stereoscopic screens (one type is called Eyephones). The gloves have sensors that collect data about your hand movements (one type is called DataGlove). Coupled with software (such as a program called Body Electric), this interactive sensory equipment lets you immerse yourself in a computer-generated world. See Figure 4-20.

Virtual reality modeling language (VRML) is used to create real-time animated 3-D scenes. Hundreds of sites exist on the Web with virtual reality applications. Users are able to experience these applications with browsers that support VRML.

Figure 4-20   Virtual reality

Creating virtual reality programs once required very high end software costing several thousands of dollars. Recently, several lower-cost yet powerful authoring programs have been introduced. These programs utilize VRML and are widely used to create Web-based virtual reality applications. One of the best known is Cosmo Worlds from Cosmo Software.

There are any number of possible applications for virtual reality. The ultimate recreational use might be something resembling a giant virtual amusement park. More serious applications can simulate important experiences or training environments such as in aviation, surgical operations, spaceship repair, or nuclear disaster cleanup. Modern virtual reality strives to be an **immersive experience,** allowing a user to walk into a virtual reality room or view simulations on a **virtual reality wall.** (See Figure 4-21.)

Figure 4-21   Virtual reality wall

KNOWLEDGE-BASED (EXPERT) SYSTEMS

People who are expert in a particular area—certain kinds of law, medicine, accounting, engineering, and so on—are generally well paid for their specialized knowledge. Unfortunately for their clients and customers these experts are expensive, not always available, and hard to replace when they move on.

What if you were to somehow capture the knowledge of a human expert and make it accessible to everyone through a computer program? This is exactly what is being done with so-called knowledge-based or expert systems. **Knowledge-based systems,** also known as **expert systems,** are a type of artificial intelligence that uses a database to provide assistance to users. These systems use a database, or **knowledge base,** that contains specific facts, rules to relate these facts, and user input to formulate recommendations and decisions. The sequence of processing is determined by the interaction of the user and the knowledge base. Many expert systems use so-called **fuzzy logic,** which allows users to respond to questions in a very humanlike way. For example, if an expert

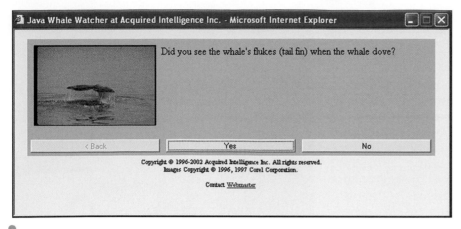

Figure 4-22 Whale identification using an expert system

system asked how your classes were going, you could respond, "great," "OK," "terrible," and so on.

Over the past decade, expert systems have been developed in areas such as medicine, geology, architecture and nature. (See Figure 4-22.) There are expert systems with such names as Oil Spill Advisor, Bird Species Identification, and even Midwives Assistant. A system called Grain Marketing Advisor helps farmers select the best way to market their grain.

ROBOTICS

Robotics is the field of study concerned with developing and using robots. **Robots** are computer-controlled machines that mimic the motor activities of living things. Some robots can solve unstructured problems using artificial intelligence. You may have seen household robots used for mowing the lawn or for entertainment purposes, like Sony's AIBO robotic dog. (See Figure 4-23.)

Robots are used in factories, manufacturing, home security, the military, and many other fields of human endeavor. They differ from other assembly-line machines because they can be reprogrammed to do more than one task. Robots are often used to handle dangerous, repetitive tasks. There are three types of robots.

Figure 4-23 AIBO

- **Perception systems: Perception system robots** imitate some of the human senses. For example, robots with television-camera vision systems are particularly useful. They can guide machine tools, inspect products, and secure homes.

- **Industrial robots: Industrial robots** are used to perform a variety of tasks. Examples are machines used in automobile plants to do welding, polishing, and painting. Some types of robots have claws for picking up objects and handling dangerous materials. (See Figure 4-24.)

- **Mobile robots: Mobile robots** act as transports and are widely used for a variety of different tasks. For example, the police and military use them to locate and disarm explosive devices. Mobile robots have entered the world of entertainment with their own television program called "Battlebots." You can even build your own personal robot using special robot building kits. (See Figure 4-25.)

Figure 4-24 Industrial robot

▼ CONCEPT CHECK

▶ Define artificial intelligence.

▶ What is virtual reality? What is VRML?

▶ Describe knowledge-based systems and fuzzy logic.

▶ Describe three types of robots.

Site	Description
battlebot.com	Offers a variety of information including links to sites offering different types of robot kits
robotkits.com	Sells beginner as well as advanced robot creation kits
roboticsonline.com	Offers news and advice for the robot enthusiast
lynxmotion.com	Sells robotic equipment and software

Figure 4-25   Robot kits

A Look to the Future

The Future of Artificial Intelligence Is Emotional

Would you like to voice conference with your mom through robots that resemble you both and demonstrate your emotions on their rubber faces? What if you received a companion robot with a set of moral values? Would you trust a robot to trade the stocks in your portfolio? Researchers are currently at work on robots with the artificial intelligence needed to perform these tasks and more.

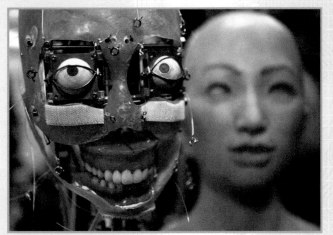

The Saya robot, with its artificial skin and muscles, is currently under development in Tokyo. Researchers hope that eventually it will be used as a communication device similar to a current Web cam. For example, you could connect to a robot that resembles you at your mother's house and communicate through it with her. You would see your mother through the robot's visual system. Your mother would hear your voice come from the robot and your emotions would be displayed on its face.

Other research is being conducted that will give robots a sense of values. It is hoped that these robots will be able to make decisions independently based on this set of values. Researchers in California are creating robots that act as surveillance instruments, capable of following a target without direction from a human. The robots can predict potential escape routes and pursue a subject through crowded areas.

At the Sociable Machines Project at MIT, students are working on a robot named Kismet that detects human emotions through social and audio cues and responds with emotions of its own. Kismet recognizes faces and responds to stimuli like an infant would with emotions ranging from surprise to disgust. Researchers believe that robots such as Kismet can interact with and learn from humans better than traditional computer interfaces.

All of these projects are designed to move beyond simple computing and into a decidedly human realm of emotional intelligence. Some experts have even suggested that human intelligence relies on emotional input for all important decision-making. Thus, by definition, for a machine to approximate human intelligence it would have to understand and rely on emotions. If computers could read human emotions, and had emotional intelligence of their own, it could be possible for your computer to act as a stress counselor when you stay up all night working on a project.

Computers with their own emotional intelligence could be the ultimate human companions. Computer scientists have suggested they may read your mood and play music accordingly. Or they could search through audio and video files for media you would find moving, funny, or dramatic. If computers had their own emotional sense, it is possible that they, like the humans they emulate, would require interaction for mental health.

Would you use a robot as a communication device? Do you think we should build robots with a sense of moral values? Some researchers have suggested that robots with artificial intelligence could serve as ideal supervisors and managers. What do you think? Would you like to have an "emotional" robot for a boss?

Specialized Application Software

www.olearyseries.com/CE06   **109**

VISUAL SUMMARY

SPECIALIZED APPLICATION SOFTWARE

GRAPHICS

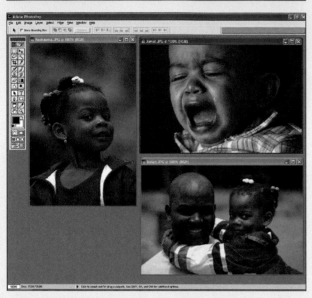

Professionals in graphic arts use specialized graphics programs.

Desktop Publishers
Desktop publishers (page layout programs) mix text and graphics to create professional publications.

Image Editors
Image editors create and modify **bitmap (raster) image** files. Images are recorded as dots or **pixels.**

Illustration Programs
Illustration programs, also known as **drawing programs,** modify **vector images (vector illustrations).** In a vector file, images are recorded as a collection of objects such as lines, rectangles, and ovals.

Image Galleries
Image galleries are libraries of electronic images, widely available from the Web. Two types are **stock photographs** and **clip art.**

Graphics Suites
A **graphics suite** is a collection of individual graphics programs sold as a unit.

AUDIO AND VIDEO

Recent advances in video and audio technology allow individuals to assemble near-professional quality video and audio footage.

Video Software
Video editing software allows you to reorganize, add effects, and more to digital video.

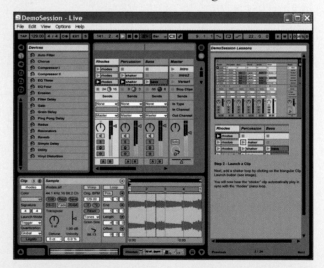

Audio Software
Audio editing software allows you to create and edit audio clips. You can add audio effects, like filters, to your tracks. You can create MP3s.

To be a competent end user you need to be aware of specialized applications. You need to know who uses them, what they are used for, and how they are used. Specialized applications include graphics programs, audio and video editing software, multimedia, Web authoring, and the field of artificial intelligence.

MULTIMEDIA

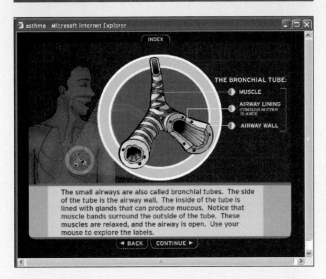

Multimedia integrates all sorts of media, including video, music, voice, graphics, and text into one presentation. An essential feature is user participation or **interactivity.**

Links and Buttons
A multimedia presentation is organized as a series of related pages. Pages are **linked,** or connected, by clicking **buttons.**

Developing Multimedia Presentations
The creation of multimedia presentations involves four steps:
- **Plan and analyze**—determine objectives, resources required, and project team.
- **Design**—use **story boards** to record the intended overall logic, flow, and structure.
- **Create**—use multimedia authoring programs to create a presentation and integrate various media elements.
- **Support**—identify errors, evaluate effectiveness, and revise as needed.

Multimedia Authoring Programs
Multimedia authoring programs are special programs to create multimedia presentations. They bring together video, audio, graphics, and text elements in an interactive framework.

WEB AUTHORING

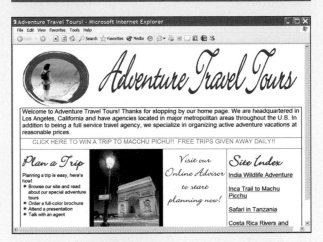

Web logs (blogs) are personal Web sites. Creating Web sites is called **Web authoring.** It begins with Web site design followed by creating a document file that displays the Web site content.

Web Site Design
Web sites are an interactive multimedia form of communication.

Graphical maps use linked blocks to represent a Web site's overall content. Typically, blocks represent individual Web pages and links indicate relationships between related pages.

The first Web page usually introduces the site and supplies a table of contents. Multimedia elements are added to pages. **Animations** are moving graphics. **Flash** is a widely used type of Web animation. **Morphing** is a special effect that seems to melt one image into another.

Web Authoring Programs
Web sites can be created using a simple text editor or word processor. **Web authoring programs,** also known as **Web page editors** or **HTML editors,** are specifically designed to create Web sites. They provide support for Web site design and HTML coding.

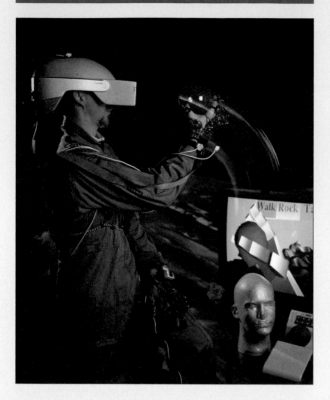

The common thread of emerging applications is the inclusion of artificial intelligence concepts.

Artificial Intelligence

Artificial intelligence (AI) attempts to develop computer systems that mimic human senses, thought processes, and actions.

Most applications address **structured problems** that can be broken down into a series of well-defined steps. Less defined or **unstructured problems** are being addressed. Three areas are virtual reality, knowledge-based systems, and robotics.

Virtual Reality

Virtual reality (VR, artificial reality, or **virtual environments)** creates computer-generated simulated environments. It involves the use of interactive sensory equipment, including head gear and gloves. **VRML (virtual reality modeling language)** is used to create or program real-time virtual reality applications.

Applications include recreational and other areas such as aviation, surgical operations, spaceship repair, and nuclear disaster cleanup. Modern applications strive for **immersive experiences** and can be viewed on **virtual reality walls.**

Knowlege-based Systems

Knowledge-based (expert) systems are programs that duplicate the knowledge that humans use to perform specific tasks.

Knowledge bases are databases containing facts and rules that relate facts to user input. **Fuzzy logic** allows users to respond to questions in a very humanlike way.

Some application areas include medicine, geology, architecture, and nature.

Robotics

Robotics is a field of study concerned with developing and using robots. **Robots** are computer-controlled machines that mimic the motor activities of living things. Three types of robots are:

- **Perception system**—imitate human senses. Used to guide tools, inspect products, secure homes.
- **Industrial robots**—perform a variety of tasks including welding, polishing, painting, and handling dangerous materials.
- **Mobile robots**—transport and are used in a variety of tasks. Military and police applications include locating, removing, and disarming explosive devices.

animation   (104)
artificial reality   (107)
artificial intelligence (AI)   (106)
audio editing software   (97)
bitmap image   (95)
button   (99)
clip art   (96)
desktop publishing program   (95)
drawing program   (95)
expert system   (107)
Flash   (104)
fuzzy logic   (107)
graphical map   (104)
graphics suite   (97)
HTML editor   (105)
illustration program   (95)
image gallery   (95)
immersive experience   (107)
industrial robot   (108)
interactivity   (99)
knowledge base   (107)
knowledge-based system   (107)
link   (99)
mobile robot   (108)
morphing   (104)
multimedia   (98)

multimedia authoring program   (102)
page layout program   (95)
perception system   (108)
pixel   (95)
raster image   (95)
robotics   (108)
robot   (108)
story board   (102)
stock photograph   (96)
structured problem   (106)
unstructured problem   (106)
vector   (95)
vector illustration   (95)
vector image   (95)
video editing software   (97)
virtual environment   (107)
virtual reality   (107)
virtual reality modeling language
    (VRML)   (107)
virtual reality wall   (107)
VR   (107)
Web authoring   (104)
Web authoring program   (105)
Web log   (104)
Web page editor   (105)

FEATURES

Animations

Careers in IT

DVD Direct

Expansions

Making IT Work for You

On the Web Explorations

TechTV

Tips

CHAPTER REVIEW

Key Terms

Crossword

Multiple Choice

Matching

Open-ended

Using Technology

Expanding Your Knowledge

Building Your Portfolio

To test your knowledge of these key terms with animated flash cards, consult your Computing Essentials CD or visit our Web site at www.olearyseries.com/CE06 and select Key Terms.

COMPUTING ESSENTIALS 2006

CROSSWORD PUZZLE

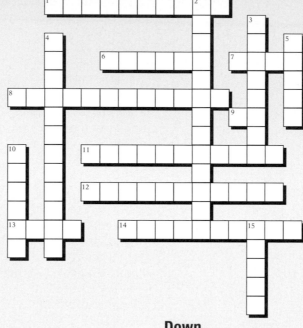

Across

1 Allows responses like "OK" and "Great!"

6 Type of robot used by police and military.

7 Used to create real-time 3D animation.

8 Representation of overall site design.

9 Attempt to develop computers that mimic human senses.

11 Image recorded as a collection of objects.

12 Composed of thousands of pixels.

13 Connection between pages in a multi-media presentation.

14 Design tool used to plan multimedia presentations.

Down

2 User participation.

3 Special effect that blends images together.

4 Creating a site.

5 Widely used type of Web animation.

10 Dots that make up an image.

15 Editing software used to create MP3s.

For an interactive version of this crossword, consult your Computing Essentials CD or visit our Web site at **www.olearyseries.com/CE06** and select Crossword.

Circle the letter or fill in the correct answer.

1. _____ focus on page design and layout and provide greater flexibility than word processors.
   a. Desktop publishers
   b. Graphics editors
   c. Web page editors
   d. Multimedia authoring programs
   e. PERT

2. Draw programs are used to modify vector images, while image editors are used to modify _____.
   a. bitmap images
   b. images buttons
   c. links
   d. HTML code
   e. VRML

3. _____ allows you to reorganize, add effects, and more to your digital video footage.
   a. Video editing software
   b. Audio editing software
   c. Paint program
   d. Browsers
   e. Animation

4. _____ connect related pages in a multimedia presentation.
   a. Robots
   b. Links
   c. Slides
   d. Pixels
   e. Vectors

5. A(n) _____ is typically organized as a series of related pages with links to related information.
   a. graphical map
   b. story board
   c. multimedia presentation
   d. image editor
   e. virtual environment

6. _____ can be simple moving text or complicated interactive features.
   a. VR
   b. Graphics editors
   c. Graphics suites
   d. Animation
   e. Vector images

7. Intuition, memory, and reasoning are used to solve _____.
   a. structured problems
   b. unstructured problems
   c. knowledge bases
   d. organization problems
   e. complex circuits

8. Expert systems use _____ that contain specific facts, rules to relate these facts, and user input to formulate decisions.
   a. robots
   b. fuzzy logic
   c. story boards
   d. knowledge bases
   e. interactivity

9. Many expert systems use _____ to allow human-like responses.
   a. packets
   b. fuzzy logic
   c. robots
   d. story boards
   e. vector images

10. Police and military use _____ to locate and disarm explosive devices.
    a. mobile robots
    b. OSI
    c. industrial robots
    d. perception systems
    e. fuzzy logic

For an interactive version of these multiple choice questions, consult your Computing Essentials CD or visit our Web site at www.olearyseries.com/CE06 and select Multiple Choice.

MATCHING

Match each numbered item with the most closely related lettered item. Write your answers in the spaces provided.

a. AI
b. bitmap
c. desktop publishing
d. expert system
e. Flash
f. fuzzy logic
g. graphical map
h. graphics suite
i. interactivity
j. image editor
k. morphing
l. multimedia
m. pixel
n. perception system
o. multimedia authoring programs
p. robots
q. story board
r. structured problems
s. vector image
t. Web authoring

1. Integrates all sorts of media into one presentation. _____
2. User participation in multimedia. _____
3. Graphics program for creating and editing bitmap images. _____
4. Tool for planning and structuring a multimedia presentation. _____
5. Programs used to create multimedia presentations. _____
6. Creating a Web site. _____
7. Diagram of a Web site's overall design. _____
8. Program that allows you to mix text and graphics to create publications of professional quality. _____
9. Dots used to represent images. _____
10. Group of graphics programs offered at lower cost than if purchased separately. _____
11. Special effect in which one image seems to melt into another. _____
12. Graphics file made up of thousands of pixels. _____
13. Graphics file made up of a collection of objects, such as rectangles, lines, and ovals. _____
14. Problems that can be broken down into well-defined steps. _____
15. Attempts to develop computer systems that mimic or simulate human thought processes and actions. _____
16. Gives advice to decisionmakers who normally rely on humans. _____
17. Animation that is usually full-screen and interactive. _____
18. Allows users to respond using terms such as great and OK. _____
19. Machines that mimic the motor activities of living things. _____
20. System that relies on sense of touch or other human senses. _____

For an interactive version of this matching exercise, consult your Computing Essentials CD or visit our Web site at **www.olearyseries.com/CE06** and select Matching.

OPEN-ENDED

On a separate sheet of paper, respond to each question or statement.

1. Describe graphics, including desktop publishers, image editors, illustration programs, image galleries, and graphics suites.
2. Discuss audio and video editing software.
3. What is multimedia? How are multimedia presentations developed?
4. Describe Web authoring, including Web site design and Web authoring programs.
5. Discuss three areas of artificial intelligence.

Digital Video Editing

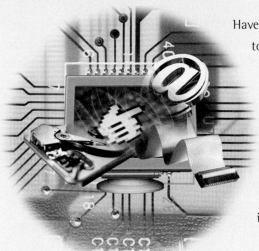

Have you ever thought of making your own movie? Would you like to edit some home videos and distribute them to family and friends on DVDs? It's easy with the right equipment and software. To learn more about digital video editing, review Making IT Work for You: Digital Video Editing, on pages 100 and 101. Then answer the following questions: (a) What program is used to capture video from your camcorder to your computer? (b) Where can you preview your movie in Windows Movie Maker? (c) What is Sonic MyDVD and what is it used for?

Shockwave

Web sites aren't all just text and pictures anymore. Many are taking advantage of browser plug-ins that add new functionality and display abilities to Web browsers, as we discussed in Chapter 2. One of the most popular plug-ins is Macromedia's Shockwave. Visit our Web site at www.olearyseries.com/CE06 and select Using

Technology to link to the Macromedia site. Once connected, read about Shockwave and answer the following questions: (a) What is Shockwave? What types of content can it display? (b) How is the Shockwave plug-in obtained? (c) What types of companies are using Shockwave in their Web page designs? (d) Do you think Shockwave is a valuable Web page addition, or just a flashy distraction? Explain your answer.

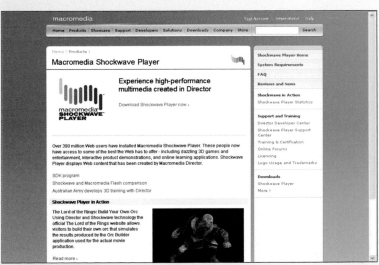

1

How Digital Video Editing Works

The falling prices of digital camcorders and improvements in computer technology have made digital video editing affordable for individuals. Families can now save their home movies on DVDs with titles and special effects that would impress Hollywood directors. Study the Expansion "Digital Video Editing" on your Computing Essentials CD or on our Web site at www. olearyseries.com/CE06. Then answer the following questions. (a) What hardware is needed to capture video from a VCR tape? Why is this hardware necessary? (b) How can video editing software be used to improve a video? (c) What are some common ways to share videos? How do these ways differ?

2

Personal Web Site

Do you have something to share with the world? Would you like a personal Web site but don't want to deal with learning HTML? Creating your own home page on the Internet is easy, and there are many services available to get you started. To learn more about "Personal Web Sites," consult your Computing Essentials CD or visit our Web site at www.olearyseries.com/ CE06 and select Expansions. Then answer the following questions: (a) What are Web logs? What are they used for? (b) What is Blogger.com? Describe the following features provided by Blogger.com: templates, upload file, hyperlink, post, publish, and view Web page. (c) Have you ever created a Web log or other types of personal Web site? If you have, describe how you created it and what you used it for. If you have not, discuss why and how you might use one.

1

Artificial Intelligence

Artificial Intelligence attempts to simulate human senses, thought processes, and actions with an eye toward productivity. Write a one-page paper titled "Artificial Intelligence" that addresses the following issues: (a) Define and describe artificial intelligence. (b) How is it currently used? How can software exhibit artificial intelligence? (c) With advancing developments in artificial intelligence, what can we expect from operating systems in the future?

2

HTML Source Code

One way to learn how to create interesting and dynamic Web sites is to examine how professionals create their sites. Once connected to a Web site, you can typically display the HTML source code used to create that site. With Netscape, for example, select Document Source from the View submenu. Try this out on your own for your favorite Web site, and then answer the following questions in a one-page paper: (a) Do you see any ethical issues that relate to examining the HTML code? (b) What about copying parts of the code for your own Web site? (c) What about copying all the code? Defend your answers.

COMPETENCIES

After you have read this chapter, you should be able to:

1 **Describe the differences between system software and application software.**

2 **Discuss the four types of system software.**

3 **Discuss the basic functions, features, and categories of operating systems.**

4 **Describe the Windows, Mac OS, UNIX, and Linux operating systems.**

5 **Describe the purpose of utilities and utility suites.**

6 **Identify the five most essential utilities.**

7 **Discuss Windows utility programs.**

8 **Describe device drivers, including printer drivers.**

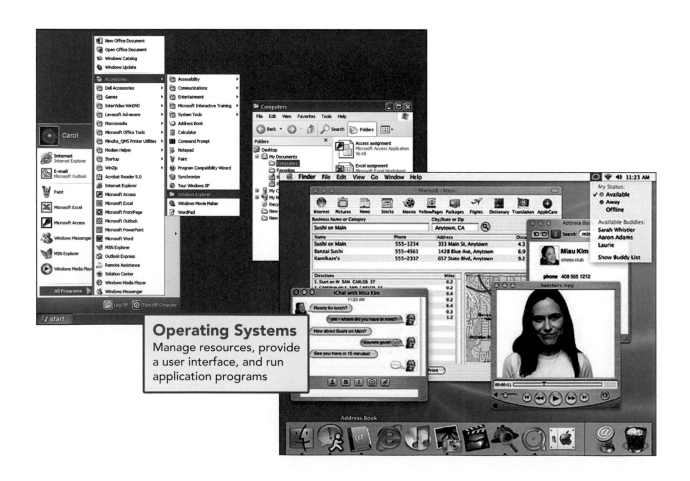

Operating Systems
Manage resources, provide a user interface, and run application programs

When most people think about computers, they think about surfing the Web, creating reports, analyzing data, storing information, making presentations, and any number of other valuable applications. We typically think about applications and application software. Computers and computer applications have become a part of the fabric of our everyday lives. Most of us agree that they are great . . . as long as they are working.

We usually do not think about the more mundane and behind-the-scenes computer activities: loading and running programs, coordinating networks that share resources, organizing files, protecting our computers from viruses, performing periodic maintenance to avoid problems, and controlling hardware devices so that they can communicate with one another. Typically, these activities go on behind the scenes without our help.

That is the way it should be, and the way it is, as long as everything is working perfectly. But what if new application programs are not compatible and will not run on our current computer system? What if we get a computer virus? What if our hard disk fails? What if we buy a new digital video camera and can't store and edit the images on our computer system? What if our computer starts to run slower and slower?

These issues may seem mundane, but they are critical. This chapter covers the vital activities that go on behind the scenes. A little knowledge about these activities can go a long way to making your computing life easier. To effectively use computers, competent end users need to understand the functionality of system software, including operating systems, utility programs, and device drivers.

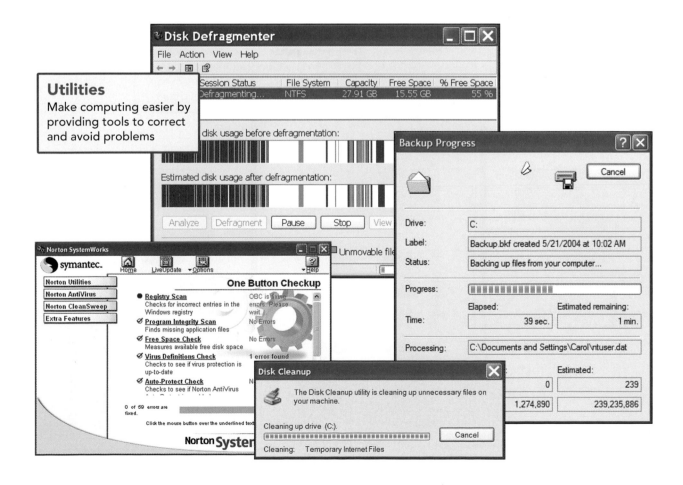

Utilities
Make computing easier by providing tools to correct and avoid problems

SYSTEM SOFTWARE

System software handles technical details. Operating systems, utilities, device drivers, and language translators are types of system software programs.

End users use application software to accomplish specific tasks. For example, we use word processors to create brochures, letters, and reports. However, end users also use system software. **System software** works with end users, application software, and computer hardware to handle the majority of technical details. For example, system software controls where a word processing program is stored in memory, how commands are converted so that the system unit can process them, and where a completed document or file is saved. See Figure 5-1.

System software is not a single program. Rather it is a collection or a system of programs that handle hundreds of technical details with little or no user intervention. System software consists of four types of programs:

- **Operating systems** coordinate computer resources, provide an interface between users and the computer, and run applications.
- **Utilities,** also known as **service programs,** perform specific tasks related to managing computer resources.
- **Device drivers** are specialized programs that allow particular input or output devices to communicate with the rest of the computer system.
- **Language translators** convert the programming instructions written by programmers into a language that computers understand and process.

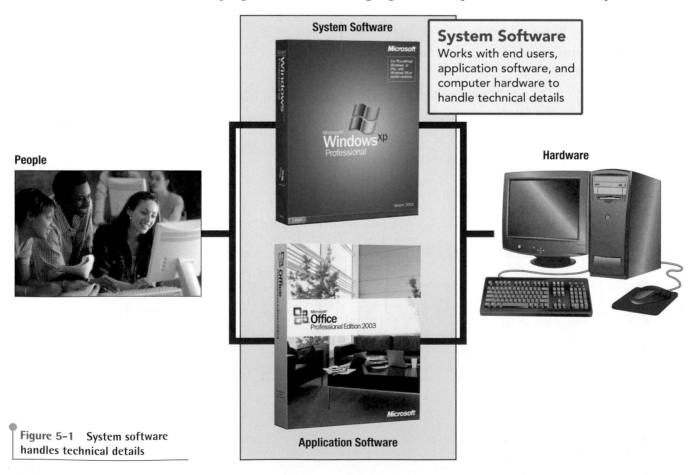

Figure 5–1   System software handles technical details

OPERATING SYSTEMS

> Operating systems are programs that manage resources, provide user interface, and run applications. Three categories of operating systems are embedded, network, and stand-alone. Windows, Mac OS, UNIX, and Linux are operating systems.

An **operating system** is a collection of programs that handle many of the technical details related to using a computer. In many ways, an operating system is the most important type of computer program. Without it your computer would be useless.

FUNCTIONS

Every computer has an operating system and every operating system performs a variety of functions. These functions can be classified into three groups:

- **Managing resources:** These programs coordinate all the computer's resources including memory, processing, storage, and devices such as printers and monitors. They also monitor system performance, schedule jobs, provide security, and start up the computer.

- **Providing user interface:** Users interact with application programs and computer hardware through a user interface. Many older operating systems used a **character based interface** in which users communicated with the operating system through written commands such as "Copy A: assign.doc to C:". Almost all newer operating systems use a **graphical user interface (GUI).** As we discussed in Chapter 3, a graphical user interface uses graphical elements such as icons and windows.

- **Running applications:** These programs load and run applications such as word processors and spreadsheets. Most operating systems support **multitasking,** or the ability to switch between different applications stored in memory. With multitasking, you could have Word and Excel running at the same time and switch easily between the two applications. The program that you are currently working on is described as running in the **foreground.** The other program or programs are running in the **background.**

FEATURES

Starting or restarting a computer is called **booting** the system. There are two ways to boot a computer: a warm boot and a cold boot. A **warm boot** occurs when the computer is already on, and you restart it without turning off the power. A warm boot can be accomplished in several ways. For example, in Windows XP, a running computer can be restarted by pressing a sequence of keys. Starting a computer that has been turned off is called a **cold boot.** To learn more about booting your computer system and POST, consult your Computing Essentials CD or visit our Web site at www.olearyseries.com/CE06 and select Expansions.

You typically interact with the operating system through the graphical user interface. Most provide a place, called the **desktop,** which provides access to computer resources. (See Figure 5-2.) Operating systems have several features in common with application programs including:

- **Icons**—graphic representations for a program or function.
- **Pointer**—controlled by a mouse and changes shape depending upon its current function. For example, when shaped like an arrow, the pointer can be used to select items such as an icon.

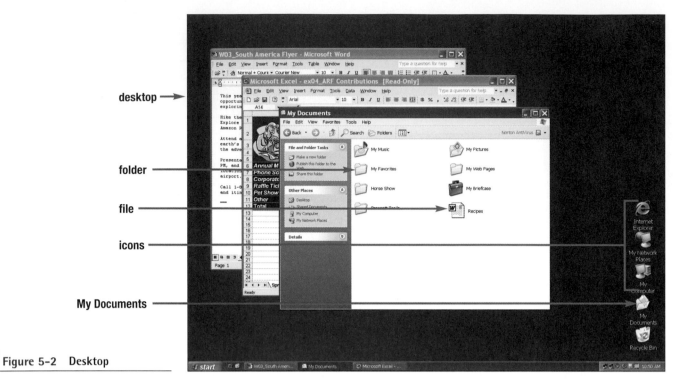

desktop →

folder →

file →

icons →

My Documents →

Figure 5-2 Desktop

- **Windows**—rectangular areas for displaying information and running programs.
- **Menus**—provide a list of options or commands.
- **Dialog boxes**—provide information or request input.
- **Help**—provides online assistance for operating system functions and procedures.

Most operating systems store data and programs in a system of files and folders. Unlike the traditional filing cabinet, computer files and folders are stored on a secondary storage device such as your hard disk. **Files** are used to store data and programs. Related files are stored within a **folder,** and for organizational purposes, a folder can contain other folders. For example, you might organize your electronic files in the *My Documents* folder on your hard disk. This folder could contain other folders, each named to indicate their contents. One might be "Computers" and could contain all the files you have created (or will create) for this course.

CATEGORIES

While there are hundreds of different operating systems, there are only three basic categories: embedded, network, or stand-alone.

Figure 5-3 PDAs have embedded operating systems

- **Embedded operating systems** are used for handheld computers and smaller devices like PDAs. (See Figure 5-3.) The entire operating system is stored within or embedded in the device. The operating system programs are permanently stored on ROM or read only memory chips. Popular embedded operating systems include Windows CE .NET and Palm OS.
- **Network operating systems (NOS)** are used to control and coordinate computers that are networked or linked together. Many networks are small and connect only a limited number of microcomputers. Other networks like those at colleges and universities are very large and complex. These networks may include other smaller networks and typically connect a variety of different types of computers.

Windows operating system

Figure 5-4   Stand-alone operating system

Network operating systems are typically located on one of the connected computers' hard disks. Called the **network server,** this computer coordinates all communication between the other computers. Popular network operating systems include NetWare, Windows NT Server, Windows XP Server, and UNIX.

• **Stand-alone operating systems,** also called **desktop operating systems,** control a single desktop or notebook computer. (See Figure 5-4.) These operating systems are located on the computer's hard disk. Often desktop computers and notebooks are part of a network. In these cases, the desktop operating system works with the network's NOS to share and coordinate resources. In these situations, the desktop operating system is referred to as the **client operating system.** Popular desktop operating systems include Windows, Mac OS, and some versions of UNIX.

The operating system is often referred to as the **software environment** or **platform.** Application programs are designed to run with a specific platform. For example, AppleWorks is designed to run with the Mac OS environment. There are many different types of operating systems. Windows, Mac OS, and Linux are operating systems commonly used by individuals.

Most operating systems are **proprietary operating systems;** that is, they are owned and licensed by a corporation. The Windows operating system is a proprietary operating system owned by the Microsoft Corporation. Some individuals and organizations have developed **nonproprietary operating systems** in which the operating system program or source code is provided to outside individuals. These individuals are encouraged to use, improve, and modify the programs. The objective is to produce better and more useful programs in the long run. Programs released in this way are called **open source.** For example, Linux is an open source program currently provided to software developers under an open source agreement.

▼ CONCEPT CHECK

▶ What is system software? What are the four kinds of system software programs?

▶ What is an operating system? Discuss operating system functions and features.

▶ Describe each of the three categories of operating systems.

WINDOWS

Microsoft's **Windows** is by far the most popular microcomputer operating system today with over 90 percent of the market. Because its market share is so large, more application programs are developed to run under Windows than any other operating system. Windows comes in a variety of different versions and is designed to run with Intel and Intel-compatible microprocessors such as the Pentium IV. For a summary of Microsoft's desktop operating systems, see Figure 5-5.

The latest release of the Windows operating system is **Windows XP.** It provides a new user interface called **Luna.** Compared to other user interfaces, Luna emphasizes functions over programs. For example, the new **Start menu** displays categories like E-mail and Internet, rather than individual programs such as Outlook and Internet Explorer. This menu displays a list of commands that can be used to access information, change hardware settings, find information, get online help, run programs, log off a network, and shut down your computer system.

For example, you could use the Start menu to run the Internet Explorer program as shown in Figure 5-6.

Name	Description
Windows NT Workstation	Client operating system designed to work with the Windows NT Server
Windows 98	Stand alone operating system
Windows 2000 Professional	Upgrade to Windows NT Workstation
Windows ME	Upgrade to Windows 98 specifically designed for home users
Windows XP	One of Microsoft's newest and most powerful desktop operating systems
Windows XP Tablet PC Edition	Version of Windows XP designed to support tablet PC functions such as converting handwritten input to digital form

Figure 5-5   Microsoft desktop operating systems

1 ● Click *Start* on the task bar to open the Start Menu.

2 ● Click the Internet Explorer icon to open your home page.

Internet Explorer icon

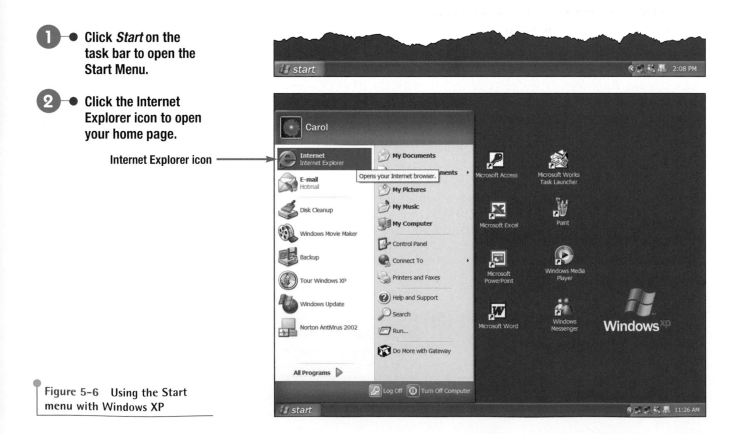

Figure 5-6   Using the Start menu with Windows XP

MAC OS

Macintosh introduced its first operating system and microcomputer in 1984. It provided one of the first GUIs, making it easy even for novice computer users to move and delete files. Designed to run with Apple computers, **Mac OS** is not nearly as widely used as the Windows operating system. As a result, fewer application programs have been written for it. Nonetheless, Mac OS is considered to be one of the most innovative operating systems. It is a powerful, easy-to-use operating system that is popular with professional graphic designers, desktop publishers, and many home users.

Aqua →

Sherlock

Figure 5-7   Mac OS X

One of the latest versions of the Macintosh operating system, **Mac OS X,** features a new user interface called **Aqua.** It is an intuitive interface providing photo-quality icons and easy-to-use menus. The desktop features **Dock,** a tool for visually organizing files. Additionally, Mac OS X provides an updated version of its **Sherlock** search tool for locating information on the Web as well as on the user's computer system. (See Figure 5-7.)

UNIX AND LINUX

The **UNIX** operating system was originally designed to run on minicomputers in network environments. Now, it is also used by powerful microcomputers and by servers on the Web. There are a large number of different versions of UNIX. One receiving a great deal of attention today is **Linux.**

While Windows, Mac OS, and many versions of UNIX are proprietary operating systems, Linux is not. It is open source software free and available from many sources, including the Web. As a graduate student at the University of Helsinki, Linus Torvalds developed Linux in 1991. He has allowed distribution of the operating system code and has encouraged others to modify and further develop the code. Linux is one of the most popular and powerful alternatives to the Windows operating system. (See Figure 5-8.)

Figure 5-8   Recent version of Linux

▼ CONCEPT CHECK

▶   What is Windows? What is Luna? How is it different from the classic interface?

▶   What is Mac OS? What is Aqua? Dock? Sherlock?

▶   What is UNIX? What is Linux?

UTILITIES

Backup, Disk Cleanup, and Disk Defragmenter are Windows utilities. McAfee Office, Norton SystemWorks, and V Communications System Suite are utility suites.

Ideally, microcomputers continuously run without problems. However, that simply is not the case. All kinds of things can happen—internal hard disks can crash, computers can freeze up, operations can slow down, and so on. These events can make computing very frustrating. That's where utilities come in. **Utilities** are specialized programs designed to make computing easier. There are hundreds of different utility programs. The most essential are:

- **Troubleshooting** or **diagnostic** programs that recognize and correct problems, ideally before they become serious.
- **Antivirus** programs that guard your computer system against viruses or other damaging programs that can invade your computer system.
- **Uninstall** programs that allow you to safely and completely remove unneeded programs and related files from your hard disk.
- **Backup** programs that make copies of files to be used in case the originals are lost or damaged.
- **File compression** programs that reduce the size of files so they require less storage space and can be sent more efficiently over the Internet.

Most operating systems provide some utility programs. Even more powerful utility programs can be purchased separately or in utility suites.

WINDOWS UTILITIES

The Windows operating systems are accompanied by several utility programs, including Backup, Disk CleanUp, and Disk Defragmenter. These utilities can be accessed from the System Tools menu. (See Figure 5-9.)

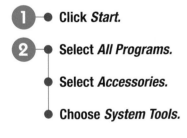

1 ● Click *Start.*

2 ● Select *All Programs.*

● Select *Accessories.*

● Choose *System Tools.*

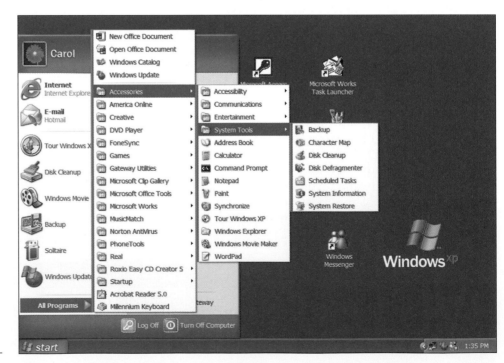

Figure 5-9 Accessing Windows XP utilities

Backup is a utility program included with the many versions of Windows that makes a copy of all files or selected files that have been saved onto a disk. It helps to protect you from the effects of a disk failure. For example using the Professional edition of XP, you can select Backup from the Windows XP System Tools menu to create a backup for your hard disk as shown in Figure 5-10. (While most versions of XP include the Backup utility, the XP Home edition does not.)

When you surf the Web, a variety of programs and files are saved on your hard disk. Many of these and other files are not essential. **Disk CleanUp** is a trouble-shooting utility that identifies and eliminates nonessential files. This frees up valuable disk space and improves system performance.

1 ● Click *Start.*

● Select *Accessories* from the *All Programs* menu.

● Select *Backup* from the *System Tools* menu.

2 ● Run the Restore Wizard and specify your settings.

● Choose *Backup* and choose the files you want to include.

● Choose the destination for the backup.

3 ● Finish the Restore Wizard to back up the selectcd drive.

● Close the B*ackup Progress* window or view the report.

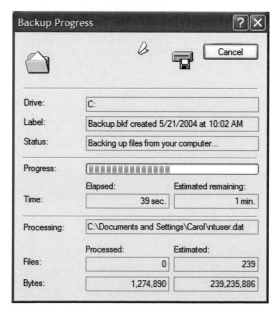

Figure 5-10 Backup utility

For example, by selecting Disk Cleanup from the Windows XP System Tools menu, you can eliminate unneeded files on your hard disk as shown in Figure 5-11.

As we will discuss in detail in Chapter 8, files are stored and organized on a disk according to tracks and sectors. A **track** is a concentric ring. Each track is divided into wedge-shaped sections called **sectors.** (See Figure 5-12.) The operating system tries to save a file on a single track across contiguous sectors. Often, however, this is not possible and the file has to be broken up, or **fragmented,** into small parts that are stored wherever space is available. Whenever

1 • Click *Start.*

• Select *Accessories* from the *All Programs* menu.

• Select *Disk Cleanup* from the *System Tools* menu.

2 • Verify the files suggested for cleanup.

• Click *OK.*

• Click *Yes* to begin disk cleanup.

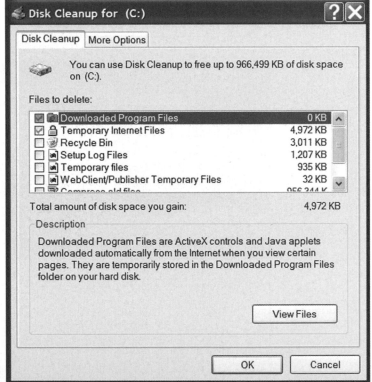

3 • The utility cleans the selected files.

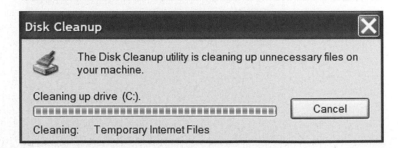

Figure 5-11   Disk CleanUp utility

a file is retrieved, it is reconstructed from the fragments. After a period of time, a hard disk becomes highly fragmented, slowing operations.

Disk Defragmenter is a utility program that locates and eliminates unnecessary fragments and rearranges files and unused disk space to optimize operations. For example, by selecting Disk Defragmenter from the Windows XP Systems Tool menu, you can defrag your hard disk as shown in Figure 5-13.

UTILITY SUITES

Like application software suites, **utility suites** combine several programs into one package. Buying the package is less expensive than buying the programs separately. The three best known utility suites are McAfee Office, Norton SystemWorks, and V Communications SystemSuite. These suites provide a variety of utilities, including programs that will protect your system from dangerous programs called **computer viruses.** You can "catch" a computer virus many ways, including by

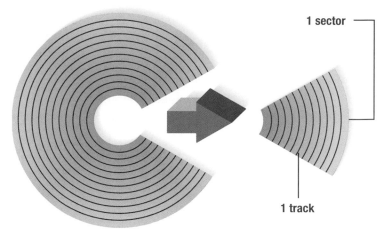

Figure 5-12   Tracks and sectors

---

1 ● Click *Start.*

● Select *Accessories* from the *All Programs* menu.

● Select *Disk Defragmenter* from the *System Tools* menu.

Figure 5-13   Disk Defragmenter utility

2 ● If necessary, choose the drive you want to analyze and defragment.

● Click the *Analyze* button to determine whether defragging is needed.

● View the report or, if necessary, defragment the drive.

● Click the *Defragment* button to begin defragging.

● When defragmentation is complete for the selected drive, view the report or close the window.

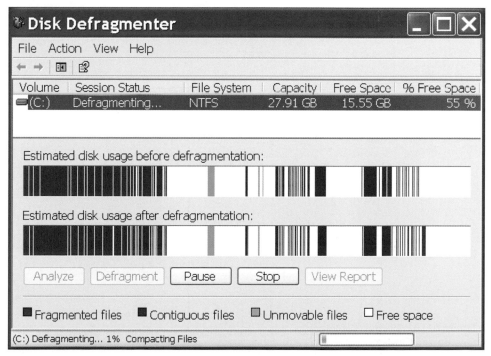

System Software

opening attachments to e-mail messages and downloading software from the Internet. (We will discuss computer viruses in detail in Chapter 10.)

To learn more about virus protection, consult your Computing Essentials CD or visit our Web site at www.olearyseries.com/CE06 and select Animations. Also see Making IT Work for You: Virus Protection and Internet Security on pages 134 and 135.

Norton SystemWorks is one of the most widely used utility suites. It includes the following:

On the Web
Explorations

Utility software can make your computer faster, safer, and more productive. To learn more about a market leader of utility software, visit our Web site at

www.olearyseries.com/CE06 and select On the Web Explorations.

- **Norton AntiVirus** is a collection of antivirus programs that can protect your system from over 21,000 different viruses, quarantine or delete existing viruses, and automatically update its virus list to check for the newest viruses.

- **Norton CleanSweep** is a collection of programs that guide you through the process of safely removing programs and files you no longer need. Additionally, they will archive, move, and make backups of programs as well as clean up your hard disk. They can also protect your existing files from damage when you install new programs.

- **Web CleanUp** is a collection of programs that check your computer system for unnecessary files, including temporary files created by application programs, cache files, history files, and cookies. You can then eliminate these files with a click of a button.

- **Connection Keep Alive** prevents dial-up Internet connections from timing out by simulating online user activity during periods of inactivity.

- **GoBack Personal Edition** will restore system configurations, help to locate lost files, and repair damaged files.

- **Norton Utilities** is a collection of several separate troubleshooting utilities. These programs can be used to find and fix problems, improve system performance, prevent problems from occurring, and troubleshoot a variety of other problems. One of the programs, **One Button Checkup,** integrates several of the separate troubleshooting utilities. (See Figure 5-14.)

▼ CONCEPT CHECK

▶ What is the difference between a utility and a utility suite?

▶ Describe Backup, Disk CleanUp, and Disk Defragmenter.

▶ What is a computer virus? How you can you protect yourself against them?

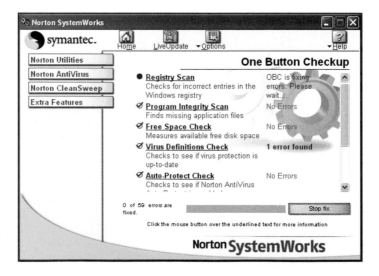

Figure 5-14   Norton SystemWorks' One Button Checkup

DEVICE DRIVERS

Device drivers are specialized programs that allow devices such as a mouse, keyboard, and printer to communicate with the rest of the computer system.

Every device, such as a mouse or printer, that is connected to a computer system, has a special program associated with it. This program, called a **device driver** or simply a **driver,** works with the operating system to allow communication between the device and the rest of the computer system. Each time the computer system is started, the operating system loads all of the device drivers into memory.

Whenever a new device is added to a computer system, a new device driver must be installed before the device can be used. Windows supplies hundreds of different device drivers with its system software. For many devices, the appropriate drivers are automatically selected and installed when the device is first connected to the computer system. For others, the device driver must be manually installed. Fortunately, Windows provides wizards to assist in this process. For example, Windows **Add Printer Wizard** provides step-by-step guidance for selecting the appropriate printer driver and installing that driver. (See Figure 5-15.) If a particular device driver is not included with the Windows system software, the product's manufacturer will supply one. Many times these drivers are available directly from the manufacturer's Web site.

You probably never think about the device drivers in your computer. However, when your computer behaves unpredictably, you may find reinstalling or updating your device drivers solves your problems. Windows makes it easy to update the drivers on your computer using **Windows Update,** as shown in Figure 5-16.

▼ CONCEPT CHECK

▶ What are device drivers? What does the Window's Add Printer Wizard do?

▶ What is Windows Update? When would you use it?

To access the Add Printer Wizard

- Select *Control Panel* from the *Start* menu.

- Click *Printers and faxes.*

- Click *Add a printer.*

Figure 5–15   Add Printer Wizard

MAKING (IT) WORK FOR YOU:

VIRUS PROTECTION AND INTERNET SECURITY

Are you worried that a computer virus will erase your personal files? Did you know that others could be intercepting your private e-mail? It is even possible for others to gain access to and control over your computer system. Fortunately, Internet security suites are available to help ensure your safety while you are on the Internet.

Getting Started   The first step is to install an Internet security suite. Once installed, the software will continually work to ensure security and privacy. One of the best known suites is McAfee Internet Security Suite, which can be installed by following the instructions below.

1 ● Connect to *www.mcafee.com* and follow the on-screen instructions to subscribe to this Internet security suite.

2 ● The security suite is downloaded and installed to your computer directly from the Web site.

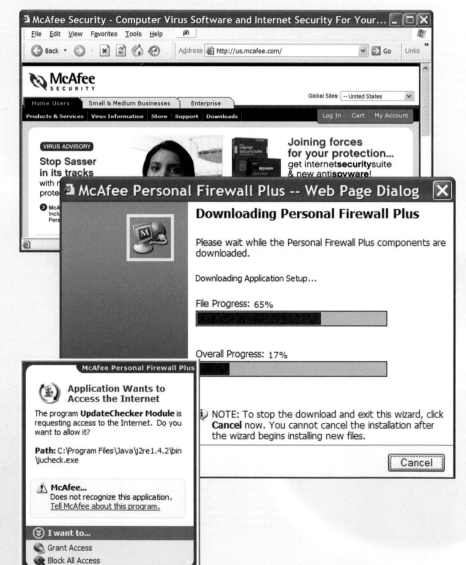

Once installed, the security suite will automatically be activated each time you start your computer. An alert similar to the one on the right is displayed when any privacy or security vulnerabilities are detected.

134

Internet Security Suite   Internet Security Suite runs a number of programs continually to monitor your computer. Some of Internet Security Suite's most powerful programs include VirusScan, PersonalFirewall, and PrivacyService. You can modify the way these programs run with the McAfee SecurityCenter.

VirusScan   VirusScan controls how frequently the computer system is searched for computer viruses. When a file is checked, it is compared to the profile of known viruses. Once a virus is detected, the infected file is quarantined or deleted.

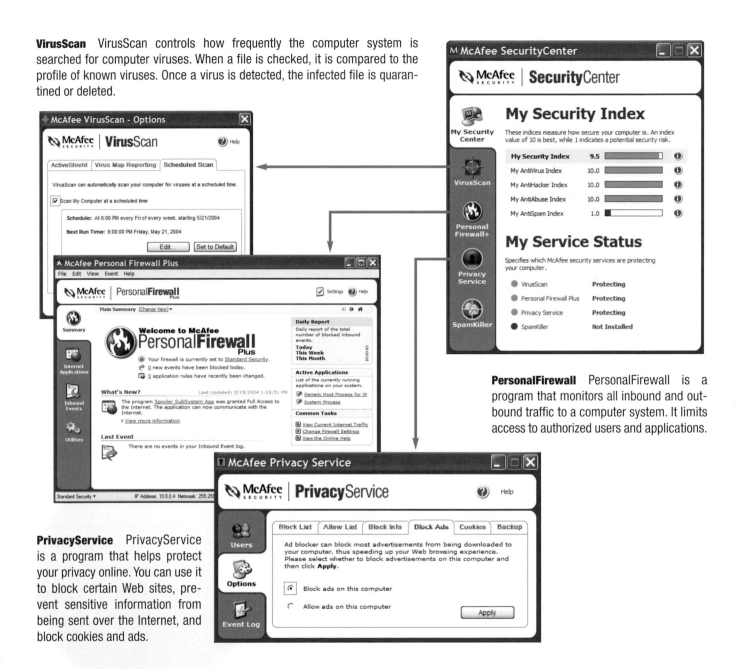

PersonalFirewall   PersonalFirewall is a program that monitors all inbound and outbound traffic to a computer system. It limits access to authorized users and applications.

PrivacyService   PrivacyService is a program that helps protect your privacy online. You can use it to block certain Web sites, prevent sensitive information from being sent over the Internet, and block cookies and ads.

The Web is continually changing, and some of the specifics presented in this Making IT Work for You may have changed. To learn more about other ways to make information technology work for you, visit our Web site at www.olearyseries.com/CE06 and select Making IT Work for You.

1 Access *Windows Update* from the *All Programs* list of the *Start* menu.

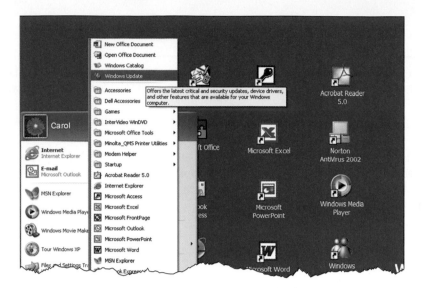

2 Click *Scan for updates.*

Click *Driver Updates.*

3 Click *Add.*

Click *Review and Install Drivers.*

Click *Install Now* and *Accept* the license agreement.

Click *OK* to restart the computer.

Figure 5-16   Using Windows Update

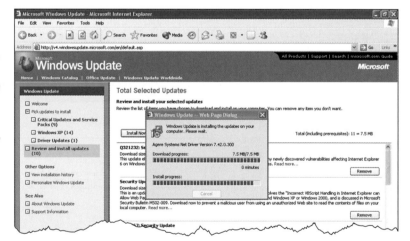

A Look to the Future

IBM Builds an Aware Supercomputer

Wouldn't it be nice if computers could fix themselves? What if you never had to worry about installing or updating software? What if your computer could continually fine-tune its operations to maintain peak performance? What if your computer could fight off viruses and malicious attacks from outsiders? For many people this sounds too good to be true. Maintenance and security tasks like these can be time consuming and frustrating.

Now imagine you run a business and unless these tasks are performed, you will lose valuable time and money. It is not a pleasant daydream and it quickly becomes a nightmare without properly trained systems administrators to keep servers running smoothly. Yet many experts predict that supercomputers and business systems are not far from becoming too complex for humans to oversee. Recent news from IBM makes the dream of a self-repairing, self-updating, and self-protecting server seem ever closer.

IBM has announced plans to concentrate research efforts on developing just such a server. The project, called the Autonomic Computing Initiative (ACI), hopes to free businesses from the time-consuming maintenance and the complexity of business infrastructure. IBM hopes the new system will be self-regulating and virtually invisible. They believe ACI has the potential to revolutionize the way businesses run.

Autonomic computing is a system that allows machines to run with little human intervention. Such computers would not have self-awareness, but rather would be self-correcting. Autonomic processes in machines are modeled after autonomic processes in the human body. For example, you are not consciously breathing as you read this. Instead, your body monitors and maintains your respiration without your constant input. Scientists hope autonomic computing will behave in a similar manner and maintain self-regulating systems without intervention.

Autonomic machines would be able to sense security flaws and repair them. They would be able to sense slow operation's programs and take corrective action. They would be able to sense new equipment, format it, and test it. These goals are impressive and the autonomic computer is still in development.

As technology continues to develop, many computer systems have become too complex for human maintenance. This progress makes autonomic computing more valuable now than ever. However, it is important to note that autonomic computing is not artificial intelligence, because autonomic machines do not have human cognitive abilities or intelligence. Instead, these machines have knowledge of their own systems and the capability to learn from experiences to correct errors in such systems.

Given the potential for a self-maintaining server, the possibility of a similar system designed for a microcomputer seems less like a dream and more like a reality. What do you think—will microcomputers someday care for themselves?

VISUAL SUMMARY

SYSTEM SOFTWARE

SYSTEM SOFTWARE

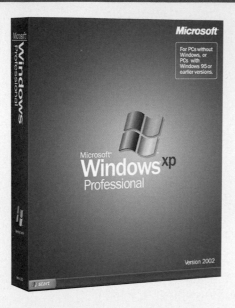

System software works with end users, application programs, and computer hardware to handle many details relating to computer operations.

Not a single program but a collection or system of programs, these programs handle hundreds of technical details with little or no user intervention.

Four kinds of systems programs are operating systems, utilities, device drivers, and language translators.

- **Operating systems** coordinate resources, provide an interface between users and the computer, and run programs.

- **Utilities (service programs)** perform specific tasks related to managing computer resources.

- **Device drivers** allow particular input or output devices to communicate with the rest of the computer system.

- **Language translators** convert programming instructions written by programmers into a language that computers can understand and process.

OPERATING SYSTEMS

Operating systems (software environments, platforms) handle technical details.

Functions

Functions include managing **resources,** providing a **user interface** (**character based interface** uses written commands; **graphical user interface (GUI)** uses graphical elements; **desktop** is interface provided by Windows), and running **applications** (**multitasking** allows switching between applications; current program in **foreground,** others in **background**).

Features

Booting starts **(cold)** or restarts **(warm)** a computer system. The **desktop** provides access to computer resources. Common features of application programs and operating systems include **icons, pointers, windows, menus, dialog boxes,** and **help.** Data and programs stored in a system of **files** and **folders.**

Categories

The three basic categories are **embedded, network (NOS; network server coordinates),** and **stand-alone (desktop,** called **client operating systems** in networked environments).

Operating systems are often called **software environment (platform). Propriety operating systems** are owned and licensed by a corporation; **non-proprietary** are free **(open source)** programs.

To effectively use computers, competent end users need to understand the functionality of system software, including operating systems, utility programs, and device drivers.

OPERATING SYSTEMS

UTILITIES

Windows

Windows is the most widely used operating system with over 90 per cent of the market. It is designed to run with Intel and Intel-compatible microprocessors. There are numerous versions of Windows. The latest, **Windows XP,** provides a new interface **(Luna)** that emphasizes functions over programs. For example, the **Start menu** displays categories such as E-mail and Internet rather than programs such as Outlook and Internet Explorer.

Mac OS

Macintosh introduced one of the first GUIs. **Mac OS** is an innovative, powerful, easy-to-use operating system; designed to run with Macintosh computers. The latest version is **Mac OS X,** has a new interface **(Aqua)** and includes **Dock** (tool for visually organizing files) and **Sherlock** (search tool for locating information on the Web and user's computer system).

UNIX and Linux

UNIX was originally designed to run on minicomputers in network environments. Now, it is used by powerful microcomputers and servers on the Web. There are many different versions of UNIX. One version, **Linux,** is non-proprietary, free, and available on the Web. It is one of the most popular and powerful alternatives to the Windows operating system.

Utilities are specialized programs designed to make computing easier. The most essential utilities are **troubleshooting (diagnostic), antivirus, uninstall, backup,** and **file compression.**

Windows Utilities

The Windows operating systems come with several utility programs accessible from the Systems Tools menu. Three such utilities are **Backup, Disk CleanUp,** and **Disk Defragmenter** (eliminates unnecessary **fragments; tracks** are concentric rings; **sectors** are wedge-shaped).

Utility Suites

Utility suites combine several programs into one package. **Computer viruses** are dangerous programs **One Button Checkup** integrates several Norton utilities.

DEVICE DRIVERS

Device drivers (drivers) are specialized programs to allow communication between hardware devices. **Add Printer Wizard** gives step-by-step guidance to install printer drivers. **Windows Update** automates the process of updating device drivers.

COMPUTING ESSENTIALS 2006

KEY TERMS

Add Printer Wizard (133)
antivirus program (128)
application (138)
Aqua (127)
background (123)
Backup (129)
booting (123)
character based interface (123)
client operating system (125)
cold boot (123)
computer virus (131)
desktop (123)
desktop operating system (125)
device driver (122)
diagnostic program (128)
dialog box (124)
Disk CleanUp (129)
Disk Defragmenter (131)
Dock (127)
driver (133)
embedded operating systems (124)
file (124)
file compression program (128)
folder (124)
foreground (123)
fragmented (130)
graphical user interface (GUI) (123)
Help (124)
icon (123)
language translator (122)
Linux (127)
Luna (126)
Mac OS (127)

Mac OS X (127)
menu (124)
multitasking (123)
network operating systems (NOS) (124)
network server (125)
nonproprietary operating system (125)
One Button Checkup (132)
open source (125)
operating system (122)
platform (125)
pointer (123)
proprietary operating system (125)
resources (138)
sectors (130)
service program (122)
Sherlock (127)
software environment (125)
software platform (138)
stand-alone operating system (125)
Start menu (126)
system software (122)
tracks (130)
troubleshooting program (128)
uninstall program (128)
UNIX (127)
user interface (138)
utility (122)
utility suite (131)
warm boot (123)
window (124)
Windows (126)
Windows Update (133)
Windows XP (126)

To test your knowledge of these key terms with animated flash cards, consult your Computing Essentials CD or visit our Web site at www.olearyseries.com/CE06 and select Key Terms.

COMPUTING ESSENTIALS 2006

CROSSWORD PUZZLE

Across

1 Location to store related files.

4 Starting or restarting a computer.

6 Broken up file stored in different sectors.

8 Uses graphical elements to communicate with the operating system.

11 Server that coordinates all communication between other computers.

13 Place where current programs run.

15 Combination of several utility programs in one package.

16 Used to control and coordinate networked computers.

Down

2 Allows communication between devices and the operating system.

3 Boot that occurs when the computer is already on.

5 Nonproprietary operating system.

7 Program that makes copies of files in case of damage or loss.

9 Also known as service program.

10 Operating system with over 90 percent of the market.

12 Concentric ring on a disk.

14 Latest version of Macintosh operating system.

For an interactive version of this crossword, consult your Computing Essentials CD or visit our Web site at **www.olearyseries.com/CE06** and select Crossword.

Circle the letter or fill in the correct answer.

1. Service programs are another name for _____.
   a. operating systems
   b. utilities
   c. device drivers
   d. language translators
   e. interfaces

2. Language translators convert human language into _____.
   a. machine language
   b. UNIX
   c. service programs
   d. operating systems
   e. EBCDIC

3. The process of starting or restarting a computer is called _____.
   a. booting
   b. docking
   c. embedding
   d. fragmenting
   e. tracking

4. Desktop operating systems are also called _____ operating systems.
   a. network
   b. embedded
   c. server
   d. Mac
   e. stand-alone

5. _____ provides online assistance for operating system functions.
   a. Menu
   b. The platform
   c. Explorer
   d. Utility
   e. Help

6. The _____ operating system was originally designed to run on minicomputers in network environments.
   a. Windows
   b. Mac OS
   c. UNIX
   d. Sherlock
   e. Norton

7. To remove unneeded programs and related files from a hard disk you would use a(n) _____ program.
   a. backup
   b. troubleshooting
   c. file compression
   d. antivirus
   e. uninstall

8. Files that are broken into small parts and stored wherever space is available are said to be _____.
   a. compressed
   b. fragmented
   c. lost
   d. uninstalled
   e. sectored

9. _____ is a Windows program that locates and eliminates unnecessary fragments and rearranges files and unused disk space to optimize operations.
   a. Disk CleanUp
   b. Active Desktop
   c. Sherlock
   d. Disk Defragmenter
   e. Resource Locator

10. Norton SystemWorks is a _____.
   a. Web service
   b. troubleshooting program
   c. utility
   d. utility suite
   e. none of the above

For an interactive version of these multiple choice questions, consult your Computing Essentials CD or visit our Web site at www.olearyseries.com/CE06 and select Multiple Choice.

Match each numbered item with the most closely related lettered item. Write your answers in the spaces provided.

a. antivirus program
b. backup program
c. desktop OS
d. embedded OS
e. file compression program
f. folders
g. foreground
h. GUI
i. icons
j. Linux
k. Mac OS
l. multitasking
m. NOS
n. network server
o. open source
p. operating systems
q. proprietary OS
r. sector
s. track
t. utilities

1. Software that deals with the complexities of computer hardware. _____
2. Programs that coordinate computer resources. _____
3. Concentric ring on a disk. _____
4. Wedge-shaped section. _____
5. Where the active program runs. _____
6. Graphic elements that represent commonly used features. _____
7. A computer's ability to run more than one application at a time. _____
8. Operating systems completely stored within ROM memory. _____
9. Operating system used to control and coordinate computers that are linked together. _____
10. Operating system whose code is made available to outside individuals for improvements. _____
11. A computer that coordinates all communication between other computers. _____
12. An operating system located on a single stand-alone hard disk. _____
13. Operating system used by Macintosh computers. _____
14. Uses graphical elements like icons. _____
15. Along with files, a component of the system that Windows stores information in. _____
16. One popular, and free, version of the UNIX operating system. _____
17. Operating system owned and operated by a company. _____
18. Guards computer systems against damaging and invasive programs. _____
19. Makes copies of files to be used if originals are lost or damaged. _____
20. Program that reduces the size of files for efficient storage. _____

For an interactive version of this matching exercise, consult your Computing Essentials CD or visit our Web site at **www.olearyseries.com/CE06** and select Matching.

OPEN-ENDED

On a separate sheet of paper, respond to each question or statement.

1. Describe system software. What are the four types of system programs?
2. What are the basic functions of every operating system? What are the three basic operating system categories?
3. Explain the differences and similarities between Windows, Mac OS, and Linux.
4. Discuss utilities. What are the five most essential utilities? What is a utility suite?
5. Explain the role of device drivers. Discuss the Add Printer Wizard and Windows Update.

1

Virus Protection

Worried about computer viruses? Did you know that others could be intercepting your private e-mail? It is even possible for them to gain access and control over your computer systems. Fortunately, Internet security suites are available to help ensure your safety while you are on the Internet. To learn more about virus protection, review Making IT Work for You: Virus Protection and Internet Security on pages 134 and 135. Then answer the following questions: (a) What are viruses? What are Internet security suites? What do they do? (b) Have you ever experienced a computer virus? If you have, describe the virus, how you got it, and what you did to get rid of it. If you have not, have you taken any special precautions? Discuss the precautions. Do you think it's possible that you may have one now and not know it, or do you think that you have just been lucky? (c) What is a personal firewall? What does it do?

2

Windows Update

Windows Update is a utility built into Windows that monitors and controls the process of keeping the computer up-to-date. Connect to our Web site at www.olearyseries.com/CE06 and select Using Technology to link to the Windows Update Web site. Read the information about Windows Update. Then answer the following questions: (a) How does Windows Update work? (b) How does a user know when he or she requires an update? (c) What is the process for initiating an update using Windows Update? (d) In what ways can Windows Update be automated?

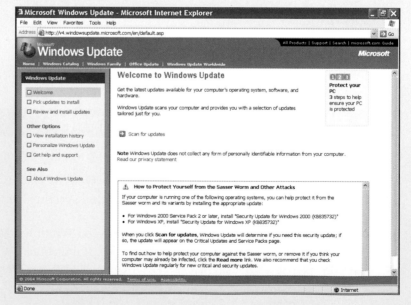

1   How Virus Protection Programs Work

Computer viruses are destructive and dangerous programs that can migrate through networks and operating systems. They often attach themselves to other programs, e-mail messages, and databases. It is essential to protect your computer system from computer viruses. After viewing the animation "How Virus Protection Programs Work" from your Computing Essentials CD or from our Web site at www.olearyseries.com/CE06, answer the following questions: (a) Briefly describe the four steps taken by virus protection programs. (b) What is signature scanning? (c) What is heuristic detection and how is it different from signature scanning. (d) Do you use a virus protection program? If yes, what program(s) do you use and has it been effective? If no, do you plan to in the near future? Why or why not?

2   Booting and POST

Computers do a considerable amount of work before a user even hits a key. Knowing how a computer starts up can be an invaluable tool for fixing a broken computer or getting working computers to run at peak efficiency. After reading the Expansion "Booting and Post" from your Computing Essentials CD or from our Web site at www.olearyseries.com/CE06, answer the following questions: (a) Briefly describe the four steps of a cold boot. (b) When booting up, what does the microprocessor do first? (c) What does BIOS stand for? (d) Advanced users often customize their BIOS and POST. What benefits can users achieve by modifying their BIOS or POST?

1

Linux

Linux is a powerful operating system used by many computer professionals. Research Linux and then write a one-page paper titled "Linux" that covers the following points: (a) What is Linux? (b) How was it developed originally? (c) How is Linux currently used? (d) How might it be used in the future? (e) Why has Linux received so much attention recently?

2

Antitrust

Much attention has been focused on Microsoft's legal battles over antitrust issues. It has been argued that Microsoft has an unfair market advantage because its Windows operating system has been tailored to use Microsoft applications. Write a one-page paper responding to the following questions: (a) Do you think Microsoft has an unfair advantage in the software market? (b) How can the decisions in the Microsoft antitrust case affect the software available for consumers to buy? (c) What ethical obligations do you think Microsoft has to other software developers? (d) What ethical obligations does it have to the consumer? Explain your answer.

COMPETENCIES

After you have read this chapter, you should be able to:

1 **Describe the four basic types of system units.**

2 **Discuss how a computer uses binary codes to represent data in electronic form.**

3 **Describe each of the major system unit components.**

4 **Discuss microprocessors, including specialty processors.**

5 **Describe the different types of memory.**

6 **Discuss expansion slots and boards.**

7 **Describe the five principal types of expansion buses.**

8 **Discuss the four standard ports.**

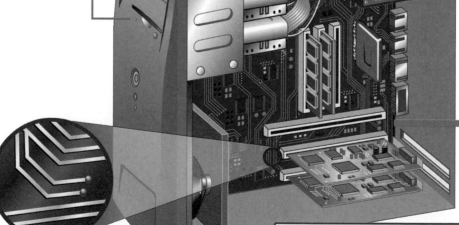

Disk Drives
Are secondary storage devices for saving data, programs, and information

Power Supply Unit
Converts AC to DC, providing power to the system unit

Systems Board
Connects all system components to one another

System Unit
Contains most of the computer's electronic components

Bus Lines
Provide data pathways that connect various system components

CHAPTER

6

Why are some microcomputers more powerful than others? The answer lies in three words: speed, capacity, and flexibility. After reading this chapter, you will be able to judge how fast, powerful, and versatile a particular microcomputer is. As you might expect, this knowledge is valuable if you are planning to buy a new microcomputer system or to upgrade an existing system. (The Buyer's Guide and the Upgrader's Guide at the end of this book provide additional information.) It will also help you to evaluate whether or not an existing microcomputer system is powerful enough for today's new and exciting applications. For example, with the right hardware, you can use your computer to watch TV while you work and to capture video clips for class presentations.

Sometime you may get the chance to watch when a technician opens up a microcomputer. You will see that it is basically a collection of electronic circuitry. While there is no need to understand how all these components work, it is important to understand the principles. Once you do, you will be able to determine how powerful a particular microcomputer is. This will help you judge whether it can run particular kinds of programs and can meet your needs as a user.

Competent end users need to understand the functionality of the basic components in the system unit, including the system board, microprocessor, memory, system clock, expansion slots and cards, bus lines, ports, cables, and power supply units.

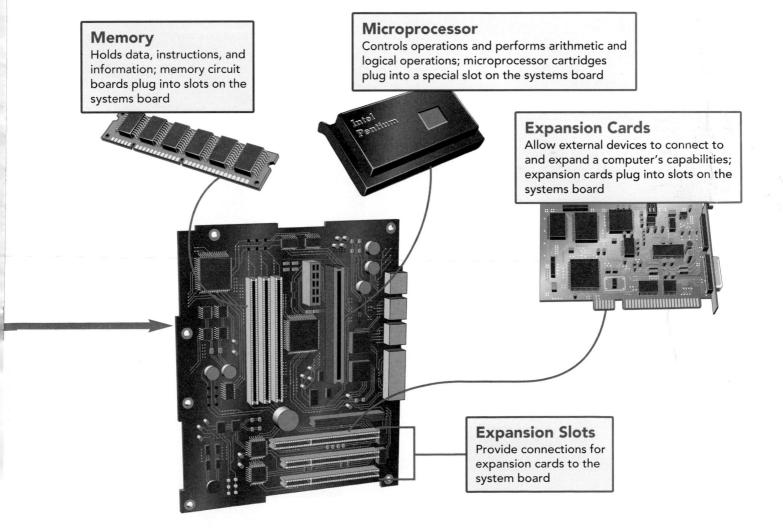

Memory
Holds data, instructions, and information; memory circuit boards plug into slots on the systems board

Microprocessor
Controls operations and performs arithmetic and logical operations; microprocessor cartridges plug into a special slot on the systems board

Expansion Cards
Allow external devices to connect to and expand a computer's capabilities; expansion cards plug into slots on the systems board

Expansion Slots
Provide connections for expansion cards to the system board

System components are housed within the system unit or system cabinet. Desktop, notebook, tablet PC, and handheld are four types of system units.

The **system unit,** also known as the **system cabinet** or **chassis,** is a container that houses most of the electronic components that make up a computer system. All computer systems have a system unit. For microcomputers, there are four basic types (see Figure 6-1):

- **Desktop system units** typically contain the system's electronic components and selected secondary storage devices. Input and output devices, such as a mouse, keyboard, and monitor, are located outside the system unit. This type of system unit is designed to be placed either horizontally or vertically. Vertical units are often called **tower models.**

- **Notebook system units** are portable and much smaller. These system units contain the electronic components, selected secondary storage devices, and input devices (keyboard and pointing device). Located outside the system unit, the monitor is attached by hinges. Notebook system units are often called **laptops.**

Figure 6-1   Basic types of system units

Desktop (tower model)

PDA

Notebook

Tablet PC

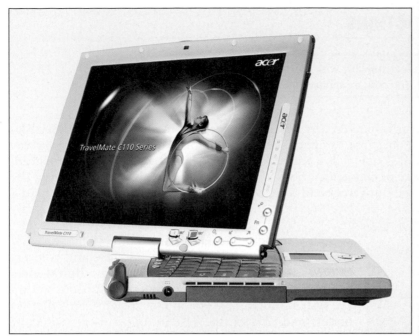
Convertible tablet PC

Figure 6-2 Tablet PCs

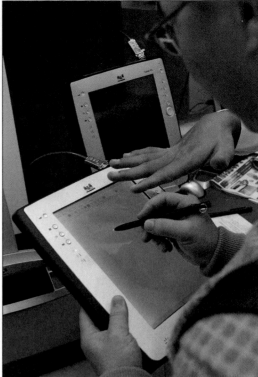
Slate tablet PC

- **Tablet PC system units** are similar to notebook system units. **Tablet PCs** are highly portable devices that support the use of a stylus or pen to input commands and data. There are two basic categories: convertible and slate. The **convertible tablet PC** is effectively a notebook computer with a monitor that swivels and folds onto its keyboard. The **slate tablet PC** is similar to a notebook computer except that its monitor is attached to the system unit and does not have a keyboard integrated into the system unit. (See Figure 6-2.)
- **Handheld computer system units** are the smallest and are designed to fit into the palm of one hand. Also known as **palm computers,** these systems contain an entire computer system, including the electronic components, secondary storage, and input and output devices. **Personal digital assistants (PDAs)** are the most widely used handheld computers.

While the actual size may vary, each type of system unit has the same basic system components including system board, microprocessor, and memory. Before considering these components, however, a more basic issue must be addressed. How do we as human beings communicate with and control all this electronic circuitry?

▼ CONCEPT CHECK

▶ What is the system unit?

▶ Describe the four basic types of microcomputer system units.

▶ What is a tablet PC? Describe the two basic categories.

ELECTRONIC DATA AND INSTRUCTIONS

> Data and instructions are represented electronically with a binary, or two-state, numbering system. ASCII, EDCDIC, and Unicode are binary coding schemes.

Have you ever wondered why it is said that we live in a *digital world?* (See Figure 6-3.) It's because computers cannot recognize information the same way you and I can. People follow instructions and process data using letters, numbers, and special characters. For example, if we wanted someone to add the numbers 3 and 5 together and record the answer, we might say "please add 3 and 5." The system unit, however, is electronic circuitry and cannot directly process such a request.

Our voices create **analog,** or continuous signals, that vary to represent different tones, pitches, and volume. Computers, however, can recognize only **digital** electronic signals. Before any processing can occur within the system unit, a conversion must occur from what we understand to what the system unit can electronically process.

What is the most fundamental statement you can make about electricity? It is simply this: It can be either on or off. Indeed, there are many forms of technology that can make use of this **two-state** on/off, yes/no, present/absent arrangement. For instance a light switch may be on or off, or an electric circuit open or closed. A specific location on a tape or disk may have a positive charge or a negative charge. This is the reason, then, that a two-state or binary system is used to represent data and instructions.

Figure 6-3 The digital world. Data and information in digital form can be processed and sent almost anywhere in the world in seconds.

The decimal system that we are all familiar with has 10 digits (0, 1, 2, 3, 4, 5, 6, 7, 8, 9). The **binary system,** however, consists of only two digits—0 and 1. Each 0 or 1 is called a **bit**—short for binary digit. In the system unit, the 0 can be represented by electricity being off, and the 1 by electricity being on. In order to represent numbers, letters, and special characters, bits are combined into groups of eight called **bytes.** Each byte typically represents one character.

BINARY CODING SCHEMES

Now let us consider an important question. How are characters represented as 0s and 1s ("off" and "on" electrical states) in the computer? The answer is in the use of **binary coding schemes.** (See Figure 6-4.) Two of the most popular binary coding schemes use eight bits or one byte. These two codes are ASCII and EBCDIC. (See Figure 6-5.) A recently developed code, unicode, uses sixteen bits.

Code	Uses
ASCII	Microcomputers
EBCDIC	Large computers
Unicode	International languages

Figure 6-4 Binary codes

- **ASCII,** pronounced "as-key," stands for **A**merican **S**tandard **C**ode for **I**nformation **I**nterchange. This is the most widely used binary code for microcomputers. For example, the number 3 is represented in ASCII code as 0011 0011.
- **EBCDIC,** pronounced "eb-see-dick," stands for **E**xtended **B**inary **C**oded **D**ecimal **I**nterchange **C**ode. It was developed by IBM and is used primarily for large computers. For example, the number 3 is represented in EBCDIC code as 1111 0011.

Symbol	ASCII	EBCDIC	Symbol	ASCII	EBCDIC
A	0100 0001	1100 0001	X	0101 1000	1110 0111
B	0100 0010	1100 0010	Y	0101 1001	1110 1000
C	0100 0011	1100 0011	Z	0101 1010	1110 1001
D	0100 0100	1100 0100	!	0010 0001	0101 1010
E	0100 0101	1100 0101	"	0010 0010	0111 1111
F	0100 0110	1100 0110	#	0010 0011	0111 1011
G	0100 0111	1100 0111	$	0010 0100	0101 1011
H	0100 1000	1100 1000	%	0010 0101	0110 1100
I	0100 1001	1100 1001	&	0010 0110	0101 0000
J	0100 1010	1101 0001	(	0010 1000	0100 1101
K	0100 1011	1101 0010	)	0010 1001	0101 1101
L	0100 1100	1101 0011	*	0010 1010	0101 1100
M	0100 1101	1101 0100	+	0010 1011	0100 1110
N	0100 1110	1101 0101	0	0011 0000	1111 0000
O	0100 1111	1101 0110	1	0011 0001	1111 0001
P	0101 0000	1101 0111	2	0011 0010	1111 0010
Q	0101 0001	1101 1000	3	0011 0011	1111 0011
R	0101 0010	1101 1001	4	0011 0100	1111 0100
S	0101 0011	1110 0010	5	0011 0101	1111 0101
T	0101 0100	1110 0011	6	0011 0110	1111 0110
U	0101 0101	1110 0100	7	0011 0111	1111 0111
V	0101 0110	1110 0101	8	0011 1000	1111 1000
W	0101 0111	1110 0110	9	0011 1001	1111 1001

ASCII code for +

ASCII code for 3

ASCII code for 5

Figure 6-5 ASCII and EBCDIC binary coding schemes

- **Unicode** is a 16-bit code designed to support international languages like Chinese and Japanese. These languages have too many characters to be represented by the eight-bit ASCII and EBCDIC codes.

When you press a key on the keyboard, a character is automatically converted into a series of electronic pulses that the system can recognize. For example, pressing the number 3 on a keyboard causes an electronic signal to be sent to the microcomputer's system unit where it is converted to the ASCII code of 0011 0011.

Coding schemes are particularly important to computer specialists for tracking down errors and other types of problems. But why are coding schemes important to end users? There are several reasons. One of the most important is that data created by one computer system using one coding scheme cannot be directly accessed and used by another computer system using a different coding scheme. Generally, this is not a problem if both computers are microcomputers since both would most likely use ASCII code. And most microcomputer applications store data using this code. However, problems occur when data is shared between microcomputers and larger computers that use EBCDIC code. The data must be translated from one coding scheme to the other before processing can begin. Fortunately, special conversion programs are available to help with this translation.

▼ CONCEPT CHECK

▶ What are decimal and binary systems? How are they different?

▶ What are binary coding schemes? Name and describe three.

▶ Describe how ASCII code is used to represent numbers and letters.

SYSTEM BOARD

The system board connects all system components and allows input and output devices to communicate with the system unit. Sockets, slots, and bus lines are components of the system board.

On the Web Explorations

Improvements in system unit components are being made every day. To learn more about a company on the forefront of these technologies, visit our Web site at

www.olearyseries.com/CE06

and select On the Web Explorations.

The **system board** is also known as the **main board** or **motherboard**. The system board is the communications medium for the entire computer system. Every component of the system unit connects to the system board. It acts as a data path allowing the various components to communicate with one another. External devices such as the keyboard, mouse, and monitor could not communicate with the system unit without the system board.

On a desktop computer, the system board is located at the bottom of the systems unit or along one side. (See Figure 6-6.) It is a large flat circuit board covered with a variety of different electronic components including sockets, slots, and bus lines. (See Figure 6-6.)

- **Sockets** provide a connection point for small specialized electronic parts called chips. **Chips** consist of tiny circuit boards etched onto squares of sandlike material called silicon. These circuit boards can be smaller than the tip of your finger. (See Figure 6-7.) A chip is also called a **silicon chip, semiconductor,** or **integrated circuit.** Chips are mounted on **carrier packages.** (See Figure 6-8.) These packages either plug directly into sockets on the system board or onto cards that are then plugged into slots on the system board. Sockets are used to connect the system board to a variety of different types of chips, including microprocessor and memory chips.

- **Slots** provide a connection point for specialized cards or circuit boards. These cards provide expansion capability for a computer system. For example, a modem card plugs into a slot on the system board to provide a connection to the Internet.

- Connecting lines called **bus lines** provide pathways that support communication among the various electronic components that are either located on the system board or attached to the system board. (See Figure 6-9.)

Notebook, tablet PC, and handheld system boards are smaller than desktop system boards. However, they perform the same functions as desktop system boards.

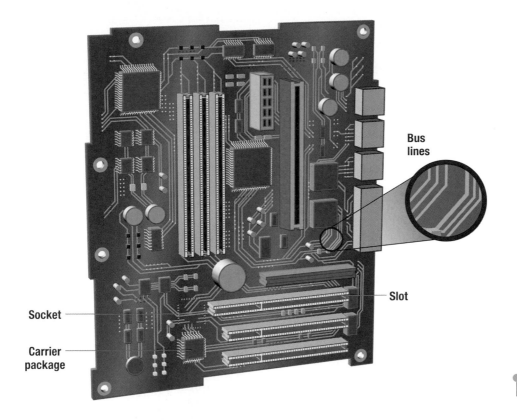

Bus lines

Socket

Carrier package

Slot

Figure 6-6   System board

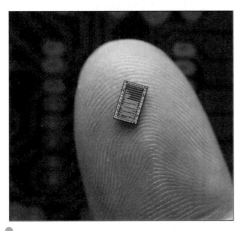

Figure 6-7   Chip

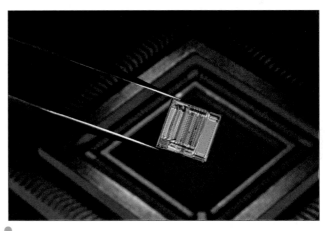

Figure 6-8   Chip being mounted onto a carrier package

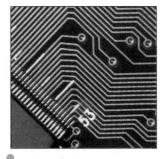

Figure 6-9   Bus lines

▼ CONCEPT CHECK

► What is the system board and what does it do?

► Define and describe sockets, slots, and bus lines.

► What are chips? How are chips attached to the system board?

MICROPROCESSOR

Microprocessors have two components—control and arithmetic-logic units. RISC and CISC are types of microprocessor chips. Coprocessors, parallel processors, and smart cards are specialty processors.

In a microcomputer system, the **central processing unit (CPU)** or **processor** is contained on a single chip called the **microprocessor.** The microprocessor is either mounted onto a carrier package that plugs into the system board or contained within a cartridge that plugs in to a special slot on the system board. (See Figure 6-10.) The microprocessor is the "brains" of the computer system. It has two basic components: the control unit and the arithmetic-logic unit.

- **Control unit:** The **control unit** tells the rest of the computer system how to carry out a program's instructions. It directs the movement of electronic signals between memory, which temporarily holds data, instructions, and processed information, and the arithmetic-logic unit. It also directs these control signals between the CPU and input and output devices.

- **Arithmetic-logic unit:** The **arithmetic-logic unit,** usually called the **ALU,** performs two types of operations—arithmetic and logical. **Arithmetic operations** are, as you might expect, the fundamental math operations: addition, subtraction, multiplication, and division. **Logical operations** consist of comparisons. That is, two pieces of data are compared to see whether one is equal to (=), less than (<), or greater than (>) the other.

MICROPROCESSOR CHIPS

Chip capacities are often expressed in word sizes. A **word** is the number of bits (such as 16, 32, or 64) that can be accessed at one time by the CPU. The more bits in a word, the more powerful—and the faster—the computer is. As mentioned previously, eight bits group together to form a byte. A 32-bit-word computer can access 4 bytes at a time. A 64-bit-word computer can access 8 bytes at a time. Therefore, the computer designed to process 64-bit-words is faster.

Older microcomputers typically process data and instructions in millionths of a second, or **microseconds.** Newer microcomputers are much faster and process data and instructions in billionths of a second, or **nanoseconds.** Super-

Figure 6-10 Microprocessor carrier package and cartridge

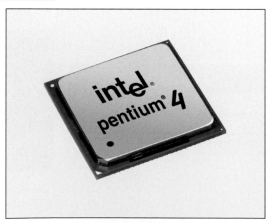

Carrier package

Cartridge

computers, by contrast, operate at speeds measured in **picoseconds**—1,000 times as fast as microcomputers. (See Figure 6-11.)

There are two types of microprocessor chips.

Unit	Speed
Microsecond	Millionth of a second
Nanosecond	Billionth of a second
Picosecond	Trillionth of a second

Figure 6-11   Processing speeds

- **CISC chips:** The most common type of microprocessor is the **complex instruction set computer (CISC) chip.** This design was popularized by Intel and is the basis for its line of microprocessors. It is the most widely used chip design with thousands of programs written specifically for it. Intel's Pentium microprocessors are CISC chips. While Intel is the leading manufacturer of microprocessors, other manufacturers produce microprocessors using a nearly identical design. These chips, referred to as **Intel-compatible** processors, are able to process programs originally written specifically for Intel chips. For example, AMD Corporation produces Intel-compatible chips known as Athlon and Hammer.
- **RISC chips: Reduced instruction set computer (RISC) chips** use fewer instructions. This design is simpler and less costly than CISC chips. The PowerPC is a RISC chip produced by Motorola. SPARC is a RISC chip produced by Sun. These chips are used in many of today's most powerful microcomputers known as **workstations.**

See Figure 6-12 for a table of popular microprocessors.

On the Web Explorations

RISC chips run some of today's most powerful computers. To learn more about one of the manufacturers of RISC chips, visit our Web site at

www.olearyseries.com/CE06

and select On the Web Explorations.

SPECIALTY PROCESSORS

In addition to microprocessor chips, a variety of more specialized processing chips have been developed. One of the most common is coprocessors. **Coprocessors** are specialty chips designed to improve specific computing operations. One of the most widely used is the **graphics coprocessor.** These processors are specifically designed to handle the processing requirements related to displaying and manipulating 2-D and 3-D graphics images.

Another specialty processor is the **parallel processor.** These processors work with one or more other parallel processor chips to run or process large programs. The processors use special software that takes a large program, breaks it down into parts, and assigns the parts to separate processors. The processors then work on their respective parts simultaneously and share results as required by the program. This approach is called **parallel processing.** Although not commonly used with microcomputers, parallel processing is commonly used by supercomputers to run very large and complex programs.

Smart cards use another type of specialty processor. A **smart card** is essentially a plastic card the size of a regular credit card that has an embedded chip. While most current smart cards can store 80 times the information stored on the magnetic strip of a regular credit card, larger capacity cards are expected soon. Visa, MasterCard, and American Express have introduced their smart cards to millions of users. (See Figure 6-13.) Many colleges and universities are distributing smart cards to their students

Manufacturer	Processor	Type	Typical Use
Intel	Pentium	CISC	Microcomputers
AMD	Athlon	CISC	Microcomputers
	Hammer	CISC	Workstations
Motorola	PowerPC	RISC	Apple computers
Sun	SPARC	RISC	Workstations

Figure 6-12   Popular microprocessors

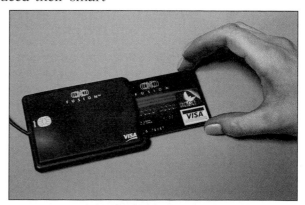

Figure 6-13   Smart card

for identification. The University of Michigan, for example, provides its students with a smart card called the Mcard that allows them to access their dorms and use their meal plans.

▼ **CONCEPT CHECK** //

► Name and describe the two components of a microprocessor.

► Name and describe the two types of microprocessor chips.

► What are specialty chips? Name and discuss two types of specialty processors.

MEMORY

> Memory holds data, instructions, and information. RAM, ROM, and CMOS are three types of memory chips.

Memory is a holding area for data, instructions, and information. Like microprocessors, **memory** is contained on chips connected to the system board. There are three well-known types of memory chips: random-access memory (RAM), read-only memory (ROM), and complementary metal-oxide semiconductor (CMOS).

RAM

Random-access memory (RAM) chips hold the program (sequence of instructions) and data that the CPU is presently processing. (See Figure 6-14.) RAM is called temporary or **volatile storage** because everything in most types of RAM is lost as soon as the microcomputer is turned off. It is also lost if there is a power failure or other disruption of the electric current going to the microcomputer. Secondary storage, which we shall describe in Chapter 8, does not lose its contents. It is permanent or **nonvolatile storage,** such as the data stored on diskettes. For this reason, as we mentioned earlier, it is a good idea to save your work in progress to a secondary storage device. That is, if you are working on a document or a spreadsheet, every few minutes you should save, or store, the material.

Figure 6-14 RAM chips mounted on circuit board

Cache (pronounced "cash") **memory** or **RAM cache** improves processing by acting as a temporary high-speed holding area between the memory and the CPU. In a computer with a cache (not all machines have one), the computer detects which information in RAM is most frequently used. It then copies that information into the cache. When needed, the CPU can quickly access the information from the cache.

Flash RAM or **flash memory** chips can retain data even if power is disrupted. This type of RAM is the most expensive and used primarily for special applications such as for digital cell telephones, digital video cameras, and portable computers.

Having enough RAM is important! For example, to effectively use Excel requires 32 MB of RAM and additional RAM is needed to hold any data or other applications. Some microcomputers—particularly older ones—do not have this much memory. Additional RAM, however, can be added to these computer systems. The capacity or amount of RAM is expressed in bytes. There are three commonly used units of measurement to describe memory capacity. (See Figure 6-15.)

Other types of RAM include DRAM, SDRAM, DDR, SDRAM, and Direct RDRAM. To learn more about these other types of RAM, consult your Computing Essentials CD or visit us on the Web at www.olearyseries.com/CE06 and select Expansions.

Even if your computer does not have enough RAM to hold a program, it might be able to run the program using **virtual memory.** Most of today's operating systems support virtual memory. With virtual memory, large programs are divided into parts and the parts are stored on a secondary device, usually a hard disk. Each part is then read into RAM only when needed. In this way, computer systems are able to run very large programs. To learn more about how virtual memory works, consult your Computing Essentials CD or visit our Web site at www.olearyseries.com/CE06 and select Expansions.

Unit	Capacity
Megabyte (MB)	1 million bytes
Gigabyte (GB)	1 billion bytes
Terabyte (TB)	1 trillion bytes

Figure 6-15   Memory capacity

ROM

Read-only memory (ROM) chips have programs built into them at the factory. Unlike RAM chips, ROM chips are not volatile and cannot be changed by the user. "Read only" means that the CPU can read, or retrieve, data and programs written on the ROM chip. However, the computer cannot write—encode or change—the information or instructions in ROM.

ROM chips typically contain special instructions for detailed computer operations. For example, ROM instructions are needed to start a computer, give keyboard keys their special control capabilities, and put characters on the screen. ROMs are also called **firmware.**

CMOS

A **complementary metal-oxide semiconductor (CMOS)** chip provides flexibility and expandability for a computer system. It contains essential information that is required every time the computer system is turned on. The chip supplies such information as the current date and time, amount of RAM, type of keyboard, mouse, monitor, and disk drives. Unlike RAM, it is powered by a battery and does not lose its contents when the power is turned off. Unlike ROM, its contents can be changed to reflect changes in the computer system such as increased RAM and new hardware devices.

See Figure 6-16 for a summary of the three types of memory.

Type	Use
RAM	Programs and data
ROM	Fixed start-up instructions
CMOS	Flexible start-up instructions

Figure 6-16   Memory

▼ CONCEPT CHECK

▶ What is memory? Name and describe the three types of memory chips.

▶ Define cache memory, flash RAM, and virtual memory.

The System Unit

SYSTEM CLOCK

The system clock is like a bass drum. Clock speed is measured in gigahertz or billions of beats per second.

The **system clock** is located on a small specialized chip that produces precisely timed electrical beats or impulses. The system clock performs a function similar to the bass drum in a marching band. Just as the bass drum determines the cadence, or how fast the band marches, the system clock emits a beat or pulse that sets the operating pace for all of the components in the system unit.

Unlike a bass drum, which can beat faster to increase cadence, a computer's system clock has a fixed speed that cannot be varied. For that reason, a computer system's clock speed is an important measurement indicating the speed of processing or power of a computer system. The **clock speed** or **clock rate** for powerful microcomputers is measured in **gigahertz (GHz)** or billions of beats per second. The faster the clock speed, the faster the computer can process instructions.

▼ CONCEPT CHECK

▶ What is a system clock? How is it like a bass drum?

▶ What is clock speed? How is it measured?

TIPS Does your computer seem to be getting slower and slower? Perhaps it's so slow you are thinking about buying a new one. Before doing that, consider the following suggestions that might add a little zip to your current system.

1 **Uninstall programs you no longer need.** Explore the contents of your hard disk and identify programs that you no longer need. If you have Windows XP, use Start/Control Panel/Add/Remove Programs (for Windows 2000 use Start/Settings/Control Panel/Add/Remove Programs) to access the Uninstall feature.

2 **Remove unneeded fonts.** If you have Windows XP use Start/Control Panel/Fonts in the classic view (for Windows 2000 use Start/Settings/Control Panel/Fonts) to determine the different font types stored on your system. To see a sample of any font type, double-click it. Review the fonts and delete those you will not need.

3 **Empty the Recycle Bin.** If you have either Windows 2000 or Windows XP, files are not removed from your hard disk when you delete them. Rather, they are moved to the Recycle Bin. To empty or remove files from the Recycle Bin, open the Recycle Bin and use File/Empty Recycle Bin.

EXPANSION SLOTS AND CARDS

Expansion slots provide an open architecture. Expansion cards provide connections for video, network, TV tuner cards, and more. Plug and play is a set of standards. PC cards are for notebook and handheld computers.

Computers are known for having different kinds of "architectures." Machines that have **closed architecture** are manufactured in such a way that users cannot easily add new devices. Most microcomputers have **open architecture.** They allow users to expand their systems by providing **expansion slots** on the

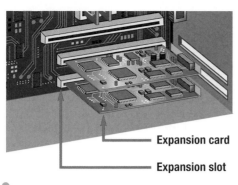

Ports to
connect to
outside devices

Connections that
fit into slots on the
system board

Figure 6-17   Expansion cards fit
into slots on the system board

Figure 6-18   Expansion card

system board. Users can insert optional devices known as **expansion cards** into these slots. (See Figure 6-17.)

Expansion cards are also called **plug-in boards, controller cards, adapter cards,** and **interface cards.** They plug into slots located on the system board. Ports on the cards allow cables to be connected from the expansion cards to devices outside the system unit. (See Figure 6-18.) There are a wide range of different types of expansion cards. Some of the most commonly used expansion cards are:

Figure 6-19   Modem card

- **Video cards:** Also known as **graphics cards,** these cards connect the system board to the computer's monitor. The cards convert the internal electronic signals to video signals so they can be displayed on the monitor.
- **Sound cards:** These cards accept audio input from a microphone and convert it into a form that can be processed by the computer. Also, these cards convert internal electronic signals to audio signals so they can be heard from external speakers.
- **Modem cards:** Also known as **internal modems,** these cards allow distant computers to communicate with one another by converting electronic signals from within the system unit into electronic signals that can travel over telephone lines and other types of connections. (See Figure 6-19.)
- **Network interface cards (NIC):** These cards, also known as **network adapter cards,** are used to connect a computer to one or more other computers. This forms a communication network whereby users can share data, programs, and hardware. The network adapter card typically connects the system unit to a cable that connects to the network.
- **TV tuner cards:** Now you can watch television, capture video, and surf the Internet at the same time. TV tuner cards, also known as **television boards, video recorder cards,** and **video capture cards,** contain a TV tuner and a video converter that changes the TV signal into one that can be displayed on your monitor. To see how TV tuner cards work, consult your Computing Essentials CD or visit our Web site at www.olearyseries. com/CE06 and select Animations. (To learn more about using TV tuner cards, see Making IT Work for You: TV Tuner Cards and Video Clips on pages 162 and 163.)

Plug and Play is a set of hardware and software standards developed by Intel, Microsoft, and others. It is an effort by hardware and software vendors to create operating systems, processing units, and expansion boards, as well as other devices that are able to configure themselves. Ideally, to install a new

The System Unit

TV TUNER CARDS AND VIDEO CLIPS

Want to watch your favorite television program while you work? Perhaps you would like to include a video clip from television and include it in a class presentation. It's easy using a TV tuner card.

Viewing   Once a TV tuner card has been installed, you can view your favorite TV shows, even while running other applications such as Excel, by taking the steps shown here.

1 ● Click the *TV icon* on the desktop.

● Size and move the television window and control box window.

● Select the channel.

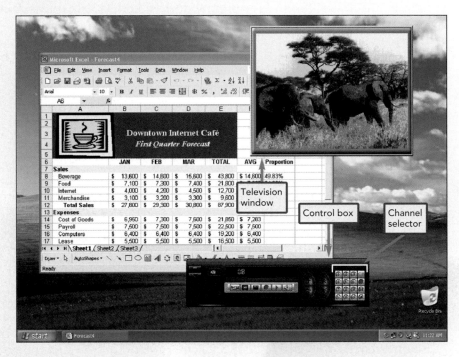

Capturing   You can capture the video playing in the TV window into a digital file by taking the steps shown here.

1 ● Specify where to save the video clip on your computer by clicking the *Properties* button.

● Click the *Record* button to start recording.

● Click the *Stop* button to stop recording.

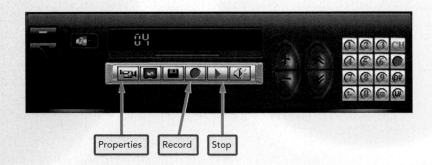

Using Once captured in a file, a video can be used in any number of ways. It can be added to a Web page, attached to an e-mail, or added to a class presentation. For example, you could include a video clip in a PowerPoint presentation by taking the steps shown here.

1 Insert the video clip into a page in the presentation by clicking *Insert/Movies and Sounds/Movie from File.*

2 Click on the image of the inserted video clip anytime during your presentation to play it.

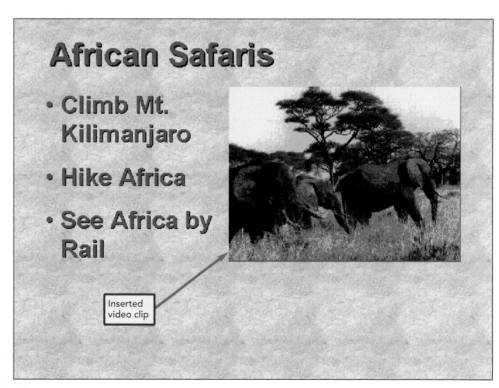

TV tuner cards are relatively inexpensive and easy to install. Some factors limiting their performance on your computer are the speed of your processor, the amount of memory, and secondary storage capacity.

TV tuner cards are continually changing, and some of the specifics presented in this Making IT Work for You may have changed. To learn about other ways to make information technology work for you, consult your Computing Essentials CD or visit our Web site at www.olearyseries.com/CE06 and select Making IT Work.

expansion board all you have to do is insert the board and turn on the computer. As the computer starts up, it will search for these Plug and Play devices and automatically configure the devices and the computer system. Unfortunately, not all computer systems and expansion cards have this capability. For those devices that do not, reconfiguration involves installing device drivers as discussed in Chapter 5.

To meet the size constraints of notebook and handheld computers, credit card-sized expansion cards have been developed. These cards can be easily inserted and removed. They are called **PC cards** or **Personal Computer Memory Card International Association (PCMCIA) cards.** (See Figure 6-20.)

▼ **CONCEPT CHECK**

▶ What does open versus closed architecture mean?

▶ What are expansion slots and cards? Name five expansion cards.

▶ What is Plug and Play? What are PC cards?

Figure 6-20 **Inserting a PC card into a notebook computer**

BUS LINES

Bus lines provide data pathways that connect various system components. System and expansion are two categories of buses.

bus line—also known simply as a **bus**—connects the parts of the CPU to each other. Buses also link the CPU to various other components on the system board. (See Figure 6-21.) A bus is a pathway for bits representing data and instructions. The number of bits that can travel simultaneously down a bus is known as the **bus width.**

A bus is similar to a multilane highway that moves bits rather than cars from one location to another. The number of traffic lanes determines the bus width. A highway (bus line) with more traffic lanes (bus width) can move traffic (data and instructions) faster. For example, a 64-bit bus is twice as fast as a 32-bit bus. Why should you even care about what a bus line is? Because as microprocessor chips have changed, so have bus lines. Bus design or bus architecture is an important factor relating to the speed and power for a particular computer. Additionally, many devices, such as expansion boards, will work with only one type of bus.

EXPANSION BUSES

Every computer system has two basic categories of buses. One category, called **system buses,** connects the CPU to memory on the system board. The other category, called **expansion buses,** connects the CPU to other components on the system board, including expansion slots.

Computer systems typically have a combination of different types of expansion buses. The principal types are ISA, PCI, AGP, USB, and HPSB.

• **Industry standard architecture (ISA)** was developed for the first IBM Personal Computer. Originally, it had an 8-bit bus width. Later, it was expanded to 16 bits. Although too slow for many of today's applications, the ISA bus is still widely used.

- **Peripheral component interconnect (PCI)** was originally developed to meet the video demands of graphical user interfaces. PCI is a high-speed 32-bit or 64-bit bus that is over 20 times faster than ISA buses.
- **Accelerated graphics port (AGP)** is over twice as fast as the PCI bus. While the PCI bus is used for a variety of purposes, the AGP bus is dedicated to the acceleration of graphics performance. Widely used for graphics and 3-D animations, the AGP is replacing the PCI bus for the transfer of video data.
- **Universal serial bus (USB)** combines with a PCI bus on the system board to support several external devices without using expansion cards or slots. External USB devices are connected from one to another and then onto the USB bus. The USB bus then connects to the PCI bus on the motherboard. The first universal serial bus was called USB 1.1 and is over twice as fast as the AGP bus. Recently, a new version called USB 2.0 has been introduced that is 40 times faster than USB 1.1.
- **FireWire buses,** also known as **high performance serial bus (HPSB),** operate much like USB buses and perform at speeds comparable to USB 2.0. FireWire and USB 2.0 buses are used for special applications that provide support for digital camcorders and video editing software.

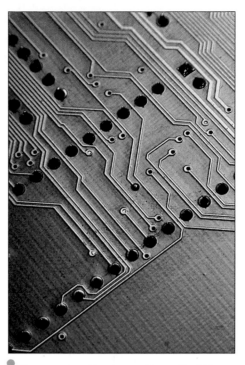

Figure 6-21   Bus is a pathway for bits

PORTS

Ports are connecting sockets on the systems unit. Serial, parallel, USB, and FireWire are standard ports. Cables connect external devices to ports.

A **port** is a socket for external devices to connect to the system unit. (See Figure 6-22.) Some ports connect directly to the systems board while others connect to cards that are inserted into slots on the systems board. Some ports are standard features of most computer systems and others are more specialized.

STANDARD PORTS

Many ports, like the mouse, keyboard, and video ports, are for specific devices. Others, like those listed below, can be used for a variety of different devices.

- **Serial ports** are used for a wide variety of purposes. They are often used to connect a mouse, keyboard, modem, and many other devices to the system unit. Serial ports send data one bit at a time and are very good for sending information over a long distance.
- **Parallel ports** are used to connect external devices that need to send or receive a lot of data over a short distance. These ports typically send eight bits of data simultaneously across eight parallel wires. Parallel ports are mostly used to connect printers to the system unit.
- **Universal serial bus (USB) ports** are gradually replacing serial and parallel ports. They are faster, and one USB port can be used to connect several devices to the system unit.
- **FireWire ports,** also known as **high performance serial bus (HPSB) ports,** are as fast as USB 2.0 ports and provide connections to specialized FireWire devices such as camcorders.

Figure 6-22   Ports

CABLES

Cables are used to connect exterior devices to the system unit via the ports. One end of the cable is attached to the device and the other end has a connector that is attached to a matching connector on the port.

POWER SUPPLY

> DC powers computers. Desktop computers use power supply units. Notebook and handheld computers use AC adapters and batteries.

omputers require **direct current (DC)** to power their electronic components and to represent data and instructions. DC power can be provided indirectly by converting **alternating current (AC)** from standard wall outlets or directly from batteries.

- Desktop computers have a **power supply unit** located within the system unit. (See Figure 6-23.) This unit plugs into a standard wall outlet, converts AC to DC, and provides the power to drive all of the system unit components.
- Notebook computers use **AC adapters** that are typically located outside the system unit. (See Figure 6-24.) AC adapters plug into a standard wall outlet, convert AC to DC, provide power to drive the system unit components, and can recharge batteries. Notebook computers can be operated either using an AC adapter plugged into a wall outlet or using battery power. Notebook batteries typically provide sufficient power for 2 to 4 hours before they need to be recharged.
- Like notebook computers, handheld computers use AC adapters located outside the system unit. Unlike notebook computers, however, handheld computers typically operate only using battery power. The AC adapter is used to recharge the batteries.

Figure 6-23   Power supply unit

Figure 6-24   AC adapter

▼ CONCEPT CHECK

▶   What is a bus and what is its function? Describe five types.

▶   What are ports? What do they do? Describe four standard ports.

▶   What is a power supply unit? What is an AC adaptor?

A Look to the Future

Xybernaut Corporation Makes Wearable Computers a Reality

Wouldn't it be nice if you could conveniently access the Internet wirelessly at any time during the day? What if you could send and receive e-mail from your waist-mounted computer? What if you could maintain your personal schedule book, making new appointments with others on the fly? What if you could play interactive games, and surf the Web from anywhere?

Of course you can do all this and more using wireless technology and PDAs. Many people currently use this technology when they are away from their home or office. What if these users could accomplish these tasks with an even smaller, more portable, and less intrusive system? Will people be wearing computers rather than carrying them? What if your computer featured a head-mounted display?

Xybernaut Corporation is currently marketing a personal wearable computer called POMA®. The device is described as a personal multimedia appliance. It is composed of a processor that runs Windows CE, a wireless pointing device, and a head-mounted display. The display allows you to see the equivalent of a desktop monitor via a small screen that is worn in front of one eye. This screen is only one inch square and weighs a mere 3 ounces. The device includes an MP3 player that plays songs and displays videos, and abridged versions of Windows Office programs.

Devices made by Xybernaut® are currently being evaluated for use in airports by security personnel. These devices are currently being used by the U.S. Department of Defense for military applications and by the Toronto Blue Jays to end long lines at ticket windows. When coupled with face recognition technology, Xybernaut's Mobile Assistant® V provides security personnel portable and instant communication with the command center. Police and security officers may someday use this technology to check IDs and verify your identity. Experts say that wearable computers will be used by surgeons in operating rooms to "view" their patients.

Will we be wearing computers soon? Some of us already are. And some experts predict the majority of us will employ a wearable computer before the end of the decade. Many computer manufacturers are currently working on wearable computers, and there is even a wearable computer fashion show that showcases the latest designs. Many people are already wearing their computers, and making use of this mobile technology to read e-mail while waiting in lines or even studying their notes for the next exam. What do you think? Will Americans someday grab their keys and their computers before they leave the house? Will your computer one day be housed in your jacket?

VISUAL SUMMARY

THE SYSTEM UNIT

SYSTEM UNIT

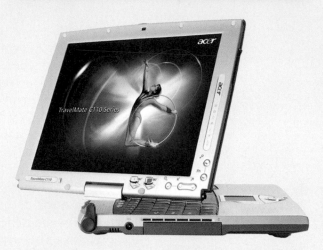

System unit (system cabinet or **chassis)** contains electronic components. Four basic types are: **desktop (tower models** positioned vertically), **notebook, tablet PC (convertible** and **slate),** and **handheld. PDA (personal digital assistant)** is the most widely used handheld computer.

Electronic Representation

Our voices create continuous **analog** signals. A conversion to **digital** signals is necessary before processing. Data and instructions can be represented electronically with a **two-state** or **binary system** of numbers (0 and 1). Each 0 or 1 is called a **bit.** A **byte** consists of eight bits and represents one character.

Binary Coding Schemes

Binary coding schemes convert binary data into characters. Three such schemes are:

- **ASCII**—the most widely used for microcomputers.
- **EBCDIC**—developed by IBM; used primarily by large computers.
- **Unicode**—16-bit code; designed to support international languages like Chinese and Japanese.

SYSTEM BOARD

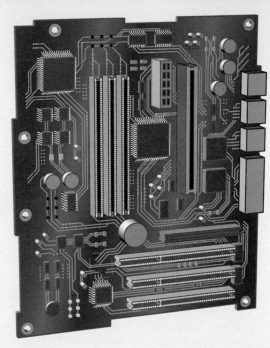

The **system board (main board** or **motherboard)** connects all system components and allows input and output devices to communicate with the system unit. It is a flat circuit board covered with these electronic components:

- **Sockets** provide connection points for **chips (silicon chips, semiconductors, integrated circuits).** Chips are mounted on **carrier packages.**
- **Slots** provide connection points for specialized cards or circuit boards.
- **Bus lines** provide pathways to support communication.

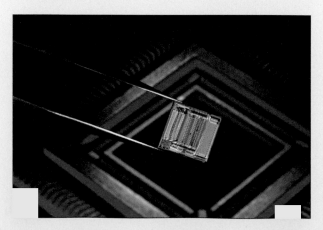

To be a competent end user, you need to understand how data and programs are represented electronically. Additionally, you need to understand the functionality of the basic components in the system unit: system board, microprocessor, memory, system clock, expansion slots and cards, bus lines, and ports and cables.

MICROPROCESSOR

The **microprocessor** is a single chip that contains the **central processing unit (CPU)** or **microprocessor.** It has two basic components:

- **Control unit** tells the computer system how to carry out program instructions.
- **Arithmetic-logic unit (ALU)** performs **arithmetic** and **logical operations.**

Microprocessor Chips

A **word** is the number of bits that can be accessed by the microprocessor at one time. Older microprocessors process data and instructions in **microseconds;** newer ones process in **nanoseconds.** Supercomputers process in **picoseconds.**

Two types of microprocessor chips are **complex instruction set computer (CISC)** and **reduced instruction set computer** (**RISC,** used in powerful microcomputers known as **workstations**).

Specialty Processors

Specialty processors include **graphics coprocessors** (handle processing requirements for 2-D and 3-D graphic images), **parallel processors** (work together to run large programs, **parallel processing**), and **smart cards** (plastic cards containing embedded chips).

Unit	Speed
Microsecond	Millionth of a second
Nanosecond	Billionth of a second
Picosecond	Trillionth of a second

MEMORY

Memory holds data, instructions, and information. There are three types of memory chips: RAM, ROM, and CMOS.

RAM

RAM (random access memory) chips are called temporary or **volatile storage** because their contents are lost if power is disrupted.

- **Cache memory** or **RAM cache** is a high-speed holding area for frequently used data and information.
- **Flash RAM** or **flash memory** is a special type of RAM that does not lose its contents when power is disrupted.
- **Virtual memory** divides large programs into parts that are read into RAM as needed.

ROM

ROM (read only memory) chips, also called **firmware,** are **nonvolatile storage** and control essential system operations.

CMOS

CMOS (complementary metal-oxide semiconductor) chips provide flexibility and expandability to computer systems.

SYSTEM CLOCK

System clock controls the speed of operations. **Clock speed (clock rate)** is measured in **gigahertz (GHz).**

EXPANSION SLOTS AND CARDS

Computers with **closed architecture** are not easily expanded. **Open architecture** computers have **expansion slots** on their system boards to accept **expansion cards (plug-in boards, controller cards, adapter cards,** or **interface cards).**

Examples of **expansion cards** include:

- **Video cards**—also known as **graphics cards,** connect to monitors.
- **Sound cards**—convert audio signals for processing and output.
- **Modem cards**—also known as **internal modems,** connect over a telephone line.
- **Network interface cards (NIC)**—also known as **network adapter cards,** connect to a network.
- **TV tuner cards**—contain TV tuner and video capture capabilities, also known as **television boards** and **video recorder cards.**
- **PC cards**—credit card-size expansion cards for portable computers, also known as **PCMCIA (Personal Computer Memory Card International Association) cards.**

Plug and Play is a set of hardware and software standards designed to assist with the installation of expansion cards.

BUS LINES

Bus lines, also known as **buses,** provide data pathways that connect various system components. **Bus width** is the number of bits that can travel simultaneously.

Expansion Buses

System buses connect CPU and memory. **Expansion buses** connect CPU and slots. Five principal expansion bus types are **ISA (Industry Standard Architecture), PCI (Peripheral Component Interconnect), AGP (Accelerated Graphics Port), USB (Universal Serial Bus),** and **FireWire bus (HPSB or High Performance Serial Bus).**

PORTS

Ports are connecting sockets on the outside of the system unit.

Standard Ports

Four standard ports are **serial, parallel, USB (universal serial bus),** and **FireWire (HPSB or high performance serial bus).**

Cables

Cables are used to connect external devices to the system unit via ports.

POWER SUPPLY

Computers require **direct current (DC)**. DC power is supplied by either converting **alternating current (AC)** from standard wall outlets or directly from batteries. **Power supply units** convert AC to DC; they are located within the desktop computer's system unit. **AC adapters** power notebook computers and tablet PCs and recharge batteries.

AC adapter (166)
accelerated graphics port (AGP) (165)
adapter card (161)
alternating current (AC) (166)
analog (152)
arithmetic operation (156)
arithmetic-logic unit (ALU) (156)
ASCII (152)
binary coding scheme (152)
binary system (152)
bit (152)
bus (164)
bus line (154)
bus width (164)
byte (152)
cable (166)
cache memory (158)
carrier package (154)
central processing unit (CPU) (156)
chassis (150)
chip (154)
clock speed (160)
clock rate (160)
closed architecture (160)
complementary metal-oxide semiconductor (CMOS) (159)
complex instruction set computer (CISC) chip (157)
control unit (156)
controller card (161)
convertible tablet PC (151)
coprocessor (157)
desktop system unit (150)
digital (152)
direct current (DC) (166)
EBCDIC (152)
expansion bus (164)
expansion card (161)
expansion slot (160)
FireWire bus (165)
FireWire port (165)

firmware (159)
flash RAM (158)
flash memory (158)
gigahertz (GHz) (160)
graphics card (161)
graphics coprocessor (157)
handheld computer system unit (151)
high performance serial bus (HPSB) (165)
high performance serial bus (HPSB) port (165)
industry standard architecture (ISA) (164)
integrated circuit (154)
Intel-compatible (157)
interface card (161)
internal modem (161)
laptop computer (150)
logical operation (156)
main board (154)
memory (158)
microprocessor (156)
microsecond (156)
modem card (161)
motherboard (154)
nanosecond (156)
network adapter card (161)
network interface card (NIC) (161)
nonvolatile storage (158)
notebook system unit (150)
open architecture (160)
palm computer (151)
parallel port (165)
parallel processing (157)
parallel processor (157)
PC card (164)
peripheral component interconnect (PCI) (165)
Personal Computer Memory Card International Association (PCMCIA) card (164)
personal digital assistant (PDA) (151)

picosecond (157)
Plug and Play (161)
plug-in board (161)
port (165)
power supply unit (166)
processor (156)
RAM cache (158)
random-access memory (RAM) (158)
read-only memory (ROM) (159)
reduced instruction set computer (RISC) chip (157)
semiconductor (154)
serial port (165)
silicon chip (154)
slate tablet PC (151)
slot (154)
smart card (157)
sound card (161)
socket (154)
system board (154)
system bus (164)
system cabinet (150)
system clock (160)
system unit (150)
tablet PC (151)
tablet PC system unit (151)
television board (161)
tower model (150)
TV tuner card (161)
two-state system (152)
Unicode (152)
universal serial bus (USB) (165)
universal serial bus (USB) port (165)
video card (161)
video capture card (161)
video recorder card (161)
volatile storage (158)
virtual memory (159)
word (156)
workstation (157)

To test your knowledge of these key terms with animated flash cards, consult your Computing Essentials CD or visit our Web site at www.olearyseries.com/CE06 and select Key Terms.

COMPUTING ESSENTIALS 2006

CROSSWORD PUZZLE

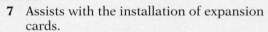

Across

7 Assists with the installation of expansion cards.

9 Type of architecture that users cannot easily add devices to.

12 Most widely used microprocessor binary coding scheme.

13 Controls the speed of operations.

15 Holding area for data, instructions, and information.

16 Used to connect external devices to system unit via ports.

Down

1 Connect the system board to a computer's monitor.

2 The number of bits that can be accessed by the microprocessor at one time.

3 Another name for ROM chips.

4 Container that houses most electronic computer components.

5 Provide connection points for chips.

6 Connects the parts of the CPU to each other.

8 Temporary high-speed holding area between the memory and CPU.

10 The number of bits that can travel simultaneously down a bus.

11 Binary digit.

12 Over twice as fast as the PCI bus.

14 Connection point for specialized cards or circuit boards.

For an interactive version of this crossword, consult your Computing Essentials CD or visit our Web site at **www.olearyseries.com/CE06** and select Crossword.

MULTIPLE CHOICE

Circle the letter or fill in the correct answer.

1. The system unit is also called the _____.
   - a. PDA
   - b. system board
   - c. system cabinet and chassis
   - d. mother board
   - e. chassis

2. _____ are the most widely used handheld computer.
   - a. RAMs
   - b. Notebooks
   - c. PDAs
   - d. CPUs
   - e. Tower units

3. ASCII, EBCDIC, and Unicode are examples of _____.
   - a. analog systems
   - b. integrated circuits
   - c. binary coding schemes
   - d. adapter cards
   - e. slots

4. _____ connect special cards or circuit boards to the system board.
   - a. Slots
   - b. Carrier packages
   - c. Unicodes
   - d. PC cards
   - e. Ports

5. Random-access memory (RAM) is a kind of _____ storage.
   - a. permanent
   - b. temporary
   - c. flash
   - d. smart
   - e. expansion

6. _____ is a temporary high-speed holding area between memory and the CPU.
   - a. Flash
   - b. ALU
   - c. ASCII
   - d. Cache
   - e. CMOS

7. ROM is also known as _____.
   - a. semiconductor
   - b. slot
   - c. adapter
   - d. network
   - e. firmware

8. A(n) _____ chip provides flexibility and expandability for a computer system; it contains essential information that is required every time the computer system is turned on.
   - a. ROM
   - b. RAM
   - c. TCP/IP
   - d. CMOS
   - e. ALU

9. _____ is a set of hardware and software standards that allows expansion boards and other devices to install themselves.
   - a. Plug and Play
   - b. Unicode
   - c. System unit
   - d. Industry standard architecture
   - e. EBCDIC

10. A(n) _____, also called a bus, connects the parts of the CPU together.
    - a. adapter card
    - b. parallel port
    - c. serial port
    - d. ISA
    - e. bus line

For an interactive version of these multiple choice questions, consult your Computing Essentials CD or visit our Web site at **www.olearyseries.com/CE06** and select Multiple Choice.

COMPUTING
ESSENTIALS
2006

MATCHING

Match each numbered item with the most closely related lettered item. Write your answers in the spaces provided.

a. analog

b. bus width

c. cables

d. cache memory

e. chip

f. CISC chip

g. closed architecture

h. control unit

i. expansion card

j. flash RAM

k. firmware

l. graphics coprocessor

m. parallel port

n. PC card

o. port

p. RAM

q. smart card

r. system board

s. system clock

t. system unit

1. Houses most of the electronic components in a computer system. _____

2. The number of bits that can travel down a bus at the same time. _____

3. The communications web for the entire computer system. _____

4. Consists of a circuit board etched on a stamp-sized square of silicon. _____

5. Tells the computer system how to carry out a program's instructions. _____

6. Type of signal created by our voices. _____

7. The most common type of microprocessor. _____

8. A credit card size piece of plastic with an embedded chip. _____

9. Volatile storage that holds the program and data the CPU is currently processing. _____

10. Fast, temporary holding area between the memory and CPU. _____

11. Produces precisely timed electrical beats as a timing mechanism. _____

12. Machines that users cannot easily add new devices to. _____

13. Also called plug-in boards, controller cards, adapter cards, and interface cards. _____

14. Also called ROMs. _____

15. Credit card-sized expansion boards used by portable computers. _____

16. Handles computations related to graphics images. _____

17. Connecting socket on the outside of the system unit. _____

18. Connects external devices that need to send lots of data a short distance. _____

19. Another name for flash memory. _____

20. Connects input and output devices to the system unit via the ports. _____

For an interactive version of this matching exercise, consult your Computing Essentials CD or visit our Web site at **www.olearyseries.com/CE06** and select Matching.

OPEN-ENDED

On a separate sheet of paper, respond to each question or statement.

1. Describe the four basic types of system units.

2. Describe the two basic components of the CPU.

3. What are the differences and similarities between the three types of memory?

4. Identify five expansion cards and describe the function of each.

5. Identify and describe four standard ports.

TV Tuner Cards and Video Clips

1

Want to watch your favorite television program while you work? Perhaps you would like to include a video clip in a class presentation. It's easy using a video TV card. To learn more about this technology, review Making IT Work for You: TV Tuner Cards and Video Clips on pages 162 and 163. Then visit our Web site at www.olearyseries.com/CE06 and select Using Technology. Play the video and answer the following questions: (a) Describe the two windows that open when the TV icon is selected. (b) What are the basic functions of the control box? (c) What is the command sequence to insert a video clip into a PowerPoint presentation?

Desktop and Notebook Computers

2

Have you recently purchased a new computer? Are you thinking about purchasing one? The Web is an excellent source for reviewing, comparing, and purchasing computers. Visit our Web site at www. olearyseries.com/CE06 and select Using Technology to link to several sites that present information about the newest desktop and notebook computers. Connect to these sites to check out different desktop and notebook

models, and then answer the following questions: (a) If you were to purchase a desktop computer, which one would you select? Describe how it would fit your needs and print out its specifications. (b) If you were to purchase a notebook computer, which one would you select? Describe how it would fit your needs and print out its specifications. (c) If you had to choose between the desktop and notebook, which one would you choose? Defend your selection in one paragraph by discussing the relative advantages and disadvantages of each type.

1

How TV Tuner Cards Work

The advent of digital TV and the success of digital video recorders has made TV tuner cards a popular addition to many computers. TV tuner cards allow you to watch and record TV shows on your computer, even while running other applications. After viewing the Animation "How TV Tuner Cards Work" from your Computing Essentials CD or from our site at www. olearyseries.com/CE06, answer the following questions: (a) What are some examples of inputs to a TV tuner card? (b) What is the function of a TV tuner card? (c) Where can the TV tuner card send the video signal once it is converted?

How Virtual Memory Works

Typically before a program can be executed, it must be read into RAM. Many programs, however, are too large to fit into many computer systems' RAM. One option is to increase the RAM in the system. Another way is to use virtual memory. To learn more about "How Virtual Memory Works," consult your Computing Essentials CD or visit our Web site at www.olearyseries.com/CE06 and select animations. Then answer the following questions: (a) What is virtual memory? (b) Define page file, page, and paging. (c) What is thrashing?

1 Microprocessors

The microprocessor is the "brains" of the system unit. It has two basic components: control unit and arithmetic-logic unit. Microprocessors approximately double their speed every year and a half. New technologies make faster chips and faster PCs. Research the latest microprocessors from industry leaders Intel, AMD, and Cyrix. Then write a one-page paper titled "Current Microprocessors" that addresses the following points: (a) Describe the chips you located. (b) How does each of these chips differ from its last generation? What improvements have been made? (c) Describe any special features that these chips offer and explain each.

2 Processor Serial Numbers

When the Intel Pentium III microprocessor was released, each unit originally contained a unique Processor Serial Number, or PSN. This PSN could be used by online e-commerce sites to identify and to track individuals by the computer they used. This tracking would be similar to keeping track of car owners by their license plate numbers. Write a one-page paper that addresses the following items: (a) What are the benefits of a PSN for a computer user? For society? Explain your answers. (b) What privacy issues does a PSN raise for a computer user? (c) Describe how a PSN could be misused.

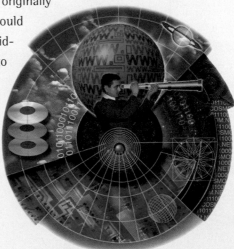

COMPETENCIES

After you have read this chapter, you should be able to:

1 **Define input.**

2 **Describe keyboard entry, pointing devices, and scanning devices.**

3 **Discuss image capturing devices, including digital cameras, digital video cameras, and audio input devices.**

4 **Define output.**

5 **Describe monitors, printers, and audio output devices.**

6 **Discuss combination input and output devices, including fax machines, multifunctional devices, Internet telephones, and terminals.**

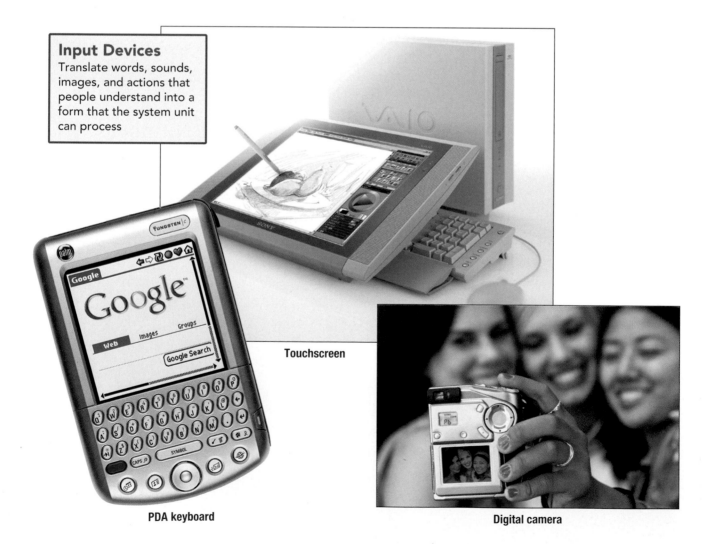

Input Devices
Translate words, sounds, images, and actions that people understand into a form that the system unit can process

Touchscreen

PDA keyboard

Digital camera

CHAPTER

How do you get data to the CPU? How do you get information out? Here we describe one of the most important places where the computer interfaces with people. We input text, music, and even speech, but we probably never think about the relationship between what we enter and what the computer processes. People understand language, which is constructed of letters, numbers, and punctuation marks. However, computers can understand only the binary machine language of 0s and 1s. Input devices are essentially translators. Input devices translate numbers, letters, and actions that people understand into a form that computers can process.

Have you ever wondered how information processed by the system unit is converted into a form that you can use? That is the role of output devices.

While input devices convert what we understand into what the system unit can process, output devices convert what the system unit has processed into a form that we can understand. Output devices translate machine language into letters, numbers, sounds, and images that people can understand.

Competent end users need to know about the most commonly used input devices, including keyboards, mice, scanners, digital cameras, digitizing tablets, voice recognition, and MIDI devices. Additionally, they need to know about the most commonly used output devices, including monitors, printers, and audio output devices. And, end users need to be aware of combination input and output devices such as fax machines, multifunctional devices, Internet telephones, and terminals.

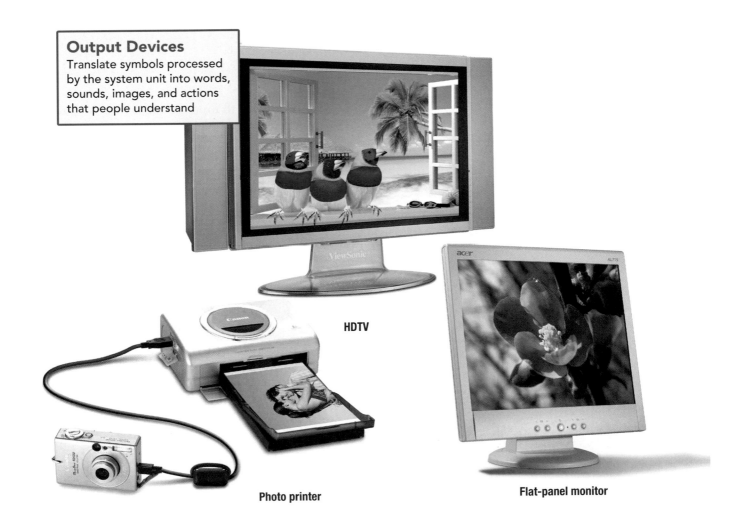

Output Devices
Translate symbols processed by the system unit into words, sounds, images, and actions that people understand

HDTV

Photo printer

Flat-panel monitor

WHAT IS INPUT?

Input consists of data and instructions. Input devices translate what people understand into a form that computers can process.

Input is any data or instructions that are used by a computer. They can come directly from you or from other sources. You provide input whenever you use system or application programs. For example, when using a word processing program, you enter data in the form of numbers and letters and issue commands such as to save and to print documents. You also can enter data and issue commands by pointing to items, or using your voice. Other sources of input include scanned or photographed images.

Input devices are hardware used to translate words, sounds, images, and actions that people understand into a form that the system unit can process. For example, when using a word processor, you typically use a keyboard to enter text and a mouse to issue commands. In addition to keyboards and mice, there are a wide variety of other input devices. These include pointing, scanning, image capturing, and audio-input devices.

KEYBOARD ENTRY

Keyboards translate numbers, letters, and special characters. Traditional, ergonomic, flexible, wireless, and PDA are types of keyboards. Numeric keypads, toggle and combination keys are keyboard features.

Figure 7-1   Flexible keyboard

Figure 7-2   Ergonomic keyboard

One of the most common ways to input data is by **keyboard.** As mentioned in Chapter 6, keyboards convert numbers, letters, and special characters that people understand into electrical signals. These signals are sent to, and processed by, the system unit. Most keyboards use an arrangement of keys given the name QWERTY. This name reflects the keyboard layout by taking the letters of the first six alphabetic characters found on the fourth row of keys.

KEYBOARDS

There are a wide variety of different keyboard designs. They range from the full-sized to miniature and from rigid to flexible. The most common types are:

- **Traditional keyboards**—full-sized, rigid, rectangular keyboards that include function, navigational, and numeric keys.
- **Flexible keyboards**—fold or roll up for easy packing or storage. They are designed to provide mobile users with a full-sized keyboard with minimal storage requirements. (See Figure 7-1.)
- **Ergonomic keyboards**—similar to traditional keyboards. The keyboard arrangement, however, is not rectangular and a palm rest is provided. They are designed specifically to alleviate wrist strain associated with the repetitive movements of typing. (See Figure 7-2.)

- **Wireless keyboards**—transmit input to the system unit through the air. By eliminating connecting wires to the system unit, these keyboards provide greater flexibility and convenience.
- **PDA keyboards**—miniature keyboards for PDAs used to send e-mail, create documents, and more. (See Figure 7-3.)

FEATURES

A computer keyboard combines a typewriter keyboard with a **numeric keypad,** used to enter numbers and arithmetic symbols. It also has many special-purpose keys. Some keys, such as the Caps Lock key, are **toggle keys.** These keys turn a feature on or off. Others, such as the *Ctrl* key, are **combination keys,** which perform an action when held down in combination with another key. To learn more about keyboard features see Figure 7-4.

Figure 7-3 PDA keyboard

CONCEPT CHECK

▶ What is input? What are input devices?

▶ Discuss the five common types of keyboard designs.

▶ What are some common keyboard features?

Figure 7-4 Traditional keyboard

Escape Key
Typically cancels a selection or a procedure.

Function Keys
Shortcut for specific tasks. F1, for example, typically displays online Help.

Numeric Keypad
Enters numbers and arithmetic symbols and controls cursor or insertion point.

Windows Key
Displays the Start menu.

Spacebar
Enters blank spaces between characters.

Navigation Keys
Control the cursor or insertion point on the screen.

Input and Output

POINTING DEVICES

A mouse controls a pointer on the monitor. Joysticks are used primarily for games. Touch screens are pressure-sensitive monitors. Light pens close circuits on special monitors. Tablet PCs and PDAs use styluses.

Pointing, of course, is one of the most natural of all human gestures. **Pointing devices** provide a comfortable interface with the system unit by accepting pointing gestures and converting them into machine-readable input. There is a wide variety of different pointing devices, including the mouse, joystick, touch screen, light pen, and stylus.

MOUSE

A **mouse** controls a pointer that is displayed on the monitor. The **mouse pointer** usually appears in the shape of an arrow. It frequently changes shape, however, depending on the application. A mouse can have one, two, or more buttons, which are used to select command options and to control the mouse pointer on the monitor. Some mice have a **wheel button** that can be rotated to scroll through information that is displayed on the monitor. Although there are several different mouse types, there are three basic designs:

- **Mechanical mouse** is generally considered the traditional type and is currently the most widely used. It has a ball on the bottom and is attached with a cord to the system unit. As you move the mouse across a smooth surface, or **mouse pad,** the roller rotates and controls the pointer on the screen.

- **Optical mouse** has no moving parts. It emits and senses light to detect mouse movement. This newer type of mouse has some advantages compared to the mechanical mouse: it can be used on any surface, is more precise, and does not require periodic cleaning. (See Figure 7-5.)

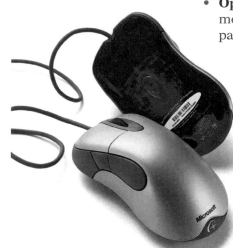

- **Cordless** or **wireless mouse** is a battery-powered device that typically uses radio waves or infrared light waves to communicate with the system unit. These devices eliminate the mouse cord and free up desk space.

Three devices similar to a mouse are trackballs, touch surfaces, and pointing sticks. You can use the **trackball,** also known as the **roller ball,** to control the pointer by rotating a ball with your thumb. (See Figure 7-6.) You can use **touch surfaces,** or **touch pads,** to control the pointer by moving and tapping your finger on the surface of a pad. (See Figure 7-7.) You can use a **pointing stick,** located in the middle of the keyboard, to control the pointer by directing the stick with your finger. (See Figure 7-8.)

Figure 7–5 Optical mouse

Figure 7.6 Trackball

Figure 7.7 Touch surface

Figure 7.8 Pointing stick

JOYSTICK

A **joystick** is the most popular input device for computer games. You control game actions by varying the pressure, speed, and direction of the joystick. Additional controls, such as buttons and triggers, are used to specify commands or initiate specific actions. (See Figure 7-9.)

TOUCH SCREEN

A **touch screen** is a particular kind of monitor with a clear plastic outer layer. Behind this layer are crisscrossed invisible beams of infrared light. This arrangement enables someone to select actions or commands by touching the screen with a finger. Touch screens are easy to use, especially when people need information quickly. They are commonly used at restaurants, automated teller machines (ATMs), and information centers. (See Figure 7-10.)

LIGHT PEN

A **light pen** is a light-sensitive penlike device. The light pen is placed against the monitor. This closes a photoelectric circuit and identifies the spot for entering or modifying data. For example, light pens are used to edit digital images. (See Figure 7-11.)

Figure 7-9   A joystick: a computer game application

Figure 7-10   A touch screen: a consumer application

Figure 7-11   A light pen: a home application

STYLUS

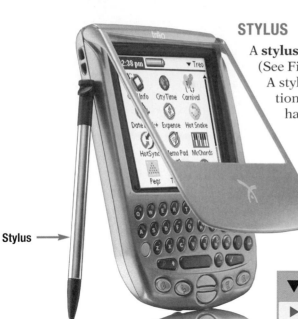

A **stylus** is a penlike device commonly used with tablet PCs and PDAs. (See Figure 7-12.) A stylus uses pressure to draw images on a screen. A stylus interacts with the computer through handwriting recognition software. **Handwriting recognition software** translates handwritten notes into a form that the system unit can process.

Graphics tablets use a special graphics surface or tablet and a stylus. Either the user sketches directly on the tablet or traces images that have been placed on the tablet. Graphics tablets are very specialized devices used by artists for creating illustrations, by mapmakers to record or trace maps, and by engineers to save mechanical drawings digitally.

Stylus ⟶

▼ CONCEPT CHECK

▶ What is a pointing device? Describe five pointing devices.

▶ Describe three basic mouse designs.

▶ Describe trackballs, touch surfaces, and pointing sticks.

Figure 7-12   Stylus

SCANNING DEVICES

Optical scanners copy or reproduce text and images. Bar code readers identify and price products. Character and mark recognition devices recognize special characters and marks.

Scanners move across text and images. **Scanning devices** convert scanned text and images into a form that the system unit can process. There are three types of scanning devices: optical scanners, bar code readers, and character and mark recognition devices.

OPTICAL SCANNERS

An **optical scanner,** also known simply as a scanner, accepts documents consisting of text and/or images and converts them to machine-readable form. These devices do not recognize individual letters or images. Rather, they recognize light, dark, and colored areas that make up individual letters or images. Typically, scanned documents are saved in files that can be further processed, displayed, printed, or stored for later use. There are two basic types of optical scanners: flatbed and portable. (See Figure 7-13.)

- **Flatbed scanner** is much like a copy machine. The image to be scanned is placed on a glass surface and the scanner records the image from below.
- **Portable scanner** is typically a handheld device that slides across the image, making direct contact.

Optical scanners are powerful tools for a wide variety of end users, including graphics and advertising professionals who scan images and combine them with text. Lawyers and students use portable scanners as a valuable research tool to record information.

Flatbed scanner

Portable scanner

Figure 7-13 Two types of scanners

BAR CODE READERS

You are probably familiar with **bar code readers** or scanners from grocery stores. (See Figure 7-14.) These devices are either handheld **wand readers** or **platform scanners.** They contain photoelectric cells that scan or read **bar codes,** or the vertical zebra-striped marks printed on product containers.

Almost all supermarkets use electronic cash registers and a bar code system called the **Universal Product Code (UPC).** At the checkout counter, electronic cash registers use a bar code reader to scan each product's UPC code. The codes are sent to the supermarket's computer, which has a description, the latest price, and an inventory level for each product. The computer processes this input to update the inventory level and to provide the electronic cash register with the description and price for each product. These devices are so easy to use that many supermarkets are offering customers self-checkout stations.

Figure 7-14 A bar code reader is used to record product codes

CHARACTER AND MARK RECOGNITION DEVICES

Character and **mark recognition devices** are scanners that are able to recognize special characters and marks. They are specialty devices that are essential tools for certain applications. Three types are:

- **Magnetic-ink character recognition (MICR)**—used by banks to automatically read those unusual numbers on the bottom of checks and deposit slips. A special-purpose machine known as a **reader/sorter** reads these numbers and provides input that allows banks to efficiently maintain customer account balances.

- **Optical-character recognition (OCR)**—uses special preprinted characters that can be read by a light source and changed into machine-readable code. A common OCR device is the handheld wand reader. (See Figure 7-15.) These are used in department stores to read retail price tags by reflecting light on the printed characters.

- **Optical-mark recognition (OMR)** is also called **mark sensing.** An OMR device senses the presence or absence of a mark, such as a pencil mark. OMR is often used to score multiple-choice tests such as the College Board's Scholastic Aptitude Test (SAT) and the Graduate Record Examination (GRE).

Figure 7-15 A wand reader is used to record product codes

Input and Output

IMAGE CAPTURING DEVICES

Digital cameras capture still images. Digital video cameras capture motion. WebCams are specialized digital video cameras.

Optical scanners, like traditional copy machines, can make a copy from an original. For example, an optical scanner can make a digital copy of a photograph. **Image capturing devices,** on the other hand, create or capture original images. These devices include digital cameras and digital video cameras.

DIGITAL CAMERA

Digital cameras are similar to traditional cameras except that images are recorded digitally on a disk or in the camera's memory rather than on film and then **downloaded,** or transferred, to your computer. (See Figure 7-16.) You can take a picture, view it immediately, and even place it on your own Web page, within minutes.

To learn more about how digital photography works, consult your Computing Essentials CD or visit us on the Web at www.olearyseries. com/CE06 and select Animations. Digital photographs can be shared easily with others over the Internet.

Figure 7-16   A digital camera

DIGITAL VIDEO CAMERA

Unlike traditional video cameras, **digital video cameras** record motion digitally on a disk or in the camera's memory. Most have the capability to take still images as well. **Web-Cams (Web cameras)** are specialized digital video cameras that capture images and send them to a computer for broadcast over the Internet. (See Figure 7-17.) To learn more about WebCams, consult your Computing Essentials CD or visit our Web site at www.olearyseries.com/CE06 and select Expansions. To learn how you can videoconference, see Making IT Work for You: Web-Cams and Instant Messenging on pages 188 and 189.

Figure 7-17   A WebCam

Are you having trouble getting the kind of photos you want with a digital camera? Would you like to make the most of digital technology in your photos? Here are some tips to help you get started:

1 **Buttons and Knobs.** Get to know the functions of your camera before you begin. Most cameras have an automatic mode, but be sure you know how to turn on the flash, zoom the lens, and set the image resolution.

2 **Photography Basics.** Many digital cameras have an LCD screen on the back. You can use it to help frame your shots more accurately. Just be aware that using the LCD screen uses more battery power.

3 **Red-eye Reduction.** Many digital cameras have a red-eye reduction feature. When photographing people in low light, you can use this setting to eliminate glassy red eyes in photos. Consult your owner's manual to learn more about this feature.

▼ CONCEPT CHECK

▶ How are digital cameras different from traditional cameras?

▶ What is a WebCam?

AUDIO-INPUT DEVICES

> Audio-input devices convert sounds for processing. Voice recognition systems accept voice commands to control computer operations and to create documents. MIDI is a standard for connecting musical instruments to the system unit.

Audio-input devices convert sounds into a form that can be processed by the system unit. By far the most widely used audio-input device is the microphone. **Audio-input** can take many forms, including the human voice and music.

VOICE

Voice recognition systems use a microphone, a sound card, and special software. These systems allow users to operate computers and to create documents using voice commands. Portable voice recognition systems are widely used by doctors, lawyers, and others to record dictation. (See Figure 7-18.) These devices are able to record for several hours before connecting to a computer system to edit, store, and print the dictated information. Some systems are even able to translate dictation from one language to another, such as from English to Japanese.

As we discussed in Chapter 3, voice recognition is a common feature with many of today's newest software applications. For example, recent versions of Microsoft's Word support voice recognition. Using the **Language bar,** you can switch between voice command mode and dictation mode. (See Figure 7-19.)

• **Voice command mode** allows the user to select menu items, toolbars, and dialog box options. For example, to specify the use of the Times New Roman font requires this command sequence:

Format>Font>Times New Roman>OK

Figure 7-18   **A portable voice recognition system**

WEBCAMS AND INSTANT MESSAGING

Do you enjoy chatting with your friends? Are you working on a project and need to collaborate with others in your group? What if you could see and hear your group online? Perhaps instant messaging is just what you're looking for. It's easy and free with an Internet connection and the right software.

Sending Messages and Transferring Files   After installing free instant messaging software, you can exchange messages and files with friends. Your friends are added to a list of contacts that shows you when your friends are online and available to chat. For example, you could use Windows Messenger as follows:

1
- Add contacts by clicking *Add a Contact* and following the on-screen instructions.

- Double-click the name of a friend who appears in the *Online* section.

- Enter your message in the window that appears.

- Click the *Send* button.

Your message appears on your friend's screen instantly. Your friend can then continue the conversation by following the steps above.

2
- Click *Send a File or Photo* in the *I want to...* menu in the sidebar.

- Browse for the file you would like to share, and click *Open*.

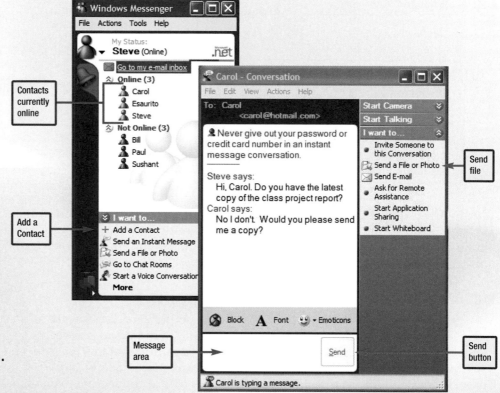

Your friend is given an option to accept the file. Once your friend accepts, you can continue your conversation without interruption while the file is transferred.

Using a WebCam In addition to typing text messages, some instant messaging software allows you to have voice or video conversations over the Internet so you can see and hear the person you are collaborating with. To do this, both users must have a microphone and speakers, as well as Web cameras for video conferencing. You could hold a video conference using Windows Messenger by following these steps.

1 ● **Start a conversation with a contact as shown in the Sending Messages and Transferring Files section.**

● **Click** *Start Camera* **in the sidebar.**

Your friend is given the option to accept the video conference. Once he or she accepts, the video conference begins.

2 ● **As you speak, adjust the** *Speakers* **and** *Microphone* **sliders to comfortable levels.**

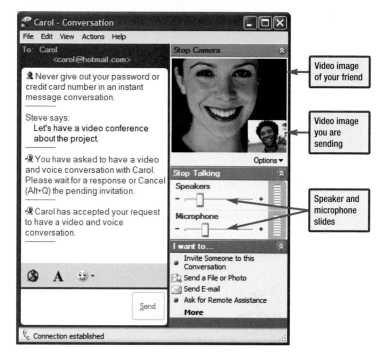

Video image of your friend

Video image you are sending

Speaker and microphone slides

Sharing an Application Sharing applications is another way to collaborate using instant messaging software. Sharing applications allows you to surf the Web or edit a document over the Internet while working with a friend. For example, you could collaborate with a friend on a Microsoft Word document by following the steps below:

1 ● **Start a conversation with a contact as shown in the Sending Messages and File Transfer section.**

● **Click** *Start Application Sharing* **in the sidebar.**

Your friend is given the option to accept the application sharing session. Once he or she accepts, the application sharing session begins.

2 ● **Select the application you want to share in the Share Programs list, and click the** *Share* **button.**

● **Click the** *Allow Control* **button to allow your friends to control the shared application.**

● **Click the** *Close* **button.**

Share Programs List

Your application can be controlled by you and your friend simultaneously.

The Web is continually changing, and some of the specifics presented in this Making IT Work for You may have changed. To learn more about other ways to make information technology work for you, visit our Web site at www.olearyseries.com/CE06 and select Making IT Work for You.

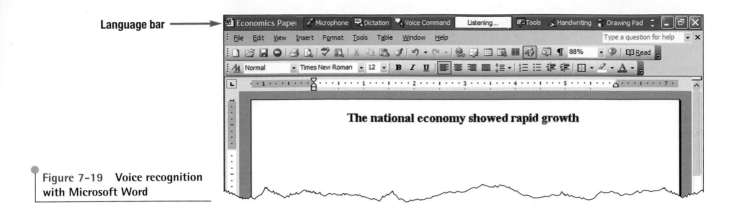

Language bar ——►

Figure 7-19 Voice recognition with Microsoft Word

The national economy showed rapid growth

Figure 7-20 Yamaha MIDI Silent Cello

You could issue this command using a mouse, or you could use a microphone and state:

> *"Format font Times New Roman OK"*

- **Dictation mode** allows the user to dictate text directly into a Word document. For example, consider the following sentence:

> **The national economy showed rapid growth.**

You could enter this text using a keyboard or you could use a microphone and state:

> *"The national economy showed rapid growth"*

MUSIC

Musical instrument digital interface or **MIDI** is a standard that allows musical instruments to connect to the system unit using a special MIDI port. **MIDI devices** are specialized musical instruments that provide input in the form of encoded digital signals representing musical sounds. MIDI devices can be used to create, record, and play back musical compositions. The most commonly used MIDI device is an electronic keyboard. Others include MIDI violins, guitars, and even cellos. (See Figure 7-20.)

▼ CONCEPT CHECK

► Describe voice recognition systems.

► What is MIDI? What are some common MIDI devices?

WHAT IS OUTPUT?

Output is processed data or information. Text, graphics, audio, and video are types of output. Output devices translate processed information into a form humans can understand.

Output is processed data or information. Output typically takes the form of text, graphics, photos, audio, and/or video. For example, when you create a presentation using a presentation graphics program, you typically input text and graphics. You could also include photographs and even add voice narration. The output would be the completed presentation.

Output devices are any hardware used to provide or to create output. They translate information that has been processed by the system unit into a form that humans can understand. There are a wide range of output devices. The most widely used are monitors, printers, and audio-output.

MONITORS

> Monitor features include resolution, dot pitch, refresh rate, and size. CRT and flat-panel are types of monitors. E-books, data projectors, and HDTV are specialty monitors.

The most frequently used output device is the **monitor.** Also known as **display screens** or simply as **screens,** monitors present visual images of text and graphics. The output is often referred to as **soft copy.** Monitors vary in size, shape, and cost. Almost all, however, have some basic distinguishing features.

FEATURES

The most important characteristic of a monitor is its clarity. **Clarity** refers to the quality and sharpness of the displayed images. It is a function of several monitor features, including resolution, dot pitch, refresh rate, and size.

- **Resolution** is one of the most important features. Images are formed on a monitor by a series of dots or **pixels (picture elements).** (See Figure 7-21.) Resolution is expressed as a matrix of these dots or pixels. For example, many monitors today have a resolution of 1,280 pixel columns by 1,024 pixel rows for a total of 1,310,720 pixels. The higher a monitor's resolution (the more pixels) the clearer the image produced. See Figure 7-22 for the most common monitor resolutions.

- **Dot pitch** is the distance between each pixel. Most newer monitors have a dot pitch of .31 mm (31/100th of a millimeter) or less. The lower the dot pitch (the shorter the distance between pixels), the clearer the images produced.

- **Refresh rate** indicates how often a displayed image is updated or redrawn on the monitor. Most monitors operate at a rate of 75 hertz, which means that the monitor is redrawn 75 times each second. Images displayed on monitors with refresh rates lower than 75 hertz appear to flicker and can cause eye strain. The faster the refresh rate (the more frequently images are redrawn), the better the quality of images displayed.

- **Size** or **viewable size** is measured by the diagonal length of a monitor's viewing area. Common sizes are 15, 17, 19, and 21 inches. The smaller the monitor size the better the quality of images displayed.

Figure 7-21 Monitor resolution

Standard	Pixels
SVGA	800 × 600
XGA	1,024 × 768
SXGA	1,280 × 1,024
UXGA	1,600 × 1,200

Figure 7-22 Resolution standards

CATHODE-RAY TUBE

The most common type of monitor for the office and the home is the **cathode-ray tube (CRT).** (See Figure 7-23.) These monitors are typically placed directly on the system unit or on the desktop. CRTs are similar in size and technology to televisions. Compared to other types of monitors, their primary advantages are low cost and excellent resolution. Their primary disadvantage is that they are bulky and occupy a considerable amount of space on the desktop.

FLAT-PANEL MONITOR

Because CRTs are too bulky to be transported easily, portable monitors, known as **flat-panel monitors,** were developed. Flat-panel monitors are much thinner and require less power to operate than CRTs. These monitors are widely used with desktop, tablet PC, and handheld computers. (See Figure 7-24).

There are two basic types of flat-panel monitors: passive-matrix and active-matrix. **Passive-matrix,** or **dual-scan monitors,** create images by scanning the entire screen. This type requires very little power, but the clarity of the images is not as sharp. **Active-matrix** or **thin film transistor (TFT)** monitors do not scan down the screen; instead, each pixel is independently activated. They can display more colors with better clarity. Active-matrix monitors are more expensive and require more power.

OTHER MONITORS

There are several other types of monitors. These monitors are used for more specialized applications, such as reading books, making presentations, and watching television. Three of these specialized devices are e-books, data projectors, and high-definition television.

- **E-books,** also known as **e-book readers,** are handheld, book-sized devices that display text and graphics. Using content downloaded from the Web or from special cartridges, these devices are used to read newspapers, magazines, and entire books. (See Figure 7-25.)

- **Data projectors** are specialized devices similar to slide projectors. These devices, however, connect to microcomputers and project computer output just as it would appear on a monitor. Data projectors are commonly used for presentations almost anywhere from the classroom to the boardroom.

Figure 7-23   CRT monitor

Figure 7-24   A flat-panel monitor

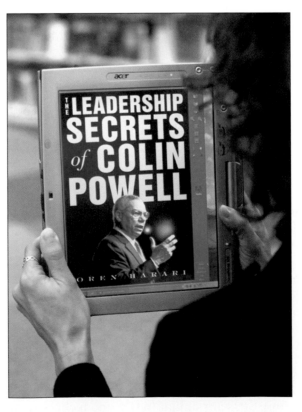

Figure 7-25   E-book

- **High-definition television (HDTV)** is a recent development in the merger of microcomputers and television, called **PC/TV.** HDTV delivers a much clearer and more detailed wide-screen picture than regular television. (See Figure 7-26.) Because the output is digital, users can readily freeze video sequences to create high-quality still images. The video and still images can then be digitized, edited, and stored on disk for later use. This technology is very useful to graphic artists, designers, and publishers.

Figure 7-26   HDTV

On the Web Explorations

HDTV is expected to be the standard in television broadcasting by 2006. To learn more about HDTV visit our Web site at

www.olearyseries.com/CE06

and select On the Web Explorations.

▼ CONCEPT CHECK

▶   What is output? What are output devices?

▶   Define these monitor features: resolution, dot pitch, refresh rate, and size.

▶   Describe CRTs, flat-panel, and specialty monitors.

PRINTERS

Printer features include resolution, color capability, speed, and memory. Ink-jet, laser, and thermal are common types of printers. Other types include dot-matrix, plotter, photo, and portable.

You probably use a printer with some frequency to print homework assignments, photographs, and Web pages. **Printers** translate information that has been processed by the system unit and present the information on paper. Printer output is often called **hard copy.**

FEATURES

There are many different types of printers. Almost all, however, have some basic distinguishing features, including resolution, color capability, speed, and memory.

- **Resolution** for a printer is similar to monitor resolution. It is a measure of the clarity of images produced. Printer resolution, however, is measured in **dpi (dots per inch).** (See Figure 7-27.) Most printers designed for personal use average 1,200 dpi. The higher the dpi, the better the quality of images produced.

- **Color capability** is provided by most printers today. Users typically have the option to print either with just black ink or with color. Because it is more expensive to print in color, most users select black ink for letters, drafts, and homework. Color is used more selectively for final reports containing graphics and for photographs.

- **Speed** is measured in the number of pages printed per minute. Typically, printers for personal use average 15 to 19 pages per minute for single color (black) output and 13 to 15 pages per minute for color output.

300 dpi

1200 dpi

Figure 7-27   Dpi comparison

- **Memory** within a printer is used to store printing instructions and documents waiting to be printed. The more memory in a printer, the faster it will be able to create large documents.

Figure 7-28   A special application ink-jet printer

INK-JET PRINTER

Ink-jet printers spray ink at high speed onto the surface of paper. This process not only produces a letter-quality image but also permits printing to be done in a variety of colors making them ideal for select special applications. (See Figure 7-28.) Ink-jet printers are the most widely used printers. They are reliable, quiet, and relatively inexpensive. The most costly aspect of ink-jet printers is replacing the ink cartridges. For this reason, most users specify black ink for the majority of print jobs and use the more expensive color printing for select applications. Typical ink-jet printers produce 17 to 19 pages per minute of black-only output and 13 to 15 pages of color output.

LASER PRINTER

The **laser printer** uses a technology similar to that used in a photocopying machine. Laser printers use a laser light beam to produce images with excellent letter and graphics quality. More expensive than ink-jet printers, laser printers are faster and are used in applications requiring high-quality output. (See Figure 7-29.)

TIPS Do you find extra pages in the printer when you try to print from the Web? Would you like to print your favorite articles without all the ads and hyperlinks? There are several ways to get what you want in a printout. Here are a few suggestions you can use with Internet Explorer:

1. **Preview.** To see what will be printed, choose *Print Preview* from the *File* menu. You can scroll through the pages and make sure the items you want will be printed.

2. **Choose Printer Friendly.** Many Web pages have a Printer Friendly button that removes all the ads and sidebars. Look for the button at the conclusion of most Web articles.

3. **Print Selection.** You can highlight and print only the text you would like to print. Highlight the text and graphics you would like to print and choose *File/Print* and check the *Selection* option under the *Page range* box.

There are two categories of laser printers. **Personal laser printers** typically do not support color, are less expensive, and are used by many single users. They typically can print 15 to 17 pages a minute. **Shared laser printers** typically support color, are more expensive, and are used (shared) by a group of users. Shared laser printers typically print over 50 pages a minute.

THERMAL PRINTER

A **thermal printer** uses heat elements to produce images on heat-sensitive paper. Originally these printers were only used in scientific labs to record data. More recently, color thermal printers have been widely used to produce very high-quality color artwork and text.

Color thermal printers are not as popular because of their cost and the requirement of specially treated paper. They are special-use printers that produce near-photographic output. They are widely used in professional art and design work where very high-quality color is essential.

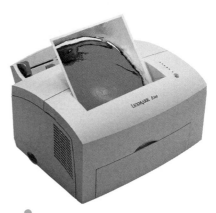

Figure 7-29   A laser printer

OTHER PRINTERS

There are several other types of printers. These printers include dot-matrix printers, chain printers, plotters, photo printers, and portable printers:

- **Dot-matrix printers** form characters and images using a series of small pins on a print head. Once a widely used microcomputer printer, they are inexpensive and reliable but quite noisy. In general, they are used for tasks where high-quality output is not required.

- **Plotters** are special-purpose printers for producing a wide range of specialized output. Using output from graphics tablets and other graphical input devices, plotters can create maps, images, and architectural and engineering drawings. Plotters are widely used by graphic artists, engineers, and architects to print out designs, sketches, and drawings.

- **Photo printers** are special-purpose printers designed to print photo-quality images from digital cameras. (See Figure 7-30.) Most photo printers print 3 × 5″ or 4 × 6″ images on glossy, photo-quality paper.

- **Portable printers** are usually small and lightweight printers designed to work with a notebook computer. Portable printers may be ink-jet or laser printers, print in black and white or color, and connect with USB or parallel port connections.

Figure 7-30   Photo printer

▼ CONCEPT CHECK

▶ Discuss these printer features: resolution, color capability, speed, and memory.

▶ What are the three printer types commonly used with microcomputers?

▶ Discuss dot-matrix, plotter, photo, and portable printers.

AUDIO-OUTPUT DEVICES

> Audio-output devices produce sounds for people. Speakers and headphones are the most common types.

Figure 7-31   Headphones

Audio-output devices translate audio information from the computer into sounds that people can understand. The most widely used audio-output devices are **speakers** and **headphones.** (See Figure 7-31) These devices are connected to a sound card in the system unit. The sound card is used to capture as well as play back recorded sounds. Audio-output devices are used to play music, vocalize translations from one language to another, and communicate information from the computer system to users.

Creating voice output is not anywhere near as difficult as recognizing and interpreting voice input. In fact, voice output is quite common. It is used with many soft-drink machines, telephones, and cars. It is used as a reinforcement tool for learning, such as to help students study a foreign language. It is also used in many supermarkets at the checkout counter to confirm purchases. One of its most powerful capabilities is to assist the physically challenged.

COMBINATION INPUT AND OUTPUT DEVICES

> Fax machines send and receive images over telephone lines. Multifunction devices have input and output capabilities. Internet telephones use telephony to connect people. Dumb, intelligent, network, or Internet are types of terminals.

Many devices combine input and output capabilities. Sometimes this is done to save space. Other times it is done for very specialized applications. Common **combination devices** include fax machines, multifunction devices, Internet telephones, and terminals.

FAX MACHINES

A **fax machine,** also known as a **facsimile transmission machine,** is a standard tool in nearly every office. At one time, all fax machines were separate stand-alone devices for sending and receiving images over telephone lines. Now, most computer systems have that capability with the simple addition of a fax/modem board. To send a fax, these devices scan the image of a document converting the light and dark areas into a format that can be sent electronically over standard telephone lines. To receive a fax, these devices reverse the process and print the document (or display the document on your monitor) using signals received from the telephone line.

MULTIFUNCTION DEVICES

Multifunctional devices (MFD), also known as **all in one (AIO)** devices, typically combine the capabilities of a scanner, printer, fax, and copy machine. These multifunctional devices offer a cost and space advantage. They cost

**On the Web
Explorations**

Multifunctional devices save space and money, making them a favorite in home offices and small businesses. To learn more about MFDs, visit our Web site at
www.olearyseries.com/CE06
and select On the Web Explorations.

about the same as a good printer or copy machine but require much less space than the single-function devices they replace. Their disadvantage is that the quality and functionality are not quite as good as those of the separate single-purpose devices. Even so, multifunctional devices are widely used in home and small business offices.

INTERNET TELEPHONE

Internet telephones are specialized input and output devices for receiving and sending voice communication. Typically, these devices connect to the system unit through a USB port and operate much like a traditional telephone.

Telephony is the transmission of telephone calls over computer networks. Also known as **Internet telephony, IP telephony,** and **Voice-over IP (VoIP),** telephony uses the Internet rather than traditional communication lines to support voice communication. To place telephone calls using telephony requires a high speed Internet connection and special software and/or hardware. The three most popular approaches are:

- **Computer-to-computer** communications allow individuals to place free long-distance calls. This application requires that both parties have a computer and that their computers are on and connected to the Internet when a call is placed. The required software is available from a variety of sources for free or at very low cost. MSN Explorer is one of the most widely used.

- **Computer-to-traditional telephone** communications allow a user to call almost any traditional telephone from his or her computer. Only the person making the call needs to have a computer connected to the Internet. The calling party subscribes to a special Internet phone service provider that supplies the required software and charges a small monthly and/or per-minute fee. To see how this works, consult your Computing Essentials CD or visit our Web site at www.olearyseries.com/CE06 and select Animations.

- **Traditional telephone-to-traditional telephone** communications do not require a computer. The calling party subscribes to a special Internet phone service provider that supplies a special hardware adapter that connects a traditional telephone to the Internet. The cost for this service is similar to the computer-to-traditional telephone approach.

Compared to traditional telephone calls, Internet supported calls may have a lower sound quality. However, most users report that this difference is not significant. Telephony promises to dramatically impact the telecommunications industry and to reduce our costs for telephone communications.

Figure 7-32   Dumb terminal

TERMINALS

A **terminal** is an input and output device that connects you to a mainframe or other type of computer called a **host computer** or **server.** There are four kinds of terminals:

- A **dumb terminal** can be used to input and receive data, but it cannot process data independently. It is used to gain access and to send information to a computer. Such a terminal is often used by airline reservation clerks to access a mainframe computer for flight information. (See Figure 7-32.)

- Essentially, an **intelligent terminal** is a microcomputer with communications software and a telephone hookup (modem) or other communications link. These connect the terminal to the larger computer or to the Internet. An increasingly popular type is the **Net PC,** also known as the **Net Personal Computer.** These low-cost and limited microcomputers typically have only one type of secondary storage (an internal hard disk drive), a sealed system unit, and no expansion slots.
- A **network terminal,** also known as a **thin client** or **network computer,** is a low-cost alternative to an intelligent terminal. Most network terminals do not have a hard-disk drive and must rely on a host computer or server for application and system software. These devices are becoming increasingly popular in many organizations.
- An **Internet terminal,** also known as a **Web terminal** or **Web appliance,** provides access to the Internet and typically displays Web pages on a standard television set. These special-purpose terminals offer Internet access without a microcomputer. Unlike the other types of terminals, Internet terminals are used almost exclusively in the home.

▼ **CONCEPT CHECK**

▶ What are the two most widely used audio-output devices?

▶ Describe the three most popular Internet telephony approaches.

▶ Describe the following combination devices: fax machine, MFD, Internet telephone, and terminal.

A Look to the Future

Electronic Translators May Be in Your Future

Have you ever wished you could speak more than one language fluently? What if you could speak hundreds of languages instantly? Would you like to have your own personal interpreter to accompany you whenever you traveled to a foreign country? What if you could take a picture of a foreign road sign or restaurant menu and have it immediately translated for you? Technology called electronic interpretation may soon exist to do all of these things. The military and private sector are funding a variety of research projects on electronic interpreters, and the commercial opportunities are enormous. The worldwide translation services market is already a $5 billion a year industry and is expected to grow to $7.6 billion by 2006.

Prototype portable handheld electronic interpreters are currently in a testing phase at the U.S. Office of Naval Research. In fact, it is expected that these devices will be widely used within the next year. The company SpeechGear has developed a machine called Interact that takes verbal statements in one language, converts the statements to text, translates that text to another language, and then vocalizes the translated text. And it does all this in two seconds! The military is particularly interested in electronic interpreters as they focus on peacekeeping objectives. More than ever before, U.S. soldiers find themselves needing to communicate with non-English-speaking civilians to settle disputes and maintain order.

Despite the achievements of Interact and other translation hardware, several challenges remain that plague all translation hardware. Current translation techniques are labor intensive; they require linguists and programmers to create large lists of words and their corresponding meanings. Unfortunately, computers have a difficult time understanding idioms, such as "It is raining cats and dogs." They may also have difficulty correctly identifying words by their context. For example, the sentences "The refrigerator is cool" and "The Fonz is cool" use the same word, *cool,* but it has a very different meaning in each sentence. Entrepreneurs in New York City may have a solution to these problems with the EliMT project. Instead of translating from word to word, EliMT compares books that have been translated in different languages, looking for sentence fragment patterns. By comparing sentence fragments, it is hoped that translation programs will be able to identify word groupings and translate them into another language's comparable word grouping, essentially translating concepts instead of individual words.

What are the uses for such a device? Will the average person want or need an electronic translator? What type of professions and professionals will use them? What industries would benefit most from electronic translators? How could you use this technology?

VISUAL SUMMARY

INPUT

Input is any data or instructions used by a computer. **Input devices** translate words, images, and actions into a form a computer can process.

Keyboards

Keyboards are the most common way to input data. The most common types are:

- **Traditional**—full-sized, rigid, rectangular.
- **Flexible**—roll up for easy packing.
- **Ergonomic**—designed to minimize wrist strain.
- **Wireless**—no wire provides greater flexibility.
- **PDA**—miniature keyboards for PDAs.

Features include **numeric keypads, toggle,** and **combination keys.**

Pointing Devices

Pointing devices accept pointing gestures and convert them to machine-readable input.

- **Mouse** controls a **mouse pointer.** A **wheel button** rotates to scroll through information. Three basic mouse designs are **mechanical** (**mouse pad** provides smooth rolling surface), **optical,** and **cordless (wireless).** Similar devices include: **trackball (roller ball), touch surface (touch pad),** and **pointing stick.**

INPUT

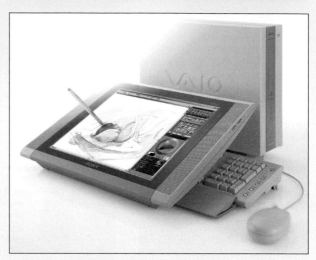

- **Joysticks** are popular for computer games. Operations are controlled by varying pressure, speed, and direction.
- **Touch screens** have a clear plastic layer over crisscrossed invisible beams. Operations are controlled by touching the screen with a finger.
- **Light pens** are light-sensitive pen-like devices. Operations are controlled by placing light pen against monitor.
- **Stylus** are penlike devices used with tablet PCs, PDAs, and **graphic tablets. Handwriting recognition software** translates handwritten notes.

Scanners

Scanners move across text and graphics. **Scanning devices** convert scanned text and images into a form that can be processed by the system unit.

- **Optical scanners** record light, dark, and colored areas of scanned text or images. There are two types: **flatbed and portable.**
- **Bar code readers** are used with electronic cash registers in supermarkets. **Wand readers** or **platform scanners** read **UPC** codes that are used to determine product descriptions and prices and to update inventory levels.

To be a competent end user you need to be aware of the most commonly used input and output devices. These devices are translators for information into and out of the system unit. Input devices translate words, sounds, and actions into symbols the system unit can process. Output devices translate symbols from the system unit into words, images, and sounds that people can understand.

INPUT

- **Character** and **mark recognition devices** recognize special characters and marks. Three types: **MICR (read by readers/sorters), OCR,** and **OMR (mark sensing).**

Image Capturing Devices

Image capturing devices create or capture original images. These devices include: **digital cameras** (images **downloaded** to system unit for further processing and/or printing) and **digital video cameras** (**Webcams** or **Web cameras** capture and send images over the Internet).

Audio-Input Devices

Audio-input devices convert sounds into a form that can be processed by the system unit. **Audio-input** takes many forms including the human voice and music.

- **Voice—voice recognition systems** use a combination of a microphone, a sound card, and special software. Microsoft Word's language bar allows users to switch between **voice command** and **dictation modes.**

- **Music—Musical Instrument Digital Interface (MIDI)** standards allows musical instruments to connect to MIDI ports in the system unit. **MIDI devices** send encoded digital signals representing musical sounds.

OUTPUT

Output is data or information processed by a computer. **Output devices** translate processed text, graphics, audio and video into a form humans can understand.

Monitors

Monitors (display screens, screens) present visual images of text and graphics. Monitor output is described as **soft copy.**

Clarity is a function of several monitor features including **resolution** (expressed as matrix of **pixels** or **picture elements**), **dot pitch, refresh rate,** and **size (viewable size).**

- **Cathode ray tubes (CRTs)** use technology similar to a television. Low cost with excellent resolution. However, bulky and occupy considerable space on the desktop.

- **Flat-panel monitors** compared to CRTs are thinner, require less power, and used with all types of computers especially portable computers. Two types are **passive-matrix (dual-scan)** and **active matrix (thin film transistor, TFT).**

Three specialized types of monitors are **e-books (e-book readers), data projectors,** and **high-definition television (HDTV).** HDTV is a merger of microcomputers and television called **PC/TV.**

Printers

Printers translate information processed by system unit and present the information on paper. Output from printers is described as **hard copy.** Some distinguishing features of printers include **resolution** (measured in **dpi** or **dots per inch**), **color capability, speed,** and **memory.**

- **Ink-jet printers** spray ink to produce high quality output. These printers are inexpensive and the most widely used type of printer.
- **Laser printers** use technology similar to photocopying machines. Two categories are **personal** and **shared.**
- **Thermal printers** use heat elements and heat-sensitive paper. Used to record data and to provide very high-quality artwork and text.

Other printers include **dot-matrix printers, plotters, photo printers,** and **portable printers.**

Audio-Output Devices

Audio-output devices translate audio information from the computer into sounds that people can understand. **Speakers** and **headphones** are the most widely used audio-output devices.

Combination devices combine input and output capabilities. Common types include:

Fax Machines

Fax machines (facsimile transmission machines) send and receive images via standard telephone lines.

Multifunction Devices

Multifunctional devices (MFD, all in one, AIO) typically combine the capabilities of a scanner, printer, fax, and copy machine.

Internet Telephone

Internet telephones receive and send voice communication. **Telephony (Internet telephony, IP Telephony,** and **Voice-over IP, VoIP)** uses networks (Internet) to place long distance calls. Three approaches are computer-to-computer, computer-to-traditional telephone, and traditional telephone-to-traditional telephone.

Terminals

Terminals connect to a **host computer** or **server.** There are four kinds: **dumb** (no processing), **intelligent** (microcomputer with communication software and communication link), **network** (low-cost alternative, also known as **thin client** or **network computer**), and **Internet** (access Internet without microcomputer, also known as **Web terminal** or **Web appliance**).

active-matrix monitor (192)
all in one (AIO) device (196)
audio input (187)
audio input device (187)
audio output (196)
audio-output device (196)
bar code (185)
bar code reader (185)
bar code scanner (185)
cathode-ray tube monitor (CRT) (191)
character recognition device (185)
clarity (191)
color capability (193)
combination device (196)
combination key (181)
cordless mouse (182)
data projector (192)
dictation mode (190)
digital camera (186)
digital video camera (186)
dot pitch (191)
dots-per-inch (dpi) (193)
dot-matrix printer (195)
download (186)
dual-scan monitor (192)
dumb terminal (197)
e-book (192)
e-book reader (192)
ergonomic keyboard (180)
facsimile (fax) transmission machine (196)
flatbed scanner (184)
flat-panel monitor (192)
flexible keyboard (180)
graphics tablet (184)
handwriting recognition software (184)
hard copy (193)
headphones (196)
high-definition television (HDTV) (193)
host computer (197)
image capturing device (186)
ink-jet printer (194)
input (180)
input device (180)

intelligent terminal (198)
Internet telephone (197)
Internet telephony (197)
Internet terminal (198)
IP Telephony (197)
joystick (183)
keyboard (180)
Language bar (187)
laser printer (194)
light pen (183)
magnetic-ink character recognition (MICR) (185)
mark recognition device (185)
mark sensing (185)
mechanical mouse (182)
memory (194)
MIDI (190)
MIDI device (190)
monitor (191)
mouse (182)
mouse pad (182)
mouse pointer (182)
multifunctional device (MFD) (196)
musical instrument digital interface (190)
Net Personal Computer (Net PC) (198)
network computer (198)
network terminal (198)
numeric keypad (181)
optical mouse (182)
optical scanner (184)
optical-character recognition (OCR) (185)
optical-mark recognition (OMR) (185)
output (190)
output device (191)
passive-matrix monitor (192)
PC/TV (193)
PDA keyboard (181)
personal laser printer (195)
photo printer (195)
platform scanner (185)
picture elements (191)
pixel (191)

plotter (195)
pointing stick (182)
pointing device (182)
portable printer (195)
portable scanner (184)
printer (193)
reader/sorter (185)
refresh rate (191)
resolution (191)
roller ball (182)
scanner (184)
scanning device (184)
server (197)
shared laser printer (195)
size (191)
soft copy (191)
speakers (196)
speed (193)
stylus (184)
telephony (197)
terminal (197)
thermal printer (195)
thin client (198)
thin film transistor monitor (TFT) (192)
toggle key (181)
touch pad (182)
touch screen (183)
touch surface (182)
trackball (182)
traditional keyboard (180)
Universal Product Code (UPC) (185)
viewable size (191)
voice command mode (187)
Voice-over IP (VoIP) (197)
voice recognition system (187)
wand reader (185)
Web appliance (198)
WebCam (186)
Web camera (186)
Web terminal (198)
wheel button (182)
wireless keyboard (181)
wireless mouse (182)

To test your knowledge of these key terms with animated flash cards, consult your Computing Essentials CD or visit our Web site at www.olearyseries.com/CE06 and select Key Terms.

COMPUTING
ESSENTIALS
2006

CROSSWORD

Across

3 Bar code system used in supermarkets.

5 Used to grade multiple choice exams.

6 Keys that turn features on and off.

9 Use special surface and stylus to create digital illustrations.

10 Measure of resolution.

13 Most popular input device used for computer games.

14 Keyboard that rolls up for storage and transport.

15 Button rotated to scroll through information displayed on the monitor.

16 Delivers much clearer picture than regular TV.

17 Most commonly used way to input data.

18 The distance between each pixel.

19 Number of times a screen is redrawn each second.

Down

1 Translates processed information into hard copy.

2 Description of monitor output.

4 Resolution is expressed as a matrix of these dots.

7 Letters, words, sentences, and paragraphs.

8 Records images digitally on a disk.

10 Type of terminal that does no processing.

11 Most widely used type of mouse.

12 Specialized digital camera that broadcasts images over the Internet.

For an interactive version of this crossword, consult your Computing Essentials CD or visit our Web site at **www.olearyseries.com/CE06** and select Crossword.

COMPUTING
ESSENTIALS
2006

MULTIPLE CHOICE

Circle the letter or fill in the correct answer.

1. A(n) _____ mouse emits and senses light to detect movement.
   a. mechanical
   b. cordless
   c. wireless
   d. pointer
   e. optical

2. A _____ allows you to control the pointer by moving and tapping your finger on the surface of a pad.
   a. touch surface
   b. touch pad
   c. MICR
   d. mouse
   e. digitizer

3. A wand reader is a type of _____ reader.
   a. MICR
   b. Bar code
   c. OMR
   d. touch surface
   e. MIDI

4. _____ are specialized digital video cameras that capture images and send them to a computer for broadcast over the Internet.
   a. OMR devices
   b. Mark sensing devices
   c. WebCams
   d. Graphics tablets
   e. Digital cameras

5. Voice recognition systems use a microphone, a _____, and special software.
   a. sound card
   b. keyboard shortcut
   c. toggle key
   d. MIDI device
   e. scanner

6. A handheld, book-sized device used to read downloaded content is a(n) _____.
   a. wand reader
   b. e-book
   c. light pen
   d. graphic tablet
   e. stylus

7. Printers convert information output to human language or symbols and transfer it onto paper as _____.
   a. soft copy
   b. hard copy
   c. TFT
   d. dot-matrix
   e. facsimile

8. _____ use a technology similar to that used in a photocopier.
   a. Laser printers
   b. Ink-jet printers
   c. Plotters
   d. MIDI
   e. Dot-matrix printers

9. _____ uses the Internet rather than traditional communication lines to connect two or more people via telephone.
   a. A multifunctional device
   b. A fax machine
   c. A dumb terminal
   d. Telephony
   e. An output device

10. A network computer is also known as a(n) _____.
    a. thin client
    b. intelligent terminal
    c. dumb terminal
    d. Net PC
    e. Web terminal

For an interactive version of these multiple choice questions, consult your Computing Essentials CD or visit our Web site at www.olearyseries.com/CE06 and select Multiple Choice.

MATCHING

Match each numbered item with the most closely related lettered item. Write your answers in the spaces provided.

a. clarity

b. cordless mouse

c. CRT

d. digital camera

e. dpi

f. ergonomic keyboard

g. HDTV

h. input

i. joystick

j. MFD

k. output

l. plotter

m. pointing stick

n. stylus

o. TFT

p. thermal

q. thin client

r. toggle

s. UPC

t. wand reader

1. Any data or instruction used by a computer. _____

2. Alleviates wrist strain from typing. _____

3. These keys turn a feature on or off. _____

4. Also known as a wireless mouse. _____

5. Similar to a mouse, this device is located in the middle of the keyboard. _____

6. A pointing device widely used for computer games. _____

7. Penlike device commonly used with tablet PCs and PDAs. _____

8. Scanners with photoelectric cells that read bar codes. _____

9. Type of bar code used in supermarkets. _____

10. Similar to traditional cameras but images are recorded digitally. _____

11. Processed data or information from a computer. _____

12. Refers to quality and sharpness of displayed images. _____

13. Type of monitor similar to a television set. _____

14. Multifunctional device. _____

15. Monitors that have independently activated pixels. _____

16. Delivers a much clearer wide-screen picture than regular television. _____

17. Measurement used to determine a printer's resolution. _____

18. Printer that uses heat to produce images on heat-sensitive paper. _____

19. Used to create maps, and architectural and engineering drawings. _____

20. Terminal that typically relies on host computer or server for application and system software. _____

For an interactive version of this matching exercise, consult your Computing Essentials CD or visit our Web site at www.olearyseries.com/CE06 and select Matching.

OPEN-ENDED

On a separate sheet of paper, respond to each question or statement.

1. Define input and output devices.

2. Describe the different types of pointing, scanning, image capturing, and audio-input devices.

3. Describe the three categories of output devices.

4. Define output and output devices.

5. What are combination input and output devices? Describe four such devices.

WebCams and Instant Messenging

1

Do you enjoy chatting with friends? Are you working on a project and need to collaborate with others in your group? What if you could see and hear your group online? Perhaps instant messaging and WebCams are just what you're looking for. It's easy and free with an Internet connection and the right software. To learn more about WebCams and instant messaging, review Making IT Work for You: WebCams and Instant Messaging on pages 188 and 189. Then answer the following questions: (a) How do you add a new friend to Windows Messenger? (b) What hardware is necessary to video conference with Windows Messenger? (c) When sharing an application, how do you give control of the application to a friend?

Internet Telephones

2

Do you need a cheaper way to stay in touch with friends and family? Did you know you can use your computer and the Internet to make long-distance calls to regular phones? All you need is some software and an Internet connection to get started. To learn more about this technology, consult your Computing Essentials CD or visit our Web site at www.olearyseries.com/CE06 and select Making IT Work for You. Then answer the following questions: (a) Which Internet phone service provider is featured in the examples? (b) What are the sliders used for in the Setup Wizard? (c) Which button is clicked to end a call?

1

Digital Cameras

While traditional cameras capture images on film, digital cameras capture images, then convert them into a digital form. These images can be viewed immediately and saved to a disk or into the camera's memory. To learn more about "How Digital Cameras Work," consult your Computing Essentials CD or visit our Web site at www.olearyseries.com/CE06 and select Animations. Then answer the following questions: (a) What is a CCD and what is its function? (b) What is an ADC and what is its function? (c) How are images transported from a digital camera to a computer?

2

How Internet Telephones Works

Internet telephones offer a low cost alternative to making long-distance calls. Using the Internet telephone (or other appropriate audio-input and output devices), the Internet, a special service provider, a sound card, and special software, you can place long-distance calls to almost anywhere in the world. To learn more about "How Internet Telephony Works," consult your Computing Essentials CD or visit our Web site at www. olearyseries.com/CE06 and select Expansions. Then answer the following questions: (a) What input and output devices are used? (b) What advantages and disadvantages would these devices have compared to an Internet telephone? (c) If Chris were to place a call to Steve, would she incur traditional long-distance charges? Why or why not? (d) Create a drawing similar to the animation that would represent computer-to-computer telephony. Be sure to include and number the appropriate steps.

1

Digital Input

Digitizing devices convert sketches, figures, or images into a form that can be processed by a computer. These devices typically record the movement of a writing device as a series of points and send this information to the computer. Write a one-page paper titled "Digital Input" that answers the following questions: (a) Define digitizer, digital camera, and digital video camera. (b) Give examples of ways that you would use the devices above. (c) Give examples of ways that individuals in corporations use the devices above.

2

Electronic Security

Electronic monitoring equipment is becoming more widely used in stores, the workplace, and in public. Consider the following questions and discuss your answers. Write a one-page summary of your analysis that answers the following questions: (a) What common applications of electronic monitoring or surveillance equipment have you noticed recently? (b) Does knowing that an electronic security device is in place make you feel more secure? (c) Have you ever felt that electronic surveillance equipment was an invasion of your privacy? (d) Consider the trade-off between security and privacy. In what cases is one more important than the other? Are these cases the same for everyone? Explain your answer.

COMPETENCIES

After you have read this chapter, you should be able to:

1 **Distinguish between primary and secondary storage.**

2 **Describe the traditional floppy disk and compare it to high capacity floppy disks.**

3 **Compare internal hard disks, hard-disk cartridges, and hard-disk packs.**

4 **Describe ways to improve hard-disk operations, including disk caching, redundant arrays of inexpensive disks, and data compression and decompression.**

5 **Discuss the different types of optical disks.**

6 **Describe solid-state storage, Internet drives, and magnetic tape.**

7 **Discuss mass storage and mass storage devices.**

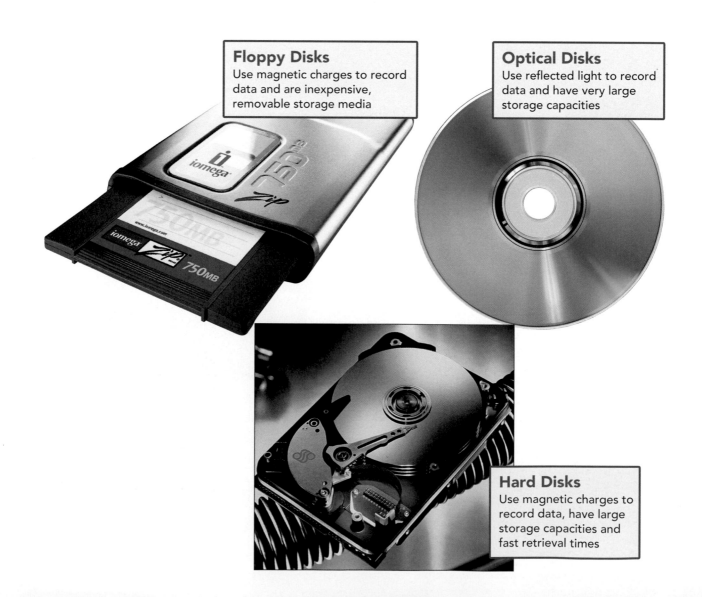

Floppy Disks
Use magnetic charges to record data and are inexpensive, removable storage media

Optical Disks
Use reflected light to record data and have very large storage capacities

Hard Disks
Use magnetic charges to record data, have large storage capacities and fast retrieval times

Secondary storage devices are used to save, to back up, and even to transport files consisting of data or programs from one location or computer to another. Not long ago, almost all files contained only numbers and letters. The demands for saving these files were easily met with low capacity floppy and hard-disk drives. For example, to save a 100-page research paper might require 400 KB of storage, which easily fits onto a single floppy disk.

In the past five years, however, secondary storage devices have been required to service much greater demands. Data storage has expanded from text and numeric files to include digital music files, photographic files, video files, and much more. These new types of files require secondary storage devices that have much greater capacity. For example, a 10-minute video might require 100 MB of storage.

Today's secondary storage devices are routinely used for a variety of tasks that were impossible just a few years ago. CDs and DVDs, for example, store data that can be used over and over again. You can download music from the Internet, play it on your computer, and create custom CDs with the right hardware and software.

Secondary storage devices have always been an indispensable element in any computer system. They have similarities to output and input devices. Like output devices, secondary storage devices receive information from the system unit in the form of the machine language of 0s and 1s. Rather than translating the information, however, secondary storage devices save the information in machine language for later use. Like input devices, secondary storage devices send information to the system unit for processing. However, the information, since it is already in machine form, does not need to be translated. It is sent directly to memory (RAM), where it can be accessed and processed by the CPU.

Competent end users need to be aware of the different types of secondary storage. They need to know the capabilities, limitations, and uses of floppy disks, hard disks, optical disks, and other types of secondary storage. Additionally, they need to be aware of specialty storage devices for portable computers and to be knowledgeable about how large organizations manage their extensive data resources.

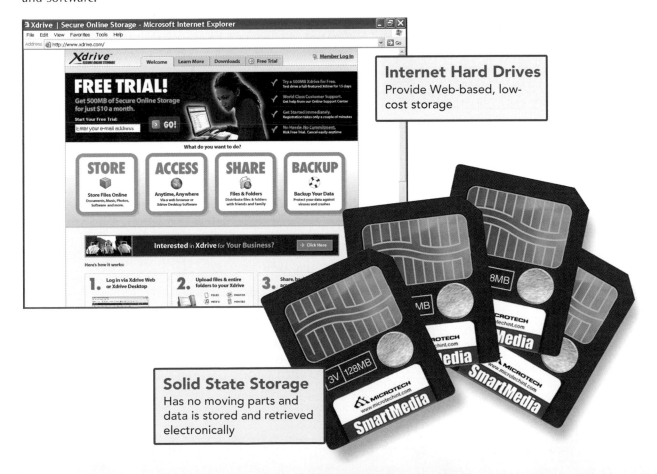

Internet Hard Drives
Provide Web-based, low-cost storage

Solid State Storage
Has no moving parts and data is stored and retrieved electronically

STORAGE

Primary storage is volatile. Secondary storage is nonvolatile. Important storage characteristics include media, capacity, storage devices, and access speed.

An essential feature of every computer is the ability to save, or store, information. As discussed in Chapter 6, random-access memory (RAM) holds or stores data and programs that the CPU is presently processing. Before data can be processed or a program can be run, it must be in RAM. For this reason, RAM is sometimes referred to as **primary storage.**

Unfortunately, most RAM provides only temporary or **volatile storage.** That is, it loses all of its contents as soon as the computer is turned off. Its contents are also lost if there is a power failure that disrupts the electric current going into the system unit. This volatility results in a need for more permanent or **nonvolatile storage** for data and programs. We also need external storage because users need much more storage capacity than is typically available in a computer's primary or RAM memory.

Secondary storage provides permanent or nonvolatile storage. Using **secondary storage devices,** such as a floppy disk drive, data and programs can be retained after the computer has been shut off. This is accomplished by *writing* files to and *reading* files from secondary storage devices. **Writing** is the process of saving information *to* the secondary storage device. **Reading** is the process of accessing information *from* secondary storage. This chapter focuses on secondary storage devices.

Some important characteristics of secondary storage include:

- **Media** or **medium,** which is the actual physical material that holds the data and programs. (See Figure 8-1.)
- **Capacity** measures how much a particular storage medium can hold.
- **Storage devices** are hardware that reads data and programs from storage media. Most also write to storage media.
- **Access speed** or **access time** measures the amount of time required by the storage device to retrieve data and programs.

Figure 8-1   Secondary storage media

Most desktop microcomputer systems have floppy, hard, and optical disk drives.

FLOPPY DISKS

Floppy disks are removable storage media. The traditional floppy disk is 1.44 MB. Data is recorded on tracks and sectors. Zip, SuperDisk, and HiFD are high capacity floppy disks.

Floppy disks, often called **diskettes** or simply **disks,** are portable or removable storage media. They are typically used to store and transport word processing, spreadsheet, and other types of files. They use flat circular pieces of Mylar plastic that have been coated with a magnetic material. **Floppy disk**

drives (FDD) store data and programs by altering the electromagnetic charges on the disk's surface to represent 1s and 0s. Floppy disk drives retrieve data and programs by reading these charges from the magnetic disk. Characters are represented by positive (+) and negative (−) charges using the ASCII, EBCDIC, or Unicode binary codes. For example, the number 3 would require a series of 8 charges. (See Figure 8-2.)

Floppy disks are also called **flexible disks** and **floppies.** This is because the plastic disk inside the diskette cover is flexible, not rigid. There are several types of floppy disks with different capacities ranging from the traditional floppy disk to a variety of high capacity floppy disks.

Figure 8–2 How charges on a disk surface store the number 3

TRADITIONAL FLOPPY DISK

The traditional floppy disk is the **1.44 MB 3½-inch disk.** (See Figure 8-3.) Although introduced over 20 years ago, they are still widely used. The most common type is labelled **2HD,** which means "two-sided, high-density." Two-sided indicates that data can be stored on both sides of the disk. **Density** refers to how tightly the bits (electromagnetic charges) can be packed next to one another. These disks have a capacity of 1.44 megabytes—the equivalent of over 350 typewritten pages.

Floppy disks have a thin exterior jacket made of hard plastic to protect the flexible disk inside. (See Figure 8-4.) A **shutter** on the disk slides to the side to expose the recording surface. **Labels** provide users with an area to write or document the contents of the disk. The **write-protection notch** has a slide that opens and closes. In either position, files can be read from the floppy disk. When the notch is closed, files can be saved to the disk. If you save a file with the same name as a file already on the disk, the original file is lost. As a protection against accidentally losing important files, the write-protection notch can be set to the open position as shown in Figure 8-4. In this position, files cannot be saved to the floppy disk.

As we discussed in Chapter 5, files are stored and organized on the flexible disk according to tracks and sectors. **Tracks** are rings of concentric circles without visible grooves. Each track is divided into invisible wedge-shaped sections called **sectors.** Each track's sector can store up to 512 bytes or characters.

To see how a floppy disk drive works, consult your Computing Essentials CD or visit our Web site at www.olearyseries.com/CE06 and select Animations.

Figure 8–3 A 1.44 MB 3½-inch floppy disk

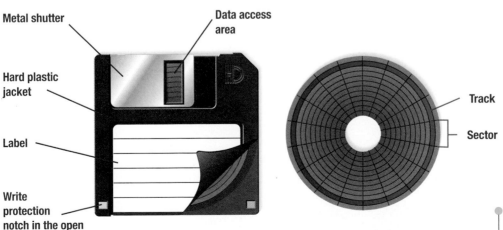

Metal shutter

Data access area

Hard plastic jacket

Label

Write protection notch in the open position

Front of disk

Inside of disk

Track

Sector

Figure 8–4 The parts of a 3½-inch floppy disk

HIGH CAPACITY FLOPPY DISKS

Figure 8-5 Zip disk and drive

While the traditional floppy disk is very reliable and still widely used to store data, it has very limited capacity. While 1.44 MB is fine for many text and spreadsheet files, it is not sufficient to hold larger files. For example, many PowerPoint presentation files far exceed 1.44 MB. Most multimedia applications require even greater capacity. **High capacity disks,** also known as **floppy-disk cartridges,** are rapidly replacing the traditional floppy disk. Like the traditional floppy, the high capacity disks are 3½ inches in diameter. However, they are able to store more information, are thicker, and require special disk drives. The three best known high capacity disks are Zip, HiFD, and SuperDisks.

- **Zip disks** are produced by Iomega and typically have a 100 MB, 250 MB, or 750 MB capacity—over 500 times as much as today's standard floppy disk. Internal Zip drives are a standard feature on many of today's system units. External Zip drives are generally connected to the system unit using parallel or USB ports. Zip disks are widely used to store multimedia, database, large text, and spreadsheet files. (See Figure 8-5.)

- **HiFD disks** from the Sony Corporation have a capacity of 200 MB or 720 MB. They have one major advantage over Zip disks. HiFD drives are able to read and store data on today's 1.44 MB traditional disk as well as on their own higher capacity disks. For this reason, HiFD are popular for use with notebook computers.

- **SuperDisks** are produced by Imation and have a 120 MB or 240 MB capacity. Like HiFD drives, SuperDisk disk drives are able to use today's 1.44 MB standard disks.

Each of these will likely improve its capacity and speed in the near future. Will one of them become the next standard floppy disk? While most observers believe one will become the next standard, they are less certain which one and when this will occur. For a summary of floppy disk capacities, see Figure 8-6.

On the Web Explorations

As more people share digital music and video, the need for high capacity disks is increasing. To learn more about a company in this field, visit our Web site at

www.olearyseries.com/CE06

and select On the Web Explorations.

Description	Capacity
2HD	1.44 MB
Zip	100/250/750 MB
HiFD	200/720 MB
SuperDisk	120/240 MB

Figure 8-6 Typical floppy disk capacities

TIPS

Are you concerned about losing the data stored on your floppy disks? Actually, floppy disks are quite durable, and taking care of them boils down to just a few basic rules.

1 **Don't bend.** Don't bend them, flex them, or put heavy weights on them.

2 **Don't touch.** Don't touch anything visible through the protective jacket.

3 **Don't remove.** Never attempt to remove a disk when it is rotating and in use.

4 **Avoid extreme conditions.** Keep disks away from strong magnetic fields, extreme heat, and any chemicals such as alcohol and other solvents.

5 **Use storage boxes.** Store disks in a sturdy plastic storage box.

Of course the best protection is to make a backup or duplicate copy of your disk.

▼ CONCEPT CHECK

▶ Discuss four important characteristics of secondary storage.

▶ What is the traditional floppy disk? Why is it likely to be replaced in the future?

HARD DISKS

Hard disks store files using tracks, sectors, and cylinders. Internal hard disks are fixed. Hard-disk cartridges are removable. Hard-disk packs are high capacity and removable. Disk caching, RAID, and file compression/decompression improve hard disk performance.

Like floppy disks, hard disks save files by altering the magnetic charges of the disk's surface. While a floppy disk uses a thin flexible plastic disk, a **hard disk** uses thicker, rigid metallic **platters** that are stacked one on top of another. Hard disks store and organize files using tracks, sectors, and cylinders. A **cylinder** runs through each track of a stack of platters. Although not needed by floppy disks that have a single platter, cylinders are necessary to differentiate files stored on the same track and sector of different platters. When a hard disk is formatted, tracks, sectors, and cylinders are assigned.

Compared to floppy disks, hard disks are able to store and retrieve information much faster and have a greater capacity. They are, however, sensitive instruments. Their read/write heads ride on a cushion of air about 0.000001 inches thick. It is so thin that a smoke particle, fingerprint, dust, or human hair could cause what is known as a head crash. (See Figure 8-7.)

A **head crash** occurs when a read/write head makes contact with the hard disk's surface or with particles on its surface. A head crash is a disaster for a hard disk. The disk surface is scratched and some or all of the data is destroyed. At one time, head crashes were commonplace. Now, fortunately, they are rare.

There are three types of hard disks: internal hard disk, hard-disk cartridge, and hard-disk pack.

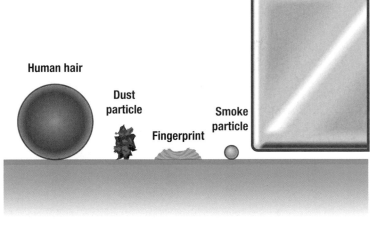

Figure 8-7 Materials that can cause a head crash

INTERNAL HARD DISK

An **internal hard disk,** also known as a **fixed disk,** is located inside the system unit. For most microcomputer systems, the internal hard disk drive is designated as the **C drive.** It is used to store programs and large data files. For example, nearly every microcomputer uses its internal hard disk to store its operating system and major applications such as Word and Excel.

Internal hard disks have two advantages over floppy disks: capacity and access speed. A 200-gigabyte internal hard disk, for instance, can hold almost as much information as 140,000 standard floppy disks. Because hard disks rotate faster and their read/write heads are closer to the recording surface, the time required to find and retrieve information (access speed) is much faster than floppy disks. For these reasons, almost all of today's powerful applications are designed to be stored on and run from an internal hard disk. Adequate internal hard disk capacity is essential.

To see how a hard disk works, consult your Computing Essentials CD or visit our Web site at www.olearyseries.com/CE06 and select Animations.

To ensure adequate performance of your internal hard disk, you should perform routine maintenance and periodically make backup copies of all important files. For hard disk maintenance and backup procedures, refer to Chapter 5's coverage of the Windows utilities Backup, Disk CleanUp, and Disk Defragmenter.

HARD-DISK CARTRIDGES

While internal hard disks provide fast access, they have a fixed amount of storage and cannot be easily removed from the system cabinet. **Hard-disk cartridges,** also known as **removable hard disks,** are as easy to remove as a cassette from a videocassette recorder. The amount of storage available to a computer system is limited only by the number of cartridges.

Hard-disk cartridges are used primarily to complement an internal hard disk. Because the cartridges are easily removed, they are particularly useful to protect or secure sensitive information. Other uses for hard-disk cartridges include backing up the contents of the internal hard disk and providing additional hard disk capacity.

Hard-disk cartridges for desktop computers have typical capacities of 10 to 20 GB (gigabytes). One of the most widely used hard-disk cartridges is Peerless disks from Iomega. (See Figure 8-8.) Credit card size hard-disk cartridges called **PC Card hard disks** are available for notebook computers with typical capacities up to 5 gigabytes. Two well-known PC Card hard disks are IBM's Microdrive and Toshiba's MK5002. (See Figure 8-9.)

HARD-DISK PACKS

Hard-disk packs are removable storage devices used to store massive amounts of information. (See Figure 8-10.) Their capacity far exceeds the other types of hard disks. Although you may never have seen one, it is almost certain that you have used them. Microcomputers that have access to the Internet, minicomputers, or mainframes often have access to external hard-disk packs through communication lines. Banks and credit card companies use them to record financial information.

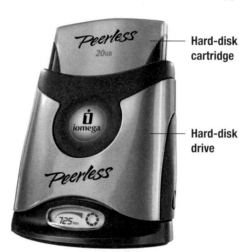

Hard-disk cartridge

Hard-disk drive

Figure 8-8 Hard-disk cartridge and card from Iomega

Figure 8-9   PC card hard disk from Toshiba

Figure 8-10   Hard-disk pack enclosed in a plastic cover

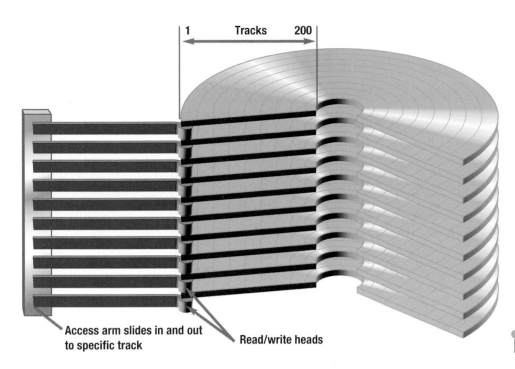

1 ← Tracks → 200

Access arm slides in and out to specific track

Read/write heads

Figure 8-11 Hard-disk pack

Like internal hard disks, hard-disk packs have multiple recording platters aligned one above the other. Hard-disk packs, however, use much larger platters, use more platters, and are not enclosed in a special container. Hard-disk packs are stored in a hard plastic cover that is removed when the pack is mounted onto special drives. The drive rotates the pack and access arms move in and out between the rotating platters. Each access arm has two read/write heads. One reads the disk surface above it; the other reads the disk surface below it. All the access arms move in and out together. However, only one of the read/write heads is activated at a given moment. A disk pack with 11 disks provides 20 recording surfaces. This is because the top and bottom outside surfaces of the pack are not used. (See Figure 8-11.)

For a summary of the different types of hard disks, see Figure 8-12.

Type	Description
Internal	Fast access to applications, fixed
Cartridge	Complement to internal hard disk, removable
Disk pack	Massive storage capacity, removable

Figure 8-12 Types of hard disks

PERFORMANCE ENHANCEMENTS

Three ways to improve the performance of hard disks are disk caching, redundant arrays of inexpensive disks, and file compression/decompression.

Disk caching improves hard-disk performance by anticipating data needs. It performs a function similar to RAM caching discussed in Chapter 6. While RAM caching improves processing by acting as a temporary high-speed holding area between memory and the CPU, disk caching improves processing by acting as a temporary high-speed holding area between a secondary storage device and the CPU. Disk caching requires a combination of hardware and software. During idle processing time, frequently used data is read from the hard disk into memory (cache). When needed, the data is then accessed directly from memory. The transfer rate from memory is much faster than from the hard disk. As a result, overall system performance is often increased by as much as 30 percent.

Redundant arrays of inexpensive disks (RAID) improve performance by expanding external storage, improving access speed, and providing reliable storage. Several inexpensive hard-disk drives are connected to one another

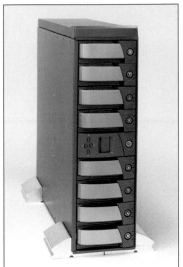

Figure 8-13 RAID storage device

These connections can be by a network or within specialized RAID devices. (See Figure 8-13.) Using special software, the connected hard-disk drives are related or grouped together, and the computer system interacts with the RAID system as though it were a single large capacity hard disk drive. Files written to a RAID system are saved using more than one hard disk and are automatically duplicated. The result is expanded storage capability, fast access speed, and high reliability. For these reasons RAID is often used by Internet servers and large organizations.

File compression and **file decompression** increase storage capacity by reducing the amount of space required to store data and programs. File compression is not limited to hard-disk systems. It is frequently used to compress files on floppy disks as well. File compression also helps to speed up transmission of files from one computer system to another. Sending and receiving compressed files across the Internet is a common activity.

File compression programs scan files for ways to reduce the amount of required storage. One way is to search for repeating patterns. The repeating patterns are replaced with a token, leaving enough tokens so that the original can be rebuilt or decompressed. These programs often shrink files to a quarter of their original size. To learn more about file compression, consult your Computing Essentials CD or visit our Web site at www.olearyseries.com/CE06 and select Expansions.

You can compress and decompress files using specialized utilities such as WinZip from Nico Mak Computing and PKZip from PKWare. Or, if these specialized utilities are not available, you can use utility programs in Windows XP.

For a summary of performance enhancement techniques, see Figure 8-14.

Technique	Description
Disk caching	Uses cache and anticipates data needs
RAID	Linked, inexpensive hard-disk drives
File compression	Reduces file size
File decompression	Expands compressed files

Figure 8-14 Performance enhancement techniques

TIPS Are you running short of hard-disk storage space? Want to send a large file or several files at once over the Internet? You can save both space and valuable connection time by compressing the files first. Compression/decompression utility programs are available in Windows XP. If you don't have Windows XP, consider using WinZip, a popular compression program:

1 **Start.** Start the WinZip program.

2 **Create file.** Click the *New* button on the toolbar to create and name a zip file.

3 **Select.** Locate and select the file(s) you want to compress.

4 **Compress.** Click the *Add* button to compress and add the selected file(s) to the zip file.

You can now replace the selected file(s) with the much smaller zip file. To access the original files at any time, start the WinZip program, select the file(s) to decompress and click the WinZip *Extract* button.

▼ CONCEPT CHECK

▶ Compare floppy and hard disks. What is a head crash?

▶ What are the three types of hard disks? Briefly describe each.

▶ List and describe three ways to improve the performance of hard disks.

OPTICAL DISKS

> Optical disks use laser technology to provide high capacity storage. Basic CDs include read only, write once, rewriteable, Picture CD, and Photo CD. DVDs are replacing CDs. Basic DVDs include read only, write once, and rewriteable.

Today's **optical disks** can hold over 17 gigabytes of data. (See Figure 8-15.) That is the equivalent of over several million typewritten pages or a medium-sized library all on a single disk. Optical disks are having a great impact on storage today, but we are probably only beginning to see their effects.

In optical-disk technology, a laser beam alters the surface of a plastic or metallic disk to represent data. Unlike floppy and hard disks, which use magnetic charges to represent 1s and 0s, optical disks use reflected light. The 1s and 0s are represented by flat areas called **lands** and bumpy areas called **pits** on the disk surface. The disk is read by an **optical disk drive** using a laser that projects a tiny beam of light on these areas. The amount of reflected light determines whether the area represents a 1 or a 0. To see how an optical disk drive works, consult your Computing Essentials CD or visit our Web site at www.olearyseries.com/CE06 and select Animations.

Like floppy and hard disks, optical disks use tracks and sectors to organize and store files. Unlike the concentric tracks and wedge-shaped sectors used for floppy and hard disks, however, optical disks typically use a single track that spirals toward the center of the disk. This single track is divided into equally sized sectors.

Optical disks come in many different sizes, including 3½, 4¾, 5¼, 8, 12, and 14 inches. The most common size is 4¾ inches. These disks are typically stored in clear protective boxes called **jewel boxes.** Data is stored on these disks in different ways or different formats. The two most common are CD and DVD.

Figure 8-15 Optical disk

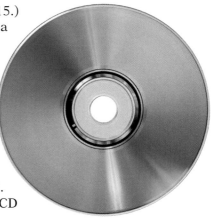

COMPACT DISC

Compact disc, or as it is better known, **CD,** is one of the most widely used optical formats. CD drives are standard on many microcomputer systems. Typically, CD drives can store from 650 MB (megabytes) to 1 GB (gigabyte) of data on one side of a CD. One important characteristic of CD drives is their **rotational speed.** This speed is important because it determines how fast data can be transferred from the CD. For example, a 24X or 24-speed CD drive can transfer 3.6 MB per second, while a 48X drive can transfer 7.2 MB per second. The faster the drive, the faster data can be read from the CD and used by the computer system.

There are four basic types of CDs: read only, write once, rewritable, and Picture and Photo CDs:

Are you concerned about damaging your optical disks? Actually, they are quite durable, and taking care of them boils down to just a few basic rules.

TIPS

1. **Don't stack.** Don't stack or bend disks.

2. **Don't touch.** Don't touch the recording surfaces. Hold only by their edges.

3. **Don't remove.** Never attempt to remove a disk when it is rotating and in use.

4. **Avoid extreme conditions.** Keep disks from extreme heat and direct sunlight.

5. **Use storage boxes.** Store disks in plastic storage boxes.

Of course the best protection is to make a backup or duplicate copy of your disk.

- **Read only—CD-ROM,** which stands for **compact disc-read only memory,** is similar to a commercial music CD. *Read only* means it cannot be written on or erased by the user. Thus, you as a user have access only to the data imprinted by the publisher. CD-ROMs are used to distribute large databases and references. They are also used to distribute large software application packages.

- **Write once—CD-R,** which stands for **CD-recordable,** can be written to once. After that they can be read many times without deterioration but

cannot be written on or erased. CD-R drives, also known as **CD burners,** are often used to archive data and to record music downloaded from the Internet. To learn about how music is downloaded from the Internet, consult your Computing Essentials CD or visit our Web site at www. olearyseries.com/CE06 and select Animations. To learn more about the specifics of finding music on the Internet, creating custom CDs, and uploading to a portable player, see Making IT Work for You: Music from the Internet on pages 222 and 223.

- **Rewriteable—CD-RW** stands for **compact disc rewritable.** Also known as **erasable optical disks,** these disks are very similar to CD-Rs except that the disk surface is not permanently altered when data is recorded. Because they can be changed, CD-RWs are often used to create and edit multimedia presentations. One limitation of CD-R and CD-RW disks is that older CD-ROM drives may not be able to read them. Most newer CD-ROM drives are **multiread** or able to read both CD-R and CD-RW disks.

- **Picture CDs** and **Photo CDs** use a special format developed by Eastman Kodak to store digital images. Picture CDs are less expensive and typically are used by nonprofessionals. Today, most film developers provide traditional printed pictures and digital images. The digital images are delivered by the Internet or by Picture CD. These disks are typically **single-session,** meaning that all images must be transferred at one time to the CD. Photo CDs, however, are **multisession,** meaning that new images can be added at any time.

DIGITAL VERSATILE DISC

DVD stands for **digital versatile disc** or **digital video disc.** This is a newer format that is rapidly replacing CDs as the standard optical disk. DVD drives are very similar to CDs except that more data can be packed into the same amount of space. DVD discs can store 4.7 GB to 17 GB on a single DVD disk—17 times the capacity of CDs.

Today's more powerful microcomputer systems come with DVD drives. There are three basic types of DVDs similar to CDs: read only, write once, and rewriteable.

- **Read only—DVD-ROM** stands for **digital versatile disc-read only memory.** DVD-ROM drives are also known as **DVD players.** DVD-ROMs are having a major impact on the video market. While CD-ROMs are effective for distributing music, they can only contain just over an hour of fair-quality video. DVD-ROMs can provide over two hours of very high-quality video and sound comparable to that found in motion picture theatres. The motion picture industry has rapidly shifted video distribution from video cassettes to DVD-ROMs.

- **Write once—DVD+R** and **DVD-R** are two competing write once formats. Both stand for **DVD recordable.** Each has a slightly different way in which they format their disks. Fortunately, most new DVD players can use either format. These drives are typically used to create permanent archives for large amounts of data and to record videos. DVD recordable drives are rapidly replacing CD-R drives due to their massive capacity.

- **Rewriteable—DVD+RW, DVD-RW,** and **DVD-RAM** are the three most widely used formats. DVD+RW and DVD-RW stand for **DVD rewriteable. DVD-RAM** stands for **DVD random-access memory.** Each format has a unique way of storing data. Unfortunately, older DVD players typically can only read one type of format. Newer DVD players, however, are able to read and to use any of the formats. Rewriteable DVD disc drives have rapidly replace CD rewriteable drives. Applications range from recording

Format	Typical Capacity	Type	Description
CD	650 MB to 1 GB	CD-ROM	Read only, used to distribute databases, reference books, and software
		CD-R	Write one time only, used to archive large amounts of data
		CD-RW	Rewriteable, used to create and edit large multimedia presentations
		Picture CD	Single-session CD, used to store images
		Photo CD	Multisession CD, used to store images
DVD	17 GB to 17 GB	DVD-ROM	Read only, distribute theater-quality video and sound presentations
		DVD-R and DVD+R	Written-to one time only, used to archive very large amounts of data
		DVD-RW, DVD+RW and DVD-RAM	Rewriteable, able to create and read CD disks, used to create and edit large-scale multimedia presentations

Figure 8–16   Types of optical disks

video from camcorders to developing large multimedia presentations that include extensive graphics and video. For a summary of optical disk storage capacities, see Figure 8-16.

▼ CONCEPT CHECK

▶   How is data represented on optical disks?

▶   Compare CD and DVD formats. Why are DVDs replacing CDs?

▶   What are DVD-RW, DVD+RW, and DVD-RAM?

OTHER TYPES OF SECONDARY STORAGE

Solid–state storage does not have moving parts. Internet drives use the Internet to store data and information. Magnetic tape provides sequential access for backup.

For the typical microcomputer user, the three basic storage options—floppy disk, hard disk, and optical disk—are complementary, not competing. Almost all microcomputers today have at least one floppy-disk drive, one hard-disk drive, and one optical drive. For many users, these secondary storage devices are further complemented with more specialized storage such as solid state storage, Internet hard drives, and magnetic tape.

SOLID-STATE STORAGE

Each of the secondary storage devices discussed thus far has moving parts. For example, hard disks rotate and read/write heads move in and out. Unlike these devices, **solid-state storage** devices have no moving parts. Data and information are stored and retrieved electronically directly from these devices much as they would be from conventional computer memory. While this type of storage is more expensive than the others, it is more reliable and requires less power.

MUSIC FROM THE INTERNET

Did you know you can use the Internet to locate and play music? You can even create your own compact discs, or transfer music to a portable player. All you need is the right software, hardware, and a connection to the Internet.

Finding Music   There are many services on the Internet for finding music. The first step is to download software that connects with a music service. You can use this software to search for songs, create a playlist of songs you will listen to frequently, and play them. For example, to create a playlist using Apple iTunes:

1 ● Connect to
   www.apple.com and
   follow the on-screen
   instructions for
   downloading and
   installing the iTunes
   software.

2 ● Select *Music Store* from
   the Source List and
   follow the on-screen
   instructions to locate
   and purchase music
   files.

● Click the *Create a
   Playlist* button and enter
   a name for your playlist.

● Click *Library* in the
   Source list to view your
   songs.

● Drag songs you would
   like to hear to your
   playlist.

● Select your playlist and
   click the *Play* button to
   hear your music.

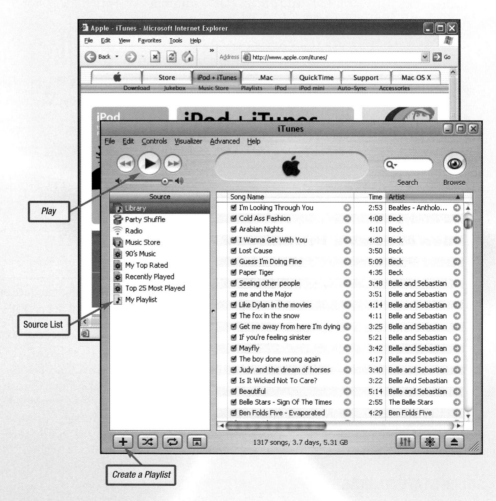

Creating a Custom CD   If your computer is equipped with a CD-R or CD-RW drive, creating a custom CD is one way to take your favorite tunes with you. To create a CD using iTunes:

1 ● Create a playlist as shown in the previous step.

● Select your playlist from the Source list.

● Click the *Burn Disc* button.

● Insert a blank CD into your CD drive.

● Click the *Burn Disc* button once more to create the CD.

Uploading to a Portable Player   Another popular way to take your favorite tunes with you is to upload them to a portable music player. Portable music players are lightweight digital storage devices that do not require cassettes or discs but that store music files internally. For example, you could transfer music to an iPod portable music player using iTunes software by following the steps below:

1 ● Connect your iPod to your computer. iTunes starts automatically and synchronizes with the songs in the iTunes library.

● To transfer individual music files, select them from the Library and drag them to *iPod* in the source list.

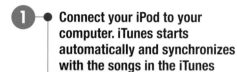

The Web is continually changing, and some of the specifics presented in this Making IT Work for You may have changed. To learn more about other ways to make information technology work for you, visit our Web site at www.olearyseries.com/CE06 and select Making IT Work for You.

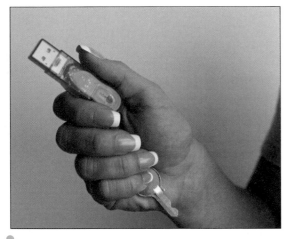

Figure 8-17   Flash memory cards

Figure 8-18   Key chain flash
memory

For these reasons, this technology is becoming widely used for specialized secondary storage.

Flash memory cards, are credit card sized solid-state storage devices widely used in notebook computers. (See Figure 8-17.) Flash memory is also used in a variety of specialized input devices to capture and transfer data to desktop computers. For example, flash memory is used to store images captured from digital cameras and then to transfer the images to desktop and other computers. Flash memory also is used to record MP3 music files and to transfer those files to computers and other devices.

Key chain hard drives have recently been introduced. These devices, also known as **key chain flash memory devices,** are so compact that they can be transported on a key ring or a necklace. (See Figure 8-18.) Key chain hard drives conveniently connect directly to a computer's USB port to transfer files and have typical capacities of 1 GB. Due to their convenient size and large capacities, some predict that key chain hard drive devices may replace the floppy disk for transporting data and information between computers and a variety of specialty devices.

INTERNET HARD DRIVES

Special service sites on the Web provide users with storage. This storage is called an **Internet hard drive,** also known as **i-drive** or **online storage.** (See Figure 8-19.)

Advantages of Internet hard drives compared to other types of secondary storage include low cost and the flexibility to access information from any location using the Internet. Because all information must travel across the Internet, however, access speed is slower. Another consideration is that users are dependent on the availability and security procedures of the service site. Because of these limitations, Internet hard drives are typically used as a specialized secondary storage device and not for storing highly personalized or sensitive information.

Figure 8-19   An Internet hard drive site

Typically, Internet hard drive sites focus on supplying their services either to businesses or to individuals. The business-oriented sites provide faster access and greater security for a fee. The individual-focused sites provide limited storage for much lower cost and some sites are free. (See Figure 8-20.)

Focus	Company	Location
Individual	Apple	itools.mac.com
Individual	Freedrive	www.freedrive.com
Individual	Yahoo	briefcase.yahoo.com
Business	Amerivault	www.amerivault.com
Business	Connected TLM	connected.com

Figure 8-20   Internet hard drive sites

MAGNETIC TAPE

To find a particular song on an audiotape, you may have to play several inches of tape. Finding a song on an audio compact disc, in contrast, can be much faster. You select the track, and the disc player moves directly to it. That, in brief, represents the two different approaches to external storage. The two approaches are called **sequential access** and **direct access.**

Disks provide fast direct access. Tapes provide slower sequential access. With tape, information is stored in sequence, such as alphabetically. For example, all the grades of students at your school could be recorded on tape arranged alphabetically by their last names. To find the grades for one student, say Chris Reed, the search would begin at the start of the tape and search alphabetically past all the last names beginning with A to Q before ultimately reaching Reed. This may involve searching several inches or feet, which takes time.

Like floppy and hard disks, **magnetic tape** stores data and programs by altering the electromagnetic charges on a recording surface. Although slower to access specific information, magnetic tape is an effective and commonly used tool for backing up data. At one time mainframe computers used **magnetic tape reels** exclusively. This type of tape is typically ½-inch wide and 1½-mile long and provides massive storage capacity. Now, most mainframes as well as microcomputers use **tape cartridges** or **magnetic tape streamers** to back up data. (See Figure 8-21.)

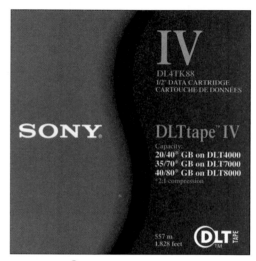

Figure 8-21   Magnetic tape cartridge

▼ CONCEPT CHECK

► What is solid-state storage? What are key chain hard drives?

► What are Internet hard drives? What are they used for?

► Discuss magnetic tape reels and tape cartridges.

MASS STORAGE DEVICES

> Mass storage devices are specialized high capacity secondary storage devices. Mass storage devices include file servers, RAID systems, tape libraries, optical juke boxes, and organizational Internet storage.

It is natural to think of secondary storage media and devices as they relate to us as individuals. It may not be as obvious how important these matters are to organizations. **Mass storage** refers to the tremendous amount of secondary storage required by large organizations. **Mass storage devices** are specialized high capacity secondary storage devices designed to meet organizational demands for data.

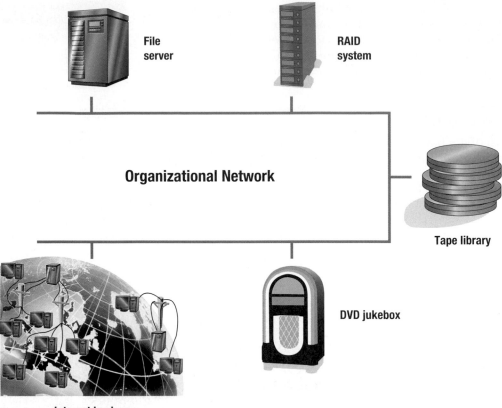

File
server

RAID
system

Organizational Network

Tape library

DVD jukebox

Internet back up

Figure 8-22   Enterprise storage system

Most large organizations have established a strategy called an **enterprise storage system** to promote efficient and safe use of data across the networks within their organizations. (See Figure 8-22.) Some of the mass storage devices that support this strategy are:

- **File servers**—dedicated computers with very large storage capacities that provide users access to fast storage and retrieval of data.
- **RAID systems**—larger version of the specialized devices discussed earlier in this chapter that enhances organizational security by constantly making backup copies of files moving across the organization's networks.
- **Tape library**—device that provides automatic access to data archived on a large collection or library of tapes.
- **DVD-ROM** and **CD-ROM jukeboxes**—provide automatic access to a large collection or library of optical disks.
- **Organizational Internet storage**—high speed Internet connection to a dedicated remote organizational Internet drive site.

The availability, security, and organization of data are essential to the efficient operations of any organization.

▼ CONCEPT CHECK

▶ Define mass storage and mass storage devices.

▶ What is an enterprise storage system?

▶ List and describe five mass storage devices.

A Look to the Future

Blu-Ray Technology and Plastic Memory Expected to Replace DVD

Have you ever run out of space on a disk? How would you like to store hours of music on one disk? Would you like to record 13 hours of broadcast television or several movies on a single disk? What if you could record an entire library on a single disk? Blu-Ray and plastic memory are emerging storage technologies that promise to do that and much more.

Nine of the largest manufacturers of electronics, including Hitachi, Pioneer, and Sony, have recently agreed to support new optical disk technology that will allow users to record and play back much more information than is currently possible. This new storage is called Blu-Ray, because the new discs use blue laser light instead of the red laser light used in traditional CD players. Blu-Ray discs may ultimately hold over 50 GB on a single disk.

Existing CD and DVD players and recorders, however, will not be able to play or record on the new optical disks. In the near future, new players and recorders will likely incorporate both red and blue laser technology to accommodate both technologies. Manufacturers and media developers hope that cooperation on the Blu-Ray project will help prevent the incompatibility problems that limited the expansion of the DVD in its early development. They hope that this new larger and easy-to-use format will expedite the transition to these new discs.

Further into the future, the next great leap in data storage may be nano devices that store information on plastic sheets. IBM has already successfully tested these memory plastics. Tiny prongs, less than a nanometer (one billionth of a meter) in length, press small dimples onto a plastic sheet. A dimple indicates a zero, no dimple indicates a one. Compared to optical and metallic disks, these plastic sheets have a far greater capacity, are more durable, require less energy to operate, and are unaffected by power surges and magnetic fields.

While Blu-Ray disks are just around the corner, widespread use of memory plastics likely will be years away. What impact do you think these new technologies will have on businesses and individuals? How could these ultra high capacity secondary storage technologies affect you?

VISUAL SUMMARY

SECONDARY STORAGE

STORAGE

RAM is **primary storage.** Most RAM is **volatile,** meaning that it loses its contents whenever power is disrupted. **Secondary storage** provides **nonvolatile** storage. Secondary storage retains data and information after the computer system is turned off.

Writing is the process of saving information to **secondary storage devices. Reading** is the process of accessing information from secondary storage devices.

Important characteristics of secondary storage include:

- **Media** or **medium**—actual physical material that retains data and programs.
- **Capacity**—how much a particular storage medium can hold.
- **Storage devices** are hardware that read and write to storage media.
- **Access time** or **access speed**—time required to retrieve data from a secondary storage device.

Writing is process of saving data and information to secondary storage. **Reading** is process of accessing data and information.

FLOPPY DISKS

Floppy disks are also known as **diskettes, disks, flexible disks,** and **floppies. Floppy disk drives (FDD)** store data and programs by charging the disk surface.

Traditional Floppy Disk
The traditional floppy disk is the **1.44 MB 3½-inch disk. 2DH** indicates two-sided high **density** disk. Disks have **shutters** that open to provide access to the recording surface, **labels** to record disk content, and **write-protection notches** to allow or prohibit writing to the disk.

Files are stored and organized according to **tracks** (concentric circles) and **sectors** (wedge-shapes).

High Capacity Floppy Disks
High capacity disks (floppy-disk cartridges) have greater capacity and are replacing the traditional floppy disk. The three best known are:

- **Zip disks**—typical capacities are 100MB, 250MB, and 750MB.
- **HiFD disks**—typical capacities are 200MB and 720MB; HiFD drives can read traditional floppy disks.
- **SuperDisks**—typical capacities are 120MB and 240MB; SuperDisk drives can read traditional floppy disks.

To be a competent end user you need to be aware of the different types of secondary storage. You need to know their capabilities, limitations, and uses. There are four widely used storage media: floppy disk, hard disk, optical disk, and other types of secondary storage.

HARD DISKS

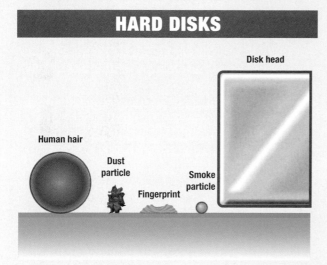

Disk head

Human hair

Dust particle

Fingerprint

Smoke particle

Compared to floppy disks, **hard disks** use rigid metallic **platters** that provide much greater capacity. Files are organized according to **tracks, sectors,** and **cylinders.**

A **head crash** occurs when the hard disk makes contact with the drive's read/write heads.

Three types of hard disks are internal hard disks, hard-disk cartridges, and hard-disk packs.

Internal Hard Disk
Internal hard disks (fixed disk) are located within the system unit and typically identified as the **C drive.**

Hard-Disk Cartridge
Unlike internal hard disks, **hard-disk cartridges (removable hard disks)** are removable and their capacity is limited only by the number of cartridges. **PC Card hard disks** are for notebooks.

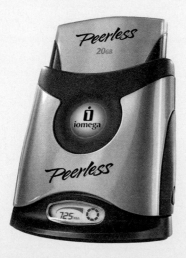

HARD DISKS

Hard-Disk Pack
Hard-disk packs are removable and have several platters and extensive capacity. A disk pack typically has 11 platters with 20 recording surfaces.

Performance Enhancements
Three ways to improve hard disk performance are disk caching, RAIDS, and file compression and file decompression.

- **Disk caching**—provides a temporary high speed holding area between memory and the CPU; improves performance by anticipating data needs and reducing time to access data from secondary storage.

- **RAIDS (redundant array of inexpensive disks)**—several inexpensive hard-disk drives are connected together; improves performance by providing expanded storage, fast access, and high reliability.

- **File compression** and **decompression**—files compressed before storing and then decompressed before being used again; improves performance through efficient storage.

Secondary Storage

www.olearyseries.com/CE06   **229**

OPTICAL DISKS

Optical disks use laser technology. 1s and 0s are represented by **pits** and **lands. Jewel boxes** protect optical disks. **Rotational speed** of **optical disk drives** affects access speed.

Compact Discs
Compact discs (CDs) have typical capacity of 650 MB to 1 GB. Four types are:

- **CD-ROM—compact disc-read only memory;** used to distribute databases, reference, and software.
- **CD-R—CD-recordable;** CD-R drives also known as **CD burners;** used to create custom music CDs and to archive data.
- **CD-RW—compact disk rewritable (erasable optical disks);** used for large multimedia presentations. **Multiread** CD-ROM drives can use CD-R and CD-RW disks.
- **Picture** and **Photo CD**—Picture CDs are **single-session.** Photo CDs are **multisession.**

Digital Versatile Discs
DVDs (digital versatile discs, digital video discs) have far greater capacity than CDs. Three types are: **DVD-ROM (digital versatile disc-read only memory; DVD players** are drives), write once **(DVD+RW, DVD-R),** and rewriteable **(DVD+RW, DVD-RW, DVD-RAM).**

OTHER TYPES

The three basic storage options (floppy, hard, and optical) are complementary and not competitive. Many users complement with more specialized devices including:

- **Solid-state storage**—no moving parts. **Flash memory cards** are solid-state storage devices. **Key chain hard drives (key chain flash memory devices)** provide very compact storage.
- **Internet hard drives (i-drive, online storage)**—Web-based, low-cost storage. Accessible from any Internet connection, these drives are often slow and security is an issue.
- **Magnetic tape—sequential access** (disks provide **direct access**) used primarily for backing up data. **Magnetic tape reels** were widely used with mainframes. Now **tape cartridges (magnetic tape streamers)** are most widely used for mainframes and microcomputers.

MASS STORAGE

Mass storage refers to the tremendous amount of secondary storage required by large organizations. **Mass storage devices** are specialized high capacity secondary storage devices designed to meet organizational demands for data.

Most large organizations have established a strategy called an **enterprise storage system** to promote efficient and safe use of data across the networks within their organizations.

Mass storage devices that support this strategy are: **file servers, RAID systems, tape libraries, DVD-ROM and CD-ROM jukeboxes, and organizational Internet storage.**

1.44 MB 3½-inch disk   (213)
2HD   (213)
access time   (212)
access speed   (212)
C drive   (215)
capacity   (212)
CD (compact disc)   (219)
CD burner   (220)
CD-R (CD-recordable)   (219)
CD-ROM (compact disc-read only
   memory)   (219)
CD-ROM jukebox   (226)
CD-RW (compact disc rewritable)   (220)
cylinder   (215)
density   (213)
direct access   (225)
disk   (212)
disk caching   (217)
diskette   (212)
DVD (digital versatile disc or digital
   video disc)   (220)
DVD player   (220)
DVD-R (DVD recordable)   (220)
DVD+R (DVD recordable)   (220)
DVD-RAM (DVD random-access
   memory)   (220)
DVD-ROM (DVD read only memory)   (220)
DVD-ROM jukebox   (226)
DVD-RW (DVD rewritable)   (220)
DVD+RW (DVD rewritable)   (220)
enterprise storage system   (226)
file compression   (218)
file decompression   (218)
file server   (226)
fixed disk   (215)
flash memory card   (224)
flexible disk   (213)
floppies   (213)
floppy disk   (212)
floppy disk drive (FDD)   (212–213)
floppy-disk cartridge   (214)
hard disk   (215)
hard-disk cartridge   (216)
hard-disk pack   (216)
head crash   (215)
HiFD disk   (214)
high capacity disk   (214)
i-drive   (224)
internal hard disk   (215)

Internet hard drive   (224)
jewel box   (219)
key chain hard drive   (224)
key chain flash memory device   (224)
label   (213)
land   (219)
magnetic tape   (225)
magnetic tape reel   (225)
magnetic tape streamer   (225)
mass storage   (225)
mass storage devices   (225)
media   (212)
medium   (212)
multiread   (220)
multisession   (220)
nonvolatile storage   (212)
online storage   (224)
optical disk   (219)
optical disk drive   (219)
organizational internet storage   (226)
PC Card hard disk   (216)
Photo CD   (220)
Picture CD   (220)
pit   (219)
platters   (215)
primary storage   (212)
read only   (219)
reading   (212)
redundant arrays of inexpensive disks
   (RAID)   (217)
removable hard disk   (216)
rewriteable   (220)
rotational speed   (219)
secondary storage   (212)
sccondary storage device   (212)
sector   (213)
sequential access   (225)
shutter   (213)
single-session   (220)
solid-state storage   (221)
storage device   (212)
SuperDisk   (214)
tape cartridge   (225)
track   (213)
volatile storage   (212)
write once   (219)
write-protection notch   (213)
writing   (212)
Zip disk   (214)

To test your knowledge of these key terms with animated flash cards, consult your Computing Essentials CD or visit our Web site at www.olearyseries.com/CE06 and select Key Terms.

COMPUTING ESSENTIALS 2006

CROSSWORD

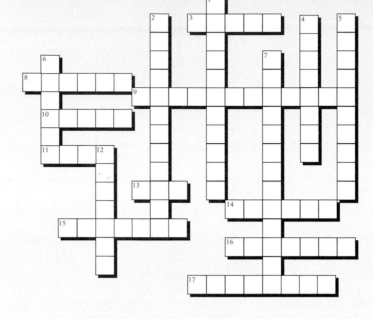

Across

3 Also known as the internal hard disk.
8 Invisible wedge-shaped division of a track.
9 Represent 1s and 0s.
10 Rings of concentric circles without visible grooves.
11 Grouped disk drives treated as one hard disk by the computer system.
13 Disk with 500 times the storage as a standard floppy.
14 Portable and removable storage device.
15 The process of saving information to the secondary storage device.
16 Rigid metallic part of a hard disk.
17 Storage medium that contains a flexible plastic disk.

Down

1 Improves hard-disk performance by anticipating data needs.
2 Meaning new images can be added to a CD at any time.
4 Runs through each track of a stack of platters.
5 Measures the amount of time required to retrieve data.
6 Invisible wedge-shaped section.
7 Web based storage.
12 How tightly the bits can be packed next to each other.

For an interactive version of this crossword, consult your Computing Essentials CD or visit our Web site at **www.olearyseries.com/CE06** and select Crossword.

COMPUTING ESSENTIALS 2006

MULTIPLE CHOICE

Circle the letter or fill in the correct answer.

1. _____ is permanent storage used to preserve data and programs.
   a. Nonvolatile storage
   b. Volatile storage
   c. Internal storage
   d. File compression
   e. Read only memory

2. _____ is the process of accessing files from a disk.
   a. Reading
   b. Writing
   c. Printing
   d. Spanning
   e. Caching

3. _____ measures the amount of time required by a storage device to retrieve data and programs.
   a. Capacity
   b. Media
   c. Reading
   d. Access time
   e. Primary storage

4. Another name for floppy disks is _____.
   a. diskettes
   b. disks
   c. flexible disks
   d. floppies
   e. all of the above

5. _____ refers to how tightly bits can be packed.
   a. Density
   b. Pit
   c. Multithread
   d. Section
   e. Zip

6. Files cannot be written onto a floppy disk when the write-protection notch is _____ .
   a. zipped
   b. open
   c. closed
   d. sealed
   e. crossed

7. The internal hard disk is typically referred to as the _____ drive.
   a. A
   b. B
   c. C
   d. alternate
   e. secondary

8. An internal hard disk is also known as a _____ because it is located inside the system unit.
   a. hard-disk pack
   b. fixed disk
   c. PC Card hard disk
   d. removable disk
   e. hard disk cartridge

9. _____ can provide over two hours of high-quality video and sound comparable to that found in theaters.
   a. CD-RW
   b. CD
   c. CD-ROM
   d. DVD-ROM
   e. Picture CD

10. _____ is exclusively a sequential-access storage media.
    a. A floppy disk
    b. A hard disk
    c. Magnetic tape
    d. Photo CD
    e. WORM

For an interactive version of these multiple choice questions, consult your Computing Essentials CD or visit our Web site at www.olearyseries.com/CE06 and select Multiple Choice.

MATCHING

Match each numbered item with the most closely related lettered item. Write your answers in the spaces provided.

a. access speed
b. CD burner
c. cylinder
d. disk caching
e. disks
f. file compression
g. fixed disk
h. flash memory card
i. floppy disk
j. floppy-disk cartridge
k. hard-disk pack
l. tapes
m. jewel box
n. sector
o. i-drive
p. Picture CD
q. RAM
r. solid-state storage
s. track
t. writing

1. A type of storage that is volatile. _____
2. The process of saving a file to a secondary storage device. _____
3. Time required to retrieve data and programs. _____
4. Also known as a diskette or disk. _____
5. Closed concentric ring on a disk on which data is recorded. _____
6. Wedge-shaped section of a track. _____
7. Zip disks, SuperDisks, HiFD disks. _____
8. Runs through each track of a stack of platters. _____
9. Several platters aligned one above the other, allowing greater storage capacity. _____
10. Hardware and software that anticipates data needs. _____
11. Increases storage capacity by reducing the amount of space required to store data and programs. _____
12. Used to protect optical disks. _____
13. CD-R drive. _____
14. Special CD format for storing digital pictures. _____
15. Stores data electronically and has no moving parts. _____
16. Solid-state storage device used in portable computers. _____
17. Free or low-cost storage available at special service Web sites. _____
18. Provide fast direct access. _____
19. Provide slower sequential access. _____
20. Also known as an internal hard disk. _____

For an interactive version of this matching exercise, consult your Computing Essentials CD or visit our Web site at www.olearyseries.com/CE06 and select Matching.

OPEN-ENDED

On a separate sheet of paper, respond to each question or statement.

1. Discuss the three most likely successors to the 1.44 MB 3½-inch floppy.
2. What are the three types of hard disks? Describe three ways to improve hard disk performance.
3. What are the two most common optical disk formats? Describe the basic types for each format.
4. Discuss solid-state storage, Internet hard drives, and magnetic tape. What are the advantages and disadvantages of each?
5. Discuss mass storage, enterprise storage systems, and mass storage devices.

Music from the Internet

1

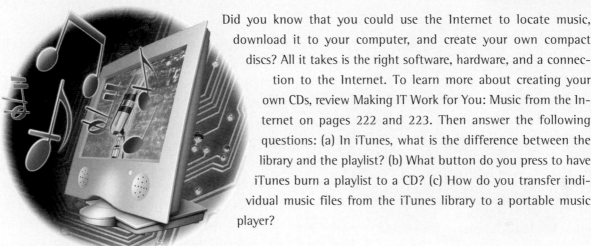

Did you know that you could use the Internet to locate music, download it to your computer, and create your own compact discs? All it takes is the right software, hardware, and a connection to the Internet. To learn more about creating your own CDs, review Making IT Work for You: Music from the Internet on pages 222 and 223. Then answer the following questions: (a) In iTunes, what is the difference between the library and the playlist? (b) What button do you press to have iTunes burn a playlist to a CD? (c) How do you transfer individual music files from the iTunes library to a portable music player?

iPod

2

Apple's iPod is a personal portable music player that stores a large number of digital music files. Connect to our Web site at www.olearyseries.com/CE06 and select Using Technology to link to the iPod Web site.

Once connected, read about the features and capabilities of iPod, and then answer the following questions: (a) How are music files transferred to iPod? (b) What type of secondary storage does iPod use? (c) What is iPod's storage capacity?

1

How Music is Downloaded from the Internet

One of the most popular activities on the Internet is to locate and download music files. Using a CD burner, the files are saved onto an optical disk. These disks can then be played in a variety of different types of devices. After viewing the Animation "How Music is Downloaded" from your Computing Essentials CD or our Web site at www.olearyseries.com/CE06, answer the following questions: (a) Go to the Web and find a Web site where you can download music from the Internet. What Web site did you find? How much do they charge to download music? (b) When you download music from the Internet, where is it stored on your computer? (c) Name three ways you can play music from the Internet.

2

File Compression

A common problem for computer users is that they run out of hard disk space. File compression software can open up space on a full hard drive, improve system performance, and make files easier to find and organize. To learn more about "File Compression" consult your Computing Essentials CD or visit our Web site at www. olearyseries.com/CE06 and select Expansions. Then answer the following questions: (a) What are the two types of file compression? How do they differ? (b) What type of file compression is used for home movies? Why? (c) What type of file compression is used for a resume? Why? (d) Research a compression/decompression utility on the Web. What types of files does your utility create? Is this a lossy or lossyless file compression?

1 DVD

DVD is a newer optical format that is rapidly replacing CDs as the standard in optical disks. DVDs can store 17 gigabytes, more than 30 times the capacity of a CD. Many of today's microcomputers come with DVD drives. Write a one-page paper titled "DVD Technology" that addresses the following: (a) Define DVD-ROM, DVD-R, and DVD-RW. (b) Compare DVD technology to other types of secondary storage in terms of speed, portability, and capacity. (c) Give examples of applications where a DVD would be the best choice for storage. (d) What are some applications where a DVD would not be the best choice? Explain your answers.

2 CD-R and Music Files

Burning a custom CD of your favorite music is a popular use of secondary storage. Many sites on the Web offer free music that you can download. However, not all music files that are available on the Internet are freely distributable. Consider the following questions and write a one-page paper addressing them: (a) Is it fair to make a copy on your computer of a CD you have purchased? (b) Would it be fair to give a burned copy of a CD to a friend? What if the friend would not have otherwise purchased that CD? (c) People have been making illegal copies of music cassette tapes for some time. How is using the Internet to make and distribute copies of music receiving so much attention?

COMMUNICATIONS AND NETWORKS

COMPETENCIES

After you have read this chapter, you should be able to:

1 Discuss connectivity, the wireless revolution, and communication systems.

2 Describe physical and wireless communications channels.

3 Discuss connection devices, including modems, T1, DSL, cable modem, and satellite connections.

4 Describe data transmission factors, including bandwidths and protocols.

5 Discuss networks and key network terminology.

6 Describe different types of networks, including local area, metropolitan area, and wide area networks.

7 Describe network architectures, including configurations and strategies.

8 Describe organizational uses of Internet technologies, including intranets, extranets, and firewalls.

Connectivity
Provides incredible power to you while at and away from your desk

Communication Channels
Carry data via telephone lines, coaxial cables, microwave, and satellite.

Connection Devices
Convert analog and digital signals. Modems, DSL, cable, and satellites provide connections.

CHAPTER 9

Communications has extended our uses for the microcomputer enormously. The mobile telephone and other wireless technologies are revolutionizing how we use computers today. You can connect your microcomputer to the other people's microcomputers, to the Internet, and to other, larger computers located throughout the world. As we've mentioned earlier, this connectivity puts incredible power on your desk. The result is increased productivity—for you as an individual and for the groups and organizations of which you are a member. Connectivity has become particularly important in business, where individuals now find themselves connected in networks to other individuals and departments.

Communication systems are the electronic systems that transmit data over communications lines from one location to another. You might use a wearable computer and a satellite communication system to access the Internet from almost anywhere. You might work for an organization whose computer system is spread throughout a building, or even throughout the country or world. Or you might use telecommunications lines—telephone lines—to tap into information located in an outside data bank. You could then transmit it to your microcomputer for your own reworking and analysis.

You can even set up a network in your home or apartment using existing telephone lines. Or you can set up a wireless network. Then you can share files, use one Internet connection, and play interactive games with others in your home.

Competent end users need to understand the concept of connectivity, the impact of the wireless revolution, and the elements of a communications system. Additionally, they need to understand the basics of communication channels, connection devices, data transmission, networks, network architectures, and network types.

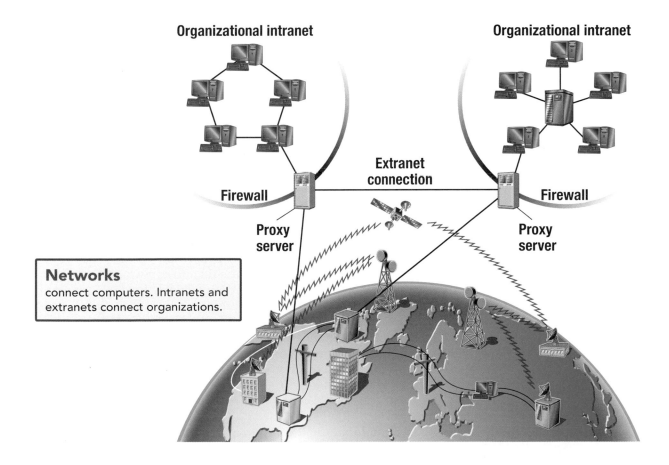

Organizational intranet

Organizational intranet

Extranet connection

Firewall

Firewall

Proxy server

Proxy server

Networks
connect computers. Intranets and extranets connect organizations.

COMMUNICATIONS

Connectivity relates to linking people and resources by networks. The wireless revolution allows Web-enabled devices to connect to the Internet from almost anywhere in the world. Communication systems comprise sending and receiving devices, a communication channel, connection devices, and transmission specifications.

Computer **communications** is the process of sharing data, programs, and information between two or more computers. We have discussed numerous applications that depend on communication systems, including:

- **E-mail**—provides a fast, efficient alternative to traditional mail by sending and receiving electronic documents.
- **Instant messaging**—supports direct, "live" electronic communication between two or more friends or buddies.
- **Internet telephone**—provides a very low cost alternative to long-distance telephone calls using electronic voice delivery.
- **Electronic commerce**—buying and selling goods electronically.

In this chapter, we will focus on the communication systems that support these and many other applications. Connectivity, the wireless revolution, and communication systems are key concepts and technologies for the 21st century.

CONNECTIVITY

Connectivity is a concept related to using computer networks to link people and resources. For example, connectivity means that you can connect your microcomputer by telephone or other telecommunications links to other computers and information sources almost anywhere. With this connection, you are linked to the world of larger computers and the Internet. This includes minicomputers and mainframes and their extensive information resources. Thus, becoming computer competent and knowledgeable becomes a matter of knowing not only about connectivity through networks to microcomputers, but also about larger computer systems and their information resources.

THE WIRELESS REVOLUTION

The single most dramatic change in connectivity and communications in the past five years has been the widespread use of mobile or wireless telephones. Students, parents, teachers, business people, and others routinely talk and communicate with these devices. It is estimated that over 600 million mobile telephones are in use worldwide. This wireless technology allows individuals to stay connected with one another from almost anywhere at any time.

So what's the revolution? While this wireless technology was originally intended for voice communication, it is now becoming widely used to support all kinds of communication, especially computer communication. In addition, recently released wireless technology promises to allow a wide variety of nearby devices to communicate with one another without any physical connection. You can share a high-speed printer, share data files, and collaborate on working documents with a nearby coworker without having your computers connected by cables or telephone—wireless communication. Other wireless technology allows individuals to connect to the Internet and share information from almost anywhere in the world. (See Figure 9-1.) But is it a revolution? Most experts say yes and that the revolution is just beginning.

COMMUNICATION SYSTEMS

Communication systems are electronic systems that transmit data from one location to another. Whether wired or wireless, every communication system has four basic elements. (See Figure 9-2.)

- **Sending** and **receiving devices.** These are often a computer or specialized communication device. They originate (send) as well as accept (receive) messages in the form of data, information, and/or instructions.
- **Communication channel.** This is the actual connecting or **transmission medium** that carries the message. This medium can be a physical wire or cable, or it can be wireless.
- **Connection devices.** These devices, also known as **communication devices,** act as an interface between the sending and receiving devices and the communication channel. They convert outgoing messages into a form and format that can travel across the communication channel. They also reverse the process for incoming messages.
- **Data transmission specifications.** These are rules and procedures that coordinate the sending and receiving devices by precisely defining how the message will be sent across the communication channel.

Figure 9-1 Connectivity options

For example, if you wanted to send an e-mail to a friend, you could create and send the message using your computer, the *sending device.* Your modem, a *connection device,* would modify and format the message so that it could travel efficiently across *communication channels,* such as telephone lines. The specifics describing how the message is modified, reformatted, and sent would be described in the *data transmission specifications.* After your message traveled across the channel, the receiver's modem, a connection device, would reform it so that it could be displayed on your friend's computer, the *receiving device.* (Note: This example presents the basic communication system elements involved in sending e-mail. It does not and is not intended to demonstrate all the specific steps and equipment involved in an e-mail delivery system.)

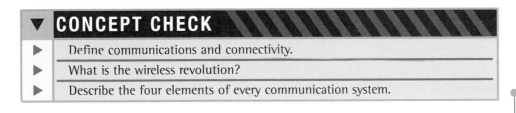

▼ CONCEPT CHECK

▶ Define communications and connectivity.

▶ What is the wireless revolution?

▶ Describe the four elements of every communication system.

Figure 9-2 Basic elements of a communication system

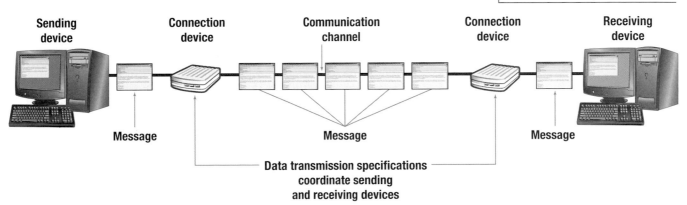

Communication channels carry data. Telephone lines, coaxial cables, and fiber–optical cable are physical channels. Infrared, broadcast radio, microwave, and satellite are wireless channels.

Communication channels are an essential element of every communication system. These channels actually carry the data from one computer to another. There are two categories of communication channels. One category connects sending and receiving devices by providing a physical connection, such as a wire or cable. The other category is wireless.

PHYSICAL CONNECTIONS

Physical connections use a solid medium to connect sending and receiving devices. These connections include telephone lines (twisted pair), coaxial cable, and fiber-optic cable.

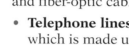

Figure 9-3   Twisted pair cable

Figure 9-4   Coaxial cable

Figure 9-5   Fiber-optic cable

- **Telephone lines** you see strung on poles consist of **twisted pair cable,** which is made up of hundreds of copper wires. A single twisted pair culminates in a wall jack into which you can plug your phone and computer. (See Figure 9-3.) Telephone lines have been the standard transmission medium for years for both voice and data. However, they are now being phased out by more technically advanced and reliable media.

- **Coaxial cable,** a high-frequency transmission cable, replaces the multiple wires of telephone lines with a single solid-copper core. (See Figure 9-4.) In terms of the number of telephone connections, a coaxial cable has over 80 times the transmission capacity of twisted pair. Coaxial cable is used to deliver television signals as well as to connect computers in a network.

- **Fiber-optic cable** transmits data as pulses of light through tiny tubes of glass. (See Figure 9-5.) In terms of the number of telephone connections, fiber-optic cable has over 26,000 times the transmission capacity of twisted pair cable. Compared to coaxial cable, they are lighter and more reliable at transmitting data. They transmit information using beams of light at light speeds instead of pulses of electricity, making them far faster than copper cable. Fiber-optic cable is rapidly replacing twisted pair cable telephone lines.

WIRELESS CONNECTIONS

Wireless connections do not use a solid substance to connect sending and receiving devices. Rather, they use the air itself. Primary technologies used for wireless connections are infrared, broadcast radio, microwave, and satellite.

- **Infrared** uses infrared light waves to communicate over short distances. It is sometimes referred to as **line of sight communication** because the light waves can only travel in a straight line. This requires that sending and receiving devices must be in clear view of one another without any obstructions blocking that view. One of the most common applications is to transfer data and information from a portable device such as a notebook computer or PDA, to a desktop computer.

- **Broadcast radio** communication uses special sending and receiving towers called **transceivers.** These transceivers send and receive radio signals from wireless devices. For example, cellular telephones and many

Web-enabled devices use broadcast radio to place telephone calls and/or to connect to the Internet. Some end users connect their notebook or handheld computers to a cellular telephone to access the Web from remote locations. Most of these Web-enabled devices follow a standard known as **Wi-FI (wireless fidelity).** Also known as **802.11,** this wireless standard is widely used to connect computers to each other and to the Internet.

- **Microwave** communication uses high-frequency radio waves. Like infrared, microwave communication provides line of sight communication because microwaves travel in a straight line. Because the waves cannot bend with the curvature of the earth, they can be transmitted only over relatively short distances. Thus, microwave is a good medium for sending data between buildings in a city or on a large college campus. For longer distances, the waves must be relayed by means of **microwave stations** with **microwave dishes** or antennas. (See Figure 9-6.) These stations can be installed on towers, high buildings, and mountaintops.

Figure 9-6   Microwave dish

    Bluetooth is a short range wireless communication standard that uses microwaves to transmit data over short distances of up to approximately 33 feet. Unlike traditional microwaves, Bluetooth does not require line of sight communication. Rather it uses radio waves that can pass through nearby walls and other nonmetal barriers. It is anticipated that within the next few years, this technology will be widely used to connect a variety of different communication devices.

- **Satellite** communication uses satellites orbiting about 22,000 miles above the earth as microwave relay stations. (See Figure 9-7.) Many of these are offered by Intelsat, the International Telecommunications Satellite Consortium, which is owned by 114 governments and forms a worldwide communications system. Satellites rotate at a precise point and speed above the earth. They can amplify and relay microwave signals from one transmitter on the ground to another. Satellites can be used to send and receive large volumes of data. **Uplink** is a term relating to sending data to a satellite. **Downlink** refers to receiving data from a satellite. The major drawback to satellite communication is that bad weather can sometimes interrupt the flow of data.

Figure 9-7   Satellite

    One of the most interesting applications of satellite communications is for **global positioning.** A network of 24 satellites owned and managed by the Defense Department continuously sends location information to earth. **Global positioning system (GPS)** devices use that information to uniquely determine the geographic location of the device. Available in some automobiles to provide navigational support, these systems are often mounted into the dash with a monitor to display maps and speakers to provide spoken directions. (See Figure 9-8.)

For a summary of communication channels, see Figure 9-9.

Figure 9-8   GPS navigation

CONCEPT CHECK

▶ What are communication channels?

▶ Compare telephone, coaxial, and fiber-optic cables.

▶ Compare physical and wireless channels.

▶ What is Wi-FI? Bluetooth? GPS?

Channel	Description
Twisted pair	Copper wire, standard voice telephone line
Coaxial cable	Solid copper core, more than 80 times the capacity of twisted pair
Fiber-optic cable	Light carries data, more than 26,000 times the capacity of twisted pair
Infrared	Infrared light travels in a straight line
Broadcast radio	Radio waves used by cellular telephones and other wireless devices
Microwave	High-frequency radio waves, travels in straight line through the air
Satellite	Microwave relay station in the sky, used by GPS devices

Figure 9-9   Types of communication channels

CONNECTION DEVICES

Conventional modems convert analog and digital signals. External, internal, PC Card, and wireless are types of modems. Leased high speed telephone lines, DSL, cable modems, and satellites are types of connections.

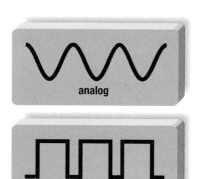

Figure 9-10   Analog versus digital signals

A great deal of computer communication takes place over telephone lines. However, because the telephone was originally designed for voice transmission, telephones typically send and receive **analog signals,** which are continuous electronic waves. Computers, in contrast, send and receive **digital signals.** (See Figure 9-10.) These represent the presence or absence of an electronic pulse—the on/off binary signals we mentioned in Chapter 6. To convert the digital signals to analog signals and vice versa, you need a modem.

MODEMS

The word **modem** is short for *modulator-demodulator.* **Modulation** is the name of the process of converting from digital to analog. **Demodulation** is the process of converting from analog to digital. The modem enables digital microcomputers to communicate across analog telephone lines. This communication includes both voice and data communications.

The speed with which modems transmit data varies. This speed, called **transfer speed** or **transfer rate,** is typically measured in **bits per second (bps).** (See Figure 9-11.) The higher the speed, the faster you can send and receive information. For example, transferring an image like Figure 9-10, might take 75 seconds with a 33.6 kbps modem and only 45 seconds with a 56 kbps modem.

There are four basic types of modems: external, internal, PC Card, and wireless. (See Figure 9-12.)

Unit	Speed
bps	bits per second
kbps	thousand bits per second
mbps	million bits per second
gbps	billion bits per second

Figure 9-11   Transfer speeds

- The **external modem** stands apart from the computer and typically is connected by a cable to the computer's serial port. Another cable connects the modem to the telephone wall jack.
- The **internal modem** consists of a plug-in circuit board inside the system unit. A telephone cable connects the modem to the telephone wall jack.

Figure 9-12 Basic types of modems

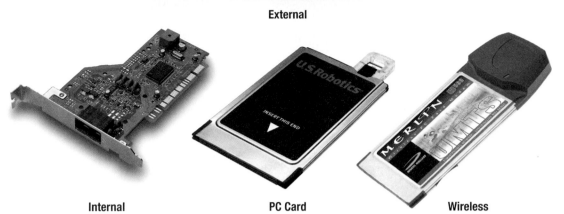

| Internal | PC Card | Wireless |

External

- The **PC Card modem** is a credit card-size expansion board that is inserted into portable computers. A telephone cable connects the modem to the telephone wall jack.
- A **wireless modem** may be internal, external, or a PC Card. Unlike the other modems, it does not use cables. Instead, wireless modems send and receive through the air.

CONNECTION SERVICE

Standard telephone lines and conventional modems provide what is called a **dial-up service.** Although still the most popular type of connection service, dial-up service is quite slow, and many users find it inadequate to meet their communication needs.

For years, large corporations have been leasing special high-speed lines from telephone companies. These lines—known as **T1, T2, T3,** and **T4 lines**—support all digital communications, do not require conventional modems, and provide very high capacity. Unfortunately, this type of connection is very expensive. For example, T1 lines provide a speed of 1.5 mbps (over 26 times as fast as a conventional modem) and cost several thousand dollars.

While the special high-speed lines are too costly for most individuals, there are affordable connections that provide significantly higher capacity than standard dial-up service. These include DSL, cable modems, and satellite. For a comparison of typical user connection costs and speeds, see Figure 9-13.

- **Digital subscriber line (DSL)** uses existing telephone lines to provide high-speed connections. **ADSL (asymmetric digital subscriber line)** is one of the most widely used types of DSL. This technology is widely available in most areas.

Type	Monthly Fee	Speed	Seconds to Receive Image
Dial-up	$16	56 kbps	45.0 seconds
DSL	50	1.5 mbps	1.7 seconds
Cable modem	45	1.5 mbps	1.7 seconds
Satellite	60	900 kbps	2.8 seconds

- **Cable modems** use existing television cables to provide high-speed connections as fast as a T1 or DSL connection, at a lower cost. Although cable connections reach 90 percent of the homes in America, all cable companies do not support cable modems.

Figure 9-13 Typical user connection costs and speeds

Industry observers, however, predict 100 percent availability within the next few years.

- **Satellite/air connection services** use satellites and the air to download (down link) or send data to users at a rate seven times faster than dial-up connections. While older satellite services could not upload (uplink) or send data to satellites and had to rely on slow dial-up connections, newer two-way satellite connections are now available. While slower than DSL and cable modems, satellite/air connections are available almost anywhere that a satellite-receiving disk can be aimed at the southern skies.

▼ CONCEPT CHECK

▶ What is the function of a modem?

▶ Compare the four types of modems.

▶ Describe the high-speed Internet connection options affordable to most users.

DATA TRANSMISSION

Bandwidth measures capacity of communication channel. Protocols are rules for exchanging data.

Several factors affect how data is transmitted. These factors include bandwidth and protocols.

BANDWIDTH

Bandwidth is a measurement of the width or capacity of the communication channel. Effectively, it means how much information can move across the communication channel in a given amount of time. For example, to transmit text documents, a slow bandwidth would be acceptable. However, to effectively transmit video and audio, a wider bandwidth is required. There are three categories of bandwidth.

- **Voiceband,** also known as **voice grade** and **low bandwidth,** is used for standard telephone communication. Microcomputers with standard modems and dial-up service use this bandwidth. While effective for transmitting text documents, it is too slow for many types of transmission including high-quality audio and video. Typical speeds are 56 to 96 kbps.
- **Medium band** is the bandwidth used in special leased lines to connect minicomputers and mainframes as well as to transmit data over long distances. Unlike voice band and broadband, medium band is not typically used by individuals.
- **Broadband** is the bandwidth used for high-capacity transmissions. Microcomputers with DSL, cable, and satellite connections as well as other more specialized high-speed devices use this bandwidth. It is capable of effectively meeting most of today's communication needs, including transmitting high-quality audio and video. Speeds are typically 1.5 mbps, although much higher speeds are possible.

PROTOCOLS

For data transmission to be successful, sending and receiving devices must follow a set of communication rules for the exchange of information. These rules for exchanging data between computers are known as **protocols.**

The standard protocol for the Internet is **TCP/IP (transmission control protocol/Internet protocol).** The essential features of this protocol involve (1) identifying sending and receiving devices and (2) reformatting information for transmission across the Internet.

- **Identification:** Every computer on the Internet has a unique numeric address called an **IP address (Internet Protocol address).** Similar to the way a postal service uses addresses to deliver mail, the Internet uses IP addresses to deliver e-mail and to locate Web sites. Because these numeric addresses are difficult for people to remember and use, a system was developed to automatically convert text-based addresses to numeric IP addresses. This system uses a **domain name server (DNS)** that converts text-based addresses to IP addresses. For example, whenever you enter a URL, say www.mcgraw-hill.com, a DNS converts this to an IP address before a connection can be made. (See Figure 9-14.)

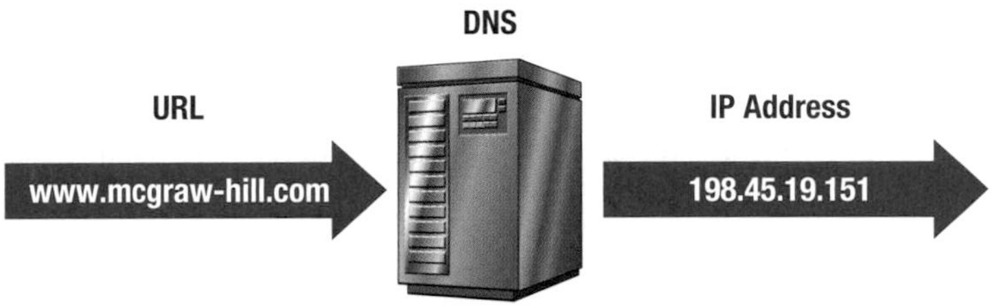

Figure 9-14   DNS converts text-based addresses to numeric IP addresses

- **Reformatting:** Information sent or transmitted across the Internet usually travels through numerous interconnected networks. Before the message is sent, it is reformatted or broken down into small parts called **packets.** Each packet is then sent separately over the Internet, possibly traveling different routes to one common destination. At the receiving end, the packets are reassembled into the correct order.

▼ CONCEPT CHECK

▶   What is bandwidth? Describe the three categories.

▶   What are protocols? What is TCP/IP? What is DNS? What are packets?

NETWORKS

> Computer networks connect computers. A node may be a client, server, hub, or host computer. Node, client, server, hub, NIC, NOS, distributed processing, host computer, and network manager are specialized network terms.

A **computer network** is a communication system that connects two or more computers so that they can exchange information and share resources. Networks can be set up in different arrangements to suit users' needs. (See Figure 9-15.)

TERMS

There are a number of specialized terms that describe computer networks. These terms include:

- **Node**—any device that is connected to a network. It could be a computer, printer, or data storage device.

Figure 9-15   Computer network

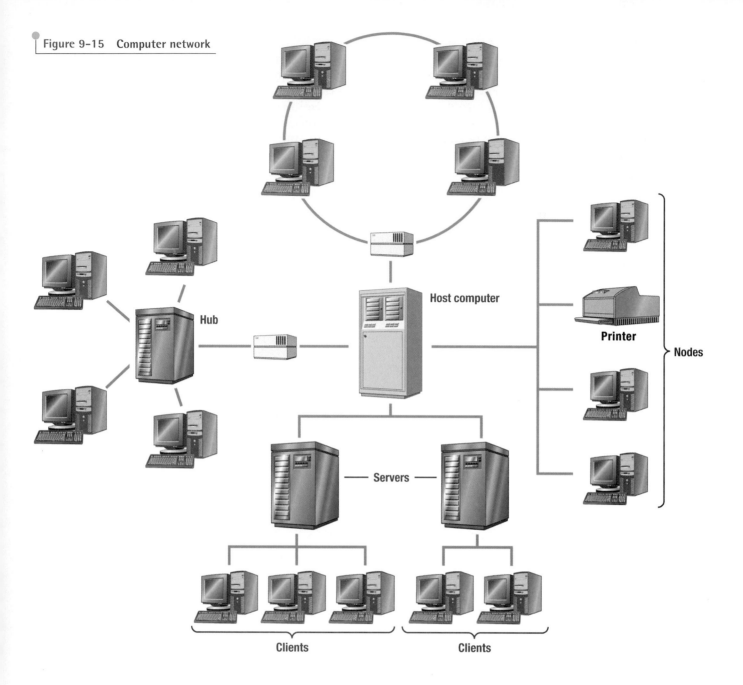

- **Client**—a node that requests and uses resources available from other nodes. Typically, a client is a user's microcomputer.
- **Server**—a node that shares resources with other nodes. **Dedicated servers** specialize in performing specific tasks. Depending on the specific task, they may be called an **application server, communication server, database server, file server, printer server,** or **Web server.**
- **Hub**—the center or central node for other nodes. This device can be a server or simply a connection point for cables from other nodes.
- **Network interface cards (NIC)**—as discussed in Chapter 6, these are expansion cards located within the system unit that connect the computer to a network. Sometimes referred to as a **LAN adapter.**
- **Network operating systems (NOS)**—control and coordinate the activities of all computers and other devices on a network. These activities include electronic communication and the sharing of information and resources.

- **Distributed processing**—a system in which computing power is located and shared at different locations. This type of system is common in decentralized organizations where divisional offices have their own computer systems. The computer systems in the divisional offices are networked to the organization's main or centralized computer.
- **Host computer**—a large centralized computer, usually a minicomputer or a mainframe.
- **Network manager**—a computer specialist, also known as **network administrator,** responsible for efficient network operations and implementation of new networks.

A network may consist only of microcomputers, or it may integrate microcomputers or other devices with larger computers. Networks can be controlled by all nodes working together equally or by specialized nodes coordinating and supplying all resources. Networks may be simple or complex, self-contained or dispersed over a large geographical area.

▼ CONCEPT CHECK

▶ What is a computer network? What are nodes, clients, servers, hubs, and host computers?

▶ What is the function of an NIC and an NOS?

▶ What is distributed processing and what is a network manager?

NETWORK TYPES

> Communications networks differ in geographical size. LANs, including home networks, connect nearby devices. MANs connect buildings in a city. WANs are countrywide and worldwide networks.

Clearly, different types of channels—cable or air—allow different kinds of networks to be formed. Telephone lines, for instance, may connect communications equipment within the same building or within a home. Networks may also be citywide and even international, using both cable and air connections. Local area, metropolitan area, and wide area networks are distinguished by the geographic area they serve.

LOCAL AREA NETWORKS

Networks with nodes that are in close physical proximity—within the same building, for instance—are called **local area networks (LANs).** Typically, LANs span distances less than a mile and are owned and operated by individual organizations. LANs are widely used by colleges, universities, and other types of organizations to link microcomputers and to share printers and other resources. For a simple LAN, see Figure 9-16.

The LAN represented in Figure 9-16 is a typical arrangement and provides two benefits: economy and flexibility. People can share costly equipment. For instance, the four microcomputers share the laser printer and the file server, which are expensive pieces of hardware. Other equipment or nodes may also be added to the LAN—for instance, more microcomputers, a mainframe computer, or optical-disk storage devices. Additionally, the **network gateway** is a

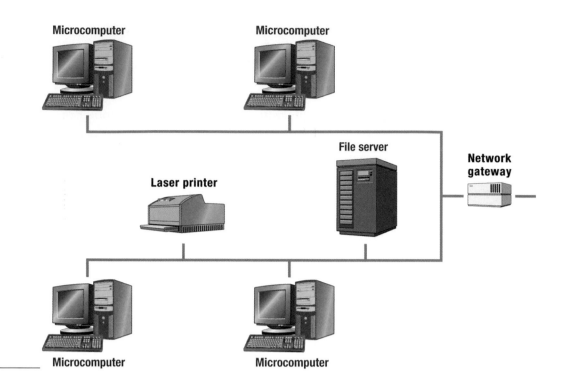

Microcomputer   Microcomputer

File server

Network gateway

Laser printer

Figure 9-16 Local area network

Microcomputer   Microcomputer

On the Web Explorations

Wireless home networks are becoming fast, cheap, and popular. To learn more about a company helping to "unwire" our homes, visit our Web site at

www.olearyseries.com/CE06

and select On the Web Explorations.

device that allows one LAN to be linked to other LANs or to larger networks. For example, the LAN of one office group may be connected to the LAN of another office group.

There are a variety of different standards or ways in which nodes can be connected to one another and ways in which their communications are controlled in a LAN. The most common standard is known as **Ethernet.** LANs using this standard are sometimes referred to as **Ethernet LANs.**

HOME NETWORKS

While LANs have been widely used within organizations for years, they are now being commonly used by individuals in their homes and apartments. These LANs, called **home networks,** allow different computers to share resources, including a common Internet connection. Computers can be connected in a variety of ways, including electrical wiring, telephone wiring, and special cables. One of the simplest ways, however, is without cables, or wireless.

A wireless local area network is typically referred to as a **wireless LAN (WLAN).** It uses radio frequencies to connect computers and other devices. All communications pass through the network's centrally located **wireless receiver** or **base station.** This receiver interprets incoming radio frequencies and routes communications to the appropriate devices. To see how home networks work, consult your Computing Essentials CD or visit our Web site at www.olearyseries.com/CE06 and select Animations.

To learn more about how to set up and use a wireless home network, see Making IT Work for You: Home Networking on page 252 and 253.

METROPOLITAN AREA NETWORKS

The next step up from the LAN is the **MAN**—the **metropolitan area network.** Also known as **regional networks,** MANs span distances up to 100 miles. These networks are frequently used as links between office buildings that are located throughout a city.

Unlike a LAN, a MAN is typically not owned by a single organization. Rather, it is either owned by a group of organizations who jointly own and operate the network or by a single network service provider who provides network services for a fee. **Cellular phone systems** expand the flexibility of MANs by allowing links to car phones and portable phones.

WIDE AREA NETWORKS

Wide area networks (WANs) are countrywide and worldwide networks. These networks provide access to regional service (MAN) providers and typically span distances greater than 100 miles. They use microwave relays and satellites to reach users over long distances—for example, from Los Angeles to Paris. Of course, the widest of all WANs is the Internet, which spans the entire globe.

The primary difference between a LAN, MAN, and WAN is the geographical range. Each may have various combinations of hardware, such as microcomputers, minicomputers, mainframes, and various peripheral devices.

▼ CONCEPT CHECK

▶ What are the three types of networks? What is their primary difference?

▶ What is a home network?

▶ What is a WLAN? What is a wireless receiver?

NETWORK ARCHITECTURE

> Network architecture describes how a computer network is configured and what strategies are employed. Configurations include star, bus, ring, and hierarchical. Strategies include terminal, client-server, and peer-to-peer.

Network architecture describes how a network is arranged and how resources are coordinated and shared. It encompasses a variety of different network specifics, including network configurations and strategies. Network configurations describe the physical arrangement of the network. Network strategies define how information and resources are shared.

Figure 9-17   Star network

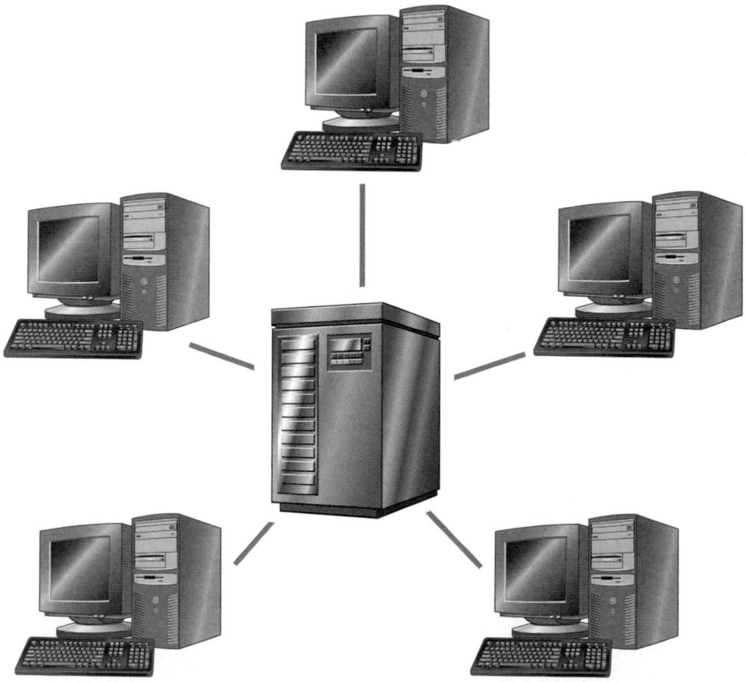

CONFIGURATIONS

A network can be arranged or configured in several different ways. This arrangement is called the network's **topology.** The four principal network topologies are star, bus, ring, and hierarchical.

In a **star network,** a number of small computers or peripheral devices are linked to a central unit. (See Figure 9-17.) The central unit is the **network hub** and is typically a host computer or file server.

All communications pass through this central unit. Control is maintained by **polling.** That is, each connecting device is asked ("polled") whether it has a message to send. Each device is then in turn allowed to send its message.

Communications and Networks

HOME NETWORKING

Computer networks are not just for corporations and schools anymore. If you have more than one computer, you can use a home network to share files and printers, to allow multiple users access to the Internet at the same time, and to play multiplayer computer games.

Installing the Network   Each computer on a wireless network requires a wireless network card. Cards are often available in kits that also include a base station. Once the cards are installed in each computer, the base station must be configured for sharing the Internet. Then, each computer can be configured to share files and printers. For example, to set up a wireless network using Agere System's Residential Gateway and Windows XP:

1 ● Install a compatible wireless card in each computer. In most cases, simply plugging the card in is all that is required.

● Run the included software to set up the base station for accessing and sharing the Internet.

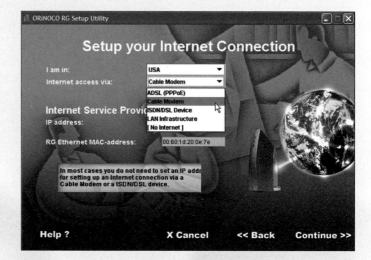

2 ● Click *Start/My Network Places* and click *Set up a home or small office network.*

● Follow the instructions in the wizard to set up your computer for file and printer sharing and to access the Internet through the residential gateway.

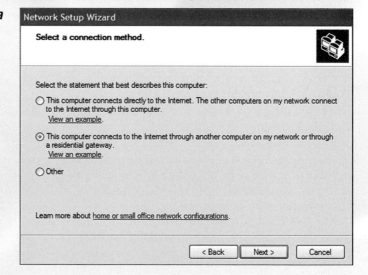

Using the Network   Now your computers are ready to share their resources. The four most common uses of a home network are to share files, printers, and Internet access and to run multiplayer computer games.

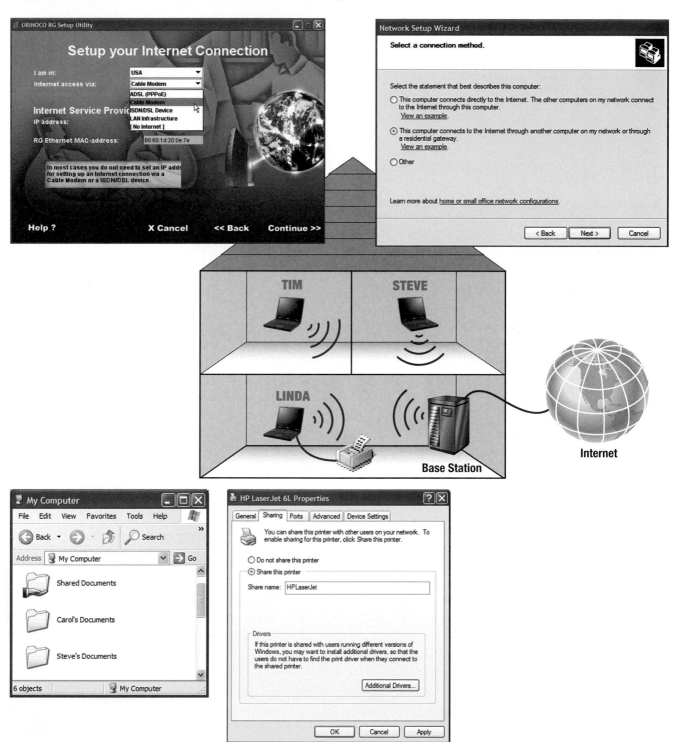

Home networks are continually changing, and some of the specifics presented in this Making IT Work for You may have changed. To learn about other ways to make information technology work for you, consult your Computing Essentials CD or visit our Web site at www.olearyseries/CE06 and select Making IT Work for You.

printer

Figure 9–18   Bus network

One particular advantage of the star topology is that it can be used to support a **time-sharing system.** That is, several users can share resources (time) on a central computer. The star is a common topology for linking microcomputers to a mainframe that allows access to an organization's database.

In a **bus network** each device in the network handles its own communications control. There is no host computer. All communications travel along a common connecting cable called a **bus** or **backbone.** (See Figure 9-18.) As the information passes along the bus, it is examined by each device to see if the information is intended for it.

The bus network is typically used when only a few microcomputers are to be linked together. This arrangement is common for sharing data stored on different microcomputers. Because a star network typically provides a more direct path to shared resources, it is more efficient than a bus network for sharing these resources. However, a bus network is easy to install and is less expensive.

Figure 9–19   Ring network

In a **ring network,** each device is connected to two other devices, forming a ring. (See Figure 9-19.) There is no central file server or computer. Messages are passed around the ring until they reach the correct destination. With microcomputers, the ring arrangement is the least frequently used of the four networks. However, it often is used to link mainframes, especially over wide geographical areas. These mainframes tend to operate fairly autonomously. They perform most or all of their own processing and only occasionally share data and programs with other mainframes.

A ring network is useful in a decentralized organization because it makes possible a **distributed data processing system.** That is, computers can perform processing tasks at their own dispersed locations. However, they also can share programs, data, and other resources with each other.

The **hierarchical network**—also called a **hybrid network**—consists of several computers linked to a central host computer, just like a star network. However, these other computers are also hosts to other, smaller computers or to peripheral devices. (See Figure 9-20.)

Thus, the host at the top of the hierarchy could be a mainframe. The computers below the mainframe could be minicomputers, and those below, microcomputers. The hierarchical network allows various computers to share databases, processing power, and different output devices.

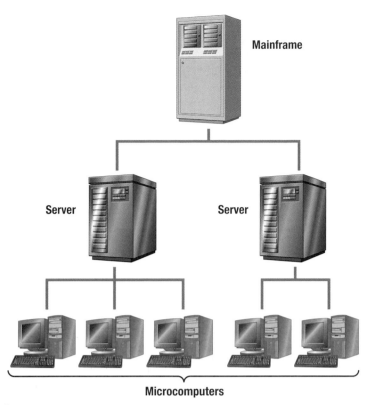

Figure 9-20   Hierarchical network

Topology	Description
Star	Several computers connected to a central server or host; all communications travel through central server; good for sharing common resources
Bus	Computers connected by a common line; communication travels along this common line; less expensive than star
Ring	Each computer connected to two others forming a ring; communications travel around ring; often used to link mainframe computers in decentralized organizations
Hierarchical	One top-level host computer connected to next-level computers, which are connected to third-level computers; often used in centralized organizations

Figure 9-21   Principal network configurations

A hierarchical network is useful in centralized organizations. For example, different departments within an organization may have individual micro-computers connected to departmental minicomputers. The minicomputers in turn may be connected to the corporation's mainframe, which contains data and programs accessible to all.

For a summary of the network configurations, see Figure 9-21.

▼ CONCEPT CHECK

► What is a network topology? What are the four principal network topologies?

► What is a time-sharing system? What is a distributed data processing system?

STRATEGIES

Every network has a **strategy,** or way of coordinating the sharing of informa-tion and resources. The most common network strategies are terminal, client/server, and peer-to-peer systems.

In a **terminal network system,** processing power is centralized in one large computer, usually a mainframe. The nodes connected to this host computer are either terminals with little or no processing capabilities or microcomputers running special software that allows them to act as terminals. (See Figure 9-22.) The star and hierarchical networks are typical configurations with UNIX as the operating system.

Many airline reservation systems are terminal systems. A large central com-puter maintains all the airline schedules, rates, seat availability, and so on. Travel agents use terminals to connect to the central computer and to schedule reservations. Although the tickets may be printed along with travel itineraries

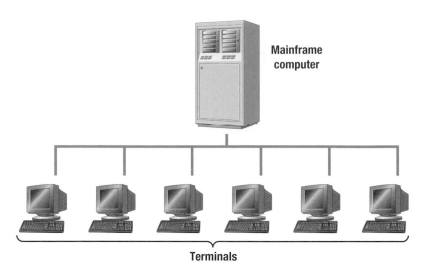

Mainframe computer

Terminals

Figure 9-22 Terminal network system

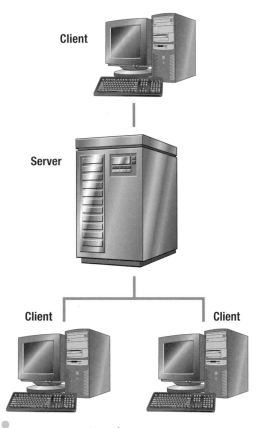

Client

Server

Client Client

Figure 9-23 Client/server network system

at the agent's desk, nearly all processing is done at the central computer.

One advantage of terminal network systems is the centralized location and control of technical personnel, software, and data. One disadvantage is the lack of control and flexibility for the end user. Another disadvantage is that terminal systems do not use the full processing power available with microcomputers. Though the terminal strategy was once very popular, most new systems do not use it.

Client/server network systems use one computer to coordinate and supply services to other nodes on the network. The server provides access to resources such as Web pages, databases, application software, and hardware. (See Figure 9-23.) This strategy is based on specialization. Server nodes coordinate and supply specialized services, and client nodes request the services. Commonly used network operating systems are Novell's NetWare, Microsoft's Windows NT, IBM's LAN Server, and Banyan Vines.

Client/server network systems are widely used on the Internet. For example, **Napster** (the once popular music service) employed a version of this strategy. Music enthusiasts used the Internet to connect to Napster servers. The Napster servers provided lists of music files (some of which were copyrighted) that were available to be copied from participating Napster users. The music enthusiasts were clients requesting services (information regarding the location of others willing to share music files) from Napster servers. To learn more about Napstar, consult your Computing Essentials CD or visit our Web site at www.olearyseries.com/CE06 and select Expansions.

One advantage of the client/server network strategy is the ability to handle very large networks efficiently. Another advantage is the availability of powerful network management software to monitor and control network activities. The major disadvantages are the cost of installation and maintenance.

In a **peer-to-peer network system,** nodes have equal authority and can act as both clients and servers. For example, one microcomputer can obtain files located on another microcomputer and can also provide files to other microcomputers. (See Figure 9-24.) A typical configuration for a peer-to-peer system is the bus network. Commonly used network operating systems are Novell's NetWare Lite, Microsoft's Windows NT, and Apple's Macintosh Peer-to-Peer LANs.

Many current popular music sharing services use this network strategy. In fact, the Napster approach was actually a hybrid network in which the Napster server worked in a client-server environment providing a service to clients. Once a Napster user had the location of requested music files, he or she could sign off the network and then connect directly to the source forming a very simple peer-to-peer network. Each node could act as a server by providing access to music files and a client by receiving copies of music files. Today, **Gnutella** is a widely used peer-to-peer network system for sharing all kinds of files, including music files. Unlike the Napster approach, Gnutella networks directly connect users without a central server acting as the focal point for operations. There are various different versions of Gnutella. To learn more about one of the most popular versions, consult your Computing Essentials CD or visit our Web site at www.olearyseries.com/CE06 and select Expansions.

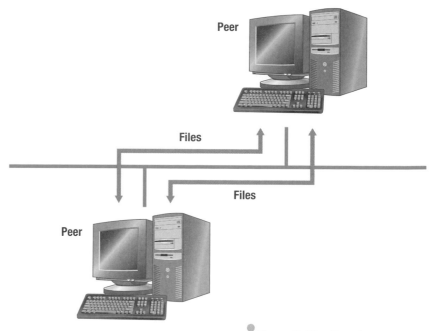

Figure 9-24 Peer-to-peer network system

There are several advantages to the peer-to-peer network strategy. The networks are inexpensive and easy to install, and they usually work well for smaller systems with fewer than 10 nodes. Unlike the client/server network strategy, network operations are not dependent upon a single central node. As the number of nodes increases, however, the performance of the network declines. Another disadvantage is the lack of powerful management software to effectively monitor a large network's activities. For these reasons, peer-to-peer networks are typically used by smaller networks within organizations and for sharing files on the Internet.

▼ CONCEPT CHECK

▶ What is a network strategy? Discuss the three most common network strategies.

▶ Compare the network strategies employed by Napster and Gnutella.

ORGANIZATIONAL INTERNETS: INTRANETS AND EXTRANETS

Intranets are private networks within an organization. Extranets are private networks connecting organizations. Organizational firewalls typically use proxy servers to provide security.

Computer networks in organizations have evolved over time. Most large organizations have a complex and wide range of different network configurations, operating systems, and strategies. Integrating or connecting all of these networks has been a very challenging task. One way is to apply Internet technologies to support communication within and between organizations using intranets and extranets.

INTRANETS

An **intranet** is a *private* network within an organization that resembles the Internet. Like the *public* Internet, intranets use browsers, Web sites, and Web pages. Intranets typically provide e-mail, mailing lists, newsgroups, and FTP services accessible only to those within the organization.

Organizations use intranets to provide information to their employees. Typical applications include electronic telephone directories, e-mail addresses, employee benefit information, internal job openings, and much more. Employees find surfing their organizational intranets to be as easy and as intuitive as surfing the Internet.

EXTRANETS

An **extranet** is a *private* network that connects *more than one* organization. Many organizations use Internet technologies to allow suppliers and others limited access to their networks. The purpose is to increase efficiency and reduce costs. For example, General Motors has thousands of suppliers for the parts that go into making an automobile. By having access to the production schedules, suppliers can schedule and deliver parts as they are needed at the General Motors assembly plants. In this way, General Motors can be assured of having adequate parts without maintaining large inventories.

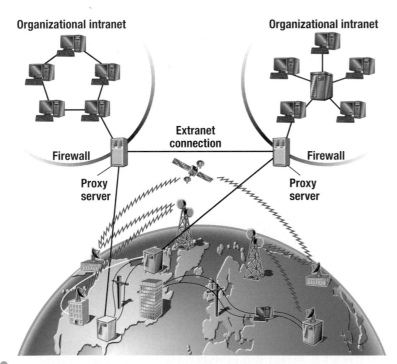

Figure 9-25 Intranets, extranets, firewalls, and proxy servers

FIREWALLS

Organizations have to be very careful to protect their information systems. A **firewall** is a security system designed to protect an organization's network against external threats. It consists of hardware and software that control access to a company's intranet or other internal networks.

Typically organizational firewalls include a special computer called a **proxy server.** This computer is a gatekeeper. All communications between the company's internal networks and the outside world must pass through it. By evaluating the source and the content of each communication, the proxy server decides whether it is safe to let a particular message or file pass into or out of the organization's network. (See Figure 9-25.)

Of course, end users have security issues as well. We are subject to many of the same types of security concerns that face organizations. Additionally, we need to be concerned about the privacy of our personal information. In the next chapter, we will discuss personal firewalls and other ways to protect personal privacy and security.

▼ **CONCEPT CHECK**

▶ What are intranets? Compare intranets to the Internet.

▶ What are extranets? Compare intranets and extranets.

▶ What are firewalls? What is a proxy server?

A Look to the Future

Toyota and Sony Create Wireless Robotic Car

Have you ever found yourself driving around lost in an unfamiliar city, wishing you could connect to the Internet and download driving directions? Have you ever longed for access to your favorite Internet radio station while you drive around? What if you could send and receive e-mail while you wait in traffic? Wouldn't it be convenient if your car would just send an e-mail whenever it needed maintenance? Toyota and Sony are collaborating on a car called "Pod" that does all this and more.

Pod stands for personalization on demand. Toyota hopes this new car will predict and respond to your moods, likes, and dislikes. It features lighting that may display red if you drive erratically or orange if you seem happy. It features voice recognition technology and responds to verbal commands. Pod is designed to learn and adapt to your driving habits and needs. Some say it is the car equivalent of the Sony AIBO robotic pet.

The Pod connects wirelessly to a portable terminal called the Mini Pod to share data and serve the user's needs. For example, Pod might use the information stored in the PDA-like Mini Pod to download songs from the Internet it thinks you might like. The Pod also uses GPS information and the Internet to make recommendations concerning local restaurants as you drive around.

Pod uses technology developed by Suzuki Motors to phone the owner if it is broken into or needs mechanical attention. Pod can communicate with other cars by using a horn messaging system. It also locates pedestrians and warns the driver to correct speed or course to avoid them. Pod can also phone ahead to your destination to advise those waiting if it detects you will be delayed. It may even alert you when you drive by restaurants that it thinks you may like.

Do these new features appeal to you? Do you think Americans will someday be driving cars that can connect to the Internet? Many new cars come equipped with wireless technology and GPS devices. Some car enthusiasts look forward to a car that senses your mood and downloads songs to match it. For now Pod is a concept vehicle, but many of the features it includes may soon be found in your next car. What do you think? Would you buy a car that communicates with other cars, the Internet, and you?

COMMUNICATIONS AND NETWORKS

COMMUNICATIONS

Communications is the process of sharing data, programs, and information between two or more computers. Applications include **e-mail, instant messaging, Internet telephones,** and **electronic commerce.**

Connectivity

Connectivity is a concept related to using computer networks to link people and resources. You can link or connect to large computers and the Internet providing access to extensive information resources.

The Wireless Revolution

Mobile or wireless telephones have brought dramatic changes in connectivity and communications. These wireless devices are becoming widely used for computer communication.

Communication Systems

Communication systems transmit data from one location to another. Four basic elements are:

- **Sending and receiving devices**
- **Communication channel (transmission medium)**
- **Connection (communication) devices**
- **Data transmission specifications**

COMMUNICATION CHANNELS

Communication channels carry data from one computer to another.

Physical Connections

Physical connections use a solid medium to connect sending and receiving devices. These connections include **telephone lines (twisted pair), coaxial cable,** and **fiber-optic cable.**

Wireless Connections

Wireless connections use air rather than solid substance to connect devices.

- **Infrared**—uses light waves over a short distance; **line of sight communication.**
- **Broadcast radio**—uses **transceivers** to collect radio waves. **Wi-FI (wireless fidelity, 802.11)** is widely used standard.
- **Microwave**—uses high-frequency radio waves; line of sight communication; uses **microwave stations** and **dishes; Bluetooth** is a widely used short range standard.
- **Satellite**—microwave relay station in the sky to **uplink** and **downlink** data; **GPS** provides **global positioning** to track geographic locations.

To be a competent end user you need to understand the concepts of connectivity, the wireless revolution, and communication systems. Additionally, you need to know the essential parts of communications technology, including channels, connection devices, data transmission, networks, network architectures, and network types.

CONNECTION DEVICES

External

Internal   **PC Card**   **Wireless**

Many communication systems use standard telephone lines and **analog signals.** Computers use **digital signals.**

Modems

Modems modulate (convert digital signals to analog) and **demodulate. Transfer speed (rate)** is measured in **bits per second.** Four types of conventional modems are **external, internal, PC Card modem,** and **Wireless.**

Connections Service

Dial-up services use standard telephone lines and conventional modems. **T1, T2, T3,** and **T4** support very high speed, all-digital transmission. More affordable technologies include **DSL (digital subscriber line, ADSL** widely used), **cable modems,** and **satellite/air (satellites** to download data).

DATA TRANSMISSION

Bandwidth is a measure of a communication channel's width or capacity. Three bandwidths are: **voiceband (voice grade** or **low bandwidth), medium band** (uses special leased lines), **broadband** (high-capacity transmissions). **Protocols** are rules for exchanging data. **TCP/IP** is standard Internet protocol. **IP addresses** are unique numeric Internet addresses. **DNS** converts text-based addresses to numeric IP addresses. **Packets** are small parts of messages.

NETWORKS

Computer networks connect two or more computers.

Some specialized network terms include:

- **Node**—any device connected to a network.
- **Client**—node requesting resources.
- **Server**—node providing resources; specialized servers such as **application, communication, database, file, printer,** and **Web servers** are called **dedicated servers.**
- **Hub**—center or central node.
- **NIC (network interface cards)—LAN adapter** card for connecting to a network.
- **NOS (network operating system)**—controls and coordinates network operations.
- **Distributed processing**—system where processing is located and shared at different locations.
- **Host computer**—large centralized computer.
- **Network manager (administrator)**—network specialist responsible for network operations.

NETWORK TYPES

Networks can be citywide or even international, using both cable and air connections.

- **Local area networks (LAN)** connect nearby devices. **Network gateways** connect networks to one another. **Ethernet** is a LAN standard. These LANs are called **Ethernet LANs.**
- **Home networks** are LANs used in homes. **Wireless LANs (WLAN)** use a **wireless receiver (base station)** as a hub.
- **Metropolitan area networks (MANs, regional networks)** link office buildings within a city. **Cellular phone systems** link car phones and portable phones.
- **Wide Area Networks** or **WANs** are the largest type. They span states and countries or form worldwide networks. The Internet is the largest wide area network in the world.

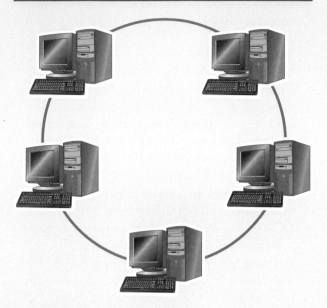

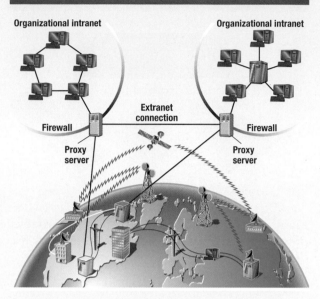

Network architecture describes how a computer network is configured and what strategies are employed.

Configurations

A network's configuration is called its **topology.** Principal topologies are: **star network** (each device is linked to the **network hub;** control maintained by **polling;** often used for **time-sharing systems), bus network** (nodes connect by cable called a **bus** or **backbone**), **ring network** (often used in **distributed data processing systems**), **hierarchical network (hybrid network).**

Strategies

Every network has a **strategy,** or way of sharing information and resources. Common **strategies** include:

- **Terminal network system**—a centralized computer distributes power to several terminals.
- **Client/server network system**—client computers request resources from a server computer; **Napster** servers operated with client/server strategy.
- **Peer-to-peer network system**—each computer acts as both a server and a client. **Gnutella** supports peer-to-peer file sharing.

Many organizations use Internet technologies to support communication within and between organizations using intranets and extranets.

Intranets

Intranets are *private* networks within an organization that resemble the Internet. Like the Internet, they use browsers, Web sites, and Web pages. Unlike the Internet, intranets are available only to those within the organization.

Extranets

Extranets are similar to intranets, except that extranets connect more than one organization. Extranets are often used to connect suppliers and producers to increase efficiency.

Firewalls

A **firewall** is a security system to protect against external threats. It consists of both hardware and software. All communications into and out of an organization pass through a special security computer called a **proxy server.**

802.11   (243)
analog signal   (244)
application server   (248)
asymmetric digital subscriber
   line (ADSL)   (245)
backbone   (254)
bandwidth   (246)
base station   (250)
bits per second (bps)   (244)
Bluetooth   (243)
broadcast radio   (242)
broadband   (246)
bus   (254)
bus network   (254)
cable modem   (245)
cellular phone system   (251)
client   (248)
client/server network
   system   (256)
coaxial cable   (242)
communication   (240)
communication channel   (241)
communication device   (241)
communication server   (248)
communication system   (241)
computer network   (247)
connection device   (241)
connectivity   (240)
data transmission
   specification   (241)
database server   (248)
dedicated server   (248)
demodulation   (244)
dial-up service   (245)
digital signal   (244)
digital subscriber line
   (DSL)   (245)
distributed data processing
   system   (254)
distributed processing   (249)
domain name server
   (DNS)   (247)
downlink   (243)
electronic commerce   (240)
e-mail   (240)

Ethernet   (250)
Ethernet LAN   (250)
external modem   (244)
extranet   (258)
fiber-optic cable   (242)
file server   (248)
firewall   (258)
global positioning   (243)
global positioning system
   (GPS)   (243)
Gnutella   (257)
hierarchical network   (254)
home network   (250)
host computer   (249)
hub   (248)
hybrid network   (254)
infrared   (242)
instant messaging   (240)
internal modem   (244)
Internet telephone   (240)
intranet   (258)
IP address (Internet Protocol
   address)   (247)
line of sight
   communication   (242)
local area network
   (LAN)   (249)
low bandwidth   (246)
medium band   (246)
metropolitan area network
   (MAN)   (250)
microwave   (243)
microwave dish   (243)
microwave station   (243)
modem   (244)
modulation   (244)
Napster   (256)
network administrator   (249)
network architecture   (251)
network gateway   (249)
network hub   (251)
network interface card
   (NIC)   (248)
network manager   (249)

network operating system
   (NOS)   (248)
node   (247)
packet   (247)
PC Card modem   (245)
peer-to-peer network
   system   (256)
polling   (251)
printer server   (248)
protocol   (247)
proxy server   (258)
receiving device   (241)
regional network   (250)
ring network   (254)
satellite   (243)
satellite/air connection
   service   (246)
sending device   (241)
server   (248)
star network   (251)
strategy   (255)
telephone line   (242)
terminal network system   (255)
time-sharing system   (254)
T1, T2, T3, T4 lines   (245)
topology   (251)
transceiver   (242)
transfer speed   (244)
transfer rate   (244)
transmission control
   protocol/Internet
   protocol (TCP/IP)   (247)
transmission medium   (241)
twisted pair cable   (242)
uplink   (243)
voiceband   (246)
voice grade   (246)
Web server   (248)
wide area network (WAN)   (251)
Wi-FI (wireless fidelity)   (243)
wireless LAN (WLAN)   (250)
wireless modem   (245)
wireless receiver   (250)

To test your knowledge of these key terms with animated flash cards, consult your Computing
Essentials CD or visit our Web site at www.olearyseries.com/CE06 and select Key Terms.

CROSSWORD

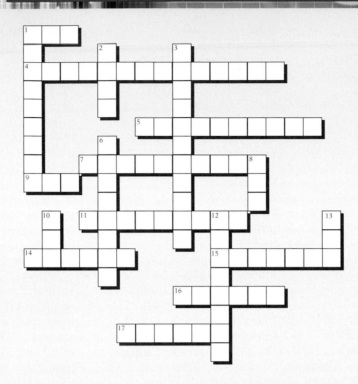

Across

1 Transfer speed or transfer rate.
4 Device that allows links between LANs.
5 Each device in the network handles its own communications.
7 Process that converts digital to analog.
9 Central node for other nodes.
11 Short range wireless communication standard.
14 Node that requests and uses resources available from other nodes.
15 Pieces of a message sent over the Internet.
16 Relating to sending data to a satellite.
17 Not digital.

Down

1 Measurement of the width of the communication channel.
2 Any device that is connected to a network.
3 Interprets and routes incoming radio frequencies.
6 Relating to receiving data from a satellite.
8 Network Interface Card.
10 Uses existing telephone lines to provide high-speed connections.
12 Configuration of a network.
13 Global Positioning System.

For an interactive version of this crossword, consult your Computing Essentials CD or visit our Web site at **www.olearyseries.com/CE06** and select Crossword.

Circle the letter or fill in the correct answer.

1. _____ use satellites to determine geographic locations.
   a. TCP/IP
   b. OSI
   c. GPS
   d. DSL
   e. NOS

2. Standard telephone lines and conventional modems provide what is called _____.
   a. network architecture
   b. broadband
   c. dial-up service
   d. data transmission
   e. channels

3. Modulation and demodulation are the processes of a(n) _____.
   a. connection device
   b. node
   c. modulator
   d. modem
   e. OSI

4. _____ is a measurement of the capacity of the communication channel.
   a. Protocol
   b. Packet
   c. Network architecture
   d. IP address
   e. Bandwidth

5. Every computer on the Internet has a unique numeric address called a(n) _____.
   a. packet
   b. protocol
   c. network bridge
   d. bandwidth
   e. IP address

6. _____ controls and coordinates the activities of all computers and devices on a network.
   a. TCP/IP
   b. NOS
   c. DNS
   d. OSI
   e. DSL

7. _____ use wireless receivers as a hub.
   a. WLANs
   b. Microwaves
   c. LANs
   d. MANs
   e. Satellites

8. _____ describes how the network is arranged and how the resources are coordinated and shared.
   a. Topology
   b. Communication channel
   c. Sharing system
   d. Domain name system
   e. Network architecture

9. In a _____ network, each device in the network handles its own communications control.
   a. bus
   b. client
   c. host
   d. sharing
   e. polling

10. Gnutella uses a _____ network strategy.
    a. terminal
    b. peer-to-peer
    c. client/server
    d. wireless
    e. NIC

For an interactive version of these multiple choice questions, consult your Computing Essentials CD or visit our Web site at www.olearyseries.com/CE06 and select Multiple Choice.

COMPUTING ESSENTIALS 2006

MATCHING

Match each numbered item with the most closely related lettered item. Write your answers in the spaces provided.

a. ADSL
b. bandwidth
c. Bluetooth
d. client
e. coaxial cable
f. communication system
g. computer network
h. dedicated
i. distributed processing
j. firewall
k. host
l. hybrid network
m. infrared
n. packets
o. protocol
p. star
q. TCP/IP
r. topology
s. transfer speed
t. wide area network

1. Transmits data over communication lines between locations. _____
2. Wireless connection that uses light waves over short distances. _____
3. High-frequency transmission cable with a single solid-copper core. _____
4. Uses microwaves to transmit data over short distances up to 33 feet. _____
5. Measured in bits per second. _____
6. Type of DSL. _____
7. Measurement of the width of a communication channel. _____
8. Rules for exchanging data between computers. _____
9. Standard protocol for the Internet. _____
10. Broken-down parts of a message sent over the Internet. _____
11. A large centralized computer. _____
12. The type of server that performs specific tasks. _____
13. Communications system connecting two or more computers that work together to exchange information and share resources. _____
14. A node that requests resources from other nodes. _____
15. Countrywide and worldwide networks. _____
16. The configuration of a network. _____
17. This type of network links computers and other devices to a central unit. _____
18. System in which computing power is located and shared at different locations. _____
19. Also known as a hierarchical network. _____
20. Protects network from external threats. _____

For an interactive version of this matching exercise, consult your Computing Essentials CD or visit our Web site at www.olearyseries.com/CE06 and select Matching.

OPEN-ENDED

On a separate sheet of paper, respond to each question or statement.

1. Define and discuss connectivity, the wireless revolution, and communications.
2. Identify and describe the various physical and wireless communication channels.
3. Identify the standard Internet protocol and discuss its essential features.
4. Define and discuss the four principal network topologies.
5. Define and discuss the three most common network strategies.

Home Networking

1

Computer networks are not just for corporations and schools anymore. If you have more than one computer, you can use a home network to share files and printers, to allow multiple users access to the Internet at the same time, and to play multiplayer computer games. To learn more about this technology, review Making IT Work for You: Home Networking on pages 252 and 253. Then answer the following questions: (a) Describe the window shown for the setup of the wireless base station. (b) What are the four most common uses of a home network? (c) What are the names of the folders displayed in the My Computer window?

Distributed Computing

2

When networked computers are not in use, their processing power can be combined with other networked computers to perform a common task. In some cases, the problems that can be solved by many individual computers are far too large to be solved by any single computer. Connect to our site at www.olearyseries.com/CE06 and select Using Technology to link to a site that features distributed computing. Explore the site and answer the following questions: (a) What type of problem does this site solve with distributed computing? (b) How do users donate unused computer time to this project? (c) Would you donate your extra computer time to a distributed computing project? Why or why not?

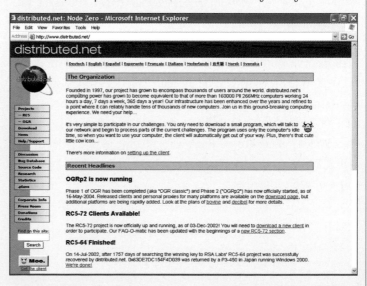

1 How Wireless Home Networks Work

Wireless home networks are becoming very popular. These LANs are easy to set up and use. They allow different computers to share resources including a common Internet connection and printer. To learn "How Home Networks Work," consult your Computing Essentials CD or visit our Web site at www.olearyseries.com/CE06 and select Animations. Then answer the following questions. (a) What is a node? (b) What is a base station and what is its function? (c) What is a wireless card and what is its function? (d) If one or more requests to print a document are made at exactly the same time, what node determines which document is printed first? (e) Can the Nodes TIM, LINDA, and STEVE access and use the Internet at the same time? If yes, how can this be done with a single Internet connection?

2 Napster and Gnutella

Many popular file sharing services use different strategies to allow users to share files. Study the "Napster and Gnutella" Expansion on your Computing Essentials CD or from our Web site at www. olearyseries.com/CE06. Then answer the following questions: (a) Describe how Napster used a client/server network system. (b) Describe how Gnutella uses a peer-to-peer network system. (c) Both network systems connect users willing to share files. Which system do you think would be the most efficient? Defend your answer. (d) Discuss the advantages and disadvantages of each strategy.

User Connection

One of the key determinants to enjoyable and effective use of the Internet is available bandwidth. As bandwidth increases, Internet content becomes richer and more varied. Write a one-page paper titled "Internet Connections" that addresses the following topics: (a) Define voiceband, medium band, and broadband. (b) Describe the four types of connections that are commonly available. (c) Discuss how faster Internet connections are shaping the way in which the Internet is used. (d) Research and discuss three specific examples.

Digital Rights Management

In response to the issue of sharing copyrighted material over computer networks discussed in this chapter, many different forms of Digital Rights Management, or DRM, have been proposed. However, DRM is controversial, and hotly debated by industry groups and consumer advocates. Use the Web to research DRM, and then write a one-page paper titled "Digital Rights Management" that addresses the following topics: (a) Define "Digital Rights Management." (b) What systems have been proposed for DRM? (c) Why are some consumers opposed to these systems? (d) Do you think DRM is a fair solution to online piracy? Justify your answer.

COMPETENCIES

After you have read this chapter, you should be able to:

1 Discuss the privacy issues related to the presence of large databases, private networks, the Internet, and the Web.

2 Describe the major privacy laws and the Code of Fair Information Practice.

3 Describe the security threats posed by computer criminals, computer crime, and other hazards.

4 Discuss ways that individuals and organizations protect their security.

5 Describe the common types of physical and mental risks associated with computer use and ways to protect yourself against these risks.

6 Discuss what the computer industry is doing, and what you can do to protect the environment.

Privacy
Concerns collection and use of data

Ergonomics
Human factors related to the devices people use

The tools and products of the information age do not exist in a world by themselves. As we said in Chapter 1, a computer system consists not only of software, hardware, data, and procedures but also of people. Because of people, computer systems may be used for both good and bad purposes.

There are more than 300 million microcomputers in use today. What are the consequences of the widespread presence of this technology? Does technology make it easy for others to invade our personal privacy? When we apply for a loan or for a driver's license, or when we check out at the supermarket, is that information about us being distributed and used without our permission? When we use the Web, is information about us being collected and shared with others?

Does technology make it easy for others to invade the security of business organizations like our banks or our employers? What about health risks to people who use computers? What about the environment? Do computers pose a threat to our ecology?

This technology prompts lots of questions—very important questions. Perhaps these are some of the most important questions for the 21st century. Competent end users need to be aware of the potential impact of technology on people and how to protect themselves on the Web. They need to be sensitive to and knowledgeable about personal privacy, organizational security, ergonomics, and the environmental impact of technology.

Environment
Discovering ways to discourage waste in the microcomputer industry

Security
Keeping private information safe from criminals, natural hazards, and civil unrest

PEOPLE

Information systems consist of people, procedures, software, hardware, and data. The most significant concerns for people are privacy, security, ergonomics, and the environment.

As we have discussed, information systems consist of people, procedures, software, hardware, and data. (See Figure 10-1.) This chapter focuses on people. While most everyone agrees that technology has had a very positive impact on people, it is important to recognize the negative, or potentially negative, impacts as well.

Effective implementation of computer technology involves maximizing its positive effects while minimizing its negative effects. The most significant concerns are:

- **Privacy:** What are the threats to personal privacy and how can we protect ourselves?
- **Security:** How can access to sensitive information be controlled and how can we secure hardware and software?
- **Ergonomics:** What are the physical and mental risks to technology and how can these risks be eliminated or controlled?
- **Environment:** What can individuals and organizations do to minimize the impact of technology on our environment?

Let us begin by examining privacy.

Software
Provides step-by-step instructions for computer hardware

People
Are end users who use computers to make themselves more productive

Procedures
Specify rules or guidelines for computer operations

Figure 10–1   The parts of an information system

> Computer ethics provide guidelines for computer use. Privacy relates to the collection and use of personal information. Privacy concerns include large databases, private networks, the Internet, and the Web. While privacy laws exist, privacy remains primarily an ethical issue.

What do you suppose controls how computers can be used? You probably think first of laws. Of course that is right, but technology is moving so fast that it is very difficult for our legal system to keep up. The essential element that controls how computers are used today is *ethics*.

Ethics, as you may know, are standards of moral conduct. **Computer ethics** are guidelines for the morally acceptable use of computers in our society. There are four primary computer ethics issues:

- **Privacy** concerns the collection and use of data about individuals.
- **Accuracy** relates to the responsibility of those who collect data to ensure that the data is correct.
- **Property** relates to who owns data and rights to software.
- **Access** relates to the responsibility of those who have data to control who is able to use that data.

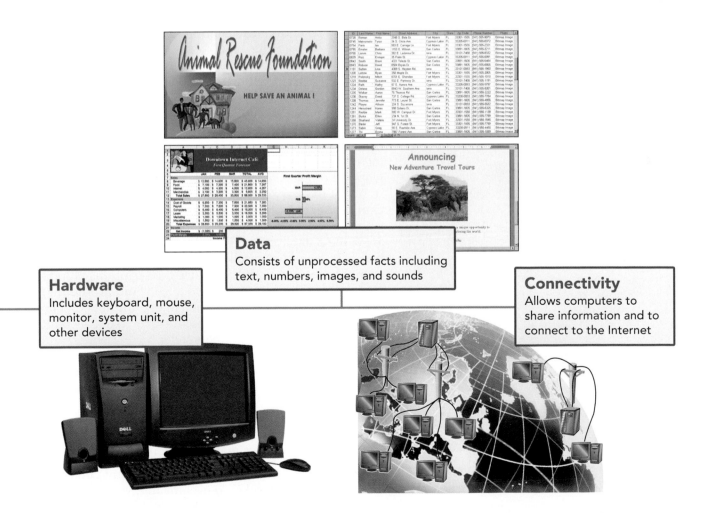

Data
Consists of unprocessed facts including text, numbers, images, and sounds

Hardware
Includes keyboard, mouse, monitor, system unit, and other devices

Connectivity
Allows computers to share information and to connect to the Internet

We are all entitled to ethical treatment. This includes the right to keep personal information, such as credit ratings and medical histories, from getting into unauthorized hands. Many people worry that this right is severely threatened. Let us examine some of the concerns.

LARGE DATABASES

Large organizations are constantly compiling information about us. The federal government alone has over 2,000 databases. Our Social Security numbers have become a national identification number. This number has become a standard field in all kinds of databases, including employment records, medical records, credit card records, and on and on. The vast majority of forms we fill out today require our Social Security number. Indeed, even children are now required to have Social Security numbers. Shouldn't we be concerned that cross-referenced information might be used for the wrong purposes?

Every day, data is gathered about us and stored in large databases. For example, for billing purposes, telephone companies compile lists of the calls we make, the numbers called, and so on. A special telephone directory (called a

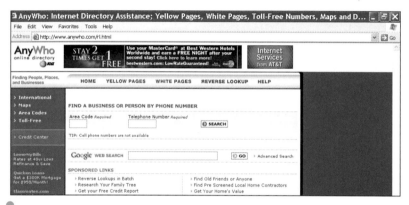

Figure 10-2   Reverse directory Web site

reverse directory) lists telephone numbers sequentially. Using it, government authorities and others can easily get the names, addresses, and other details about the persons we call. Numerous sites on the Web provide access to these reverse directories. (See Figure 10-2.) Additionally, some of the reverse directory Web sites will provide maps to the addresses associated with any telephone.

Credit card companies keep similar records. Supermarket scanners in grocery checkout counters record what we buy, when we buy it, how much we buy, and the price. (See Figure 10-3.) Financial institutions, including banks and credit unions, record how much money we have, what we use it for, and how much we owe. Publishers of magazines, newspapers, and mail-order catalogues have our names, addresses, phone numbers, and what we order.

A vast industry of data gatherers known as **information resellers** or **information brokers** now exists that collects and sells such personal data. Using publicly available databases and in many cases nonpublic databases, information resellers create **electronic profiles** or highly detailed and personalized descriptions of individuals. Very likely, you have an electronic profile that includes your name, address, telephone number, Social Security number, driver's license number, bank account numbers, credit card numbers, telephone records, and shopping and purchasing patterns. Information resellers sell these electronic profiles to direct marketers, fund-raisers, and others. Many provide these services on the Web for free or for a nominal cost. (See Figure 10-4.)

Your personal information, including preferences, habits, and financial data, has become a marketable commodity. This raises many issues, including:

Figure 10-3   Large organizations are constantly compiling information about us, such as the kinds of products we buy.

- **Spreading information without personal consent:** How would you feel if your name and your taste in movies were made available nation-wide? For a while, Blockbuster, a large video rental company, considered doing just this.

What if a great deal of information about your shopping habits—collected about you without your consent—was made available to any microcomputer user who wanted it? Before dropping the project, Lotus Development Corporation and Equifax Inc. planned to market disks containing information on 120 million American consumers. (Lotus claimed it was providing small businesses with the same information currently available to larger organizations.)

How would you feel if an employer were using your medical records to make decisions about hiring, placement, promotion, and firing? A University of Illinois survey found that half the Fortune 500 companies were using medical records for just these purposes.

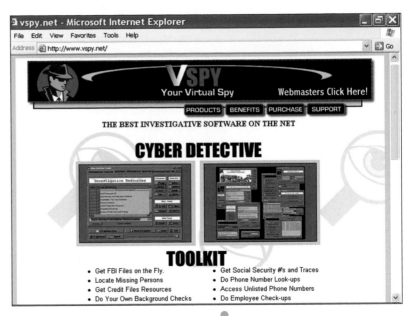

Figure 10-4 Information reseller's Web site

How would you feel if someone obtained a driver's license and credit cards in your name? What if that person then assumed your identity to buy clothes, cars, and a house? It happens every day. Last year, well over 10 million people were victimized in this way. It is called **identify theft.** Identity theft is the illegal assumption of someone's identity for the purposes of economic gain. It is one of the fastest growing crimes in the country. To learn more about identity theft and how to minimize your risk, consult your Computing Essentials CD or visit our Web site at www.olearyseries.com/CE06 and select Expansions.

- **Spreading inaccurate information:** How would you feel if inaccurate information about you were being used to make important decisions? Simple recording mistakes happen all the time and an error in one file can be quickly spread to other files. Unfortunately, even if an error is located and corrected in one file, it is often very difficult to locate and correct in all files.

How would you like to be turned down for a home loan because of an error in your credit history? This is much more common than you might expect. What if you could not find a job or were fired from a job because of an error giving you a serious criminal history? This can and has happened due to simple clerical errors. In one case, an arresting officer while completing an arrest warrant incorrectly recorded the Social Security number of a criminal. From that time forward, this arrest and the subsequent conviction became part of another person's electronic profile. This is an example of **mistaken identity** in which the electronic profile of one person is switched with another.

It's important to know that you have some recourse. The law allows you to gain access to those records about you that are held by credit bureaus. Under the **Freedom of Information Act,** you are also entitled to look at

Have you been a victim of identify theft? If you have or if you ever are, here are some suggestions on what you should do.

TIPS

1. Contact local and federal police authorities to report the crime.

2. Call the Federal Trade Commission's (FTC) free Identity Theft Hotline at 1-877-IDTHEFT (438-4338) to obtain current advice relating to resolving credit-related problems.

3. Visit the ID Theft Web site at www.consumer.gov/idtheft for additional information and advice.

4. Obtain and file the ID Theft Affidavit available at the ID Theft Web site.

your records held by government agencies. (Portions may be deleted for national security reasons.)

To learn more about mistaken identity, consult your Computing Essentials CD or visit our Web site at www.olearyseries.com/CE06 and select Expansions.

▼ CONCEPT CHECK

► What are four primary computer ethics issues?

► What is identity theft? What is mistaken identity? How are they different?

► What is the Freedom of Information Act?

PRIVATE NETWORKS

Suppose you use your company's electronic mail system to send a co-worker an unflattering message about your supervisor. Later you find the boss has been spying on your exchange. Or suppose you are a subscriber to an online discussion group. You discover that the company that supports the discussion group screens all your messages and rejects those it deems inappropriate. Both these situations have actually happened.

The first instance, of firms eavesdropping on employees, has inspired attempts at federal legislation. One survey revealed that nearly 75 percent of all businesses search employees' electronic mail and computer files using so-called **snoopware**. (See Figure 10-5.) These programs record virtually everything you do on your computer. Currently this is legal. One proposed law would not prohibit this type of electronic monitoring but would require employers to provide prior written notice. Employers would also have to alert employees during the monitoring with some sort of audible or visual signal.

The second instance, in which online information services screen and reject messages, is a common activity with most commercial services. In one case, the Prodigy Information Service terminated the accounts of eight members who had been using the electronic mail system to protest Prodigy's rate hikes. Prodigy executives argued that the U.S. Constitution does not give members of someone's private network the right to express their views without restrictions. Opponents say that the United States is becoming a nation linked by electronic mail. Therefore, the government has to provide protection for users against other people reading or censoring their messages.

Figure 10-5 Snoopware

On the Web Explorations

Several organizations monitor the legislation on privacy issues. To learn more about one such organization, visit our Web site at

www.olearyseries.com/CE06 and select On the Web Explorations.

THE INTERNET AND THE WEB

When you send e-mail on the Internet or browse the Web, do you have any concerns about privacy? Most people do not. They think that as long as they are selective about disclosing their names or other personal information, then little can be done to invade their personal privacy. Experts call this the **illusion of anonymity** that the Internet brings.

As discussed earlier, many organizations monitor e-mail content of all messages sent within their private electronic networks. Likewise, for some unscrupulous individuals, it is also a common practice to eavesdrop or snoop into the content of e-mail sent across the Internet.

Furthermore, when you browse the Web, your activity is monitored. Whenever you visit a Web site, your browser stores critical information onto your hard disk, typically without your explicit permission or knowledge. For example, your browser creates a **history file** that includes the locations of sites visited by your computer system.

Another way your Web activity is monitored is by **cookies** or specialized programs that are deposited on your hard disk from Web sites you have visited. Typically, these programs are deposited without your explicit knowledge or consent. They record what sites you visit, what you do at the sites, and other information you provide, such as passwords and credit card numbers.

There are two basic types of cookies: traditional and ad network.

- **Traditional cookies** monitor your activities at a single site. When you first visit a site, a cookie is deposited and begins to monitor your activities. When you leave the site, the cookie becomes dormant. When you revisit, the cookie is reactivated and sends the previously collected information back to the site and then continues recording your activities. These cookies are intended to provide customized service. For example, when you revisit an electronic commerce site, you can be greeted by name, presented with customized advertising banners, and directed to Web pages promoting items you have previously purchased.

- **Ad network** or **adware cookies** monitor your activities across all sites you visit. Once deposited onto your hard drive, they continue to actively collect information on your Web activities. These cookies are secretly deposited on your hard disk by organizations that compile and market the information, including individual personal profiles, mailing lists, and e-mail addresses. Two such organizations are DoubleClick and Avenue A.

Most browsers are able to control many types of cookies. For example, Internet Explorer version 6.0 provides settings to selectively block cookies from being deposited onto a system's hard disk. A more effective way to control unwanted cookies, however, is to use specialized programs. These programs, called **cookie-cutter programs,** allow users to selectively filter or block the most intrusive cookies while allowing selective traditional cookies to operate. For a list of some of the most widely used cookie-cutter programs, see Figure 10-6.

The term **spyware** is used to describe a wide range of programs that are designed to secretly record and report an individual's activities on the Internet. Ad network cookies are just one type of spyware. Two other types are Web bugs and computer monitoring software.

Program	Web Site
AdSubtract	adsubtract.com
Cookie Cleanup	softadd.com
Cookie Crusher	thelimitsoft.com
Cookie Pal	kburra.com
WebWasher	webwasher.com

Figure 10-6 Cookie-cutter programs

- **Web bugs** are small programs typically hidden within the HTML code for a Web page or e-mail message as a graphical image. Web bugs migrate whenever an unsuspecting user visits a Web site containing a Web bug or opens an infected e-mail message. Web bugs often work with cookies on the user's computer to collect and report information back to a predefined server on the Web. Web bugs can even be used to secretly read a user's e-mail messages. To see how Web bugs can work, consult your Computing Essentials CD or visit our Web site at www.olearyseries.com/CE06 and select Animations.

- **Computer monitoring software** is the most invasive and dangerous type of spyware. These programs record every activity and keystroke made on your computer system, including credit card numbers, bank account

Figure 10-7 Protect your privacy

Program	Web Site
Ad-aware	lavasoftusa.com
PestPatrol	pestpatrol.com
Spybot-S&D	spybot.com
Spy Sweeper	spysweeper.com

Figure 10-8 Spyware removal programs

numbers, and e-mail messages. Also known as **sniffer programs** and **keystroke loggers,** computer monitoring software can be deposited onto your hard drive without your knowledge either from the Web or by someone installing the programs directly onto your computer. The previously mentioned snoopware is a type of computer monitoring software used by businesses to monitor their employees. Computer monitoring software has also been used by the FBI and the CIA to collect incriminating evidence on suspected terrorists and organized crime members. These programs are also widely used by private investigators, criminals, and spouses.

Unfortunately, it is more difficult to remove Web bugs and computer monitoring software than ad network cookies because they are more difficult to detect. There are over 78,000 active spyware programs, and chances are you have one of them on your computer. A new category of programs known as **spy removal programs,** which are designed to detect Web bugs and monitoring software, has evolved recently. (See Figure 10-7.) For a list of some of these programs, see Figure 10-8.

To learn more about protecting yourself from Spyware, see Making IT Work for You: Spyware Removal on pages 280 and 281.

MAJOR LAWS ON PRIVACY

Some federal laws governing privacy matters have been created (see Figure 10-9). However, most of the information collected by private organizations is not covered by existing laws. As a result, privacy remains primarily an ethical issue. Increasingly, more and more individuals have become concerned about controlling who has the right to personal information and how that information is used.

To respond to these privacy concerns, a Code of Fair Information Practice has been established. (See Figure 10-10.) The code was

TIPS What can you do to protect your privacy while on the Web? Here are a few suggestions.

1 Encrypt sensitive e-mail. Encrypt or code sensitive e-mail using special encryption programs.

2 Shield your identity. Use an anonymous remailer or special Web site that forwards your e-mail without disclosing your identity.

3 Block cookies. Use your browser or a cookie-cutter program to block unwanted cookies.

4 Check for Web bugs and computer monitoring software. Use spy removal programs to check for Web bugs and computer monitoring software.

5 Notify providers. Instruct your service provider or whomever you use to link to the Internet not to sell your name or any other personal information.

6 Be careful. Never disclose your telephone number, passwords, or other private information to strangers.

Law	Year	Protection
Fair Credit Reporting Act	1970	Gives right to review and correct personal credit records; restricts sharing of personal credit histories.
Freedom of Information Act	1970	Gives right to see personal files collected by federal agencies.
Privacy Act	1974	Prohibits use of federal information for purposes other than original intent.
Right to Financial Privacy Act	1979	Limits federal authority to examine personal bank records.
Computer Fraud and Abuse Act	1986	Allows prosecution of individuals who access computers and databases without authorization.
Electronic Communications Privacy Act (ECPA)	1986	Protects privacy on public electronic mail systems.
Video Privacy Protection Act	1988	Prevents sale of video rental records.
Computer Matching and Privacy Protection Act	1988	Limits government's authority to match an individual's data.
Computer Abuse Amendments Act	1994	Outlaws transmission of viruses.
National Information Infrastructure Protection Act	1996	Protects computer systems, networks, and information.
No Electronic Theft (NET) Act	1997	Prevents unauthorized distribution of copyrighted software on the Internet.
Child Online Protection Act (COPA)	1998	Prohibits commercial distribution of materials harmful to minors.
Digital Millennium Copyright Act (DMCA)	1998	Protects software manufacturers against sale of devices that illegally copy software. Prohibits tampering with antiprivacy schemes.
Provide Appropriate Tools Required to Intercept and Obstruct Terrorism (PATRIOT) Act	2001	Provides for legal monitoring of people's activities.

Figure 10-9   Summary of privacy laws

Principle	Description
No secret databases	There must be no record-keeping systems containing personal data whose very existence is kept secret.
Right of individual access	Individuals must be able to find out what information about them is in a record and how it is used.
Right of consent	Information about individuals obtained for one purpose cannot be used for other purposes without their consent.
Right to correct	Individuals must be able to correct or amend records of identifiable information about them.
Assurance of reliability and proper use	Organizations creating, maintaining, using, or disseminating records of identifiable personal data must make sure the data is reliable for its intended use. They must take precautions to prevent such data from being misused.

Figure 10-10   Principles of the Code of Fair Information Practice

SPYWARE REMOVAL

Have you installed any free software from the Internet? Did you know seemingly harmless software might actually be spying on you, even sending personal information to advertisers or worse? Fortunately, spyware removal software is available to help keep your personal information private.

Finding and Removing Spyware   Once spyware removal software is installed on your system, you can scan your system for known spyware and remove it. Follow the steps below to find and remove spyware using Ad-aware.

1 ● Connect to *www.lavasoftusa.com* and follow the on-screen instructions to download and install the Ad-aware software.

2 ● Launch the Ad-aware application.

● Click the *Scan now* button.

● Click the *Next* button to begin scanning for spyware.

● After the scan is complete, click the *Next* button to see the results.

● Click the *Next* button to remove all the components Ad-aware has identified as spyware.

Automating Spyware Removal   To protect your system from spyware, you should run your spyware removal software automatically. Follow the steps below to set Ad-aware to run each time you start your system.

1 ● Click the *Settings* button.

2 ● Click *Run at Windows start up*.

● Click the *Proceed* button.

Ad-aware will now run automatically each time you start your system and alert you to any new spyware detected.

Staying Up To Date   Now that your system is protected from spyware, you'll want to keep it that way. Spyware removal programs keep a profile of known spyware, which must be updated from time to time. Follow the steps below to update the spyware profile in Ad-aware.

1 ● Click the *Open WebUpdate* button.

2 ● Click the *Connect* button.

Ad-aware connects to the Internet and updates its spyware profile.

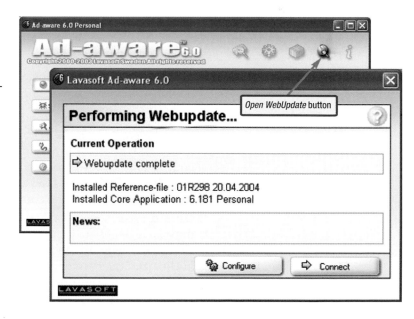

The newest Ad-aware reference file is installed automatically. You can now follow the steps in the "Finding and Removing Spyware" section to rid your system of the latest known spyware. The Web is continually changing, and some of the specifics presented in this Making IT Work for You may have changed. To learn about other ways to make information technology work for you, consult your Computing Essentials CD or visit our Web site at www.olearyseries.com/CE06 and select Making IT Work for You.

recommended by a committee established by former Secretary of Health, Education, and Welfare Elliott Richardson. While this code has been adopted by many information-collecting businesses it is not a law. Privacy advocates strongly support legislation that makes this code an enforceable law.

▼ CONCEPT CHECK

▶ What are history files? What are cookies?

▶ What are Web bugs? What is computer monitoring software? What is spyware?

▶ Describe the Code of Fair Information Practice.

SECURITY

Threats to computer security are computer criminals, computer crime, and other hazards. Measures to protect security include encryption, restricting access, anticipating disasters, and making backup copies.

We are all concerned with having a safe and secure environment to live in. We are careful to lock our car doors and our homes. We are careful about where we walk at night and whom we talk to. This is personal security. What about computer security? What if someone gains unauthorized access to our computer or other computers that contain information about us? What if someone steals our computer or other computers that contain information about us? What are the major threats to computer security, and how can we be protected?

THREATS TO COMPUTER SECURITY

Keeping information private depends on keeping computer systems safe from criminals, natural hazards, and other threats. (See Figure 10-11.)

COMPUTER CRIMINALS

A **computer crime** is an illegal action in which the perpetrator uses special knowledge of computer technology. Computer criminals are of five types:

- **Employees:** The largest category of computer criminals consists of those with the easiest access to computers—namely, employees. Sometimes the employee is simply trying to steal something from the employer—equipment, software, electronic funds, proprietary information, or computer time. Sometimes the employee is acting out of resentment and is trying to get back at the company.

- **Outside users:** Not only employees but also some suppliers or clients may have access to a company's computer system. Examples are bank customers who use an automated teller machine. Like employees, these authorized users may be able to obtain confidential passwords or find other ways of committing computer crimes.

- **Hackers and crackers:** Some people think of these two groups as being the same, but they are not. **Hackers** are people who gain unauthorized access to a computer system for the fun and challenge of it. **Crackers** do the same thing but for malicious purposes. They may intend to steal technical information or to introduce what they call a **bomb**—a destructive computer program—into the system.

Natural hazards

Civil unrest

Computer theft

Figure 10-11 There are numerous threats to computer security

- **Organized crime:** Members of organized crime groups have discovered that they can use computers just as people in legitimate businesses do, but for illegal purposes. For example, computers are useful for keeping track of stolen goods or illegal gambling debts. In addition, counterfeiters and forgers use microcomputers and printers to produce sophisticated-looking documents such as checks and driver's licenses.

- **Terrorists:** Knowledgeable terrorist groups and hostile governments could potentially crash satellites and wage economic warfare by disrupting navigation and communication systems. The Department of Defense reports that its computer systems are probed approximately 250,000 times a year by unknown sources.

COMPUTER CRIME

The FBI estimates that businesses lost $1.5 trillion in the past year from computer crimes. The number of these crimes has tripled in the past two years. Computer crime can take various forms including the creation of malicious programs, denial of service attacks, Internet scams, theft, and data manipulation.

Malicious Programs

Hackers and crackers are notorious for creating and distributing malicious programs. These programs are called **malware,** which is short for **mal**icious soft**ware.** They are specifically designed to damage or disrupt a computer system. The three most common types of malware are viruses, worms, and Trojan horses.

- **Viruses** are programs that migrate through networks and operating systems, and most attach themselves to different programs and databases. While most viruses are relatively harmless, some can be quite destructive. Once activated, these destructive viruses can alter and/or delete files. Some delete all files on the hard disk and can damage system components. Creating and knowingly spreading a virus is a very serious crime and a federal offense punishable under the **Computer Abuse Amendments Act of 1994.**

See Figure 10-12 for a list of common viruses.

- **Worms** are a special type of virus that does not attach itself to programs and databases. Rather it fills a computer system with self-replicating information, clogging the system so that its operations are slowed or stopped. A recent worm traveled across the world within hours stopping tens of thousands of computers along its way. Internet worms can also be carriers of more traditional viruses. Once the traditional virus has been deposited by a worm onto an unsuspecting computer system, the virus will either activate immediately or lie dormant until some future time.

  See Figure 10-13 for a list of common worms, each with different variations.

Viruses and worms typically find their way into microcomputers through e-mail attachments, copied floppy disks, or programs downloaded from the Internet. Because viruses can be so serious—certain "disk-killer" viruses can destroy all the information on a person's system—computer users are advised to exercise care in accepting new programs and data from other sources.

As we discussed in Chapter 5, detection programs called **virus checkers** are available to alert users when certain kinds of viruses and worms enter their system. Four of the most widely used virus checkers are Dr. Solomon's Anti-Virus, McAfee VirusScan, eSafe, and Norton AntiVirus. Unfortunately, new viruses are being developed all the time, and not all viruses can be detected. (See Making IT Work for You: Virus Protection and Internet Security on pages 134 and 135 in Chapter 5.)

To learn more about viruses and how you could get one, study Figure 10-14.

- **Trojan horses** are programs that come into a computer system disguised as something else. Trojan horses are not viruses. Like worms, however, they are carriers of viruses. The most common types of Trojan horses appear as free computer games and free screen saver programs that can

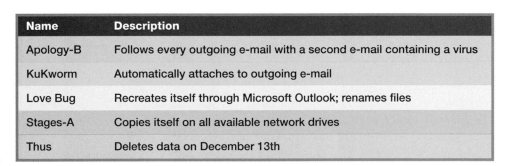

Name	Description
Apology-B	Follows every outgoing e-mail with a second e-mail containing a virus
KuKworm	Automatically attaches to outgoing e-mail
Love Bug	Recreates itself through Microsoft Outlook; renames files
Stages-A	Copies itself on all available network drives
Thus	Deletes data on December 13th

Figure 10-12 Commonly encountered viruses

Name	Description
Bugbear	Most deposit viruses; some are e-mail viruses, others deposit computer monitoring software
Fizzer	Most deposit an e-mail virus; others locate and disable the infected computer system's virus protection programs
Klez	Duplicates itself through mass-mailing of e-mail; however, most do not deposit traditional viruses
Yaha	Most are activated when an infected e-mail is opened; unsuspecting recipients are enticed to open the e-mail by subject lines such as free screen saver and one way to love

Figure 10-13 Commonly encountered worms

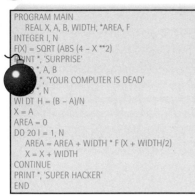

```
PROGRAM MAIN
   REAL X, A, B, WIDTH, *AREA, F
INTEGER I, N
F(X) = SQRT (ABS (4 – X **2)
PRINT *, 'SURPRISE'
   *, A, B
   *, 'YOUR COMPUTER IS DEAD'
   *, N
WI DT H = (B – A)/N
X = A
AREA = 0
DO 20 I = 1, N
   AREA = AREA + WIDTH * F (X + WIDTH/2)
   X = X + WIDTH
CONTINUE
PRINT *, 'SUPER HACKER'
END
```

1 A virus begins when a cracker or programmer writes a program that attaches itself to an operating system, another program, or piece of data.

2 The virus travels via floppy disk, downloading from the Internet, or other networks or bulletin boards to anywhere that the operating system, program, or data travels.

3 The virus is set off. A nondestructive virus may simply print a message ("Surprise!"). A destructive virus may erase data, destroy programs, and even (through repeated reading and writing to one location) wear out a hard disk. The virus may be set off either by a time limit or by a sequence of operations the user performs.

Figure 10-14   How a computer virus can spread

be downloaded from the Internet. Once the Trojan horse is downloaded onto a computer system, the viruses are deposited and ready to activate. One of the most dangerous types of Trojan horse claims to provide free antivirus programs. These programs begin by locating and disabling any existing virus protection programs and then deposit the virus.

Denial of Service

Like a worm, a **denial of service (DoS) attack** attempts to slow down or stop a computer system or network. Unlike a worm that self-replicates, a DoS attack floods a computer or network with requests for information and data. The targets of these attacks are usually Internet service providers (ISP) and specific Web sites. Once under attack, the servers at the ISP or the Web site become overwhelmed with these requests for service and are unable to respond to legitimate users. As a result, the ISP or Web site is effectively shut down.

Internet Scams

A **scam** is a fraudulent or deceptive act or operation designed to trick individuals into spending their time and money for little or no return. An **Internet scam** is simply a scam using the Internet. Internet scams are becoming a serious problem and have created financial and legal problems for thousands of people. Almost all of the scams are initiated by a mass mailing to unsuspecting individuals.

See Figure 10-15 for a list of common types of Internet scams.

Are you concerned about catching a virus? Here are a few suggestions that might help:

1 **Use an antivirus program.** Install antivirus programs on all computer systems you use and run them frequently.

2 **Check disks.** Before using any floppy or CD, check for viruses.

3 **Enable write protection.** Protect data and programs on floppy disks by enabling write protection.

4 **Check all downloads.** Check all files downloaded from the Internet.

5 **Update your antivirus program.** New viruses are being developed daily, and the virus programs are continually being revised. Update your antivirus program frequently.

Type	Description
Identity theft	Individual(s) pose as ISPs, bank representatives, or government agencies requesting personal information. Once obtained, criminal(s) assume a person's identity for a variety of financial transactions.
Chain letter	Classic chain letter instructing recipient to send a nominal amount of money to each of five people on a list. The recipient removes the first name on the list, adds their name at the bottom and mails the chain letter to five friends. Almost all chain letters are fraudulent and illegal.
Auction fraud	Merchandise is selected and payment is sent. Merchandise is never delivered.
Vacation prize	"Free" vacation has been awarded. Upon arrival at vacation destination, the accommodations are dreadful but can be upgraded for a fee.
Advance fee loans	Guaranteed low rate loans available to almost anyone. After applicant provides personal loan-related information, the loan is granted subject to payment of an "insurance fee."

Figure 10-15   Common Internet scams

Theft

Theft can take many forms—of hardware, of software, of data, of computer time. Thieves steal equipment and programs, of course, but there are also white-collar crimes. These crimes include the theft of data in the form of confidential information such as preferred-client lists. Another common crime is the use (theft) of a company's computer time by an employee to run another business.

Unauthorized copying of programs for personal gain is a form of theft called **software piracy.** According to the **Software Copyright Act of 1980,** it is legal for a program owner to make only his or her own backup copies of that program. *It's important to note that none of these copies may be legally resold or given away. This may come as a surprise to those who copy software from a friend, but that's the law. It is also illegal to download copyright-protected music and videos from the Internet.*

Pirated software accounts for over 40 percent of software used in the United States. The incidence of pirated software is even higher overseas in such countries as Italy (82 percent) and Thailand (92 percent). Penalties for violating this law are up to $250,000 in fines and five years in prison.

Data Manipulation

Finding entry into someone's computer network and leaving a prankster's message may seem like fun, which is why hackers do it. It is still against the law. Moreover, even if the manipulation seems harmless, it may cause a great deal of anxiety and wasted time among network users.

The **Computer Fraud and Abuse Act of 1986** makes it a crime for unauthorized persons even to view—let alone copy or damage—data using any computer across state lines. It also prohibits unauthorized use of any government computer or a computer used by any federally insured financial institution. Offenders can be sentenced to up to 20 years in prison and fined up to $100,000.

For a summary of computer crimes, see Figure 10-16.

Computer Crime	Description
Malicious programs	Include viruses, worms, and Trojan horses
DoS	Cause computer systems to slow down or stop
Internet scams	Are scams over the Internet initiated by e-mail
Theft	Includes hardware, software, and computer time
Data manipulation	Involves changing data or leaving prank messages

Figure 10-16   Computer crimes

OTHER HAZARDS

There are plenty of other hazards to computer systems and data besides criminals. They include the following:

- **Natural hazards:** Natural forces include fires, floods, wind, hurricanes, tornadoes, and earthquakes. Even home computer users should store backup disks of programs and data in safe locations in case of fire or storm damage.
- **Civil strife and terrorism:** Wars, riots, and terrorist activities are real risks in all parts of the world. Even people in developed countries must be mindful of these acts.
- **Technological failures:** Hardware and software don't always do what they are supposed to do. For instance, too little electricity, caused by a brownout or blackout, may cause the loss of data in primary storage. Too much electricity, as when lightning or some other electrical disturbance affects a power line, may cause a **voltage surge,** or **spike.** This excess of electricity may destroy chips or other electronic components of a computer.

  Microcomputer users should use a **surge protector,** a device that separates the computer from the power source of the wall outlet. When a voltage surge occurs, it activates a circuit breaker in the surge protector, protecting the computer system.

  Another technological catastrophe occurs when a hard-disk drive suddenly crashes, or fails (as discussed in Chapter 8), perhaps because it has been bumped inadvertently. If the user has forgotten to make backup copies of data on the hard disk, data may be lost. (See Figure 10-17.)
- **Human errors:** Human mistakes are inevitable. Data-entry errors are probably the most commonplace and, as we have discussed, can lead to mistaken identity. Programmer errors also occur frequently. Some mistakes may result from faulty design, as when a software manufacturer makes a deletion command closely resembling another command. Some errors may be the result of sloppy procedures. One such example occurs when office workers save important documents under file names that are not descriptive and not recognizable by others.

Figure 10–17   Crashes can result in lost data

▼ CONCEPT CHECK

▶ Describe malware, including viruses, worms, and Trojan horses.

▶ Compare a worm to a denial of service attack. How are they similar? How are they different?

▶ Describe the five most common types of Internet scams.

MEASURES TO PROTECT COMPUTER SECURITY

Security is concerned with protecting information, hardware, and software from unauthorized use as well as from damage from intrusions, sabotage, and natural disasters. (See Figure 10-18.) Considering the numerous ways in which computer systems and data can be compromised, we can see why security is a growing field. Some of the principal measures to protect computer security are encryption, restricting access, anticipating disasters, and backing up data.

Figure 10-18 Disasters—both natural and manmade—can play havoc with computers

Encrypting Messages

Whenever information is sent over a network, the possibility of unauthorized access exists. The longer the distance the message has to travel, the higher the security risk is. For example, an e-mail message on a LAN meets a limited number of users operating in controlled environments such as offices. An e-mail message traveling across the country on the Internet affords greater opportunities for the message to be intercepted.

Businesses have been **encrypting,** or coding, messages for years. They have become so good at it that some law enforcement agencies are unable to wiretap messages from suspected criminals. Some federal agencies have suggested that a standard encryption procedure be used so that law enforcement agencies can monitor suspected criminal communications. Individuals are also using encryption programs to safeguard their private communications. One of the most widely used personal encryption programs is Pretty Good Privacy. (See Figure 10-19.)

Figure 10-19 Encrypted e-mail

Restricting Access

Security experts are constantly devising ways to protect computer systems from access by unauthorized persons. Sometimes security is a matter of putting guards on company computer rooms and checking the identification of everyone admitted. Other times it is using **biometric scanning** devices such as fingerprint and iris (eye) scanners. (See Figure 10-20.)

Oftentimes it is a matter of being careful about assigning passwords to people and of changing the passwords when people leave a company. **Passwords** are secret words or numbers that must be keyed into a computer system to gain access. In some dial-back computer systems, the user telephones the computer, punches in the correct password, and then hangs up. If the password is verified by the computer system, it then calls the user back at a certain preauthorized telephone number. For many applications on the Web, users assign their own passwords.

As mentioned in previous chapters, most major corporations today use special hardware and software called firewalls to control access to their internal computer networks. **Firewalls** act as a security buffer between the corporation's private network and all external networks, including the Internet. All electronic

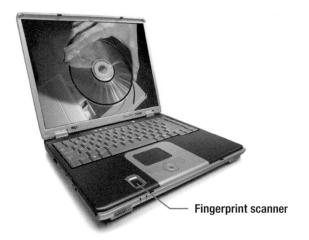

Fingerprint scanner

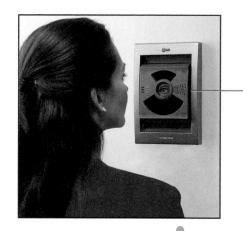

Iris scanner

Figure 10-20   Biometric scanning devices

communications coming into and leaving the corporation must be evaluated by the firewall. Security is maintained by denying access to unauthorized communications. To learn how to use Windows XP's built-in firewall, consult your Computing Essentials CD or visit our Web site at www.olearyseries.com/CE06 and select Expansions.

Anticipating Disasters

Companies (and even individuals) should prepare themselves for disasters. **Physical security** is concerned with protecting hardware from possible human and natural disasters. **Data security** is concerned with protecting software and data from unauthorized tampering or damage. Most large organizations have a **disaster recovery plan** describing ways to continue operating until normal computer operations can be restored.

Hardware can be kept behind locked doors, but often employees find this restriction a hindrance to their work. As a result, security is often lax. Fire and water (including the water from ceiling sprinkler systems) can do great damage to equipment. Many companies therefore will form a cooperative arrangement to share equipment with other companies in the event of a catastrophe. Special emergency facilities called **hot sites** may be created that are fully equipped backup computer centers. They are called **cold sites** if they are empty shells in which hardware must be installed.

Backing Up Data

Equipment can always be replaced. A company's *data,* however, may be irreplaceable. Most companies have ways of trying to keep software and data from being tampered with in the first place. They include careful screening of job applicants, guarding of passwords, and auditing of data and programs from time to time. An essential procedure, however, is to make frequent backups of data and to store them in safe remote locations.

On the Web Explorations

Encryption is the only thing between criminals and private information on the Internet, such as bank accounts, passwords, and even tax returns. To learn more about one encryption company, visit our Web site at

www.olearyseries.com/CE06 and select On the Web Explorations.

▼ CONCEPT CHECK

▶ What is encryption? What is Pretty Good Privacy?

▶ Discuss biometric scanning, passwords, and firewalls.

▶ Discuss ways to anticipate disasters, including physical and data security, disaster recovery plans, hot sites, and cold sites.

ERGONOMICS

Ergonomics is the study of human factors related to things people use. Physical risks include eyestrain, backache, neck pain, and RSI. Mental risks include noise and electronic monitoring.

Computers have become a common business tool because they increase productivity. Unfortunately, there are certain ways in which computers may actually make people less productive. Many of those affected are in positions that involve intensive data entry, such as clerks and word processor operators. However, anyone whose job involves heavy use of the computer may be affected. As a result, there has been great interest in a field known as **ergonomics.**

Ergonomics (pronounced "er-guh-nom-ix") is defined as the study of human factors related to things people use. It is concerned with fitting the job to the worker rather than forcing the worker to contort to fit the job. As computer use has increased, so has interest in ergonomics. People are devising ways that computers can be designed and used to increase productivity and avoid health risks.

PHYSICAL HEALTH

Sitting in front of a screen in awkward positions for long periods may lead to physical problems such as eyestrain, headaches, and back pain. Computer users can alleviate these problems by taking frequent rest breaks and by using well-designed computer furniture. Some recommendations by ergonomics experts for the ideal microcomputer setup are illustrated in Figure 10-21.

The physical health matters related to computers that have received the most attention recently are the following:

- **Eyestrain and headache:** Our eyes were made for most efficient seeing at a distance. However, monitors require using the eyes at closer range for a long time, which can create eyestrain, headaches, and double vision.

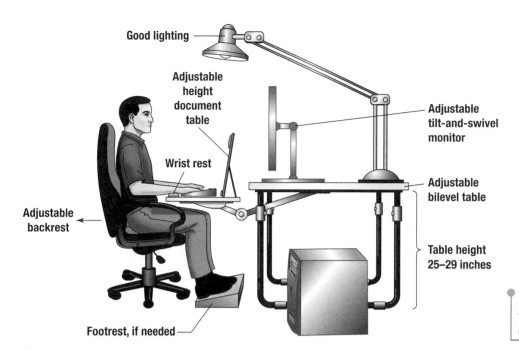

Good lighting

Adjustable height document table

Adjustable tilt-and-swivel monitor

Wrist rest

Adjustable bilevel table

Adjustable backrest

Table height 25–29 inches

Footrest, if needed

Figure 10-21 Recommendations for the ideal microcomputer work environment

To make the computer easier on the eyes, take a 15-minute break every hour or two. Avoid computer screens that flicker. Keep computer screens away from windows and other sources of bright light to minimize reflected glare on the screen. Special antiglare screen coatings and glare shields are also available. Make sure the screen is three to four times brighter than room light. Keep everything you're focusing on at about the same distance. For example, the computer screen, keyboard, and a document holder containing your work might be positioned about 20 inches away. Clean the screen of dust from time to time.

- **Back and neck pain:** Many people work at monitors and keyboards that are in improper positions. The result can be pains in the back and neck. (See Figure 10-22.)

To avoid such problems, make sure equipment is adjustable. You should be able to adjust your chair for height and angle, and the chair should have good back support. The table on which the monitor stands should also be adjustable, and the monitor itself should be of the tilt-and-swivel kind. The monitor should be at eye level or slightly below eye level. Keyboards should be detachable. Document holders should be adjustable. Use a footrest, if necessary, to reduce leg fatigue.

- **Repetitive strain injury:** Data-entry operators may make as many as 23,000 keystrokes a day. Some of these workers and other heavy keyboard users have fallen victim to a disorder known as repetitive strain injury.

Repetitive strain injury (RSI)—also called **repetitive motion injury** and **cumulative trauma disorder**—is the name given to a number of injuries. These result from fast, repetitive work that can cause neck, wrist, hand, and arm pain. RSI is by far the greatest cause of workplace illnesses in private industry. It accounts for billions of dollars in compensation claims and lost productivity every year. Some RSI sufferers are slaughterhouse, textile, and automobile workers, who have long been susceptible to the disorder. One particular type of RSI, **carpal tunnel syndrome,** found among heavy computer users, consists of damage to nerves and tendons in

On the Web Explorations

Computer-related eyestrain is a painful and increasingly common problem. To learn more about organizations devoted to helping those with this condition, visit our Web site at

www.olearyseries.com/CE06

and select On the Web Explorations.

Figure 10-22 Back and neck pain

Figure 10-23 **Carpal tunnel syndrome**

Figure 10-24 **Ergonomic keyboard**

the hands. (See Figure 10-23.) Some victims report the pain is so intense that they cannot open doors or shake hands and that they require corrective surgery.

Ergonomically correct keyboards have recently been developed to help prevent injury from heavy computer use. (See Figure 10-24.) In addition to using ergonomic keyboards, you should take frequent short rest breaks and gently massage your hands. Experts also advise getting plenty of sleep and exercise, watching your weight, sitting up straight, and learning and using stress-management techniques.

MENTAL HEALTH

Computer technology offers many ways of improving productivity, but it also creates some irritants that may be counterproductive.

*   **Noise:** Computing can be quite noisy. Voice input and output can be distracting for coworkers. Working next to some types of printers can leave one with ringing ears. Also, users may develop headaches and tension from continual exposure to the high-frequency, barely audible squeal produced by cooling fans and vibrating parts inside the system unit. This is particularly true for women who, according to recent studies, hear high-frequency sounds better than men do.

    Head-mounted microphones and earphones greatly reduce the effect of voice input and output. Acoustical tile and sound-muffling covers are available for reducing the noise from coworkers and impact printers. Tightening loose system unit components will reduce high-frequency noise.

*   **Electronic monitoring:** Research shows that workers whose performance is monitored electronically suffer more health problems than do those watched by human supervisors. For instance, a computer may monitor the number of keystrokes a data-entry clerk completes in a day. It might tally the time a customer-service person takes to handle a call. The company might then decide to shorten the time allowed and to continue monitoring to ensure compliance. By so doing, it may force a pace leading to physical problems, such as RSI, and mental health difficulties. One study found that electronically monitored employees reported more tension, extreme anxiety, depression, anger, and severe fatigue than those who were not electronically monitored.

    Recently it has been shown that electronic monitoring actually is not necessary. For instance, both Federal Express and Bell Canada replaced electronic monitoring with occasional monitoring by human managers, and they found that employee productivity stayed up and even increased.

A new word—*technostress*—has been proposed to describe the stress associated with computer use that is harmful to people. **Technostress** is the tension that arises when we have to adapt unnaturally to computers rather than having computers adapt to us.

DESIGN

Electronic products from microcomputers to microwave ovens to VCRs offer the promise of more efficiency and speed. Often, however, the products are so overloaded with features that users cannot figure them out. Because a microprocessor chip handles not just one operation but several, some manufacturers feel obliged to pile on the bells and whistles. Thus, many home and office products, while being fancy technology platforms, are difficult for humans to use.

A recent trend among manufacturers is to deliberately strip down the features offered, rather than to constantly do all that is possible. In appliances, this restraint is shown among certain types of high-end audio equipment, which comes with fewer buttons and lights. In computers, there are similar trends.

Surveys show that consumers want plug-and-play equipment—machines that they can simply turn on and with which they can quickly start working. Thus, computers are being made easier to use, with more menus, windows, icons, and pictures.

For a summary of ergonomic concerns, see Figure 10-25.

Problem	Remedy
Eyestrain and headache	Take frequent breaks, avoid screen glare, place object at fixed focal distance
Back and neck pain	Use adjustable equipment
Repetitive strain injury	Use ergonomically correct keyboards, take frequent breaks
Noise	Use head-mounted microphones and earphones, install acoustical tile and sound-muffling covers, tighten system unit components
Stress from excessive monitoring	Remove electronic monitoring

Figure 10-25 Summary of ergonomic concerns

▼ CONCEPT CHECK

► What is ergonomics and why is it important?

► Discuss some of the most significant physical concerns created by frequent computer use and how they can be avoided.

► Discuss some of the most significant mental concerns created by frequent computer use and how they can be avoided.

THE ENVIRONMENT

The computer industry has responded to the Energy Star program with the Green PC. You can help by conserving, recycling, and educating.

What do you suppose uses the greatest amount of electricity in the workplace? Microcomputers do. They account for five percent of the electricity used. Increased power production translates to increased air pollution, depletion of nonrenewable resources, and other environmental hazards.

The Environmental Protection Agency (EPA) has created the **Energy Star** program to discourage waste in the microcomputer industry. Along with over 50 manufacturers, the EPA has established a goal of reducing power requirements for system units, monitors, and printers. The industry has responded with the concept of the **Green PC.** (See Figure 10-26.)

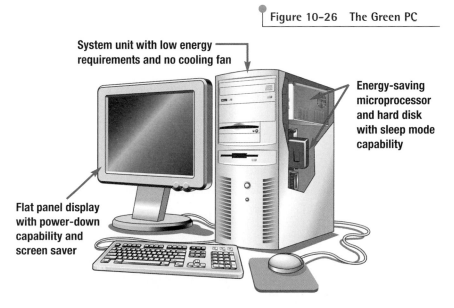

Figure 10-26 The Green PC

System unit with low energy requirements and no cooling fan

Energy-saving microprocessor and hard disk with sleep mode capability

Flat panel display with power-down capability and screen saver

THE GREEN PC

The basic elements of the Green PC are:

- **System Unit:** Using existing technology from portable computers, the system unit (1) uses an energy-saving microprocessor that requires a minimal amount of power, (2) employs microprocessor and hard-disk drives that shift to an energy-saving or sleep mode when not in operation, (3) replaces the conventional power supply unit with an adapter that requires less electricity, and (4) eliminates the cooling fan.

- **Display:** Displays have been made more energy efficient by using (1) flat panels that require less energy than the traditional monitors, (2) special power-down monitors that automatically reduce power consumption when not in use, and (3) screen-saver software that clears the display whenever it is not in use.

- **Manufacturing:** Computer manufacturers such as Intel, Apple, Compaq, and others are using fewer harmful chemicals in production. Particular attention is given to **chlorofluorocarbons (CFCs)** in solvents and cleaning agents. (CFCs can travel into the atmosphere and are suspected by some in the scientific community of depleting the earth's ozone layer.) Toxic nickel and other heavy metals are being eliminated or reduced in the manufacturing processes.

Of course, not all of these technologies and manufacturing processes are used for all microcomputers. But more and more of them are.

PERSONAL RESPONSIBILITY

Some of the things that you, as a computer user, can do to help protect the environment are the following:

- **Conserve:** The EPA estimates that 30 to 40 percent of computer users leave their machines running days, nights, and weekends. When finished working for the day, turn off all computers and other energy-consuming devices. The EPA also estimates that 80 percent of the time a monitor is on, no one is looking at it. Use screen-saver programs that blank the computer screen after three to five minutes of inactivity.

- **Recycle:** U.S. businesses use an enormous amount of paper each year—a pile 48,900 miles high. Much of that, as well as the paper we throw out at home, can be recycled. Other recyclable items include computer boxes, packaging material, printer cartridges, and floppy disks. Last year over 24 million computers were thrown away. (See Figure 10-27.) Only 14 percent were recycled. Recycle discarded computers by contacting any one of the groups listed in Figure 10-28.

- **Educate:** Be aware of and learn more about ecological dangers of all types. Make your concerns known to manufacturers and retail agencies. Support ecologically sound products.

Figure 10-27   Discarded computer components

▼ CONCEPT CHECK

▶ What is the Energy Star program?

▶ What is a Green PC? What are the basic elements of the Green PC?

▶ What actions can you take to help protect the environment?

Organization	Web Site
Computers for Schools Association	www.detwiler.org
Computers for Youth	www.cfy.org
National Cristina Foundation	www.cristinak.org
Share Technology	www.sharetechnology.org

Figure 10-28   Computer recycling groups

A Look to the Future

Presence Technology Makes Finding People Easy

How would you like the devices you use to alert others when you are using them? What if you sat down to watch television and a message popped up alerting you that a friend wants to chat? What if you could instantly know what is the best way to get in touch with someone you know? Presence technology is designed to meet all of these needs, and many more.

Many people are currently exposed to presence technology through their instant messaging software. When a user signs on to a system, friends are alerted to his or her presence. Many manufacturers of personal computing devices and cellular phones are currently developing presence technology. Analysts expect presence technology to become a feature of everything from your computer to your car. Some even anticipate that your friends will be able to tell where you are and which device (PDA, television, telephone) is the best way to contact you. While there are many advantages to such a system, the potential loss of privacy is of concern to many. They argue the potential abuse by advertisers and others makes presence technology a threat to privacy. Supporters of this technology suggest that the user would have control over when and where they are "seen."

What do you think? Would you like to know that you are always available to those who need to get in touch with you? What are the potential advantages of this type of technology? Some experts suggest presence technology will become a standard feature of new cars, phones, and appliances. What do you think? Would you buy a television that lets everyone know you are watching TV instead of working on homework or studying for exams?

PRIVACY AND SECURITY

PRIVACY

Computer ethics are guidelines for moral computer use. Four computer ethics issues are **privacy, accuracy, property, and access.**

Large Databases

Large organizations are constantly compiling information about us. **Reverse directories** list telephone numbers followed by subscriber names. **Information resellers (information brokers)** collect and sell personal data. **Electronic profiles** compiled from databases to provide highly detailed and personalized descriptions of individuals

Identity theft is the illegal assumption of someone's identity for the purposes of economic gain. **Mistaken identity** occurs when an electronic profile of one person is switched with another. The **Freedom of Information Act** entitles individuals access to governmental records relating to them.

Private Networks

Many organizations monitor employee e-mail and computer files using special software called **snoopware.**

Internet and the Web

Many people believe that while using the Web as long as they are selective about disclosing their name and other personal information, little can be done to invade their privacy. This is called the **illusion of anonymity.**

PRIVACY

Created by browsers, **history files** record locations of sites visited by a computer system. **Cookies** are specialized programs deposited onto your computer system that records sites visited, activity at sites, and other information. Two basic types of cookies, **traditional cookies** and **Ad network cookies (adware cookies)** monitor activities across all sites visited. **Cookie-cutter programs** allow users to selectively filter or block the most intrusive cookies while allowing selective traditional cookies to operate.

The term **spyware** is used to describe a wide range of programs that are designed to secretly record and report an individual's activities on the Internet. Ad network cookies are just one type of spyware. Two other types are **Web bugs** and **Computer monitoring (sniffer programs, keystroker loggers).** A new category of programs known as **spy removal programs** has recently evolved that is designed to detect Web bugs and monitoring software.

Major Privacy Laws

There are numerous federal laws governing privacy matters. Nonetheless, privacy remains primarily an ethical issue. To respond to privacy concerns, a Code of Fair Information Practice has been established.

To be a competent end user you need to be aware of the potential impact of technology on people. You need to be sensitive to and knowledgeable about personal privacy, organizational security, ergonomics, and the environmental impact of technology.

SECURITY

Computer Criminals

Computer criminals include employees, outside users, hackers and crackers (**hackers** gain access for the fun and challenge while **crackers** do it for malicious purposes, **bomb** is a destructive program), organized crime, and terrorists.

Computer Crime

Computer crime is an illegal action with which a criminal uses special knowledge of computer technology.

- Malicious programs or **malware,** include **viruses** (**Computer Abuse Amendments Act of 1994** makes spreading a virus a federal offense), **worms** (self-replicate to slow or stop a computer's operations), and **Trojan horses** (enter a computer system disguised as something else). **Virus checkers** alert users when certain viruses and worms enter their systems.

- **Denial of service attack (DoS)** is an attempt to shut down or stop a computer system or network. It floods a computer or network with requests for information and data. Servers under attack are unable to respond to legitimate users.

SECURITY

- **Scams** are fraudulent or deceptive acts or operations designed to trick individuals into spending their time and money with little or no return. Common **Internet scams** include identity theft, chain letters, auction fraud, vacation prizes, and advance fee loans.

- **Theft** takes many forms including stealing hardware, software, data, and computer time. Unauthorized copying of programs is called **software piracy** and protected by the **Software Copyright Act of 1980.**

- **Data manipulation** involves changing data or leaving prank messages. The **Computer Fraud and Abuse Act of 1986** helps protect against data manipulation.

- Other hazards include natural disasters, civil strife, terrorism, technological failures (**surge protectors** protect against **voltage surges** or **spikes**), and human error.

Measures to Protect Computer Security

Security is concerned with keeping hardware, software, data, and programs safe from unauthorized personnel. Some measures are **encrypting,** restricting access by using **biometric scanning** devices, **passwords** and **firewalls,** and anticipating disasters (**physical** and **data security, disaster recovery plans, hot sites** and **cold sites**), and backing up data.

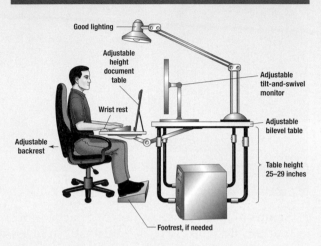

Good lighting

Adjustable height document table

Adjustable tilt-and-swivel monitor

Wrist rest

Adjustable bilevel table

Adjustable backrest

Table height 25–29 inches

Footrest, if needed

Ergonomics is the study of human factors related to things people use, including computers.

Physical Health

Physical health problems and their solutions include:

- Eyestrain and headache—take frequent breaks; avoid glare on the monitor.
- Back and neck pains—use adjustable chairs, tables, monitor stands, keyboards, footrests.
- **Repetitive strain injury (RSI, repetitive motion injury, cumulative trama disorder)** includes **carpal tunnel syndrome**—take frequent breaks; use good posture; adopt healthy lifestyle; use ergonomic keyboards.

Mental Health

Counterproductive mental irritations include:

- Noise from clattering printers and high-frequency squeals from computers.
- Stress from electronic monitoring.

Unnatural adaptation to computers can cause **technostress.**

Design

Computers are being designed for easier and healthier use. There is a trend toward simplifying features offered on new models.

Organization	Web Site
Computers for Schools Association	www.detwiler.org
Computers for Youth	www.cfy.org
National Cristina Foundation	www.cristinak.org
Share Technology	www.sharetechnology.org

Microcomputers are the greatest users of electricity in the workplace. The EPA has established the **Energy Star program** to promote energy-efficient computer use. The computer industry has responded with the concept of the **Green PC.**

The Green PC

The basic elements of the Green PC include:

- System units with energy-saving processors, sleep-mode capability, efficient adapters, and no cooling fans.
- Display units that replace CRT displays with flat panels, use special power-down monitors and screen-saver software.
- Manufacturing that eliminates or reduces the use of harmful chemicals such as **chlorofluorocarbons (CFCs),** nickel, and other heavy metals.

Personal Responsibility

As a responsible computer user, you can help protect the environment by:

- Conserving energy by turning off computer systems at night and using screen savers.
- Recycling paper, computer boxes, packaging materials, printer cartridges, and floppy disks.
- Educating yourself and others about ecological dangers and using ecologically sound products.

access (273)
accuracy (273)
ad network cookie (277)
adware cookie (277)
biometric scanning (288)
bomb (282)
carpal tunnel syndrome (291)
chlorofluorocarbons (CFCs) (294)
cold site (289)
Computer Abuse Amendments Act
  of 1994 (284)
computer crime (282)
computer ethics (273)
Computer Fraud and Abuse Act
  of 1986 (286)
computer monitoring software (277)
cookie-cutter program (277)
cookies (277)
cracker (282)
cumulative trauma disorder (291)
data security (289)
denial of service (DoS) attack (285)
disaster recovery plan (289)
electronic monitoring (292)
electronic profile (274)
encrypting (288)
Energy Star (293)
ergonomics (290)
ethics (273)
firewall (288)
Freedom of Information Act (275)
Green PC (293)
hacker (282)
history file (277)
hot site (289)

identity theft (275)
illusion of anonymity (276)
information broker (274)
information reseller (274)
Internet scam (285)
keystroke logger (278)
malware (283)
mistaken identity (275)
password (288)
physical security (289)
privacy (272)
property (273)
repetitive motion injury (291)
repetitive strain injury (RSI) (291)
reverse directory (274)
scam (285)
security (287)
sniffer program (278)
snoopware (276)
Software Copyright Act of 1980 (286)
software piracy (286)
spike (287)
spy removal program (278)
spyware (277)
surge protector (287)
technostress (292)
traditional cookies (277)
Trojan horse (284)
virus (283)
virus checker (284)
voltage surge (287)
Web bug (277)
worm (284)

To test your knowledge of these key terms with animated flash cards, consult your Computing Essentials CD or visit us at www.olearyseries.com/CE06 and select Key Terms.

COMPUTING ESSENTIALS 2006

CROSSWORD

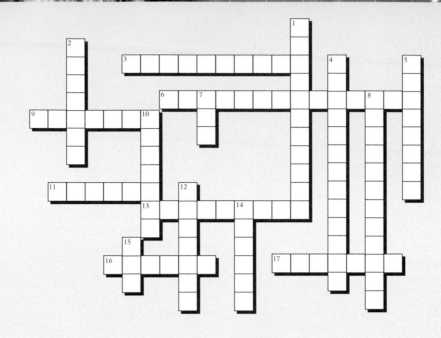

Across

3 Study of human factors related to the things people use.

6 Device that separates the computer from the power source.

9 Those who gain access to systems for malicious purposes.

11 Those who gain access to systems for the fun and challenge.

13 Used to record virtually everything done on a computer.

16 Specialized program deposited by a Web site on your computer.

17 Program that records keystrokes and activities.

Down

1 Includes the locations of sites visited by your browser.

2 Malicious software.

4 Illegal assumption of someone's identity.

5 Acts as a security buffer between networks.

7 Repetitive strain injury.

8 Tension that arises when users unnaturally adapt to computers.

10 Directory used to obtain addresses from a list of phone numbers.

12 Fully equipped backup center.

14 Small program hidden in HTML code.

15 Attempts to slow down or stop a computer system or network.

For an interactive version of this crossword, consult your Computing Essentials CD or visit us at **www.olearyseries.com/CE06** and select Crossword.

Circle the letter or fill in the correct answer.

1. The ethical issue that relates to the responsibility of those who collect data to ensure that the data is correct is _____.
   a. privacy
   b. accuracy
   c. property
   d. access
   e. ethics

2. The ethical issue that concerns the collection and use of data about individuals is _____.
   a. privacy
   b. accuracy
   c. property
   d. access
   e. ethics

3. _____ is a term used to describe a wide range of programs that secretly record and report an individual's activities on the Internet.
   a. Worm
   b. Utility
   c. Virus
   d. Suite
   e. Spyware

4. The largest category of computer criminals is _____.
   a. crackers
   b. hackers
   c. agents
   d. organized criminals
   e. employees

5. _____ is/are concerned with protecting information, hardware, and software.
   a. Users
   b. FBI agents
   c. Security
   d. The Department of Defense
   e. Protection programs

6. _____ is concerned with protecting hardware from possible human and natural disasters.
   a. Physical security
   b. Data security
   c. The FBI
   d. Encryption
   e. Energy Star

7. _____ is concerned with fitting the job to the worker rather than forcing the worker to contort to fit a job.
   a. Human Resources
   b. Ergonomics
   c. Energy Star
   d. RSI
   e. An HMO

8. _____ is also called repetitive motion injury and cumulative trauma disorder.
   a. BRM
   b. ARD
   c. TVT
   d. EMI
   e. RSI

9. _____ describes the stress that is associated with computers.
   a. RSI
   b. EMI
   c. Technostress
   d. Computer Use Distress
   e. Cumulative TechStress

10. Environmentally friendly system units, displays, and manufacturing are the basic elements of the _____.
    a. Energy Star
    b. Green PC
    c. Standard System
    d. Millennium Plan
    e. EarthTech Program

For an interactive version of these multiple choice questions, consult your Computing Essentials CD or visit us at www.olearyseries.com/CE06 and select Multiple Choice.

MATCHING

Match each numbered item with the most closely related lettered item. Write your answers in the spaces provided.

a. ad network
   cookies
b. cold site
c. computer
   crime
d. cookie
e. cookie-cutter
f. cracker
g. DoS
h. hot site
i. encrypting
j. ethics
k. firewall
l. hacker
m. illusion of
   anonymity
n. property
o. reverse
   directory
p. snoopware
q. spike
r. virus
   checkers
s. viruses
t. worm

1. Standards of moral conduct. _____
2. Relates to who owns data and rights to software. _____
3. Lists subscriber names followed by telephone numbers. _____
4. Programs that record virtually every activity on a computer system. _____
5. Belief that there is little threat to personal privacy via the Internet. _____
6. Specialized programs that record information on Web site visitors. _____
7. Monitor Web activity and send reports to marketing groups. _____
8. Program that blocks the most intrusive ad network cookies. _____
9. Illegal action involving special knowledge of computer technology. _____
10. Gains unauthorized access to a system for the fun and challenge. _____
11. Gains unauthorized access to a system for malicious purposes. _____
12. Hidden instructions that migrate through networks and operating systems and become embedded in different programs. _____
13. Fills a computer system with self-replicating information. _____
14. An attack that overwhelms Web sites with data, making them inaccessible. _____
15. Programs that alert users when certain viruses enter a system. _____
16. Electricity surge that may destroy chips or electronic components. _____
17. Coding information so that only authorized users can read or use it. _____
18. Security hardware and software that controls access to internal computer networks. _____
19. Fully equipped backup computer center. _____
20. Emergency facility that is a shell in which hardware must be installed. _____

For an interactive version of this matching exercise, consult your Computing Essentials CD or visit our Web site at www.olearyseries.com/CE06 and select Matching.

OPEN-ENDED

On a separate sheet of paper, respond to each question or statement.

1. Discuss the relationship between databases and privacy.
2. Discuss the Code of Fair Information Act. Why has this act not been made into law?
3. Discuss the various kinds of computer criminals.
4. What are the principal measures used to protect computer security? What is encryption? How is it used by corporations and individuals?
5. What is ergonomics? How does computer use impact mental health? Physical health?

Spyware

1

Have you installed any free software from the Internet? Did you know that seemingly harmless software might actually be spying on you, even sending personal information to advertisers or worse? Fortunately, spyware removal programs can help. After reviewing Making IT Work for You: Spyware Removal on pages 280 and 281, answer the following questions: (a) Define spyware and discuss how it works. (b) Describe the process for downloading and installing Lavasoft's Ad-aware. (c) Describe the capabilities of Ad-aware. (d) Do you think that spyware might be on your computer? If yes, how do suppose the spyware was deposited onto your system? If no, why are you so confident?

Personal Firewalls

2

At one time, firewalls were used only for large servers. Today firewalls are available for almost any device that connects to the Internet, and are essential to ensure security. Connect to our Web site at www.olearyseries.com/CE06 and select Using Technology to link to a personal firewall product for home users. Once connected, read about the firewall, and then answer the following questions: (a) Is this firewall a hardware or software solution? (b) Describe the procedure for installing the firewall. (c) What types of security risks does this firewall protect against? (d) Are there any security risks the firewall does not cover? If so, how can those risks be reduced?

1

How Web Bugs Work

The Internet is popular because it is fast, cheap, and open to everyone. These qualities also make it an ideal tool for criminals. Unscrupulous people can use programs called Web bugs to spy on you when you use the Internet. To learn more about "How Web Bugs Work," consult your Computing Essentials CD or visit our Web site at www.olearyseries.com/CE06, and select Animations. Then answer the following questions: (a) How can a Web bug infect your computer? (b) When a Web bug is delivered by e-mail, it typically sends a copy of that e-mail back to the server. What is the significance or purpose of this activity? (c) Do you think Web bugs are really a privacy concern? Do you think your computer may have one? How could you find out?

2

Mistaken Identity

A simple typo can result in mistaken identity. Such mistakes can have a tremendous impact on a person's career, family, and future. To learn more about "Mistaken Identity," consult your Computing Essentials CD or visit our Web site at www. olearyseries.com/CE06, and select Expansions. Then answer the following questions: (a) Have you been a victim of mistaken identity? If so, please discuss. (b) If your response was "yes", how would you verify that mistaken identity has occurred? (c) Perhaps you have been a victim without knowing it. List the questions that should be considered.

FEATURES

Animations

Careers in IT

DVD Direct

Expansions

Making IT Work for You

On the Web Explorations

TechTV

Tips

CHAPTER REVIEW

Key Terms

Crossword

Multiple Choice

Matching

Open-ended

Using Technology

Expanding Your Knowledge

Building Your Portfolio

Firewalls

1

Firewalls are a necessary component of complete computer security. They consist of hardware and software that control access to internal networks. A firewall usually includes a proxy server as a gatekeeper. Research firewalls and computer crime and write a one-page paper titled "Firewall Security" that addresses the following questions: (a) Define the term firewall. (b) What types of computer crime do firewalls protect against? (c) What types of computer crime are firewalls unable to protect against? Why? (d) What type of firewall protection might a corporation use? (e) What firewall protection is available for home users?

Facial Recognition

2

As new technologies emerge that promise to enhance our security, our privacy may be at stake. A recent example is the introduction of facial recognition systems in public places for use by police officers. Such systems have recently caught the attention of privacy advocates, as well as the ACLU. Research facial recognition systems on the Web, and then write a one-page paper titled "Facial Recognition" that addresses the following topics: (a) Describe how facial recognition technology works. (b) How can facial recognition technology enhance security? (c) In what ways might facial recognition technology compromise privacy? (Hint: Consider security cameras in department or grocery stores.) (d) Do you approve of facial recognition technology? Explain your answer.

COMPETENCIES

After you have read this chapter, you should be able to:

1 **Explain how organizations can be structured according to five functions and three management levels.**

2 **Describe how information flows in an organization.**

3 **Distinguish among a transaction processing system, a management information system, a decision support system, and an executive support system.**

4 **Distinguish between office automation systems and knowledge work systems.**

5 **Explain the difference between data workers and knowledge workers.**

Information Flow
Flows vertically and horizontally throughout an organization

Information Flow

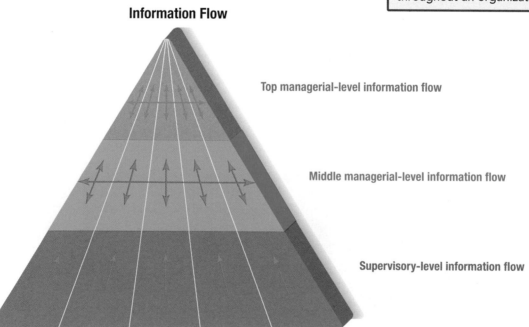

Top managerial-level information flow

Middle managerial-level information flow

Supervisory-level information flow

CHAPTER

An information system is a collection of people, procedures, software, hardware, and data (as we discussed in Chapter 1). They all work together to provide information essential to running an organization. This is information that will successfully produce a product or service and, for profit-oriented enterprises, derive a profit.

Why are computers used in organizations? No doubt you can easily state one reason: to keep records of events. However, another reason might be less obvious: to help make decisions. For example, point-of-sale terminals record sales as well as which salesperson made each sale. This information can be used for decision making. For instance, it can help the sales manager decide which salespeople will get year-end bonuses for doing exceptional work.

The Internet, communication links, and databases connect you with information resources as well as information systems far beyond the surface of your desk. The microcomputer offers you access to a greater quantity of information than was possible a few years ago. In addition, you also have access to better quality information. As we show in this chapter, when you tap into a computer-based information system, you not only get information—you also get help in making decisions.

Competent end users need to understand how the information flows as it moves through an organization's different functional areas and management levels. They need to be aware of the different types of computer-based information systems, including transaction processing systems, management information systems, decision support systems, and executive support systems. They also need to understand the role and importance of databases to support each level or type of information system.

Information Systems
Support the natural flow of information within an organization

Information Systems

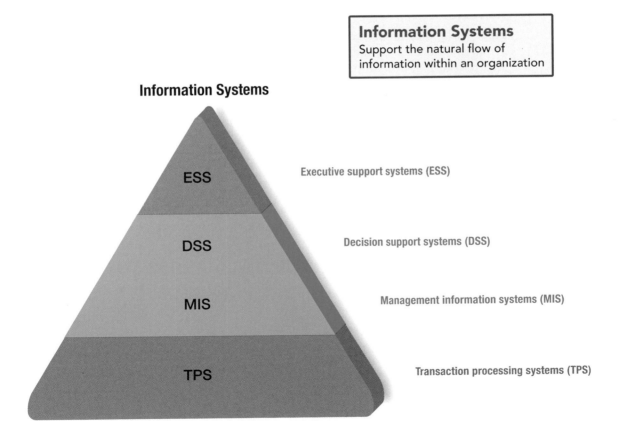

- Executive support systems (ESS)
- Decision support systems (DSS)
- Management information systems (MIS)
- Transaction processing systems (TPS)

Organizations can be viewed from a functional perspective. Management has three levels. Information flows up, down, and across among managers and departments.

In large and medium-sized organizations, computerized information systems do not just keep track of transactions and day-to-day business operations. They also support the flow of information within the organization. This information flows both vertically and horizontally. To understand this, we need to understand how an organization is structured. One way to examine an organization's structure is to view it from a functional perspective. That is, you can study the different basic functional areas in organizations and the different types of people within these functional areas.

As we describe these, you might consider how they apply to any organization you are familiar with. Or consider how they apply to a hypothetical manufacturer of sporting goods, the HealthWise Group. Think of this as a large company that manufactures equipment for sports and physical activities, including those that interest you. These goods range from every type of ball imaginable (from golf to tennis to soccer) to hockey pads, leotards, and surf boards. (See Figure 11-1.)

Like many organizations, HealthWise Group can be viewed from a functional perspective with various management levels. Effective operations require an efficient and coordinated flow of information throughout the organization.

FUNCTIONS

Depending on the services or products they provide, most organizations have departments that specialize in one of five basic functions. These are accounting, marketing, human resources, production, and research. (See Figure 11-2.)

- **Accounting** records all financial activity from billing customers to paying employees. For example, at HealthWise, the accounting department tracks

Figure 11-1 Manufacturing surf boards

Figure 11-2   The five functions
of an organization

Human resources finds and hires people and handles matters such as sick leave and retirement benefits. In addition, it is concerned with evaluation, compensation, and professional development.

Accounting tracks all financial activity. At HealthWise, this department records bills and other financial transactions with sporting goods stores. It also produces financial statements, including budgets and forecasts of financial performance.

Research conducts basic research and relates new discoveries to the firm's current or new products department. Research people at HealthWise explore new ideas from exercise physiologists about muscle development. They use this knowledge to design new physical fitness machines.

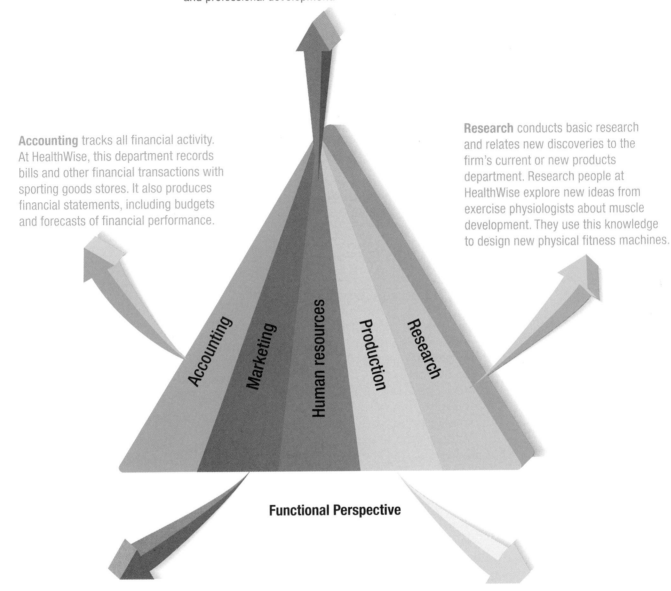

Functional Perspective

Marketing handles planning, pricing, promoting, selling, and distributing goods and services to customers. At HealthWise, they even get involved with creating a customer newsletter that is distributed via the corporate Web page.

Production takes in raw materials and people work to turn out finished goods (or services). It may be a manufacturing activity or—in the case of a retail store—an operations activity. At HealthWise, this department purchases steel and aluminum to be used in weight-lifting and exercise machines.

all sales, payments, and transfers of funds. It also produces reports detailing the financial condition of the company.

- **Marketing** plans, prices, promotes, sells, and distributes the organization's goods and services. At HealthWise, goods include a wide range of products related to sports and other types of physical activity.

- **Human resources** focuses on people—hiring, training, promoting, and any number of other human-centered activities within the organization. This function relates to people in each of the functional areas, including accountants, sales representatives, human resource specialists, production workers, and research scientists.

- **Production** actually creates finished goods and services using raw materials and personnel. At HealthWise, this includes manufacturing a variety of sports equipment, including surf boards.

- **Research** identifies, investigates, and develops new products and services. For example, at HealthWise, scientists are investigating a light, inexpensive alloy for a new line of weight training equipment.

Although the titles may vary, nearly every large and small organization has departments that perform these basic functions. Whatever your job in an organization, it is likely to be in one of these functional areas.

MANAGEMENT LEVELS

Most people who work in an organization are not managers, of course. At the base of the organizational pyramid are the assemblers, painters, welders, drivers, and so on. These people produce goods and services. Above them are various levels of managers—people with titles such as supervisor, director, regional manager, and vice president. These are the people who do the planning, leading, organizing, and controlling necessary to see that the work gets done. At HealthWise, for example, the northwest district sales manager directs and coordinates all the salespeople in her area. Other job titles might be vice president of marketing, director of human resources, or production manager. In smaller organizations, these titles are often combined.

Management in many organizations is divided into three levels: supervisors, middle-level, and top-level. (See Figure 11-3.)

- **Supervisors:** Supervisors manage and monitor the employees or workers—those who actually produce the goods and services. Thus, these managers have responsibility relating to *operational matters*. They monitor day-to-day events and immediately take corrective action, if necessary. (See Figure 11-4.)

- **Middle management:** Middle-level managers deal with *control, planning* (also called *tactical planning*), and *decision making*. They implement the long-term goals of the organization.

- **Top management:** Top-level managers are concerned with *long-range planning* (also called *strategic planning*). They need information that will help them to plan the future growth and direction of the organization.

INFORMATION FLOW

Each level of management has different information needs. Top-level managers need information that is summarized in capsule form to reveal the overall condition of the business. They also need information from outside the organization, because top-level managers need to forecast and plan for long-range events. Middle-level managers need summarized information—weekly

Managerial Levels

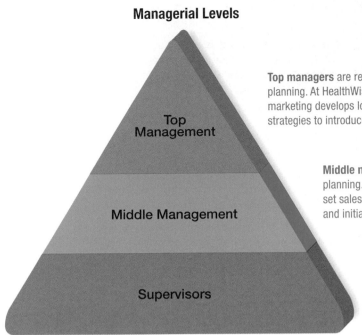

Top managers are responsible for long-range planning. At HealthWise, the vice president of marketing develops long-term marketing strategies to introduce newly developed products.

Middle managers are responsible for tactical planning. At HealthWise, regional sales managers set sales goals, monitor progress to meet goals, and initiate corrective action as needed.

Supervisors are responsible for operational matters. At HealthWise, a production supervisor monitors the inventory for parts and reorders when low.

Figure 11-3 Three levels of management

or monthly reports. They need to develop budget projections and to evaluate the performance of supervisors. Supervisors need detailed, very current, day-to-day information on their units so that they can keep operations running smoothly.

To support these different needs, information *flows* in different directions. (See Figure 11-5.) For top-level managers, the flow of information from within the organization is both vertical and horizontal. The top-level managers, such as the chief executive officer (CEO), need information from below and from all departments. (See Figure 11-6.) They also need information from outside the organization. For example, at HealthWise, they are deciding whether to introduce a line of hockey equipment in the southwestern United States. The vice president of marketing must look at relevant data. Such data might include availability of ice rinks and census data about the number of young people. It might also include sales histories on related cold-weather sports equipment.

Figure 11-4 Supervisors monitor day-to-day events

For middle-level managers, the information flow is both vertical and horizontal across functional lines within the organization. For example, the regional sales managers at HealthWise set their sales goals by coordinating with middle managers in the production department. They are able to tell sales managers what products will be produced, how many, and when. An example of a product might be an exercise bicycle. The regional sales managers also must coordinate with the strategic goals set by the top managers. They must set and monitor the sales goals for the supervisors beneath them.

For supervisory managers, information flow is primarily vertical. That is, supervisors communicate mainly with their middle managers and with the workers beneath them. For instance, at HealthWise, production supervisors rarely communicate with people in the accounting department. However, they are constantly communicating with production line workers and with their own managers.

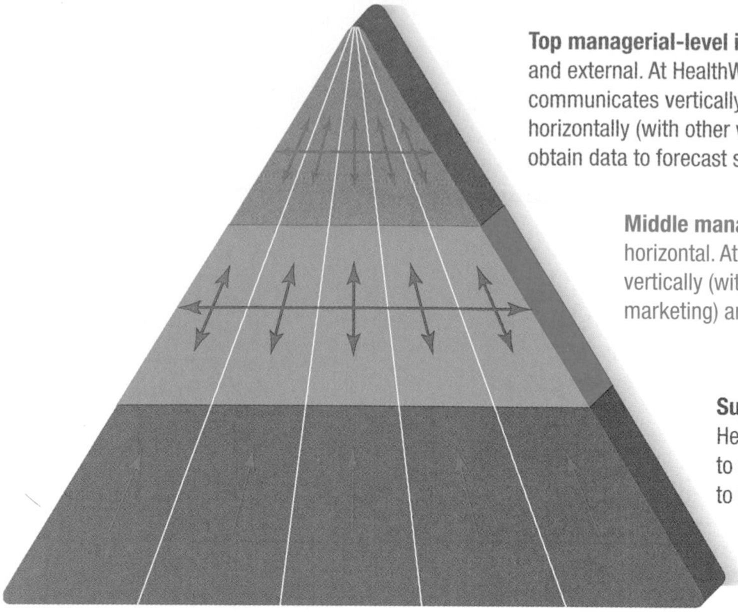

Information Flow

Top managerial-level information flow is vertical, horizontal, and external. At HealthWise, the vice president of marketing communicates vertically (with regional sales managers), horizontally (with other vice presidents), and externally to obtain data to forecast sales.

Middle managerial-level information flow is vertical and horizontal. At HealthWise, regional sales managers communicate vertically (with district sales managers and the vice president of marketing) and horizontally with other middle-level managers.

Supervisory-level information flow is primarily vertical. At HealthWise, production supervisors monitor worker activities to ensure smooth production. They provide daily status reports to middle-level production managers.

Figure 11-5 Information flow within an organization

Now we know how a large organization is usually structured and how information flows within the organization. But how is a computer-based information system likely to be set up to support its needs? And what do you, as a microcomputer user, need to know to use it?

▼ **CONCEPT CHECK**

▶ What are the five basic functions within an organization?

▶ What are the three levels of management? Discuss each level.

▶ Describe the flow of information within an organization.

Figure 11-6 Top-level managers handle both vertical and horizontal information flow

COMPUTER-BASED INFORMATION SYSTEMS

There are four kinds of computer-based information systems: transaction processing system, management information system, decision support system, and executive support system.

Almost all organizations have computer-based **information systems.** Large organizations typically have formal names for the systems designed to collect and use the data. Although different organizations may use different names, the most common names are transaction processing, management information, decision support, and executive support systems. (See Figure 11-7.)

Information Systems

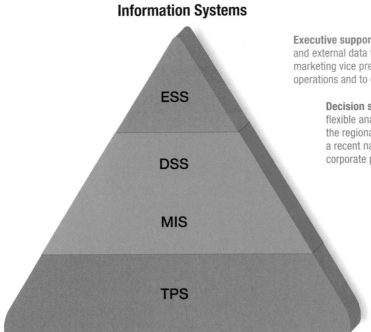

Executive support systems (ESS) use internal data from MIS and TPS and external data to support top-level managers. At HealthWise, the marketing vice president uses his ESS to view current marketing operations and to develop long-term marketing strategies.

Decision support systems (DSS) use data from TPS and a set of flexible analytical tools to support middle managers. At HealthWise, the regional sales managers use the DSS to evaluate the impact of a recent national promotion campaign on regional sales and corporate profit.

Management information systems (MIS) use data from the TPS to support middle-level managers. At HealthWise, regional sales managers use their MIS reports to monitor weekly divisional sales and to compare actual sales to established sales goals.

Transaction processing systems (TPS) record day-to-day transactions to support middle managers. At HealthWise, production supervisors use their TPS to record and to monitor current inventory levels and production line output.

Figure 11–7 **Four kinds of computer–based information systems**

- **Transaction processing system:** The **transaction processing system (TPS)** records day-to-day transactions, such as customer orders, bills, inventory levels, and production output. The TPS helps supervisors by generating databases that act as the foundation for the other information systems.

- **Management information system:** The **management information system (MIS)** summarizes the detailed data of the transaction processing system in standard reports for middle-level managers. Such reports might include weekly sales and production schedules.

- **Decision support system:** The **decision support system (DSS)** provides a flexible tool for analysis. The DSS helps middle-level managers and others in the organization analyze a wide range of problems, such as the effect of events and trends outside the organization. Like the MIS, the DSS draws on the detailed data of the transaction processing system.

- **Executive support system:** The **executive support system (ESS),** also known as the **executive information system (EIS),** is an easy-to-use system that presents information in a very highly summarized form. It helps top-level managers oversee the company's operations and develop strategic plans. The ESS combines the internal data from TPS and MIS with external data.

▼ CONCEPT CHECK

▶ What are the four most common computer-based information systems? Describe each.

▶ Compare and contrast management information systems with decision support systems.

A transaction processing system tracks operations and creates databases. Accounting TPS have six activities involving sales order processing, accounts receivable, inventory, accounts payable, payroll, and general ledger.

Figure 11-8 Transaction processing system database

A *transaction processing system (TPS)* helps an organization keep track of routine operations and records these events in a database. (See Figure 11-8.) For this reason, some firms call this the **data processing system (DPS).** The data from operations—for example, customer orders for HealthWise's products—makes up a database that records the transactions of the company. This database of transactions is used to support an MIS, DSS, and ESS.

One of the most essential transaction processing systems for any organization is in the accounting area. (See Figure 11-9.) Every accounting department handles six basic activities. Five of these are sales order processing, accounts receivable, inventory and purchasing, accounts payable, and payroll. All of these are recorded in the general ledger, the sixth activity.

Let us take a look at these six activities. They will make up the basis of the accounting system for almost any office you might work in.

- The **sales order processing** activity records the customer requests for the company's products or services. When an order comes in—a request for a set of barbells, for example—the warehouse is alerted to ship a product. (See Figure 11-10.)

- The **accounts receivable** activity records money received from or owed by customers. HealthWise keeps track of bills paid by sporting goods stores and by gyms and health clubs to which it sells directly.

- The parts and finished goods that the company has in stock are called **inventory**—all exercise machines in the warehouse, for example. (See Figure 11-11.) An **inventory control system** keeps records of the number of each kind of part or finished good in the warehouse. **Purchasing** is the buying of materials and services. Often a **purchase order** is used. This is a form that shows the name of the company supplying the material or service and what is being purchased.

- **Accounts payable** refers to money the company owes its suppliers for materials and services it has received—steel and aluminum, for example.

- The **payroll** activity is concerned with calculating employee paychecks. Amounts are generally determined by the kind of job, hours worked, and

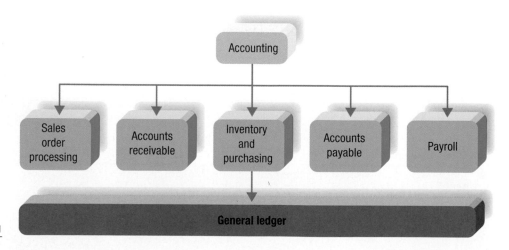

Figure 11-9 Transaction processing system for accounting

Figure 11-10 Customer orders are sent to the warehouse via sales order processing

Figure 11-11 Inventory control systems manage the merchandise in the warehouse

kinds of deductions (such as taxes, social security, medical insurance). Paychecks may be calculated from employee time cards or, in some cases, supervisors' time sheets.

- The **general ledger** keeps track of all summaries of all the foregoing transactions. A typical general ledger system can produce income statements and balance sheets. **Income statements** show a company's financial performance—income, expenses, and the difference between them for a specific time period. **Balance sheets** list the overall financial condition of an organization. They include assets (for example, buildings and property owned), liabilities (debts), and how much of the organization (the equity) is owned by the owners.

There are many other transaction systems that you come into contact with every day. These include automatic teller machines, which record cash withdrawals; online registration systems, which track student enrollments; and supermarket discount cards, which track customer purchases.

▼ CONCEPT CHECK

▶ What is the purpose of a transaction processing system?

▶ Describe the six activities of a TPS for accounting.

MANAGEMENT INFORMATION SYSTEMS

A management information system produces summarized, structured reports. Periodic, exception, and demand are three types of reports.

A *management information system (MIS)* is a computer-based information system that produces standardized reports in summarized structured form. (See Figure 11-12.) It is used to support middle managers. An MIS differs from a transaction processing system in a significant way. Whereas a transaction processing system *creates* databases, an MIS *uses* databases. Indeed, an MIS can draw from the databases of several departments. Thus, an MIS requires a *database management system* that integrates the databases of the different

The Sports Company
Regional Sales Report

Region	Actual Sales	Target	Difference
Central	$166,430	$175,000	($8,570)
Northern	137,228	130,000	7,228
Southern	137,772	135,000	2,772
Eastern	152,289	155,000	(2,711)
Western	167,017	160,000	7,017

Figure 11-12   Management information system report

Figure 11-13   Reports can be shared by regional managers with a management information system

departments. Middle managers need summary data often drawn from across different functional areas.

An MIS produces reports that are *predetermined*. That is, they follow a predetermined format and always show the same kinds of content. Although reports may differ from one industry to another, there are three common categories of reports: periodic, exception, and demand.

- **Periodic reports** are produced at regular intervals—weekly, monthly, or quarterly, for instance. Examples are HealthWise's monthly sales and production reports. The sales reports from district sales managers are combined into a monthly report for the regional sales managers. For comparison purposes, a regional manager is also able to see the sales reports of other regional managers. (See Figure 11-13.)

- **Exception reports** call attention to unusual events. An example is a sales report that shows that certain items are selling significantly above or below marketing department forecasts. For instance, if fewer exercise bicycles are selling than were predicted for the northwest sales region, the regional manager will receive an exception report. That report may be used to alert the district managers and salespeople to give this product more attention.

- The opposite of a periodic report, a **demand report,** is produced on request. An example is a report on the numbers and types of jobs held by women and minorities. Such a report is not needed periodically, but it may be required when requested by the U.S. government. At HealthWise, many government contracts require this information. It is used to certify that HealthWise is within certain government equal-opportunity guidelines.

▼ **CONCEPT CHECK**

▶ What is the purpose of a management information system?

▶ Describe the three common categories of MIS reports.

DECISION SUPPORT SYSTEMS

A DSS helps decision makers analyze unanticipated situations. Four parts of a DSS are user, system software, data, and decision models. GDSS supports collective work.

Managers often must deal with unanticipated questions. For example, the HealthWise manager in charge of manufacturing might ask how a strike would affect production schedules. A *decision support system (DSS)* enables managers to get answers to such unexpected and generally nonrecurring kinds of problems. Frequently, a team is formed to address large problems. A **group decision support system (GDSS)** is then used to support this collective work.

A DSS, then, is quite different from a transaction processing system, which simply records data. It is also different from a management information system, which summarizes data in predetermined reports. A DSS is used to analyze data. Moreover, it produces reports that do not have a fixed format. This makes the DSS a flexible tool for analysis.

At one time, most DSSs were designed for large computer systems. Now, microcomputers, with their increased power and sophisticated software, such as spreadsheet and database programs, are widely used for DSS. Users of a DSS are managers, not computer programmers. Thus, a DSS must be easy to use—or most likely it will not be used at all. A HealthWise marketing manager might want to know which territories are not meeting their monthly sales quotas. To find out, the executive could query the database for all "SALES < QUOTA." (See Figure 11-14.)

How does a decision support system work? Essentially, it consists of four parts: the user, system software, data, and decision models.

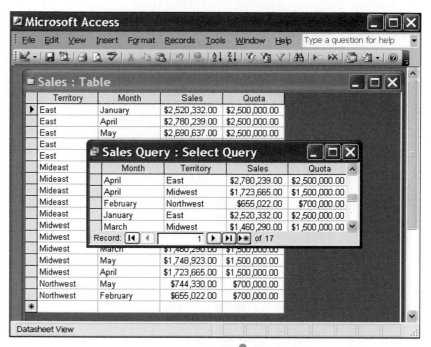

Figure 11-14 Decision support system query results for SALES < QUOTA

- The **user** could be you. In general, the user is someone who has to make decisions—a manager, often a middle-level manager.

- **System software** is essentially the operating system—programs designed to work behind the scenes to handle detailed operating procedures. In order to give the user a good, comfortable interface, the software typically is menu- or icon-driven. That is, the screen presents easily understood lists of commands or icons, giving the user several options.

- **Data** in a DSS is typically stored in a database and consists of two kinds. **Internal data**—data from within the organization—consists principally of transactions from the transaction processing system. **External data** is data gathered from outside the organization. Examples are data provided by marketing research firms, trade associations, and the U.S. government (such as customer profiles, census data, and economic forecasts).

- **Decision models** give the DSS its analytical capabilities. There are three basic types of models: strategic, tactical, and operational. **Strategic models** assist top-level managers in long-range planning, such as stating company objectives or planning plant locations. **Tactical models** help middle-level managers control the work of the organization, such as financial planning and sales promotion planning. **Operational models** help lower-level managers accomplish the organization's day-to-day activities, such as evaluating and maintaining quality control.

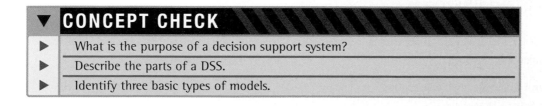

▼ CONCEPT CHECK

► What is the purpose of a decision support system?

► Describe the parts of a DSS.

► Identify three basic types of models.

EXECUTIVE SUPPORT SYSTEMS

> Executive support systems include sophisticated software, are specifically designed for easy use, require little training, and use graphics extensively.

Using a DSS requires some training. Many top managers have other people in their offices running DSSs and reporting their findings. Top-level executives also want something more concise than an MIS—something that produces very focused reports.

Executive support systems (ESSs) consist of sophisticated software that, like an MIS or a DSS, can present, summarize, and analyze data from an organization's databases. However, an ESS is specifically designed to be easy to use. This is so that a top executive with little spare time, for example, can obtain essential information without extensive training. Thus, information is often displayed in very condensed form with informative graphics. (See Figure 11-15.)

Consider an executive support system used by the president of Health-Wise. It is available on his microcomputer. The first thing each morning, the president calls up the ESS on his display screen, as shown in Figure 11-16. Note that the screen gives a condensed account of activities in the five different areas of the company. (These are Accounting, Marketing, Production, Human Resources, and Research.) On this particular morning, the ESS shows business in four areas proceeding smoothly. However, in the first area, Accounting, the percentage of late-paying customers—past due accounts—has increased by 3 percent. Three percent may not seem like much, but HealthWise has had a history of problems with late payers, which has left the company at times strapped for cash. The president decides to find out the details. To do so, he selects 1. Accounting.

Within moments, the display screen displays a graph of the past due accounts. (See Figure 11-17.) The status of today's late payers is shown in red. The status of late payers at this time a year ago is shown in yellow. The differences between today and a year ago are significant and clearly presented. For example, approximately $60,000 was late 1 to 10 days last year. This year, over

Figure 11-15   An ESS is designed for the executive

Information in condensed text form

Figure 11-16   Opening screen for an executive information system

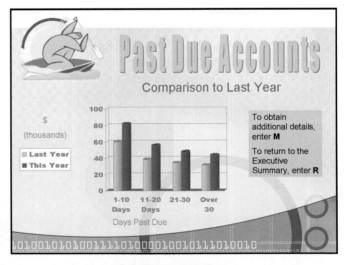

Details in graphic form

Figure 11-17   Graphic representation of Past Due Accounts

$80,000 was late. The president knows that he must take some action to speed up customer payments. (For example, he might call this to the attention of the vice president of accounting. The vice president might decide to implement a new policy that offers discounts to early payers or charge higher interest to late payers.)

ESSs permit a firm's top executives to gain direct access to information about the company's performance. Most provide direct electronic communication links to other executives. Some systems provide structured forms to help managers streamline their thoughts before sending electronic memos. In addition, an ESS may be organized to retrieve information from databases outside the company, such as business-news services. This enables a firm to watch for stories on competitors and stay current on relevant news events that could affect its business. For example, news of increased sports injuries caused by running and aerobic dancing, and the consequent decrease in people's interest in these activities, might cause HealthWise to alter its sales and production goals for its line of fitness-related shoes.

For a summary of the different types of information systems, see Figure 11-18.

Type	Description
TPS	Tracks routine operations and records events in databases, also known as data processing systems
MIS	Produces standardized reports (periodic, exception, and demand) using databases created by TPS
DSS	Analyzes unanticipated situations using data (internal and external) and decision models (strategic, tactical, and operational)
ESS	Presents summary information in a flexible, easy-to-use, graphical format designed for top executives

Figure 11-18   Summary of information systems

▼ CONCEPT CHECK

► What is the purpose of an executive support system?

► How is an ESS similar to and different from an MIS or DSS?

OTHER INFORMATION SYSTEMS

Information workers include data workers and knowledge workers. Data workers distribute and communicate information and use office information systems. Knowledge workers create information and use knowledge work systems.

We have discussed only four information systems: TPS to support lower-level managers, MIS and DSS to support middle-level managers, and ESS to support top-level managers. There are many other information systems to support different individuals and functions. The fastest-growing are information systems designed to support information workers.

Information workers distribute, communicate, and create information. They are the organization's secretaries, clerks, engineers, and scientists, to name a few. Some are involved with distribution and communication of information (like the secretaries and clerks; see Figure 11-19). They are called **data workers.** Others are involved with the creation of information (like the engineers and scientists). They are called **knowledge workers.**

Figure 11-19   Secretaries and clerks are data workers

Figure 11–20   Videoconferencing: Individuals and groups can see and share information

Two systems to support information workers are:

- **Office automation systems: Office automation systems (OASs)** are designed primarily to support data workers. These systems focus on managing documents, communicating, and scheduling. Documents are managed using word processing, Web authoring, desktop publishing, and other image technologies. **Project managers** are programs designed to schedule, plan, and control project resources. Microsoft Project is the most widely used project manager. **Videoconferencing systems** are computer systems that allow people located at various geographic locations to communicate and have in-person meetings. (See Figure 11-20.) To see how you can videoconference using your computer and the Internet, see Making IT Work for You: WebCams and Instant Messaging on pages 188 and 189.

- **Knowledge work systems: Knowledge workers** use OAS systems. Additionally, they use specialized information systems called **knowledge work systems (KWSs)** to create information in their areas of expertise. For example, engineers involved in product design and manufacturing use **computer-aided design/computer-aided manufacturing (CAD/CAM) systems.** (See Figure 11-21.) These KWSs consist of powerful microcomputers running special programs that integrate the design and manufacturing activities. CAD/CAM is widely used in the manufacture of automobiles and other products.

Figure 11–21   CAD/CAM: Knowledge work systems used by design and manufacturing engineers

▼ CONCEPT CHECK

▶ What is an information worker?

▶ Who are data workers? What type of information system is designed to support them?

▶ Who are knowledge workers? What type of information system is design to support them?

A Look to the Future

Information Overload

Have you ever questioned the value of technology? Has it really helped us and made us more productive? Is it possible that the various devices intended to increase our productivity have actually had the opposite effect?

E-mail, cell phones, notebook computers, and the Web are great. They allow us to communicate, work almost anywhere, and have access to vast amounts of data. However, unless we are careful, they can create "information overload" and have a negative effect on our ability to get work done.

Several recent studies have found that e-mail is the major source of information overload. It was recently reported that a typical knowledge worker in a large corporation sends and receives over 100 e-mail messages a day. Furthermore, the study concluded that the majority of these messages are not necessary. Here are some tips to control e-mail overload:

- **Be selective.** Look first at the subject line in an e-mail—read only those of direct and immediate interest to you. Look next at the sender line—read only those from people important to you; postpone or ignore the others.

- **Remove.** After reading an e-mail, respond if necessary; then either file it in the appropriate folder or delete it.

- **Protect.** Limit your e-mail by giving your address only to those who need it.

- **Be brief.** When responding, be concise and direct.

- **Stop spam.** Spam is unwanted e-mail advertisements. Avoid mailing lists, complain to those who send spam, and ask to have your name removed from their mailing list.

- **Don't respond.** You do not have to respond to an e-mail. Be selective; respond only to those worthy of your time.

Is information overload part of your future? If you are like today's busy executives, it probably will be. Don't let it get you down!

USING IT AT DVD DIRECT—A CASE STUDY

INFORMATION SYSTEMS AT DVD DIRECT

DVD Direct, a factitious organization, is an entirely Web-oriented movie rental business. Unlike traditional movie rental businesses like Blockbuster, DVD Direct conducts all business over the Web at its Web storefront. For a monthly fee, their customers are able to order up to three movies at a time from a listing posted at the company Web site. The movies the customers select are delivered to them on DVD disks by mail within three working days. After viewing, customers return one or more disks by mail. They are allowed to keep the disks as long as they wish but can never have more than three disks in their possession at one time.

Although in operation for only three years, DVD Direct has experienced rapid growth. To help manage and to accelerate this growth, the company has just hired Alice, a recent college graduate. To follow Alice on her first day and to learn about DVD Direct's information systems, consult your Computing Essentials CD or visit us on the Web at www.olearyseries.com/CE06 and select DVD Direct and then select Information Systems.

VISUAL SUMMARY

INFORMATION SYSTEMS

INFORMATION FLOW

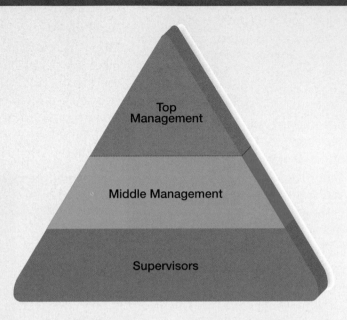

Information flows in an organization through functional areas and between management levels.

Functions

Most organizations have separate departments to perform five functions:

- **Accounting**—tracks all financial activities and generates periodic financial statements.
- **Marketing**—advertises, promotes, and sells the product (or service).
- **Production**—makes the product (or service) using raw materials and people to turn out finished goods.
- **Human resources**—finds and hires people, handles such matters as sick leave, retirement benefits, evaluation, compensation, and professional development.
- **Research**—conducts product research and development, monitors and troubleshoots new products.

Management Levels

The three basic management levels are:

- **Top-level**—concerned with long-range planning and forecasting.
- **Middle-level**—deals with control, planning, decision-making, and implementing long-term goals.
- **Supervisors**—control operational matters, monitoring day-to-day events, and supervising workers.

Information Flow

Information flows within an organization in different directions.

- For **top-level managers** the information flow is primarily upward from within the organization and into the organization from the outside.
- For **middle-level managers** the information flow is horizontal and vertical within departments.
- For **supervisors** the information flow is primarily vertical.

To be a competent end user you need to understand how information flows through functional areas and management levels. You need to be aware of the different types of computer-based information systems, including transaction processing systems, management information systems, decision support systems, and executive support systems.

INFORMATION SYSTEMS

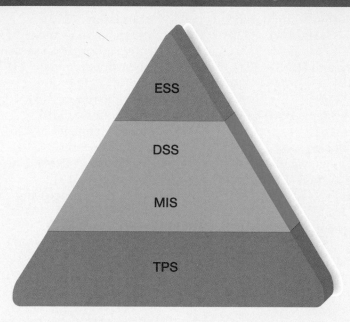

All organizations have computer-based **information systems,** including the following.

Transaction Processing Systems

Transaction processing systems (TPS), also known as **data processing systems (DPS),** record day-to-day transactions. An example is in accounting, which handles six activities: **sales order processing, accounts receivable, inventory (inventory control systems) and purchasing, accounts payable, payroll,** and **general ledger.** General ledger is used to produce **income statements** and **balance sheets.**

Management Information Systems

Management information systems (MIS) produce predetermined **periodic, exception,** and **demand reports.** Management information systems use database management systems to integrate the databases of different departments.

Decision Support Systems

Decision support systems (DSS) enable managers to get answers for unanticipated questions. Teams formed to address large problems use **group decision support systems (GDSS).** A decision support system consists of the **user, sys-**tem software, (data—**internal** and **external**), and **decision models.** Three types of decision models are **strategic, tactical,** and **operational.**

Executive Support Systems

Executive support systems (ESS) assist top-level executives. An executive support system is similar to MIS or DSS but easier to use. ESSs are designed specifically for top-level decision makers.

Other Systems

Many other systems are designed to support **information workers** who create, distribute, and communicate information. Two such systems are:

- **Office automation systems (OAS)** support **data workers** who are involved with distribution and communication of information. **Project managers** and **videoconferencing systems** are OAS.
- **Knowledge work systems (KWS)** support **knowledge workers,** who create information. Many engineers use **computer-aided design/computer-aided manufacturing system (CAD/CAM)** KWS.

KEY TERMS

accounting   (308)
accounts payable   (314)
accounts receivable   (314)
balance sheet   (315)
computer-aided design/computer-aided
   manufacturing (CAD/CAM)   (320)
data   (317)
data processing system (DPS)   (314)
data worker   (319)
decision model   (317)
decision support system (DSS)   (313)
demand report   (316)
exception report   (316)
executive information system (EIS)   (313)
executive support system (ESS)   (313)
external data   (317)
general ledger   (315)
group decision support system (GDSS)   (316)
human resources   (310)
income statement   (315)
information system   (312)
information worker   (319)
internal data   (317)
inventory   (314)
inventory control system   (314)

knowledge work system (KWS)   (320)
knowledge worker   (319)
management information system
   (MIS)   (313)
marketing   (310)
middle management   (310)
office automation system (OAS)   (320)
operational model   (317)
payroll   (314)
periodic report   (316)
production   (310)
project manager   (320)
purchase order   (314)
purchasing   (314)
research   (310)
sales order processing   (314)
strategic model   (317)
supervisor   (310)
system software   (317)
tactical model   (317)
top management   (310)
transaction processing system
   (TPS)   (313)
user   (317)
videoconferencing system   (320)

To test your knowledge of these key terms with animated flash cards, consult your Computing Essentials CD or visit our Web site at www.olearyseries.com/CE06 and select Key Terms.

COMPUTING
ESSENTIALS
2006

CROSSWORD

Across

3 Level of management concerned with strategic planning.

5 Identifies, investigates, and develops new products and services.

9 Report produced upon request.

10 Someone who makes decisions in a DSS.

11 Model that helps middle-level managers in long range planning.

12 Information worker involved in the creation of information.

14 Concerned with calculating employee paychecks.

16 Specialized information system that knowledge workers use.

17 Keeps track of summaries of all foregoing transactions.

Down

1 The buying of materials and services.

2 Plans, prices, promotes, sells, and distributes goods and services.

4 Form that shows supply and order information.

6 Report that calls attention to unusual events.

7 Help top-level managers oversee operations and develop plans.

8 Information worker that distributes information.

13 Use data from TPS to support middle managers.

15 Level of management concerned with decision making.

For an interactive version of this crossword, consult your Computing Essentials CD or visit our Web site at **www.olearyseries.com/CE06** and select Crossword.

MULTIPLE CHOICE

Circle the letter or fill in the correct answer.

1. The _____ department focuses on hiring, training, and promoting.
   a. marketing
   b. production
   c. research
   d. accounting
   e. human resources

2. The level of manager whose information flow is primarily vertical is _____.
   a. vice president
   b. executive
   c. top-level manager
   d. supervisor
   e. data worker

3. A(n) _____ is a collection of people, procedures, software, hardware, and data.
   a. corporation
   b. information system
   c. knowledge work system
   d. office automation system
   e. data processing system

4. Because it helps an organization keep track of routine operations and records these events in a database, some firms call a TPS a(n) _____.
   a. decision support system
   b. executive support system
   c. executive information system
   d. data processing system
   e. management information system

5. Purchasing, accounts receivable, and inventory are examples of _____ activities.
   a. executive
   b. managerial
   c. clerical
   d. accounting
   e. human resources

6. A typical general ledger can produce income statements and _____.
   a. balance sheets
   b. accounts receivable
   c. purchasing forms
   d. payroll records
   e. DSS

7. _____ help lower-level managers accomplish the organization's day-to-day activities, such as evaluating and maintaining quality control.
   a. Tactical models
   b. Operational models
   c. Strategic models
   d. Exception reports
   e. Periodic reports

8. Information workers who create information are known as _____.
   a. supervisors
   b. managers
   c. data workers
   d. knowledge workers
   e. executives

9. People involved in distribution and communication of information are called _____.
   a. knowledge workers
   b. users
   c. data workers
   d. managers
   e. secretaries

10. _____ are designed primarily to support data workers.
    a. Office automation systems
    b. Knowledge work systems
    c. CAD/CAM systems
    d. Decision support systems
    e. Management information systems

For an interactive version of these multiple choice questions, consult your Computing Essentials CD or visit our Web site at www.olearyseries.com/CE06 and select Multiple Choice.

MATCHING

Match each numbered item with the most closely related lettered item. Write your answers in the spaces provided.

a. computer-aided design (CAD)
b. demand report
c. DPS
d. DSS
e. EIS
f. exception report
g. GDSS
h. general ledger
i. internal data
j. inventory
k. knowledge workers
l. MIS
m. payroll
n. periodic report
o. purchasing
p. research department
q. strategic models
r. supervisor
s. tactical models
t. TPS

1. Manager responsible for administration and monitoring workers. _____
2. Department that identifies, investigates, and develops new products and services. _____
3. System that records day-to-day transactions. _____
4. Computer-based information system that produces standardized reports in summarized, structured form. _____
5. TPS that keeps track of routine operations and records these events in a database. _____
6. The parts and finished goods that a company has in stock. _____
7. Buying of raw materials and services. _____
8. Activity concerned with calculating employee paychecks. _____
9. Activity that produces income statements and balance sheets based on all transactions of a company. _____
10. Report generated at regular intervals. _____
11. Report that calls attention to unusual events. _____
12. The opposite of a scheduled report. _____
13. Flexible tool for analysis that helps managers make decisions about unstructured problems. _____
14. System used to support the collective work of a team addressing large problems. _____
15. Data gathered from within an organization. _____
16. Models that assist top-level managers in long-range planning. _____
17. Models that help middle managers control the work of the organization. _____
18. Sophisticated software that can draw together data from an organization's databases in meaningful patterns. _____
19. Individuals involved in the creation of information. _____
20. Program that integrates design and manufacturing activity. _____

For an interactive version of this matching exercise, consult your Computing Essentials CD or visit our Web site at www.olearyseries.com/CE06 and select Matching.

OPEN-ENDED

On a separate sheet of paper, respond to each question or statement.

1. Name and discuss the five common functions of most organizations.
2. Discuss the roles of the three kinds of management in a corporation.
3. What are the four most common computer-based information systems?
4. Describe the different reports and their roles in managerial decision making.
5. What is the difference between an office automation system and a knowledge work system?

1 CAD

Many companies model plans or products using computer-aided design, or CAD. One of the most popular CAD applications is AutoCAD from Autodesk. To learn more about one of these products, visit our Web site at www.olearyseries.com/CE06 and select Using Technology. Connect to the products site and read about the features of the product. Then answer the following questions: (a) What type of modeling is the product used for? (b) What are its basic features? (c) Cite some specific applications for the product. (d) Are there any special or advanced features that set it apart from other CAD software?

2 Knowledge Work Systems

Companies always want to tailor their Web sites to the needs of their customers to stay competitive; sites that are easier to navigate or provide the desired information quicker will be most in demand by consumers. One way to accomplish this is with Web site knowledge work software that monitors traffic on a Web server and pro-

vides reports that summarize visitors' activities. Visit our Web site at www.olearyseries.com/CE06 and select Using Technology to link to a company that delivers such software. Once connected, review the company's products, and then answer the following questions: (a) What events can the software monitor for? Briefly describe each. (b) How are reports about Web site usage delivered? What information do they include? (c) How can a company apply this information to improve its Web site? Provide specific examples.

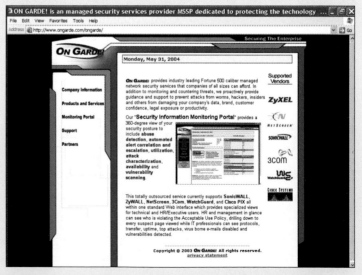

DVD Rental Companies

1

To learn abut DVD Direct, consult your Computing Essentials CD or visit us on the Web at www.olearyseries.com/CE06, and select DVD Direct and then select Information Systems. DVD Direct is similar to several real-world DVD rental companies. Connect to one of these companies' Web sites by visiting our Web site at www.olearyseries.com/CE06 and selecting Expanding Your Knowledge. Once connected, explore the site and then answer the following questions: (a) How are DVD Direct and this company similar? (b) How are they different? (c) Does this company offer streaming video downloads? (d) If DVD Direct wanted to provide delivery via streaming video, what would you anticipate would be their greatest challenges?

Executive Support Systems

2

Research at least three different executive support systems using a Web search. Review each, and then answer the following questions: (a) Which ESSs did you review? (b) What are the common features of ESSs? (c) What specific types of decisions was each ESS designed to aid in? (d) What type of company is likely to use each? Provide some examples.

COMPUTING
ESSENTIALS
2006

BUILDING YOUR PORTFOLIO

1

Office Automation Systems

Office Automation Systems are often used to minimize human error and enhance productivity in a variety of business disciplines. Used primarily to support data workers, these systems focus on managing documents, communicating, and scheduling. Write a one-page paper titled "Office Automation Systems" that addresses the following topics: (a) Define and describe an Office Automation System. (b) Describe the type of worker that an OAS supports. What is the role of an OAS in a company? (c) Describe how OASs are used. Give specific examples.

2

Identity Theft

Identity theft occurs when someone acquires your personal information and uses it to hijack your finances. A common scenario is a thief using your Social Security number opens a credit card account in your name. When the thief does not pay, it is your credit history that is blemished. Consider this scam thoroughly, and then answer the following questions in a one-page paper: (a) List three steps an individual should take to avoid identity theft. (b) List three steps a corporation that maintains your personal data in their information system should take to safeguard your data. (c) How can Internet activities contribute to the likelihood of identity theft? How can this be prevented?

COMPETENCIES

After you have read this chapter, you should be able to:

1 **Distinguish between the physical and logical view of data.**

2 **Describe how data is organized: characters, fields, records, files, and databases.**

3 **Describe databases, database issues, and database management systems (DBMS).**

4 **Describe five data models: hierarchical, network, relational, multidimensional, and object-oriented.**

5 **Distinguish among individual, company, distributed, proprietary, and Web databases.**

6 **Recognize strategic database uses and security concerns.**

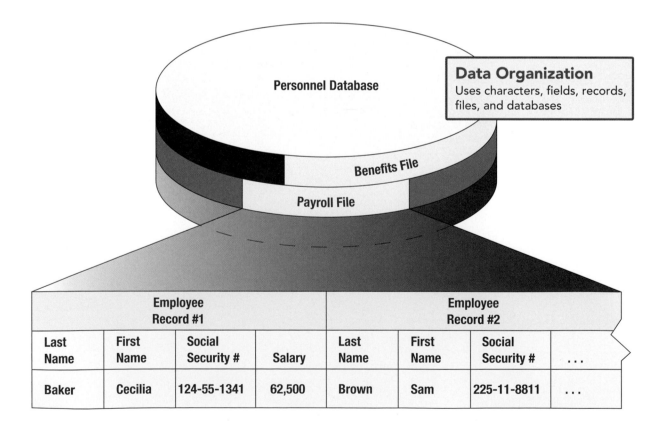

Personnel Database

Data Organization
Uses characters, fields, records, files, and databases

Benefits File

Payroll File

Employee Record #1				Employee Record #2			
Last Name	First Name	Social Security #	Salary	Last Name	First Name	Social Security #	...
Baker	Cecilia	124-55-1341	62,500	Brown	Sam	225-11-8811	...

Like a library, secondary storage is designed to store information. How is such stored information organized? What are files and databases and why do you need to know anything about them? Perhaps the answer is this: To be a competent user of information in the information age, you have to know how to find information, and so you have to understand how it is stored.

At one time, it was not important for microcomputer users to know much about data files and databases. However, the recent arrival of very powerful microcomputers and their connectivity to communications networks and the Internet has changed that. Communications lines and the Internet extend the reach of your microcomputer well beyond the desktop.

Competent end users need to understand data fields, records, files, and databases. They need to be aware of the different ways in which a database can be structured and the different types of databases. Also, they need to know the most important database uses and issues.

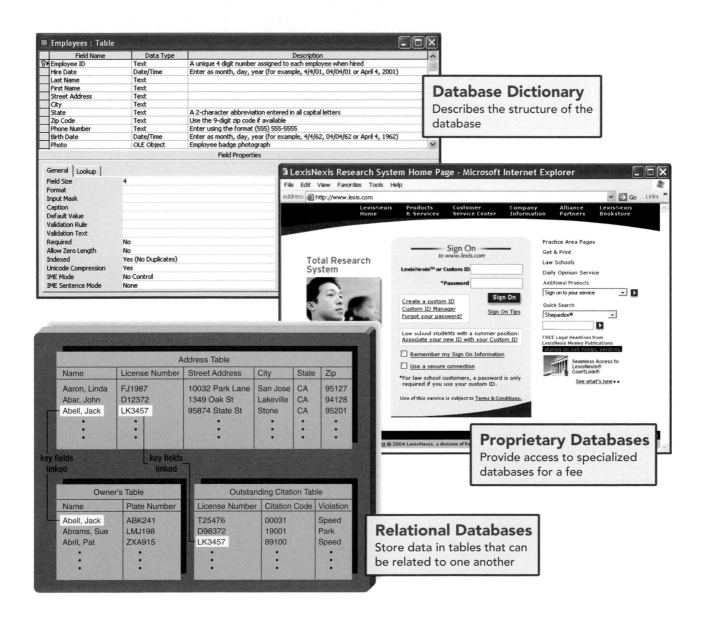

Database Dictionary
Describes the structure of the database

Proprietary Databases
Provide access to specialized databases for a fee

Relational Databases
Store data in tables that can be related to one another

DATA

Data is defined as facts or observations about people, places, things, and events. Physical view focuses on the actual format and location of data. Logical view focuses on the meaning and content of data.

As we have discussed throughout this book, information systems consist of people, procedures, software, hardware, and data. This chapter focuses on the last element, **data,** which can be defined as facts or observations about people, places, things, and events. More specifically, this chapter focuses on how databases are used to store, organize, and use data.

Not long ago, data was limited to numbers, letters, and symbols recorded by keyboards. Now, as depicted in Figure 12-1, data is much richer and includes:

- Audio captured, interpreted, and saved using microphones and voice recognition systems.
- Music captured from the Internet, from MIDI devices, and other sources.
- Photographs captured by digital cameras, edited by image editing software, and shared with others over the Internet.
- Video captured by digital video cameras, TV tuner cards, and WebCams.

There are two ways or perspectives to view data. These perspectives are the *physical view* and the *logical view*. The **physical view** focuses on the actual format and location of the data. As discussed in Chapter 6, data is recorded as digital bits that are typically grouped together into bytes that represent characters using a coding scheme such as ASCII. Typically, only very specialized computer professionals are concerned with the physical view. The other perspective, the **logical view,** focuses on the meaning and content of the data. End users and most computer professionals are concerned with this view. They are involved with actually using the data with application programs. This chapter presents the logical view of data and how data is stored in databases.

▼ CONCEPT CHECK

▶ Describe some of the different types of data.

▶ What is the physical view of data?

▶ What is the logical view of data?

DATA ORGANIZATION

Character, field, record, file, and database are logical data groups. Key fields uniquely identify records. Batch processing processes data later. Real-time processing processes data now.

You want to know your final grades for the semester. You call your school's registrar after your last final exam to find out your grade point average. Perhaps you are told, "Sorry, that's not in the computer yet." Why can't they tell you? How is the school's computer system different from, say, your bank's, where deposits and withdrawals seem to be recorded right away?

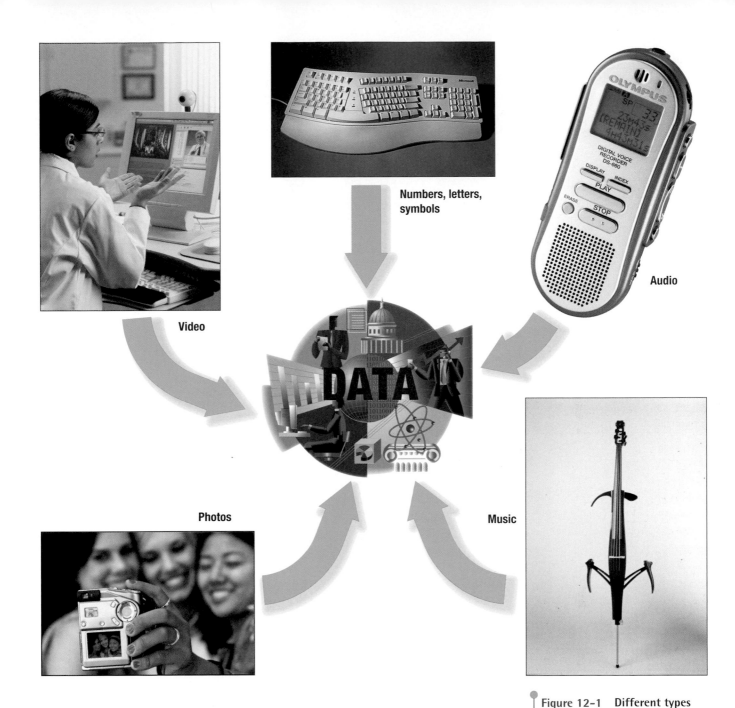

Video

Numbers, letters, symbols

Audio

Photos

Music

Figure 12–1   Different types of data

The answers to these questions lie in part in how the data is organized into logical groups or categories. Each group is more complex than the one before. (See Figure 12-2.)

- **Character:** A **character** is the most basic logical data element. It is a single letter, number, or special character, such as a punctuation mark, or a symbol, such as $. For example, in Figure 12-2 the letter *B* is the first letter of an employee's last name.
- **Field:** The next higher level is a **field** or group of related characters. In our example, Baker is in the data field for the Last Name of an employee. It consists of the individual letters (characters) that make up the last name. A data field represents an **attribute** (description or characteristic) of some **entity** (person, place, thing, or object). For example, an employee is an **entity** with many attributes, including his or her last name.

Databases

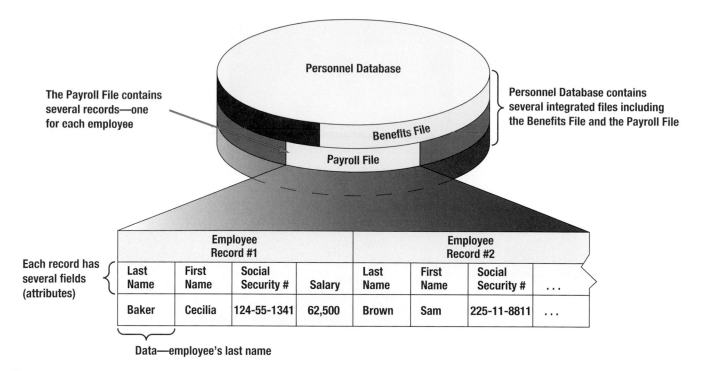

The Payroll File contains several records—one for each employee

Personnel Database

Benefits File

Payroll File

Personnel Database contains several integrated files including the Benefits File and the Payroll File

Each record has several fields (attributes)

	Employee Record #1				Employee Record #2			
Last Name	First Name	Social Security #	Salary	Last Name	First Name	Social Security #	. . .
Baker	Cecilia	124-55-1341	62,500	Brown	Sam	225-11-8811	. . .

Data—employee's last name

Figure 12-2 Logical data organization

- **Record:** A **record** is a collection of related fields. A record represents a collection of attributes that describe an entity. In our example, the payroll record for an employee consists of the data fields describing the attributes for one employee. These attributes are First Name, Last Name, Social Security Number, and Salary.
- **File:** A **file** is a collection of related records. For example, the payroll file would include payroll information (records) for all the employees (entities).
- **Database:** A **database** is an integrated collection of logically related records or objects. For example, the Personnel Database would include all related employee files, including payroll file and benefits file.

KEY FIELD

Each record in a database has at least one distinctive field, called the **key field.** Also known as the **primary field,** this field uniquely identifies the record. For many employee and university databases, the key field is Social Security number. Key fields in different files can be used to integrate the data in a database. For example, in the Personnel Database, both the Payroll and the Benefits files include the field Social Security #. Data from the two files could be related by combining all records with the same key field (Social Security number). While Social Security number is the most commonly used key field, other widely used key fields are student identification numbers, employee identification numbers, part numbers, and inventory numbers.

BATCH VERSUS REAL-TIME PROCESSING

Traditionally data is processed in one of two ways. These are batch processing, or what we might call "later," and real-time processing, or what we might call "now." These two methods have been used to handle common record-keeping activities such as payroll and sales orders.

- **Batch processing:** In **batch processing,** data is collected over several hours, days, or even weeks. It is then processed all at once as a "batch." If you have a bank credit card, your bill probably reflects batch processing. That is, during the month, you buy things and charge them to your credit card. Each time you charge something, an electronic copy of the transaction is sent to the credit card company. At some point in the month, the company's data processing department puts all those transactions (and those of many other customers) together and processes them at one time. The company then sends you a single bill totaling the amount you owe. (See Figure 12-3.)

- **Real-time processing:** Totaling up the sales charged to your bank credit card is an example of batch processing. You might use another kind of card—your bank's automated teller machine (ATM) card—for the second kind of processing. **Real-time processing,** also known as **online processing,** occurs when data is processed at the same time the transaction occurs. As you use your ATM card to withdraw cash, the system automatically computes the balance remaining in your account. (See Figure 12-4.)

At one time, only magnetic tape storage, and therefore only sequential access storage (as we discussed in Chapter 8), was available. All processing then was batch processing and was done on mainframe computers. Even today, a great deal of mainframe time is dedicated to this kind of processing. Many smaller organizations, however, use microcomputers for this purpose.

Real-time processing is made possible by the availability of disk packs and direct access storage (as we described in Chapter 8). Direct access storage makes it possible to go quickly and directly to a particular record. (In sequential access storage, by contrast, the user must wait for the computer to scan several records one at a time. It continues scanning until the desired record is located.)

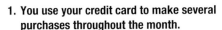

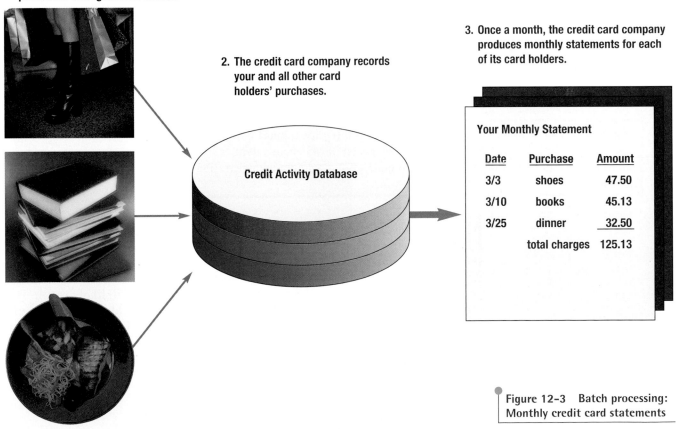

1. You use your credit card to make several purchases throughout the month.

2. The credit card company records your and all other card holders' purchases.

Credit Activity Database

3. Once a month, the credit card company produces monthly statements for each of its card holders.

Your Monthly Statement

Date	Purchase	Amount
3/3	shoes	47.50
3/10	books	45.13
3/25	dinner	32.50
	total charges	125.13

Figure 12–3 Batch processing: Monthly credit card statements

Databases

1. You request a $200 withdrawal at an ATM.

2. The ATM immediately sends the electronic request to your bank.

3. The bank processes the request by first verifying that you have sufficient funds to cover the request.

Request

Approval

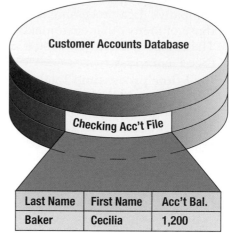

Customer Accounts Database

Checking Acc't File

Last Name	First Name	Acc't Bal.
Baker	Cecilia	1,200

6. The ATM dispenses $200 to you.

5. The bank sends an electronic approval and reduces your account balance by $200.

4. The bank determines your account balance is $1,200.

Figure 12-4 Real-time processing: ATM withdrawal

▼ CONCEPT CHECK

► Describe how data is organized.

► What are key fields and how are they used?

► Compare batch processing and real-time processing.

DATABASES

Databases reduce data redundancy, enhance data integrity, support data sharing, and provide security. DBMS software has five parts: DBMS engine, data definition, data manipulation, application generation, and data administration subsystems.

Many organizations have multiple files on the same subject or person. For example, records for the same customer may appear in different files in the sales department, billing department, and credit department. This is called **data redundancy.** If the customer moves, then the address in each file must be updated. If one or more files are overlooked, problems will likely result. For example, a product ordered might be sent to the new address, but the bill might be sent to the old address. This situation results from a lack of **data integrity.**

Moreover, data spread around in different files is not as useful. The marketing department, for instance, might want to offer special promotions to customers who order large quantities of merchandise. However, they may be unable to do so because the information they need is in the billing department. A database can make the needed information available.

NEED FOR DATABASES

For both individuals and organizations, there are many advantages to having databases:

- **Sharing:** In organizations, information from one department can be readily shared with others. Billing could let marketing know which customers ordered large quantities of merchandise.

- **Security:** Users are given passwords or access only to the kind of information they need. Thus, the payroll department may have access to employees' pay rates, but other departments would not.

- **Less data redundancy:** With several departments having access to one file, there are fewer files. Excess storage is reduced. Microcomputers linked by a network to a file server, for example, could replace the hard disks located in several individual microcomputers.

- **Data integrity:** Older filing systems many times did not have "integrity." That is, a change made in the file in one department might not be made in the file in another department. As you might expect, this can cause serious problems and conflicts when data is used for important decisions affecting both departments.

DATABASE MANAGEMENT

In order to create, modify, and gain access to a database, special software is required. This software is called a **database management system,** which is commonly abbreviated **DBMS.**

Some DBMSs, such as Access, are designed specifically for microcomputers. Other DBMSs are designed for mainframes and for specialized database or file servers. DBMS software is made up of five parts or subsystems: *DBMS engine, data definition, data manipulation, application generation,* and *data administration.*

- The **DBMS engine** provides a bridge between the logical view of the data and the physical view of the data. When users request data (logical perspective), the DBMS engine handles the details of actually locating the data (physical perspective).

- The **data definition subsystem** defines the logical structure of the database by using a **data dictionary.** This dictionary contains a description of the structure of data in the database. For a particular item of data, it defines the names used for a particular field. It defines the type of data for each field (text, numeric, time, graphic, audio, and video). An example of an Access data dictionary form is presented in Figure 12-5.

- The **data manipulation subsystem** provides tools for maintaining and analyzing data. Maintaining

Figure 12-5   Access data dictionary form

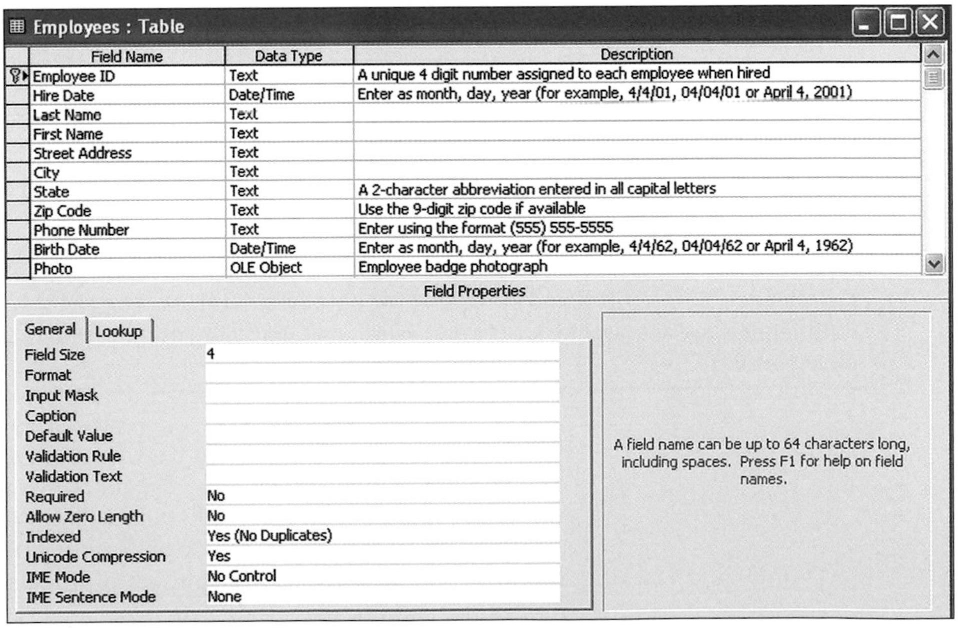

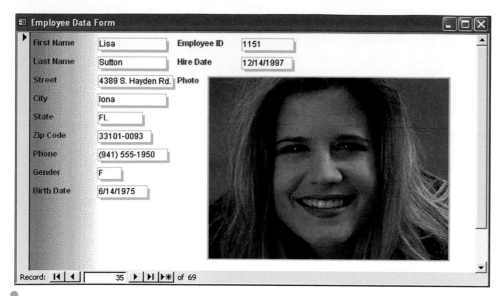

Figure 12-6 Access data entry form

data is known as **data maintenance.** It involves adding new data, deleting old data, and editing existing data. Analysis tools support viewing all or selected parts of the data, querying the database, and generating reports. Specific tools include **query-by-example** and specialized programming languages called **structured query languages (SQL).** (Structured query languages and other types of programming languages will be discussed in Chapter 14.)

- The **application generation subsystem** provides tools to create data entry forms and specialized programming languages that interface or work with common and widely used programming languages such as COBOL. See Figure 12-6 for a data entry form created by the application generation subsystem in Access.

- The **data administration subsystem** helps to manage the overall database, including maintaining security, providing disaster recovery support, and monitoring the overall performance of database operations. Larger organizations typically employ highly trained computer specialists, called **database administrators (DBAs),** to interact with the data administration subsystem. Additional duties of database administrators include determining **processing rights** or determining which people have access to what kinds of data in the database.

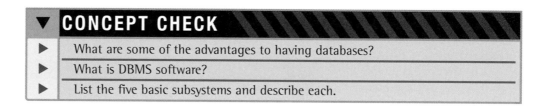

▼ CONCEPT CHECK

▶ What are some of the advantages to having databases?

▶ What is DBMS software?

▶ List the five basic subsystems and describe each.

DBMS STRUCTURE

Data models define rules and standards for data in a database. The five data models are hierarchical, network, relational, multidimensional, and object-oriented.

DBMS programs are designed to work with data that is logically structured or arranged in a particular way. This arrangement is known as the **data model.** These models define rules and standards for all the data in a database. For example, Access is designed to work with databases using the relational data model. There are five widely used data models: *hierarchical, network, relational, multidimensional,* and *object-oriented.*

HIERARCHICAL DATABASE

At one time, nearly every DBMS designed for mainframes used the hierarchical data model. In a **hierarchical database,** fields or records are structured in nodes. **Nodes** are points connected like the branches of an upside-down tree. Each entry has one **parent node,** although a parent may have several **child nodes.** This is sometimes described as a **one-to-many relationship.** To find a particular field you have to start at the top with a parent and trace down the tree to a child.

The nodes farther down the system are subordinate to the ones above, like the hierarchy of managers in a corporation. An example of a hierarchical database is a nationwide airline reservations system. (See Figure 12-7.) The parent node is the "departure" city, Los Angeles. This parent has four children, labeled "arrival." New York, one of the children, has three children of its own. They are labeled "flight number." Flight 110 has three children, labeled "passenger." (See Figure 12-8.)

The problem with a hierarchical database is that if one parent node is deleted, so are all the subordinate child nodes. Moreover, a child node cannot be added unless a parent node is added first. The most significant limitation is the rigid structure: one parent only per child, and no relationships or connections between the child nodes themselves.

Figure 12-7   Airlines may use a hierarchical database for their reservations system

NETWORK DATABASE

Responding to the limitations of the hierarchical data model, network models were developed. A **network database** also has a hierarchical arrangement of nodes. However, each child node may have more than one parent node. This is sometimes described as a **many-to-many relationship.** There are additional connections—called **pointers**—between parent nodes and child nodes. Thus, a node may be reached through more than one path. It may be traced down through different branches.

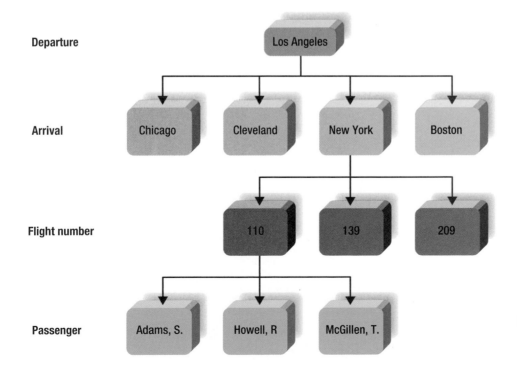

Figure 12-8   Hierarchical database

Databases

Figure 12–9 Universities may use a network database

For example a university could use this type of organization to record students taking classes. (See Figure 12-9.) If you trace through the logic of this organization, you can see that each student can have more than one teacher. (See Figure 12-10.) Each teacher can also teach more than one course. Students may take more than a single course. This demonstrates how the network arrangement is more flexible and in many cases more efficient than the hierarchical arrangement.

RELATIONAL DATABASE

A more flexible type of organization is the **relational database.** In this structure, there are no access paths down a hierarchy. Rather, the data elements are stored in different tables, each of which consists of rows and columns. A table is called a **relation.**

An example of a relational database is shown in Figure 12-11. The address table contains the names, driver's license numbers, and addresses for all registered drivers in a particular state. Within the table, a row resembles a record—

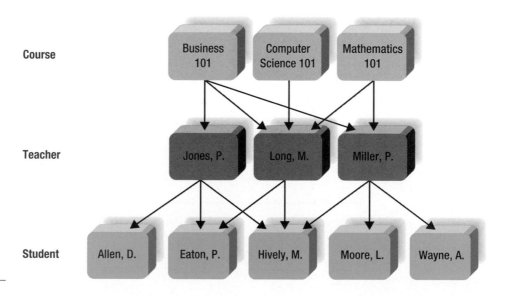

Figure 12–10 Network database

Address Table					
Name	License Number	Street Address	City	State	Zip
Aaron, Linda	FJ1987	10032 Park Lane	San Jose	CA	95127
Abar, John	D12372	1349 Oak St	Lakeville	CA	94128
Abell, Jack	LK3457	95874 State St	Stone	CA	95201
•	•	•	•	•	•

key fields linked   **key fields linked**

Owner's Table	
Name	Plate Number
Abell, Jack	ABK241
Abrams, Sue	LMJ198
Abril, Pat	ZXA915
•	•

Outstanding Citation Table		
License Number	Citation Code	Violation
T25476	00031	Speed
D98372	19001	Park
LK3457	89100	Speed
•	•	•

Figure 12-11   Relational database

for example, information about one driver. A column entry resembles a field. The driver's name is one field; the driver's license number is another field. All related tables must have a **common data item** (key field). Thus, information stored on one table can be linked with information stored on another. One common field might be a person's Social Security number. Another might be a driver's license number.

Thus, police officers who stop a speeding car can radio the driver's license number and the car's license plate number to the Department of Motor Vehicles. They can use the driver's license number as the key field. With it they can find out about any unpaid traffic violations (such as parking tickets) or outstanding arrest warrants. Also, using the license plate number, they can obtain the car owner's name and address. If the owner's name and address do not match the driver who has been stopped, the police officer may check further for a stolen vehicle. (See Figure 12-12.)

The most valuable feature of relational databases is their simplicity. Entries can be easily added, deleted, and modified. The hierarchical and network databases are more rigid. The relational organization is common for microcomputer DBMSs, such as Access, Paradox, dBASE, and R: Base. Relational databases are also widely used for mainframe and minicomputer systems.

MULTIDIMENSIONAL DATABASE

The multidimensional data model is a variation and an extension of the relational data model. While relational databases use tables consisting of rows and columns, **multidimensional databases** extend this two-dimensional data model to include additional or multiple dimensions sometimes called a **hyper cube.** Data can be viewed as a cube having three or more sides and consisting of cells. Each side of the cube is considered a dimension of the data. In this way, complex relationships between data can be represented and efficiently analyzed.

Figure 12-12   The Department of Motor Vehicles may use a relational database

Multidimensional databases provide several advantages over relational databases. Two of the most significant advantages are:

- **Conceptualization.** Multidimensional databases and hyper cubes provide users with an intuitive model in which complex data and relationships can be conceptualized.
- **Processing speed.** Analyzing and querying a large multidimensional database is much faster. For example, a query requiring just a few seconds on a multidimensional database could take minutes or hours to perform on a relational database.

OBJECT-ORIENTED DATABASE

The other data structures are primarily designed to handle structured data such as names, addresses, pay rates, and so on. **Object-oriented databases** are more flexible, store data as well as instructions to manipulate the data, and are able to handle unstructured data such as photographs, audio, and video.

Object-oriented databases organize data using objects, classes, entities, attributes, and methods.

- **Objects** are items that contain both data and instructions to manipulate the data.
- **Classes** are similar objects grouped together.
- **Entities** are a person, place, thing, or event that is to be described.
- **Attributes** are the description of entities. They are similar to fields.
- **Methods** are descriptions of how the data is to be manipulated.

For example, a health club might use an object-oriented employment database. (See Figure 12-13.)

The objects Trainers, Front desk, and Managers describe the three types of employees at the health club. These objects are grouped together to form the class Employees. Time cards are another class. Each object in a class has some common attributes. In the case of the Employees class, the common attributes are PHOTO, LAST NAME, FIRST NAME, and ADDRESS. YEARLY SALARY is a unique attribute assigned to the Managers object. The object-oriented database also contains methods for calculating weekly payroll checks for trainers, front desk, and manager employees. (See Figure 12-14.) While hierarchical

Figure 12-13   A fitness club may use an object-oriented database to organize employee and member data

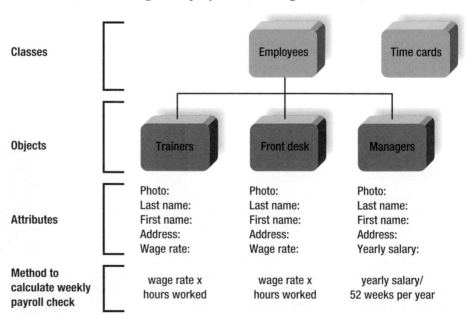

Figure 12-14   Object-oriented database

	Trainers	Front desk	Managers
Classes	Employees		Time cards
Objects	Trainers	Front desk	Managers
Attributes	Photo: Last name: First name: Address: Wage rate:	Photo: Last name: First name: Address: Wage rate:	Photo: Last name: First name: Address: Yearly salary:
Method to calculate weekly payroll check	wage rate x hours worked	wage rate x hours worked	yearly salary/ 52 weeks per year

Organization	Description
Hierarchical	Data structured in nodes organized like an upside-down tree; each parent node can have several children; each child node can have only one parent
Network	Like hierarchical except that each child can have several parents
Relational	Data stored in tables consisting of rows and columns
Multidimensional	Data stored in hyper cubes with three or more dimensions
Object-oriented	Organizes data using objects, classes, entities, attributes, and methods

Figure 12-15 Summary of DBMS organization

and network databases are still widely used, the relational, multidimensional, and object-oriented data models are more popular today.

For a summary of DBMS organization, see Figure 12-15.

TYPES OF DATABASES

There are five classifications of databases: individual, company, distributed, proprietary, and Web.

Databases may be small or large, limited in accessibility or widely accessible. Databases may be classified into five types: *individual, company (or shared), distributed, proprietary,* and *Web.*

INDIVIDUAL

The **individual database** is also called a **microcomputer database.** It is a collection of integrated files primarily used by just one person. Typically, the data and the DBMS are under the direct control of the user. They are stored either on the user's hard-disk drive or on a LAN file server.

There may be many times in your life when you will find this kind of database valuable. If you are in sales, for instance, a microcomputer database can be used to keep track of your customers. If you are a sales manager, you can keep track of your salespeople and their performance. If you are an advertising account executive, you can keep track of what work and how many hours to charge each client.

COMPANY OR SHARED

Companies, of course, create databases for their own use. The **company (shared) database** may be stored on a mainframe and managed by a database administrator. Users throughout the company have access to the database through their microcomputers linked to local area networks or wide area networks.

Company databases are of two types:

- The **common operational database** contains details about the operations of the company, such as inventory, production, and sales. It contains data describing the day-to-day operations of the organization.

- The **common user database** contains selected information both from the common operational database and from outside private (proprietary) databases. Managers can tap into this information on their microcomputers or terminals and use it for decision making.

As we discussed in Chapter 11, company databases are the foundation for management information systems. For instance, a department store can record all sales transactions in the database. A sales manager can use this information to see which salespeople are selling the most products. The manager can then determine year-end sales bonuses. Or the store's buyer can learn which products are selling well or not selling and make adjustments when reordering. A top executive might combine overall store sales trends with information from outside databases about consumer and population trends. This information could be used to change the whole merchandising strategy of the store.

DISTRIBUTED

Many times the data in a company is stored not in just one location but in several locations. It is made accessible through a variety of communications networks. The database, then, is a **distributed database.** That is, it is located in a place or places other than where users are located. Typically, database servers on a client/server network provide the link between users and the distant data.

For instance, some database information can be at regional offices. Some can be at company headquarters, some down the hall from you, and some even overseas. Sales figures for a chain of department stores, then, could be located at the various stores. But executives at district offices or at the chain's headquarters could have access to these figures.

PROPRIETARY

A **proprietary database** is generally an enormous database that an organization develops to cover particular subjects. It offers access to this database to the public or selected outside individuals for a fee. Sometimes proprietary databases are also called **information utilities** or **data banks.** An example is LexisNexis, which offers a variety of financial services. (See Figure 12-16.)

Some important proprietary databases are the following:

- **CSi:** Offers consumer and business services, including electronic mail.
- **Dialog Information Services:** Offers business information, as well as technical and scientific information.
- **Dow Jones Interactive Publishing:** Provides world news and information on business, investments, and stocks.
- **LexisNexis:** Offers news and information on legal, public records, and business issues.

Most of the proprietary databases are designed for organizational as well as individual use. Organizations typically pay a membership fee plus hourly use fees. Often, individuals are able to search the database to obtain a summary of available information without charge. They pay only for those items selected for further investigation.

WEB DATABASE

While a **Web database** is similar to the other types of databases, its distinguishing feature is that it is available over the Web. Nearly every Web site you visit collects data about you and enters that data into a Web database. Specialized search sites use their Web databases to provide information to you.

As we discussed in Chapter 2, when you surf the Web, traditional and ad network cookies are collecting data about you. This data is sent back to a Web site that uses a Web database to store, organize, and use your data. One common use is by Web site developers who collect visitor information to better serve their customers and to improve the effectiveness of their Web sites. Another use is by information resellers who collect and market the data to others.

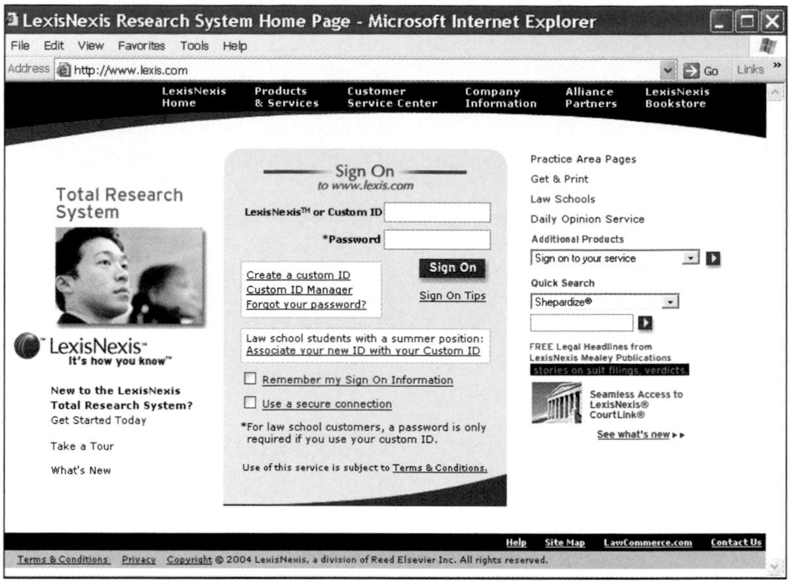

As we discussed in Chapter 2, whenever you use a search engine on the Web, you are interacting with a database. For example, if you connect to the Yahoo! site and search using a keyword such as "travel," the site searches its Web database to locate all pages containing that keyword.

Whenever you complete a form or provide any information at a Web site, the data is recorded by that Web site's Web database. Typically, this is accomplished by special interface programs that create the input forms, accept your input, and send the data to the Web database. Typically, these programs consist of **CGI (Common Gateway Interface) scripts.**

See Figure 12-17 for a summary of the five types of databases.

Figure 12-16 Proprietary database (LexisNexis)

Type	Description
Individual	Integrated files used by just one person
Company	Common operational or commonly used files shared in an organization
Distributed	Database spread geographically and accessed using database server
Proprietary	Information utilities or databanks available to users on a wide range of topics for a fee
Web	Used by Web sites collecting data and search sites providing data

Figure 12-17 Summary of the five types of databases

▼ CONCEPT CHECK

▶ What are the five types of databases?

▶ Give a brief example of each type of database.

▶ What distinguishes Web databases from the other types of databases?

Databases

DATABASE USES AND ISSUES

Data warehouse is a type of database. Data mining is a technique to locate related information and patterns. Firewalls are hardware and software to control access.

Databases offer great opportunities for productivity. In fact, in corporate libraries, electronic databases are now considered more valuable than books and journals. However, maintaining databases means users must make constant efforts to keep them from being tampered with or misused.

STRATEGIC USES

Databases help users to keep up to date and to plan for the future. To support the needs of managers and other business professionals, many organizations collect data from a variety of internal and external databases. This data is then stored in a special type of database called a **data warehouse.** A technique called **data mining** is often used to search these databases to look for related information and patterns.

There are hundreds of databases available to help users with both general and specific business purposes, including:

- *Business directories* providing addresses, financial and marketing information, products, and trade and brand names.
- *Demographic data,* such as county and city statistics, current estimates on population and income, employment statistics, census data, and so on.
- *Business statistical information,* such as financial information on publicly traded companies, market potential of certain retail stores, and other business data and information.
- *Text databases* providing articles from business publications, press releases, reviews on companies and products, and so on.
- *Web databases* covering a wide range of topics, including all of the above. As mentioned earlier, Web search sites like Yahoo! maintain extensive databases of available Web sites.

SECURITY

Precisely because databases are so valuable, their security has become a vital issue. As we discussed in Chapter 10, there are several database security concerns. One concern is that personal and private information about people stored in databases may be used for the wrong purposes. For instance, a person's credit history or medical records might be used to make hiring or promotion decisions. Another concern is unauthorized users gaining access to a database. For example, there have been numerous instances in which a computer virus has been launched into a database or network.

Security may require putting guards in company computer rooms and checking the identification of everyone admitted. Some security systems electronically check fingerprints. (See Figure 12-18.) Security is particularly

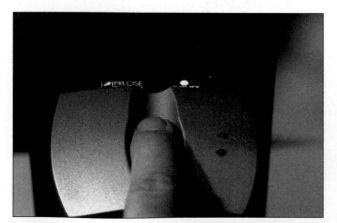

Figure 12–18 Security: Electronic fingerprint pads

important to organizations using WANs. Violations can occur without actually entering secured areas. As mentioned in previous chapters, most major corporations today use special hardware and software called **firewalls** to control access to their internal networks.

▼ CONCEPT CHECK

► What is a data warehouse? What is data mining?

► What are some database security concerns?

► What is a firewall?

USING ⒤ AT DVD DIRECT—A CASE STUDY

DATABASES AT DVD DIRECT

DVD Direct is an entirely Web-oriented movie rental business. Its members order movies from DVD Direct's Web site and the movies are delivered on DVD disks by mail. Members can keep the movies as long as they wish before returning them by mail. However, a member can have at most three movies out at one time.

A recent internal study at DVD Direct discovered that many current and potential customers with high bandwidth Internet connections would prefer to have movies delivered over the Internet. Further, the study indicated that current customers who recently switched to high bandwidth connections were very likely to drop their DVD Direct membership. Top management has become concerned that if DVD Direct does not address these findings it will continue to lose high bandwidth members and it may no longer be able to compete in the online movie rental business. This has led Carol, DVD Direct's CEO, to consider some dramatic changes to its business model—the way it does business.

So far, this issue has been formally discussed only in high-level meetings. However, the rumor mill has been working and almost everyone in the company knows that some type of change is in the works. Alice, a recently hired market analyst, has joined the company at this critical moment for DVD Direct and is about to learn more about the proposed changes. To follow Alice as she meets with Bob, the vice president of marketing, consult your Computing Essentials CD or visit us on the Web at www.olearyseries.com/CE06 and select DVD Direct and then select Databases.

A Look to the Future

Xperanto Makes Database Searches Easier

Have you ever been frustrated by the results of a Web search? Have you ever wished you could search all the Word files on your computer for a specific word or phrase? Businesses with multiple databases and many types of data are even more frustrated with limited searches and unreachable data. IBM has recently announced technology it hopes will help businesses access many kinds of data from many locations from one database interface.

Xperanto is designed to make both structured (relational databases) and unstructured data (word processing or spreadsheet files, for example) searchable in a database. For example, an organization might use a database that accesses all employee Word files. Xperanto might also be used to examine audio transcripts of phone calls. Using this technology an organization has access to all of its files, on all computers, and in all locations through a database.

Xperanto combines various technological breakthroughs to make this possible, but the project relies heavily on XML. XML allows information in Web pages to be accessed by a database. XML uses special notation in the code to identify parts of the page, including names and dates.

What do you think of this development? Do you think this kind of easy access to data has benefits for the general public? Some privacy advocates worry that connected databases are a danger to individual privacy. What do you think?

Client

XML/XQuery

W

WebSphere

W

W

Open client

Sginet

Informix

Xperanto

SOAP

Sybase

Oracle

DRDA

Informix

Text documents

XML documents

DB2

VISUAL SUMMARY

DATABASES

DATA

Data consist of facts or observations about people, places, things, and events.

Data Types
Not long ago, data was limited to numbers, letters, and symbols. Now data includes:

- Audio—captured, interpreted, and saved using microphones and voice recognition systems.
- Music—captured from the Internet and other sources, rearranged, and used to create customized CDs.
- Photographs—captured by digital cameras, edited by image editing software, and shared with others over the Internet
- Video—captured by digital video cameras and TV tuner cards, saved, and used in presentations.

Data Views
There are two ways or perspectives to view data: the *physical view* and the *logical view*.

- **Physical view** focuses on actual format and location of data; very specialized computer professionals are concerned with this view.
- **Logical view** focuses on meaning and content of data; end users and most computer professionals are concerned with this view.

DATA ORGANIZATION

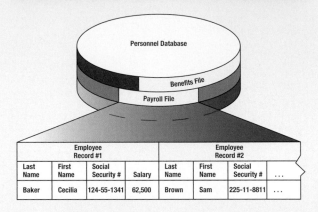

Data is organized by the following groups:

- **Character**—the most basic logical element, for example, characters can consist of individual letters, for example the letter *B*.
- **Field**—next level consisting of a set of related characters, for example, a person's last name. A data field represents an **attribute** (description or characteristic) of some **entity** (person, place, thing, or object).
- **Record**—a collection of related fields, for example, a payroll record consisting of fields of data relating to one employee.
- **File**—a collection of related records, for example, a payroll file consisting of all the employee records.
- **Database**—an integrated collection of related files, for example, a personnel database contains all related employee files, including the payroll file.

Key Field
A **key field (primary field)** is the field in a record that uniquely identifies each record.

- Key fields in different files can be used to integrate the data in a database.
- Common key fields are Social Security numbers and driver's license numbers.

To be a competent end user you need to understand data fields, records, files, and databases. You need to be aware of the different ways in which a database can be structured and the different types of databases. Also, you need to know the most important database uses and issues.

DATA ORGANIZATION

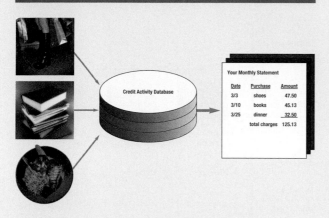

Batch versus Real-Time Processing

Traditionally, data is processed in one of two ways: batch or real-time processing.

- **Batch processing**—data is collected over time and then processed later all at one time (batched).
- **Real-time processing (online processing)**—data is processed at the same time the transaction occurs; direct access storage devices make real-time processing possible.

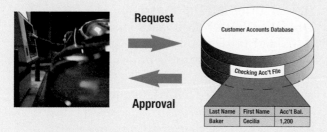

DATABASES

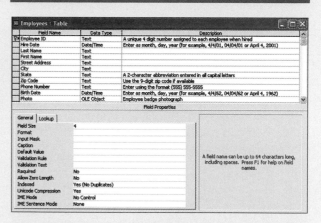

A **database** is a collection of integrated data—logically related files and records.

Need for Databases

Advantages of databases are sharing data, improved security, reduced **data redundancy,** and higher **data integrity.**

Database Management

A **database management system (DBMS)** is the software for creating, modifying, and gaining access to the database. A DBMS consists of five subsystems:

- **DBMS engine** provides a bridge between logical and physical data views.
- **Data definition subsystem** defines the logical structure of a database using a **data dictionary.**
- **Data manipulation subsystem** provides tools for **data maintenance** and data analysis; tools include **query-by-example** and **structured query languages (SQL).**
- **Application generation subsystem** provides tools for data entry forms and specialized programming languages.
- **Data administration subsystem** manages database; **database administrators (DBAs)** are computer professionals who help define **processing rights.**

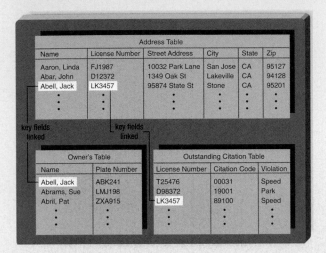

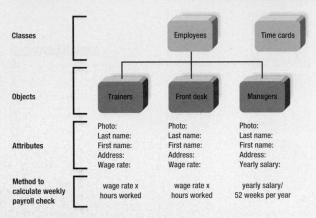

DBMS programs are designed to work with specific data structures or **data models.** These models define rules and standards for all the data in the database. Five principal data models are *hierarchical, network, relational, multidimensional,* and *object-oriented.*

Hierarchical Database

Hierarchical database uses **nodes** to link and structure fields and records; entries may have one **parent node** with several **child nodes** in a **one-to-many relationship.**

Network Database

Network database is like hierarchical except a child node may have more than one parent in a **many-to-many relationship;** additional connections are called **pointers.**

Relational Database

Relational database data is stored in tables **(relations);** related tables must have a **common data item** (key field).

Multidimensional Database

Multidimensional databases extend two-dimensional relational tables to three or more dimensions, sometimes called a **hyper cube.** Advantages include:

- Conceptualization—database provides an intuitive model for complex data and relationships.

- Processing speed—analyzing and querying is faster.

Object-Oriented Database

Object-oriented databases store data, instructions and unstructured data. Data is organized using *objects, classes, entities, attributes,* and *methods.*

- **Objects** contain both data and instructions to manipulate data.

- **Classes** are similar to objects grouped together.

- **Entities** are a person, place, thing, or event.

- **Attributes,** similar to fields; are descriptions or characteristics of entities.

- **Methods** describe how data is to be manipulated.

TYPES OF DATABASES

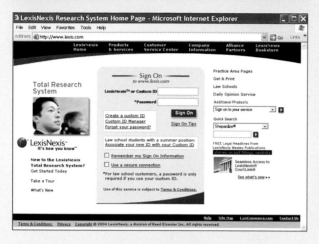

There are five types of databases:

Individual
Individual database or **microcomputer database** is used by one person.

Company or Shared
Two types of **company (shared) databases** are **common operational database** (contains data on company operations) and **common user database** (contains selected data from common operational and outside private databases).

Distributed
Distributed database is spread out geographically; accessible by communications links.

Proprietary
Proprietary database is available by subscription, also known as **information utilities** and **data banks.**

Web
Web databases are used by Web sites to record data collected from users and by Web search engines; **CGI (Common Gateway Interface)** scripts used in interface programs.

DATABASE USES AND ISSUES

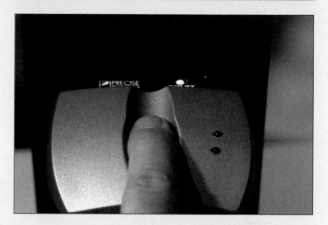

Databases offer a great opportunity for increased productivity; however, security is always a concern.

Strategic Uses
Data warehouses are a new type of database that support data mining. **Data mining** is a technique for searching and exploring databases for related information and patterns.

Databases available for general and specific business purposes include:
- Business directories
- Demographic data
- Business statistical information
- Text databases
- Web databases

Security
Two important security concerns are illegal use of data and unauthorized access. Most organizations use **firewalls** to protect their internal networks.

FEATURES

Animations

Careers in IT

DVD Direct

Expansions

Making IT Work for You

On the Web Explorations

TechTV

Tips

CHAPTER REVIEW

Key Terms

Crossword

Multiple Choice

Matching

Open-ended

Using Technology

Expanding Your Knowledge

Building Your Portfolio

application generation subsystem   (340)
attribute   (335)
batch processing   (336)
CGI (Common Gateway Interface)
   script   (347)
character   (335)
child node   (341)
class   (344)
common data item   (343)
common operational database   (346)
common user database   (346)
company database   (345)
data   (334)
data administration subsystem   (340)
data bank   (346)
data definition subsystem   (339)
data dictionary   (339)
data integrity   (338)
data maintenance   (340)
data manipulation subsystem   (339)
data mining   (348)
data model   (340)
data redundancy   (338)
data warehouse   (348)
database   (336)
database administrator (DBA)   (340)
database management system (DBMS)   (339)
DBMS engine   (339)
distributed database   (346)
entity   (335)
field   (335)
file   (336)

firewall   (349)
hierarchical database   (341)
hyper cube   (343)
individual database   (345)
information utility   (346)
key field   (336)
logical view   (334)
many-to-many relationship   (341)
method   (344)
microcomputer database   (345)
multidimensional database   (343)
network database   (341)
node   (341)
object   (344)
object-oriented database   (344)
one-to-many relationship   (341)
online processing   (337)
parent node   (341)
physical view   (334)
pointers   (341)
primary field   (336)
processing rights   (340)
proprietary database   (346)
query-by-example   (340)
real-time processing   (337)
record   (336)
relation   (342)
relational database   (342)
shared database   (345)
structured query language (SQL)   (340)
Web database   (347)

To test your knowledge of these key terms with animated flash cards, consult your Computing Essentials CD or visit our Web site at www.olearyseries.com/CE06 and select Key Terms.

Across

1 Used to control access to internal networks.

3 Items that contain both data and instructions to manipulate the data.

6 Proprietary database.

7 Type of processing where data collected over time is processed at one time.

8 Facts or observations about people, places, things, and events.

13 Data captured or saved used a microphone.

16 Multiple files on the same subject or person.

17 Points connected like the branches of a tree.

Down

2 Type of database available over the Web.

4 Similar objects grouped together.

5 A collection of related fields.

6 Problems that occur when one or more files is overlooked.

9 Uniquely identifies each record.

10 Technique used to search databases for information and patterns.

11 Focuses on the meaning and content of the data.

12 Distinctive field in each record of a database.

14 Descriptions of how data is to be manipulated.

15 Person, place, thing, or object.

For an interactive version of this crossword, consult your Computing Essentials CD or visit our Web site at **www.olearyseries.com/CE06** and select Crossword.

MULTIPLE CHOICE

Circle the letter or fill in the correct answer.

1. A _____ is a collection of related fields.
   a. field
   b. class
   c. file
   d. record
   e. character

2. In _____ processing data is collected over time and then processed later all at one time.
   a. real-time
   b. relational
   c. batch
   d. database
   e. direct

3. _____ provide(s) tools for maintaining and analyzing data.
   a. Child nodes
   b. Data redundancy
   c. Data manipulation subsystem
   d. DBMS
   e. Security

4. The person responsible for determining processing rights and which people have access to data is called a _____.
   a. database manager
   b. database administrator
   c. database operator
   d. pointer
   e. hasher

5. The arrangement used in a network database is an example of a _____.
   a. one-to-one relationship
   b. one-to-many relationship
   c. many-to-many relationship
   d. many-to-one relationship
   e. none of the above

6. A common data item is also known as a _____.
   a. field
   b. transaction file
   c. pointer
   d. node
   e. key field

7. _____ are persons, places, things, or events that are to be described in an object-oriented database.
   a. Methods
   b. Fields
   c. Classes
   d. Entities
   e. Attributes

8. A collection of integrated records useful mainly to one person is a(n) _____.
   a. common user database
   b. individual database
   c. company database
   d. common operational database
   e. distributed database

9. An enormous database an organization develops to cover certain objects is called a _____.
   a. data warehouse
   b. company database
   c. common operational database
   d. distributed database
   e. proprietary database

10. _____ are special hardware and software designed to control access to internal networks.
    a. Firewalls
    b. Data models
    c. DBMS
    d. Relations
    e. Pointers

For an interactive version of these multiple choice questions, consult your Computing Essentials CD or visit our Web site at www.olearyseries.com/CE06 and select Multiple Choice.

Match each numbered item with the most closely related lettered item. Write your answers in the spaces provided.

FEATURES

Animations

Careers in IT

DVD Direct

Expansions

Making IT Work for You

On the Web Explorations

TechTV

Tips

CHAPTER REVIEW

Key Terms

Crossword

Multiple Choice

Matching

Open-ended

Using Technology

Expanding Your Knowledge

Building Your Portfolio

a. batch processing
b. character
c. child node
d. class
e. data dictionary
f. data mining
g. data redundancy
h. DBMS
i. DBMS engine
j. distributed database
k. file
l. hierarchical database
m. key field
n. logical
o. multi-dimensional
p. network database
q. pointer
r. SQL
s. real-time processing
t. relational database

1. End users and most computer professionals use this data view. _____
2. A single letter or number. _____
3. A collection of records. _____
4. The common field by which tables in a database are related. _____
5. Processing performed all at once on data collected over several days. _____
6. Processing that occurs where data is processed when the transaction occurs. _____
7. Database problem in which data is duplicated and stored in different files. _____
8. DBMS subsystem that bridges logical and physical data views. _____
9. Software required to create, modify, and gain access to a database. _____
10. Dictionary with a description of the data structure in a database. _____
11. Database in which fields or records are structured in nodes. _____
12. Most widely used query language. _____
13. A node one level below the node being considered in a hierarchical database. _____
14. Database with hierarchical arrangement of nodes in which each child node may have more than one parent node. _____
15. Connection between parent node and a child node in a hierarchical database. _____
16. Database structure, in which data is organized into related tables. _____
17. Similar objects grouped together. _____
18. DBMS structure that extends the two-dimensional relational data model. _____
19. Database that can be made accessible through a variety of communications networks. _____
20. Technique of searching data warehouses for related information. _____

For an interactive version of this matching exercise, consult your Computing Essentials CD or visit our Web site at www.olearyseries.com/CE06 and select Matching.

OPEN-ENDED

On a separate sheet of paper, respond to each question or statement.

1. Describe the five logical data groups or categories.
2. What is the difference between batch processing and real-time processing?
3. Identify and define the five parts of DBMS programs.
4. What are the five types of databases? Why does more than one kind of database exist?
5. What are some of the benefits and limitations of databases? Why is security a concern?

1

Free Database Software

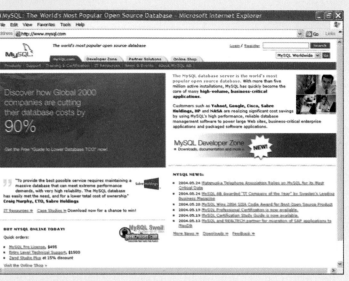

Software to manage relational databases is a key component in many corporate IS departments. Database software like Microsoft Access and Oracle can be money well spent when fast, reliable information retrieval is a must. But did you know that advanced database management software can be obtained for free? Visit our Web site at www.olearyseries.com/CE06 and select Using Technology to connect to a site that features free database software. Read about this software, and then answer the following questions: (a) What is MySQL? What is its basic functionality? (b) How does MySQL compare to commercial software like Microsoft Access in terms of performance? (c) What support is available to users of MySQL? How is it provided? (d) Would you recommend MySQL as an IT solution? Why or why not?

2

Internet Movie Database

One popular Web database is the Internet Movie Database, or IMDB. Connect to our Web site at www.olearyseries.com/CE06 and select Using Technology to link to the IMDB site. Once connected, try making a couple of queries and then answer the following questions: (a) What types of information does the IMDB contain? (b) What queries did you try? What were the results? (c) Based on your knowledge of databases, would you expect the IMDB to be relational or object-oriented? Justify your answer.

DVD Direct

1

DVD Direct customers currently use the Internet to order videos. The videos are sent and returned by mail. DVD Direct is exploring the use of streaming video to deliver videos through the Internet. This change would significantly impact the way it does business. To learn more about DVD Direct, consult your Computing Essentials CD or visit us on the Web at www.olearyseries/ CE06 and select DVD Direct and then select Databases. (1) Describe how DVD Direct currently stores movie data. (2) Create a drawing similar to Figure 12-3 that shows how DVD Direct uses batch processing. (3) What changes would be required to support online delivery of movies? (4) Create a drawing similar to Figure 12-4 that shows how DVD Direct could use real-time processing. (5) Compare the advantages and disadvantages of batch and real-time processing.

Internet Movie

2

DVD Direct's MOVIE database is similar to the Internet Movie Database (IMDB). To learn about the Movie database, consult your Computing Essentials CD or visit us on the Web at www. olearyseries.com/CE06 and select DVD Direct and then select Databases. Then using the Web, locate and connect to the IMDB. Once connected, explore the site and then answer the following questions: (a) Compare the fields in the IMDB to those in the DVD Direct MOVIE database. (b) Which fields are similar? (c) Are any unique? (d) Based on your knowledge of databases, would you expect the IMDB to be relational or object-oriented? Justify your answer.

1 — Web Databases

Web databases are a convenient way to deliver information access to a large audience. Write a one-page paper titled "Web Databases" that addresses the following: (a) What type of data is well suited for Web delivery? (b) What type of data would not be a good candidate for Web delivery? Why? (c) What are the benefits for a company to allow its users online access to information instead of through a DBMS application? (d) What are the benefits to the user?

2 — Personal Information

Corporations currently collect information about the purchases you make and your personal spending habits. Sometimes corporations will share information to build a more informative profile about you. There have been proposals for legislation to regulate or halt this type of exchange. Consider how you feel about this exchange of information, and then answer the following questions in a one-page paper: (a) What ethics and privacy concerns are related to corporations sharing personal data? (b) How might the consumer benefit from this? (c) Could this harm the consumer? What could happen if your grocery store shared information about your purchases with your life insurance carrier? (d) What rights do you feel consumers should have with regard to privacy of information collected about them? How should these rights be enforced? Defend your answer.

SYSTEMS ANALYSIS AND DESIGN

COMPETENCIES

After you have read this chapter, you should be able to:

1 **Describe the six phases of the systems life cycle.**

2 **Identify information needs and formulate possible solutions.**

3 **Analyze existing information systems and evaluate the feasibility of alternative systems.**

4 **Identify, acquire, and test new system software and hardware.**

5 **Switch from an existing information system to a new one with minimal risk.**

6 **Perform system audits and periodic evaluations.**

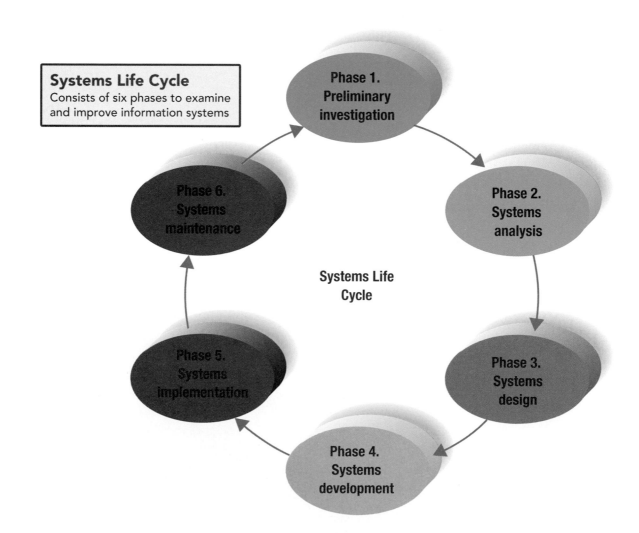

Systems Life Cycle
Consists of six phases to examine and improve information systems

Phase 1.
Preliminary investigation

Phase 2.
Systems analysis

Phase 3.
Systems design

Phase 4.
Systems development

Phase 5.
Systems implementation

Phase 6.
Systems maintenance

Systems Life Cycle

Most people in an organization are involved with an information system of some kind, as we saw in the previous chapter. For an organization to create a system and for users to make it truly useful require considerable thought and effort. Fortunately, there is a six-step problem-solving process for accomplishing this. It is known as systems analysis and design.

Big organizations can make big mistakes. For example, General Motors spent $40 billion putting in factory robots and other high technology in its auto making plants. It then removed much of this equipment and reinstalled that basic part of the assembly line, the conveyor belt. Why did the high-tech production systems fail? The probable reason was that GM did not devote enough energy to training its workforce in using the new systems.

The government also can make big mistakes. In one year, the Internal Revenue Service computer system was so overwhelmed it could not deliver tax re-funds on time. How did this happen? Despite extensive testing of much of the system, not all testing was completed. Thus, when the new system was phased in, the IRS found it could not process tax returns as quickly as it had hoped.

Both of these examples show the necessity for thorough planning—especially when an organization is trying to implement a new kind of system. Systems analysis and design reduces the chances for such spectacular failures.

Competent end users need to understand the importance of systems analysis and design. They need to be aware of the relationship of an organization's chart to its managerial structure. Additionally, they need to know the six phases of the systems development life cycle: preliminary investigation, systems analysis, systems design, systems development, systems implementation, and systems maintenance.

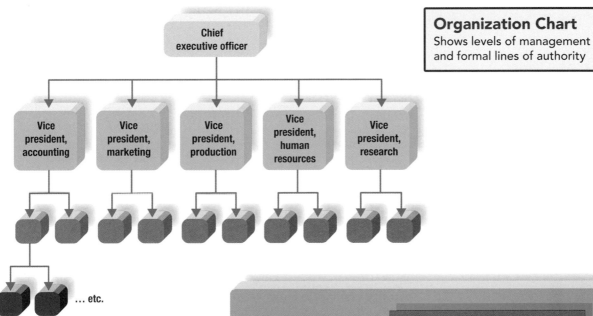

Organization Chart
Shows levels of management and formal lines of authority

Decision Table
Shows the decision rules that apply when certain conditions occur

		Decision rules		
Conditions	1	2	3	4
1. Project less than $10,000	Y	Y	N	N
2. Good credit history	Y	N	Y	N
Actions	1	2	3	4
1. Accept project	✓	✓	✓	
2. Require deposit		✓	✓	
3. Reject project				✓

Systems analysis and design is a six-phase problem-solving procedure for examining and improving an information system.

We described different types of information systems in the last chapter. Now let us consider: What, exactly, is a **system?** We can define it as a collection of activities and elements organized to accomplish a goal. As we saw in Chapter 11, an *information system* is a collection of hardware, software, people, procedures, and data. These work together to provide information essential to running an organization. This information helps to produce a product or service and, for profit-oriented businesses, derive a profit.

Information about orders received, products shipped, money owed, and so on, flows into an organization from the outside. Information about what supplies have been received, which customers have paid their bills, and so on, also flows within the organization. To avoid confusion, the flow of information must follow a route that is defined by a set of rules and procedures. However, from time to time, organizations need to change their information systems. Reasons include organizational growth, mergers and acquisitions, new marketing opportunities, revisions in governmental regulations, and availability of new technology.

Systems analysis and design is a six-phase problem-solving procedure for examining and improving an information system.

The six phases make up the **systems life cycle.** (See Figure 13-1.) The phases are as follows:

1. *Preliminary investigation:* The information problems or needs are identified.
2. *Systems analysis:* The present system is studied in depth. New requirements are specified.
3. *Systems design:* A new or alternative information system is designed.
4. *Systems development:* New hardware and software are acquired, developed, and tested.
5. *Systems implementation:* The new information system is installed and adapted to the new system, and people are trained to use it.
6. *Systems maintenance:* In this ongoing phase, the system is periodically evaluated and updated as needed.

In organizations, this six-phase systems life cycle is used by computer professionals known as **systems analysts.** These people study an organization's systems to determine what actions to take and how to use computer technology to assist them. A recent survey by *Money* magazine compared salary, prestige, and security of 100 widely held jobs. The top job classification was computer engineer, followed by computer systems analyst.

As an end user, working alone or with a systems analyst, it is important that you understand how the systems life cycle works. In fact, you may *have* to use the procedure. More and more end users are developing their own information systems. This is because in many organizations there

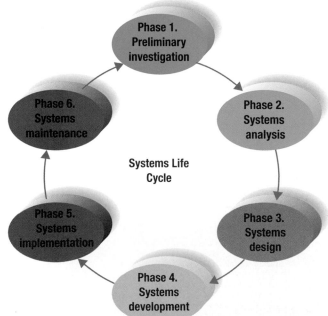

Figure 13-1   The six-phase systems life cycle

is a three-year backlog of work for systems analysts. For instance, suppose you recognize that there is a need for certain information within your organization. Obtaining this information will require the introduction of new hardware and software. You go to seek expert help from systems analysts in studying these information needs. At that point you discover that the systems analysts are so overworked it will take them three years to get to your request! You can see then, why many managers are learning to do these activities themselves. In any case, learning the six steps described in this chapter will raise your computer competency. It will also give you skills to solve a wide range of problems. These skills can make you more valuable to an organization.

▼ CONCEPT CHECK

▶ What is a system?

▶ Name the six phases of the systems life cycle.

▶ What do systems analysts do?

PHASE 1: PRELIMINARY INVESTIGATION

> In the preliminary investigation phase, the problems are briefly identified and a few solutions are suggested.

The first phase of the systems life cycle is a **preliminary investigation** of a proposed project to determine the need for a new information system. This usually is requested by an end user or a manager who wants something done that is not presently being done. For example, suppose you work for Advantage Advertising, a fast-growing advertising agency. Advantage Advertising produces a variety of different ads for a wide range of different clients. The agency employs both regular staff workers and on-call freelancers. One of your responsibilities is keeping track of the work performed for each client and the employees who performed the work. In addition, you are responsible for tabulating the final bill for each project. (See Figure 13-2.)

Figure 13-2 Preliminary investigation

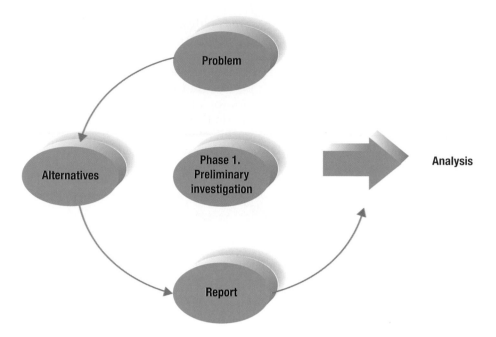

Figure 13–3 Phase 1:
Preliminary investigation

How do you figure out how to charge which clients for which work done by which employees? This kind of problem is common to many service organizations (such as lawyers' and contractors' offices). Indeed, it is a problem in any organization where people charge for their time and clients need proof of hours worked.

In Phase 1, the systems analyst—or the end user—is concerned with three tasks: (1) briefly defining the problem, (2) suggesting alternative solutions, and (3) preparing a short report. (See Figure 13-3.) This report will help management decide whether to pursue the project further. (If you are an end user employing this procedure for yourself, you may not produce a written report. Rather, you would report your findings directly to your supervisor.)

DEFINING THE PROBLEM

Defining the problem means examining whatever current information system is in use. Determining what information is needed, by whom, when, and why is accomplished by interviewing and making observations. If the information system is large, this survey is done by a systems analyst. If the system is small, the survey can be done by the end user.

For example, suppose Advantage Advertising account executives, copywriters, and graphic artists currently just record the time spent on different jobs on their desk calendars. (Examples might be "Client A, telephone conference, 15 minutes"; "Client B, design layout, 2 hours.") After interviewing several account executives and listening to their frustrations, it becomes clear that the approach is somewhat helter-skelter. (See Figure 13-4.) Written calendar entries are too unprofessional to be shown to clients. Moreover, a large job often has many people working on it. It is difficult to pull together all their notations to make up a bill for the client. Some freelancers work at home, and their time slips are not readily available. These matters constitute a statement of the problem: The company has a manual time-and-billing system that is slow and difficult to implement.

As an end user, you might experience difficulties with this system yourself. You're in someone else's office, and a telephone call comes in for you from a client. Your desk calendar is back in your own office. You have two choices. You can always carry your calendar with you, or you can remember to note the

Figure 13-4 One step in defining problems with the current system is to interview executives

time you spent on various tasks when you return to your office. The secretary to the account executive is continually after you (and everyone else at Advantage) to provide photocopies of your calendar. This is so that various clients can be billed for the work done on various jobs. Surely, you think, there must be a better way to handle time and billing.

SUGGESTING ALTERNATIVE SYSTEMS

This step is simply to suggest some possible plans as alternatives to the present arrangement. For instance, Advantage could hire more secretaries to collect the information from everyone's calendars (including telephoning those working at home). Or it could use the existing system of network-linked microcomputers that staffers and freelancers presently use. Perhaps, you think, there is already some off-the-shelf packaged software available that could be used for a time-and-billing system. At least there might be one that would make your own job easier.

PREPARING A SHORT REPORT

For large projects, the systems analyst writes a report summarizing the results of the preliminary investigation and suggesting alternative systems. (See Figure 13-5.) The report also may include schedules for further development of the project. This document is presented to higher management, along with a recommendation to continue or discontinue the project. Management then decides whether to finance the second phase, the systems analysis.

For Advantage Advertising, your report might point out that billing is frequently delayed. It could say that some tasks may even "slip through the cracks" and not get charged at all. Thus, as the analyst has noted, you suggest the project might pay for itself merely by eliminating lost or forgotten charges.

Figure 13-5 Management meets to evaluate the preliminary investigation report

▼ **CONCEPT CHECK**

▶ What is the purpose of the preliminary investigation phase?

▶ What are the three tasks the systems analyst is concerned with during this
   phase?

PHASE 2: ANALYSIS

> In the systems analysis phase, the present system is studied in depth, and new
> requirements are specified.

In Phase 2, **systems analysis,** data is collected about the present system. This
data is then analyzed, and new requirements are determined. We are not concerned with a new design here, only with determining the *requirements* for a
new system. Systems analysis is concerned with gathering and analyzing the
data. This usually is completed by documenting the analysis in a report. (See
Figure 13-6.)

GATHERING DATA

When gathering data, the systems analyst—or the end user doing systems
analysis—expands on the data gathered during Phase 1. He or she adds details
about how the current system works. Data is obtained from observation and
interviews. In addition, data may be obtained from questionnaires given to
people using the system. Data is also obtained from studying documents that
describe the formal lines of authority and standard operating procedures. One
document is the **organization chart,** which shows levels of management and
formal lines of authority. (See Figure 13-7.) You might note that an organization chart resembles the hierarchy of three levels of management we described
in Chapter 11. The levels are top managers, middle managers, and supervisors.

Note in our illustration in Figure 13-7 that we have preserved the department labeled "Production." However, the name in an advertising agency might

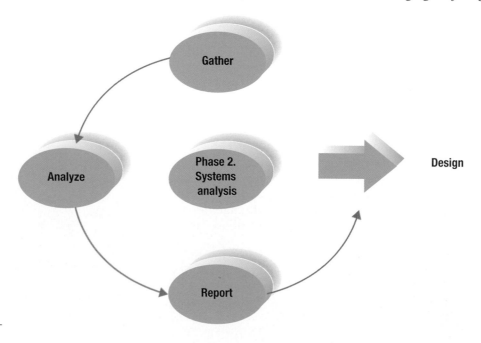

Figure 13–6   Phase 2: Systems
analysis

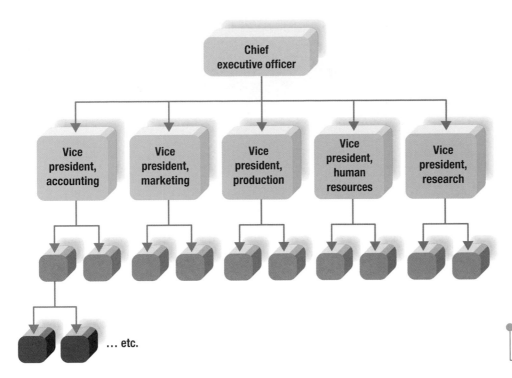

Figure 13-7   Example of an organization chart

be something like "Creative Services." Obviously, the products an advertising agency produces are ads: radio and television commercials, magazine and newspaper ads, billboard ads, and so on. In any case, if the agency is working on a major advertising campaign, people from several departments might be involved. There might also be people from different management levels within the departments. Their time charges will vary, depending on how much they are paid.

ANALYZING THE DATA

In the data analysis step, the idea is to learn how information currently flows and to pinpoint why it isn't flowing appropriately. The whole point of this step is to apply logic to the existing arrangement to see how workable it is. Many times the current system is not operating correctly because prescribed procedures are not being followed. That is, the system may not really need to be redesigned. Rather, the people in it may need to be shown how to follow correct procedures.

Many different tools are available to assist systems analysts and end users in the analysis phase. Some of the principal ones are as follows:

- **Checklists:** Numerous checklists are available to assist in this stage. A checklist is a list of questions. It is helpful in guiding the systems analyst and end user through key issues for the present system.

   For example, one question might be "Can reports be prepared easily from the files and documents currently in use?" Another might be "How easily can the present time-and-billing system adapt to change and growth?"

- **Top-down analysis method:** The top-down analysis method is used to identify the top-level components of a complex system. Each component is then broken down into smaller and smaller components. This approach makes each component easier to analyze and deal with.

   For instance, the systems analyst might look at the present kind of bill submitted to a client for a complex advertising campaign. The analyst

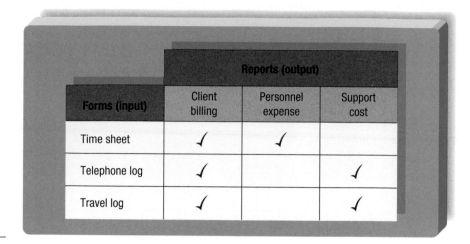

Figure 13-8   Example of a grid chart

Forms (input)	Reports (output)		
	Client billing	Personnel expense	Support cost
Time sheet	✓	✓	
Telephone log	✓		✓
Travel log	✓		✓

Conditions	Decision rules			
	1	2	3	4
1. Project less than $10,000	Y	Y	N	N
2. Good credit history	Y	N	Y	N
Actions	1	2	3	4
1. Accept project	✓	✓	✓	
2. Require deposit		✓	✓	
3. Reject project				✓

Figure 13-9   Example of a decision table

might note the categories of costs—employee salaries, telephone and mailing charges, travel, supplies, and so on.

- **Grid charts:** A grid chart shows the relationship between input and output documents. An example is shown in Figure 13-8 that indicates the relationship between the data input and the outputs.

    For instance, a time sheet is one of many inputs that produces a particular report, such as a client's bill. Other inputs might be forms having to do with telephone conferences and travel expenses. On a grid sheet, rows represent inputs, such as time sheet forms. Columns represent output documents, such as different clients' bills. A check mark at the intersection of a row and column means that the input document is used to create the output document.

- **Decision tables:** A decision table shows the decision rules that apply when certain conditions occur. Figure 13-9 shows a decision table to evaluate whether to accept a client's proposed advertising project. The first decision rule applies if both conditions are met. If the project is less than $10,000 and if the client has a good credit history, the firm will accept the project without requiring a deposit.

- **System flowcharts:** System flowcharts show the flow of input data to processing and finally to output, or distribution of information. An example of a system flowchart keeping track of time for advertising "creative people" is shown in Figure 13-10. The explanation of the symbols used appears in Figure 13-11. Note that this describes the present manual, or non-computerized, system. (A system flowchart is not the same as a program flowchart, which is very detailed. Program flowcharts are discussed in Chapter 14.)

- **Data flow diagrams:** Data flow diagrams show the data or information flow within an information system. The data is traced from its origin through processing, storage, and output. An example of a data flow diagram is shown in Figure 13-12. The explanation of the symbols used appears in Figure 13-13.

- **Automated design tools:** Automated design tools are software packages that evaluate hardware and software alternatives according to requirements given by the systems analyst. They are also called **computer-aided software engineering (CASE) tools.** These tools are not limited to system analysis. They are used in system design and development as well. CASE tools relieve the system analysts of many repetitive tasks, develop clear documentation, and, for larger projects, coordinate team member activities.

For a summary of the analysis tools, see Figure 13-14.

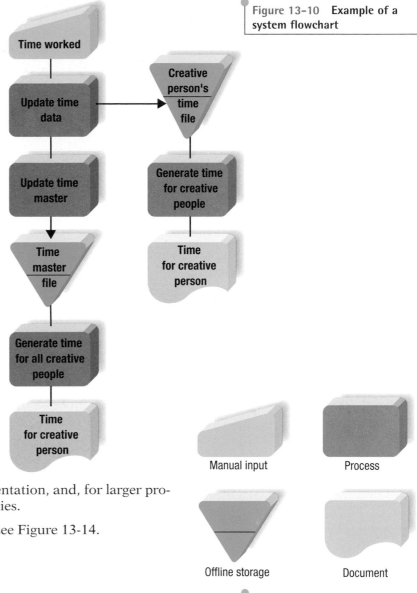

Figure 13-10   Example of a system flowchart

Manual input   Process

Offline storage   Document

Figure 13-11   System flowchart symbols

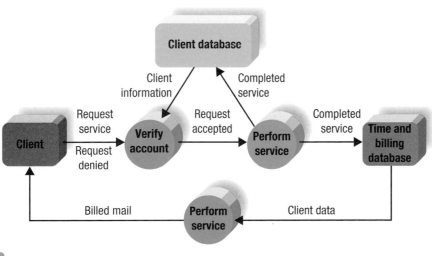

Figure 13-12   Example of a data flow diagram

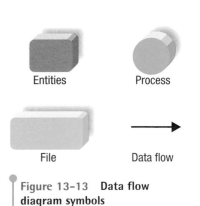

Entities   Process

File   Data flow

Figure 13-13   Data flow diagram symbols

Systems Analysis and Design

Tool	Description
Checklist	Provides a list of questions about key issues
Top-down analysis	Divides a complex system into components, beginning at the top
Grid chart	Shows relationships between inputs and outputs
Decision table	Specifies decision rules and circumstances when specific rules are to be applied
System flowchart	Shows movement of input data, processing, and output or distribution of information
Data flow diagram	Shows data flow within an organization or application
Automated design tools	Automates the analysis, design, and development of information systems

Figure 13-14   Summary of analysis tools

Figure 13-15   Systems analysis documentation

DOCUMENTING SYSTEMS ANALYSIS

In larger organizations, the systems analysis stage is typically documented in a report for higher management. The **systems analysis report** describes the current information system, the requirements for a new system, and a possible development schedule. For example, at Advantage Advertising, the system flowcharts show the present flow of information in a manual time-and-billing system. Some boxes in the system flowchart might be replaced with symbols showing where a computerized information system could work better.

Management studies the report and decides whether to continue with the project. Let us assume your boss and higher management have decided to continue. You now move on to Phase 3, systems design. (See Figure 13-15.)

▼ CONCEPT CHECK

- ► What is the purpose of the analysis phase?
- ► List and describe the common analysis tools.
- ► What is a systems analysis report?

PHASE 3: DESIGN

In the systems design phase, a new or alternative information system is designed.

Phase 3 is **systems design.** It consists of three tasks: (1) designing alternative systems, (2) selecting the best system, and (3) writing a systems design report. (See Figure 13-16.)

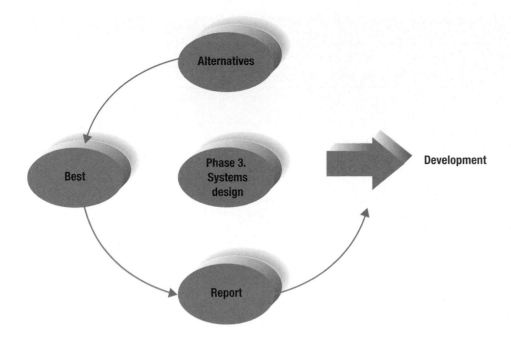

Figure 13–16   Phase 3: Systems design

DESIGNING ALTERNATIVE SYSTEMS

In almost all instances, more than one design can be developed to meet the information needs. Systems designers evaluate each alternative system for feasibility. By feasibility we mean three things:

- **Economic feasibility:** Will the costs of the new system be justified by the benefits it promises? How long will it take for the new system to pay for itself?
- **Technical feasibility:** Are reliable hardware, software, and training available to make the system work? If not, can they be obtained?
- **Operational feasibility:** Can the system actually be made to operate in the organization, or will people—employees, managers, clients—resist it?

SELECTING THE BEST SYSTEM

When choosing the best design, managers must consider these four questions. (1) Will the system fit in with the organization's overall information system? (2) Will the system be flexible enough so it can be modified in the future? (3) Can it be made secure against unauthorized use? (4) Are the benefits worth the costs?

For example, one aspect you have to consider at Advantage Advertising is security. Should freelancers and outside vendors enter data directly into a computerized time-and-billing system, or should they keep submitting time sheets manually? In allowing these outside people to input information directly, are you also allowing them access to files they should not see? Do these files contain confidential information, perhaps information of value to rival advertising agencies?

WRITING THE SYSTEMS DESIGN REPORT

The **systems design report** is prepared for higher management and describes the alternative designs. It presents the costs versus the benefits and outlines the effect of alternative designs on the organization. It usually concludes by recommending one of the alternatives.

▶ What is the purpose of the design phase?

▶ Distinguish between economic, technical, and operational feasibility.

▶ Identify the factors that need to be considered when choosing the best systems design.

PHASE 4: DEVELOPMENT

> **In the systems development phase, software and hardware are acquired and tested.**

Phase 4 is **systems development.** It has three steps: (1) acquiring software, (2) acquiring hardware, and (3) testing the new system. (See Figure 13-17.)

ACQUIRING SOFTWARE

Application software for the new information system can be obtained in two ways. It can be purchased as off-the-shelf packaged software and possibly modified, or it can be custom designed. If any of the software is being specially created, the programming steps we will outline in Chapter 14 should be followed.

With the systems analyst's help, you have looked at time-and-billing packaged software designed for service organizations. Unfortunately, you find that none of the packaged software will do. Most of the packages seem to work well for one person (you). However, none seem to be designed for many people working together. It appears, then, that software will have to be custom designed. (We discuss the process of developing software in Chapter 14, on programming.)

ACQUIRING HARDWARE

Some new systems may not require new computer equipment, but others will. The equipment needed and the places they are to be installed must be deter-

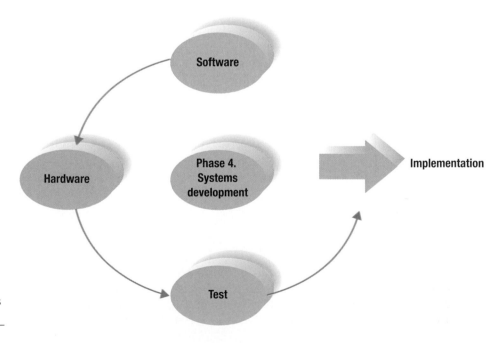

Figure 13–17 Phase 4: Systems development

mined. This is a very critical area. Switching or upgrading equipment can be a tremendously expensive proposition. Will a microcomputer system be sufficient as a company grows? Are networks expandable? Will people have to undergo costly training?

The systems analyst tells you that there are several different makes and models of microcomputers currently in use at Advantage Advertising. Fortunately, all are connected by a local area network to a file server that can hold the time-and-billing data. To maintain security, the systems analyst suggests that an electronic mailbox be installed for freelancers and others outside the company. They can use this electronic mailbox to post their time charges. Thus, it appears that existing hardware will work just fine.

TESTING THE NEW SYSTEM

After the software and equipment have been installed, the system should be tested. Sample data is fed into the system. The processed information is then evaluated to see whether results are correct. Testing may take several months if the new system is complex.

For this step, you ask some people in Creative Services to test the system. (See Figure 13-18.) You observe that some of the people have problems knowing where to enter their times. To solve the problem, the software is modified to display an improved user entry screen. After the system has been thoroughly tested and revised as necessary, you are ready to put it into use.

Figure 13–18 To test a system, sample data is entered and problems are resolved

▼ CONCEPT CHECK

- ▶ What is the purpose of the development phase?
- ▶ What are the ways by which application software can be obtained?

PHASE 5: IMPLEMENTATION

> In the systems implementation phase, the new information system is installed, and people are trained to use it.

Another name for Phase 5, **systems implementation,** is **conversion.** It is the process of changing—converting—from the old system to the new one and training people to use the new system. (See Figure 13-19.)

TYPES OF CONVERSION

There are four approaches to conversion: *direct, parallel, pilot,* and *phased.*

- In the **direct approach,** the conversion is done simply by abandoning the old and starting up the new. This can be risky. If anything is still wrong with the new system, the old system is no longer available to fall back on.

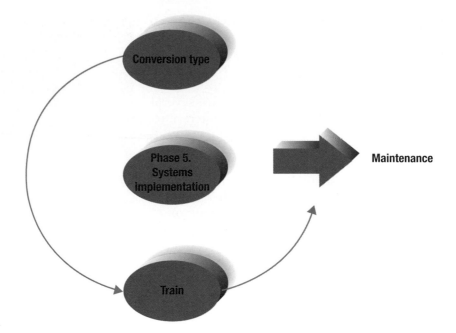

Figure 13-19 Phase 5: Systems implementation

The direct approach is not recommended precisely because it is so risky. Problems, big or small, invariably crop up in a new system. In a large system, a problem might just mean catastrophe.

- In the **parallel approach,** old and new systems are operated side by side until the new one proves to be reliable.

  This approach is low-risk. If the new system fails, the organization can just switch to the old system to keep going. However, keeping enough equipment and people active to manage two systems at the same time can be very expensive. Thus, the parallel approach is used only in cases in which the cost of failure or of interrupted operation is great.

- In the **pilot approach,** the new system is tried out in only one part of the organization. Once the system is working smoothly in that part, it is implemented throughout the rest of the organization.

  The pilot approach is certainly less expensive than the parallel approach. It also is somewhat riskier. However, the risks can be controlled because problems will be confined only to certain areas of the organization. Difficulties will not affect the entire organization.

- In the **phased approach,** the new system is implemented gradually over a period of time.

  The entire implementation process is broken down into parts or phases. Implementation begins with the first phase, and once it is successfully implemented, the second phase begins. This process continues until all phases are operating smoothly. This is an expensive proposition because the implementation is done slowly. However, it is certainly one of the least risky approaches.

In general, the pilot and phased approaches are the favored methods. Pilot is preferred when there are many people in an organization performing similar operations—for instance, all sales clerks in a department store. Phased is more appropriate for organizations in which people are performing different operations. For a summary of the different types of conversions, see Figure 13-20.

You and the systems analyst, with top management support, have decided on a pilot implementation. This approach was selected in part based on cost and the availability of a representative group of users. The Creative Services

Type	Description	Discussion
Direct	Abandon the old	Very risky; not recommended
Parallel	Run old and new side by side	Very low risk; however, very expensive; not generally recommended
Pilot	Convert part of organization first	Less expensive but riskier than parallel conversion; recommended for situations with many people performing similar operations
Phased	Implement gradually	Less risky but more expensive than parallel conversion; recommended for situations with many people performing different operations

Figure 13-20 Types of conversion

department previously tested the system and has expressed enthusiastic support for it. A group from this department will pilot the implementation of the time-and-billing system. (See Figure 13-21.)

TRAINING

Training people is important, of course. Unfortunately, it is one of the most commonly overlooked activities. Some people may begin training early, even before the equipment is delivered, so that they can adjust more easily. In some cases, a professional software trainer may be brought in to show people how to operate the system. However, at Advantage Advertising, the time-and-billing software is simple enough that the systems analyst can act as the trainer.

Figure 13-21 A pilot group from Creative Services tests the new system

▼ CONCEPT CHECK

▶ What is the goal of the implementation phase?

▶ Briefly describe the four approaches to conversion.

PHASE 6: MAINTENANCE

Systems maintenance is first a systems audit and then an ongoing evaluation to see whether a system is performing productively.

After implementation comes **systems maintenance,** the last step in the systems life cycle. This phase is a very important, ongoing activity. Most organizations spend more time and money on this phase than on any of the others. Maintenance has two parts—a *systems audit* and a *periodic evaluation.* (See Figure 13-22.)

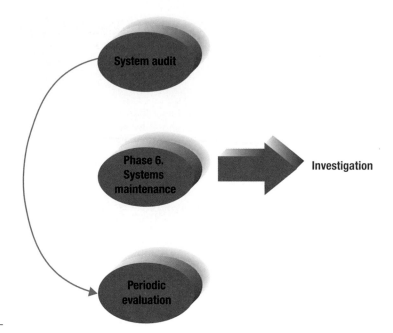

Figure 13–22 Phase 6: Systems maintenance

Phase	Activity
1 Preliminary investigation	Define problem, suggest alternatives, prepare short report
2 Systems analysis	Gather data, analyze data, document
3 Systems design	Design alternatives, select best alternative, write report
4 Systems development	Develop software, acquire hardware, test system
5 Systems implementation	Convert, train
6 Systems maintenance	Perform system audit, evaluate periodically

Figure 13–23 Summary of systems life cycle

In the **systems audit,** the system's performance is compared to the original design specifications. This is to determine whether the new procedures are actually furthering productivity. If they are not, some redesign may be necessary.

After the systems audit, the new information system is further modified, if necessary. All systems should be evaluated from time to time to determine whether they are meeting the goals and providing the service they are supposed to.

The six-step systems life cycle is summarized in Figure 13-23.

▼ CONCEPT CHECK

▶ What is the purpose of the maintenance phase?

▶ Name the two parts of the maintenance phase.

PROTOTYPING AND RAPID APPLICATIONS DEVELOPMENT

Prototyping and RAD are two alternatives to the systems life cycle approach.

Is it necessary to follow every phase of the systems life cycle? It may be desirable, but often there is no time to do so. For instance, hardware may change so fast that there is no opportunity for evaluation, design, and testing as just described. Two alternative approaches that require much less time are *prototyping* and *rapid applications development*.

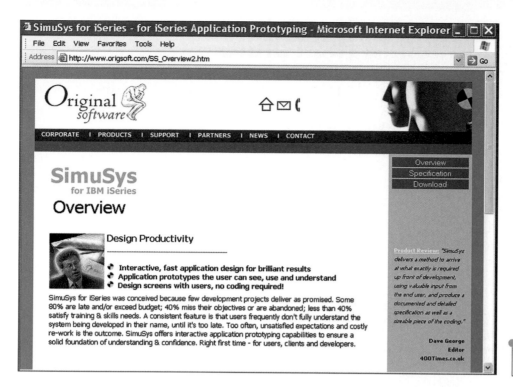

Figure 13-24 SimuSys prototyping software from IBM

PROTOTYPING

Prototyping means to build a *model* or *prototype* that can be modified before the actual system is installed. For instance, the systems analyst for Advantage Advertising might develop a proposed or prototype menu as a possible screen display for the time-and-billing system. Users would try it out and provide feedback to the systems analyst. The systems analyst would revise the prototype until the users felt it was ready to put into place. Typically, the development time for prototyping is shorter; however, it is sometimes more difficult to manage the project and to control costs. (See Figure 13-24.)

RAPID APPLICATIONS DEVELOPMENT

Rapid applications development (RAD) involves the use of powerful development software, small specialized teams, and highly trained personnel. For example, the systems analyst for Advantage Advertising would use specialized development software like CASE, form small teams consisting of select users and managers, and obtain assistance from other highly qualified analysts. Although the resulting time-and-billing system would likely cost more, the development time would be shorter and the quality of the completed system would be better.

▼ CONCEPT CHECK

► What is meant by prototyping?

► What is involved in RAD?

A Look to the Future

Rapid Change

Most observers firmly believe that the pace of business is now faster than ever before. The time to develop a product and bring it to market in many cases is now months rather than years. Internet technologies, in particular, have provided tools to support the rapid introduction of new products and services.

To stay competitive, corporations must integrate these new technologies into their existing way of doing business. Existing systems are being modified, and entirely new systems are being developed. In most cases, the traditional systems life cycle approach takes too long—sometimes years—to develop a system. Many organizations are responding by aggressively implementing prototyping and RAD. Others are enlisting the services of outside consulting groups that specialize in system development.

One such company is Drapkin Technology. Drapkin provides technical expertise and managerial experience to the systems analysis and design process. Working with corporations such as Gateway and Sony, the company provides project assessment, analysis, design, development, implementation, and administration. Drapkin can also step in and quickly reorganize projects when the systems life cycle fails—a crucial service in and of itself.

As the pace of business continues to increase, more and more organizations are expected to move to prototyping and RAD approaches and to enlist the services of outside consulting groups.

SYSTEMS ANALYSIS AND DESIGN AT DVD DIRECT

DVD Direct is an entirely Web-oriented movie rental business. Its customers order movies from DVD Direct's Web site and the movies are delivered on DVD disks by mail. While business has been good, some recent indications have pointed to possible trouble ahead. Specifically, an internal study discovered that many current and potential customers with high bandwidth Internet connections prefer to have movies delivered over the Internet rather than by mail. Further, the study reported that current customers who recently switched to high bandwidth connections were very likely to drop their DVD Direct membership.

In response, top management has committed to expanding DVD Direct's business model to include online delivery of movies using streaming video technology. Once an order is placed, the Internet-delivered movies would be immediately downloaded onto the member's hard disk. The movie would remain there for a week, or until the movie was played, whichever occurs first.

Alice, a recently hired marketing analyst, has proposed the creation of a Frequent Renters Club that gives members points for each streaming movie they order. As a member's points accumulate, the points can be redeemed for gifts and for free rentals. To follow Alice as she meets with Bob, the vice president of marketing, to discuss the proposed Frequent Renters Club, consult your Computing Essentials CD or visit us on the Web at www.olearyseries.com/CE06 and select DVD Direct and then select System Analysis and Design.

VISUAL SUMMARY

SYSTEMS ANALYSIS AND DESIGN

SYSTEM ANALYSIS AND DESIGN

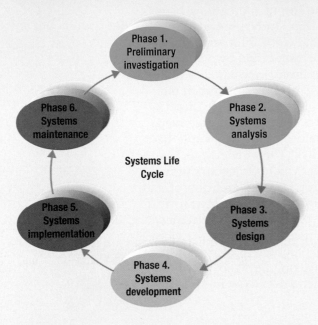

A **system** is a collection of activities and elements organized to accomplish a goal. **System analysis and design** is a six-phase problem solving procedure that makes up the **systems life cycle.**

The phases are:

- *Preliminary investigation*—identifying problems or needs.
- *Systems analysis*—studying present system and specifying new requirements.
- *Systems design*—designing new or alternative system to meet new requirements.
- *Systems development*—acquiring, developing, and testing needed hardware and software.
- *Systems implementation*—installing new system and training people.
- *Systems maintenance*—periodically evaluating and updating system as needed.

Systems analysts are computer professionals who typically conduct system analysis and design.

PHASE 1: PRELIMINARY INVESTIGATION

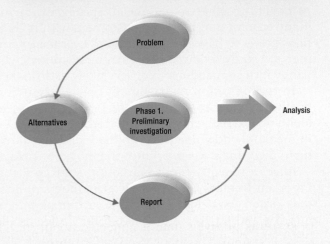

The **preliminary investigation** determines the need for a new information system. It is typically requested by an end user or a manager. Three tasks of this phase are defining the problem, suggesting alternative systems, and preparing a report.

Defining the Problem

The current information system is examined to determine who needs what information, when the information is needed, and why.

If the existing information system is large, then a **systems analyst** conducts the survey. Otherwise, the end user conducts the survey.

Suggesting Alternative Systems

Some possible alternative systems are suggested. Based on interviews and observations made in defining the problem, alternative information systems are identified.

Preparing a Short Report

To document and to communicate the findings of Phase 1, preliminary investigation, a short report is prepared and presented to management.

To be a competent end user you need to understand the importance of systems analysis and design. You need to know the six phases of the systems development life cycle: preliminary investigation, analysis, design, development, implementation, and maintenance. Additionally, you need to understand prototyping and RAD.

PHASE 2: ANALYSIS

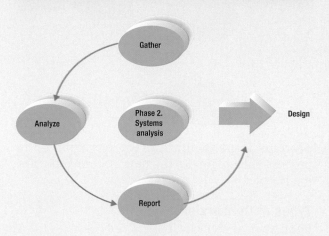

In **systems analysis** data is collected about the present system. The focus is on determining the requirements for a new system. Three tasks of this phase are gathering data, analyzing the data, and documenting the analysis.

Gathering Data

Data is gathered by observation, interviews, questionnaires, and looking at documents. One helpful document is the **organization chart,** which shows a company's functions and levels of management.

Analyzing the Data

There are several tools for the analysis of data, including **checklists, top-down analysis, grid charts, decision tables,** and **system flowcharts.**

Documenting Systems Analysis

To document and to communicate the findings of Phase 2, a **systems analysis report** is prepared for higher management.

PHASE 3: DESIGN

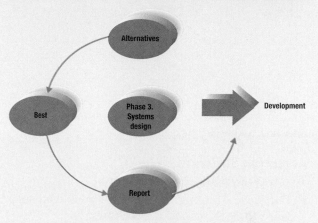

In the **systems design** phase, a new or alternative information system is designed. This phase consists of three tasks:

Designing Alternative Systems

Alternative information systems are designed. Each alternative is evaluated for:

- **Economic feasibility**—cost versus benefits; time for the system to pay for itself.
- **Technical feasibility**—hardware and software reliability; available training.
- **Operational feasibility**—will the system work within the organization?

Selecting the Best System

Four questions should be considered when selecting the best system:

- Will the system fit into an overall information system?
- Will the system be flexible enough to be modified as needed in the future?
- Will it be secure against unauthorized use?
- Will the system's benefits exceed its costs?

Writing the System Design Report

To document and to communicate the findings of Phase 3, a **systems design report** is prepared for higher management.

Systems Analysis and Design

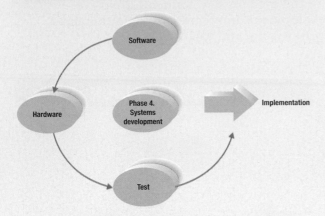

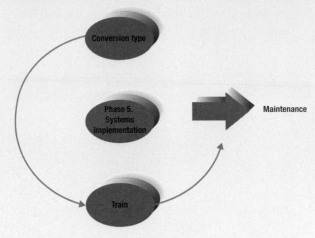

In the **systems development** phase, software and hardware are acquired and tested.

Acquiring Software

Two ways to acquire software are:

- Purchase—buying off-the-shelf packaged software to be modified if necessary.
- Custom designed—create programs following programming steps presented in Chapter 14.

Acquiring Hardware

Acquiring hardware is very critical and involves consideration for future company growth, existing networks, communication capabilities, and training.

Testing the New System

Using sample data, the new system is tested. This step can take several months for a complex system.

Systems implementation (conversion) is the process of changing to the new system and training people.

Types of Conversion

Four ways to convert are:

- **Direct approach**—abandoning the old and starting up the new; can be very risky and not recommended.
- **Parallel approach**—operating the old and new side by side until the new one proves its worth; low risk but expensive.
- **Pilot approach**—trying out the new system in only one part of an organization. Compared to parallel, pilot is riskier and less expensive.
- **Phased approach**—implementing the new system gradually; low risk but expensive.

Training

A software trainer may be used to train end users to use the new system.

PHASE 6: MAINTENANCE

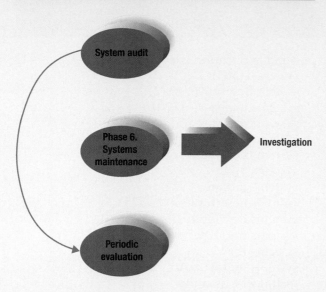

Systems maintenance is the final phase. It consists of a system audit followed by periodic evaluation.

System Audit

Once the system is operational, the systems analyst performs a **system audit** by comparing the new system to its original design specifications. If the system does not meet these specifications, some further redesign of the system may be required.

Periodic Evaluation

The new system is periodically evaluated to ensure that it is operating efficiently. If it is not, some redesign may be required.

PROTOTYPING AND RAD

Due to time pressures, it is not always feasible to follow every phase of the systems life cycle. Two alternatives that require less time are *prototyping* and *RAD*.

Prototyping

Prototyping means to build a model or prototype that can be modified before the actual system is installed. Typically, the development time for prototyping is shorter; however, it can be more difficult to manage the project and to control costs.

Rapid Application Development

Rapid application development (RAD) uses powerful development software, small specialized teams, and highly trained personnel. Typically, the development costs more. However, the time is much less and the quality is often better.

Phase	Activity
1 Preliminary investigation	Define problem, suggest alternatives, prepare short report
2 Systems analysis	Gather data, analyze data, document
3 Systems design	Design alternatives, select best alternative, write report
4 Systems development	Develop software, acquire hardware, test system
5 Systems implementation	Convert, train
6 Systems maintenance	Perform system audit, evaluate periodically

Systems Analysis and Design

COMPUTING
ESSENTIALS
2006

KEY TERMS

automated design tools   (373)
checklist   (371)
computer-aided software engineering
    (CASE) tools   (373)
conversion   (377)
data flow diagram   (373)
decision table   (372)
direct approach   (377)
economic feasibility   (375)
grid chart   (372)
operational feasibility   (375)
organization chart   (370)
parallel approach   (378)
phased approach   (378)
pilot approach   (378)
preliminary investigation   (367)
prototyping   (381)

rapid applications development (RAD)   (381)
system   (366)
system flowchart   (372)
systems analysis   (370)
systems analysis and design   (366)
systems analysis report   (374)
systems analyst   (366)
systems audit   (380)
systems design   (374)
systems design report   (375)
systems development   (376)
systems implementation   (377)
systems life cycle   (366)
systems maintenance   (379)
technical feasibility   (375)
top-down analysis method   (371)

To test your knowledge of these key terms with animated flash cards, consult your Computing Essentials CD or visit our Web site at www.olearyseries.com/CE06 and select Key Terms.

FEATURES

Animations

Careers in IT

DVD Direct

Expansions

Making IT Work for You

On the Web Explorations

TechTV

Tips

CHAPTER REVIEW

Key Terms

Crossword

Multiple Choice

Matching

Open-ended

Using Technology

Expanding Your Knowledge

Building Your Portfolio

Across

3 Systems implementation.

8 Collection of activities and elements organized to accomplish a goal.

9 Build a model that can be modified before the system is installed.

10 Automated design tool.

12 Approach where new system is tried in only one part of an organization.

14 Shows levels of management and formal lines of authority.

15 List of questions.

Down

1 1st step in the design phase.

2 Study an organization's systems.

4 System's performance is compared to the original specifications.

5 Approach where new system is implemented slowly over time.

6 Conversion done by abandoning old system and starting the new.

7 Diagram that shows the information flow within an organization.

11 Shows the relationship between input and output documents.

12 Old and new systems are operated side by side.

13 The most commonly overlooked activity in the Implementation phase.

For an interactive version of this crossword, consult your Computing Essentials CD or visit our Web site at **www.olearyseries.com/CE06** and select Crossword.

Circle the letter or fill in the correct answer.

1. Preliminary investigation, systems analysis, systems design, systems development, systems implementation, and systems maintenance are elements of the _____.
   a. systems checklist
   b. systems life cycle
   c. technical feasibility chart
   d. parallel approach
   e. pilot approach

2. A(n) _____ is usually requested by an end user or manager who wants something done.
   a. prototype
   b. systems audit
   c. top-down analysis
   d. organization chart
   e. preliminary investigation

3. Defining the problem, suggesting alternative systems, and preparing a report are part of the _____ phase.
   a. preliminary investigation
   b. analysis
   c. design
   d. development
   e. implementation

4. A _____ studies an organization's systems to determine what actions to take and how to use technology to assist them.
   a. RAD
   b. data worker
   c. CASE
   d. systems analyst
   e. data flow diagram

5. A(n) _____ shows the formal lines of authority.
   a. systems audit
   b. organization chart
   c. grid chart
   d. decision table
   e. RAD

6. Checklists, grid charts, decision tables, and system flowcharts are part of the _____ phase.
   a. preliminary investigation
   b. analysis
   c. design
   d. development
   e. implementation

7. Automated design tools are also called _____.
   a. data flow diagrams
   b. decision tables
   c. grid charts
   d. CASE tools
   e. system flowcharts

8. The _____ describes the current information system, the requirements for a new system, and a possible development schedule.
   a. systems analysis report
   b. systems design report
   c. system flowchart
   d. systems implementation report
   e. operational feasibility report

9. _____ determines whether or not reliable hardware, software, and training are available to make a new system work.
   a. Economic feasibility
   b. Operational feasibility
   c. Technical feasibility
   d. Systems audit
   e. Top-down analysis

10. In the _____, conversion to a new system is done simply by abandoning the old and starting up the new.
   a. parallel approach
   b. direct approach
   c. pilot approach
   d. phased approach
   e. pilot and direct approaches

For an interactive version of these multiple choice questions, consult your Computing Essentials CD or visit our Web site at www.olearyseries.com/CE06 and select Multiple Choice.

MATCHING

Match each numbered item with the most closely related lettered item. Write your answers in the spaces provided.

a. automated design tools
b. checklist
c. data flow diagram
d. decision table
e. direct approach
f. economic feasibility
g. grid chart
h. operational feasibility
i. organization chart
j. phased approach
k. preliminary investigation
l. prototyping
m. RAD
n. system
o. systems analysis and design
p. systems analysis
q. systems analyst
r. systems audit
s. systems design report
t. systems development

1. Activities and elements designed to accomplish a goal. ____
2. Six-phase procedure for examining and improving information systems. ____
3. Computer professional who studies an organization's systems. ____
4. The first phase of the systems life cycle. ____
5. Data is collected about the present system. ____
6. Chart showing management levels and formal lines of authority. ____
7. Record of questions that guides the systems analyst and end user through key issues for the present system. ____
8. Shows the relationship between input and output documents. ____
9. Table showing decision rules applying when certain conditions occur. ____
10. Shows the data or information flow within an information system. ____
11. Software package that evaluates hardware and software alternatives according to requirements given by the systems analyst. ____
12. Condition where cost of designing a system are justified by the benefits. ____
13. Condition where new system will be able to function within the existing framework of an organization. ____
14. Report for higher management describing the alternative designs suggested in the design phase. ____
15. Phase consisting of developing software, acquiring hardware, and testing the new system. ____
16. Implementation that abandons the old system for the new. ____
17. Implementation gradually over a period of time. ____
18. System comparison that determines if new procedures improve productivity. ____
19. Building a modifiable model before the actual system is installed. ____
20. Use of powerful software and specialized teams as alternative to systems development life cycle approach. ____

For an interactive version of this matching exercise, consult your Computing Essentials CD or visit our Web site at **www.olearyseries.com/CE06** and select Matching.

OPEN-ENDED

On a separate sheet of paper, respond to each question or statement.

1. What is a system? What are the six phases of the systems life cycle? Why do corporations undergo this process?
2. What are the tools used in the analysis phase? What is top-down analysis? How is it used?
3. Describe each type of system conversion. Which is the most commonly used?
4. What is system maintenance? When does it occur?
5. Explain prototyping and RAD. When might they be used by corporations?

1

System Design Software

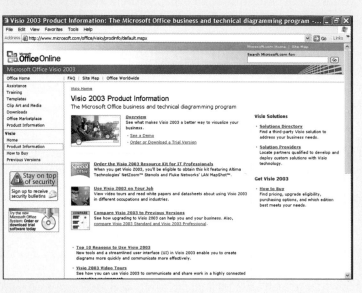

Software tools are often used to enhance understanding of the different phases of system design. To learn more about one of these tools, visit our Web site at www.olearyseries.com/CE06 and select Using Technology. Once connected, select one of these tools and read about it. Then answer the following questions: (a) What is the product, and what does it do? (b) What types of projects could you use it for? (c) What types of professionals could use this product? Provide specific examples.

2

Systems Analysis Software

There are several companies that specialize in systems analysis support software. Connect to our Web site at

www.olearyseries.com/CE06 and select Using Technology to link to one of these organizations. Explore the products the company offers. Then answer the following questions: (a) Describe the products designed to enhance systems analysis. (b) For each product you described, list the phase or phases of the systems life cycle it applies to. (c) Review the DVD Direct case study in the chapter. Pick a product that could assist Alice and Mia, and describe how. Be specific.

DVD Direct

1

DVD Direct is planning to implement a Frequent Renters Club. The key to successful implementation of this program is the development of an information system that accurately and consistently records reward points. They are going to use systems analysis and design to develop the information system. To learn more about DVD Direct's plans, consult your Computing Essentials CD or visit us on the Web at www.olearyseries.com/CE06 and select DVD Direct and then select Systems Analysis and Design. (1) Describe the six sequential phases of systems analysis and design as they relate to the Frequent Renters Club information system. (2) If you were developing this information system, would you use prototyping rather than the full systems analysis and design approach? Why or why not? (3) If you were developing this information system, would you use rapid applications development rather than the full systems analysis and design approach? Why or why not?

Conversion

2

To learn more about how DVD Direct plans to convert to its new information system, consult your Computing Essentials CD or visit us on the Web at www.olearyseries.com/CE06 and select DVD Direct and then select Systems Analysis and Design. Then answer the following questions: (a) Define the term *conversion*, and briefly describe each conversion type. (b) Which phase of the systems life cycle does conversion occur in? (c) What type of conversion do Alice and Mia use for implementing the new DVD Direct system? (d) Do you agree that this was the best choice for DVD Direct? Why or why not?

1

CASE Tools

Sometimes described as a CAD system for systems analysts, CASE tools are primarily used to automate and manage the elements of the analysis phase. In a one-page paper entitled "CASE tools," address the following: (a) Define CASE. (b) Give specific examples of how CASE tools can be used in each of the following instances: system analysis, system development, and system design.

2

Managing Choices

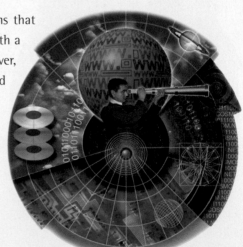

Consider the following scenario, and then answer the questions that follow in a one-page paper: You're a manager who comes up with a new system that will make your company more efficient. However, implementing this system would make several tasks obsolete and cost many of your coworkers their jobs. (a) What is your ethical obligation to your company in this situation? (b) What is your ethical obligation to your coworkers? (c) What would you do in this situation? Defend your answer.

PROGRAMMING AND LANGUAGES

COMPETENCIES

After you have read this chapter, you should be able to:

1 **Describe the six steps of programming.**

2 **Discuss design tools including top-down design, pseudocode, flowcharts, and logic structures.**

3 **Describe program testing and the tools for finding and removing errors.**

4 **Describe CASE tools and object-oriented software development.**

5 **Explain the five generations of programming languages.**

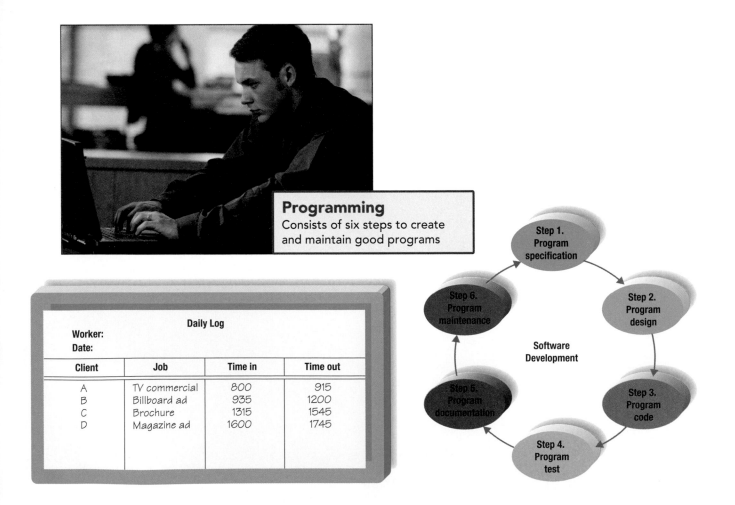

Programming
Consists of six steps to create and maintain good programs

	Daily Log		
Worker:			
Date:			
Client	**Job**	**Time in**	**Time out**
A	TV commercial	800	915
B	Billboard ad	935	1200
C	Brochure	1315	1545
D	Magazine ad	1600	1745

Software Development

- Step 1. Program specification
- Step 2. Program design
- Step 3. Program code
- Step 4. Program test
- Step 5. Program documentation
- Step 6. Program maintenance

How do you go about getting a job? You might look through newspaper classified ads, check with employment services, write to prospective employers, and so on. In other words, you do some general problem solving to come up with a broad plan. This is similar to what you do in systems analysis and design. Once you have determined a particular job, then you do some specific problem solving. That is what you do in programming. In this chapter, we describe programming in two parts: (1) the steps in the programming process and (2) some of the programming languages available.

Why should you need to know anything about programming? The answer is simple. You might need to deal with programmers in the course of your work. You also may be required to do some programming yourself in the future. A new field has emerged known as end user application development. In this field, users like you create their own business application programs, without the assistance of a programmer. Thus, organizations avoid paying high software development costs, and you and other end users avoid waiting months for programmers to get around to projects important to you.

In Chapter 13, we described the six phases of the systems life cycle. Programming is part of phase 4, systems development. Competent end users need to understand the relationship between systems development and programming. Additionally, they need to know the six steps of programming, including program specification, program design, program code, program test, program documentation, and program maintenance.

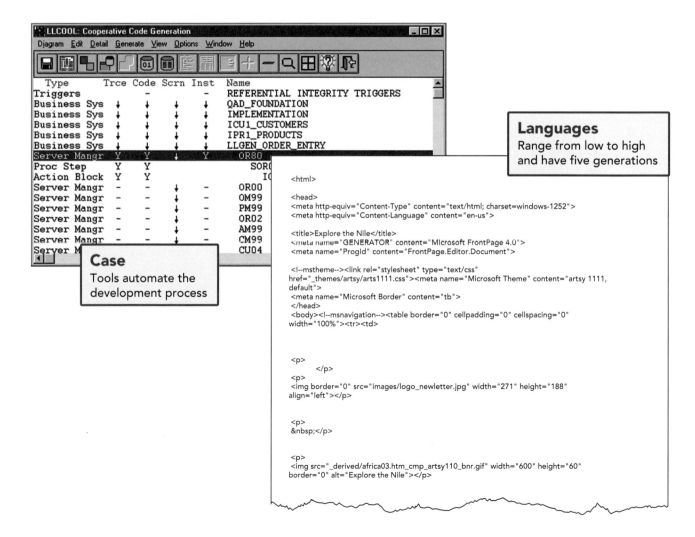

Languages
Range from low to high and have five generations

Case
Tools automate the development process

PROGRAMS AND PROGRAMMING

A program is a list of instructions. Programming is a six-step procedure for creating programs. Programmers use this six-step procedure.

What exactly is programming? Many people think of it as simply typing words into a computer. That may be part of it, but that is certainly not all of it. Programming, as we've hinted before, is actually a *problem-solving procedure*.

WHAT IS A PROGRAM?

To see how programming works, think about what a program is. A **program** is a list of instructions for the computer to follow to accomplish the task of processing data into information. The instructions are made up of statements used in a programming language, such as BASIC, C, or Java.

You are already familiar with some types of programs. As we discussed in Chapters 1 and 3, application programs are widely used to accomplish a variety of different types of tasks. For example, we use word processors to create documents and spreadsheets to analyze data. System programs, on the other hand, focus on tasks necessary to keep the computer running smoothly. These can be purchased and are referred to as prewritten or packaged programs. Programs can also be created or custom-made. In Chapter 13, we saw that the systems analyst looked into the availability of time-and-billing software for Advantage Advertising. Will off-the-shelf software do the job, or should it be custom written? This is one of the first things that needs to be decided in programming.

WHAT IS PROGRAMMING?

A program is a list of instructions for the computer to follow to process data. **Programming,** also known as **software development,** is a six-step procedure for creating that list of instructions. Only one of those steps consists of typing (keying) statements into a computer. (See Figure 14-1.)

The six steps are as follows:

1. *Program specification:* The program's objectives, outputs, inputs, and processing requirements are determined.
2. *Program design:* A solution is created using programming techniques such as top-down program design, pseudocode, flowcharts, and logic structures.
3. *Program code:* The program is written or coded using a programming language.
4. *Program test:* The program is tested or debugged by looking for syntax and logic errors.
5. *Program documentation:* Documentation is an ongoing process throughout the programming process. This phase focuses on formalizing the written description and processes used in the program.
6. *Program maintenance:* Completed programs are periodically reviewed to evaluate their accuracy, efficiency, standardization, and ease of use. Changes are made to the program's code as needed.

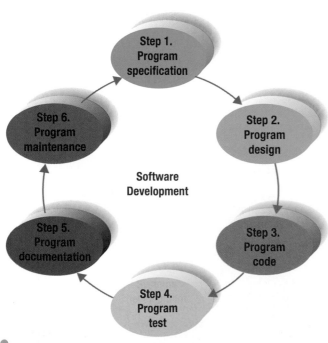

Figure 14-1 Software development

In organizations, computer professionals known as **software engineers** or **programmers** use this six-step procedure. Working closely with systems analysts in systems development, phase 4 of the systems life cycle, programmers create software required for information systems. In a recent survey by *Money* magazine, software engineers were ranked at the top of over 100 widely held jobs based on salary, prestige, and security.

You may well find yourself working directly with a programmer or indirectly through a systems analyst. Or you may actually do the programming for a system that you develop. Whatever the case, it's important that you understand the six-step programming procedure.

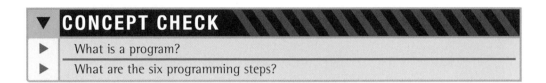

▼ CONCEPT CHECK

▶   What is a program?

▶   What are the six programming steps?

STEP 1: PROGRAM SPECIFICATION

> In the program specification step, the objectives, outputs, inputs, and processing requirements are determined. This step concludes with documentation.

Program specification is also called **program definition** or **program analysis.** It requires that the programmer—or you, the end user, if you are following this procedure—specify five items: (1) the program's objectives, (2) the desired output, (3) the input data required, (4) the processing requirements, and (5) the documentation. (See Figure 14-2)

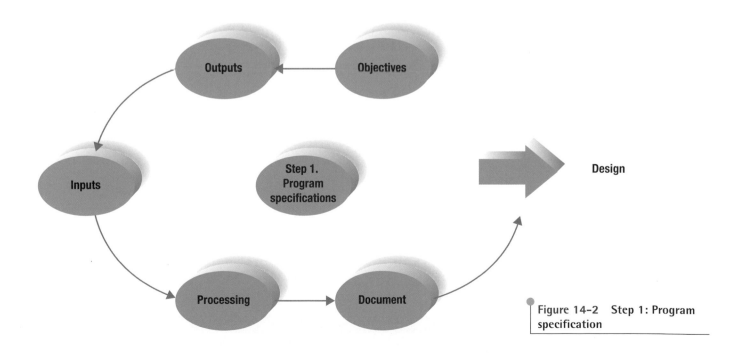

Figure 14-2   Step 1: Program specification

Figure 14–3 Problem
definition: Make a clear
statement of the problem

PROGRAM OBJECTIVES

You solve all kinds of problems every day. A problem might be deciding how to commute to school or work or which homework or report to do first. Thus, every day you determine your **objectives**—the problems you are trying to solve. Programming is the same. You need to make a clear statement of the problem you are trying to solve. (See Figure 14-3.) An example would be "I want a time-and-billing system to record the time I spend on different jobs for different clients of Advantage Advertising."

DESIRED OUTPUT

It is best always to specify outputs before inputs. That is, you need to list what you want to *get out* of the computer system. Then you should determine what will *go into it*. The best way to do this is to draw a picture. You—the end user, not the programmer—should sketch or write how you want the output to look when it's done. It might be printed out or displayed on the monitor.

For example, if you want a time-and-billing report, you might write or draw something like Figure 14-4. Another form of output from the program might be bills to clients.

INPUT DATA

Once you know the output you want, you can determine the input data and the source of this data. For example, for a time-and-billing report, you can specify

Client name: Allen Realty			Month and year: Jan' 00	
Date	Worker	Regular Hours & Rate	Overtime Hours & Rate	Bill
1/2	M. Jones	5 @ $10	1 @ $15	$65.00
	K. Williams	4 @ $30	2 @ $45	$210.00

Figure 14–4 End user's sketch of desired output

Daily Log

Worker:

Date:

Client	Job	Time in	Time out
A	TV commercial	800	915
B	Billboard ad	935	1200
C	Brochure	1315	1545
D	Magazine ad	1600	1745

Figure 14-5 Example of statement of hours worked—manual system; hours are expressed in military time

that one source of data to be processed should be time cards. These are usually logs or statements of hours worked submitted on paper forms. The log shown in Figure 14-5 is an example of the kind of input data used in Advantage Advertising's manual system. Note that military time is used. For example, instead of writing "5:45 P.M.," people would write "1745."

PROCESSING REQUIREMENTS

Here you define the processing tasks that must happen for input data to be processed into output. For Advantage, one of the tasks for the program will be to add the hours worked for different jobs for different clients.

DOCUMENT PROGRAM SPECIFICATIONS

As in the systems life cycle, ongoing documentation is essential. You should record program objectives, desired outputs, needed inputs, and required processing. This leads to the next step, program design.

▼ CONCEPT CHECK

► What is program specification?

► What are the five tasks of the program specification phase?

STEP 2: PROGRAM DESIGN

In the program-design step, a solution is created using programming techniques such as top-down program design, pseudocode, flowcharts, and logic structures.

After program specification, you begin **program design.** (See Figure 14-6.) Here you plan a solution, preferably using **structured programming techniques.** These techniques consist of the following: (1) top-down program design, (2) pseudocode, (3) flowcharts, and (4) logic structures. (See Figure 14-7.)

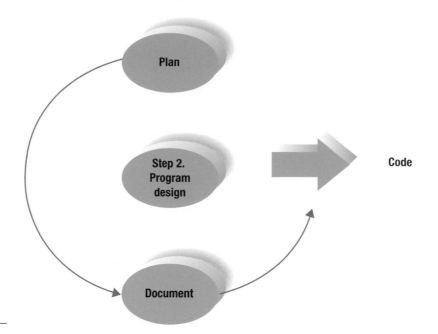

Figure 14-6   Step 2: Program design

Figure 14-7   Program design: Plan the solution

TOP-DOWN PROGRAM DESIGN

First you determine the outputs and inputs of the computer program you will create. Then you can use **top-down program design** to identify the program's processing steps. Such steps are called **program modules** (or just **modules**). Each module is made up of logically related program statements.

An example of a top-down program design for a time-and-billing report is shown in Figure 14-8. Each of the boxes shown is a module. Under the rules of top-down design, each module should have a single function. The program must pass in sequence from one module to the next until all modules have been processed by the computer. Three of the boxes—"Obtain input," "Compute hours for billing," and "Produce output"—correspond to the three principal computer system operations: *input, process,* and *output.*

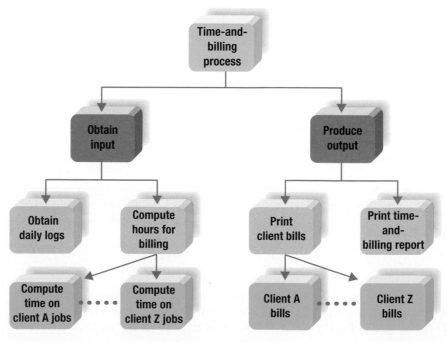

Figure 14-8   Example of top-down program design

PSEUDOCODE

Pseudocode (pronounced "soo-doh-code") is an outline of the logic of the program you will write. It is like doing a summary of the program before it is written. Figure 14-9 shows the pseudocode you might write for one module in the time-and-billing program. This shows the reasoning behind determining hours—including overtime hours—worked for different jobs for one client, Client A. Again, note this expresses the *logic* of what you want the program to do.

Compute time for Client A

Set total regular hours and total overtime hours to zero.

Get time in and time out for a job.

If worked past 1,700 hours, then compute overtime hours.

Compute regular hours.

Add regular hours to total regular hours.

Add overtime hours to total overtime hours.

If there are more jobs for that client, go back and compute for that job as well.

Figure 14–9 Example of pseudocode

FLOWCHARTS

We mentioned system flowcharts in the previous chapter. Here we are concerned with **program flowcharts.** These graphically present the detailed sequence of steps needed to solve a programming problem. Figure 14-10 presents the standard flowcharting symbols. An example of a program flowchart is presented in Figure 14-11. This flowchart expresses all the logic for just one module—"Compute time on Client A jobs"—in the top-down program design.

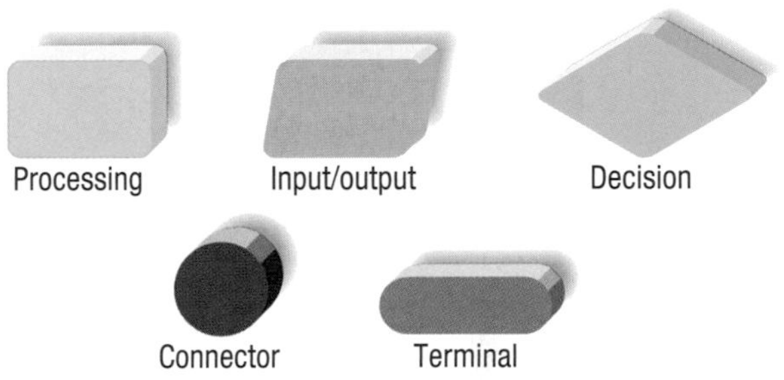

Perhaps you can see from this flowchart why a computer is a computer, and not just a fancy adding machine. A computer does more than arithmetic. It also *makes comparisons*—whether something is greater than or less than, equal to or not equal to.

But have we skipped something? How do we know which kind of twists and turns to put in a flowchart so that it will work logically? The answer is based on the use of logic structures, as we will explain.

Processing   Input/output   Decision

Connector   Terminal

Figure 14–10 Flowchart symbols

LOGIC STRUCTURES

How do you link the various parts of the flowchart? The best way is a combination of three **logic structures** called *sequence, selection,* and *loop.* Using these arrangements enables you to write so-called structured programs, which take much of the guesswork out of programming. Let us look at the logic structures.

- In the **sequence structure,** one program statement follows another. (See Figure 14-12.) Consider, for example, the "compute time" flowchart. (Refer back to Figure 14-11.) The two "add" boxes are "Add regular hours to total regular hours" and "Add overtime hours to total overtime hours." They logically follow each other. There is no question of "yes" or "no," of a decision suggesting other consequences.

- The **selection structure** occurs when a decision must be made. The outcome of the decision determines which of two paths to follow. (See Figure 14-13.) This structure is also known as an **IF-THEN-ELSE structure,** because that is how you can formulate the decision. Consider, for example, the selection structure in the "compute time" flowchart, which is concerned about computing overtime hours. (Refer back to Figure 14-11.) It might be expressed in detail as follows:

  IF hour finished for this job is later than 1,700 hours (5:00 P.M.),
  THEN overtime hours equal the number of hours past 1,700 hours,
  ELSE overtime hours equal zero.

- The **loop structure** describes a process that may be repeated as long as a certain condition remains true. The structure is called a "loop" or "iteration" because the program loops around (iterates or repeats) again and

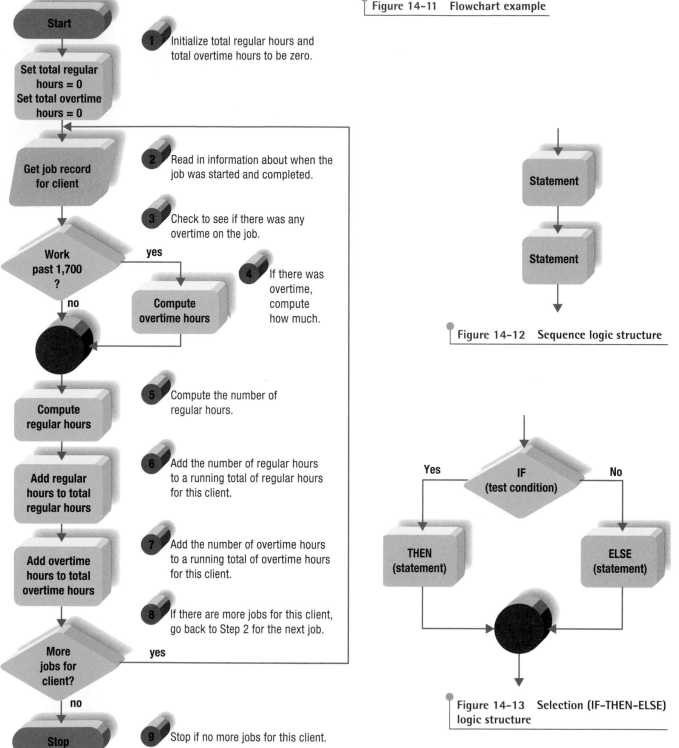

Figure 14–11   Flowchart example

Start

1 Initialize total regular hours and total overtime hours to be zero.

Set total regular hours = 0 Set total overtime hours = 0

Get job record for client

2 Read in information about when the job was started and completed.

3 Check to see if there was any overtime on the job.

Work past 1,700 ?

yes

Compute overtime hours

4 If there was overtime, compute how much.

no

Compute regular hours

5 Compute the number of regular hours.

Add regular hours to total regular hours

6 Add the number of regular hours to a running total of regular hours for this client.

Add overtime hours to total overtime hours

7 Add the number of overtime hours to a running total of overtime hours for this client.

8 If there are more jobs for this client, go back to Step 2 for the next job.

More jobs for client?

yes

no

Stop

9 Stop if no more jobs for this client.

Statement

Statement

Figure 14–12   Sequence logic structure

Yes   **IF (test condition)**   No

THEN (statement)

ELSE (statement)

Figure 14–13   Selection (IF-THEN-ELSE) logic structure

again. The loop structure has two variations: *DO UNTIL* and *DO WHILE*. (See Figure 14-14.) An example of the **DO UNTIL structure** follows.

DO read in job information UNTIL there are no more jobs.

An example of the **DO WHILE structure** is:

DO read in job information WHILE (that is, as long as) there are more jobs.

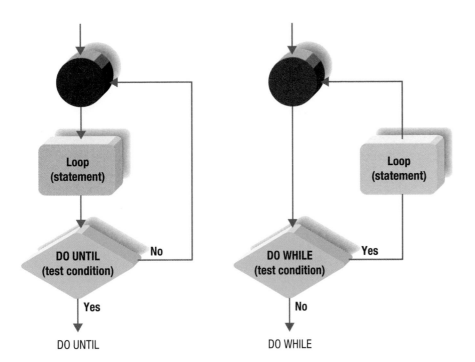

Figure 14-14 **Loop logic structures: DO UNTIL and DO WHILE**

There is a difference between the two loop structures. You may have several statements that need to be repeated. If so, the decision when to *stop* repeating them can appear at the *beginning* of the loop (DO WHILE). Or it can appear at the *end* of the loop (DO UNTIL). The DO UNTIL loop means that the loop statements will be executed at least once. This is because the loop statements are executed before you are asked whether to stop.

A summary of the structured programming techniques is presented in Figure 14-15.

The last thing to do before leaving the program design step is to document the logic of the design. This report typically includes pseudocode, flowcharts, and logic structures. Now you are ready for the next step, program code.

Technique	Description
Top-down design	Major processing steps, called program modules, are identified
Pseudocode	A narrative expression of the logic of the program is written
Program flowcharts	Graphic representation of the steps needed to solve the programming problem is drawn
Logic structures	Three arrangements are used in program flowcharts to write structured programs

Figure 14-15 **Summary of structured programming techniques**

▼ CONCEPT CHECK

► Define the goal of the program design step.

► Discuss top-down program design, pseudocode, flowcharts, and logic structures.

► Describe three logic structures.

STEP 3: PROGRAM CODE

Coding is the actual writing of a program. Good programs are structured programs. Formatting languages control the display of information. Programming languages specify the processing of data for specific operations.

Writing the program is called **coding.** Here you use the logic you developed in the program design step to actually write the program. (See Figure 14-16.) That is, you write out—using pencil and paper or typing on a computer keyboard—the letters, numbers, and symbols that make up the program. This is the "program code" that instructs the computer what to do. Coding is what many people think of when they think of programming. As we've pointed out, however, it is only one of the six steps in the programming process. (See Figure 14-17.)

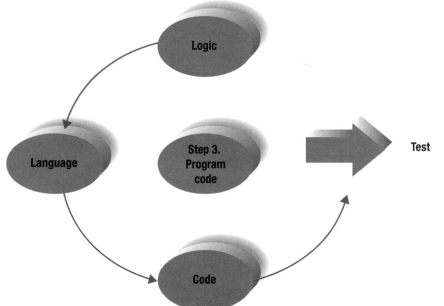

Figure 14–16   Step 3: Program code

Figure 14–17   Program code: Write the program

THE GOOD PROGRAM

What are the qualities of a good program? Above all, it should be reliable—that is, it should work under most conditions. It should catch obvious and common input errors. It should also be well documented and understandable by programmers other than the person who wrote it. After all, someone may need to make changes in the program in the future. The best way to code effective programs is to write so-called **structured programs,** using the logic structures described in Step 2.

CODING

After the program logic has been formulated, the next step is to **code** or write the program using the appropriate computer language. There are numerous formatting and programming languages. A **formatting,** or **presentation language** uses symbols, words, and phrases that instruct a computer how to display information to the user. For example, HTML is a widely used formatting language to display Web pages. See Figure 14-18 for a partial listing of the HTML code used to display The Adventure Traveler's Explore the Nile Web page. Some of the most popular formatting languages are presented in Figure 14-19.

A **programming language** uses a collection of symbols, words, and phrases that instruct a computer to perform specific operations. While formatting languages focus on displaying information primarily for Web pages, programming languages focus on processing data and information for a wide variety of different types of applications. Figure 14-20 presents the programming code using C++, a widely used programming language, to calculate the compute time

```
<html>

<head>
<meta http-equiv="Content-Type" content="text/html; charset=windows-1252">
<meta http-equiv="Content-Language" content="en-us">

<title>Explore the Nile</title>
<meta name="GENERATOR" content="Microsoft FrontPage 4.0">
<meta name="ProgId" content="FrontPage.Editor.Document">

<!--mstheme--><link rel="stylesheet" type="text/css"
href="_themes/artsy/arts1111.css"><meta name="Microsoft Theme" content="artsy 1111,
default">
<meta name="Microsoft Border" content="tb">
</head>
<body><!--msnavigation--><table border="0" cellpadding="0" cellspacing="0"
width="100%"><tr><td>


<p>
        </p>
<p>
<img border="0" src="images/logo_newletter.jpg" width="271" height="188"
align="left"></p>


<p>
 </p>


<p>
<img src="_derived/africa03.htm_cmp_artsy110_bnr.gif" width="600" height="60"
border="0" alt="Explore the Nile"></p>
```

Figure 14–18   Portion of HTML code to display Explore the Nile Web page

Language	Description
HTML	Stands for HyperText Markup Language and is the most common formatting language to present Web pages
DHTML	Stands for Dynamic HTML and improves HTML by including animations, interaction, and dynamic updating
XHTML	Stands for eXtended HTML; combines HTML and XML to add structure and flexibility to HTML
XML	Stands for eXtensible Markup Language; assists sharing of data and interactivity
WML	Stands for Wireless Markup Language; provides a standard for describing data in wireless applications

Figure 14–19   Widely used formatting languages

```
#include <fstream.h>

void main (void)
{
    ifstream input_file;

    float total_regular, total_overtime, regular, overtime;
    int hour_in, minute_in, hour_out, minute_out;
    input_file.open("time.txt",ios::in);

    total_regular = 0;
    total_overtime = 0;

    while (input_file != NULL)
    {
        input_file >> hour_in >> minute_in >> hour_out >> minute_out;

        if (hour_out > 17)
            overtime = (hour_out-17) +(minute_out/(float)60);
        else
            overtime = 0;
            regular = ((hour_out - hour_in) +(minute_out
                        - minute_in)/(float)60)    - overtime;
        total_regular += regular;
        total_overtime += overtime;
    }

    cout <<"Regular: " << total_regular <<endl;
    cout <<"Overtime " << total_overtime <<endl;
}
```

Figure 14-20   C++ code for computing regular and overtime hours

Language	Description
C	Widely used programming language, often associated with the UNIX operating system
C++	Extends C to use objects or program modules that can be reused and interchanged between programs
C#	Extends C++ to include XML functionality and support for a new Microsoft initiative called .Net
Java	Primarily used for Internet applications, similar to C++, runs with a variety of operating systems
JavaScript	Embedded into Web pages to provide dynamic and interactive content
Visual Basic	Uses a very graphical interface making it easy to learn and to rapidly develop Windows and other applications

Figure 14-21   Widely used programming languages

module. For a description of C++ and some other widely used programming languages, see Figure 14-21.

Once the program has been coded, the next step is testing, or debugging, the program.

▼ CONCEPT CHECK

► What is coding?

► What makes a good program?

► What is the difference between a formatting and a programming language?

STEP 4: PROGRAM TEST

> Debugging is testing a program and eliminating errors. Syntax errors are violations of a programming language's rules. Logic errors are created by incorrect or missing specifications. The testing process is designed to identify and remove syntax and logic errors.

Debugging is a programmer's word for testing and then eliminating errors ("getting the bugs out"). (See Figure 14-22.) It means running the program on a computer and then fixing the parts that do not work. (See Figure 14-23.) Programming errors are of two types: *syntax errors* and *logic errors*.

SYNTAX ERRORS

A **syntax error** is a violation of the rules of the programming language. For example, in C++, each statement must end with a semicolon (;). If the semicolon is omitted, the program will not run due to a syntax error. For example, Figure 14-24 shows testing of the compute time module in which a syntax error was identified.

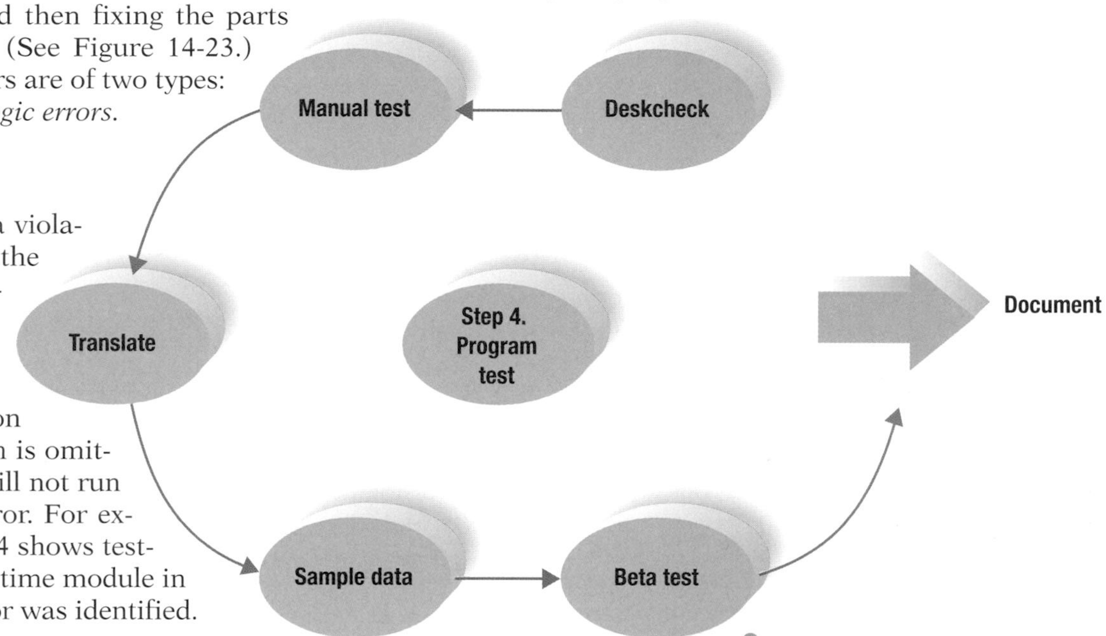

Manual test ← Deskcheck

Translate

Step 4. Program test

Document

Sample data → Beta test

Figure 14-22 Step 4: Program test

LOGIC ERRORS

A **logic error** occurs when the programmer uses an incorrect calculation or leaves out a programming procedure. For example, a payroll program that did not compute overtime hours would have a logic error.

TESTING PROCESS

Several methods have been devised for finding and removing both types of errors:

- **Desk checking:** In desk checking, a programmer sitting at a desk checks (proofreads) a printout of the program. The programmer goes through the listing line by line looking for syntax and logic errors.
- **Manually testing with sample data:** Using a calculator and sample data, a programmer follows each program statement and performs every calculation. Looking for programming logic errors, the programmer compares the manually calculated values to those calculated by the programs.
- **Attempt at translation:** The program is run through a computer, using a translator program. The translator attempts to translate the written program from the programming language (such as C++) into the machine language. Before the program will run, it must be free of syntax errors. Such errors will be identified by the translating program. (See Figure 14-24.)

Figure 14-23 Program test: Locate errors

Programming and Languages

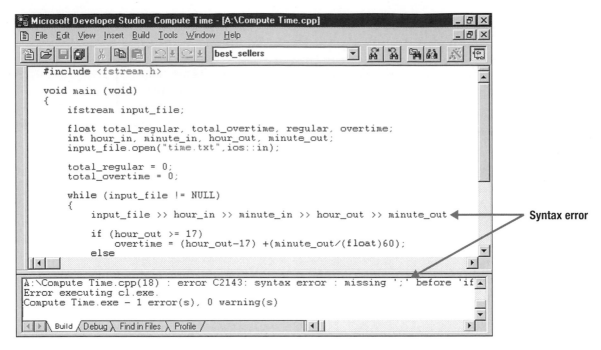

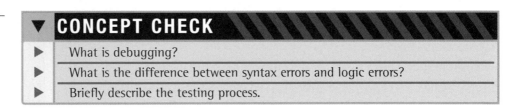

Figure 14–24   Syntax error
identified

Task	Description
1	Desk-check for syntax and logic errors
2	Manually test with sample data
3	Translate program to identify syntax errors
4	Run program with sample data
5	Beta test with potential users

Figure 14–25   Step 4: Program
testing process

- **Testing sample data on the computer:** After all syntax errors have been corrected, the program is tested for logic errors. Sample data is used to test the correct execution of each program statement.

- **Testing by a select group of potential users:** This is sometimes called **beta testing.** It is usually the final step in testing a program. Potential users try out the program and provide feedback.

For a summary of Step 4: Program test, see Figure 14-25.

▼ CONCEPT CHECK ////////////////////////////

▶ What is debugging?

▶ What is the difference between syntax errors and logic errors?

▶ Briefly describe the testing process.

STEP 5: PROGRAM DOCUMENTATION

Documentation consists of written descriptions and procedures. Program documentation occurs throughout the programming process.

Documentation consists of written descriptions and procedures about a program and how to use it. (See Figure 14-26.) It is not something done just at the end of the programming process. **Program documentation** is carried on throughout all the programming steps. This documentation is typically within the program itself and in printed documents. In this step, all the prior docu-

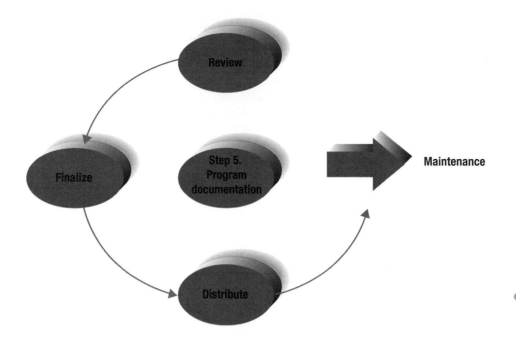

Figure 14–26 Step 5: Program documentation

mentation is reviewed, finalized, and distributed. Documentation is important for people who may be involved with the program in the future. (See Figure 14-27.) These people may include the following:

Figure 14–27 Program documentation: An ongoing process

- **Users:** Users need to know how to use the software. Some organizations may offer training courses to guide users through the program. However, other organizations may expect users to be able to learn a package just from the written documentation. Two examples of this sort of documentation are the manuals that accompany the software and the help option within most microcomputer applications.

- **Operators:** Documentation must be provided for computer operators. If the program sends them error messages, for instance, they need to know what to do about them.

- **Programmers:** As time passes, even the creator of the original program may not remember much about it. Other programmers wishing to update and modify it—that is, perform program maintenance—may find themselves frustrated without adequate documentation. This kind of documentation should include text and program flowcharts, program listings, and sample output. It might also include system flowcharts to show how the particular program relates to other programs within an information system.

▼ CONCEPT CHECK

▶ What is documentation?

▶ When does program documentation occur?

▶ Who is affected by documentation?

STEP 6: PROGRAM MAINTENANCE

Maintenance programmers are specialists in program maintenance. Operations activities focus on locating and correcting errors and standardizing software. Maintenance is also needed to adapt to the changing needs of an organization.

The final step is **program maintenance.** (See Figure 14-28.) As much as 75 percent of the total lifetime cost for an application program is for maintenance. This activity is so commonplace that a special job title, **maintenance programmer,** exists. (See Figure 14-29.)

The purpose of program maintenance is to ensure that current programs are operating error free, efficiently, and effectively. Activities in this area fall into two categories: operations and changing needs.

OPERATIONS

Operations activities concern locating and correcting operational errors, making programs easier to use, and standardizing software using structured programming techniques. For properly designed programs these activities should be minimal.

CHANGING NEEDS

The category of changing needs is unavoidable. All organizations change over time, and their programs must change with them. Programs need to be adjusted for a variety of reasons, including new tax laws, new information needs, and new company policies. Significant revisions may require that the entire programming process begin again with program specification.

Figure 14-30 summarizes the six steps of the programming process.

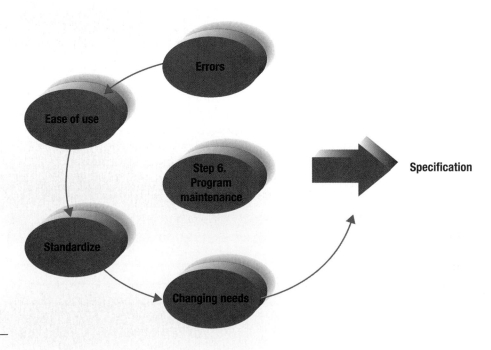

Figure 14-28   Step 6: Program maintenance

Figure 14-29 Program maintenance: Ensure program operating correctly

Step	Primary Activity
1. Program specification	Determine program objectives, desired output, required input, and processing requirements
2. Program design	Use structured programming techniques
3. Program code	Select programming language; write the program
4. Program test	Perform desk check and manual checks; attempt translation; test using sample data; beta test with potential users
5. Program documentation	Write procedure for users, operators, and programmers
6. Program maintenance	Adjust for errors, inefficient or ineffective operations, nonstandard code, and changes over time

Figure 14-30   Summary of six steps in programming

▼ CONCEPT CHECK

▶ What is the purpose of program maintenance?

▶ Discuss operational activities.

▶ What are changing needs and how do they affect programs?

CASE AND OOP

CASE tools automate the development process. Object-oriented software development focuses on relationships between procedures and objects. Object-oriented programming organizes a program into objects.

You hear about efficiency and productivity everywhere. They are particularly important for software development. Two resources that promise to help are *CASE tools* and *object-oriented software development*.

CASE TOOLS

Professional programmers are constantly looking for ways to make their work easier, faster, and more reliable. One tool we mentioned in Chapter 13, CASE, is meeting this need. **Computer-aided software engineering (CASE) tools** provide some automation and assistance in program design, coding, and testing. (See Figure 14-31.)

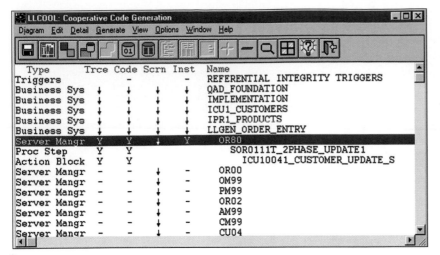

Type	Trce	Code	Scrn	Inst	Name
Triggers		-		-	REFERENTIAL INTEGRITY TRIGGERS
Business Sys	↓	↓	↓	↓	QAD_FOUNDATION
Business Sys	↓	↓	↓	↓	IMPLEMENTATION
Business Sys	↓	↓	↓	↓	ICU1_CUSTOMERS
Business Sys	↓	↓	↓	↓	IPR1_PRODUCTS
Business Sys	↓	↓	↓	↓	LLGEN_ORDER_ENTRY
Server Mangr	Y	Y	↓	Y	OR80
Proc Step	Y	Y			SOR0111T_2PHASE_UPDATE1
Action Block	Y	Y			ICU10041_CUSTOMER_UPDATE_S
Server Mangr	-	-	↓	-	OR00
Server Mangr	-	-	↓	-	OM99
Server Mangr	-	-	↓	-	PM99
Server Mangr	-	-	↓	-	OR02
Server Mangr	-	-	↓	-	AM99
Server Mangr	-	-	↓	-	CM99
Server Mangr	-	-	↓	-	CU04

Figure 14-31 **CASE tool:** Providing code-generation assistance

OBJECT-ORIENTED SOFTWARE DEVELOPMENT

Traditional systems development is a careful, step-by-step approach focusing on the procedures needed to complete a certain objective. **Object-oriented software development** focuses less on the procedures and more on defining the relationships between previously defined procedures or "objects." **Object-oriented programming (OOP)** is a process by which a program is organized into objects. Each **object** contains both the data and processing operations necessary to perform a task. Let's explain what this means.

In the past, programs were developed as giant entities, from the first line of code to the last. This has been compared to building a car from scratch. Object-oriented programming is like building a car from prefabricated parts—carburetor, alternator, fenders, and so on. Object-oriented programs use objects that are reusable, self-contained components. Programs built with these objects assume that certain functions are the same. For example, many programs, from spreadsheets to database managers, have an instruction that will sort lists of names in alphabetical order. A programmer might use this object for alphabetizing in many other programs. There is no need to invent this activity anew every time. C++ is one of the most widely used object-oriented programming languages.

▼ CONCEPT CHECK

► What are CASE tools?

► What is object-oriented software development?

► What is object-oriented programming?

GENERATIONS OF PROGRAMMING LANGUAGES

> Low-level languages are closer to computer languages consisting of 0s and 1s. High-level languages are closer to human language. Programming language generations include: machine, assembly, high level, problem-oriented, and natural and visual programming.

Computer professionals talk about **levels** or **generations** of programming languages, ranging from "low" to "high." Programming languages are called **lower level** when they are closer to the language the computer itself uses. The computer understands the 0s and 1s that make up bits and bytes. Programming languages are called **higher level** when they are closer to the language humans use—that is, for English speakers, more like English.

There are five generations of programming languages. These are (1) machine languages, (2) assembly languages, (3) procedural languages, (4) problem-oriented languages, and (5) natural languages.

MACHINE LANGUAGES: THE FIRST GENERATION

We mentioned in Chapter 6 that a byte is made up of bits, consisting of 1s and 0s. These 1s and 0s may correspond to electricity's being on or off in the computer. They may also correspond to a magnetic charge being present or absent on storage media such as disk or tape. From this two-state system, coding schemes have been developed that allow us to construct letters, numbers, punctuation marks, and other special characters. Examples of these coding schemes, as we saw, are ASCII and EBCDIC.

Data represented in 1s and 0s is said to be written in **machine language.** To see how hard this is to understand, imagine if you had to code this:

11110010011100111101001000010000011100000101011

Machine languages also vary according to make of computer—another characteristic that makes them hard to work with.

ASSEMBLY LANGUAGES: THE SECOND GENERATION

Before a computer can process or run any program, the program must be converted or translated into machine language. **Assembly languages** use abbreviations or mnemonics such as ADD that are automatically converted to the appropriate sequence of 1s and 0s. Compared to machine languages, assembly languages are much easier for humans to understand and to use. The machine language code we gave above could be expressed in assembly language as

ADD 210(8,13),02B(4,7)

This is still pretty obscure, of course, and so assembly language is also considered low level.

Assembly languages also vary from computer to computer. With the third generation, we advance to high-level languages, many of which are considered **portable languages.** That is, they can be run on more than one kind of computer—they are "portable" from one machine to another.

HIGH-LEVEL PROCEDURAL LANGUAGES: THE THIRD GENERATION

People are able to understand languages that are more like their own (e.g., English) than machine languages or assembly languages. These more English-like programming languages are called "high-level" languages. However, most people still require some training to use higher-level languages. This is particularly true of procedural languages.

Procedural languages, also known as **3GLs (third generation languages),** are designed to express the logic—the procedures—that can solve general problems. Procedural languages, then, are intended to solve general problems. C++ is a procedural language widely used by today's programmers. For example, C++ was used in Advantage's time-and-billing report. (See again Figure 14-20 for the "compute time" module of this program.)

Consider the following C++ statement from a program that assigns letter grades based on the score of an exam.

if (score > = 90) grade = 'A' ;

This statement tests whether the score is greater than or equal to 90. If it is, then the letter grade of A is assigned.

Like assembly languages, procedural languages must be translated into machine language so that the computer processes them. Depending on the language, this translation is performed by either a *compiler* or an *interpreter.*

- A **compiler** converts the programmer's procedural language program, called the **source code,** into a machine language code, called the **object**

code. This object code can then be saved and run later. Examples of procedural languages using compilers are the standard versions of Pascal, COBOL, and FORTRAN.

- An **interpreter** converts the procedural language one statement at a time into machine code just before it is to be executed. No object code is saved. An example of a procedural language using an interpreter is the standard version of BASIC.

What is the difference between using a compiler and using an interpreter? When a program is run, the compiler requires two steps. The first step is to convert the entire program's source code to object code. The second step is to run the object code. The interpreter, in contrast, converts and runs the program one line at a time. The advantage of a compiler language is that once the object code has been obtained, the program executes faster. The advantage of an interpreter language is that programs are easier to develop.

PROBLEM-ORIENTED LANGUAGES: THE FOURTH GENERATION

Third generation languages are valuable, but they require training in programming. Problem-oriented languages, also known as **4GLs** and **very high level languages,** require little special training on the part of the user.

Unlike general-purpose languages, **problem-oriented languages** are designed to solve specific problems. While 3GLs focus on procedures and *how* a program will accomplish a specific task, 4GLs are nonprocedural and focus on specifying *what* the program is to accomplish. 4GLs are more Englishlike, easier to program, and widely used by nonprogrammers. Some of these fourth generation languages are used for very specific applications. For example, **IFPS (interactive financial planning system)** is used to develop financial models. Many 4GLs are part of a database management system. 4GLs include query languages and application generators:

- **Query languages: Query languages** enable nonprogrammers to use certain easily understood commands to search and generate reports from a database. One of the most widely used query languages is SQL (structured query language). For example, let's say that Advantage Advertising has a database containing all customer calls for service and that their management would like a listing of all clients who incurred overtime charges. The SQL command to create this list is:

  SELECT client FROM dailyLog WHERE serviceEnd > 17

  This SQL statement selects or identifies all clients (a field name from the dailyLog table) that required service after 17 (military time for 5:00 P.M.). Microsoft Access can generate SQL commands like this one by using its Query wizard.

- **Application generators:** An **application generator** or a **program coder** is a program that provides modules of prewritten code. When using an application generator, a programmer can quickly create a program by referencing the appropriate module(s). This greatly reduces the time to create an application. For example, Access has a report generation application and a Report wizard for creating a variety of different types of reports using database information.

NATURAL LANGUAGES AND VISUAL PROGRAMMING LANGUAGES: THE FIFTH GENERATION

As they have evolved through the generations, computer languages have become more humanlike. Clearly the fourth generation query languages using commands that include words like SELECT, FROM, and WHERE are much more humanlike than the 0s and 1s of machine language. However, 4GLs are still a long way from the natural languages such as English and Spanish that people use.

The standard definition of a **fifth generation language (5GL)** is a computer language that incorporates the concepts of artificial intelligence to allow direct human communication. Additionally, these languages would enable a computer to *learn* and to *apply* new information as people do. Rather than coding by keying in specific commands, we would communicate more directly to a computer using **natural languages** or human languages such as English or Spanish.

Consider the following natural language statement that might appear in a 5GL program for recommending medical treatment.

If patient is dizzy, then check temperature and blood pressure.

Recently, the definition of 5GL has been expanded to include **visual programming languages** that provide a natural visual interface for program development. This interface provides intuitive icons, menus, and drawing tools for creating program code. Under this definition, programs such as Microsoft's Visual Basic are fifth generation programming languages.

See Figure 14-32 for a summary of the generations of programming languages.

Generation	Sample Statement
First: Machine	1111001001110011110100100001000001110000000101011
Second: Assembly	ADD 210(8, 13),02B(4, 7)
Third: Procedural	if (score > = 90) grade = 'A';
Fourth: Problem	SELECT client FROM dailyLog WHERE serviceEnd > 17
Fifth: Natural and Visual	If patient is dizzy, then check temperature and blood pressure.

Figure 14-32 Summary of five programming generations

▼ CONCEPT CHECK

▶ What distinguishes a lower-level language from a higher-level language?

▶ Outline the five generations of programming languages.

▶ Distinguish between natural and visual programming languages.

A Look to the Future

MI-tech Takes the Pain Out of Programming

What if you could instruct a computer to code a program with a simple wish list written in English? What if syntax errors didn't happen? What if the computer asked you to clarify your meaning rather than just report an error? What if you could create a program that would run on a Windows PC, an Apple Mac, or even a Linux computer? At Synapse Solutions they believe they have created a system that meets these needs.

Traditional programming relies on a compiler and a translator to communicate the desires of the programmer to the computer. There are also precise rules that must be followed to correctly communicate with the computer. Natural language programming (using a human language to talk to the computer) has been the dream of programmers for a long time. Human language can be confusing to a machine because it is possible to have double meanings and uncertainty.

Synapse Solutions has created a system called MI-tech that has an understanding of word order and meaning in English. To program using the system, you enter a "wish list" and the computer translates these sentences into machine language. If the system does not understand a "wish," it makes a request for clarification. It also uses a dictionary to look up words it doesn't recognize.

Would you like to create your own applications? What if you could create a Web page using a list of what you would like to appear on the page? Synapse Solutions believes it will soon be possible to use its system to do just that. What other programs do you think could utilize this system? Do you think someday all computer users will be programmers?

PROGRAMMING AT DVD DIRECT

DVD Direct is an entirely Web-oriented movie rental business in which customers select movies to rent from the company's Web site and choose the delivery method. One way is to receive selected movies on DVD disks by mail. This is how the business originally started out. The other way is to immediately download the movies onto the member's hard disk. Online delivery is a recent innovation. To encourage the choice of online delivery (which is more cost effective for DVD Direct), a Frequent Renters Club has been established. Whenever members select online delivery, they receive reward points that can be redeemed for a variety of items.

To support the record keeping of the Frequent Renters Club, an information system was developed by Alice, a marketing analyst, and Mia, a systems analyst. The hardware needed to support the system was leased, and most of the software was purchased from an outside vendor. Mia created one program that integrated a login screen to the Frequent Renters Club Web site. After some initial modifications, the Frequent Renters Club has been successfully operating for the past two months.

One morning Mia receives a telephone call from Bob, the vice president of marketing, asking her to come to the meeting room to discuss the login program she wrote for the Frequent Renters Club Web site and to bring all her documentation from the project. This is a bit of a surprise, and Mia wonders what it could be about. The system has been up and running for two months without problems. The login program is quite simple. Could that in itself somehow be the problem? Why aren't they meeting in Bob's office? To follow Alice into the meeting, consult your Computing Essentials CD or visit us on the Web at www.olearyseries.com/CE06 and select DVD Direct and then select Programming and Languages.

PROGRAMMING AND LANGUAGES

PROGRAMS AND PROGRAMMING

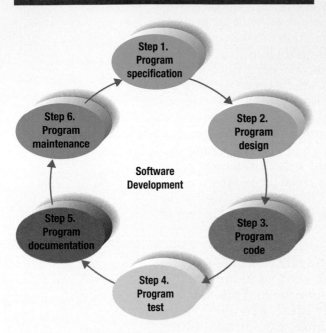

A **program** is a list of instructions for a computer to follow. **Programming (software development)** is a six-step procedure for creating programs.

The steps are:

- Program specification—defining objectives, inputs, outputs, and processing requirements.
- Program design—creating a solution using structured programming techniques.
- Program code—writing or coding the program.
- Program test—testing or debugging program.
- Program documentation—ongoing process throughout programming process.
- Program maintenance—evaluating and modifying program code as needed.

STEP 1: PROGRAM SPECIFICATION

Program specification, also called **program definition** or **program analysis,** consists of specifying five tasks related to objectives, outputs, inputs, requirements, and documentation.

Program Objectives

The first task is to clearly define the problem to solve in the form of program **objectives.**

Desired Output

Next, focus on the desired output before considering the required inputs.

Input Data

Once outputs are defined, determine the necessary input data and the source of the data.

Processing Requirements

Next, determine the steps necessary (processing requirements) to use input to produce output.

Program Specifications Document

The final task is to create a specifications document to record this step's program objectives, outputs, inputs, and processing requirements.

To be a competent end user, you need to understand the six steps of programming: program specification, program design, program coding, program test, program documentation, and program maintenance. Additionally, you need to be aware of CASE, OOP, and the generations of programming languages.

STEP 2: PROGRAM DESIGN

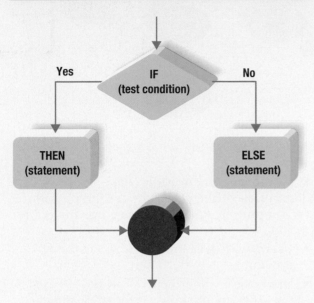

In **program design,** a solution is designed using, preferably, **structured programming techniques,** including the following.

Top-Down Design
In **top-down design,** major processing steps, called **program modules,** are identified.

Pseudocode
Pseudocode is an outline of the logic of the program you will write.

Flowcharts
Program flowcharts are graphic representations of the steps necessary to solve a programming problem.

Logic Structures
Logic structures are arrangements of programming statements. Three types are:

- **Sequence**—one program statement followed by another.
- **Selection (IF-THEN-ELSE)**—when a decision must be made.
- **Loop (DO UNTIL and DO WHILE)**—when process is repeated until condition is true.

STEP 3: PROGRAM CODE

Coding is writing a program. There are several important aspects of writing a program. Two are writing good programs and actually writing or coding:

Good Programs
Good programs are reliable, detect obvious and common errors, and are well documented. The best way to create good programs is to write **structured programs** using the three basic logic structures presented in step 2.

Coding
There are hundreds of different programming languages. Two types are:

- **Formatting languages** that instruct a computer how to display information for the user. Widely used formatting languages include HTML.
- **Programming languages** that instruct a computer to perform specific operations. C++ is a widely used programming language.

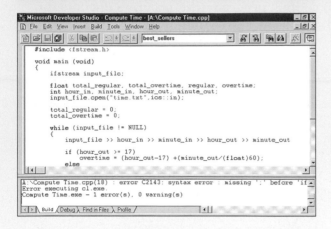

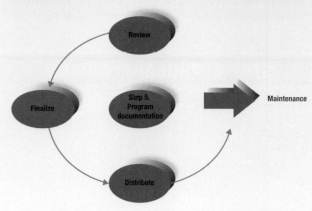

Debugging is a process of testing and eliminating errors in a program. Syntax and logic are two types of programming errors.

Syntax Errors

Syntax errors are violations of the rules of a programming language. For example, omitting a semicolon at the end of a C++ statement is a syntax error.

Logic Errors

Logic errors are incorrect calculations or procedures. For example, failure to include calculation of overtime hours in a payroll program is a logic error.

Testing Process

Five methods for testing for syntax and logic errors are:

- **Desk checking**—careful reading of a printout of the program.
- **Manual testing**—using a calculator and sample data to test for correct programming logic.
- **Attempt at translation**—running the program using a translator program to identify syntax errors.
- **Testing sample data**—running the program and testing the program for logic errors using sample data.
- **Testing by users (beta testing)**—final step in which potential users try the program and provide feedback.

Program documentation consists of a written description of the program and the procedures for running it. People who use documentation include:

- **Users,** who need to know how to use the program.
- **Operators,** who need to know how to execute the program and how to recognize and correct errors.
- **Programmers,** who may need to update and maintain the program in the future.

STEP 6: PROGRAM MAINTENANCE

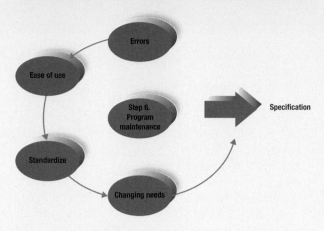

Program maintenance is designed to ensure that the program operates correctly, efficiently, and effectively. Two categories of maintenance activities are the following.

Operations

Operations activities include locating and correcting errors, improving usability, and standardizing software.

Changing Needs

Organizations change over time and their programs must change with them.

CASE AND OOP

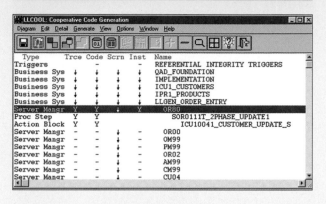

CASE

Computer-aided software engineering (CASE) tools provide automation and assistance in program design, coding, and testing.

OOP

Traditional systems development focuses on procedure to complete a specific objective.

Object-oriented software development focuses less on procedures and more on defining relationships between previously defined procedures or objects. **Object-oriented programming (OOP)** is a process by which a program is divided into **modules** called objects. Each object contains both the data and processing operations necessary to perform a task.

These modules are reusable and self-contained components. C++ is one of the most widely used object-oriented programming languages.

PROGRAMMING GENERATIONS

Programming languages have **levels** or **generations** ranging from low to high. **Lower-level** languages are closer to the 0s and 1s language of computers. **Higher-level** languages are closer to the languages of humans.

Generation	Sample Statement
First: Machine	1111001001110011110
Second: Assembly	ADD 210(8, 13),02B(4, 7)
Third: Procedural	if (score > = 90) . . .
Fourth: Problem	SELECT client FROM . . .
Fifth: Natural and Visual	If patient is dizzy, then . . .

application generator   (416)
assembly language   (415)
beta testing   (410)
code   (406)
coding   (406)
compiler   (415)
computer-aided software engineering
   (CASE) tools   (413)
debugging   (409)
desk checking   (409)
documentation   (410)
DO UNTIL structure   (404)
DO WHILE structure   (404)
fifth generation language (5GL)   (417)
formatting language   (406)
fourth generation language (4GL)   (416)
generations   (414)
higher level   (414)
IFPS (interactive financial planning
   system)   (416)
IF-THEN-ELSE structure   (403)
interpreter   (416)
levels   (414)
logic error   (409)
logic structure   (403)
loop structure   (403)
lower level   (414)
machine language   (415)
maintenance programmer   (412)
module   (402)
natural language   (417)
object   (414)
object code   (415–416)
objectives   (400)
object-oriented programming (OOP)   (414)

object-oriented software development   (414)
operators   (411)
portable language   (415)
presentation language   (406)
problem-oriented language   (416)
procedural language   (415)
program   (398)
program analysis   (399)
program coder   (416)
program definition   (399)
program design   (401)
program documentation   (410)
program flowchart   (403)
program maintenance   (412)
programmer   (399)
programming   (398)
programming language   (406)
program modules   (402)
program specification   (399)
pseudocode   (403)
query language   (416)
selection structure   (403)
sequence structure   (403)
software development   (398)
software engineer   (399)
source code   (415)
structured program   (406)
structured programming techniques   (401)
syntax error   (409)
third generation language (3GL)   (415)
top-down program design   (402)
user   (411)
very high level language   (416)
visual programming language   (417)

To test your knowledge of these key terms with animated flash cards, consult your Computing Essentials CD or visit our Web site at www.olearyseries.com/CE06 and select Key Terms.

FEATURES

Animations

Careers in IT

DVD Direct

Expansions

Making IT Work for You

On the Web Explorations

TechTV

Tips

CHAPTER REVIEW

Key Terms

Crossword

Multiple Choice

Matching

Open-ended

Using Technology

Expanding Your Knowledge

Building Your Portfolio

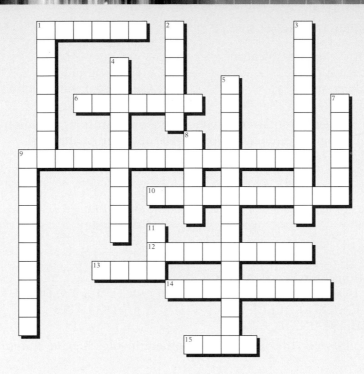

Across

1   Writing a program.
6   A list of instructions for the computer to follow.
9   Represent the steps needed to solve a programming problem.
10 Programmer that ensures current programs remain error free.
12 The problem a user is trying to solve.
13 Structure that describes a process that may be repeated while a condition is true.
14 Testing and then eliminating errors.
15 Tools that provide some automation in program design, coding, and testing.

Down

1   Converts procedural language into machine language code.
2   Error that is a violation of the rules of a programming language.
3   The final step in testing a program.
4   Software engineer.
5   Sequence, selection, and loop.
7   Processing steps used in top-down program design.
8   Error that occurs when an incorrect calculation is used.
9   Outline of the logic of the program you will write.
11 Process by which a program is organized into objects.

For an interactive version of this crossword, consult your Computing Essentials CD or visit our Web site at www.olearyseries.com/CE06 and select Crossword.

FEATURES

Animations

Careers in IT

DVD Direct

Expansions

Making IT Work for You

On the Web Explorations

TechTV

Tips

CHAPTER REVIEW

Key Terms

Crossword

Multiple Choice

Matching

Open-ended

Using Technology

Expanding Your Knowledge

Building Your Portfolio

Circle the letter or fill in the correct answer.

1. Program specification is also called _____.
   a. program definition
   b. program charting
   c. program coding
   d. program design
   e. program modeling

2. In the _____ step a solution is created using programming techniques such as top-down program design, pseudocode, flowcharts, and logic structures.
   a. program specification
   b. program design
   c. program code
   d. program test
   e. program documentation

3. Under the rules of top-down design each module should have _____ function(s).
   a. multiple
   b. two
   c. one
   d. three
   e. ten

4. The two variations of loop structure are _____ and _____.
   a. DO NOW, DO LATER
   b. DO WHILE, DO PARALLEL
   c. DO WHILE, DO UNTIL
   d. DO NOW, DO DURING
   e. DO LATER, DO UNTIL

5. Only the _____ step of software development involves keying statements into a computer.
   a. program specification
   b. program design
   c. program code
   d. program test
   e. program documentation

6. The best way to code effective programs is to write _____.
   a. top-down programs
   b. structured programs
   c. coded programs
   d. loop structured programs
   e. selection structured programs

7. The omission of a semicolon at the end of a statement in C++ is an example of a _____ error.
   a. loop
   b. direct
   c. calculation
   d. design
   e. syntax

8. _____ is carried on throughout all the programming steps.
   a. Coding
   b. Design
   c. Beta testing
   d. Documentation
   e. Desk checking

9. Languages that can run on more than one kind of computer are called _____.
   a. machine languages
   b. portable languages
   c. assembly languages
   d. problem-oriented languages
   e. query languages

10. A(n) _____ contains a number of modules that have been preprogrammed to accomplish various tasks.
    a. application generator
    b. natural language program
    c. translator
    d. interpreter
    e. compiler

For an interactive version of these multiple choice questions, consult your Computing Essentials CD or visit our Web site at www.olearyseries.com/CE06 and select Multiple Choice.

Match each numbered item with the most closely related lettered item. Write your answers in the spaces provided.

a. assembly

b. beta testing

c. coding

d. debugging

e. desk checking

f. higher-level languages

g. logic error

h. logic structure

i. loop structure

j. maintenance programmer

k. selection structure

l. objectives

m. OOP

n. procedural language

o. program specification

p. programmer

q. program

r. program flowchart

s. pseudocode

t. software development

1. A list of instructions for the computer to follow to process data. ____

2. A six-step procedure used to create a program. ____

3. Computer professional who creates new software or revises existing software. ____

4. Programming step in which objectives, outputs, inputs, and processing requirements are determined. ____

5. The problems you are trying to solve. ____

6. The logic structure that occurs when a design must be made. ____

7. An outline of the logic of the program to be written. ____

8. Graphically presents the detailed sequence of steps needed to solve a programming problem. ____

9. Structure that controls the logical sequence in which computer program instructions are executed. ____

10. Logic structure in which a process may be repeated as long as a certain condition remains true. ____

11. Actual writing of a program. ____

12. Testing and eliminating errors from a program. ____

13. Error that occurs when an incorrect calculation or incorrect procedure is used in a program. ____

14. Studying a computer program line by line looking for syntax and logic errors. ____

15. Potential users are given the opportunity to try out a program and provide feedback. ____

16. Computer specialist whose job is to ensure current programs run error free, efficiently, and effectively. ____

17. Process by which a program is organized into objects. ____

18. Programming languages closer to human languages. ____

19. Languages that use abbreviations or mnemonics. ____

20. Designed to express the logic that can solve general problems. ____

For an interactive version of this matching exercise, consult your Computing Essentials CD or visit our Web site at www.olearyseries.com/CE06 and select Matching.

OPEN-ENDED

On a separate sheet of paper, respond to each question or statement.

1. Identify and discuss each of the six steps of programming.

2. Describe CASE tools and OOP. How does CASE assist programmers?

3. What is meant by "generation" in reference to programming languages? What is the difference between low-level and high-level languages?

4. What is the difference between a compiler and an interpreter?

5. What are logic structures? Describe the differences between the three types.

FEATURES

Animations

Careers in IT

DVD Direct

Expansions

Making IT Work for You

On the Web Explorations

TechTV

Tips

CHAPTER REVIEW

Key Terms

Crossword

Multiple Choice

Matching

Open-ended

Using Technology

Expanding Your Knowledge

Building Your Portfolio

1

CVS

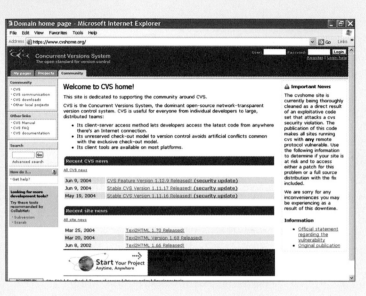

The Concurrent Versions System, or CVS, is an invaluable tool for large programming projects. Learn more about CVS by visiting our Web site at www.olearyseries.com/CE06, selecting Using Technology, and linking to the CVS Web site. Once connected, read about CVS, and then answer the following questions: (a) What is CVS? Who uses it? (b) Describe what CVS does. Be specific. (c) What is CVS useful for? (d) When is CVS not a useful choice? Why?

2

.NET Framework

Microsoft's .NET Framework is a platform for developing applications that run on computers, small devices like mobile phones and PDAs, and even across the Internet. Visit our Web site at www.olearyseries.com/CE06 and select Using Technology to link to the .NET site. Read about the .NET Framework, and then answer the following questions: (a) What are the basic components of the .NET Framework? (b) What programming languages does the .NET Framework include? (c) What are the benefits of using the .NET Framework for software developers?

DVD Direct

1

To encourage online delivery of DVD disks, DVD Direct has established a Frequent Renters Club. Whenever a member orders an online movie, he or she receives reward points that can be redeemed for a variety of items. Alice and Mia have been actively developing an information system to support the record keeping activity of the Frequent Renters Club. Mia has created a program that integrates a login screen to the Frequent Renters Club Web site. To learn more about this program, consult your Computing Essentials CD or visit us on the Web at www.olearyseries.com/CE06 and select DVD Direct and then select Programming and Languages. Describe the steps Mia followed to develop this program.

Source Code Generators

2

Generally, the human resources that are devoted to a successful software project are its greatest single expense. Programming and testing applications is a time-consuming task. Recently, source code generators have become popular for handling some of the more routine programming tasks. Research source code generators on the Web and answer the following questions: (a) What are source code generators? (b) How do source code generators work? (c) What programming tasks are source code generators best for? Why? (d) What programming tasks are beyond what source code generators can accomplish? Why?

1

Extreme Programming

Extreme Programming, also known as XP, is a newer model for the software development process. XP emphasizes simplified and accelerated development. Research Extreme Programming on the Web and then answer the following questions in a one-page paper: (a) What are the 12 principles of XP? (b) How does XP differ from other models of software development? (c) For what kinds of software projects is XP most effective? When would a different model be a better choice? Explain your answers.

2

Security and Privacy

Security and privacy are important concerns in the development of any information system. Answer the following questions in a one-page paper: (a) In the development process, who would you expect to have the responsibility of identifying security and privacy concerns? (b) In what phase of the system life cycle, would security and privacy concerns be identified? (c) To learn about security and privacy concerns for DVD Direct, consult your Computing Essentials CD or visit us on the Web at www.olearyseries.com/CE06 and select DVD Direct and then select Programming and Languages. Then identify DVD Direct's most important security and privacy concerns. Be as specific as possible.

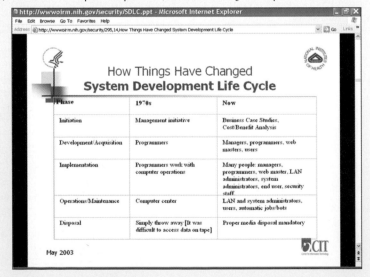

COMPETENCIES

After you have read this chapter, you should be able to:

1 Explain why it's important to have an individual strategy to be a "winner" in the information age.

2 Describe how technology is changing the nature of competition.

3 Discuss four ways people may react to new technology.

4 Describe how you can stay current with your career.

5 Describe different careers in information technology.

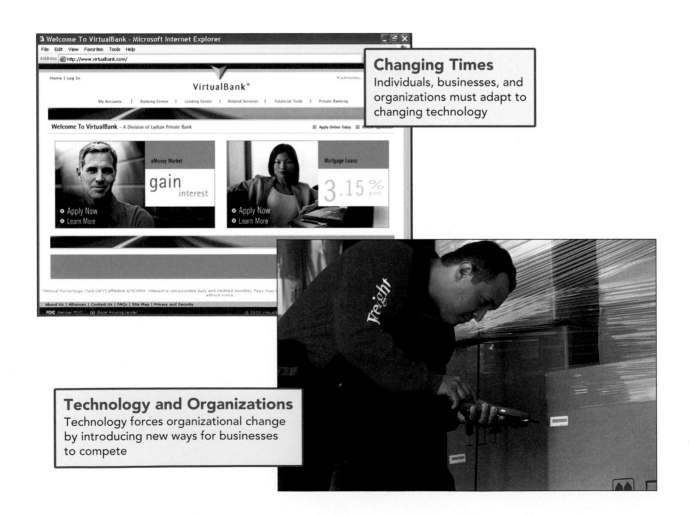

Changing Times
Individuals, businesses, and organizations must adapt to changing technology

Technology and Organizations
Technology forces organizational change by introducing new ways for businesses to compete

Throughout this book, we have emphasized practical subjects that are useful to you now or will be very soon. Accordingly, this final chapter is not about the far future, say, 10 years from now. Rather, it is about today and the near future—about developments whose outlines we can already see. It is about how organizations adapt to technological change. It is also about what you as an individual can do to keep your computer competency up to date.

Are the times changing any faster now than they ever have? It's hard to say. People who were alive when radios, cars, and airplanes were being introduced certainly lived through some dramatic changes.

Has technology made our own times even more dynamic? Whatever the answer, it is clear we live in a fast-paced age. The challenge for you as an individual is to devise ways to stay current and to use technology to your advantage. For example, you can use the Web to locate job opportunities.

To stay competent, end users need to recognize the impact of technological change on organizations and people. They need to know how to use change to their advantage and how to be winners. Although end users do not need to be specialists in information technology, they should be aware of career opportunities in the area.

Be a Winner
Stay current, develop specialties, and be alert to organizational changes and opportunities for innovation

Technology and People
Some people react negatively to technological change by being cynical, naive, or frustrated, but the most positive reaction to technological change is to be proactive

To be a winner in the information revolution, you need an individual strategy.

Almost all businesses have become aware that they must adapt to changing technology or be left behind. Most organizations are now making formal plans to keep track of technology and implement it in their competitive strategies. For example, banks have found that automated teller machines (ATMs) are vital to retail banking. (See Figure 15-1.) Not only do they require fewer human tellers, but also they are available 24 hours a day. More and more banks are also trying to go electronic, doing away with paper transactions wherever possible. ATM cards are used to buy almost anything from gas to groceries.

What's next for the banking industry? Almost all banks are also trying to popularize home banking so that customers can use microcomputers for certain financial tasks. Some banks, known as Internet banks, have even done away with physical bank buildings and conduct all business over the Web. (See Figure 15-2.) In addition, banks are exploring the use of some very sophisticated application programs. These programs will accept cursive writing (the handwriting on checks) directly as input, verify check signatures, and process the check without human intervention.

Clearly, such changes do away with some jobs—those of many bank tellers and cashiers, for example. However, they create opportunities for other people. New technology requires people who are truly capable of working with it. These are not the people who think every piece of equipment is so simple they can just turn it on and use it. Nor are they those who think each new machine is a potential disaster. In other words, new technology needs people who are not afraid to learn about it and are able to manage it. The real issue, then, is not how to make technology better. Rather, it is how to integrate the technology with people.

You are in a very favorable position compared with many other people in industry today. After reading the previous chapters, you have learned more than just the basics of hardware, software, connectivity, and the Internet. You have learned about the most current technology. You are therefore able to use these tools to your advantage—to be a winner.

How do you become and stay a winner? In brief, the answer is: You must form your own individual strategy for dealing with change. First let us look at how businesses are handling technological change. Then let's look at how people are reacting to these changes. Finally, we will offer a few suggestions that will enable you to keep up with and profit from the information revolution.

Figure 15-1   Automated teller machines are examples of technology used in business strategy

Figure 15-2 Internet banks conduct business over the Web

▼ CONCEPT CHECK

▶ Cite examples of ways computers are changing the business world.

▶ What are the human requirements of new technology?

TECHNOLOGY AND ORGANIZATIONS

Technology changes the nature of competition by introducing new products, new enterprises, and new relationships among customers and suppliers.

Technology can introduce new ways for businesses to compete with each other. Some of the principal changes are as follows.

NEW PRODUCTS

Technology creates products that operate faster, are priced cheaper, are often of better quality, or are wholly new. Indeed, new products can be individually tailored to a particular customer's needs. For example, financial services companies such as Merrill Lynch have taken advantage of technology to launch cash management accounts. (See Figure 15-3.) These accounts combine information on a person's checking, savings, credit card, and securities accounts into a single monthly statement. It automatically sets aside "idle" funds into interest-bearing money market funds. Customers can access their accounts on the Web and get a complete picture of their financial condition at any time. However, even if they don't pay much attention to their statements, their surplus funds are invested automatically.

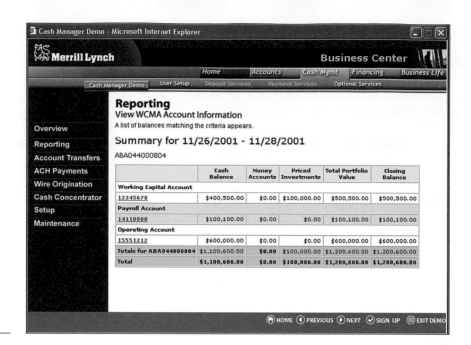

Figure 15-3   Merrill Lynch's cash management account

NEW ENTERPRISES

Information technology can build entirely new businesses. Two examples are Internet service providers and Web site development companies.

- Just a few years ago, the only computer connectivity options available to individuals were through online service providers like America Online and through colleges and universities. Now, hundreds of national service providers and thousands of local service providers are available.

- Thousands of small companies specializing in Web site development have sprung up in the past three years. These companies help small- to medium-sized organizations by providing assistance in evaluating, creating, and maintaining Web sites.

NEW CUSTOMER AND SUPPLIER RELATIONSHIPS

Businesses that make their information systems easily available may make their customers less likely to take their business elsewhere. For instance, Federal Express, the overnight package delivery service, does everything possible to make its customers dependent on it. Upon request, customers receive airbills with their name, address, and account number preprinted on them, making shipping and billing easier. Package numbers are scanned into the company's information system so that they can be tracked from pickup point to destination. (See Figure 15-4.) Thus, apprehensive customers can be informed very quickly of the exact location of their package as it travels toward its destination.

Figure 15-4   New technology helps Federal Express maintain customer loyalty

► What is the role of technology in creating new products?

► Describe two new enterprises built by information technology.

► Discuss how technology can create new customers and affect supplier relationships.

TECHNOLOGY AND PEOPLE

People may be cynical, naive, frustrated, or proactive in response to technology.

Clearly, recent technological changes, and those sure to come in the near future, will produce significant changes and opportunities in the years ahead. How should we be prepared for them?

People have different coping styles when it comes to technology. It has been suggested, for instance, that people react to changing technology in one of four ways. These ways are cynicism, naivete, frustration, and proactivity.

CYNICISM

The **cynic** feels that, for a manager at least, the idea of using a microcomputer is overrated. (See Figure 15-5.) Learning and using it take too much time, time that could be delegated to someone else. Doing spreadsheets and word processing, according to the cynic, are tasks that managers should understand. However, the cynic feels that such tasks take time away from a manager's real job of developing plans and setting goals for the people being supervised.

Cynics may express their doubts openly, especially if they are top managers. Or, they may only pretend to be interested in microcomputers, when actually they are not interested at all.

Figure 15-5   The cynic: "These gadgets are overrated."

NAIVETE

Many **naive** people are unfamiliar with computers. They may think computers are magic boxes capable of solving all kinds of problems that computers really can't handle. On the other hand, some naive persons are actually quite familiar with computers, but underestimate the difficulty of changing computer systems or of generating certain information.

FRUSTRATION

The **frustrated** person may already be quite busy and may hate having to take time to learn about microcomputers. Such a person feels it is an imposition to have to learn something new or is too impatient to try to understand the manuals explaining what hardware and software are supposed to do. The result is continual frustration. (See Figure 15-6.) Some people are frustrated because they try to do too much. Or they're frustrated because they find manuals difficult to understand. In some cases poorly written manuals are at fault.

Figure 15-6 The frustrated person: "This stuff doesn't make sense half the time."

Figure 15-7 The proactive person: "How can I use this new tool?"

PROACTIVITY

Webster's Collegiate Dictionary defines **proactive,** in part, as "acting in anticipation of future problems, needs, or changes." A proactive person looks at technology in a positive realistic way. (See Figure 15-7.) They are not cynics, underestimating the likely impact of technology on their lives. They are not naive, overestimating the ability of technology to solve the world's or their problems. They do not become frustrated easily and give up using technology. Proactive people are positive in their outlook and look at new technology as providing new tools that, when correctly applied, can positively impact their lives.

Most of us fall into one of the four categories. Cynicism, naivete, frustration, and proactivity are common human responses to change. Do you see yourself or others around you responding to technology in any of these ways? For those who respond negatively, just being aware of their reaction can help them become more positive and proactive to tomorrow's exciting new changes in technology.

▼ CONCEPT CHECK

► Describe three negative ways people cope with technological changes in the workplace.

► Describe one positive way people cope with technological change in the workplace.

► Define proactive.

HOW YOU CAN BE A WINNER

Individuals need to stay current, develop specialties, and be alert to organizational changes and opportunities for innovation.

So far we have described how progressive organizations are using technology in the information age. Now let's concentrate on you as an individual. (See Making IT Work for You: Locating Job Opportunities Online on pages 440 and 441.) How can you stay ahead? Here are some ideas.

STAY CURRENT

Whatever their particular line of work, successful professionals keep up both with their own fields and with the times. We don't mean you should try to become a computer expert and read a lot of technical magazines. Rather, you should concentrate on your profession and learn how computer technology is being used within it.

Every field has trade journals, whether the field is interior design, personnel management, or advertising. Most such journals regularly present articles about the uses of computers. It's important that you also belong to a trade or industry association and go to its meetings. Many associations sponsor seminars and conferences that describe the latest information and techniques.

Another way to stay current is by participating electronically with special-interest newsgroups on the Internet.

MAINTAIN YOUR COMPUTER COMPETENCY

Actually, you should try to stay ahead of the technology. Books, journals, and trade associations are the best sources of information about new technology that apply to your field. The general business press—*Business Week, Fortune, Inc., The Wall Street Journal,* and the business section of your local newspaper—also carries computer-related articles.

However, if you wish, you can subscribe to a magazine that covers microcomputers and information more specifically. Examples are *InfoWorld, PC World,* and *MacWorld.* You may also find it useful to look at newspapers and magazines that cover the computer industry as a whole. An example of such a periodical is *ComputerWorld.* Most of these magazines also have online versions available on the Web. (See Figure 15-8.)

Figure 15-8   PC World on the Web

Your Future and Information Technology

LOCATING JOB OPPORTUNITIES ONLINE

Did you know that you can use the Internet to find a job? You can locate and browse through job listings. You can even electronically post your resume for prospective employers to review.

How It Works   There are several Web sites designed to bring together prospective employers and employees. These sites maintain a database of available jobs and a database of resumes. Individuals are able to post resumes and to search through available jobs. Organizations are able to post job opportunities and to search through individual resumes.

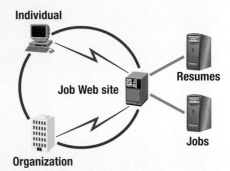

Browsing Job Listings   Three well-known job search sites on the Web are hotjobs.com, Yahoo!jobs, and monster.com. You can connect to these sites and browse through job opportunities. For example, after connecting to monster.com, you can search for a job by following steps similar to those shown below.

1
- Connect to *www.monster.com.*
- Click the *Search Jobs* link.

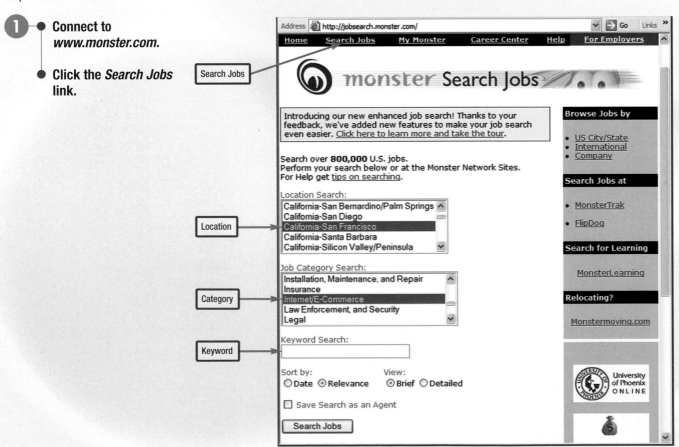

2 • Select a location to search.

• Select a category to search.

• Optionally, enter any keywords to search.

• Click *Search Jobs.*

3 • Select a job title to learn more about a job posting.

A detailed job posting, including description, company information, and contact information, is displayed.

Jobs 1 to 40 of 40		Show Jobs Posted:	Last 60 days ∨
Sort: Date | **Relevance**			View: **Brief** | Detailed
Date	**Location**	**Job Title**	**Company**
Jul 10	US-CA-San Francisco	WIN32 Developer	TRS
Jul 10	US-CA-San Francisco	Senior Software Sales Executive	Management Recruiters Intntl
Jul 9	US-CA-San Francisco	★ Software Developers Wanted!	CFH Enterprises, Inc.
Jul 9	US-CA-San Francisco	★ ASSOCIATE WEB EDITOR	CFH Enterprises, Inc.
Jul 8	US-CA-San Francisco	Director of Public Relations	Management Recruiters Intntl
Jul 8	US-CA-San Francisco	QUALITY ASSURANCE ANALYST 3	Wells Fargo

CFH Enterprises, Inc.

US-CA-San Francisco-ASSOCIATE WEB EDITOR

Will write, edit, proofread and copy edit various in house documents. Plans out and prepares articles on online newsletters. This position is part-time. A Bachelor's degree in a related field required. At least 2 years previous experience working for an Internet based company.

Please visit http://www.careersfromhome.com/internal.asp to apply.

Posting Your Resume   To make your qualifications known to prospective employers, you can post your resume at the job search site.

1 • Select *My Monster.*

• Select the *Create your new My Monster account* link.

• Follow the on-screen instructions to create an account.

| Home | Search Jobs | **My Monster** | Career Center | Help | For Employers |

My Monster

MY monster
Career Operating System

My Monster: **Build your resume and manage your career**

New account link

Create your new My Monster account today so you can:
• **Create up to five online resumes** and cover letters to use to apply online to jobs
• **Activate your resume so employers can view it** or store it privately for your own use
• Track your online job applications
• **Create automatic Job Search Agents** that email you when a

Existing Members

Enter Username:

Enter Password:

Log In

2 • Log onto your new account.

• Select the *Create a New Resume* link.

• Complete the on-screen resume form.

• Click *Submit Resume.*

MY monster
Career Operating System

| My Monster Home | Account Profile | Agents | Applications | Resumes | Letters | Career Talk |

Welcome to My Monster. Your personal home on Monster. Use all the links in this area to access your account profile, job search and career management tools and resources.

JUMPSTART your job search for less than $7 per month! ▶ CLICK HERE

My Resumes

Create a New Resume link

Create a New Resume

Profile Information
Student Name

If you're not Student Name, click here

Your agent will search new job listings and alert you to new opportunities by e-mail.

The Web is continually changing, and some of the specifics presented in this Making IT Work for You may have changed. To learn about other ways to make information technology work for you, consult your Computing Essentials CD or visit our Web site at www.oleary-series.com/ CE06 and select Making IT Work for You.

DEVELOP PROFESSIONAL CONTACTS

Besides being members of professional associations, successful people make it a point to maintain contact with others in their field. They stay in touch by telephone, e-mail, and newsgroups and go to lunch with others in their line of work. Doing this lets them learn what other people are doing in their jobs. It tells them what other firms are doing and what tasks are being automated. Developing professional contacts can keep you abreast not only of new information but also of new job possibilities. (See Figure 15-9.) It also offers social benefits. An example of a professional organization found in many areas is the local association of realtors.

Figure 15-9 Professional organizations and contacts help you keep up in your field

DEVELOP SPECIALTIES

Develop specific as well as general skills. You want to be well-rounded *within* your field, but certainly not a "jack of all trades, master of none." Master a trade or two within your profession. At the same time, don't become identified with a specific technological skill that might very well become obsolete.

The best advice is to specialize to some extent. However, don't make your specialty so tied to technology that you'll be in trouble if the technology shifts. For example, if your career is in marketing or graphics design, it makes sense to learn about desktop publishing and Web page design. (See Figure 15-10.) In this way you can learn to make high-quality, inexpensive graphics layouts. It would not make as much sense for you to become an expert on, say, the various types of monitors used to display the graphics layouts, because such monitors are continually changing.

Expect to take classes during your working life to keep up with developments in your field. Some professions require more keeping up than others—a computer

Figure 15-10 Desktop publishing: A good specialty to develop for certain careers

specialist, for example, compared to a human resources manager. Whatever the training required, always look for ways to adapt and improve your skills to become more productive and marketable. There may be times when you are tempted to start all over again and learn completely new skills. However, a better course of action may be to use emerging technology to improve your present base of skills. This way you can build on your current strong points and then branch out to other fields from a position of strength.

BE ALERT FOR ORGANIZATIONAL CHANGE

Every organization has formal lines of communication—for example, supervisor to middle manager to top manager. However, there is also the *grapevine*—informal lines of communication. (See Figure 15-11.) Some service departments will serve many layers of management and be abreast of the news on all levels. For instance, the art director for advertising may be aware of several aspects of a companywide marketing campaign. Secretaries and administrative assistants know what is going on in more than one area.

Being part of the office grapevine can alert you to important changes—for instance, new job openings—that can benefit you. However, you always have to assess the validity of what you hear on the grapevine. Moreover, it's not ad-

Figure 15-11 Informal communication can alert you to important organizational changes

visable to be a contributor to office gossip. Behind-the-back criticisms of other people have a way of getting back to the person criticized.

Be especially alert for new trends within the organization—future hiring, layoffs, automation, mergers with other companies, and the like. Notice which areas are receiving the greatest attention from top management. One tip-off is to see what kind of outside consultants are being brought in. Independent consultants are usually invited in because a company believes it needs advice in an area with which it has insufficient experience.

LOOK FOR INNOVATIVE OPPORTUNITIES

You may understand your job better than anyone—even if you've only been there a few months. Look for ways to make it more efficient. How can present procedures be automated? How can new technology make your tasks easier? Discuss your ideas with your supervisor, the training director, or the head of the information systems department. Or discuss them with someone else who can see that you get the recognition you deserve. (Co-workers may or may not be receptive and may or may not try to take credit themselves.)

A good approach is to present your ideas in terms of saving money rather than "improving information." Managers are generally more impressed with ideas that can save dollars than with ideas that seem like potential breakthroughs in the quality of decisions.

In general, it's best to concentrate on the business and organizational problems that need solving. Then look for a technological way of solving them. That is, avoid becoming too enthusiastic about a particular technology and then trying to make it fit the work situation.

▼ CONCEPT CHECK

▶ Outline the strategies you can use to stay ahead and be successful in your career.

▶ Discuss the advantages and disadvantages of specialization.

▶ Describe how you would stay alert for organizational changes.

Your Future and Information Technology

Being a winner does not necessarily mean having a career in information systems. There are, however, several jobs within information systems that you might like to consider. We have discussed several of these careers in the preceding chapters. (See Figure 15-12.)

To learn more about these careers, consult your Computing Essentials CD or visit our Web site at www. olearyseries.com/CE06 and select Careers in IT.

Figure 15-12 Careers in information systems

Career	Responsibilities
Computer support specialist	Provides technical support to customers and other users
Computer technician	Repairs and installs computer components and systems
Computer trainer	Instructs users on the latest software or hardware
Cryptographer	Designs, tests, and researches encryption procedures
Database administrator	Uses database management software to determine the most efficient ways to organize and access data
Data entry worker	Inputs customer information, lists, and other types of data
Desktop publisher	Creates and formats publication-ready material
Information systems manager	Oversees the work of programmers, computer specialists, systems analysts, and other computer professionals
Network administrator	Creates and maintains networks
Programmer	Creates, tests, and troubleshoots computer programs
Software engineer	Analyzes users' needs and creates application software
Systems analyst	Plans and designs information systems
Technical writer	Prepares instruction manuals, technical reports, and other scientific or technical documents
Webmaster	Develops and maintains Web sites and Web resources

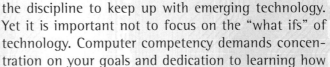

A Look to the Future

Maintaining Computer Competency and Becoming Proactive

This is not the end, it is the beginning. Being a skilled computer end user and having computer competency is not a matter of thinking "Someday I'll have to learn all about that." It is a matter of living in the present and keeping an eye on the future. Computer competency also demands

the discipline to keep up with emerging technology. Yet it is important not to focus on the "what ifs" of technology. Computer competency demands concentration on your goals and dedication to learning how the computer can aid you in obtaining these goals. Being an end user, in short, is not about trying to avoid failure. Rather, it is about always moving toward success—about taking control of the exciting new tools available to you.

NOTES

VISUAL SUMMARY

CHANGING TIMES

Individuals, businesses, and organizations must adapt to changing technology or be left behind.

Banking Industry

The banking industry uses automated teller machines (ATMs) to provide 24-hour service without incurring additional employee costs. Internet banks conduct all business over the Web.

Many changes do away with jobs. Technology, however, creates opportunities. New technology requires people who are truly capable of working with it.

To become and stay a winner, you must form your own individual strategy for dealing with changes.

TECHNOLOGY AND ORGANIZATIONS

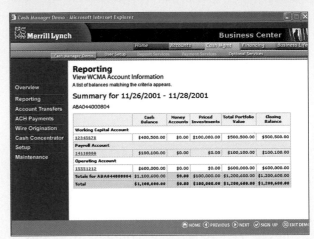

Technology can introduce new ways for businesses to compete with each other. They can compete by creating *new products, establishing new enterprises,* and *developing new customer and supplier relationships.*

New Products

Technology creates products that operate faster, are priced more cheaply, are often better quality, or are wholly new. New products can be individually tailored to a particular customer's needs.

New Enterprises

Technology can build entirely new businesses. Two examples:

- Internet service providers—just a few years ago, only a few Internet service providers were available. Now, thousands of national and local providers are available.
- Web site development companies—thousands of small companies specializing in developing Web sites have sprung up in just the past three years.

New Customer and Supplier Relationships

Businesses that make their information systems easily available may make their customers less likely to take their business elsewhere (e.g., overnight delivery services closely track packages and bills).

To stay competent, you need to recognize the impact of technological change on organizations and people. You need to know how to use change to your advantage and how to become a winner. Although you do not need to be a specialist in information technology, you should be aware of career opportunities in the area.

TECHNOLOGY AND PEOPLE

People have different coping styles when it comes to technology. Four common reactions to new technology are cynicism, naivete, frustration, and proactivity.

Cynicism
The **cynics** feel that new technology is overrated and too troublesome to learn. Some cynics openly express their doubts. Others pretend to be interested.

Naivete
Naive people may be unfamiliar or quite familiar with computers. People who are unfamiliar tend to think of computers as magic boxes. Even those familiar with technology often underestimate the time and difficulty of using technology to generate information.

Frustration
Frustrated users are impatient and irritated about taking time to learn new technology. Often these people have too much to do, find manuals difficult to understand, and/or feel stupid.

Proactivity
A **proactive** person looks at technology in a positive and realistic way. He or she is not cynical, naive, or frustrated regarding new technology. Proactive people are positive and look at new technology as providing new tools that can positively impact their lives.

HOW YOU CAN BE A WINNER

Six ongoing activities that can help you be successful are:

Stay Current
Read trade journals and the general business press, join professional associations, and participate in interest groups on the Internet.

Maintain Your Computer Competency
Stay current by reading computer-related articles in the general press and trade journals.

Develop Professional Contacts
Stay active in your profession and meet people in your field. This provides information about other people, firms, job opportunities, and social contacts.

Develop Specialties
Develop specific as well as general skills. Expect to take classes periodically to stay current with your field and technology.

Be Alert for Organizational Change
Use formal and informal lines of communication. Be alert for new trends within the organization.

Look for Innovative Opportunities
Look for ways to increase efficiency. Present ideas in terms of saving money rather than "improving information."

Network Administrator

Network administrators create and maintain networks.

Programmer

Programmers create, test, and troubleshoot computer programs.

Software Engineer

Software engineers analyze users' needs and create application software.

Systems Analyst

Systems analysts plan and design information systems.

Technical Writer

Technical writers prepare instruction manuals, technical reports, and other scientific or technical documents.

Webmaster

Webmasters develop and maintain Web sites and Web resources.

Desktop Publisher

Desktop publishers create and format publication-ready material.

Information Systems Manager

Information systems managers oversee the work of programmers, computer specialists, systems analysts, and other computer professionals.

Computer Support Specialist

Computer support specialists provide technical support to customers and other users.

Computer Technician

Computer technicians repair and install computer components and systems.

Computer Trainer

Computer trainers instruct users on the latest software or hardware.

Cryptographer

Cryptographers design, test, and research encryption procedures.

Database Administrator

Database administrators use database management software to determine the most efficient ways to organize and access data.

Data Entry Worker

Data entry workers input customer information, lists, and other types of data.

computer support specialist   (444)
computer technician   (444)
computer trainer   (444)
cryptographer   (444)
cynic   (437)
data entry worker   (444)
database administrator (DBA)   (444)
desktop publisher   (444)
frustrated   (437)

information systems manager   (444)
naive   (437)
network administrator   (444)
proactive   (438)
programmer   (444)
software engineer   (444)
systems analyst   (444)
technical writer   (444)
Webmaster   (444)

FEATURES

Animations
Careers in IT
DVD Direct
Expansions
Making IT Work for You
On the Web Explorations
TechTV
Tips

CHAPTER REVIEW

Key Terms
Crossword
Multiple Choice
Matching
Open-ended
Using Technology
Expanding Your Knowledge
Building Your Portfolio

To test your knowledge of these key terms with animated flash cards, consult your Computing Essentials CD or visit our Web site at www.olearyseries.com/CE06 and select Key Terms.

COMPUTING ESSENTIALS 2006

CROSSWORD

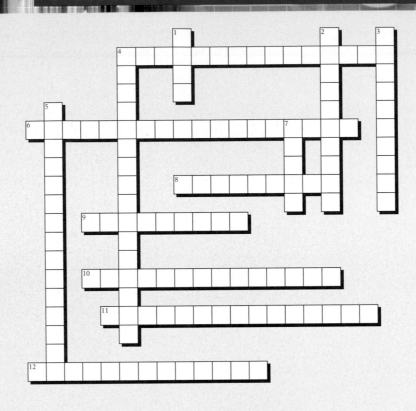

Across

4 Inputs customer information and other data.

6 Repairs and installs computer components and systems.

8 Acting in anticipation of future problems, needs, or changes.

9 Develops and maintains Web sites.

10 Plans and designs information systems.

11 Prepares instruction manuals and technical reports.

12 Designs, tests, and researches encryption procedures.

Down

1 Person that is unfamiliar with computers.

2 Creates, tests, and troubleshoots computer programs.

3 Person that feels learning about computers is an imposition.

4 Creates and formats publication-ready material.

5 Instructs users on the latest software and hardware.

7 Person that feels the idea of a using a microcomputer is overrated.

For an interactive version of this crossword, consult your Computing Essentials CD or visit our Web site at **www.olearyseries.com/CE06** and select Crossword.

COMPUTING ESSENTIALS 2006

MULTIPLE CHOICE

Circle the letter or fill in the correct answer.

1. The real issue with technology is _____.
   a. finding qualified individuals
   b. making it better
   c. integrating it with people
   d. teaching it to students
   e. summarizing it for the general society

2. The principal changes technology brings to business are _____, new enterprises, and new customer and supplier relationships.
   a. new computers
   b. new problems
   c. new agencies
   d. new laws
   e. new products

3. The _____ user believes that learning and using computers take time away from his or her real job.
   a. cynical
   b. proactive
   c. frustrated
   d. confused
   e. naive

4. The _____ user believes all problems can be solved by computers.
   a. proactive
   b. optimistic
   c. frustrated
   d. naive
   e. cynical

5. The _____ user does not become frustrated easily and give up using technology.
   a. proactive
   b. cynical
   c. naive
   d. inexperienced
   e. advanced

6. The best advice in regard to specializing is _____.
   a. don't do it
   b. it is a necessity in today's business world
   c. learn one program and learn it well
   d. learn a little about every program
   e. do so to some extent

7. _____ instruct users on the latest software or hardware.
   a. Computer support specialists
   b. Computer technicians
   c. Computer trainers
   d. Database administrators
   e. Data entry workers

8. _____ oversee the work of programmers, computer specialists, systems analysts, and other computer professionals.
   a. Data entry workers
   b. Desktop publishers
   c. Information systems managers
   d. Network administrators
   e. Programmers

9. _____ prepare instruction manuals, technical reports, and other scientific or technical documents.
   a. Programmers
   b. Software engineers
   c. Systems analysts
   d. Technical writers
   e. Webmasters

10. _____ input customer information, lists, and other types of data.
    a. Data entry workers
    b. Desktop publisher
    c. Information systems managers
    d. Network administrators
    e. Programmers create

For an interactive version of these multiple choice questions, consult your Computing Essentials CD or visit our Web site at www.olearyseries.com/CE06 and select Multiple Choice.

MATCHING

FEATURES

Animations

Careers in IT

DVD Direct

Expansions

Making IT Work for You

On the Web Explorations

TechTV

Tips

CHAPTER REVIEW

Key Terms

Crossword

Multiple Choice

Matching

Open-ended

Using Technology

Expanding Your Knowledge

Building Your Portfolio

Match each numbered item with the most closely related lettered item. Write your answers in the spaces provided.

a. database administrator

b. computer technician

c. computer trainer

d. cynic

e. software engineer

f. frustrated

g. technical writer

h. network administrator

i. proactive

j. programmer

k. systems analyst

l. data entry worker

m. Webmaster

1. Computer user who feels the idea of using microcomputers is overrated. _____

2. Computer user who feels it is an imposition to have to take the time to understand technology. _____

3. Computer user who looks at technology in a positive and realistic way. _____

4. A computer specialist employed to evaluate, create, and maintain Web sites. _____

5. Computer professional who creates, tests, and troubleshoots computer programs. _____

6. Computer specialist who inputs customer information, lists, and other types of data. _____

7. Computer specialist who uses database management software to determine the most efficient ways to organize and access data. _____

8. Computer professional who analyzes users' needs and creates application software. _____

9. Computer professional who plans and designs information systems. _____

10. Computer professional who repairs and installs computer components and systems. _____

11. Computer professional who creates and maintains networks. _____

12. Computer professional who instructs users on the latest software or hardware. _____

13. Computer professional who prepares instruction manuals, technical reports, and other scientific or technical documents. _____

For an interactive version of this matching exercise, consult your Computing Essentials CD or visit our Web site at www.olearyseries.com/CE06 and select Matching.

OPEN-ENDED

On a separate sheet of paper, respond to each question or statement.

1. Why is strategy important to individual success in the information age? What is your strategy?

2. Describe how technology changes the nature of competition.

3. How can your computer competencies and knowledge help you get ahead in today's market?

4. What does proactive mean? What is a proactive computer user? What advantages does this type of user have over the other types?

5. Discuss several different careers in information technology. Which one(s) are of interest to you?

Jobs Online

Did you know that you can use the Internet to find a job? You can browse through job listings, post resumes for prospective employers, and even use special agents to continually search for that job that's just right for you. To learn more about online job searches, review Making IT Work for You: Locating Job Opportunities Online on pages 440 and 441. Then visit our Web site at www.olearyseries.com/CE06 and select Using Technology. Once at that site, play the video and answer the following questions: (a) What locations and categories were selected for the job search? (b) Describe the process for posting a resume. (c) What search criteria were used to set up the job search agent?

Maintain Computer Competence

There are several sources of information to help keep you up to date on current computing trends. Visit our Web site at www.olearyseries.com/CE06 and select Using Technology to link to a few computing sites. Connect to and explore each and then answer the following questions: (a) List the sites you visited and describe the focus of each. (b) Which of these sites was most useful? Why? (c) Which of these sites was least useful? Why? (d) What are other ways you can stay in step with current computing issues?

1   Your Career

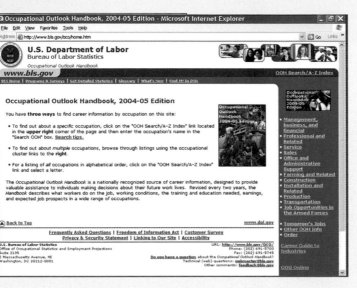

Have you thought about what your career might be? Perhaps it is in marketing, education, or information technology. If you have a career in mind, conduct a Web search to learn more about your chosen career. If you don't have a career in mind, select one of the information systems careers presented in this chapter and conduct a Web search to learn more about that career. After reviewing at least five sites, answer the following questions: (a) Describe your career of choice. (b) Why did you choose that career? (c) How is information technology used in this career? (d) How will changing technology impact your chosen career?

2   Resume Advice

There are several excellent resources available online to help you write a winning resume. Conduct a Web search using the keywords "resume help" to learn more. Review at least five sites, and then compose a sample resume for yourself, applying the information from the sites.

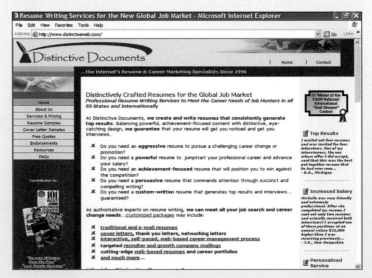

Technology Portfolio

1

As discussed in Chapter 1, a portfolio typically consists of printed material that documents an individual's competence and knowledge. Personal information technology portfolios are often submitted to prospective employers to demonstrate an individual's knowledge and understanding of information technology. Create your personal information technology portfolio by (a) compiling all your responses to the technology-oriented Building Your Portfolio questions that you have completed throughout this term (question 1 from each chapter's Building Your Portfolio is technology-oriented); (b) adding a cover page and a table of contents to the front of the paper; (c) adding a summary at the end of the paper; and (d) editing the material so that the topics flow logically (you may need to add more material) and printing your assembled personal technology portfolio.

Ethics Portfolio

2

As discussed in Chapter 1, a portfolio typically consists of printed material that documents an individual's competence and knowledge. Personal ethics portfolios relating to information technology can be presented to prospective employers to demonstrate an individual's sensitivity, understanding, and commitment to secure, private, and ethical use of computers. Create your personal ethics portfolio by (a) compiling all your responses to the ethics-oriented Building Your Portfolio questions that you have completed throughout this term (question 2 from each chapter's Building Your Portfolio is ethics oriented); (b) adding a cover page and a table of contents to the front of the paper; (c) adding a summary at the end of the paper; and (d) editing the material so that the topics flow logically (you may need to add more material) and printing your assembled personal ethics portfolio.

THE EVOLUTION OF THE COMPUTER AGE

Many of you probably can't remember a world without computers, but for some of us, computers were virtually unknown when we were born and have rapidly come of age during our lifetime.

Although there are many predecessors to what we think of as the modern computer—reaching as far back as the 18th century, when Joseph Marie Jacquard created a loom programmed to weave cloth and Charles Babbage created the first fully modern computer design (which he could never get to work)—the computer age did not really begin until the first computer was made available to the public in 1951.

The modern age of computers thus spans slightly more than 50 years (so far), which is typically broken down into five generations. Each generation has been marked by a significant advance in technology.

- **First Generation (1951–57):** During the first generation, computers were built with vacuum tubes—electronic tubes that were made of glass and were about the size of light bulbs.

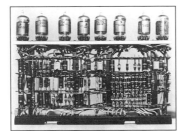

- **Second Generation (1958–63):** This generation began with the first computers built with transistors—small devices that transfer electronic signals across a resistor. Because transistors are much smaller, use less power, and create less heat than vacuum tubes, the new computers were faster, smaller, and more reliable than the first-generation machines.

- **Third Generation (1964–69):** In 1964, computer manufacturers began replacing transistors with integrated circuits. An integrated circuit (IC) is a complete electronic circuit on a small chip made of silicon (one of the most abundant elements in the earth's crust). These computers were more reliable and compact than computers made with transistors, and they cost less to manufacture.

- **Fourth Generation (1970–90):** Many key advances were made during this generation, the most significant being the microprocessor—a specialized chip developed for computer memory and logic. Use of a single chip to create a smaller "personal" computer (as well as digital watches, pocket calculators, copy machines, and so on) revolutionized the computer industry.

- **Fifth Generation (1991–2005 and beyond):** Our current generation has been referred to as the "Connected Generation" because of the industry's massive effort to increase the connectivity of computers. The rapidly expanding Internet, World Wide Web, and intranets have created an information superhighway that has enabled both computer professionals and home computer users to communicate with others across the globe.

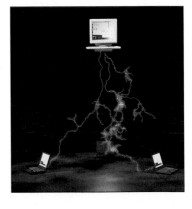

This appendix provides you with a timeline that describes in more detail some of the most significant events in each generation of the computer age.

First Generation
The Vacuum Tube Age

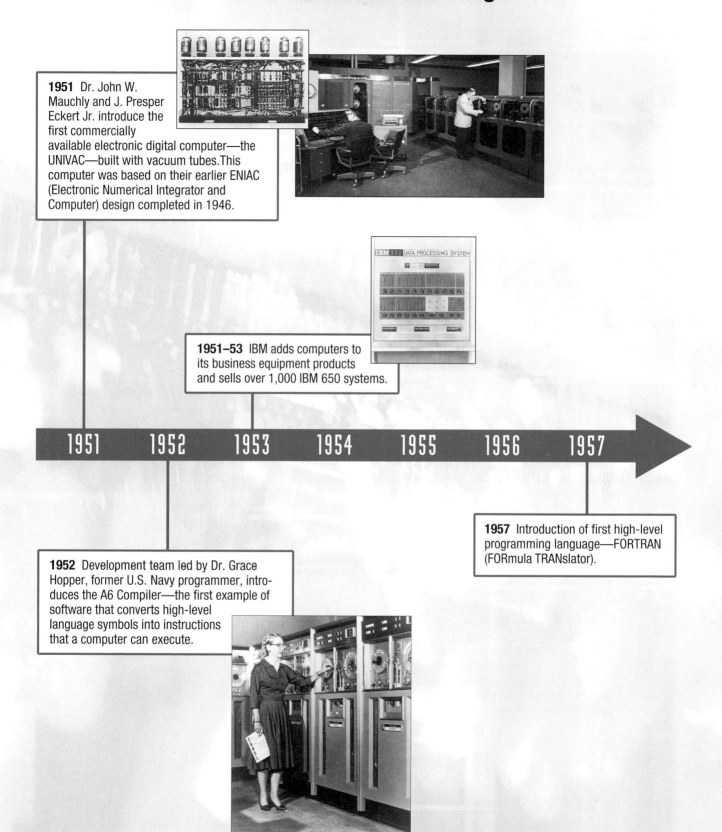

1951 Dr. John W. Mauchly and J. Presper Eckert Jr. introduce the first commercially available electronic digital computer—the UNIVAC—built with vacuum tubes. This computer was based on their earlier ENIAC (Electronic Numerical Integrator and Computer) design completed in 1946.

1951–53 IBM adds computers to its business equipment products and sells over 1,000 IBM 650 systems.

1951   1952   1953   1954   1955   1956   1957

1957 Introduction of first high-level programming language—FORTRAN (FORmula TRANslator).

1952 Development team led by Dr. Grace Hopper, former U.S. Navy programmer, introduces the A6 Compiler—the first example of software that converts high-level language symbols into instructions that a computer can execute.

Second Generation
The Transistor Age

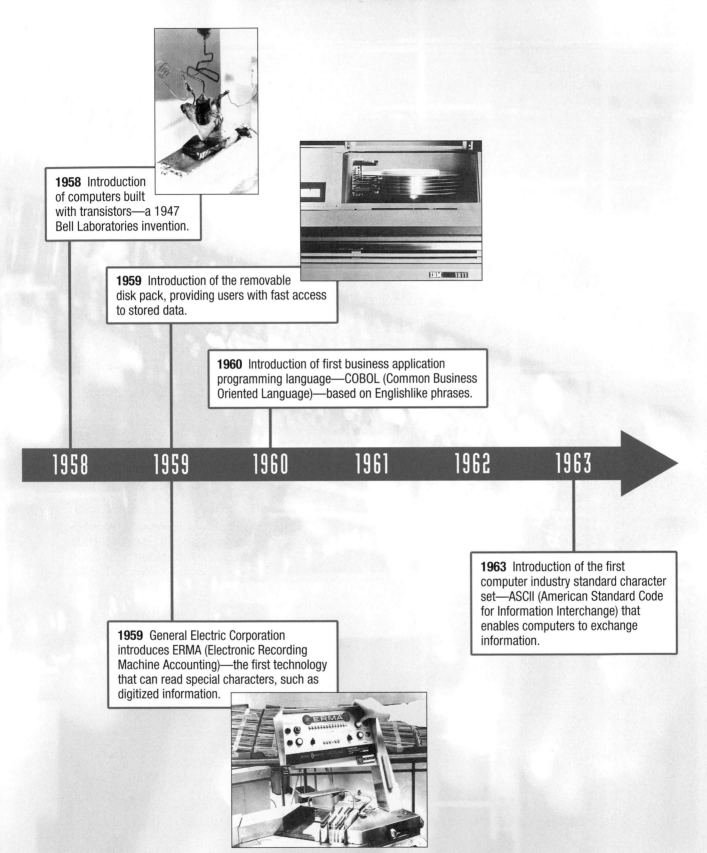

1958 Introduction of computers built with transistors—a 1947 Bell Laboratories invention.

1959 Introduction of the removable disk pack, providing users with fast access to stored data.

1960 Introduction of first business application programming language—COBOL (Common Business Oriented Language)—based on Englishlike phrases.

1958   1959   1960   1961   1962   1963

1963 Introduction of the first computer industry standard character set—ASCII (American Standard Code for Information Interchange) that enables computers to exchange information.

1959 General Electric Corporation introduces ERMA (Electronic Recording Machine Accounting)—the first technology that can read special characters, such as digitized information.

Third Generation

The Integrated Circuit Age

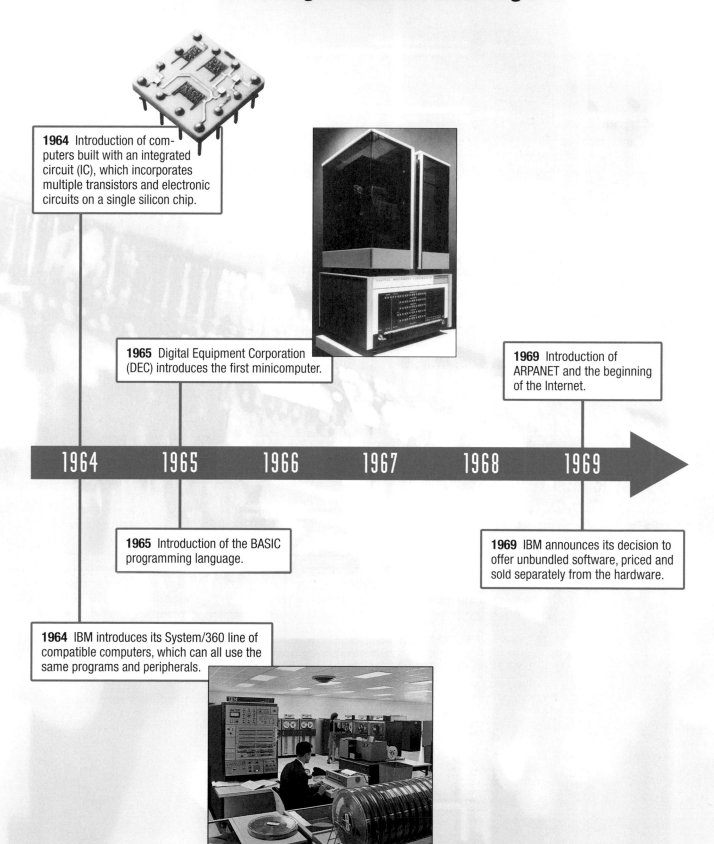

1964 Introduction of computers built with an integrated circuit (IC), which incorporates multiple transistors and electronic circuits on a single silicon chip.

1965 Digital Equipment Corporation (DEC) introduces the first minicomputer.

1969 Introduction of ARPANET and the beginning of the Internet.

1965 Introduction of the BASIC programming language.

1969 IBM announces its decision to offer unbundled software, priced and sold separately from the hardware.

1964 IBM introduces its System/360 line of compatible computers, which can all use the same programs and peripherals.

1964 1965 1966 1967 1968 1969

Fourth Generation

The Microprocessor Age

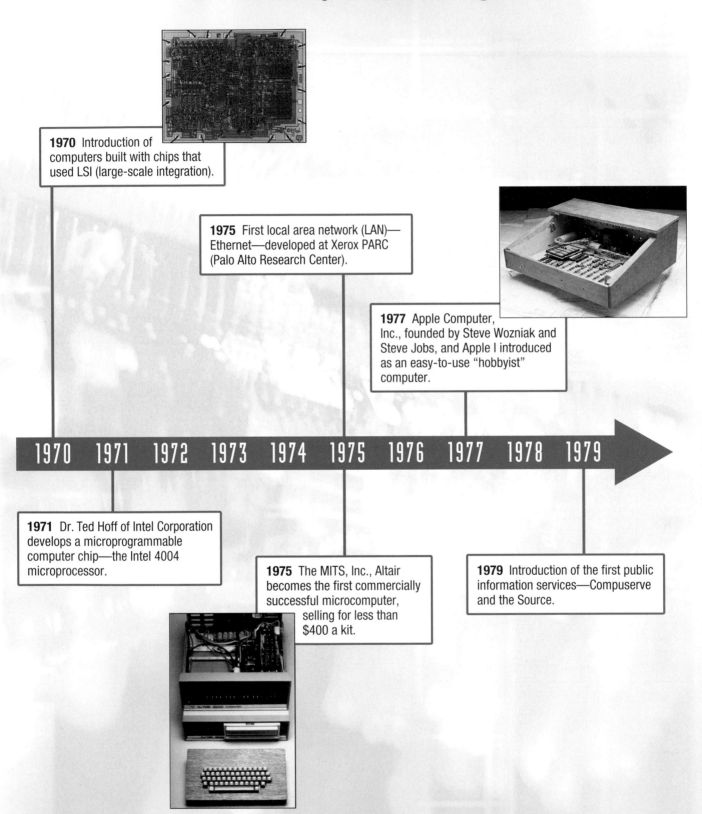

1970 Introduction of computers built with chips that used LSI (large-scale integration).

1975 First local area network (LAN)— Ethernet—developed at Xerox PARC (Palo Alto Research Center).

1977 Apple Computer, Inc., founded by Steve Wozniak and Steve Jobs, and Apple I introduced as an easy-to-use "hobbyist" computer.

1970 1971 1972 1973 1974 1975 1976 1977 1978 1979

1971 Dr. Ted Hoff of Intel Corporation develops a microprogrammable computer chip—the Intel 4004 microprocessor.

1975 The MITS, Inc., Altair becomes the first commercially successful microcomputer, selling for less than $400 a kit.

1979 Introduction of the first public information services—Compuserve and the Source.

Fifth Generation
The Age of Connectivity

1980 IBM asks Microsoft founder, Bill Gates, to develop an operating system—MS-DOS—for the soon-to-be released IBM personal computer.

1981 Introduction of the IBM PC, which contains an Intel microprocessor chip and Microsoft's MS-DOS operating system.

1989 Introduction of Intel 486—the first 1,000,000 transistor microprocessor.

1980 1981 1982 1983 1984 1985 1986 1987 1988 1989 1990

1984 Apple introduces the Macintosh Computer, with a unique, easy-to-use graphical user interface.

1985 Microsoft introduces its Windows graphical user interface.

1990 Microsoft releases Windows 3.0, with an enhanced graphical user interface and the ability to run multiple applications.

1991 Release of World Wide Web standards that describe the framework of linking documents on different computers.

1992 Apple introduces the Newton MessagePad—a personal digital assistant (PDA) that incorporates a pen interface and wireless communications.

1993 Introduction of computer systems built with Intel's Pentium microprocessor.

1995 Intel begins shipping the Pentium Pro microprocessor.

1991   1992   1993   1994   1995

1991 Linus Torvalds, a graduate student at the University of Helsinki, develops a version of UNIX called the Linux operating system.

1993 Introduction of the Mosaic graphical Web browser, which led to the organization of Netscape Communications Corporation.

1995 Microsoft releases Windows 95, a major upgrade to its Windows operating system.

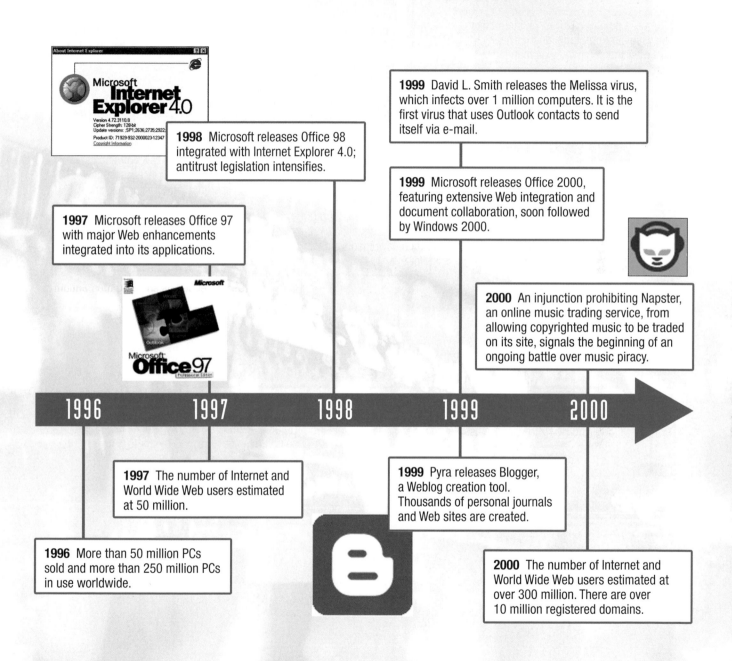

1999 David L. Smith releases the Melissa virus, which infects over 1 million computers. It is the first virus that uses Outlook contacts to send itself via e-mail.

1998 Microsoft releases Office 98 integrated with Internet Explorer 4.0; antitrust legislation intensifies.

1999 Microsoft releases Office 2000, featuring extensive Web integration and document collaboration, soon followed by Windows 2000.

1997 Microsoft releases Office 97 with major Web enhancements integrated into its applications.

2000 An injunction prohibiting Napster, an online music trading service, from allowing copyrighted music to be traded on its site, signals the beginning of an ongoing battle over music piracy.

1996   1997   1998   1999   2000

1997 The number of Internet and World Wide Web users estimated at 50 million.

1999 Pyra releases Blogger, a Weblog creation tool. Thousands of personal journals and Web sites are created.

1996 More than 50 million PCs sold and more than 250 million PCs in use worldwide.

2000 The number of Internet and World Wide Web users estimated at over 300 million. There are over 10 million registered domains.

amazon.COM.

2002 Amazon.com, the largest online retailer, announces its first profitable quarter nearly 10 years after the company was founded.

2004 CAN-SPAM Act enacted, requiring unsolicited e-mail to be labeled and making it illegal to use deceptive headers and anonymous return addresses. The law also requires unsolicited e-mail to allow recipients to opt out and authorizes the FTC to create a "do-not-e-mail" registry.

 **WiFi**™

2002 Microsoft initiates its .NET platform that allows users to create a profile for use across platforms and allows developers to create Web services quickly.

Microsoft® **.net**

2005 Wireless connections (WiFi) to the Internet, called hot spots, allow the public to access the Internet at airports, hotels, and many cafes. Many expect WiFi connections to be available almost everywhere in the next few years—from doctors' offices to airplanes. By 2007 it is expected that nearly 20 million people will use WiFi to access the Web.

2003 Apple opens the iTunes music store with a catalog of over 700,000 songs. Users can buy and then download songs for 99¢.

2001 Microsoft releases Windows XP and Office XP with enhanced user interfaces, better integration and collaboration tools, and increased stability.

2001   2002   2003   2004   2005

2002 Internet2, with over 200 university affiliates, regularly broadcasts live theatre and HDTV transmissions.

2004 Google releases invitations to test Gmail, its e-mail service that includes a search function and 1 GB of storage.

2001 Apple releases Mac OSX with a UNIX backbone and new interface.

 Mac OS X

 **Gmail**™ by Google BETA

THE BUYER'S GUIDE
How to Buy Your Own Microcomputer System

FOUR STEPS IN BUYING A MICROCOMPUTER SYSTEM

The following is not intended to make buying a microcomputer an exhausting experience. Rather, it is to help you clarify your thinking about what you need and can afford.

The four steps in buying a microcomputer system are presented on the following pages. We divide each step into two parts based on the assumptions that both your needs and the money you have to spend on a microcomputer may change.

STEP 1
What Needs Do I Want a Computer to Serve?

The trick is to distinguish between your needs and your wants. Sure, you *want* a cutting-edge system powerful enough to hold every conceivable program you'll ever need. And you want a system fast enough to process them all at the speed of light. But do you *need* this? Your main concern is to address the following two questions:

- What do I need a computer system to do for me today?
- What will I need it to do for me in another year or two?

The questionnaire at the end of this guide will help you determine the answers to both questions.

Suggestions

Consider the type of computer most available on campus. Some schools favor Apple Macintoshes, others favor IBMs or IBM-compatibles. If you own a system that's incompatible with most computers on campus, you may be stuck if your computer breaks down.

Look ahead and determine whether your major requires a computer. Business and engineering students may find one a necessity; physical education and drama majors may not. Your major may also determine the kind of computer that's best. A journalism major may want an IBM or IBM-compatible notebook. An architecture major may want a power-

ful desktop Macintosh with a laser printer that can produce elaborate drawings. Ask your academic advisor for some recommendations.

Example

Suppose you are a college student beginning your sophomore year, with no major declared. Looking at the courses you will likely take this year, you decide you will probably need a computer mainly for word processing. That is, you need a system that will help you write short (10- to 20-page) papers for a variety of courses.

By this time next year, however, you may be an accounting major. Having talked to some juniors and seniors, you find that courses in this major, such as financial accounting, will require you to use elaborate spreadsheets. Or maybe you will be a fine arts or architecture major. Then you may be required to submit projects for which drawing and painting desktop publishing software would be helpful.

STEP 2
How Much Money Do I Have to Spend on a Computer System?

When you buy your first computer, you are not necessarily buying your last. Thus, you can think about spending just the bare-bones amount for a system that meets your needs while in college. Then you might plan to get another system later on.

You know the amount of money you have to spend. Your main concern is to answer the following two questions:

- How much am I prepared to spend on a computer system today?
- How much am I prepared to spend in another year or two?

The questionnaire at the end of this guide asks you this.

Suggestions

You can probably buy a good used computer of some sort for under $300 and a printer for under $50. On the other hand, you might spend $1,000 to $2,500 on a new state-of-the-art system. When upgraded, this computer could meet your needs for the next five years.

There is nothing wrong with getting a used system if you have a way of checking it out. For a reasonable fee, a computer-repair shop can examine it prior to your purchase. Look at newspaper ads and notices on campus bulletin boards for good buys on used equipment. Also try the Internet. If you stay with recognized brands, such as Apple, IBM, Compaq, or Dell, you probably won't have any difficulties.

If you're buying new equipment, be sure to look for student discounts. Most college bookstores, for instance, offer special prices to students. Mail-order houses also steeply discount their products. These firms run ads in such periodicals as *Computer Shopper* (sold on newsstands) and other magazines as well as on the Internet. However, using mail and telephone for repairs and support can be a nuisance. Often you can use the prices advertised by a mail-order house to get local retail computer stores to lower their prices.

Example

Perhaps you have access to a microcomputer at the campus student computing center, the library, or the dormitory. Or you can borrow a friend's. However, this computer isn't always available when it's convenient for you. Moreover, you're not only going to college, but you're also working, so both time and money are tight. Having your own computer would enable you to write papers when it's convenient for you. Spending more than $350 might cause real hardship, so a new microcomputer system may be out of the question. You'll need to shop the newspaper classified ads or the campus bulletin boards to find a used but workable computer system.

Or maybe you can afford to spend more now—say, between $1,000 and $2,000—but probably only $500 next year. By this time next year, however, you'll know your major and how your computer needs have changed.

STEP 3

What Kind of Software Will Best Serve My Needs?

Most computer experts urge that you determine what software you need before you buy the hardware. The reasoning here is that some hardware simply won't run the software that is important to you. This is certainly true once you get into *sophisticated* software. Examples include specialized programs available for certain professions (such as certain agricultural or retail-management programs). However, if all you are interested in today are the basic software tools—word processing, spreadsheet, and communications programs—these are available for

nearly all microcomputers. The main caution is that some more recent versions of application software won't run on older hardware. Still, if someone offers you a free computer, don't say no because you feel you have to decide what software you need first. You will no doubt find it sufficient for many general purposes, especially during your early years in college.

That said, you are better served if you follow step 3 after step 2—namely, finding the answers to the following two questions:

- What kind of software will best serve my needs today?
- What kind will best serve my needs in another year or two?

The questionnaire at the end of this guide will help you determine your answers.

Suggestions

No doubt some kinds of application software are more available on your campus—and in certain departments on your campus—than others. Are freshman and sophomore students mainly writing their term papers in Word, WordPerfect, or Word Pro? Which spreadsheet is most often used by business students: Excel, Lotus 1-2-3, or Quattro Pro? Which desktop publishing program is most favored by graphic arts majors: PageMaker, Ventura Publisher, or Freehand? Do engineering and architecture majors use their own machines for CAD/CAM applications? Start by asking other students and your academic advisor.

If you're looking to buy state-of-the-art software, you'll find plenty of advice in various computer magazines. Several of them rate the quality of newly issued programs. Such periodicals include *PC World* and *MacWorld*.

Example

Suppose you determine that all you need is software to help you write short papers. In that case, nearly any kind of word processing program would do. But will this software be sufficient a year or two from now? Looking ahead, you guess that you'll major in theater arts and minor in screenwriting, which you may pursue as a career. At that point a simple word processing program might not do. You learn from juniors and seniors in that department that screenplays are written using special screenwriting programs. This is software that's not available for some computers. Or, as an advertising and marketing major, you're expected to turn word-processed promotional pieces into brochures. For this, you need desktop publishing software. Or, as a physics major, you discover you will need to write reports on a word processor that can handle equations. In short, you need to look at your software needs not just for today but also for the near future. You especially want to consider what programs will be useful to you in building your career.

STEP 4

What Kind of Hardware Will Best Serve My Needs?

A bare-bones hardware system might include a three-year-old desktop or notebook computer with a 3½-inch floppy disk drive and a hard-disk drive. It should also include a monitor and a printer. On the one hand, as a student—unless you're involved in some very specialized activities—it's doubtful you'll really need such things as voice-input devices, touch screens, scanners, and the like. On the other hand, you will probably need speakers and a CD-ROM or DVD-ROM drive. The choices of equipment are vast.

As with the other steps, the main task is to find the answers to the following two questions:

- What kind of hardware will best serve my needs today?
- What kind will best serve my needs in another year or two?

There are several questions on the questionnaire at the end of this guide to help you determine answers to these concerns.

Suggestions

Clearly, you should let the software be your guide in determining your choice of hardware. Perhaps you've found that the most popular software in your department runs on a Macintosh rather than an IBM-compatible computer. If so, that would seem to determine your general brand of hardware.

Whether you buy IBM or Macintosh, a desktop or a notebook, we suggest you get a 3½-inch floppy disk drive, a hard-disk drive with at least 2 gigabytes of storage, a DVD-ROM drive, at least 128 megabytes of memory, and an ink-jet printer.

As with software, several computer magazines not only describe new hardware but also issue ratings. See *PC World* and *MacWorld*, for example.

Example

Right now, let's say, you're mainly interested in using a computer to write papers, so almost anything would do. But you need to look ahead.

Suppose you find that Word seems to be the software of choice around your campus. You find that Word 2000 will run well on a Pentium machine with 8 megabytes of memory and a 1-gigabyte hard disk. Although this equipment is now outdated, you find from looking at classified ads that there are many such used machines around. Plus, they cost very little—well under $500 for a complete system.

Your choice then becomes: Should I buy an inexpensive system now that can't be upgraded, then sell it later and buy a better one? Or should I buy at least some of the components of a good system now and upgrade it over the next year or so?

As an advertising major, you see the value of learning desktop publishing. This will be a useful if not essential skill once you embark on a career. In exploring the software, you learn that Word includes some desktop publishing capabilities. However, the hardware you previously considered simply isn't sufficient. Moreover, you learn from reading about software and talking to people in your major that there are better desktop publishing programs. Specialized desktop publishing programs like Ventura Publisher are considered more versatile than Word. Probably the best software arrangement, in fact, is to have Word as a word processing program and Ventura Publisher for a desktop publishing program.

To be sure, the campus has computers that will run this software available to students. If you can afford it, however, you're better off having your own. Now, however, we're talking about a major expense. A computer running a Pentium 4 microprocessor, with 512 megabytes of memory, a DVD-ROM disk drive, and a 30-gigabyte hard disk, plus a modem, color monitor, and laser printer, could cost in excess of $1,500.

DEVELOPING A PHILOSOPHY ABOUT COMPUTER PURCHASING

It's important not to develop a case of "computer envy." Even if you buy the latest, most expensive microcomputer system, in a matter of months something better will come along. Computer technology is still in a very dynamic state, with more powerful, versatile, and compact systems constantly hitting the marketplace. So what if your friends have the hottest new piece of software or hardware? The main question is: Do you need it to solve the tasks required of you or to keep up in your field? Or can you get along with something simpler but equally serviceable?

VISUAL SUMMARY
The Buyer's Guide:
How to Buy Your Own Microcomputer System

NEEDS

What do I need a computer system to do for me today? In another year or two?

BUDGET

How much am I prepared to spend on a system today? In another year or two?

I WISH TO USE THE COMPUTER FOR:

	Today	1–2 years
Word processing—writing papers, letters, memos, or reports	❏	❏
Business or financial applications—balance sheets, sales projections, expense budgets, or accounting problems	❏	❏
Record-keeping and sorting—research bibliographies, scientific data, or address files	❏	❏
Graphic presentations of business, scientific, or social science data	❏	❏
Online information retrieval to campus networks, service providers, or the Internet	❏	❏
Publications, design, or drawing for printed newsletters, architectural drawing, or graphic arts	❏	❏
Multimedia for video games, viewing, creating, presenting, or research	❏	❏
Other (specify): _____	❏	❏

I CAN SPEND:

	Today	1–2 years
Under $500	❏	❏
Up to $1,000	❏	❏
Up to $1,500	❏	❏
Up to $2,000	❏	❏
Up to $2,500	❏	❏
Over $3,000	❏	❏
(specify): _____		

Buying a Microcomputer System	
Step	**Questions**
1	*My needs:* What do I need a computer system to do for me today? In another year or two?
2	*My budget:* How much am I prepared to spend on a system today? In another year or two?
3	*My software:* What kind of software will best serve my needs today? In another year or two?
4	*My hardware:* What kind of hardware will best serve my needs today? In another year or two?

To help clarify your thinking about buying a microcomputer system, complete the questionnaire by checking the appropriate boxes.

SOFTWARE

What kinds of software will best serve my needs today? In another year or two?

The application software I need includes:

	Today	1–2 years
Word processing—Word, WordPerfect, or other (specify): _____	❏	❏
Spreadsheet—Excel, Lotus 1-2-3, or other (specify): _____	❏	❏
Database—Access, Paradox, or other (specify): _____	❏	❏
Presentation graphics—PowerPoint, Freelance, CorelPresentations, or other (specify): _____	❏	❏
Browsers—Netscape Navigator, Microsoft Internet Explorer, or other (specify): _____	❏	❏
Other—integrated packages, software suites, graphics, multimedia, Web authoring, CAD/CAM, other (specify): _____	❏	❏

The system software I need:

	Today	1–2 years
Windows 98	❏	❏
Windows 2000	❏	❏
Windows XP	❏	❏
Mac OS	❏	❏
UNIX	❏	❏
Other (specify): _____	❏	❏

HARDWARE

What kinds of hardware will best serve my needs today? In another year or two?

The hardware I need includes:

	Today	1–2 years
Microprocessor—Pentium 4, Pentium III, Apple G4, other (specify): _____	❏	❏
Memory— (specify amount): _____	❏	❏
Monitor—size (specify): _____	❏	❏
Floppy disk drives— 3½″ and/or Zip (specify): _____	❏	❏
Optical disk drive— CD-ROM, DVD-ROM (specify type, speed, and capacity): _____	❏	❏
Hard-disk drive— (specify capacity): _____	❏	❏
Portable computer—laptop, notebook, subnotebook, personal digital assistant (specify): _____	❏	❏
Printer—ink-jet, laser, color (specify): _____	❏	❏
Other—modem, network card, speakers, fax, surge protector (specify): _____	❏	❏

THE UPGRADER'S GUIDE
How to Upgrade Your Microcomputer System

If you own a microcomputer, chances are that your machine is not the latest and greatest. Microcomputers are always getting better—more powerful and faster. While that is a good thing, it can be frustrating trying to keep up.

What can you do? If you have lots of money, you can simply buy a new one. Another alternative is to upgrade or add new components to increase the power and speed of your current microcomputer. You probably can increase your system's performance at a fraction of the cost of a new one.

THREE STEPS IN UPGRADING A MICROCOMPUTER SYSTEM

The following is not intended to detail specific hardware upgrades. Rather, it is intended to help you clarify your thinking about what you need and can afford.

The three steps in upgrading a microcomputer system are presented on the following pages. Each step begins by asking a key question and then provides some suggestions or factors to consider when responding to the question.

STEP 1

Is It Time to Upgrade?

Almost any upgrade you make will provide some benefit; the trick is determining if it is worth the monetary investment. It is rarely practical to rebuild an older computer system into a newer model piece by piece. The cost of a complete upgrade typically far exceeds the purchase price of a new system. But if your system is just a piece or two away from meeting your needs, an upgrade may be in order.

Clearly defining what you hope to gain with an upgrade of some of your system's hardware will enable you to make the most relevant and cost-effective selections. Before deciding what to buy, decide what goal you hope to accomplish. Do you want to speed up your computer's performance? Do you need more space to save your files? Do you want to add a new component such as a DVD-RW drive?

Suggestions

A good place to start is to look at the documentation on the packaging of any software you use or plan to use. Software manufacturers clearly label the minimum requirements to use their products. These requirements are usually broken down into categories that relate to specific pieces of hardware. For instance, how much RAM (random access memory) does a new program require? How much hard disk space is needed? Keep in mind these ratings are typically the bare minimum. If your system comes very close to the baseline in any particular category, you should still consider an upgrade.

Another thing to investigate is whether there is a software solution that will better serve your needs. For instance, if you are looking to enhance performance or make more room on your hard disk, there are diagnostic and disk optimization utility programs that may solve your problem. In Chapter 5, we discuss a variety of utility programs, such as Norton SystemWorks, that monitor, evaluate, and enhance system performance and storage capacity.

Typical objectives of an upgrade are to improve system performance, increase storage capacity, or add new technology.

STEP 2

What Should I Upgrade?

Once you have clearly defined your objectives, the focus shifts to identifying specific components to meet those objectives.

Suggestions

If your objective is to improve performance, three components to consider are RAM, the microprocessor, and expansion cards. If your objective is to increase storage capacity, two components to consider are hard-disk drive and Zip disk drive. If you are adding new technology, consider the capability of your current system to support new devices.

Performance

If you want to increase the speed of your computer, consider increasing the amount of RAM. In most cases, this upgrade is relatively inexpensive and will yield the highest performance result per dollar invested. How much your system's performance will increase depends on how much RAM you start with, the size of programs you run, and how often you run large programs.

Another way to increase speed is to replace your system's microprocessor. Processor speed is measured in gigahertz (GHz). This rating is not a direct measurement of how fast the processor works, but rather it gives you a general idea of how it compares to other processors. (Computing magazines such as *PC World* often publish articles comparing the relative effectiveness of different processors.) The concept behind a microprocessor upgrade is simple: A faster processor will process faster. This is often an expensive upgrade and not as cost-effective as increasing RAM.

If you are looking at upgrading for a specific type of application, perhaps an expansion card is your answer. Expansion cards connect to slots on the system board, provide specialized support, and often free up resources and increase overall system performance. For example, if you run graphics-intensive programs, such as a drafting program or a video game, a video-card upgrade may be a good buy. An upgraded video card can be used to support higher resolution displays, handle all video data, and speed up overall system performance.

Storage Capacity

It's not hard to know when it's time to upgrade your storage capacity. If you frequently have to delete old files to make way for new ones, then it is probably time for more space. A larger or an additional hard drive is usually the solution. Two things to consider when comparing new hard drives are (1) size, which is usually rated in gigabytes (GB) of data the drive can hold, and (2) seek time, which is a rating of the average time it takes the drive to access any particular piece of data.

If you are storing a lot of data that you no longer use, such as old term papers, you might consider adding a Zip drive. This is usually cheaper and is a good way to archive and transport data. Access time is slower than from a hard drive, so this is an option best suited for infrequently used data or for backing up data.

New Technology

Perhaps you are not looking to modify existing hardware, but would like to add a new device. Examples include large high-resolution monitors, DVD-RW drives, and high-speed printers.

The key consideration is whether the new device will work with your existing hardware. The requirements for these devices are typically printed on the outside packaging. If not, then refer to the product's operating manuals. Obviously, if your current system cannot support the new technology, you need to evaluate the cost of the new device plus the necessary additional hardware upgrades.

STEP 3

Who Should Do the Upgrade?

Once you've decided that the cost of the upgrade is justified and you know what you want to upgrade, the final decision is who is going to do it. Basically, there are two choices. You can either do it yourself or pay for professional installation.

Suggestions

The easiest way, and many times the best way, is to have a professional perform the upgrade. If you select this option, be sure to include the cost of installation in your analysis. If you have had some prior hardware experience or are a bit adventurous, you may want to save some money and do it yourself.

Visit a few computer stores that carry the upgrades you have selected. Most stores that provide the parts will install them as well. Talk with their technical people, describe your system (better yet, bring your system unit to the store), and determine the cost of professional installation. If you are thinking of doing it yourself, ask for their advice. Ask if they will provide assistance if you need it.

If you decide to have the components professionally installed, get the total price in writing and inquire about any guarantees that might exist. Before leaving your system be sure that it is carefully tagged with your name and address. After the service has been completed, pay by credit card and thoroughly test the upgrade. If it does not perform satisfactorily, contact the store and ask for assistance. If the store's service is not satisfactory, you may be able to have your credit card company help to mediate any disputes.

VISUAL SUMMARY
THE UPGRADER'S GUIDE: HOW TO UPGRADE YOUR MICROCOMPUTER SYSTEM

Upgrading a Microcomputer System	
Step	**Questions**
1	*Needs:* Is it time to upgrade? What do I need that my current system is unable to deliver?
2	*Analysis:* What should I upgrade? Will the upgrade meet my needs and will it be cost-effective?
3	*Action:* Who should do the upgrade? Should I pay a professional or do it myself?

NEEDS

Is it time to upgrade? What do I need that my current system is unable to deliver?

I am considering an upgrade to:
❏ **Improve performance because**
   ❏ My programs run too slowly
   ❏ I cannot run some programs I need

❏ **Increase storage capacity because**
   ❏ I don't have enough space to store all my files
   ❏ I don't have enough space to install new programs
   ❏ I need a secure place to back up important files
   ❏ I'd like to download large files from the Internet

❏ **Add new technology**
   ❏ Zip drive
   ❏ DVD-RW
   ❏ High-performance monitor
   ❏ Printer
   ❏ TV tuner card
   ❏ Enhanced video card
   ❏ Enhanced sound card
   ❏ Other _____

ANALYSIS

What should I upgrade? Will the upgrade meet my needs and will it be cost-effective?

I will improve:
❏ **Performance by**
   ❏ Adding random-access memory (RAM)
      Current RAM (MB) _____
      Upgrade to _____
      Cost $ _____
      Expected improvement _____
      Other factors _____
   ❏ Replacing the current microprocessor
      Current processor _____
      Upgrade processor _____
      Cost $ _____
      Expected improvement _____
      Other factors _____
   ❏ Adding an expansion card
      Type _____
      Purpose _____
      Cost $ _____
      Expected improvement _____
      Other factors _____

❏ Storage capacity by
   ❏ Adding a hard disk drive
      Current size (GB) _____
      Upgrade size (GB) _____
      Cost $ _____
      Expected improvement _____
      Other factors _____
   ❏ Adding a Zip disk drive
      Upgrade size (GB) _____
      Cost $ _____
      Type _____
      Expected improvement _____
      Other factors _____

❏ **Functionality by adding**
   New technology _____
   System requirements _____
   Cost $ _____
   Expected improvement _____
   Other factors _____

To help clarify your thinking about upgrading a microcomputer system, complete the questionnaire by checking the appropriate boxes.

ACTION

Who should do the upgrade? Should I do it myself or should I pay a professional?

The two choices are:

❏ **Professional installation**

The easiest way, and many times the best way, is to have a professional perform the upgrade. If you select this option, be sure to include the cost of installation in your analysis. Pay with a credit card, and make sure your system is tagged with your name and address before you part with it.

❏ **Do-it-yourself installation**

If you have had some prior hardware experience or are a bit adventurous, you may want to save some money and do it yourself. Avoid touching sensitive electronic parts and be sure to ground yourself by touching an unpainted metal surface in your computer.

Glossary

1.44 MB 3½-inch disk: The amount of data a floppy disk holds; equal to 350 typewritten pages.

2HD: Two-sided, high density. Data can be stored on both sides of the floppy disk.

3GLs (third generation languages): High-level procedural language. *See* Procedural language.

4GLs (fourth generation languages): Very high-level or problem-oriented languages. *See* Problem-oriented language.

5GLs (fifth generation languages): *See* Fifth generation language.

802.11: *See* WiFi (wireless fidelity).

A

AC adapter: Notebook computers use AC adapters that are typically outside the system unit. They plug into a standard wall outlet, convert AC to DC, provide power to drive the system components, and can recharge batteries.

Accelerated graphics port (AGP): A type of bus line that is dedicated to the acceleration of graphics performance.

Access: Refers to the responsibility of those who have data to control who is able to use that data.

Access speed: *See* Access time.

Access time: Measures the amount of time required by the storage device to retrieve data and programs.

Accounting: The organizational department that records all financial activity from billing customers to paying employees.

Accounts payable: The activity that shows the money a company owes to its suppliers for the materials and services it has received.

Accounts receivable: The activity that shows what money has been received or is owed by customers.

Accuracy: Relates to the responsibility of those who collect data to ensure that the data is correct.

Active-matrix monitor: Type of flat-panel monitor in which each pixel is independently activated. Displays more colors with better clarity; also known as thin film transistor (TFT) monitors.

Ad network cookies: Cookies that monitor your activities across all sites you visit and are continually active in collecting information on your Web activities.

Adapter card: *See* Expansion card.

Address: Located in the header of an e-mail message; the e-mail address of the persons sending, receiving, and optionally, anyone else who is to receive copies.

Advanced Research Project Agency Network (ARPANET): A national computer network from which the Internet developed.

Adware cookie: *See* Ad network cookies.

All in one (AIO) device: *See* Multifunctional devices (MFD).

Alternating current (AC): Current from standard wall outlets.

Analog signal: Signals that represent a range of frequencies, such as the human voice. They are a continuous electronic wave signal as opposed to a digital signal that is either on or off. To convert the digital signals of your computer to analog and vice versa, you need a modem. Another cable connects the modem to the telephone wall jack.

Analytical graphs or charts: Form of graphics used to put numeric data into objects that are easier to analyze, such as bar charts, line graphs, and pie charts.

Animation: Feature involving special visual and sound effects like moving pictures, audio, and video clips that play automatically when selected.

Anti-spam program: Software that uses a variety of different approaches to identify and eliminate spam or junk mail.

Antivirus utility: Programs that guard a computer system from viruses or other damaging programs.

Applets: Web pages contain links to programs called applets, which are written in a programming language called Java. These programs are used to add interest to a Web site by presenting animation, displaying graphics, providing interactive games, etc.

Application: Programs such as word processing and spreadsheets.

Application generation subsystem: Provides tools to create data entry forms and specialized programming languages that interface or work with common languages, such as COBOL.

Application generator: Also called program coder; provides modules of prewritten code to accomplish various tasks, such as calculation of overtime pay.

Application server: A dedicated server providing resources using the applications necessary to run that particular business.

Application service provider (ASP): Provides access to a wide range of application programs on the Internet and generally charges for their service.

Application software: Software that can perform useful work, such as word processing, cost estimating, or accounting tasks. The user primarily interacts with application software.

Aqua: As part of the Mac OS X operating system, Aqua is an instinctual user interface providing photo-quality icons and easy-to-use menus.

Arithmetic operation: Fundamental math operations: addition, subtraction, multiplication, and division.

Arithmetic-logic unit (ALU):   The part of the CPU that performs arithmetic and logical operations.

Artificial intelligence (AI):   A field of computer science that attempts to develop computer systems that can mimic or simulate human thought processes and actions.

Artificial reality: *See* Virtual reality.

ASCII (American Standard Code for Information Interchange):   Binary coding scheme widely used on all computers, including microcomputers. Eight bits form each byte, and each byte represents one character.

Assembly language: A step up from machine language, using names instead of numbers. These languages use abbreviations or mnemonics, such as ADD, that are automatically converted to the appropriate sequence of 1s and 0s.

Asymmetric digital subscriber line (ADSL):   One of the most widely used types of telephone high-speed connections (DSL).

Attachment: A file, such as a document or worksheet, that is attached to an e-mail message.

Attribute: A data field represents an attribute (description or characteristic) of some entity (person, place, thing, or object). For example, an employee is an entity with many attributes, including their last name, address, phone, etc.

Auction house sites: Web sites that operate like a traditional auction to sell merchandise to bidders.

Audio editing software: Allows you to create and edit audio clips like filtering out pops and scratches in an old recording.

Audio input: The human voice and music are examples of audio input. *See* Audio input device.

Audio input device: Converts sound into a form that can be processed by the computer. A microphone is an example of an audio input device.

Audio output: Converted digital signals from the system into analog sounds audible to humans, such as music played from speakers or voice output.

Audio-output device: Devices, such as speakers and headphones, that translate audio information from the computer into sounds that people can recognize and understand.

AutoContent wizard: This Microsoft wizard steps you through the process of creating a PowerPoint presentation.

Automated design tool: Software package that evaluates hardware and software alternatives according to requirements given by the systems analyst. Also called computer-aided software engineering (CASE) tools.

B

Backbone: *See* Bus.

Background: Programs you are not using are running in the background.

Backup: A utility program that helps protect you from the effects of a disk failure by making a copy of selected or all files that have been saved onto a disk.

Balance sheet: Lists the overall financial condition of an organization.

Bandwidth: Bandwidth determines how much information can be transmitted at one time. It is a measurement of the communication channel's capacity. There are three bandwidths: voiceband, medium band, and broadband.

Bar code: Code consisting of vertical zebra-striped marks printed on product containers, read with a bar code reader.

Bar code reader: Photoelectric scanner that reads bar codes for processing. *See* Scanning device.

Bar code scanner: *See* Bar code reader

Base station: *See* Wireless receiver.

Basic application: *See* General-purpose applications.

Batch processing: Processing performed all at once on data that have been collected over time.

Beta testing: Testing by a select group of potential users in the final stage of testing a program.

Binary coding schemes: The representation of characters as 0s and 1s, or "off" and "on" electrical states, in a computer. Two of the most popular Binary coding schemes use eight bits to form each byte as in the ASCII and EBCDIC codes.

Binary system: Numbering system in which all numbers consist of only two digits: 0 and 1.

Biometric scanning: Devices that check fingerprints or retinal scans.

Bit (binary digit):   Each 1 or 0 is a bit; short for binary digit.

Bitmap image: Graphic file in which an images is made up of thousands of dots (pixels).

Bits per second (bps):   Speed at which data is transferred.

Bluetooth: This is a recent wireless technology that allows nearby devices to communicate without the connection of cables or telephone systems.

Bomb: A destructive computer program.

Booting: Starting or restarting your computer.

Broadband: Bandwidth that includes microwave, satellite, coaxial cable, and fiber-optic channels. It is used for very high-speed computers.

Broadcast radio: Communication using transceivers to send and receive signals from wireless devices.

Browser: Special Internet software connecting you to remote computers; opens and transfers files, displays text and images, and provides an uncomplicated interface to the Internet and Web documents. Examples of Browsers are Internet Explorer and Netscape Navigator.

Buddy: *See* Friend.

Bulleted list: The sequence of topics arranged on a page and organized by bullets.

Bus: All communication travels along a common connecting cable called a bus or a backbone. As information passes along the bus, it is examined by each device on the system board to see if the information is intended for that device. *See* Bus line and Ethernet.

Bus line: Electronic data roadway, along which bits travel, connects the parts of the CPU to each other and links the CPU with other important hardware. The common connecting cable in a bus network.

Bus network: Also known as Ethernet. Network in which all communications travel along a common connecting cable called a bus. Each device in the network handles its own communications control. There is no host computer or file server.

Bus width: The number of bits travelling simultaneously down a bus is the bus width.

Business suite: *See* Productivity suites.

Business-to-business (B2B): A type of electronic commerce that involves the sale of a product or service from one business to another. This is typically a manufacturer-supplier relationship.

Business-to-consumer (B2C): A type of electronic commerce that involves the sale of a product or service to the general public or end users.

Button: A special area you can click to make links that "navigate" through a presentation.

Byte: Unit consisting of eight bits. There are 256 possible bit combinations in a byte and each byte represents one character.

C

C drive: For most systems the internal hard drive is designated as the C drive. Used to store programs and large data files such as the operating system and application programs like Word and Excel.

Cable: Cords used to connect input and output devices to the system unit.

Cable modem: Allows all digital communication, which is a speed of 27 million bps.

Cache memory: Area of random-access memory (RAM) set aside to store the most frequently accessed information. Cache memory improves processing by acting as a temporary high-speed holding area between memory and the CPU, allowing the computer to detect which information in RAM is most frequently used.

Capacity: Capacity is how much data a particular storage medium can hold and another characteristic of secondary storage.

Carder: Criminal who steals credit cards over the Internet.

Carpal tunnel syndrome: Disorder found among frequent computer users, consisting of damage to nerves and tendons in the hands. *See also* Repetitive strain injury.

Carrier package: The material that chips are mounted on which then plugs into sockets on the system board.

Cathode-ray tube (CRT) monitor: Desktop-type monitor built in the same way as a television set. The most common type of monitor for office and home use. These monitors are typically placed directly on the system unit or on top of a desk.

CD: *See* Compact disc.

CD Burner: Also known as CD-R drive. Used to record custom music. You can write to a CD-recordable only once.

CD-R: Stands for CD-recordable. This optical disk can be written to only once. After that it can be read many times without deterioration but cannot be written on or erased. Used to create custom music CDs and to archive data.

CD-ROM (compact disc-read only memory): Optical disk that allows data to be read but not recorded. Used to distribute large databases, references, and software application packages.

CD-RW (compact disc-rewriteable): A reusable, optical disk that is not permanently altered when data is recorded. Used to create and edit large multimedia presentations.

Cell: The space created by the intersections of a vertical column and a horizontal row within worksheets in a program like Microsoft Excel. A cell can contain text or numeric entries.

Cellular phone system: Links car phones and portable phones.

Center for European Nuclear Research (CENR): In Switzerland, where the Web was introduced in 1992.

Central processing unit (CPU): The part of the computer that holds data and program instructions for processing the data. The CPU consists of the control unit and the arithmetic-logic unit. In a microcomputer, the CPU is on a single electronic component called a microprocessor chip.

CGI (Common Gateway Interface): Whenever you complete a form or provide information at a Web site, the data is recorded by the Web site's database. Programs called CGI scripts create input forms that accept your input, and send the data to the Web database.

Channel: Topic for discussion in a chat group. You can communicate live with others by typing words on your computer once you've selected a channel or topic, and other members immediately see those words on their computer and can respond.

Character: A single letter, number, or special character, such as a punctuation mark or $.

Character recognition device: Specialty devices that are able to recognize special characters and marks.

Character based interface: In older operating systems the user communicated with the operating system through written commands such as "Copy A: assign.doc to C:".

Character effect: Change appearance of font characters by using bold, italic, shadows, and colors.

Chart: Displaying numerical data in a worksheet as a pie chart or a bar chart, making it easier to understand.

Chassis: The metal casing that houses the computer components. *See* System unit.

Chat group: An online discussion group that allows direct "live" communication.

Checklist: In analyzing data, a list of questions helps guide the systems analyst and end user through key issues for the present system.

Child node: A node one level below the node being considered in a hierarchical database or network. *See* Parent node.

Chip: A tiny circuit board etched on a small square of sandlike material called silicon. A chip is also called a silicon chip, semiconductor, or integrated circuit.

Chlorofluorocarbons (CFCs): Toxic chemicals found in solvents and cleaning agents. Chlorofluorocarbons can travel into the atmosphere and deplete the earth's ozone layer.

Clarity: Indicated by the resolution, or number of pixels, on a monitor. The greater the resolution, the better the clarity.

Class: In an object-oriented database, classes are similar objects grouped together.

Client: A node that requests and uses resources available from other nodes. Typically, a client is a user's microcomputer.

Client operating system: A type of desktop operating system that works with a network's operating system (NOS) to share and coordinate resources.

Client-server network system: Network in which one powerful computer coordinates and supplies services to all other nodes on the network. Server nodes coordinate and supply specialized services, and client nodes request the services.

Clip art: Graphic illustrations representing a wide variety of topics.

Clock rate: *See* Clock speed.

Clock speed: Also called clock rate. It is measured in gigahertz or billions of beats per second. The faster the clock speed, the faster the computer can process information and execute instructions.

Closed architecture: Computer manufactured in such a way that users cannot easily add new devices.

Coaxial cable: High-frequency transmission cable that replaces the multiple wires of telephone lines with a single solid-copper core. It is used to deliver television signals as well as to connect computers in a network.

Code: Writing a program using the appropriate computer language.

Coding: Actual writing of a computer program, using a programming language.

Cold boot: Starting the computer after it has been turned off.

Cold site: Special emergency facility in which hardware must be installed but is available to a company in the event of a disaster to its computer system. *Compare* Hot site.

Color capability: Ability to choose between printing in black and white or color.

Column: Using Microsoft Excel for example, a vertical block of cells is one cell wide all the way down the worksheet.

Combination device: Combines features of input devices, such as scanners, with features of output devices, like printers. Also known as multifunctional devices, such as fax machines, Internet telephony, and terminals.

Combination key: Keys such as the *Ctrl* key that perform an action when held down in combination with another key.

Commerce server: *See* Web storefront creation packages.

Common data item: In a relational database, all related tables must have a common data item or key field.

Common operational database: Contains details about the operations of the company, such as inventory, production, and sales.

Common user database: Company database that contains selected information from both the common operational database and from outside (proprietary) databases.

Communication: Process of sharing data, programs, and information between two or more computers.

Communication channel: The actual connecting medium that carries the message between sending and receiving devices. This medium can be a physical wire, cable, or wireless connection.

Communication device: Computer systems that communicate with other computer systems using modems. For example, it modifies computer output into a form that can be transmitted across standard telephone lines.

Communication server: Dedicated server performing specific tasks in relation to communications between computers.

Communication system: Electronic system that transmits data over communications lines from one location to another.

Compact disc (CD): Widely used optical disk format. It holds 650 MB (megabytes) to 1 GB (gigabyte) of data on one side of the CD.

Compact disc rewritable: *See* CD-RW.

Compact disc-read only memory: *See* CD-ROM.

Company database: Also called shared databases. Stored on a mainframe, users throughout the company have access to the database through their microcomputers linked by a network.

Compiler: Software that converts the programmer's procedural-language program (source code) into machine language (object code). This object code can then be saved and run later.

Complementary metal-oxide semiconductor (CMOS): A CMOS chip provides flexibility and expandability for a computer system. Unlike RAM, it does not lose its contents if power is turned off, and unlike ROM, its contents can be changed.

Complex instruction set computer (CISC) chip: The most common type of microprocessor that has thousands of programs written specifically for it. Intel's Pentium and Itanium are CISC chips.

Computer Abuse Amendments Act of 1994: Outlaws transmission of viruses and other harmful computer code.

Computer-aided design (CAD): Type of program that manipulates images on a screen.

Computer-aided design/computer-aided manufacturing (CAD/CAM): Knowledge work systems that run programs to integrate the design and manufacturing activities. CAD/CAM is widely used in manufacturing automobiles.

Computer-aided software engineering (CASE) tool: A type of software development tool that helps provide some automation and assistance in program design, coding and testing. *See* Automated design tool.

Computer competency: Becoming proficient in computer-related skills.

Computer crime: Illegal action in which a perpetrator uses special knowledge of computer technology. Criminals may be employees, outside users, hackers and crackers, and organized crime members.

Computer ethics: Guidelines for the morally acceptable use of computers in our society.

Computer Fraud and Abuse Act of 1986: Law allowing prosecution of unauthorized access to computers and databases.

Computer monitoring software: The most invasive and dangerous type of spyware. These programs record every activity made on your computer, including credit card numbers, bank account numbers, and e-mail messages.

Computer network: Communications system connecting two or more computers and their peripheral devices to exchange information and share resources.

Computer support specialist: Specialists include technical writers, computer trainers, computer technicians, and help desk specialists who provide technical support to customers and other users.

Computer technician: Specialist who installs hardware and software and troubleshoots problems for users.

Computer trainer: Computer professional who provides classes to instruct users.

Computer virus: Destructive programs that can come in e-mail attachments and spam.

Connection device: A device that acts as an interface between sending and receiving devices and the communication channel.

Connectivity: Capability of the microcomputer to use information from the world beyond one's desk. Data and information can be sent over telephone or cable lines and through the air so that computers can talk to each other and share information.

Consumer-to-consumer (C2C): A type of electronic commerce that involves individuals selling to individuals.

Contact: *See* Friend.

Contacts: Electronic address book that is linked to other parts of a PIM to save you time and energy.

Control unit: Section of the CPU that tells the rest of the computer how to carry out program instructions.

Controller card: *See* Expansion card.

Conversion: Also known as Systems implementation; four approaches to conversion: direct, parallel, pilot, and phased. *See* Systems implementation.

Convertible tablet PC: Notebook computer with a monitor that swivels and folds onto its keyboard.

Cookie-cutter programs: Specialized programs that allow users to selectively filter or block the most intrusive ad network cookies while allowing selective traditional cookies to operate.

Cookies: Programs that record information on Web site visitors.

Coprocessor: Specialized processing chip designed to improve specific computer operations, such as the graphics coprocessor.

Cordless mouse: A battery-powered mouse that typically uses radio waves or infrared light waves to communicate with the system unit. Also known as Wireless mouse.

Cracker: One who gains unauthorized access to a computer system for malicious purposes.

Cryptographer: Designs, tests, and researches encryption procedures.

Cumulative trauma disorder: *See* Repetitive strain injury.

Cybercash: *See* Electronic cash.

Cybermall: A place to visit on the Internet that provides access to a variety of different stores where you can make purchases.

Cylinder: Hard disks store and organize files using tracks, sectors, and cylinders. A cylinder runs through each track of a stack of platters. Cylinders differentiate files stored on the same track and sector of different platters.

Cynic: Individual who feels that the idea of using a microcomputer is overrated and too troublesome to learn.

D

Data: Raw, unprocessed facts that are input to a computer system that will give compiled information when the computer processes those facts. Data is also defined as facts or observations about people, places, things, and events.

Data administration subsystem: Helps manage the overall database, including maintaining security, providing disaster recovery support, and monitoring the overall performance of database operations.

Data bank: *See* Proprietary database.

Data definition subsystem: This system defines the logical structure of the database by using a data dictionary.

Data dictionary: Dictionary containing a description of the structure of data in a database.

Data entry worker: Inputs customer information, lists, and other types of data.

Data flow diagram: Diagram showing data or information flow within an information system.

Data integrity: Database characteristics relating to the consistency and accuracy of data.

Data maintenance: Maintaining data includes adding new data, deleting old data, and editing existing data.

Data manipulation subsystem: Provides tools to maintain and analyze data.

Data mining: Technique of searching data warehouses for related information and patterns.

Data model: Defines rules and standards for all data in a database. There are five data models: hierarchical, network, relational, multidimensional, and object-oriented. For example, Access uses the relational data model.

Data processing system (DPS): Transaction processing system that keeps track of routine operations and records these events in a database. Also called transaction processing system (TPS).

Data projector: Specialized device, similar to slide projector, that connects to microcomputers and projects computer output.

Data redundancy: A common database problem in which data is duplicated and stored in different files.

Data security: Protection of software and data from unauthorized tampering or damage.

Data transmission specifications: The rules and procedures that coordinate sending and receiving devices by precisely defining how messages will be sent across communication channels.

Data warehouse: Data collected from a variety of internal and external databases and stored in a database called a data warehouse. Data mining is then used to search these databases.

Data worker: Person involved with the distribution and communication of information, such as secretaries and clerks.

Database: A collection of related information, like employee names, addresses, and phone numbers. It is organized so that a computer program can quickly select the desired pieces of information and display them for you.

Database administrator (DBA): Uses database management software to determine the most efficient way to organize and access data.

Database file: File containing highly structured and organized data created by database management programs.

Database management system (DBMS): To organize, manage, and retrieve data. DBMS programs have five subsystems: DBMS engine, data definition, data manipulation, applications generation, and data administration. An example of a database management system is Microsoft Access. *See* Database manager.

Database manager: Software package used to set up, or structure, a database such as an inventory list of supplies. It also provides tools to edit, enter, and retrieve data from the database.

Database server: Dedicated server that shares resources with other computers to track and store vast amounts of information in databases.

DBMS engine: Provides a bridge between the logical view of data and the physical view of data.

Debugging: Programmer's word for testing and then eliminating errors in a program. Programming errors are of two types: syntax and logic errors.

Decision model: The decision model gives the decision support system its analytical capabilities. There are three types of models included in the decision model: tactical, operational, and strategic model.

Decision support system (DSS): Flexible analysis tool that helps managers make decisions about unstructured problems, such as effects of events and trends outside the organization.

Decision table: Table showing decision rules that apply when certain conditions occur and what action should take place as a result.

Dedicated server: Specializes in performing specific tasks like application server, database server, print server, and more.

Demand report: A demand report is produced on request. An example is a report on the numbers and types of jobs held by women and minorities done at the request of the government.

Demodulation: Process performed by a modem in converting analog signals to digital signals.

Denial of service attack (DoS): A variant virus in which Web sites are overwhelmed with data and users are unable to access the Web site. Unlike a worm that self-replicates, a DoS attack floods a computer or network with requests for information and data.

Density: Refers to how tightly the bits (electromagnetic charges) can be packed next to one another on a floppy disk.

Desk checking: Process of checking out a computer program by studying a printout of the program line-by-line, looking for syntax and logic errors.

Desktop: The screen that is displayed on the monitor when the computer starts up. All items and icons on the screen are considered to be on your desktop and are used to interact with the computer.

Desktop computer: Computer small enough to fit on top of or along the side of a desk and yet too big to carry around.

Desktop operating systems: *See* Stand-alone operating system.

Desktop publisher: One who creates and formats publication-ready material.

Desktop publishing: Program that allows you to mix text and graphics to create publications of professional quality.

Desktop system unit: A system unit that typically contains the system's electronic components and selected secondary storage devices. Input and output devices, such as the mouse, keyboard, and monitor, are located outside the system unit.

Destination file: A document in which a linked object is inserted. The object is created in the source file and then inserted into the new file, called the destination file.

Device driver: Every device that is connected to the computer has a special program associated with it called a device driver that allows communication between the operating system and the device.

Diagnostic utility: *See* Troubleshooting utility.

Dialog box: Provides additional information and requests user input.

Dial-up service: Method of accessing the Internet using a high-speed modem and standard telephone lines.

Dictation mode: Allows users to dictate text directly into a word document.

Digital: Computers are digital machines because they can only understand 1s and 0s. It is either on or off. For example, a digital watch states the exact time on the face, whereas an analog watch has the second hand moving in constant motion as it tells the time.

Digital camera: Similar to a traditional camera except that images are recorded digitally in the camera's memory rather than on film.

Digital cash: *See* Electronic cash.

Digital signal: Computers can only understand digital signals. Before processing can occur within the system unit, a conversion must occur from what we understand (analog) to what the system unit can electronically process (digital). *See* Analog signal.

Digital subscriber line (DSL): Provides high-speed connection using existing telephone lines.

Digital versatile disk (DVD): A type of optical disk similar to CD-ROMs except that more data can be packed into the same amount of space.

Digital video camera: Input device that records motion digitally.

Digital video disc: *See* DVD (digital versatile disc).

Digitizing Device: These devices convert a sketch or a figure into a form that can be processed by a computer. Examples are graphics tablets and digital notebooks.

Direct access: A fast approach to external storage, provided by disks, where information is not in a set sequence.

Direct approach: Approach for systems implementation whereby the old system is simply abandoned for the new system.

Direct current (DC): All computer hardware requires direct current (DC) to power their electronic components. DC power is provided by converting alternating current (AC) from standard outlets using a power supply or directly from batteries.

Directory search: A search engine option that provides a directory or list of categories or topics to choose from, such as Arts & Humanities, Business & Economics, or Computers & Internet, that help you narrow your search until a list of Web sites appears.

Disaster recovery plan: Plan used by large organizations describing ways to continue operations following a disaster until normal computer operations can be restored.

Discussion group: Using e-mail to communicate in groups with people you do not know but with whom you would like to share ideas and interests.

Disk: Part of a microwave station. *See* Microwave station.

Disk caching: Method of improving hard-disk performance by anticipating data needs. Frequently used data is read from the hard disk into memory (cache). When needed, data is then accessed directly from memory, which has a much faster transfer rate than from the hard disk. Increases performance by as much as 30 percent.

Disk Cleanup: A Windows troubleshooting utility that eliminates nonessential files.

Disk Defragmenter: Windows utility that optimizes disk performance by eliminating unnecessary fragments and rearranging files.

Disk drives: Secondary storage devices for saving data, programs, and information.

Diskette: *See* Floppy disk.

Display: Displaying on the computer screen the information asked for from a database.

Distributed data processing system: In a network, computers that perform processing tasks at their own dispersed locations while also sharing programs, data, and other resources with each other.

Distributed database: Database that can be made accessible through a variety of communications networks, which allow portions of the database to be located in different places.

Distributed processing: System in which computing power is located and shared at different locations.

Dock: The Mac OS X operating system features the Dock, which is a new way of visually organizing applications, documents, Web sites, and more.

Document: Any kind of text material.

Document file: File created by a word processor to save documents such as letters, research papers, and memos.

Documentation: Written descriptions and procedures about a program and how to use it. *See* Program documentation.

Domain code: Last part of an Internet address; identifies the geographical description or organizational identification. For example, using www.aol.com, the .com is the domain code and indicates it is a commercial site.

Domain name: The second part of the URL; is the name of the server where the resource is located. For example www.mtv.com.

Domain name server (DNS): Internet addressing method that assigns names and numbers to people and computers. Because the numeric IP addresses are difficult to remember, the DNS server was developed to automatically convert text-based addresses to numeric IP addresses.

Dot-matrix printer: A type of printer that forms characters and images using a series of small pins on a print head. Used where high-quality output is not required.

Dot pitch: Distance between each pixel. The lower the dot pitch, the shorter the distance between pixels, and the higher the clarity of images produced.

Dots-per-inch (dpi): Printer resolution is measured in dpi. The higher the dpi, the better the quality of images produced.

DO UNTIL structure: Loop structure in programming that appears at the end of a loop. The DO UNTIL loop means that the loop statements will be executed at least once. In other words, this program tells you to DO option one UNTIL it is no longer true.

DO WHILE structure: Loop structure in programming that appears at the beginning of a loop. The DO WHILE loop will keep executing as long as there is information to be processed. For example, DO option one WHILE (or as long as) option one remains true.

Downlink: Refers to receiving data from a satellite.

Downloading: Process of transferring information from a remote computer to the computer one is using.

Drawing program: Program used to help create artwork for publications. *See* Illustration program.

Driver: *See* Device driver.

Drop-down menu: *See* Pull-down menu.

DSL: *See* Digital subscriber line.

Dual-scan monitor: *See* Passive-matrix monitor.

Dumb terminal: Terminal that can be used to input and receive data but cannot process data independently. It is used to gain access to information. An example is the type of terminals airline reservation clerks use.

DVD (digital versatile disc or digital video disc): Similar to CD-ROMs except that more data can be packed into the same amount of space. DVD drives can store 4.7 GB to 17 GB on a single DVD disk or 17 times the capacity of CDs.

DVD player: Also known as DVD-ROM drives. *See* DVD.

DVD-R (DVD recordable): A DVD with a write-once format that differs slightly from the format of DVD+R. Typically used to create permanent archives for large amounts of data and to record videos.

DVD+R (DVD recordable): A DVD with a write-once format that differs slightly from the format of DVD-R. Typically used to create permanent archives for large amounts of data and to record videos.

DVD-RAM (DVD random-access memory): A high capacity, maximum performance disk that allows the user to read the information, write over it and erase the data if necessary. Used like a floppy disk to copy, delete files and run programs. It has up to 8 times the storage capacity of a CD and can also be used to read CD and DVD formats.

DVD-ROM (DVD read only memory): Used to distribute full-length feature films with theater-quality video and sound. Also known as DVD players. Are read-only.

DVD-RW (DVD rewritable): A type of reusable DVD disk that is more flexible than the DVD-RAM. DVD-RW is able to create and read CD disks along with creating and editing large-scale multimedia presentations.

DVD+RW (DVD rewritable): Another DVD format to record and erase repeatedly. Able to create and read CD disks along with creating and editing large-scale multimedia presentations.

E

EBCDIC (Extended Binary Coded Decimal Interchange Code): Binary coding schemes that are a standard for minicomputers and mainframe computers.

E-book: Handheld, book-sized devices that display text and graphics. Using content downloaded from the Web or special cartridges, these devices are used to read newspapers, magazines, and books.

E-book reader: *See* E-book.

E-cash: *See* Electronic cash.

E-commerce: Buying and selling goods over the Internet.

Economic feasibility: Comparing the costs of a new system to the benefits it promises.

Editing: Features that modify a document such as using a thesaurus, find and replace, or spell check.

Electronic cash (e-cash): Currency for Internet purchases. Buyers purchase e-cash from a third party (a bank that specializes in electronic currency) by transferring funds from their banks.

Electronic commerce (e-commerce): Buying and selling goods over the Internet.

Electronic mail: Transmission of electronic messages over the Internet. Also known as e-mail.

Electronic monitoring: Monitoring workers' performance electronically rather than by human supervisors.

Electronic profile: Using publicly and privately available databases, information resellers create electronic profiles, which are highly detailed and personalized descriptions of individuals.

E-mail: Communicate with anyone in the world who has an Internet address or e-mail account with a system connected to the Internet. You can include a text message, graphics, photos, and file attachments.

Embedded operating system: An operating system that is completely stored within the ROM (read only memory) of the device that it is in; used for hand-held computers and smaller devices like PDAs.

Encrypting: Coding information so that only the user can read or otherwise use it.

End user: Person who uses microcomputers or has access to larger computers.

Energy Star: Program created by the Environmental Protection Agency to discourage waste in the microcomputer industry.

Enterprise storage system: Using mass storage devices, a strategy is designed for organizations to promote efficient and safe use of data across the networks within their organizations.

Entity: In an object-oriented database, a person, place, thing, or event that is to be described.

Erasable optical disk: Optical disk on which the disk drive can write information and also erase and rewrite information. Also known as CD-RW or compact disc rewritable.

Ergonomic keyboard: Keyboard arrangement that is not rectangular with a palm rest, which is designed to alleviate wrist strain.

Ergonomics: Study of human factors related to things people use. It is concerned with fitting the job to the worker rather than forcing the worker to contort to fit the job.

Ethernet: Otherwise known as Ethernet bus or Ethernet LAN. The Ethernet bus is the pathway or arterial to which all nodes (PCs, file servers, print servers, Web servers, etc.) are connected. All of this is connected to a Local Area Network (LAN) or a Wide Area Network (WAN). *See* Bus network.

Ethernet LAN: *See* Ethernet.

Ethics: Standards of moral conduct.

Exception report: Report that calls attention to unusual events.

Executive information system (EIS): Sophisticated software that can draw together data from an organization's databases in meaningful patterns and highly summarized forms.

Executive support system (ESS): *See* Executive information system.

Expansion bus: Connects the CPU to slots on the system board. There are different types of expansion buses such as industry standard architecture (ISA), peripheral component interconnect (PCI), accelerated graphics port (AGP), universal serial bus (USB) and FireWire buses. *See* System bus.

Expansion card: Optional device that plugs into a slot inside the system unit to expand the computers' abilities. Ports on the system board allow cables to be connected from the expansion board to devices outside the system unit.

Expansion slots: Openings on a system board. Users can insert optional devices, known as expansion cards, into these slots, allowing users to expand their systems. *See* Expansion card.

Expert system: Computer program that provides advice to decision makers who would otherwise rely on human experts. It's a type of artificial intelligence that uses a database to provide assistance to users.

External data: Data gathered from outside an organization. Examples are data provided by market research firms.

External modem: Modem that stands apart from the computer and is connected by a cable to the computer's serial port.

Extranet: Private network that connects more than one organization.

F

Fiber-optic cable: Special transmission cable made of glass tubes that are immune to electronic interference. Data is transmitted through fiber-optic cables in the form of pulses of light.

Field: Each column of information within a record is called a field. A field contains related information on a specific item like employee names within a company department.

Fifth generation language (5GL): Computer language that incorporates the concept of artificial intelligence to allow direct human communication. *See* Visual programming languages.

File: A collection of related records that can store data and programs. For example, the payroll file would include payroll information (records) for all of the employees (entities).

File compression: Process of reducing the storage requirements for a file.

File compression utility: Programs that reduce the size of files so they require less storage on the computer and can be sent more efficiently over the Internet. Examples of such programs are WinZip and Wizard.

File decompression: Process of expanding a compressed file.

File server: Dedicated computer with large storage capacity providing users access to shared folders or fast storage and retrieval of information used in that business.

File transfer protocol (FTP): Internet service for uploading and downloading files.

Filter: A filter will locate or display records from a table that fit a set of conditions or criteria when using programs like Excel.

Find and replace: An editing tool that finds a selected word or phrase and replaces it with another. Click *edit, find*.

Firewall: Security hardware and software. All communications into and out of an organization pass through a special security computer, called a proxy server, to protect all systems against external threats.

FireWire bus: Operates much like USB buses on the system board but at higher speeds.

FireWire port: Used to connect high-speed printers, and even video cameras, to system unit.

Firmware: *See* ROM.

Fixed disk: *See* Internal hard disk.

Flash: An interactive animation program from Macromedia that is usually full screen and highly dynamic, displaying moving text or complicated interactive features.

Flash memory: *See* Flash RAM.

Flash memory card: A solid-state storage device widely used in notebook computers. Flash memory is also used in a variety of specialized input devices to capture and transfer data to desktop computers.

Flash RAM: RAM chips that retain data even when power is disrupted. Flash RAM is an example of solid-state storage and is typically used to store digitized images and record MP3 files.

Flat-panel monitor: Or liquid crystal display (LCD) monitor. These monitors are much thinner than CRTs and can be used for desktop systems as well.

Flatbed scanner: An input device similar to a copying machine.

Flexible disk: *See* Floppy disk.

Flexible keyboard: Fold or rollup for easy packing or storage; designed for mobile users who want a full size keyboard.

Floppies: *See* Floppy disk.

Floppy disk: Flat, circular piece of magnetically treated mylar plastic that rotates within a jacket. A floppy disk is 3½ inches and holds 1.44 MB of information. It is a portable or removable secondary storage device.

Floppy-disk cartridge: Requires special disk drives, including Zip disks, SuperDisks, and HiFD disks, all competing to become the next higher capacity floppy disk standard.

Floppy disk drive (FDD): Stores data programs by altering the electromagnetic charges on the disk's surface to represent 1s and 0s. The floppy drive retrieves the data by reading these charges from the magnetic disk.

Folder: A named area on a disk that is used to store related subfolders and files.

Font: Also known as typeface, is a set of characters with a specific design.

Font size: The height of a character measured in points with each point being ½ inch.

Foreground: Programs you are currently working in are running in the foreground.

Form: Electronic forms reflecting the contents of one record or table. Primarily used to enter new records or make changes to existing records.

Format: Features that change the appearance of a document like font, font sizes, character effects, alignment, and bulleted and numbered lists.

Formatting language: Also known as presentation language. Uses symbols, words, and phrases that instruct a computer on how to display information to the user. For example, HTML is a formatting language used to display Web pages.

Formula: Instructions for calculations in a spreadsheet. It is an equation that performs calculations on the data contained within the cells in a worksheet or spreadsheet.

Fourth generation language (4GL): Problem-oriented languages are designed to solve a specific problem and require little special training on the part of the end user.

Fragmented: Storage technique that breaks up large files and stores the parts wherever space is available in adjacent sectors and clusters.

Freedom of Information Act of 1970: Law giving citizens the right to examine data about them in federal government files, except for information restricted for national security reasons.

Friend: To use instant messaging, you specify a list of friends (also known as buddies or contacts) and register with an instant messaging server.

Frustrated: Person who feels it is an imposition to have to learn something new like computer technology.

Function: A built-in formula in a spreadsheet that performs calculations automatically.

Fuzzy logic: Used by expert systems to allow users to respond by using qualitative terms, such as *great* and *OK*.

G

General ledger: Activity that produces income statements and balance sheets based on all transactions of a company.

General-purpose applications: Applications used for doing common tasks, such as browsers and word processors, spreadsheets, databases, management systems, and presentation graphics. Also known as basic applications and productivity applications.

Generations (of programming languages): The five generations are machine languages, assembly languages, procedural languages, problem-oriented languages, and natural languages. *See* Levels.

Gigahertz (GHz): Billions of beats per second.

Global positioning: Satellite communication network of 24 satellites owned by the Defense Department that continuously sends location information to earth.

Global positioning system (GPS): Devices use location information to determine the geographic location of your car, for example.

Gnutella: Widely used peer-to-peer network system for sharing all kinds of files including music files.

Grammar checker: In word processing, a tool that identifies poorly worded sentences and incorrect grammar.

Graphic tablet: Records sketches and tracings using a special graphics surface or tablet and a special stylus.

Graphical map: Diagram of a Web site's overall design.

Graphical user interface (GUI): Special screen that allows software commands to be issued through the use of graphic symbols (icons) or pull-down menus.

Graphics: Tool for creating and importing graphic elements.

Graphics card: *See* Video card.

Graphics coprocessor: Designed to handle requirements related to displaying and manipulating 2-D and 3-D graphic images.

Graphics suite: Group of graphics programs offered at a lower cost than if purchased separately, like CorelDraw.

Graphics tablet: Tablet PC that uses a special graphics surface or tablet and a stylus. Used by artists, mapmakers, and engineers.

Green PC: Microcomputer industry concept of an environmentally friendly, low-power-consuming machine.

Grid chart: Chart that shows the relationship between input and output documents.

Group decision support system (GDSS): System used to support the collective work of a team addressing large problems.

H

Hacker: Person who gains unauthorized access to a computer system for the fun and challenge of it.

Handheld computer: *See* Personal digital assistant (PDA) and Palm computers.

Handwriting recognition software: Translates handwritten notes into a form that the system unit can process.

Hard copy: Images output on paper by a printer or plotter.

Hard disk: Enclosed disk drive containing one or more metallic disks. Hard disks use magnetic charges to record data and have large storage capacities and fast retrieval times.

Hard-disk cartridge: Hard disk that is easily removed. Used primarily to complement an internal hard disk.

Hard-disk pack: Several platters align one above the other, offering much greater storage capacity. They are removable storage devices with a massive amount of available storage. Used in big business companies.

Hardware: Equipment that includes a keyboard, monitor, printer, the computer itself, and other devices that are controlled by software programming.

Head crash: When a read-write head makes contact with the hard disk's surface or particles on its surface, the disk surface becomes scratched and some or all data is destroyed.

Header: In a typical e-mail, the header has 3 elements: header, message, and signature. The header appears first and includes addresses, subject, and attachments.

Headphones: Audio-output devices connected to a sound card in the system unit. The sound card is used to capture as well as play back recorded sound.

Help: A feature in most application software providing options that typically include an index, a glossary, and a search feature to locate reference information about specific commands.

Hierarchical database: Database in which fields or records are structured in nodes. Organized in the shape of a pyramid, and each node is linked directly to the nodes beneath it. Also called one-to-many relationship.

Hierarchical network: Also called a hybrid network. Consists of several computers linked to a central host computer. The computers linked to the host are themselves hosts to other computers or devices.

HiFD disk: High-capacity floppy disk manufactured by Sony with a capacity of 200 MB like the SuperDisk drives. HiFD, disk drives are able to read the 1.44 MB floppy disk.

High capacity disk: Also a 3½" floppy-disk cartridge. It is thicker than a floppy disk and requires a special drive. Examples are Zip disks, HiFD disks, and SuperDisks.

High performance serial bus (HPSB): *See* FireWire Bus.

High performance serial bus (HPSB) port: Also known as FireWire ports, they are faster than USB ports. They provide connections to specialized HPSB devices, such as camcorders.

High-definition television (HDTV): All-digital television that delivers a much clearer and more detailed widescreen picture.

Higher level: Programming languages that are closer to the language humans use.

History file: Created by browser to store information on Web sites visited by your computer system.

Hits: The sites that a search engine returns after running a keyword search, ordered from most likely to least likely to contain the information requested.

Home network: LAN network for homes allowing different computers to share resources, including a common Internet connection.

Home software: *See* Integrated package.

Home suite: *See* Personal suite.

Host computer: Also called a server or provider, is a large centralized computer.

Hot site: Special emergency facility consisting of a fully equipped computer center available to a company in the event of disaster to its computer system. *Compare* Cold site.

HTML: *See* Hypertext Markup Language.

HTML editor: *See* Web authoring program.

Hub: The center or central node for other nodes. This device can be a server or a connection point for cables from other nodes.

Human resources: The organizational department that focuses on the hiring, training, and promoting of people, as well as any number of human-centered activities within the organization.

Hybrid network: *See* Hierarchical network.

Hyper cube: An extension of relational databases that is able to analyze more sides of the information. Also called multidimensional databases.

Hyperlink: Connection or link to other documents or Web pages that contain related information.

Hypertext Markup Language (HTML): Programming language that creates document files used to display Web pages.

I

Icons: Graphic objects on the desktop used to represent programs and other files.

Identity theft: The illegal assumption of someone's identity for the purpose of economic gain.

I-drive: *See* Internet hard drive.

IFPS (interactive financial planning system): A 4GL language used for developing financial models.

IF-THEN-ELSE structure: Logical selection structure whereby one of two paths is followed according to IF, THEN, and ELSE statements in a program. *See* Selection structure.

Illusion of anonymity: The misconception that being selective about disclosing personal information on the Internet can prevent an invasion of personal privacy.

Illustration program: Also known as drawing programs; used to create digital illustrations and modify vector images and thus create line art, 3-D models, and virtual reality.

Image capturing device: A device, such as a digital camera or a digital video camera, that creates or captures original images.

Image gallery: Libraries of electronic images.

Immersive experience: Allows the user to walk into a virtual reality room or view simulations on a virtual reality wall.

Income statement: A statement that shows a company's financial performance, income, expenses, and the difference between them for a specific time period.

Index search: *See* Directory search.

Individual database: Collection of integrated records used mainly by just one person. Also called microcomputer database.

Industrial robot: Robot used in factories to perform a variety of tasks. For example, machines used in automobile plants to do painting and polishing.

Industry standard architecture (ISA): Bus-line standard developed for the IBM Personal Computer. It first consisted of an 8-bit-wide data path, then a 16-bit-wide data path. *See* Peripheral Component Interconnect (PCI).

Information: Data that has been processed by a computer system.

Information broker: *See* Information reseller.

Information flow: In large and medium organizations, computerized information flows both vertically and horizontally as it moves through the different functional areas and management levels.

Information reseller: Also known as information broker. It gathers personal data on people and sells it to direct markets, fund raisers, and others, usually for a fee.

Information system: Collection of hardware, software, people, data, and procedures that work together to provide information essential to running an organization.

Information systems manager: Oversees the work of programmers, computer specialists, systems analysts, and other computer professionals.

Information technology (IT): Computer and communication technologies, such as communication links to the Internet, that provide help and understanding to the end user.

Information utility: *See* Proprietary database and Data bank.

Information worker: Employee who creates, distributes, and communicates information.

Infrared: Uses infrared light waves to communicate over short distances. Sometimes referred to as line of sight communication because light waves can only travel in a straight line.

Ink-jet printer: Printer that sprays small droplets of ink at high speed onto the surface of the paper producing letter quality images and can print in color.

Input: Any data or instructions used by a computer.

Input device: Piece of equipment that translates data into a form a computer can process. The most common input devices are the keyboard and the mouse.

Instant messaging: A program allowing communication and collaboration for direct, "live," connections over the Internet between two or more people.

Integrated circuit: *See* Silicon chip.

Integrated package: A single program providing functionality of a collection of programs but is not as extensive as a specialized program like Microsoft Word. Popular with home users who are willing to sacrifice some advanced features for lower cost and simplicity.

Intel-compatible: Chips referred to as Intel-compatible processors are able to process programs originally written for Intel chips. Examples are Athlon and Hammer.

Intelligent terminal: Terminal that includes a processing unit, memory, secondary storage, communications software, and a telephone hook-up or other communication links.

Interactivity: User participation in a multimedia presentation.

Interface card: *See* Expansion card.

Internal data: Data from within an organization consisting principally of transactions from the transaction processing system.

Internal hard disk: Storage device consisting of one or more metallic platters sealed inside a container. Internal hard disks are installed inside the system cabinet of a microcomputer. It stores the operating system and major applications like Word.

Internal modem: The internal modem consists of a plug-in circuit board inside the system unit. A telephone cable connects the modem to the telephone wall jack. *See* Modem card.

Internet: A huge computer network available to everyone with a microcomputer and a means to connect to it. It is the actual physical network made up of wires, cables and satellites as opposed to the Web, which is the multimedia interface to resources available on the Internet.

Internet hard drive: A special service site on the Web providing users with free or low cost storage, allowing access to information from any computer that is connected to the Internet.

Internet relay chat (IRC): Leading type of chat group service.

Internet scam: Using the Internet, a fraudulent act or operation designed to trick individuals into spending their time and money for little or no return.

Internet service provider (ISP): Provides access to the Internet.

Internet telephone: Low cost alternative to long distance telephone calls using electronic voice delivery.

Internet telephony: *See* Telephony.

Internet terminal: Provides access to the Internet and displays Web pages on a standard television set. Also called Web terminal.

Interpreter: Software that converts a procedural language one statement at a time into machine language just before the statement is executed. No object code is saved.

Intranet: Like the Internet, it typically provides e-mail, mailing lists, newsgroups, and FTP services, but it is accessible only to those within the organization. Organizations use intranets to provide information to their employees.

Inventory: Material or products that a company has in stock.

Inventory control system: A system that keeps records of the number of each kind of part or finished goods in the warehouse.

IP address (Internet Protocol address): The unique numeric address of a computer on the Internet that facilitates the delivery of e-mail.

IP telephony: *See* Telephony.

J

Java: Programming language for creating special programs like applets. *See* Applets.

Jewel boxes: Optical disks are stored in these clear, protective boxes.

Joystick: Popular input device for computer games. You control game actions by varying the pressure, speed, and direction of the joystick.

Junk mail filter: *See* Anti-spam program.

K

Key chain hard drive: Also known as key chain flash memory devices. The size of a key chain, these hard drives connect to a computer's USB port enabling a transfer of files; has a capacity of 1GB.

Key chain flash memory device: *See* Key chain hard drive.

Key field: The common field by which tables in a database are related to each other. This field uniquely identifies the record. For example in university databases, a key field is the Social Security number. Also known as Primary field or Primary key.

Keyboard: Input device that looks like a typewriter keyboard but has additional keys.

Keystroker logger: Also known as computer monitoring software and sniffer programs. They can be loaded onto your computer without your knowledge.

Keyword search: A type of search option that causes the search engine to compare your entry against its database and return with a list of sites, or hits, that contain the keyword you entered.

Knowledge base: A system that uses a database containing specific facts, rules to relate these facts, and user input to formulate recommendations and decisions.

Knowledge work system (KWS): Specialized information system used to create information in a specific area of expertise.

Knowledge worker: Person involved in the creation of information, such as an engineer and a scientist.

Knowledge-based systems: Programs duplicating human knowledge. It's like capturing the knowledge of a human expert and making it accessible through a computer program.

L

Label: Provides structure to a worksheet by describing the contents of the rows and columns. *See* Text entry.

Land: *See* Lands and pits.

Lands and pits: Flat and bumpy areas, respectively, that represent 1s and 0s on the optical disk surface to be read by a laser.

Language bar: Microsoft word 2003 supports voice recognition. Using Word 2003's language bar, you can switch between voice command mode and dictation mode.

Language translator: Converts programming instructions into a machine language that can be processed by a computer.

Laptop computer: *See* Notebook computer and Notebook system unit.

Laser printer: Printer that creates dotlike images on a drum, using a laser beam light source.

Levels: Generations or levels of programming languages ranging from "low" to "high." *See* Generations (of programming languages).

Light pen: A light sensitive penlike device. Placing the pen against the monitor closes a photoelectric circuit and identifies the spot for entering or modifying data.

Line of sight communication: Microwave communication using high-frequency radio waves that travel in a straight line.

Link: A connection to related information.

Linux: Type of Unix operating system initially developed by Linus Torvalds designed to run on minicomputers in network environments. Now powerful microcomputers and servers on the Web use it.

List address: In discussion groups, members of a mailing list communicate by sending messages to the list address. Each message is then copied and sent via e-mail to every member of the mailing list.

Local area network (LAN): Network consisting of computers and other devices that are physically near each other, such as within the same building.

Location: For Browsers to connect to resources, location or addresses must be specified. Also known as Uniform resource locators or URL's.

Logic error: Error that occurs when a programmer has used an incorrect calculation or left out a programming procedure.

Logic structure: Programming statements or structures called sequence, selection, or loop that control the logical sequence in which computer program instructions are executed.

Logical operation: Comparing two pieces of data to see whether one is equal to (=), less than (<), or greater than (>) the other.

Logical view: Focuses on the meaning and content of the data. End users and computer professionals are concerned with this view as opposed to the physical view with which only specialized computer professionals are concerned.

Loop structure: Logic structure in which a process may be repeated as long as a certain condition remains true. This structure is called a "loop" because the program loops around or repeats again and again. There are two variations: DO UNTIL and DO WHILE.

Low bandwidth: *See* Voiceband.

Lower level: Programming language closer to the language the computer itself uses. The computer understands the 0s and 1s that make up bits and bytes.

Luna: Windows XP new user interface emphasizes functions over programs. For example, the new Start menu displays categories like e-mail and Internet, rather than individual programs such as Outlook and Internet Explorer.

Lurking: Before you submit a contribution to a discussion group, it is recommended that you observe or read the communications from others. This observing process is called lurking.

M

Mac OS: Operating system designed for Macintosh computers.

Mac OS X: Macintosh operating system featuring a user interface called Aqua.

Machine language: Language in which data is represented in 1s and 0s. Most languages have to be translated into machine language for the computer to process the data. Either a compiler or an interpreter performs this translation.

Magnetic tape: To find specific information, you will have to go through the tape sequentially until that data comes up. On the other hand, using an audio compact disk, select the song and the disk moves directly to that song. Tape may be slow, but it is effective and a commonly used tool for backing up data.

Magnetic tape reel: Typically ½-inch wide and ½-mile long, this type of magnetic tape is used by mainframe computers due to its massive storage capacity.

Magnetic tape streamer: Device that allows duplication (backup) of the data stored on a microcomputer hard disk.

Magnetic-ink character recognition (MICR): Direct-entry scanning devices used in banks. This technology is used to automatically read the numbers on the bottom of checks.

Mailing list: In discussion groups, members of a mailing list can communicate by sending messages to a list address.

Main board: *See* System board.

Mainframe computer: This computer can process several million program instructions per second. Sizeable organizations rely on these room-size systems to handle large programs and a great deal of data.

Maintenance programmer: Programmers who maintain software by updating programs to protect them from

errors, improve usability, standardize, and adjust to organizational changes.

Malware: Short for malicious software.

MAN: *See* Metropolitan area network.

Management information system (MIS): Computer-based information system that produces standardized reports in a summarized and structured form. Generally used to support middle managers.

Many-to-many relationship: In a network database, each child node may have more than one parent node and vice versa.

Mark recognition device: Scanners that are able to recognize special characters and marks.

Mark sensing: *See* Optical-mark recognition (OMR).

Marketing: The organizational department that plans, prices, promotes, sells, and distributes an organization's goods and services.

Mass storage: Refers to the tremendous amount of secondary storage required by large organizations.

Mass storage devices: Devices such as file servers, RAID systems, tape libraries, optical jukeboxes, and more.

Master slide: A special slide that does not appear in a presentation but controls all the formats and placement of all slides in a presentation. The design template can be changed for an entire presentation using a master slide.

Mechanical mouse: Traditional and most widely used type of mouse. It has a ball on the bottom and is attached with a cord to the system unit.

Media: Media is the actual physical material that holds the data, such as a floppy disk, which is one of the important characteristics of secondary storage. Also known as Medium.

Medium: *See* Media.

Medium band: Bandwidth of special leased lines, used mainly with minicomputers and mainframe computers.

Memory: Memory is contained on chips connected to the system board and is a holding area for data instructions and information (processed data waiting to be output to secondary storage). RAM, ROM, and CMOS are three types of memory chips.

Menu: List of commands.

Menu bar: Menus are displayed in a menu bar at the top of the screen.

Message: The content portion of e-mail correspondence.

Metasearch engine: Program that automatically submits your search request to several indices and search engines and then creates an index from received information. One of the best known is MetaCrawler.

Method: In an object-oriented database, description of how the data is to be manipulated.

Metropolitan area network (MAN): These networks are used as links between office buildings in a city.

Microcomputer: Small, low-cost computer designed for individual users. These include desktop, notebook, and personal digital assistant computers.

Microcomputer database: *See* Individual database.

Microprocessor: The central processing unit (CPU) of a microcomputer controls and manipulates data to produce information. The microprocessor is contained on a single integrated circuit chip and is the brains of the system.

Microsecond: One-millionth of a second. Computers process data and instructions in microseconds.

Microwave: Communication using high-frequency radio waves that travel in straight lines through the air.

Microwave dish: Can be installed on towers, high buildings, and mountains. Used to relay the high frequency radio waves of microwave communication.

Microwave station: For long line of sight distances, waves must be relayed by means of microwave stations with microwave dishes or antennas.

Middle management: Middle-level managers deal with control and planning. They implement the long-term goals of the organization.

MIDI: *See* Musical instrument digital interface.

MIDI device: Specialized musical instrument that provides input in the form of encoded digital signals representing musical sounds, like an electronic keyboard.

Midrange computer: Also known as Minicomputer.

Minicomputer: Refrigerator-sized machines falling in-between microcomputers and mainframes in processing speed and data-storing capacity. Medium-sized companies or departments of large companies use minicomputers.

Mistaken identity: When the electronic profile of one person is switched with another.

Mobile robot: Robot that acts as a transport. For example, the police use them to locate and disarm explosive devices.

Modem: Short for modulator-demodulator. It is a communications device that translates the electronic signals from a computer into electronic signals that can travel over telephone lines.

Modem card: Also known as an Internal modem, a card that allows distant computers to communicate with one another by converting electronic signals from within the system unit into electronic signals that can travel over telephone lines and other types of connections.

Modulation: Process of converting digital signals to analog signals.

Module: *See* Program module.

Monitor: Output device like a television screen that displays data processed by the computer.

Morphing: Special effect in which one image seems to melt into another.

Motherboard: Also called a System board; the communications medium for the entire system.

Mouse: Device that typically rolls on the desktop and directs the cursor on the display screen.

Mouse pad: Provides a smooth surface to roll the mouse.

Mouse pointer: Typically in the shape of an arrow. *See* Pointing device.

Multidimensional database: Data can be viewed as a cube having three or more sides consisting of cells. Each side of the cube is considered a dimension of the data, thus complex relationships between data can be represented and efficiently analyzed. Sometimes called hypercube and designed for analyzing large groups of records.

Multifunctional devices (MFD): Devices that typically combine the capabilities of a scanner, printer, fax, and copying machine.

Multimedia: Technology that can link all sorts of media into one form of presentation, such as video, music, voice, graphics, and text.

Multimedia authoring programs: Programs used to create multimedia presentations bringing together video, audio, graphics, and text elements into an interactive framework. Macromedia Director, Authorware, and Toolbook are examples of multimedia authoring programs.

Multiread: Newer CD-ROM drives are multiread or able to read both CD-R and CD-RW drives.

Multisession: Photo CDs are multisession, meaning that new images can be added to the CD at any time. *See* Single-session.

Multitasking: Operating system that allows a single user to run several application programs at the same time.

Musical instrument digital interface (MIDI): A standard that allows musical instruments to connect to the system using MIDI ports.

N

Naive: People who underestimate the difficulty of changing computer systems or generating information.

Nanosecond: Billionths of a second.

Napster: Napster was a client-server network system whereby client computers request resources from a server computer.

National service provider: Internet service providers, such as America Online (AOL), that provide access through standard telephone connections and allow users to access the Internet from almost anywhere within the country for a standard fee.

Natural language: Language designed to give people a more human connection with computers.

Net: Launched in 1969 and is a large network that connects smaller networks all over the world. Also known as the Internet.

Network: The arrangement in which various communications channels are connected through two or more computers. The largest network in the world is the Internet.

Network adapter card: Connects the system unit to a cable that connects to other devices on the network.

Network administrator: Also known as Network manager. Creates and maintains networks.

Network architecture: Describes how networks are configured and how the resources are shared.

Network computer: *See* Network terminal.

Network database: Database with a hierarchical arrangement of nodes, except that each child node may have more than one parent node. Also called many-to-many relationship.

Network gateway: Connection by which a local area network may be linked to other local area networks or to larger networks.

Network hub: The central unit in a star network where all computers and peripheral devices are linked. Typically a host computer or file server.

Network interface card (NIC):   Also known as Network adapter cards. They are used to connect a computer to one or more computers forming a communication network whereby users can share data, programs, and hardware.

Network manager: Computer professional who ensures that existing information and communication systems are operating effectively and that new ones are implemented as needed. Also responsible for meeting security and privacy requirements.

Network operating system (NOS):   Interactive software between applications and computers coordinating and directing activities between computers on a network. This operating system is located on one of the connected computer's hard disk, making that system the network server.

Network server: *See* Network operating system. This computer coordinates all communication between the other computers. Popular network operating systems include, NetWare and Windows NT Server.

Network terminal: Low-cost alternative to intelligent terminal; relies on host computer or server for software. Also called Network computer or Thin client.

Newsgroup: Newsgroups are organized by major topic areas and use the UseNet network.

Node: Any device connected to a network. For example, a node is a computer, printer, or data storage device and each device has its own address on the network. Also, within hierarchical databases, fields or records are structured in nodes.

Nonproprietary operating system: Free operating systems as opposed to being owned by a corporation. Also called Open source programs. For example Linux is an open source program.

Nonvolatile storage: Permanent storage, such as data stored on a disk, is used to preserve data and programs. Also called secondary storage because it does not lose its memory contents when the power goes off.

Notebook computer: Portable computer, also known as laptop computer, weighing between 4 and 10 pounds.

Notebook system unit: A small, portable system unit that contains electronic components, selected secondary storage devices, and input devices.

Numbered list: Sequence of steps or topics on a page organized by numbers.

Numeric entry: In a worksheet or spreadsheet; typically used to identify numbers or formulas.

Numeric keypad: Enters numbers and arithmetic symbols and is included on all computer keyboards.

O

Object: An element, such as a text box, that can be added to a workbook, which can be selected, sized, and moved. For example, if a chart (object) in an Excel workbook file (source file) is linked to a word document (destination file), the chart appears in the word document. In this manner, the object contains both data and instructions to manipulate the data.

Object code: Machine language code converted by a compiler from source code. Object code can be saved and run later.

Object embedding: The object from the source file, like a chart, is embedded and added to the destination document. It then becomes part of the destination document.

Object linking: A copy of the object from the source file that is inserted into another document or file.

Object linking and embedding (OLE):   Powerful feature of many application programs that allows sharing of information.

Objectives: In programming, it is necessary to make clear the problems you are trying to solve to create a functional program.

Object-oriented database: A more flexible type of database that stores data as well as instructions to manipulate data and is able to handle unstructured data, such as photographs, audio, and video. Object-oriented databases organize data using objects, classes, entities, attributes, and methods.

Object-oriented programming (OOP):   Methodology in which a program is organized into self-contained, reusable modules called objects. Each object contains both the data and processing operations necessary to perform a task.

Object-oriented software development: Software development approach that focuses less on the tasks and more on defining the relationships between previously defined procedures or objects.

Office automation system (OAS):   System designed primarily to support data workers. It focuses on managing documents, communicating, and scheduling.

One Button Checkup: This program integrates several of the separate troubleshooting utilities from Norton Utilities.

One-to-many relationship: In a hierarchical database, each entry has one parent node, and a parent may have several child nodes.

Online: Being connected to the Internet is described as being online.

Online processing: *See* Real-time processing.

Online storage: *See* Internet hard drive.

Open architecture: Microcomputer architecture allowing users to expand their systems by inserting optional devices known as expansion cards.

Open source: *See* Nonproprietary operating system.

Operating system: Software that interacts between application software and the computer, handling such details as running programs, storing and processing data, and coordinating all computer resources, including attached peripheral devices. It is the most important program on the computer. Windows XP and Mac OS X are examples of operating systems.

Operational feasibility: Making sure the design of a new system will be able to function within the existing framework of an organization.

Operational model: A decision model that helps lower-level managers accomplish the organization's day-to-day activities, such as evaluating and maintaining quality control.

Operators: Operators handle correcting operational errors in any programs. To do that, they need documentation, which gives them the understanding of the program, thus enabling them to fix any errors.

Optical disk: Storage device that can hold over 17 gigabytes of data, which is an equivalent of several million typewritten pages. Lasers are used to record and read data on the disk. The two basic types of optical disks are compact disks (CDs) and digital versatile or video disks (DVDs).

Optical disk drive: A disk is read by an optical disk drive using a laser that projects a tiny beam of light. The amount of reflected light determines whether the area represents a 1 or a 0.

Optical mouse: A type of mouse that emits and senses light to detect mouse movement.

Optical scanner: *See* Scanner.

Optical-character recognition (OCR): Scanning device that uses special preprinted characters, such as those printed on utility bills, that can be read by a light source and changed into machine-readable code.

Optical-mark recognition (OMR): Device that senses the presence or absence of a mark, such as a pencil mark. As an example, an OMR device is used to score multiple-choice tests.

Organization chart: Chart showing the levels of management and formal lines of authority in an organization.

Organizational Internet storage: High speed Internet connection to a dedicated remote organizational Internet drive site.

Output: Processed data or information from a computer.

Output device: Equipment that translates processed information from the central processing unit into a form that can be understood by humans. The most common output devices are monitors, or video display screens, and printers.

P

Packet: Before a message is sent on the Internet, it is broken down into small parts called packets. Each packet is then sent separately over the Internet. At the receiving end, the packets are reassembled into the correct order.

Page layout program: *See* Desktop publishing.

Palm computer: Also known as handheld computers. These systems combine pen input, writing recognition, personal organizational tools, and communications capa-

bilities. They contain an entire computer system, including the electronic components, secondary storage, and input and output devices.

Parallel approach: Systems implementation in which old and new systems are operated side by side until the new one has shown it is reliable.

Parallel port: Used to connect external devices that send or receive data over a short distance. Mostly used to connect printers to the system unit.

Parallel processing: Used by supercomputers to run large and complex programs. *See* Parallel processor.

Parallel processor: Works with one or more other parallel processor chips to run or process a large program by using software that takes a large program, breaks it down into parts, and assigns the parts to separate processors. The processors then work simultaneously and share results. *See* Parallel processing.

Parent node: Node one level above the node being considered in a hierarchical database or network. Each entry has one parent node, although a parent may have several child nodes. Also called one-to-many relationship.

Passive-matrix monitor: Monitor that creates images by scanning the entire screen. This type requires little energy but clarity of images is not sharp. Also known as dual-scan monitors.

Password: Special sequence of numbers or letters that limits access to information, such as electronic mail.

Payroll: Activity concerned with calculating employee paychecks.

PC card: *See* Personal Computer Memory Card International Association (PCMCIA) card.

PC card hard disk: A hard disk cartridge for a notebook computer that typically holds a capacity of 10 gigabytes.

PC card modem: A credit card-sized expansion board that is inserted into portable computers. A telephone cable connects the modem to the telephone wall jack.

PC/TV: Or High-definition television (HDTV). A recent development in the merger of microcomputers and television.

PDA keyboard: Miniature keyboard for PDAs used to send e-mail, create documents, and more.

Peer-to-peer network system: Network in which nodes can act as both servers and clients. For example, one microcomputer can obtain files located on another microcomputer and can also provide files to other microcomputers.

People: End users who use computers to make themselves more productive.

Perception system: Robot that imitates some of the human senses.

Periodic report: Reports for a specific time period as to the health of the company or a particular department of the company.

Peripheral component interconnect (PCI): Bus architecture that combines the capabilities of MCA and EISA with the ability to send video instructions at speeds to match the microprocessor. PCI is a 32-bit or 64-bit speed bus that is over 20 times faster than an ISA bus.

Personal Computer Memory Card International Association (PCMCIA) card: Credit card-sized expansion cards developed for portable computers.

Personal digital assistant (PDA):   A device that typically combines pen input, writing recognition, personal organizational tools, and communication capabilities in a very small package. Also called handheld PC and palm computer.

Personal laser printer: Inexpensive laser printer widely used by single users to produce black-and-white documents.

Personal software: *See* Integrated package.

Personal suite: Also known as home suites. Contain personal software applications or programs intended for home use like Microsoft Works Suite.

Person-to-person auction site: A type of Web auction site where the owner provides a forum for numerous buyers and sellers to gather.

Phased approach: System implementation whereby a new system is implemented gradually over a period of time.

Photo CD: Multisession format to store digital images on a CD.

Photo printer: A special-purpose ink jet printer designed to print photo-quality images from digital cameras.

Physical security: Activity concerned with protecting hardware from possible human and natural disasters.

Physical view: This focuses on the actual format and location of the data. *See* Logical view.

Picosecond: Trillionth of a second.

Picture CD: Single session format developed by Eastman Kodak to store digital images on a CD, which are delivered by the Internet or Picture CD.

Picture elements: *See* Pixel.

Pilot approach: Systems implementation in which a new system is tried out in only one part of the organization. Later it is implemented throughout the rest of the organization.

Pit: *See* Lands and pits.

Pixel (picture elements):   Smallest unit on the screen that can be turned on and off or made different shades. Pixels are individual dots that form images on a monitor. The greater the resolution, the more pixels and the better the clarity.

Platform: The operating system. Application programs are designed to run with a specific platform. *See* Operating system.

Platform scanner: Handheld direct-entry device used to read special characters on price tags. Also known as Wand readers.

Platters: On a hard disk, platters are where the data is stored. They are rigid, metallic, and stacked on top of each other.

Plotter: Special-purpose output device for producing bar charts, maps, architectural drawings, and three-dimensional illustrations.

Plug and Play: Set of hardware and software standards developed to create operating systems, processing units, expansion cards, and other devices that are able to configure themselves. When the computer starts up, it will search for the plug and play device and automatically configure it to the system.

Plug-in: Program that is automatically loaded and operates as part of a browser.

Plug-in board: *See* Expansion card.

Pointer: For a monitor, a pointer is typically displayed as an arrow and controlled by a mouse. For a database, a pointer is a connection between a parent node and a child node in a hierarchical database.

Pointers: Within a network database, pointers are additional connections between parent nodes and child nodes. Thus, a node may be reached through more than one path and can be traced down through different branches.

Pointing device: Accepts pointing gestures and converts them into machine-readable input. These devices include mice, joystick, touch screen, light pens, and styluses.

Pointing stick: Device used to control the pointer by directing the stick with your finger.

Polling: Process whereby a host computer or file server asks each connecting device whether it has a message to send and then allows each message, in turn, to be sent.

Port: Connecting socket on the outside of the system unit. Used to connect input and output devices to the system unit.

Portable language: Language that can be run on more than one type of computer.

Portable printer: Small and lightweight printers designed to work with notebook computers.

Power supply unit: Desktop computers have a power supply unit located within the system unit that plugs into a standard wall outlet, converting AC to DC, which becomes the power to drive all of the system unit components.

Preliminary investigation: First phase of the systems life cycle. It involves defining the problem, suggesting alternative systems, and preparing a short report.

Presentation file: A file created by presentation graphics programs to save presentation materials. For example, a file might contain audience handouts, speaker notes, and electronic slides.

Presentation graphics: Graphics used to combine a variety of visual objects to create attractive and interesting presentations.

Presentation language: *See* Formatting language.

Primary field: Also known as Primary key.

Primary storage: Holds data and program instructions for processing data. It also holds processed information before it is output. *See* Memory.

Print server: Dedicated server performing specific tasks in regard to all of the printers within that organization.

Printer: Device that produces printed paper output.

Privacy: Computer ethics issue concerning the collection and use of data about individuals.

Proactive: Person who looks at technology in a positive, realistic way.

Problem-oriented language: Programming language that is nonprocedural and focuses on specifying what the program is to accomplish. Also known as 4GLs or very high-level languages.

Procedural language: Programming language designed to focus on procedures and how a program will accomplish a specific task. Also known as 3GLs or third generation languages.

Procedures: Rules or guidelines to follow when using hardware, software, and data.

Processing rights: Refers to which people have access to what kind of data.

Processor: *See* Central processing unit.

Production: The organizational department that actually creates finished goods and services using raw materials and personnel.

Productivity application: *See* General-purpose applications.

Productivity suites: Also known as Business suites that contain professional-grade application programs, including word processing, spreadsheets, and more. A good example is Microsoft Office.

Program: Instructions for the computer to follow to process data. *See* Software.

Program analysis: *See* Program specification.

Program coder: *See* Application generator.

Program definition: *See* Program specification.

Program design: Creating a solution using programming techniques, such as top-down program design, pseudocode, flowcharts, logic structures, object-oriented programming, and CASE tools.

Program documentation: Written description of the purpose and process of a program. Documentation is written within the program itself and in printed documents. Programmers will find themselves frustrated without adequate documentation, especially when it comes time to update or modify the program.

Program flowchart: Flowchart graphically presents a detailed sequence of steps needed to solve a programming problem.

Program maintenance: Activity of updating software to correct errors, improve usability, standardize, and adjust to organizational changes.

Program module: Each module is made up of logically related program statements. The program must pass in sequence from one module to the next until the computer has processed all modules.

Program specification: Programming step in which objectives, output, input, and processing requirements are determined.

Programmer: Computer professional who creates new software or revises existing software.

Programming: A program is a list of instructions a computer will follow to process data. Programming, also known as software development, is a six-step procedure for creating that list of instructions. The six steps are program specification, program design, program code (or coding), program test, program documentation, and program maintenance.

Programming language: A collection of symbols, words, and phrases that instruct a computer to perform a specific task.

Project manager: Software that enables users to plan, schedule, and control the people, resources, and costs needed to complete a project on time.

Property: Computer ethics issue relating to who owns data and rights to software.

Proprietary database: Enormous database an organization develops to cover certain particular objects. Access to this type of database is usually offered for a fee or subscription. Also known as data bank and informational utility.

Proprietary operating system: A network operating system that is owned and licensed by a company.

Protocol: Rules for exchanging data between computers. The protocol http:// is the most common.

Prototyping: Building a model or prototype that can be modified before the actual system is installed.

Proxy server: Computer that acts as a gateway or checkpoint in an organization's firewall. *See* Firewall.

Pseudocode: An outline of the logic of the program to be written. It is the steps or the summary of the program before you actually write the program for the computer. Consequently, you can see beforehand what the program is to accomplish.

Pull-down menu: List of options or commands associated with the selected menu. Also known as drop-down menu.

Purchase order: A form that shows the name of the company supplying the material or service and what is being purchased.

Purchasing: Buying of raw materials and services.

Q

Query: A question or request for specific data contained in a database. Used to analyze data.

Query language: Easy-to-use language and understandable to most users. It is used to search and generate reports from a database. An example is the language used on an airline reservation system.

Query-by-example: A specific tool in database management that shows a blank record and lets you specify the information needed, like the fields and values of the topic you are looking to obtain.

R

RAM: *See* Random access memory.

RAM cache: *See* Cache memory.

Random access memory: Volatile, temporary storage that holds the program and data the CPU is presently processing. It is called temporary storage because its contents will be lost if electrical power to the computer is disrupted or the computer is turned off.

Range: A series of continuous cells in a worksheet.

Rapid applications development (RAD): Involves the use of powerful development software and specialized teams as an alternative to the systems development life cycle approach. Time for development is shorter and quality of the completed system development time is better, although cost is greater.

Raster image: *See* Bitmap image.

Reader/sorter: A magnetic-ink character recognition device that reads the numbers at the bottom of checks and deposit slips. This provides input allowing banks to maintain customer accounts and balances.

Read-only: Formatting that prevents the user from writing any new data onto a disc or from erasing any data imprinted by the publisher.

Read-only memory: Refers to chips that have programs built into them at the factory. The user cannot change the contents of such chips. The CPU can read or retrieve the programs on the chips but cannot write or change information. ROM stores programs that boot the computer, for example. *See* Firmware.

Real-time processing: Or Online processing. Occurs when data is processed at the same time a transaction occurs.

Recalculation: If you change one or more numbers in your spreadsheet, all related formulas will automatically recalculate and charts will be recreated.

Receiving device: A computer or specialized communication device that receives data from another location.

Record: Each row of information in a database is a record. Each record contains fields of data about some specific item, like employee name, address, phone, etc. A record represents a collection of attributes describing an entity.

Reduced instruction set computer (RISC) chip: Powerful microprocessor chip found in workstations.

Redundant arrays of inexpensive disks (RAIDs): Groups of inexpensive hard-disk drives related or grouped together using networks and special software. They improve performance by expanding external storage.

Refresh rate: How often a displayed image is updated or redrawn on the monitor.

Regional network: Span distances up to 100 miles. Typically not owned by a single organization. *See* Metropolitan area network.

Regional service provider: An Internet service provider provides access through standard telephone connections in a specific area, typically several states, for a standard fee. If users access the Internet from outside the regional area, they incur long-distance connection charges.

Relation: A table in a relational database in which data elements are stored in rows and columns.

Relational database: A widely used database structure in which data is organized into related tables. Each table is made up of rows called records and columns called fields. Each record contains fields of data about a specific item.

Removable hard disk: Also known as Hard disk cartridge.

Repetitive motion injury: *See* Repetitive strain injury.

Repetitive strain injury (RSI): Category of injuries resulting from fast, repetitive work that causes neck, wrist, hand, and arm pain.

Reports: Can be lists of fields in a table or selected fields based on a query. Typical database reports include sales summaries, phone lists, and mailing labels.

Research: The organizational department that identifies, investigates, and develops new products and services.

Resolution: A measurement in pixels of a monitor's clarity. For a given monitor, the greater the resolution, the more pixels and the clearer the image.

Resources: These programs coordinate all system resources that include the keyboard, mouse, printer, monitor, storage devices, and memory. They also monitor system performance, schedule jobs, provide security, and start the computer.

Reverse directory: A special telephone directory listing telephone numbers sequentially, followed by subscriber names.

Rewriteable: There are several rewritable formats, and few DVD players read all standards. Three most widely used formats are DVD-RW, DVD+RW, and DVD-RAM.

Ring network: Network in which each device is connected to two other devices, forming a ring. There is no host computer, and messages are passed around the ring until they reach the correct destination.

Robot: Robots are computer-controlled machines that mimic the motor activities of living things, and some robots can solve unstructured problems using artificial intelligence.

Robotics: Field of study concerned with developing and using robots.

Roller ball: *See* Trackball.

ROM: *See* Read-only memory.

Rotational speed: Important characteristic of CD drives because it determines how fast data can be transferred from the CD.

Row: A horizontal block of cells one cell high all the way across the worksheet.

S

Sales order processing: Activity that records the demands of customers for a company's products or services.

Satellite: This type of communication uses satellites orbiting about 22,000 miles above the earth as microwave relay stations.

Satellite/air connection services: Connection services that use satellites and the air to download or send data to users at a rate seven times faster than dial-up connections.

Scam: A fraudulent or deceptive act or operation designed to trick individuals into spending their time and money for little or no return.

Scanner: Device that identifies images or text on a page and automatically converts them to electronic signals that can be stored in a computer to copy or reproduce.

Scanning device: Converts scanned text and images into a form the system can process. Optical scanners, bar code readers, and character and mark recognition devices are examples of scanning devices.

Search engine: Specialized programs assisting in locating information on the Web and the Internet.

Search provider: *See* Search services.

Search services: Organizations that maintain databases relating to information provided on the Internet and also provide search engines to locate information.

Secondary storage: Permanent storage used to preserve programs and data that can be retained after the computer is turned off. These devices include floppy disks, hard disks, and magnetic tape, CDs, DVDs, and more.

Secondary storage device: These devices are used to save, backup, and transport files from one location or computer to another. *See* Secondary storage.

Sector: Section shaped like a pie wedge that divides the tracks on a disk.

Security: The protection of information, hardware, and software.

Selection structure: Logic structure that determines which of two paths will be followed when a program must make a decision. Also called IF-THEN-ELSE structures. If something is true, then do option one, or else do option two.

Semiconductor: Silicon chip through which electricity flows with some resistance.

Sending device: Often a computer or specialized communication device. They send messages in the form of data, information, and/or instructions.

Sequence structure: Logic structure in which one program statement follows another.

Sequential access: An approach to external storage, provided by magnetic tape, where information is stored in sequence. *See* Magnetic tape.

Serial port: Used to connect external devices that send or receive data one bit at a time over a long distance. Used for mouse, keyboard, modem, and many other devices.

Server: A host computer with a connection to the Internet that stores document files used to display Web pages. Depending on the resources shared, it may be called a file server, printer server, communication server, Web server, or database server.

Service program: Another word for Utilities. They perform specific tasks related to managing computer resources.

Shared database: *See* Company database.

Shared laser printer: More expensive laser printer used by a group of users to produce black-and-white docu-

ments. These printers can produce over 30 pages a minute.

Sheet: A rectangular grid of rows and columns. *See* Spreadsheet or Worksheet.

Sherlock: In the Mac OS X operating system, Sherlock locates information on the Web as well as on the user's computer system.

Shutter: The shutter on a disk slides to the side exposing the recording surface.

Signature line: Provides additional information about a sender of an e-mail message, such as name, address, and telephone number.

Silicon chip: Tiny circuit board etched on a small square of sandlike material called silicon. Chips are mounted on carrier packages, which then plug into sockets on the system board.

Single-session: Picture CD disks are single-session, meaning that all images must be transferred at one time to the CD.

Size: Also known as viewable size of a monitor, indicated by the diagonal length of the viewing area.

Slate tablet PC: Similar to a notebook computer except that its monitor is attached to the system unit and does not have a keyboard integrated into the system unit.

Slide: A PowerPoint presentation is made up of many slides shown in different views and presentation styles.

Slot: Area on a system board that accepts expansion cards to expand a computer system's capabilities.

Smart card: Card about the size of a credit card containing a tiny built-in microprocessor. It can be used to hold such information as personal identification, medical and financial knowledge, and credit card numbers. Information on this card is protected by a password, which offers security and privacy.

Sniffer programs: *See* Computer monitoring software and Keystroker logger.

Snoopware: Programs that record virtually every activity on a computer system.

Socket: Sockets provide connection points on the system board for holding electronic parts.

Soft copy: Images or characters output on a monitor screen.

Software: Computer program consisting of step-by-step instructions, directing the computer on each task it will perform.

Software Copyright Act of 1980: Law allowing owners of programs to make copies for backup purposes and to modify them to make them useful provided they are not resold or given away.

Software development: *See* Programming.

Software engineer: Programming professionals or programmers who analyze users' needs and create application software.

Software environment: Operating system, also known as software platform, consisting of a collection of programs to handle technical details depending on the type of operating system. For example, software designed to run on an Apple computer is compatible with Mac OS environment.

Software piracy: Unauthorized copying of programs for personal gain.

Software platform: *See* Software environment.

Software suite: Individual application programs that are sold together as a group.

Solid-state storage: A secondary storage device that has no moving parts. Data is stored and retrieved electronically directly from these devices, much as they would be from conventional computer memory.

Sort: Tool that rearranges a table's records numerically or alphabetically according to a selected field.

Sound card: Device that accepts audio input from a microphone and converts it into a form that can be processed by the computer. Also converts internal electronic signals to audio signals so they can be heard from external speakers.

Source code: When a programmer originally writes the code for a program in a particular language. This is called source code until it is translated by a compiler for the computer to execute the program. It then becomes object code.

Source file: The document that stores the data for the linked object.

Spam: Unwelcome and unsolicited e-mail that can carry attached viruses.

Spam blocker: *See* Anti-spam program.

Speakers: Audio-output devices connected to a sound card in the system unit. The sound card is used to capture as well as play back recorded sound.

Special purpose application: Programs that are narrowly focused on specific disciplines and occupations. Some of the best known are multimedia, Web Authoring, graphics, virtual reality, and artificial intelligence.

Specialized application: *See* Special purpose application.

Specialized search engine: Search engines that focus on subject-specific Web sites.

Specialized suite: Programs that focus on specialized applications such as graphics suites or financial planning suites.

Speech recognition: The ability to accept voice input to select menu options, and to dictate text.

Speed: Speed is measured by the number of pages printed per minute.

Spelling checker: Program used with a word processor to check the spelling of typed text against an electronic dictionary.

Spider: *See* Webcrawlers.

Spike: *See* Voltage surge.

Spreadsheet: Computer-produced spreadsheet based on the traditional accounting worksheet that has rows and columns used to present and analyze data.

Spy removal programs: Programs such as Spybot and Spysweeper, designed to detect Web bugs and monitor software.

Spyware: Wide range of programs designed to secretly record and report an individual's activities on the Internet.

Stand-alone operating system: Also called desktop operating systems; a type of operating system that controls a single desktop or notebook computer.

Standard toolbar: A collection of buttons used as shortcuts to the most frequently used menu commands, like save and print.

Star network: Network of computers or peripheral devices linked to a central computer through which all communications pass. Control is maintained by polling. The configuration of the computers looks like a star surrounding and connected to the central computer in the middle.

Start menu: A Windows menu listing commands used to gain access to information, change hardware settings, find information, get online help, run programs, log off a network, and shut down the computer system.

Stock photograph: Photographs on a variety of subject material from professional models to natural landscapes.

Storage device: Hardware that reads data and programs from storage media. Most also write to storage media.

Story board: Design tool for planning the overall logic, flow, and structure of a multimedia presentation.

Strategic model: A decision model that assists top managers in long-range planning, such as stating company objectives or planning plant locations.

Strategy: A way of coordinating the sharing of information and resources. The most common network strategies are terminal, peer-to-peer, and client/server systems.

Structured problem: A problem that can be broken down into a series of well-defined steps.

Structured program: Program that uses logic structures according to the program design and the language in which you have chosen to write the program. Each language follows techniques like pseudocode, flowcharts, and logic structures.

Structured programming techniques: Techniques consisting of top-down program design, pseudocode, flowcharts, and logic structures.

Structured query language (SQL): A program control language used to create sophisticated database applications for requesting information from a database.

Stylus: Penlike device used with tablet PCs and PDAs that use pressure to draw images on a screen. A stylus interacts with the computer through handwriting recognition software.

Subject: Located in the head of an e-mail message, a one-line description used to present the topic of the message.

Subscription address: Mailing list address. To participate in a mailing list, you must first subscribe by sending an e-mail request to the mailing list subscription address.

Supercomputer: Fastest calculating device ever invented, processing billions of program instructions per second. Used by very large organizations like NASA.

SuperDisk: High-capacity floppy disk manufactured by Imation with a capacity of 120 MB or 250 MB. SuperDisk drives are also able to read and store data on the standard 1.44 MB floppy disk.

Supervisor: Manager responsible for managing and monitoring workers. Supervisors have responsibility for operational matters.

Surfing: Moving from one Web site to another.

Surge protector: Device separating the computer from the power source of the wall outlet. When a voltage surge occurs, a circuit breaker is activated, protecting the computer system.

Syntax error: Violation of the rules of a language in which the computer program is written. For example, leaving out a semicolon would stop the entire program from working, because it is not the exact form the computer expects for that language.

System: Collection of activities and elements designed to accomplish a goal.

System board: Flat board that usually contains the CPU and memory chips connecting all system components to one another.

System bus: There are two categories of buses. One is the system bus that connects the CPU to the system board. The other is the expansion bus that connects the CPU to slots on the system board.

System cabinet: Also known as the chassis, which is a container that houses most of the electronic components that make up a computer system. *See* System unit.

System clock: Clock that controls how fast all the operations within a computer take place.

System flowchart: A flowchart that shows the flow of input data to processing and finally to output, or distribution of information.

System software: "Background" software that enables the application software to interact with the computer. System software consists of the operating system, utilities, device drivers, and language translators. It works with application software to handle the majority of technical details.

System unit: Part of a microcomputer that contains the CPU. Also known as the system cabinet or chassis and is the container that houses most of the electronic components that make up the computer system.

Systems analysis: This second phase of the systems life cycle determines the requirements for a new system. Data is collected about the present system, analyzed, and new requirements are determined.

Systems analysis and design: Six phases of problem-solving procedures for examining information systems and improving them.

Systems analysis report: Report prepared for higher management describing the current information system, the requirements for a new system, and a possible development schedule.

Systems analyst: Plans and designs information systems.

Systems audit: A systems audit compares the performance of a new system to the original design specifications to determine if the new procedures are actually improving productivity.

Systems design: Phase three of the systems life cycle, consisting of designing alternative systems, selecting the best system, and writing a systems design report.

Systems design report: Report prepared for higher management describing alternative designs, presenting cost versus benefits, and outlining the effects of alternative designs on the organization.

Systems development: Phase four of the systems life cycle, consisting of developing software, acquiring hardware, and testing the new system.

Systems implementation: Phase five of the systems life cycle is converting the old system to the new one and training people to use the new system. Also known as conversion.

Systems life cycle: The six phases of the systems analysis and design are called the systems life cycle. The phases are: preliminary investigation, systems analysis, systems design, systems development, systems implementation, and systems maintenance.

Systems maintenance: Phase six of the systems life cycle consisting of a system audit and periodic evaluation.

T

T1, T2, T3, T4 lines: High-speed lines that support all digital communications, provide very high capacity, and are very expensive.

Table (in database): The list of records in a database. Tables make up the basic structure of a database. Their columns display field data and their rows display records. *See* Field and Record.

Tablet PC: A type of notebook computer that accepts handwritten data using a stylus or pen, which is converted to standard text and can be processed by a word processor program.

Tablet PC system unit: Similar to notebook system units. Two basic categories are convertible and slate. A stylus or pen is used to input data.

Tactical model: A decision model that assists middle-level managers to control the work of the organization, such as financial planning and sales promotion planning.

Tape cartridges: *See* Magnetic tape streamer.

Technical feasibility: Making sure hardware, software, and training will be available to facilitate the design of a new system.

Technical writer: Prepares instruction manuals, technical reports, and other scientific or technical documents.

Technostress: Tension that arises when humans must unnaturally adapt to computers.

Telephone line: A transmission medium for both voice and data.

Telephony: Communication that uses the Internet rather than traditional communication lines to connect two or more people via telephone.

Television board: Contains a TV tuner card and video converter changing the TV signal into one that can be displayed on your monitor. Also known as TV tuner cards, Video recorder cards, and Video capture cards.

Telnet: Internet service that helps you to connect to another computer (host) on the Internet and log on to that computer as if you were on a terminal in the next room.

Temporary storage: Memory is sometimes referred to as temporary storage because its contents will be lost if electrical power to the computer is disrupted. RAM is this kind of memory.

Terminal: An input and output device connecting to a mainframe or other type of computer called a host computer or server.

Terminal network system: Network system in which processing power is centralized in one large computer, usually a mainframe. The nodes connected to this host computer are terminals, with little or no processing capabilities, or they are microcomputers running special software allowing them to act as terminals.

Text entry: In a worksheet or spreadsheet, a text entry is typically used to identify or label information entered into a cell as opposed to numbers and formulas. Also known as Labels.

Theme: Provides a basic layout and color scheme for Web pages.

Thermal printer: Printer that uses heat elements to produce images on heat-sensitive paper.

Thesaurus: An editing tool that provides synonyms, antonyms, and related words for a selected word or phrase.

Thin client: *See* Network terminal.

Thin film transistor (TFT) monitor: Type of flat-panel monitor activating each pixel independently.

Thread: A sequence of ongoing messages on the same subject in a discussion group.

Time-sharing system: System allowing several users to share resources in the host computer.

Toggle key: These keys turn a feature on or off like the cap lock key.

Toolbar: Bar located typically below the menu bar containing icons or graphical representations for commonly used commands.

Top level domain: *See* Domain name.

Top management: Top-level managers are concerned with long-range (strategic) planning. They supervise middle management.

Top-down analysis method: Method used to identify top-level components of a system, then break these components down into smaller parts for analysis.

Top-down program design: Used to identify the program's processing steps called program modules. The program must pass in sequence from one module to the next until the computer has processed all modules.

Topology: The configuration of a network. The four principal network topologies are *star, bus, ring,* and *hierarchical.*

Touch pad: Also known as touch surface. Used to control pointer by moving and tapping your finger on the surface of a pad.

Touch screen: Monitor screen allowing actions or commands to be entered by the touch of a finger.

Touch surface: Typically part of a portable computer, similar to a mouse.

Tower model: Vertical system units are called tower models.

Track: Closed, concentric ring on a disk on which data is recorded. Each track is divided into sections called sectors.

Trackball: Device used to control the pointer by rotating a ball with your thumb. Also called a Rollerball.

Traditional cookies: Intended to provide customized service. A program recording information on Web site visitors within a specific site. When you leave the site, the cookie becomes dormant, and is reactivated when you revisit the site.

Traditional keyboard: Full sized, rigid, rectangular keyboard that includes function, navigational, and numeric keys.

Transaction processing system (TPS): System that records day-to-day transactions, such as customer orders, bills, inventory levels, and production output. The TPS tracks operations and creates databases.

Transceiver: Sending and receiving communication tower that sends and receives radio signals from wireless devices.

Transfer rate: Or transfer speed, is the speed that modems transmit data typically measured in bits per second (bps).

Transfer speed: *See* Transfer rate.

Transmission control protocol/Internet protocol (TCP/IP): TCP/IP is the standard protocol for the Internet. The essential features of this protocol involve (1) identifying sending and receiving devices, and (2) reformatting information for transmission across the Internet.

Transmission medium: The actual connection or communication channel carrying the message. It can be a physical wire, cable, or wireless connection.

Trojan horse: Program that is not a virus but is a carrier of virus(es). The most common Trojan horses appear as free computer games, screen savers, or antivirus programs. Once downloaded they locate and disable existing virus protection and then deposit the virus.

Troubleshooting utility: A utility program that recognizes and corrects computer-related problems before they become serious. Also called diagnostic programs.

TV tuner card: *See* Television board. Also known as Video recorder cards and Video capture cards.

Twisted pair cable: Copper-wire telephone line.

2HD: Two-sided, double-density disk. Also known as a floppy disk and holds 1.44 MB of data.

Two-state system: Many forms of technology use a two-state system creating on/off, yes/no, or a present/absent arrangement. A magnetized spot on a tape or disk may have a positive or negative charge. This is the reason two-state or binary systems represent computer instructions.

Type I cards: The thinnest PC card. Used primarily to expand the notebook or handheld computer memory. These memory cards are also known as flash memory cards.

Type II cards: Thicker in size and used for communication. They include modem cards and network interface cards.

Type III cards: Thickest of the PC cards, used to expand external storage and include hard disk cards.

U

Unicode: A 16-bit code designed to support international languages, like Chinese and Japanese.

Uniform resource locator (URL):   For browsers to connect you to resources on the Web, the location or address of the resources must be specified. These addresses are called URLs.

Uninstall utility: Programs that safely and completely remove unwanted programs and related files.

Universal instant messenger: An instant messaging service that communicates with any other messaging service programs.

Universal Product Code (UPC):   A barcode system that identifies the product to the computer, which has a description and the latest price for the product.

Universal serial bus (USB):   Combines with a PCI bus on the system board to support several external devices without inserting cards for each device. USB buses are used to support high-speed scanners, printers, and video-capturing devices.

Universal serial bus (USB) port: Expected to replace serial and parallel ports. They are faster, and one USB port can be used to connect several devices to the system unit.

UNIX: An operating system originally developed for minicomputers. It is now important because it can run on many of the more powerful microcomputers.

Unstructured problem: A problem that requires the use of intuition, reasoning, and memory.

Uplink: Refers to sending data to a satellite.

Uploading: Process of transferring information from the computer the user is operating to a remote computer.

UseNet: Special network of computers that supports newsgroups.

User: Any individual who uses a computer. *See* End user.

User interface: Means by which users interact with application programs and hardware. A window is displayed with information for the user to enter or choose, and that is how users communicate with the program.

Utility: Performs specific tasks related to managing computer resources or files. Norton Utility for virus control and system maintenance is a good example of a utility. Also known as Service programs.

Utility suite: A program that combines several utilities in one package to improve system performance. McAfee Office and Norton System Works are examples.

V

Vector: Another common type of graphic file. A vector file contains all the shapes and colors, along with starting and ending points, necessary to recreate the image.

Vector Illustration: *See* Vector image.

Vector image: Graphics file made up of a collection of objects such as lines, rectangles, and ovals. Vector images are more flexible than bitmaps because they are defined by mathematical equations so they can be stretched and resized. Illustration programs create and manipulate vector graphics. Also known as Vector illustrations.

Very high-level languages: Problem-orientated languages that require little special training on the part of the user.

Video capture card: *See* Television board.

Video card: Also known as Graphic cards. They connect the system board to the computer monitor. The cards convert the internal electronic signals to video signals so they can be displayed on the monitor.

Video display screen: *See* Monitor.

Video editing software: Allows you to reorganize, add effects, and more to your video footage.

Video recorder card: Contains a TV tuner and video converter that changes the TV signal into one that can be displayed on your monitor.

Video Privacy Protection Act of 1988:   Law preventing retailers from selling or disclosing video-rental records without the customer's consent or a court order.

Videoconferencing system: Computer system that allows people located at various geographic locations to have in-person meetings.

Viewable size: Measured by the diagonal length of a monitor's viewing area.

Virtual environment: *See* Virtual reality.

Virtual library: Visit libraries on the Internet, read selected items, and check out books.

Virtual memory: Feature of an operating system that increases the amount of memory available to run programs. With large programs, parts are stored on a secondary device like your hard disk. Then each part is read in RAM only when needed.

Virtual reality: Interactive sensory equipment (headgear and gloves) allowing users to experience alternative realities generated in 3-D by a computer, thus imitating the physical world.

Virtual reality modeling language (VRML):   Used to create real-time animated 3-D scenes.

Virtual reality wall: An immersive experience whereby you are viewing simulations on a virtual reality wall in stereoscopic vision.

Virus: Hidden instructions that migrate through networks and operating systems and become embedded in different programs. They may be designed to destroy data or simply to display messages.

Virus checker: Detection programs alerting users when certain kinds of viruses enter the system.

Visual programming languages: A 5GL that provides a natural visual interface for program development, like intuitive icons, menus, and drawing tools, for creating program code. Visual Basic is a visual programming language.

Voice command mode: Allows users to select menu items, toolbars, and dialog box options using voice or a mouse.

Voice grade: *See* Voiceband.

Voice input: Entering data and issuing commands using your voice.

Voice output device: Converts digital data into speech-like sounds. For example, voice output on telephone messages, voice synthesizers that read aloud words on the screen, and mapping software for vehicle navigation devices.

Voice recognition system: Using a microphone, sound card, and speciality software, the user can operate a computer and create documents using voice commands.

Voiceband: Bandwidth of a standard telephone line. Also known as low bandwidth.

Voice-over IP (VoIP): Transmission of telephone calls over networks. *See also* Telephony.

Volatile storage: Temporary storage that destroys the current data when power is lost or new data is read, like RAM storage.

Voltage surge (spike): Excess of electricity that may destroy chips or other electronic computer components.

VR: *See* Virtual reality.

W

WAN: *See* Wide area network.

Wand reader: Special-purpose handheld device used to read OCR characters.

Warm boot: Restarting your computer while the computer is already on and the power is not turned off.

Web: A service providing a multimedia interface to resources on the Internet. *See also* World Wide Web.

Web appliance: *See* Internet terminal.

Web auction: Similar to traditional auctions except that buyers and sellers meet only on the Web. Ebay is one example.

Web authoring: Creating a Web site.

Web authoring program: Word processing program for generating Web pages. Also called HTML editor or Web page editor. Widely used Web authoring programs include Macromedia Dreamweaver and Microsoft FrontPage.

Web bug: Program hidden in the HTML code for a Web page or e-mail message as a graphical image. Web bugs can migrate whenever a user visits a Web site containing a Web bug or opens infected e-mail. They collect information on the users and report back to a predefined server.

WebCam: Specialized digital video camera for capturing images and broadcasting to the Internet.

Web camera: *See* WebCam.

Web database: Used by Web sites to record data collected from users and by Web search engines; CGI scripts used in interface programs that collect user information.

Web page: Browsers interpret HTML documents to display Web pages.

Web page editor: *See* Web authoring program.

Web server: Dedicated server that houses internal and external Web page information.

Web storefronts: Virtual stores where shoppers can go to inspect goods and make purchases.

Web storefront creation packages: Programs for creating Web sites for virtual stores.

Web terminal: *See* Internet terminal.

Web utilities: Specialized utility programs making the Internet and the Web easier and safer. Some examples are plug-ins that operate as part of a browser, and filters that block access and monitor use of selected Web sites.

Web-based applications: By using the Web to connect with an application service provider (ASP), you can copy an application program to your computer system's memory and then run the application.

Webcrawlers: Special programs that continually look for new information and update the search servers' databases.

Webmaster: Develops and maintains Web sites and Web resources.

What-if analysis: Spreadsheet feature in which changing one or more numbers results in the automatic recalculation of all related formulas.

Wheel button: Some mice have a wheel button that can be rotated to scroll through information displayed on the monitor.

Wide area network (WAN): Countrywide and worldwide networks that use microwave relays and satellites to reach users over long distances.

WiFI (wireless fidelity): Wireless standard also known as 802.11, used to connect computers to each other and to the Internet.

Window: A rectangular area containing a document or message.

Windows: An operating environment extending the capability of DOS.

Windows Update: A utility provided in the Windows platform that allows you to update the device drivers on your computer.

Windows XP: The most recent Windows operating system featuring a user interface called Luna.

Wireless keyboard: Transmits input to the system through the air providing greater flexibility and convenience.

Wireless LAN (WLAN): Uses radio frequencies to connect computers and other devices. All communications pass through the network's centrally located wireless receiver or base station and are routed to the appropriate devices.

Wireless modem: Modem connecting to the serial port but does not connect to telephone lines. It receives through the air.

Wireless mouse: *See* Cordless mouse.

Wireless receiver: Or Base station. The receiver interprets incoming radio frequencies from a wireless LAN and routes communications to the appropriate devices, which could be separate computers, a shared printer, or a modem.

Wireless revolution: A revolution that is expected to dramatically affect the way we communicate and use computer technology.

Wireless service provider: Provides Internet connections for computers with wireless modems and a wide array of wireless devices. They do not use telephone lines.

WML (Wireless Markup Language):   Provides a standard for describing data in wireless applications.

Word processor: The computer and the program allow you to create, edit, save, and print documents composed of text.

Word wrap: Feature of word processing that automatically moves the cursor from the end of one line to the beginning of the next.

Workbook file: Contains one or more related worksheets or spreadsheets. *See* Spreadsheet.

Worksheet: Also known as a spreadsheet, or sheet, and is a rectangular grid of rows and columns used in programs like Excel.

Worksheet file: Is created by electronic spreadsheets to analyze things like budgets and to predict sales.

Workstation: Usually a powerful, high-end microcomputer, but any PC can be a workstation if set up correctly. Workstations have high quality graphics capabilities that can create animations for television by using engineering applications like CAD/CAM for example. Workstations are typically connected to a network but can also be a stand-alone computer.

World Wide Web (WWW, the Web):   Introduced in 1992 and prior to the Web, the Internet was all text. The Web made it possible to provide a multimedia interface, that includes graphics, animations, sound, and video.

Worm: Virus that doesn't attach itself to programs and databases but fills a computer system with self-replicating information, clogging the system so that its operations are slowed or stopped.

Write once: DVD-R and DVD+R are competing write once formats; however, most DVD players use either format and both stand for DVD recordable.

Write protection notch: When you slide the tile on a floppy disk so you can see through the hole, none of the information on that disk can be modified or deleted and the disk is write protected. If the hole is covered, you can save or change any material on the disk.

Writing: Process of saving information to the secondary storage device.

Z

Zip disk: High capacity floppy disk manufactured by Sony. Requires a special disk drive to run this type of storage unit. They typically have 100 MB or 250 MB capacity, over 170 times as much as the standard floppy disk.

Credits

p. 2 left   Courtesy of Research in Motion (RIM)

p. 2 center   © Walter Hodges/CORBIS

p 2 right   Sony Electronics Inc.

p. 3   Courtesy of T-Mobile USA

p. 4 left   © Jose Luis Pelaez, Inc./CORBIS

p. 4   Box shots reprinted with permission from Microsoft Corporation

p. 5   Courtesy of Dell Inc.

p. 6 top left   Getty Images

p. 6 top right   © Walter Hodges/CORBIS

p. 6 bottom left   Stewart Cohen/Index Stock

p. 6 bottom right   Markus Matzel/Peter Arnold

p. 7   © Jose Luis Pelaez, Inc./CORBIS

p. 12 top left   Courtesy of Hewlett-Packard Company

p. 12 top right   © Neal and Molly Jansen/Superstock

p. 12 bottom left   Wacom Technology Corp.

p. 12 bottom right   Courtesy of Hewlett-Packard Company

p. 14 left   Sony Electronics Inc.

p. 14 top right   Getty Images

p. 14 bottom right   Victor Paris/Getty Images

p. 16 far left   Courtesy of Research in Motion (RIM)

p. 16 center left   Nokia Inc.

p. 16 center right   Sony Electronics Inc.

p. 16 far right   Courtesy of T-Mobile USA

p. 17   Getty Images

p. 18 left   © Jose Luis Pelaez, Inc./CORBIS

p. 18 top right   Getty Images

p. 18 bottom right   Markus Matzel/Peter Arnold

p. 19 left   Box shots reprinted with permission from Microsoft Corporation

p. 19 right   Courtesy of Dell Inc.

p. 20 top right   Courtesy of T-Mobile USA

p. 25   Antonio Mo/Taxi

p. 30   Getty Images

p. 46   Getty Images

p. 47   Getty Images

p. 48 left   Getty Images

p. 63   © Royalty-Free/CORBIS

p. 77   Courtesy Apple Computer

p. 78   Box shot reprinted with permission from Microsoft Corporation

p. 81   Adrian Lyon/Getty Images

p. 93 left   Roger Ressmeyer/CORBIS

p. 94 top left   Courtesy of Adobe Systems, Inc.

p. 94 top right   Courtesy Apple Computer

p. 94 center   Courtesy Macromedia

p. 94 bottom left   Box shot reprinted with permission from Microsoft Corporation

p. 97   Courtesy Corel

p. 98   Courtesy Apple Computer

p. 103   Courtesy Macromedia

p. 105   Box shot reprinted with permission from Microsoft Corporation

p. 107 top   Roger Ressmeyer/CORBIS

p. 107 bottom   Rodney White/AP

p. 108 center   Sony Electronics Inc.

p. 108 bottom   Getty Images

p. 109   Itsuo Inouye/AP

p. 110 right   Courtesy Apple Computer

p. 112 left   Roger Ressmeyer/CORBIS

p. 112 right   Sony Electronics Inc.

p. 122 left   © Jose Luis Pelaez, Inc./CORBIS

p. 122   Box shots reprinted with permission from Microsoft Corporation.

p. 124   Courtesy of Hewlett-Packard Company

p. 125   Courtesy of Dell Inc.

p. 137   EPA-Photo/EPA/Jason Szenes/AP

p. 138   Box shot reprinted with permission from Microsoft Corporation.

p. 150 top left   Sony Electronics Inc.

p. 150 top right   © Dex Images/CORBIS

p. 150 bottom left   Courtesy Acer America.

p. 150 bottom right   Courtesy Acer America.

p. 151 left   Courtesy Acer America.

p. 151 right   AFP/CORBIS

p. 152   CORBIS

p. 155 center left   Stock Photos/CORBIS

p. 155 center right   © Lawrence Manning/CORBIS

p. 155 bottom right   CORBIS

p. 155 left   Courtesy Intel

p. 157   Julia Malakie/AP Wide World

p. 158   Courtesy of Kingston Technology Company Inc.

p. 161 top right   Courtesy Creative Technology Ltd.

p. 161 center   Courtesy of Zoom Technologies Inc.

p. 164   Courtesy of Datakey, Inc.

p. 165   Getty Images

p. 166 left   Courtesy PC Power & Cooling

p. 166 right   Courtesy Toshiba America Information Systems, Inc.

p. 167   Getty Images

p. 168 left   Courtesy Acer America.

p. 168 bottom right   © Lawrence Manning/CORBIS

p. 169 left   Courtesy Intel

p. 169 right   Courtesy of Kingston Technology Company Inc.

p. 170 top   Courtesy of Creative Technology Ltd.

p. 170 bottom   Courtesy of Datakey, Inc.

p. 178 left   Courtesy of palmOne, Inc.

p. 178 center   Sony Electronics Inc.

p. 178 right   Getty Images

p. 179 right   Courtesy Acer America.

p. 179 center   Courtesy of ViewSonic Corporation

p. 179 left   Picture of Canon CP-300 dye-sublimation printer, courtesy of Canon USA. Used with permission.

p. 180 top   Courtesy Man & Machine

p. 180 bottom   Amy Etra/PhotoEdit, Inc.

p. 181   Courtesy of palmOne, Inc.

p. 182 top   Courtesy Microsoft ® Corp.

p. 182 bottom left   SuperStock

p. 182 bottom center   Bruce Avery/SuperStock

p. 182 bottom right   Getty Images

p. 183 top   Courtesy of Logitech

p. 183 bottom left   Spencer Grant/PhotoEdit, Inc.

p. 183 bottom right   Sony Electronics Inc.

p. 184   Courtesy of palmOne, Inc.

p. 185 top left   David Young-Wolff/PhotoEdit, Inc.

p. 185 top right   Courtesy of Logitech

p. 185 center   © Charles O'Rear/CORBIS

p. 185 bottom   David Young-Wolff/PhotoEdit, Inc.

p. 186 center   Getty Images

p. 186 bottom   © Ed Bock/CORBIS

p. 187   Courtesy Olympus America

p. 190   Courtesy Yamaha Band & Orchestral Division

p. 192 center left   Courtesy IBM

p. 192 center right   Courtesy Acer America

p. 192 bottom   Mark Duncan/AP

p. 193   Courtesy of ViewSonic Corporation

p. 194   CORBIS

p. 195 top   © Lexmark International, Inc.

p. 195 bottom   Picture of Canon CP-300 dye-sublimation printer, courtesy of Canon USA. Used with permission.

p. 196   David Young-Wolff/PhotoEdit, Inc.

p. 197   J P Williams/Getty Images

p. 199   Getty Images

p. 200 left   Amy Etra/PhotoEdit, Inc.

p. 200 right   Sony Electronics Inc.

p. 201 left   Getty Images

p. 201 right   Courtesy of ViewSonic Corporation

p. 202 left   CORBIS

p. 202 right   J P Williams/Getty Images

p. 210 left   Courtesy of Iomega Corporation

p. 210 right   Getty Images

p. 210 center   Courtesy of Seagate Technology

p. 211   Courtesy SCM Microsystems

p. 212   Getty Images

p. 213   Getty Images

p. 214   Courtesy of Iomega Corporation

p. 216 top   Courtesy of Iomega Corporation

p. 216 center   Courtesy of Toshiba

p. 216 bottom   IBM Corporate Archives

p. 218   Courtesy of Advance Computer & Network Group

p. 219   Getty Images

p. 224 top   Courtesy SCM Microsystems

p. 224 center   Courtesy Cyberkey Corp.

p. 225   Sony Electronics Inc.

p. 227   Sony Electronics Inc.

p. 228   Getty Images

p. 229 top right   IBM Corporate Archives

p. 229 bottom   Courtesy of Toshiba

p. 230   Getty Images

p. 238 top   Getty Images

p. 238 left   Stocktrek/CORBIS

p. 238 right   Courtesy of Novatel Wireless, Inc.

p. 241   Getty Images

p. 242 top   Getty Images

p. 242 center   Getty Images

p. 242 bottom   Getty Images

p. 243 top   Lester Lefkowitz/CORBIS

p. 243 center   Stocktrek/CORBIS

p. 243 bottom   Photo Courtesy of Lexus

p. 245 top   Courtesy of Zoom Technologies Inc.

p. 245 center left   Courtesy of U.S. Robotics, Inc.

p. 245 center   Courtesy of U.S. Robotics, Inc.

p. 245 center right   Courtesy of Novatel Wireless, Inc.

p. 259   Charles Bennett/AP Wide World

p. 260 left   Getty Images

p 260 right   Stocktrek/CORBIS

p. 261 top   Courtesy of Zoom Technologies Inc.

p. 261 left   Courtesy of U.S. Robotics, Inc.

p. 261 center   Courtesy of U.S. Robotics, Inc.

p. 261 right   Courtesy of Novatel Wireless, Inc.

p. 270 left   Neal Wilson/Getty Images

p. 270 center   © Michael A. Keller Studios, Ltd./CORBIS

p. 270 right   Eric Pearle/Getty Images

p. 271 left   Christopher Bissell/Getty Images

p. 271 right   © Mug Shots/CORBIS

p. 271 bottom   © Peter Turnley/CORBIS

p. 272 left   © Jose Luis Pelaez, Inc./CORBIS

p. 272   Box shots reprinted with permission from Microsoft Corporation.

p. 273   Courtesy of Dell Inc.

p. 274   Neal Wilson/Getty Images

p. 283 left   © A & J Verkaik/CORBIS

p. 283 center   © Peter Turnley/CORBIS

p. 283 right   © H. Prinz/CORBIS

p. 287   Christopher Bissell/Getty Images

p. 288   AP/Wide World Photos

p. 289 left   Courtesy MPC Computers

p. 289 right   Courtesy Iridian Technologies, Inc.

p. 291   © Jean-Pierre Lescourret/CORBIS

p. 292 top   © Michael A. Keller Studios, Ltd./CORBIS

p. 292 bottom   Eric Pearle/Getty Images

p. 294   © Mug Shots/CORBIS

p. 295   Getty Images

p. 296   Neal Wilson/Getty Images

p. 297   Courtesy Iridian Technologies, Inc.

p. 308   David Young-Wolff/PhotoEdit, Inc.

p. 311   Walter Hodges/Getty Images

p. 312   © Bill Varie/CORBIS

Credits

Index

C

C, 408
C#, 408
C++, 408
C drive, 215
C2C commerce, 42–43
Cable modem, 245–246
Cables, 166
Cache memory, 158
CAD, 328
CAD/CAM, 320
CAN-SPAM Act, 464
Capacity, 212
Captions, 66
Carders, 44
Career development, 438–441
   develop specialties, 442
   innovative opportunities, 443
   maintain computer
      competency, 439, 444
   networking, 442
   online job search, 440–441
   stay current, 439
   types of jobs, 444
   watch for organizational
      change, 442–443
Carpal tunnel syndrome, 291–292
Carrier package, 154–156
Case study. See DVD Direct (case study)
CASE tools, 373, 394, 413, 414
Cathode-ray tube (CRT), 191–192
CD burner, 220
CD-R, 219–220, 237
CD-ROM, 219
CD-RW, 220
Cell, 67, 69
Cellular phone systems, 251
Center aligning, 65
Center for European Nuclear Research
   (CERN), 30
Central processing unit (CPU), 156
CERN, 30
CFCs, 294
CGI (Common Gateway Interface)
   scripts, 347
Chain letter, 286
Changing times, 434
Channel, 37
Character, 335
Character based interface, 123
Character effects, 64, 65
Character recognition devices, 185
Chart, 68, 70
Chart types, 70
Chassis, 150
Chat groups, 37
Checklist, 371
Child node, 341
Child Online Protection Act
   (COPA), 279
Chip, 154, 155
Chlorofluorocarbons (CFCs), 294
CIA, 278
CISC chip, 157
Cisco Systems, 47

Civil strife, 287
Clarity, 191
Class, 344
Classroom Clipart, 97
Client, 248
Client operating system, 125
Client/server network systems, 255–256
Clip art, 96
ClipArt.com, 97
Clock rate, 160
Clock speed, 160
Closed architecture, 160
CMOS, 159
Coaxial cable, 242
COBOL, 416, 458
Code of Fair Information
   Practice, 278–279, 282
Coding, 406
Coding schemes, 152–154
Cold boot, 123
Cold site, 289
Color capability, 193
Color thermal printer, 195
Column, 67
Combination devices, 196
Combination input-output
   devices, 196–198
Combination keys, 181
Commerce servers, 43
Common data item, 343
Common operational database, 346
Common user database, 346
Communication channels, 241, 242–244
Communication devices, 241
Communication server, 248
Communication systems, 241
Communications and networks,
   238–269
   communication channels, 242–244
   communication systems, 241
   connection devices, 244–246
   connectivity, 240
   data transmission, 246–247
   network architecture, 251–257
   network types, 249–251
   networks, 247–249
   organizational internets, 257–258
   wireless revolution, 240
Compact disc (CD), 219–220, 221
Company (shared) database, 345–346
Compiler, 415–416
Complementary metal-oxide
   semiconductor (CMOS), 159
Complex instruction set computer (CISC)
   chip, 157
Compuserve, 460
Computer Abuse Amendments Act of
   1994, 279, 284
Computer-aided design/computer-aided
   manufacturing (CAD/CAM), 320
Computer-aided software engineering
   (CASE) tools, 373, 394, 413, 414
Computer based information
   systems, 312–321. See also
   Information systems

Computer communications, 240. See also
   Communications and networks
Computer competence, 3, 439, 444, 453
Computer crime, 283–286
   data manipulation, 286
   defined, 282
   DOS attack, 285
   Internet scams, 285, 286
   malicious programs, 283–285
   theft, 286
Computer ethics, 273
Computer Fraud and Abuse Act, 279, 286
Computer keyboard, 180–181
Computer Matching and Privacy
   Protection Act, 279
Computer monitoring software, 277–278
Computer network, 247–257. See also
   Communications and networks
Computer recycling groups, 295
Computer security. See Security
Computer support specialist, 444
Computer technician, 444
Computer theft, 286
Computer-to-computer
   communications, 197
Computer-to-traditional telephone
   communications, 197
Computer trainer, 444
Computer virus, 131, 283–284
ComputerWorld, 439
Concurrent version system (CVS), 428
Connection devices, 241, 244–246
Connection Keep Alive, 132
Connectivity, 240
Consumer-to-consumer (C2C)
   commerce, 42–43
Contacts, 36
Control unit, 156
Controller cards, 161
Conversion, 377
Convertible tablet PC, 151
Cookie Cleanup, 277
Cookie Crusher, 277
Cookie-cutter programs, 277
Cookie Pal, 277
Cookies, 277
COPA, 279
Coprocessor, 157
Cordless joystick, 183
Cordless mouse, 182
Corel Paradox, 72
Corel PhotoPaint, 95
Corel Presentations, 75
Corel Quattro Pro, 67
Corel WordPerfect, 64
Corel WordPerfect OfficeSuite, 78
CorelDraw, 95, 97
CorelDraw Graphics Suite, 97
Cosmos, 45
CPU, 156
Cracker, 282
Creative Suites, 97
Credit card fraud, 44
Credit card purchase, 44
Cross references, 66
CRT, 191–192

L

Labels, 67, 213
LAN, 249–250
LAN adapter, 248
LAN Server, 256
Land, 219
Language bar, 187, 190
Language translators, 122
Laptop, 150
Laser printer, 194–195
Legend, 70
Light pen, 183
Line of sight communication, 242
Link, 99
Linked object, 80
Linux, 127, 146, 462
List address, 36
Live, 97
Local area network (LAN), 249–250
Logic error, 409
Logic structures, 403–405
Logical data organization, 336
Logical operations, 156
Logical view, 334
Loop structure, 403–405
Lotus 1-2-3, 67
Lotus Approach, 72
Lotus Freelance Graphics, 75
Lotus SmartSuite, 78
Lotus Word Pro, 64
Love Bug, 284
Low bandwidth, 246
Low-level languages, 414
Luna, 126
Lurking, 37
lynxmotion.com, 109

M

Mac OS, 127
Mac OS X, 127, 464
Machine language, 415
Macintosh Computer, 461
Macintosh Peer-to-Peer LANs, 256
Macromedia Director, 102, 103
Macromedia Dreamweaver, 105
Macromedia FreeHand, 95
Macromedia Studio, 97
MacWorld, 439
Magnetic-ink character recognition (MICR), 185
Magnetic tape, 225
Magnetic tape cartridge, 225
Magnetic tape reels, 225
Magnetic tape streamers, 225
Mailing lists, 36
Main board, 154
Maintenance programmer, 412
Malicious programs, 283–285
Malware, 283
Mamma, 41
MAN, 250–251
Management information system (MIS), 315–316
Management information system report, 316
Management levels, 310, 311

Many-to-many relationship, 341
Mark recognition devices, 185
Mark sensing, 185
Marketing, 309, 310
Master slide, 75, 76
Mauchly, John W., 457
MAX, 68
MB, 159
mbps, 244
McAfee Internet Security Suite, 134–135
McAfee Office, 131
McAfee VirusScan, 284
Mcard, 158
Mechanical mouse, 182
Media (medium), 212
Media Player, 44, 45
Medium band, 246
Megabyte (MB), 159
Melissa virus, 463
Memory, 158–159
Memory capacity, 159
Mental health, 292
Menu, 60, 61, 124
Menu bar, 60
Merrill Lynch, 435, 436
MetaCrawler, 41
Metasearch engines, 41
Method, 344
Metropolitan area network (MAN), 250–251
MFD, 196–197
MI-tech, 418
MICR, 185
Microcomputer database, 345
Micrografx Designer, 95
Microprocessor, 156–158, 177
Microprocessor age, 460
Microprocessor carrier package and cartridge, 156
Microprocessor chips, 156–157
Microsecond, 156, 157
Microsoft, 146, 461–464
Microsoft Access, 72
Microsoft desktop operating systems, 126
Microsoft Excel, 67
Microsoft FrontPage, 105, 106
Microsoft Internet Explorer, 32
Microsoft Office XP, 78
Microsoft Paint, 95
Microsoft PowerPoint, 75
Microsoft Publisher, 95
Microsoft Windows, 126
Microsoft Word, 64
Microsoft Works, 77
Microsoft Works Suite, 78
Microwave, 243
Microwave dish, 243
Microwave stations, 243
Middle management, 310, 311
Middle management-level information flow, 312
MIDI, 190
MIDI devices, 190
Midwives Assistant, 108
Mini Pod, 259
MIS, 315–316
Mistaken identity, 275, 304

Mobile Assistant V, 167
Mobile robots, 108
Modem, 244–245
Modem card, 161
Modulation, 244
Module, 402
Monitor resolution, 191
Monitors, 191–193
monster.com, 440
Monthly credit card statements, 337
Morphing, 104
Mosaic, 462
Motherboard, 154
Mouse, 182
Mouse pad, 182
Mouse pointer, 182
MS-DOS, 461
MS Office clip art, 97
MSN Explorer, 197
MSN Messenger, 36
MTV web site, 33
Multidimensional database, 343–344
Multifunctional devices (MFD), 196–197
Multimedia authoring programs, 102
Multiread, 220
Multisession, 220
Multitasking, 123
Music, 190, 222–223, 235, 236
Music files, 237
Music sharing systems, 256–257
Musical instrument digital interface (MIDI), 190

N

Naive, 437
Nanosecond, 156, 157
Napster, 256, 268, 463
National Information Infrastructure Protection Act, 279
National service providers, 32
Natural hazards, 287
Natural language programming, 418
Natural languages, 417
Net 30. *See also* Internet
NET Act, 279
.NET Framework, 428
Net Nanny, 46
Net PC, 198
Net Personal Computer, 198
.NET platform, 464
.NET program, 81
NetObjects Fusion, 105
Netscape Communications Corporation, 462
Netscape Mail, 34
Netscape Navigator, 32
NetWare, 125, 256
Network, 247–257. *See also* Communications and networks
Network adapter cards, 161
Network administrator, 249, 444
Network architecture, 251–257
Network computer, 198
Network configurations, 251, 254, 255
Network database, 341–342
Network gateway, 249

Technology portfolio, 455
Technostress, 292
Telephone lines, 242
Telephony, 197
Television boards, 161
Telnet, 45
Template
   design, 75
   presentation graphics, 76
Teoma, 41
Terabyte (TB), 159
Terminal, 197–198
Terminal network system, 255
Terrorism, 283, 287
Testing
   program, 409–410
   system, 377
Text database, 348
Text entries, 67, 69
TFT monitor, 192
Theft, 286
Thermal printer, 195
Thesaurus, 64
Thin client, 198
Thin film transistor (TFT) monitor, 192
Third generation language
   (3GL), 415–416
Thread, 37
Thus, 284
Time-sharing systems, 254
Times New Roman, 64
Titling, 70
Toggle keys, 181
Toolbar, 60, 61
Toolbook, 102
Top-down analysis method, 371–372
Top-down program design, 402
Top level domain, 33
Top management, 310, 311
Top managerial-level information
   flow, 312
Topology, 251
Toronto Blue Jays, 167
Torvalds, Linus, 127, 462
Touch pad, 182
Touch screen, 183
Touch surface, 182
Tower model, 150
Toyota, 259
TPS, 314–315
Track, 130, 131, 213
Trackball, 182
Traditional cookies, 277
Traditional floppy disk, 213
Traditional keyboards, 180
Training, 379
Transaction processing system
   (TPS), 314–315
Transceivers, 242
Transfer rate, 244
Transfer speeds, 244
Transistor age, 458
Translation/translator program, 199, 409
Transmission control protocol/Internet
   protocol (TCP/IP), 247
Transmission medium, 241

Trojan horse, 284–285
Troubleshooting utility, 128
TV tuner cards, 161, 162–163, 175, 176
Twisted pair cable, 242
2HD, 213
Two-state system, 152

U

uBid.com, 44
Unicode, 153
Uniform resource locator (URL), 32, 33
Uninstall programs, 128
UNIVAC, 457
Universal instant messenger, 36
Universal Product Code (UPC), 185
Universal serial bus (USB), 165
Universal serial bus (USB) ports, 165
UNIX, 127
Unstructured problems, 106
UPC, 185
Upgrader's guide, 470–473
Uplink, 243
Uploading, 45
URL, 32, 33
U.S. Department of Defense, 167
USA PATRIOT Act, 279
USB, 165
USB 1.1, 165
USB 2.0, 165
USB ports, 165
UseNet, 37
User (DSS), 317
User interface, 60, 123
Utilities, 128–132
Utility suite, 78, 131–132
UXGA, 191

V

V Communications SystemSuite, 131
Vacation prize (scam), 286
Vacuum tube age, 457
Vector, 95
Vector illustrations, 95
Vector image, 95, 96
Video capture cards, 161
Video cards, 161, 162–163, 175
Video editing software, 97
Video Privacy Protection Act, 279
Video recorder cards, 161
Videoconferencing systems, 320
Viewable size, 191
Virtual environment, 107
Virtual libraries, 31
Virtual memory, 159, 176
Virtual reality (VR), 107
Virtual reality modeling language
   (VRML), 107
Virtual reality wall, 107
Virus checker, 284
Virus protection, 132, 134–135, 144, 145
VirusScan, 135
Visual Basic, 408
Visual programming languages, 417
Vivisimo, 41
Voice command mode, 187

Voice grade, 246
Voice input, 187
Voice output, 196
Voice-over IP (VoIP), 197
Voice recognition system, 187
Voiceband, 246
VoIP, 197
Volatile storage, 158, 212
Voltage surge, 287
VR, 107
VRML, 107

W

Wall Street Journal, 439
WAN, 251
Wand reader, 185
Warm boot, 123
Wearable computers, 167
Web. *See* World Wide Web (Web)
Web appliance, 198
Web auction, 43, 44
Web authoring programs, 104–105
Web-based applications, 61, 81, 90
Web bugs, 277, 304
Web CleanUp, 132
Web database, 347, 362
Web filtering programs, 46
Web logs, 104
Web page, 33
Web page editors, 105
Web server, 33, 248
Web site design, 104
Web sites
   auction sites, 44
   cash providers, 44
   computer recycling groups, 295
   cookie-cutter program, 277
   Flash animation, users of, 105
   fonts, 64
   image galleries, 97
   Internet hard drive sites, 225
   mailing lists, 36
   metasearch sites, 41
   newsgroups, 37
   plug-in sites, 46
   robot kits, 109
   search engines, 41
   specialized search engines, 42
   spyware removal programs, 278
Web storefront, 43
Web storefront creation packages, 43
Web terminal, 198
Web utilities, 45–46
WebCam (Web camera), 186,
   188–189, 205
Webcrawlers, 40
Webmaster, 444
WebWasher, 277
Whale identification, 108
What-if analysis, 68, 71
Wheel button, 182
Wide area networks (WAN), 251
WiFi, 243, 464
Window, 60, 61, 124

Index